BERLIOZ
Selected Letters

BERLIOZ
Selected Letters

Edited by
HUGH MACDONALD

Translated by
ROGER NICHOLS

faber and faber
LONDON · BOSTON

First published in Great Britain in 1995
by Faber and Faber Ltd
3 Queen Square London WC1N 3AU

Typography by Humphrey Stone

Photoset by Parker Typesetting Service, Leicester
Printed in England by Clays Ltd, St Ives plc

This selection © Hugh Macdonald, 1995
Translation © Roger Nichols, 1995

A CIP record for this book is available
from the British Library

ISBN 0–571–14881–6

2 4 6 8 10 9 7 5 3 1

Contents

Editor's Preface

No composer is ever free of the necessity to communicate with his fellow-beings, and success, if it comes, brings with it the baggage of fame, travel, contracts, and the public gaze. In our own time almost none of this is conducted through the medium of the hand-written letter, but in earlier centuries a busy composer, when not composing, playing, travelling or resting, would be called upon to write a myriad of letters to his friends, his family, his colleagues, his agents, not to mention strangers and fortune-seekers. Happily this activity was not simply a means of communication, it was the play of the mind and the personality on paper in a form which, unlike the sound of their music-making, makes it as alive to the reader today as it was to the original recipient. The letters of composers do not reveal the secrets of their genius – those secrets are sealed for ever – but they do illuminate the world in which the music came into being, the conditions and circumstances that shaped it, the people, places and ideas that inspired it, and the public and press that judged it. Few of us can be untouched by the reading of historical details surrounding the creation of great music, and from there it is a short step to an absorption in composers' daily doings, whether these events had any bearing on music, let alone 'great' music, or not.

For Berlioz and his contemporaries letter-writing was the flower of life, even though it could equally be a tiresome necessity. Reading the letters of Mendelssohn, Chopin, Liszt or Wagner – or their literary contemporaries – we are reminded what an enormous portion of their lives had to be given to correspondence, how writing materials and a suitable desk had always to be at hand, how efficient and reliable the delivery services were, how polished and effortless was their command of style, and how graciously their letters can take on a literary tone even when dealing with mundane matters. Letters, like conversation, provided a forum for thought, so it was no self-conscious whim that often turned letters into tracts or polemics or flights of fancy, nor was there any showing-off in the sprinkling of literary and historical allusions we find there. Although it was normal to preserve letters, particularly the letters of the famous, there was little thought for posterity or a public reader; letters, in fact, are the common bearers of confidences others were never intended to share. A letter to a friend or a colleague can rarely deceive or posture in the way that a published article often will, so that truth, if it is to be found at all, is surely more readily assembled from a man's private writings than from the judgments of his peers and contemporaries.

Berlioz, it is commonly agreed, was a master of readable prose. The French public knew him as the feuilletonist for the *Journal des débats*, providing lengthy articles at least once a month for thirty years. This was his main source of income, despite his desire to be earning money and fame as a composer. He detested his obligation to journalism and came to recognize the dismal truth that his trenchant views generated enemies and that these enemies fought back by attacking his music, not his views. Instead of winning the public to his cause, his writings helped to alienate vested interests more powerful than he realized.

One legacy of Berlioz's public writing is his group of books, the best known of which, the posthumously published *Mémoires*, is rightly appreciated as a classic autobiography. It was assembled from travel writings about Italy, Germany and Russia written at different times together with an account of his childhood and early life written in about 1848 and some updates from 1854 and 1864. Even though some chapters of the *Mémoires* are presented as letters to friends, it was written for a public readership and conveys a more sharply etched but narrower personality than that revealed in his letters. The present volume of letters can well be read in conjunction with the *Mémoires*; the account of his experiences in Italy, in particular, are closely echoed in his letters home. Berlioz's other books were collections of articles on musical topics: *Les soirées de l'orchestre* (1852), *Les grotesques de la musique* (1859) and *A travers chants* (1862). These give an excellent sampling of his best criticism and leave the reader in little doubt as to his tastes and views. It is ironical that these books were successful publications while some of his best music was never performed at all.

However much he hated journalism, he did it with extraordinary brilliance, mixing prejudice and sane judgment, wit and knowledge, tact and obstinacy. Rarely, though, do we find Berlioz complaining about writing letters. More usually he would confess to taking pleasure in writing to one of his distant friends or relations, as though the minutes spent at his desk were actual conversations with his correspondent, away from the trials of everyday life. Coming from a family that hoarded letters long before he made the name Berlioz famous, he would have expected his letters to be saved, but never published.

Although substantial two-way correspondence is missing, he saved a good many letters he received.

Berlioz usually wrote letters on folded bifolia about 7"×5" which could accommodate up to about 600 words. It is not unusual to find four or five such letters written to different people on the same day. His handwriting was elegant and beautifully legible. About 3,500 Berlioz letters have survived, and although many must be lost they provide a remarkably complete and continuous picture of his professional and private life. It is fortunate that his family preserved so much, especially from his early years. Humbert Ferrand, a friend from about 1823 until his death in 1868, preserved a remarkable series of letters reflecting an unrivalled constancy in friendship on both sides. Berlioz's letters to Liszt spread over a period of over thirty years shed invaluable light on the tumultuous musical life of the period. In his early years Berlioz preferred friends from his own part of the world, such as Edouard Rocher, and there were Frenchmen such as Morel and Duchesne with whom he kept regularly in touch. But a great many of his close friends and correspondents were foreign, including Liszt and the Princess, Hiller, Heller, Damcke, Cornelius, von Bülow, Davison, Stasov, Wagner, the Baron von Donop, and many others; having no aptitude for foreign languages, Berlioz benefited from the fact that French was then spoken by educated people everywhere. At the end of his life his circle narrowed to a group of neighbours: the Damckes, the Massarts, Reyer, Kreutzer and d'Ortigue.

The present volume offers a sampling of Berlioz's letters to these individuals without attempting to give a complete picture of their relationships. It also drops the names of grand or heroic figures with whom Berlioz came in contact, however fleetingly: Hugo, Balzac and Flaubert among writers, Queen Victoria, King Louis-Philippe and Napoleon III among rulers. There are letters to young composers, to his fellow-critics, to his publishers, to instrument-makers, to singers and to strangers. The bulk of this selection, as of his surviving correspondence as a whole, is addressed to members of his family. It is well known that Berlioz was locked in contention with his family for many years over his choice of a profession and of a wife, yet his devotion to every member of his family was profound, especially to his father. His desire to please and impress his father with reports of his music (since there never seemed any likelihood that his father would travel to hear it) is touching in its naive belief that his father would ever reconcile himself to the loss of his son. Dr Berlioz had implanted his very soul in the soil of Dauphiné and assumed that the mantle of caring for his fellow-citizens as well as his fields and vineyards would pass down within the family for generations to come. For nearly every member of his family Berlioz's affection seems to have grown with the passing years: for his elder sister Nanci, who had been very unsympathetic over Hector's marriage, for his younger sister Adèle, who clearly adored her big brother, for his colourful and slightly disreputable soldier uncle Félix Marmion, for his two brothers-in-law Pal and Suat, and for his three nieces. Even after he had lost two parents, two sisters and two wives, he was drawn ever closer to the remaining members of his family. For his son Louis, above all, we can observe the powerful burgeoning of paternal love to the point where, in the 1860s, Louis – often away at sea for long periods – became the very centre of his emotional life. We cannot begin to grasp the agony that befell Berlioz in 1867 when Louis died.

More intimately than the *Mémoires* these letters also record the nature of his relationships with women. Contrary to popular belief, Berlioz was no Don Juan. For him the appetites of the flesh were much weaker than the appetites of the mind. Harriet Smithson was for ever the embodiment of Juliet and Ophelia; Camille Moke was, at least when she played the piano, a Shakespearean 'airy spirit'; Estelle in old age was the projection of a child's vision of female prettiness. It was as if Berlioz was always looking beyond women's external features to a fantasy image which other observers could not see. There remains the mystery of Marie Recio, Berlioz's second wife, with whom he shared twenty years of his life. If he ever created any fantasies about her he did not reveal them. This is a pity, since others found her an unattractive character and we have no record of his positive feelings about her, simply the stories of his attempts to escape from her in the early years of their relationship and of his real sense of loss when she died.

After Marie's death in 1862 it is striking how swiftly he found consolation in the company of Amélie, and how, as soon as he learnt of Amélie's death, he made contact with Estelle. Estelle responded to him with great dignity and staved off the suggestion of marriage which, we may be sure, almost rose to Berlioz's lips even if it was never formally proposed. This touching friendship was conveyed almost entirely in correspondence, and whereas she asked Berlioz to burn her letters, which he did, his letters to her are happily preserved, a remarkable testament of passionate devotion in the composer's declining years.

The present selection represents about one eighth of Berlioz's surviving correspondence. The letters have been chosen to provide, as far as possible, a continuous narrative of his life, recording events large and small and offering as broad a sample of his views and thoughts as possible. The composition, performance and publication of his music is naturally a constant theme. In his early years he devoted much energy to organizing and conducting concerts at his own expense as a way of presenting his music to the Parisian public. In the 1840s he tired of this, finding the expense prohibitive and public reaction too unpredictable. His attempt to share the burdens of concert-giving by forming a Société Philharmonique in 1850–51 was successful but short-lived. In his later years only *L'enfance du Christ* brought him success in Parisian concert halls, although fragments of his music appeared on concert programmes given by other conductors. Abroad it was a different story, since he was generally engaged for a fixed fee to appear as a conductor and to present programmes which included his own music. In the 1850s he was in great demand as a conductor, in London, Hanover, Dresden, Weimar and elsewhere, and reports of wildly enthusiastic receptions in Russia, Germany and England are a commonplace of his letters to family and friends. At the same time his letters reveal just how many propositions and plans came to nothing and how much energy was consumed preparing for concerts that never too place.

In private he wrote more honestly about men's music than he did in his feuilletons, on Halévy's *La juive*, for instance, or Gounod's *Faust* or Wagner's *Tristan* Prelude. His scorn of Handel, Haydn and most Italian music was balanced by his devotion to Gluck and Spontini. His appreciation of living composers was highly selective, for although he was close to Liszt he never uttered any admiration of his music; he had little to say about Schumann and Chopin, and of Mendelssohn he liked just a few pieces. We find, by contrast, a quite disproportionate – though short-lived – admiration for Glinka and Litolff. Yet no living composer was to be imagined as even close to the thrones on which his gods (Gluck, Beethoven and Spontini) sat.

His hostility to mediocrity and triviality remained constant. He hated any tampering with composers' original scores, including his own, and fought back fiercely when accused of maltreating Weber or misunderstanding Goethe or Shakespeare. He resisted accepting any engagement where too little rehearsal was offered and discouraged performances of his works by enthusiastic conductors whom he did not trust. Whereas in his early years his campaigning on behalf of his idols and his efforts to get a hearing for his own music had the excitement of an uncertain outcome, as if he were engaged in a fair fight with the Philistines, the second half of his life is a lamentable record of struggle and disappointment, since, it has to be acknowledged, the Philistines won. The Revolutions of 1848 provide a convenient point of reckoning, since the disorder in France brought home to Berlioz the perilous state of artistic enterprise, and the surrender of institutions like the Opéra to commercial and political interests symbolized the end of a dream. From then on he knew he could never expect official recognition and support, and his struggle to get the *Te Deum* and *Les Troyens* performed and his failure ever to hear the orchestral *Nuits d'été* or the magnificent *Tristia* is a tragic confirmation of the failure of his artistic ideals. Auber, Carafa, Clapisson and Offenbach made fortunes writing catchy tunes with banal accompaniments, while Berlioz battled against indifference, ill-health and a chronic shortage of funds.

He had a number of resources to fall back on, however. Not everything in his last years was a source of gloom. He had his friends and his correspondence, which could lift him from the blackest moods. He had sympathetic audiences abroad, so that he could rely on serious music-making in Weimar or Baden-Baden, for example. He had his sense of humour, which never deserted him and which makes the reading of his feuilletons and his letters a constant delight. He had his imagination, which could transport him to a Tahitian never-never land, or back to scenes from the *Aeneid*. He had his literary passions, for Shakespeare above all. And he had his memories, of childhood, of certain unforgettable scenes of Italian landscape, and of his early trials and triumphs in Paris.

*

The present selection is based on the edition of Berlioz's *Correspondance générale* under the general editorship of Pierre Citron and published by Flammarion, Paris, as follows:

Volume 1 (1803–1832), ed. Pierre Citron, Paris 1972
Volume 2 (1832–1842), ed. Frédéric Robert, Paris 1975
Volume 3 (1842–1850), ed. Pierre Citron, Paris 1978
Volume 4 (1851–1855), ed. Pierre Citron, Yves Gérard and Hugh Macdonald, Paris 1983
Volume 5 (1855–1859), ed. Hugh Macdonald and François Lesure, Paris 1989
Volume 6 (1859–1863), ed. Hugh Macdonald, in press
Volume 7 (1864–1869 and Supplement), in preparation

Thanks to the courtesy of M. Pierre Citron and Flammarion, Paris, we have been permitted to draw on the files of this grand enterprise for the texts of letters which have yet to appear in the series. Annotations in the present edition are my own, although I freely acknowledge my considerable debt to the *Correspondance générale*. In my notes I have not included first names or dates of individuals mentioned unless this information is useful, although it is provided in the Index. The reader who desires a closer annotation of the text and a discussion of textual and dating problems is referred to that series for greater detail. I have tried to include complete letters as often as possible, but where passages have been omitted, the indication [. . .] will be found. I have put standardized dates at the start of each letter and omitted addresses unless there was some reason for Berlioz to call attention to it. Some postscripts too have been omitted without comment, and where a letter begins or ends without any salutation this is normally because the available source does not give it. Letters known only from the 1879 publication *Correspondance inédite de Hector Berlioz*, for example, generally lack the composer's signing-off formula. The spelling of names and places has been regularized, however eccentric Berlioz's spelling may have been, and Russian dates are given new style.

I wish to thank Pierre Citron for his generous co-operation and for his boundless knowledge of music and literature. I am also greatly indebted to Richard Macnutt for making available the texts of many Berlioz letters from his collection.

SELECTED LETTERS

Hector Berlioz was born on 11 December 1803 in the little town of La Côte-St-André between Lyon and Grenoble. His father's family had been lawyers and doctors in the Dauphiné for some generations, and his father established a medical practice with a consuming interest in the well-being of the town and the agriculture and viniculture of the district. His mother's family came from Meylan, a few miles east of Grenoble.

Most of the boy's schooling was at his father's hands, with a particular emphasis on Latin poetry and French Classical and Enlightenment literature. His father also taught him the rudiments of music and left his son to explore the books in his library as well as a flageolet lying in a drawer. Later he studied the guitar with a local teacher, but there was no piano in the town and the most vivid childhood experiences of music at that time were provided by the somewhat rudimentary rendering of Catholic chant in the town church, sometimes brightened by adaptations of sacred texts to tunes from popular operas, also by the more military accents of the town band and the rough, though perhaps haunting, sound of peasants singing at their work.

Berlioz's instincts as a composer were quickly formed, perhaps more by reading about music and imagining sounds than by what he heard around him, and before any decision was made about his career – for his father there could be no question of anything other than medicine – he was bold enough, at the age of fifteen, to write to music publishers in Paris offering works of his own composition. These letters are the first surviving records of an immense correspondence that spanned half a century. The first letter in our selection is the first known letter from Berlioz's hand.

1 To Janet et Cotelle[1]   La Côte, 25 March 1819

Messieurs,

I should like to have several musical works engraved and I write to you in the hope that you will be able to meet my wishes. I suggest that you

1 A successful firm of Parisian music publishers founded in 1810.

undertake the edition at your own expense, with the provision that you send me a certain number of copies; please reply as soon as possible, if you are willing to do this. I will then send you a potpourri for an ensemble of flute, horn, two violins, viola and bass. By the time you have had this work engraved I shall be able to send you some *romances* with piano accompaniment and various others, all on the same terms.[1]

Yours respectfully,
Hector Berlioz

Berlioz left La Côte-St-André in October 1821 with his cousin Alphonse Robert to become a student at the Ecole de Médecine in Paris. They took lodgings in the Rue St-Jacques, on the left bank. Berlioz reacted with mixed feelings, sometimes fascination, sometimes revulsion, to his medical studies, but was ecstatic at the musical experiences the capital offered. He saw Salieri's Les Danaïdes *and Gluck's* Iphigénie en Tauride *at the Opéra within a month of his arrival. He also found a publisher for some* romances *he had brought with him from La Côte.*

2 *To his sister Nanci Berlioz*[2]   Paris, 13 December 1821

I've taken my time, dear Nanci, in replying to your charming letter, but as you know I had to write to papa last week, and this week I've written to Uncle Félix and Uncle Auguste and to grandpapa; added to which, Sundays have been one visit after another.

You attribute to me at the start of your letter an opinion on your character which I certainly do not hold; no, dear Nanci, I've never thought you were cold or indifferent towards me. Even though you are not very demonstrative, I've never felt that and, even if I had, your letter would have been enough to persuade me otherwise. You ask me what are my pleasures and sorrows. For the latter I answer with La Fontaine: 'Absence is the greatest of ills!' But there are others too, brought on sometimes by studies that I find revolting, sometimes by the discouragement I often feel when I've been working persistently and, at

---

1 The potpourri is lost, but the *romances* Berlioz mentions here may include some of the songs later published by other publishers. Janet et Cotelle seem to have published nothing by Berlioz.
2 Anne-Marguerite Berlioz, known as Nanci, the elder of Berlioz's two surviving sisters and his younger by three years. This is the first surviving letter to his family, written six weeks after his arrival in Paris.

the end of it, realize that I know nothing, that I have everything still to learn, that perhaps papa won't be pleased with me, that perhaps ... How am I to know? If I started to tell you all the gloomy thoughts that weigh on me, there'd be no end to it.

As for my pleasures, which are few in number, they invariably come down to strong emotions and tears. The only two I've experienced so far are M. Lacretelle's history course and the Opéra.[1] The word 'course' may not give you a true impression of how enjoyable it is; but the man talks like a God. The first day I listened to him, he gave us all a really cruel description of Henri IV's assassination. First he depicted in the most vivid colours the problems that beset Louis XIII's reign at the beginning, then, to my great delight, he provided as a contrast the picture of Sully in his peaceful retirement, bemoaning in secret his country's woes. He brought the figure of Sully before my eyes, such was his dignified tone as he told how this noble friend of Henri IV was summoned to Louis XIII's court, how he appeared in an old-fashioned coat and how this prompted the young King's courtiers to sarcastic laughter. As Sully approached the throne he threw a disdainful glance at the wretches who were mocking him and said, 'Sire, when the King, your father (of respected memory) used to do me the honour of summoning me to his court, he was careful, before I was introduced, to ensure the withdrawal of the clowns and buffoons.' That is the atmosphere in which the course is always conducted; I tell you, it's extremely enjoyable to listen to, but I can hardly ever go.

The Opéra, at the moment, is something of a different order and I don't feel I can possibly describe it to you. Short of actually fainting, I couldn't have felt stronger emotions than I did seeing Gluck's masterpiece *Iphigénie en Tauride*. Imagine first of all an orchestra of eighty players whose ensemble is so good, you'd say they were a single instrument. The opera begins: in the distance you see a vast plain (the illusion is absolute) and farther off still the sea; the orchestra warns of a storm and you see black clouds slowly descending and covering the whole plain; the theatre is lit only by flashes of lightning piercing the clouds, so true to life you would have to see to believe. There's a moment of silence, no one on stage; the orchestra is murmuring quietly, like the noise of the wind (you've felt it, I'm sure, in winter when you're alone, listening to the icy blast), well, that's exactly what it's like. Imperceptibly the disturbance grows, the storm breaks and

1 Charles de Lacretelle, who taught at the Sorbonne, published a number of books on French history.

you see the arrival of Orestes and Pylades in chains. They are led by the barbarians of Tauris who intone these fearful words, 'Il faut du sang pour venger nos crimes'. It's too much to stand; I defy the most insensitive human being not to be profoundly moved, seeing these two unhappy men talking about death as the ultimate good, and when finally Orestes is the one to reject it, then it is his sister, it is Iphigenia, the priestess of Diana, who has to cut her brother's throat. It's appalling; I could never come near to giving you a true description of the horror one feels when Orestes, overwhelmed, falls to the ground with the words, 'Le calme rentre dans mon cœur'. He's in a reverie and you see the ghost of the mother he has murdered prowling around him with various spectral figures, holding two infernal torches in their hands and waving them about his head. And the orchestra! All that was in the orchestra. If you could only have heard how it describes every situation, especially when Orestes appears to be calm; the violins have a very quiet held note, a symbol of tranquillity; but underneath you can hear the basses murmuring like the remorse which, despite his apparent calm, still lurks deep in the heart of the parricide.

But I'm getting carried away; goodbye, my dear Nanci, forgive me these digressions and believe as always in my profoundest love and affection.

Hector Berlioz
Embrace everyone for me.

3 *To his sister Nanci Berlioz*   Paris, 20 February 1822

How are you spending carnival time, my dear Nanci? As though it were Lent, no doubt; so the passage from one to the other won't be all that abrupt, will it? ... The same goes for me; even so, I've received four invitations to go to balls these last few days from M. Teisseyre,[1] both at his own house and that of some people he knows. We refused the first two but as he went to call and said that we knew how to dance, he committed us for the Friday and the Sunday in such a way that we couldn't refuse. So we went. If perhaps you think that balls in Paris are different from ours at home, then you're wrong: the only difference is in the numbers, with sixty people dancing instead of sixteen, as with us, and even though the salons are large there's such a squeeze that the male dancers have to stand behind the females for want of space and concentrate every moment so as not to tread on anyone. The women all

---

1 The Teisseyre family were from Grenoble.

wear white and the men black. And if you are inclined to suppose that the orchestra is superb, well, it's not even as good as ours; just think of it, two violins and a flageolet; what a sorry show, two violins and a flageolet! I couldn't get over it. The whole evening practically, these three wretches played *contredanses* from ballets I'd heard at the Opéra; some comparison, as you can imagine. In the end we couldn't stand it any longer. We left at one o'clock and tried to think of a way of escaping Sunday evening. We found one soon enough, going to see my uncle who said we must have dinner together the next day; so we wrote to M. Teisseyre pretending that my uncle was just passing through and wanted to spend the evening with us, which solved the problem quite nicely.

We had a delightful dinner with cousin Raymond and my uncle; afterwards we went to the Feydeau theatre to hear Martin; that evening they were playing *Azémia* and *Les voitures versées* and I made up for lost time![1] I soaked up the music. I thought of you, Nanci, and how much you would have enjoyed listening to it. Perhaps you wouldn't enjoy the Opéra so much, it's too learned for you, but this music by Dalayrac is so touching and enchanting, Boieldieu's so gay, the actresses' *tours de force* so startling, Martin and Ponchard so perfect . . . I would have thrown my arms round Dalayrac's neck if I'd been standing next to his statue when I heard that aria which is beyond all description, 'Ton amour, ô fille chérie'. It was almost the same sensation I felt at the Opéra when I heard the aria from *Stratonice*,[2] 'Versez tous vos chagrins dans le sein paternel'. But I'm not going to describe that music to you again . . .

4 To his sister Nanci Berlioz   Paris, ?February 1823

My dear sister,

This reply will be much like your letter. I shall be as brief and disorganized as you, if not for the same reasons. Your agitation came from looking forward to the promised pleasure of your PICNIC, but my reasons are rather different and I haven't the time to explain them to you. The important thing is that you enjoyed yourself and that the cold pâté was good; presumably you couldn't dance for lack of male partners, since MM. Just and Laurent are in Grenoble. Unless they were

1 The Feydeau was the home of the Opéra-Comique. Jean-Blaise Martin was a celebrated baritone. Dalayrac's *Azémia* dates from 1786, Boieldieu's *Les voitures versées* from 1808.
2 Méhul's *Stratonice* (1792).

gallant enough to return for the occasion, Mlle Veyron and yourself will have found yourselves Queens without a Pawn and the evening will have been a wretched one, because you must be aware that these two gentlemen provoke hilarity wherever they go.

But enough nonsense. Papa's errands have been performed, the box was sent off, so I was assured in the office, on 26 January; it should therefore have arrived by now. The two copies of Miss Edgeworth[1] were posted the day after I received the request.

I forgot to send word to papa that the box contained two volumes for Edouard. I think I put them in an envelope with their address. There's still no sign of the works he's expecting; as soon as one of them is published, I'll post it.

Personally, I was obliged to dance twice; those two evenings would have been difficult to take *personally* but by indulging in refreshments and pastries of every variety I managed to get through them.

There's something more I have to tell you, I think, which I mustn't forget . . . What else? . . .

Ah yes, Alphonse
is
keeping
well

———

I
hope
this
finds
you
well
also

———

H. Berlioz

P.S. If you want to write nonsense to me, don't worry, it'll make it easier for me to write back.

P.P.S. In her last letter mama asked what state my trunk was in when it arrived. You can tell her that everything was in good order except two linen shirts, three fine cotton shirts, three pairs of socks, a waistcoat and a pair of underpants which were smeared with jam. One of the

———

1 Maria Edgeworth, whose novels were widely read in France.

pots broke on the journey and let its precious contents escape. But that won't happen again; there are good reasons for that.

Towards the end of 1822 the Ecole de Médecine was closed down by government order in response to political unrest, and it did not reopen for five months. During that period Berlioz became a pupil of Jean-François Le Sueur, one of France's leading composers, a move that precipitated his commitment to music. He did not resume his medical studies, although he seems to have assured his distraught father that he would hold open the possibility of some career other than music. Berlioz's mind, however, was made up, and a long period of family difficulties ensued. Le Sueur's family, on the other hand, treated him with affection.

5 *To Rodolphe Kreutzer*[1]   Paris, summer of 1823

O genius!

I succumb: I die! Tears choke me! *La mort d'Abel*: ye gods! ...

That unspeakable public! It feels nothing! What must one do for it to be moved? ...

O genius! And what shall I do if, one day, my music depicts emotions? I shall not be understood, since they do not crown the composer of all that is beautiful, nor carry him in triumph, nor prostrate themselves before him!

Sublime, heart-rending, full of pathos!

Ah! I can no more; I must write! To whom shall I write? To the genius? ... No, I dare not.

It is to the man, it is to Kreutzer ... he will laugh at me ..., never mind ...; I should die if I kept silent. Ah! Why can I not see him, speak to him? He would listen, he would see what passes in my tormented soul. Perhaps he would restore in me the courage that I have lost, seeing those unfeeling, niggardly scoundrels who are barely fit to hear that clown Rossini's pantalooneries.

If the pen did not fall from my hand, I should never finish.

AH! GENIUS!!!

H. Berlioz

pupil of Le Sueur

1 The French violinist whose name was immortalized by Beethoven's dedication of his Violin Sonata in A major op. 47. He composed over forty operas of which *La mort d'Abel*, first heard in 1810 and revived in 1823, is perhaps the finest.

My poor Adèle, your letter very nearly got lost; you'd hidden it inside a book, so well that I was convinced for three days it had been mislaid and it was only when I made another search that I discovered it. I passed on your message to Mlle Clémentine Le Sueur; she thanks you and asks me to send you all her best wishes.

I was obliged to go to the ball three weeks ago, when I was one of these ladies' squires. You can imagine how bored I was. As soon as we arrived, M. Schlösser[2] and I danced the first *contredanse* with the Le Sueur girls, then, when we asked the daughter of the house, she replied that her card was full for the next fourteen dances. So we retired from the fray and I remained a spectator for the rest of the evening; there were ten times as many dancers as there should have been.

Alphonse is well. I had a visit yesterday from M. Du Boys of Grenoble who brought me a letter from Casimir Faure. We're all having dinner tomorrow with M. Teisseyre.

Tell Nanci that I intended to write to her today, but I can't put two ideas together – it's all I can do to write legibly.

Adieu.

I'll write at greater length some other time.

Your friend,

Hector Berlioz

One of the most enduring of Berlioz's friendships was formed in 1823 with Humbert Ferrand (1805–68), a law student who spent most of his life after 1827 far from Paris in Belley and Sardinia. Ferrand had a considerable literary output of all kinds and wrote the libretto for Berlioz's opera Les francs-juges. *Their correspondence continued until Ferrand's death a few months before Berlioz's.*

Under Le Sueur's tutelage Berlioz wrote an enormous quantity of music, mostly now lost. In May 1824 he gained his first commission, for a Messe solennelle *to be performed at the church of St-Roch. He returned to La Côte that summer to visit his family for six weeks.*

---

1 Adèle-Eugénie Berlioz , Berlioz's younger sister, his younger by eleven years.
2 Probably Théodore, brother of Louis Schlösser, both musician friends of Berlioz's.

My dear Ferrand,

No sooner am I out of the capital than I can no longer resist the need to converse with you. I asked you specifically not to write to me until a fortnight after my departure, so that I would not be too long without news of you after that; but now I'm asking you to write as soon as possible, because I hope you won't be so idle as to content yourself with writing to me once and then leaving me to languish for two months, like the man of sorrow who was far from the rock of Hope and who was quite happy to go and have a vanilla ice-cream at Tortoni's (Poitier, *in lib.* Blousac, p. 32).[1]

I had a rather dull journey as far as Tarare: there I *got down* to *go up* on foot and found myself, rather against my better judgment, in conversation with two young men who had the air of being dilettanti and were, as such, to be avoided.[2] They began by explaining that they were going to Mont St-Bernard to do some landscapes and that they were learning painting from MM. Guérin and Gros; I told them in my turn that I was a pupil of Le Sueur. They expressed a host of compliments on the subject of my teacher's talent and character and, while we were talking, one of them began to hum a chorus from *Les Danaïdes*.

'*Les Danaïdes*!' I cried, 'so you're not a dilettante?'

'Me, a dilettante?' he replied, 'I've seen Dérivis and Mme Branchu[3] thirty-four times in the roles of Danaüs and Hypermnestra.'

'Ah! . . .'

And we throw our arms round each other without further ado.

'Ah, monsieur, Mme Branchu! . . . ah! . . . M. Dérivis! . . . What talent! . . . What passion!'

'I know Dérivis well', said his friend.

'So do I. And I'm lucky enough to know that sublime soprano too.'

'Ah, monsieur, how lucky you are! They say that quite apart from her prodigious talent she is well worth knowing for her wit and excellent character.'

'That is certainly true.'

'But, messieurs', I said, 'how is it that, not being musicians, you have avoided contamination by the dilettante virus, and that Rossini has not

1 Tortoni's was a well-known Paris café, but the literary reference is an invention.
2 The worst crime of the 'dilettanti', in Berlioz's opinion, was to admire Italian music to the detriment of French.
3 Dérivis was the leading bass at the Opéra in the period 1820–40. Mme Branchu sang the leading soprano roles in Gluck's and Salieri's operas until 1826.

made you turn your back on naturalness and common sense?'

'The reason is', they replied, 'that being accustomed in painting to strive for what is great, beautiful and, above all, natural, we could not mistake these qualities in the sublime tableaux of Gluck and Salieri, any more than we could in the tender, heart-rending accents of Mme Branchu and her worthy imitator. As a result, fashionable music appeals to us no more than arabesques or sketches of the Flemish school.'

A timely meeting, my dear Ferrand! Here were men of feeling, connoisseurs fit to go to the Opéra, fit to hear and understand *Iphigénie en Tauride*. We exchanged addresses and will meet again in Paris on our return.

Have you been to see *Orphée* again, with M. Nivière, and did you get something out of it? Are you still working as enthusiastically as ever at our project? Remember me to M. Berlioz;[1] I'm not surprised he's a dilettante, because you have to know about music to appreciate grand opera, whereas you have to be ignorant about it to be able to listen to a Rossini opera all the way through. He, I think, comes in the latter category. Adieu; all goes well with me. My father is totally on my side and mama is already calmly talking about my return, to Paris.

Your friend,
H. Berlioz

8 *To Edouard Rocher*[2]   La Côte-St-André, 22 June 1824

I don't know what in Heaven's name you can have been up to, but you couldn't even write to me when they were putting on *Iphigénie en Aulide*. And I wasn't there; I expect you went and this time you'll have understood it better and been more deeply moved. Who was playing Achilles? Would the Iphigenia have been Mlle Grassari, by any chance? Was Lafond passable? Answer all these questions as soon as you get my letter. The devil take me, I'm in such a state I feel I shall be all burnt up within a month. I can't get *Iphigénie en Tauride* out of my head. The other day I was singing some of the numbers and got quite carried away. I began to tremble so violently, weeping and dribbling from the mouth, and my heart began to beat so fearfully that I went up to my

---

1 Louis-Auguste Berlioz, apparently no relation, was a medical student and a friend of Berlioz and Ferrand.
2 Edouard Rocher was a friend from La Côte whose family had a number of commercial interests including the liqueur now known as Cherry Rocher. He was a student in Paris from 1823 to 1826.

room so as not to be discovered in such a state, and as soon as I got through the door I felt so ill I had to sit down. And I shan't be able to see it staged! And Mme Branchu will never again play Iphigenia! . . . Talking of which, I didn't tell you that on my last visit she explained that it was a question of the pitch; if it was lowered, she would go back to playing Alceste, Armide, etc.[1]

Ah! . . .

Alceste   Armide

Now *there* are operas for you and they have one advantage over *Orphée*: they won't please those dilettanti dogs, whereas *Orphée* has been tainted with their approval.

Young Deplagne invited me to have dinner last night at Le Pion with Victor Robert.[2] We drank white wine (ah, white wine!) and ate a first-rate leg of mutton. It was raining like the devil and we went and came back under good, large umbrellas; listening to the rain gave me gooseflesh and I said, 'Grands dieux! soyez-nous secourables. Détournez vos foudres vengeurs!'[3]

The next time you go to the Opéra and walk along the new arcade, try and have a word with M. Moulineuf, to give him my news and best wishes. Tell him that when I get back to Grenoble I'll be glad to write to him.

All the best to Laurent, Alphonse, Charles and to the two distinguished amateurs of the Rue St-Hyacinte.

Adieu. I embrace you. Your friend, as always,

H. Berlioz

9 *To Jean-François Le Sueur*   La Côte-St-André, July 1824

Monsieur,

I have for some time been tormented with the desire to write to you but did not dare to do so, for a number of reasons each of which now seems to me more ridiculous than the last. I was afraid that I might seem to be importuning you with my letters and that you might think that my desire to write to you sprang from *amour-propre*, understandable in a young man corresponding with one of those rare and outstanding figures who astonish their compatriots as much as they honour their country by their genius and knowledge. But I reasoned with myself that this distinguished man to whom I was burning to

1 The pitch at the Opéra had been raised in 1823 from A = 423 to A = 431·5.
2 Deplagne was a local friend, Victor Robert a cousin.
3 'Great Gods! Come to our aid! Hold off your vengeful lightning!' Iphigenia's aria in Act I of *Iphigénie en Tauride*, following a storm.

write would perhaps find my letters less importunate if they dealt with the art to which he brings such renown. This great composer has been kind enough to allow me to take part in his lessons, and if ever the inordinate patience and kindness of a master and the gratitude and (if I may say) the filial affection of his pupils have granted him the title of father in their regard, then I count myself as one of his children.

My family greeted me as I had been expecting, that is to say with enthusiasm; at no time did I have to counter those sad, pointless remonstrances from my mother which used only to upset both of us. Papa suggested, as a precaution, that I should never speak about music in front of her. With him, on the other hand, I speak about it quite often. I told him about the curious discoveries you were kind enough to show me in your book on ancient music. I couldn't manage to persuade him that the ancients knew about harmony: he was full of the ideas of Rousseau and other writers who have lent their authority to the opposite viewpoint. But when I quoted to him the passages in Latin (from Pliny the Elder, I think) in which there are details on ways of accompanying the voice and on how easy it is for the orchestra to depict passions by means of different rhythms from those in the vocal parts, then he was astounded and confessed that such an explanation left him with nothing to say in reply. 'Even so', he said to me, 'I should need to see the passage with my own eyes before I was convinced.'

So far I have done nothing since my arrival. To begin with my time was not my own as it was almost entirely taken up in the first few weeks with visits to and from people in the town – as it's so small, everyone knows everyone else. Then, when I wanted to start on that Mass I spoke to you about, my first reading of the *Credo* and the *Kyrie* left my brain frozen stiff. I was convinced I could never accomplish anything in such a state of mind, so I abandoned the idea. I have started to revise that oratorio *Le passage de la mer rouge*, which I showed you seven or eight months ago, parts of which I now find horribly bungled. I hope to have it performed at St-Roch when I get back to Paris, which should be before the beginning of August.

I look forward to seeing you again. In the meantime my father asks me to pass on to you his gratitude for all the kindness you have shown me, a gratitude of which I too most sincerely partake.

Your devoted servant and pupil,
Hector Berlioz

Please remember me to Mme and Mlles Le Sueur and give them my respects.

My dear papa,

You must surely realize how surprised and upset I was by your letter and there is no need for me to dwell on the fact.[1] I take the liberty of hoping that your heart disowns the cruel words it contained. I still do not understand how the letter I left with Alphonse could have had such an effect on you; I do not think there was anything in it that I have not said or communicated to you a hundred times; and I do not think that, in speaking of my parents, any word escaped me that did not belong to the feelings of a loving and respectful son.

I am being dragged involuntarily towards a magnificent career (there is no other epithet fitting for a career in the arts) and not towards my destruction. I believe I shall succeed, yes, I believe it, and considerations of modesty are no longer relevant. In order to prove to you that I am not trusting to luck, I think, in fact I am convinced that I shall distinguish myself in music, all the external signs point to it; and within me the voice of nature is stronger than the most forceful restraints of reason. Every conceivable opportunity is open to me, if you will give me your support. I am starting young, I should not have to give lessons as so many men do in order to make a living. I have some knowledge and possess the basis of yet more, which one day I can develop, and certainly my feelings are strong enough for me not to be in doubt when it comes to depicting them or giving them utterance.

If lack of success on my part were to condemn me, without leave of appeal, to die of hunger (not that I would cease to strive for the truth on that account), then your reasoning at least and your anxiety would have some foundation; but this is far from being the case and, at the lowest estimate, I can count on one day having a private income of 2000 francs. Even if we say only 1500, I could live even so on that amount, or if we said only 1200, I should be happy with that even if I was earning nothing from music. The fact is that I want to make a name for myself, I want to leave on this earth some traces of my existence; and such is the strength of this feeling, which in itself is nothing if not noble, that I would rather be Gluck or Méhul dead than who I am in the flower of my youth. Such was the ambition of the celebrated composer Marcello, who had to overcome prejudices far

1 The visit to La Côte ended in crisis when Berlioz's determination to become a musician ran headlong into his mother's disapproval of the artistic professions and his father's profound disappointment that his son was not to succeed him in his practice and patrimony.

stronger than those normally held against artists because he was the son of the Doge of Venice, and his father would rather have seen him at the bottom of the ocean than in a career which, in his eyes, covered both himself and his family with such dishonour. Well, who today would remember that there was a Doge of Venice called Marcello if his son had not immortalized the name by his sublime sacred music, heard to this day in the great churches of Italy and Germany? . . .[1]

One of your objections has often been the enormous difference between my extra-musical knowledge and that of M. Le Sueur, who knows the ancient languages and mathematics. But, as he was saying to me again yesterday, he acquired this knowledge like everyone else, at school, and then developed it over a long period afterwards when he realized the relationship that exists between some kinds of knowledge and music. He began by becoming a great composer before being a learned one; and if my preliminary plan of study finds no place for Greek or Hebrew or mathematics, there is no gainsaying the fact that this will neither increase nor diminish the opportunities open to me once I have committed myself to music.

That is my way of thinking, that is how I am and nothing on this earth will change me; you could withdraw all your support and force me to leave Paris, but I do not believe you will do so. You would not want me to lose the best years of my life, or to break the magnetic needle because you cannot change its polar attraction.

Adieu, dear papa. Read my letter again and do not think that it was written in a fit of passion; never, perhaps, have I been so calm.

My fondest embrace to you and to mama and my sisters.

Your respectful and loving son

H. Berlioz

11 *To his uncle Victor Berlioz*[2]   Paris, August or September 1824

My dear uncle,

This long delay in writing to you should not be regarded as a sign of my being remiss or forgetful of my duty. The real reason is that I did not dare to write, knowing that you were angry with me; I did not know how to excuse my departure, although papa will no doubt have explained afterwards why it was shrouded in secrecy. It was hard for

---

1 Benedetto Marcello (1686–1739) was the most popular Baroque composer in France in Berlioz's time. His father was a Venetian senator, not Doge.
2 Dr Berlioz's youngest brother and a magistrate in Grenoble.

me to leave you without acquainting you of the fresh proof I had received of his affection, and it was harder still to embrace a career which you disapprove of and which was bound to cause my family suffering. But what could I do? My fatal destiny was impelling me despite myself and any other occupation would have made me the most miserable of men. It seems to me also that with the arts one can pay society the dues she expects of us; this part of our knowledge, and music especially, elevates the soul by increasing its sensibility, and since from this quality spring those of the heart the cultivation of the fine arts cannot deprave mankind. As for the degree of celebrity one can thereby attain, I hope, with the aid and support of my great master, one day to distinguish myself. I do not suppose that you share my opinion in this matter, but I venture to hope that I have not forfeited your affection and that you do not doubt that of your respectful and loving nephew,

  H. Berlioz

12 *To Edouard Rocher*   Paris, 4 September 1824

Fear not, my dear Edouard, I never believed what I said to you in my last letter.[1] I only pushed things so far to get you to admit that you didn't go to *Les Danaïdes*. I couldn't believe that Marc[2] had lied so barefacedly and I was happy to demonstrate to you that the man who tries to prove too much ends up by proving nothing; that's the use your deceitfulness was put to. You've provided sticks to beat both yourself and Marc; he has no doubt now that all your admiration for *La mort d'Abel*, etc,[3] is just pretence. So why were you silly enough to show him your letter and to go to his house the evening they were putting on *Les Danaïdes*? If you'd done it on purpose, you couldn't have fallen more heavily into the trap.

They've just revived Piccinni's masterpiece.[4] Dido was played by a new young singer, Mlle Noël. She has a superb, immense voice, almost as good as Mme Branchu's, but she doesn't know how to use it. She has no feeling for the stage, no idea of facial expression or how to carry herself; she knows absolutely nothing about musical declamation, speaks the recitatives in a way that destroys their meaning, and I incline to the belief that she lacks sensibility. The little she showed can all be

1 See p. 12.
2 Marc Rocher, Edouard's cousin.
3 See p. 9.
4 *Didon* (1783).

attributed to Piccinni's tender, expressive melodic line which is irresistible. She sang well in the aria 'Ah, que je fus bien inspirée!', but the mad scene, dear God! I'm still trembling with rage. When she sang 'Tyriens, accourez! Embrasez les vaisseaux! Que dis-je, malheureuse!', O Mme Branchu, where were you?

All the sung part of the opera is sublime, but the recitatives are worthless, just Italian recitatives, the same thing throughout, no underlining of the meaning, no truth, no orchestral colouring.

Dérivis is superb, magnificent, admirable in the role of Iarbas. Nourrit the elder[1] played the role of Aeneas with real heroic warmth. I was dumbfounded by their sublime duet 'C'est donc toi que Didon couronne'; the effect was about three quarters of that produced on us by Cain's aria 'Abel seul est aimable'. So that gives you some idea. [. . .]

I'm working furiously on the composition of my Mass. I'm being promised marvels for its performance and I think my family's persecutions are only spurring me on; I wrote a letter back to papa the day before yesterday telling him clearly and succinctly what I think. It will produce a reaction, I'm sure. [. . .]

Ever your friend,
H. Berlioz

13 *To J.-C.-F. Letexier*[2]   Paris, 21 January 1825

Monsieur,

You must have found my behaviour at the Opéra the day before yesterday distinctly curious and if anything could justify it, it would be the delirium into which I, as well as you, was plunged by Dérivis and Sacchini. I'm afraid I committed a serious indiscretion in asking you for your address, but I shall not abuse your politeness; your business is no doubt too important and your stay in Paris too short perhaps for me to take the liberty of coming and seeing you. I dare to take that of writing to you to express my delight at finding in you that sensitivity and admiration for the truly beautiful which I had thought long since lost.

I am an artist, Monsieur, I am going to be a composer and I am a pupil of M. Le Sueur. You can imagine how painful it is for a musician who is devoured with passion for his art to see the cold insensitivity of the public when masterpieces of our school are performed, and to hear

1 Louis Nourrit, a tenor, like his illustrious son Adolphe.
2 At a performance of Sacchini's *Oedipe à Colonne* on 19 January 1825 Berlioz encountered a kindred spirit passionately moved, as was he, by the music. Berlioz took his address; he was an engineer.

continuous blasphemies against Gluck, Sacchini, Méhul, Le Sueur, Dérivis and the sublime Mme Branchu, in fact everything that is calculated to bring sensitive souls to the highest pitch of enthusiasm. So when I find one of those fiery souls who are not prevented by fanaticisim or the prejudices of fashion from being carried away by works of genius, I want not only to get to know them but to make them known to the whole world.

If you are still in Paris on 19 March, it is likely that a solemn Mass of mine with full orchestra will be performed in Ste-Geneviève.[1] I hope that Dérivis will sing the solos and if your other concerns allow you to come and hear it I should be extremely flattered.

Yours most sincerely,
Hector Berlioz

14 *To his sister Nanci Berlioz*   Paris, *c.* 2 March 1825

My dear sister,

I beg you to write and tell me as soon as possible why papa and mama should be adopting a policy of the strictest silence towards me since I replied to your letter. If you read my reply, you will have found nothing, I'm sure, that came from other than a submissive and respectful son, since I told my father that if he insisted, despite my observations and the uselessness of my spending time at La Côte, I would sacrifice a whole year's work and several years of my future to his wishes. Tell me as soon as you can if there is no hope of my being sent money, either to leave or stay, and what I should do with myself. I admit I cannot view the idea of staying at La Côte without alarm, as you yourself are ranged against me to the extent of writing me a letter in which you claim that I have to prove

1   that I can be a composer and at the same time remain a son, a brother and a friend

2   that the status of composer is not incompatible with social life

3   that I am capable of thought and reason

4   that I am not guided by instinct

5   that I am sensible of the demands of time, place, custom and manners

6   that I am not the enemy of all moral and physical order

---

1 Now the Panthéon. The first performance of the *Messe solennelle* had not taken place in December 1824 as planned, since hardly anyone attended the final rehearsal. The Ste-Geneviève plan did not work out either.

7   that I can combine the qualities of an honest man with those of a composer

8   that working to promote admiration does not bar me from being respected

It follows that if I possess all the faults which you would have me correct, I am a *bad son*, a *bad brother* and a *bad friend*, a *savage*, an *idiot* and a *madman*, a *brute beast*, an *overthrower of all moral and physical order*, a *dishonest man*, a vile and despicable being, in a word a *stupid wild animal* to be approached with the utmost caution. I strongly suggest therefore that if I do return to La Côte a kennel should be built for me at the end of the yard where I can be kept chained up as a safety measure. You see, my dear Nanci, what preposterous and absurd conclusions this high-handed attitude leads to.

I remain nonetheless your brother and your friend,

H.B.

15 *To his father Dr Louis Berlioz*   Paris, 25 April 1825

My dear papa,

The letter I have just received from mama confirms my view that you are increasingly mistaken about me; she is against me to such an extent that she claims I never really wrote that letter in March, the loss of which has led to so many misunderstandings. I never should have thought it possible that I would be accused of such shameless and protracted lying. My attempts to find the letter at the main post office have been fruitless, but I am quite sure I posted it and did not lose it; it must have been mislaid in the office at La Côte.

It seems, dear papa, as though I shall not be able to change your mind about me, so I am set to be a bad son, a bad brother, an idiot, a man unworthy of the regard of reasonable people! . . . For a father to arrive at such an opinion of his son he must have had grievous cause for complaint against him and have suffered from his behaviour more bitterly than he had ever expected to do. That I have caused the dearest of fathers such bitter suffering I can, alas, be in no doubt, and my regret is all the more profound in that I am myself incapable of alleviating it; but that my behaviour has been reprehensible I do not believe, because it has never been in my power to change it and the reasons that motivate it are nothing if not just and noble.

Believe me, dear papa, I am desolate that my destined career is not what my parents would have chosen, but I have thought long and hard about it and there is nothing I can do to choose another one. My whole being reacts against it and I am totally lacking in the strength of character necessary for any such operation. I am capable of extraordinary efforts and even of amazing perseverance in finishing something in which my passions are engaged, but a daily struggle against myself, a long labour leading to a conclusion in which I have no interest, a continual resistance to desires that would only reawaken each time I suppressed them, these are beyond me and I should find them quite impossible. Even if I did succeed in this respect, your wishes for me would not be fulfilled: I should not be happy because I should not believe I was, while no setbacks that occurred in a career of my own choosing would find me disposed to complain. There are any number of cases which prove my point. Look at Levaillant, our most celebrated explorer and naturalist, who has just died. His life was a happy one despite all the hardships and dangers he underwent. So keen was he on hunting and travelling that scarcely had he survived one danger before he was in the thick of another. He would have crossed vast deserts, suffered thirst and hunger, in short courted death in all its most terrible forms in order to catch a bird or an animal missing from his collections. When he found what he had been searching for, his joy was boundless. He himself remembered the day when, after indescribable difficulties, he killed the giraffe now in our zoo and how he was happier than any man had ever been; he rolled around on the ground, shouting.

Surely, you must agree, dear papa, that a man of that kind could not possibly turn aside from the path along which nature directed him and that it would be useless and even cruel to want to reform those who find themselves in a similar situation.

The difficulties that face anyone making a start as an operatic composer are very great, no doubt; I see them more clearly than anybody and do not blind myself as to their size or number. But they are certainly not so great that, with perseverance, prudence and talent, one cannot eventually overcome them.

The 200 francs that you were kind enough to send me at the beginning of the month will not last me beyond 3 or 4 May, because I have had to repay 50 francs which I owed for the paper and the copying I had to pay for.

I bought a hat which cost me 20 francs.

I had my boots mended, 14 francs.

I had two pairs of slippers made, 14 francs.

And now, dear papa, I am going to make a request which you will perhaps find exorbitant. I really should like to possess the complete works of Volney, made up as you know of *Les ruines, Voyage en Syrie, Tableau général des Etats-Unis, Lettres sur la Grèce* and *Recherches sur l'histoire ancienne.*[1] The existing edition is splendid but it is the only one and is on the point of being sold out; the government is not allowing it to be reprinted and the price is going up daily. Three months ago it cost 40 francs; now you cannot buy it for less than 64 francs and despite the increase in price there are only twenty copies left.

Adieu, dear papa, and please believe that I am not that far from being the son you would like me to be and that one day I shall recompense you for all the heartache I have caused you.

Your respectful and loving son,
H. Berlioz

16 *To his mother Mme Berlioz*[2]   Paris, 14 July 1825

My dear mama,

I expect you have heard from Edouard that the recent performance of my Mass was a considerable success.[3] If I have taken time in acquainting you of this fact, it is not that I had the slightest doubt of the pleasure it would give you; in spite of the desire you and papa share to see me pursuing my studies in some other direction, you love me too much to be pained by something which has caused me such joy. The sole reason, dear mama, for this delay is that I wanted to wait and see my success confirmed in the newspapers. Some half dozen of them are encouraging and enthusiastic, but unfortunately none of them can be got at La Côte: they are *L'aristarque, Le drapeau blanc, Le moniteur, Le corsaire* and *Le journal de Paris*. I'm buying them as they appear and intend to arrive home armed with the necessary documents.

It was the finest performance you can imagine, with 150 participants. I was able to overcome the most intractable problems thanks to the support of my teacher, the director of the Opéra and the conductor,[4] and especially because of the keenness they showed.

As soon as it was over, all sorts of compliments, questions and invitations fell about me like hail so that I did not know which person

1 Berlioz could count on his father's sympathy with the rationalist writings of the Count de Volney (1757–1820).
2 Marie-Antoinette-Joséphine Berlioz, née Marmion (1784–1838).
3 The *Messe solennelle* was performed in the church of St-Roch on 10 July 1825, thanks to a loan from Berlioz's friend Augustin de Pons. It was the first public performance of any of his works.
4 Valentino, assistant conductor at the Opéra.

to answer. But all this amateur enthusiasm was not what I was after: I wanted the approval of the artists and connoisseurs and I was lucky enough to obtain it. It was really wonderful to hear all these musicians, hardened critics of the current artistic scene, coming up to me and saying that I had thrilled them, that I had a demonic temperament, that my crescendos had left them breathless, that I would go far, that I needed to cultivate moderation, etc, etc, etc. I had to endure a quarter of an hour's harangue from the vicar of St-Roch, who wanted to convince me that Jean-Jacques Rousseau had perverted the public's taste in music as he had done in literature, and that I had been chosen to bring them back on to the right path; after which I escaped to go and talk to my teacher who had sent word that he was waiting for me.

As soon as M. Le Sueur appeared, he embraced me; I did not know where to put myself. I was completely overwhelmed when he began saying how happy and gratified he was, how he had even been carried away. He then told me that he had hidden himself away in a corner of the church so as not to be recognized, and had seen and heard the amazing effect my music had had on the public. Mme Le Sueur and her daughters had sat in another part of the church and they too told me what they had seen and heard and the compliments they had been asked to pass on to me, also how bitter and annoyed Berton's pupils were with it all.

So that is the first step at last successfully accomplished, but at the same time I have seen how much work I still have to do. The bulk of the audience, being swept away by the vigour of my ideas, did not notice the many faults in the work. These have been pointed out to me, I acknowledge them and will do my utmost to avoid them another time.

Adieu, dear mama, I will write again in a few days. I have not had the time today to give you more details, as I have hardly spent as much as two hours in the daytime at home.

Your affectionate son,

H. B.

In August 1825 Berlioz paid another visit to La Côte and stayed until November. Relations with his parents were still strained, even if the episode of his mother's curse, dramatically narrated in the Mémoires, *belongs not to this visit but, as is more likely, to an earlier one. Berlioz's debts were a sore point, yet his independence and determination were greater than ever when he returned to Paris to resume his career, now launched by the performance of the Mass.*

My dear Nanci,

Your letter arrived most inopportunely. Don't take umbrage at that word, but listen.

Today I'm in the middle of one of those stormy moods that I'm liable to. A multitude of ideas are crowding into my head, bumping into each other, tangling with each other, making my blood boil, in a word agitating me in an extraordinary fashion. I'm incapable of giving you a description of this state but I can give you the reasons for it. I have come to experience this species of malady only since I have been involving myself seriously with music (that's to say, since I've been capable of reflection and have attached great importance to certain ideas). In general it is occasioned by a sudden thought which appears like a flash of lightning and snatches me out of my ordinary state, bringing a blush to my cheeks and leaving me prone to an extreme exaltation of imagination and feeling. For example: I am struck with a profound admiration for some idea of vaguely human character, I need passionately to share it, I run, I fly ... I meet a cold individual who doesn't understand me or who is of an opinion contrary to mine; a truth unrecognized; a triumphant idiocy and no possibility of destroying it; the spectacle of happiness or fame that is undeserved; and above all the spectacle of a triumph justly obtained. Yes, nothing moves me so deeply or dramatically as the sight of some signal tribute paid to genius, or indeed to talent. I suddenly think again of my own case, that some day a similar tribute will be mine, that even as I am now I am capable of writing works that are great, passionate, energetic, true – in a word, beautiful.*

I'm sure that if I were well known my life would be entirely different. But reason assures me that time alone can bring about that happy state of things and that the man whose life I envy has been through the same trials as I have and has felt the same emotions. The painful, almost unbearable condition I find myself in is like that of one of a band of slaves who sees his comrades set free one by one and is aware that his own release is imminent but does not yet know the date.

These are the principal reasons for these frequent and increasingly violent attacks which occur when I am far away from the subjects of my emotion, because the impossibility of verifying facts leads of necessity to illusions and exaggerates what is true.

This language will perhaps surprise you, dear Nanci, but you don't know how I feel: my heart is the home of passions that many of my fellow men have never known and which they cannot understand without having felt them. I said that your letter arrived inopportunely and indeed the news in it is not likely to have a calming effect on me. For a start, the death of M. Rocher[1] and your reminder not to forget to write to Edouard. Did you really think, dear Nanci, that I would neglect a duty which even the most superficial friendship would have imposed? Or have you come to believe with some other people that because my friendship with Edouard is now less demonstrative than it was when I first fell under its spell, therefore it has in fact waned? In both cases you are absolutely wrong.

As far as my debts are concerned, I quite see that papa finds the uncertainty in certain areas very hard to bear; that's something we have in common. I will tell all. I owe three hundred francs to a young man in Paris whom I regard as a friend.[2] Why and how I entered into this loan I now explain. The date fixed by my father for my abandoning the study of music was approaching; only a success could rescue me; I thought this was assured as long as my Mass was well performed. The occasion for which it was to be given was not far away; all the copying was done and I was pretty well certain of all the performers when news reached me of an unbelievable calamity – the King was to be at St-Cloud on the very day of my performance, thereby removing from me all the musicians of the Chapel Royal whom I knew and could therefore count on. Cherubini, who was on duty at the time, was not the man to grant anyone leave on my account[3] and the vicar of St-Roch refused to postpone the event. I wasn't going to run the risk of inviting artists I did not know to play for nothing; they would have gone back on their word as they did the first time, and after a second failure I would have been irrevocably doomed in every sense of the word. I was in utter despair when one of my friends, seeing the terrible situation I was in, said, 'Come on, I can spare 300 francs, take them.[4] That'll pay for the most important singers and players and with a bit of energy on our part and the support of MM. Valentino and Le Sueur, the rest will follow. Don't mention the money to your parents, pay it back when you can, I don't need it.' The possibility of paying him back myself and the urgency of the situation persuaded me to accept. You can't imagine what it's like to have one foot in the stirrups and suddenly find oneself

1 Edouard Rocher's father.
2 Augustin de Pons.
3 Cherubini shared the duties with Le Sueur, who would undoubtedly have done more to help if he had been on duty.
4 The debt was actually 1200 francs.

held up by some stroke of ill fortune! I'm prepared to bet that any young man in these circumstances would have done the same. I had no intention of ever mentioning the matter and there would have been no problem either about the 80 francs Alphonse[1] lent me for the hire of instruments, which papa was kind enough to give me to pass on to him, if Alphonse had been able to wait until I had saved up enough by working. But as he could not, I had to make other arrangements. I venture to hope that papa will not regard as mistaken an action which was merely the natural consequence of the situation I was in, and one that will not recur.

Adieu, dear Nanci, I embrace you.

Your brother and friend,

H. Berlioz

* All this is rather *à la Genlis*[2], as you can see. But I'll tell you why I have such a good opinion of myself. I'm on my guard as much as anybody against the snares of conceit, and when I want to be sure whether one of my compositions is any good I finish it and then leave it on one side, giving time for a cooling off of the excitement which composition always brings with it; and when I am quite calm I read through my work as though it were not one of my own. If then it excites my admiration I remain convinced that it deserves to be admired by everyone who is sensitive and educated enough to appreciate it.

18 *To Thomas Gounet*[3]   Paris, ?1826–30

My dear Ghomas,

If you'd like to come and fetch me tomorrow, Saturday, at midday, I'm your man, or rather I'll follow you.[4]

Yours,

Bector Herlioz

Friday norming

1 Alphonse Robert.
2 The novels of Mme de Genlis were regarded as morally uplifting by such as Berlioz's mother, who gave them to her daughters to read.
3 Thomas Gounet worked at the Ministry of Education and seems to have joined Berlioz's circle in about 1826. He translated Thomas Moore's poems which Berlioz set as *Neuf mélodies* in 1829, and obviously shared Berlioz's sense of humour.
4 The French contains a pun; 'je suis votre homme ou plutôt je vous suis.'

19 *To Thomas Gounet*   Paris, 16 March 1826

My dear Gounet,

If you'd like to be at the Café Durand on the corner of the boulevard and the Rue Richelieu tomorrow, Friday, at half-past six, we can go to the Opéra together. I've got a ticket for you.[1]

Adieu.

H. Berlioz

Sometime in the winter of 1825–6 Berlioz embarked on two large compositions with texts by Humbert Ferrand. The first was Scène héroïque, *for soloists, chorus and orchestra, also known as* La révolution grecque; *the second was an opera,* Les francs-juges, *on which Berlioz pinned his hopes for success at the Opéra. He also worked with an aspiring librettist named Léon Compaignon on an adaptation of Walter Scott's* The Talisman. *This was entitled* Richard en Palestine, *but despite a nine-month correspondence (Compaignon lived at Chartres) Berlioz probably never began the music, and the project came to nothing.*

20 *To Léon Compaignon*   Paris, 29 June 1826

My dear friend,

I've not been able to answer your letter until now because of various distractions which have kept me fully occupied these last few days; it's so hot, one has to spend half the day in the Seine if one's to survive.

I'm very pleased with the three pieces you've sent me. I agree with you about the last quatrain of the invocation; change it for me, but keep the idea, only make it still more menacing if you can. The contrast with the gentleness of the prayer will make the latter stand out splendidly. I also feel you should not start the chorus with the words 'QUE la gloire' etc, etc. You've already used this formula in several of the other pieces. Don't worry if your style seems too extravagant for *opéra comique*; our story, you must remember, is very much grand opera, and in any case I have it on good authority that Pixérécourt[2] is much happier when things are grandiose – I was told so again yesterday.

---

1 If Gounet accepted the ticket he would have seen a triple bill consisting of Gyrowetz's *Les pages du duc de Vendôme*, Lebrun's *Le rossignol* and Isouard's *Cendrillon*.
2 Director of the Opéra-Comique and a celebrated playwright.

Mind you don't give me a ballad or a romance or anything light for Blondel; it's a crucial piece and it must be like Ossian and everything the Bards used to sing, dreamy and savage.

I'm still busy with the opera *Les francs-juges*. I'm just finishing the second act and I've got enough to occupy me for two or three months.

Adieu to you,

H. Berlioz

21 *To Edouard Rocher*   Paris, 15 July 1826

My dear Edouard,

I should be ashamed at not having written to you for so long if I didn't have your own example before me as justification. You've got far less to do, in fact, than I have and instead of idling away your time at Villard's or on the esplanade you could easily have picked up a pen and given me your news. The main thing that held me back was that I had so much to tell you. I'd have preferred to do so face to face, if I could only take a holiday. At the moment there's no possibility of my doing so. Even so, I won't recite in detail all the fruitless labour I had over the winter trying to get my grand Greek 'scena' performed; Figuet has given Marc a written acount of all that. I've had to fight against the particular egoism shown by those who have succeeded in preventing others from succeeding, so as not to share the cake with anyone. I'd never have thought Kreutzer was one of their number;[1] experience has proved otherwise. He said to me personally 'that I ought to be aware that the Opéra did not exist to give young men a hearing'. Mme Le Sueur was taking him to task in the Chapel some days later: 'What is to become of young composers', she said to him, 'if they are prevented from having their music heard?'

'Ah, well,' he replied jestingly, 'they'll do what they can; but what's to become of *us*, if we push them forward like that? For six months now I've been looking for a libretto to set for the Feydeau[2] and I can't find anything, they give them all to the young men.'

Tulou, who's an excellent fellow,[3] offered to have my piece played at his concert. But then it had to be cancelled. I've given up hope now of having it performed this year.

---

1 Berlioz's disappointment was doubtless the greater since he had earlier admired Kreutzer so much (see p. 9).
2 The Opéra-Comique.
3 The leading flautist of the day.

At the moment I'm finishing a three-act opera for the Odéon.¹ The director has finally got permission to put on new operas written by Frenchmen. Don't say anything about this, please, as I don't want to stir up criticism in advance. I'll hand over the score in two months' time and, if it's accepted, I don't think I'll have long to wait. The libretto is as I received it; the director of the Odéon asked for some changes, which were made. M. Le Sueur is extremely happy with the first two acts and I'll do my best with the third. He's very insistent that I should sit for the Concours of the Institut next year, and for this reason, to obtain Cherubini's support for me, he wants me to attend a counterpoint and fugue class at the Conservatoire.² With this in mind I went to see Cherubini, and when I offered to show him something of mine, so that he would know what I was capable of, he replied: 'No, no, there's no need, I know you; just bring me your birth certificate.'

Until now I appeared in the Conservatoire register only as a private pupil of Le Sueur. That's why, after the performance of my Mass, Cherubini himself asked Le Sueur to send me to him. As you can see, it's another case of teachers' pride; as soon as they see a pupil showing signs of talent, they want to grab him for themselves. When it can be said that I had counterpoint lessons at the Conservatoire, Cherubini will put all his weight behind me. If not, then not!

As a result of all that, and as M. Cherubini asked me the other day why I hadn't been to bring him my birth certificate, will you please send it to me. But I don't want anyone to know, because of the flights of imagination it might provoke in my parents. Ask Jardinet secretly or in some discreet manner and send it to me as soon as possible. Ask Marc about it but don't mention it to anybody else.

This year's Concours has already begun. The prize should go to Pâris.³ On my own behalf I'm working at the moment on another opera in three acts. It's taken from Walter Scott and we'll be offering it to the Feydeau in a month at the outside. You can see that if I left, especially over the holiday period, it would mean letting go of the thread which could lead me out of the labyrinth. Also, my father has just written to tell me that next year he would only be able to give me 600 francs; I've got to look round for some way of making ends meet. I'm sure I'll find a way. As long as my opera is performed and is a

1 *Les francs-juges.*
2 The Concours was the famous Prix de Rome. Berlioz in fact sat for the examination in this same month, July 1826, but did not pass the preliminary test. Cherubini was Director of the Conservatoire.
3 A fellow-pupil of Le Sueur who won the Prix de Rome in 1826.

success (and I have hopes of this at least as far as the libretto is concerned because it's infinitely better than the ones they've had at the Odéon until now) then I'm on my way. I think the music is the best I've written so far; but it's extremely stark and dramatic and the Odéon public is so stupid thanks to a diet of *Marguerite d'Anjou*, *Dame du lac*, etc, etc,[1] that trusting to their knowledge and good taste would be like trusting to *providence*.

Don't forget what I asked you to do, reply promptly and tell me whether Marc intends to come back next year. Give him my best wishes, and Hippolyte too. I was very sorry he wasn't here for the revival of *Armide* and *Olympie*.[2] He would have made a considerable addition to his tally of pleasurable experiences. The trouble was that the role of Armide was too heavy for Grassari. She was crushed by it. You know the details of Mme Branchu's retirement in *Olympie*; she was, if possible, more sublime than usual; and at the end, when Talma[3] and Dérivis crowned her, I thought the auditorium would burst. After the performance the Opéra chorus came to her dressing room to give her a farewell present consisting of a crown of very expensive diamonds. She assured me that this gift, made with absolutely no ulterior motives, was the one that gave her the most pleasure of all. A deputation of members of the Institut went to see M. Sosthène[4] to ask him to take her on for another year, but the entire body of our best-known composers was unable to obtain this favour from him. Spontini, who had more of a stake in this than anyone else, asked that she should sing the part of Statira in *Olympie* just three more times; when Sosthène refused, the illustrious composer cast restraint aside: 'You wanted to make me director of the Opéra', he said, 'but you don't deserve to have Spontini on your staff; here, take your contract' – so saying he tore it up and threw it at his feet – 'you are not worthy to untie the bootlaces of a man of genius; you want to kill the arts, but remember that you will perish and the arts will not.' With these words he left and, in shutting Sosthène's drawing-room door, split it from top to bottom. He went off at once to Berlin, leaving his wife here and his opera in the hands of Mlle Quiney who, with Sosthène's help, soon sank it. It's a heavenly work, worthy in every respect of the composer

---

1 *Marguerite d'Anjou* is by Meyerbeer, *La dame du lac* (*La donna del lago*) by Rossini.
2 Gluck's *Armide* was revived at the Opéra in both 1825 and 1826, Spontini's *Olympie* in February 1826, which marked Mme Branchu's retirement. She was replaced in *Armide* by Mme Grassari and in *Olympie* by Mlle Quiney.
3 The great tragic actor of the day.
4 Vicomte Sosthène de la Rochefoucauld, Minister of Fine Arts.

of *La vestale*; only there are moments when the brass are too heavy; in general, he's been too free with them all through the opera. Spontini went off in a rage, but he has the consolation that all Germany is at his feet. He's the genius of the century.

Weber has died in London,[1] after putting on his opera *Oberon*. He perished wreathed in laurels.

Talma, who was supposed to be dead, is much better since yesterday.

Adieu. Your friend,

H. Berlioz

22 *To Edouard Rocher*   Paris, *c.* 10 September 1826

My dear Edouard,

I've just finished my opera, with only the overture left to write. I'm hoping more than ever that the Odéon will get permission to play new works.[2] As a result I'm having to copy out a large number of parts so that the main sections of my score can be heard on full orchestra, with a view to getting it accepted. So there, despite wind and flood, is a work completed. Has it been played? . . . Not yet, dammit. Is it likely to appeal to the public? . . . That I doubt. Ah, my dear Edouard, what effects it contains! The devil take me if wilder music has been seen for years. All the difficulties I've had to confront right and left have built up torrents of bile inside me which burst out in this composition. Among others, the 'fanatical duet' in the first act seethes with rage. That's just between ourselves, of course.

Something you can talk about is my family's persecutions. My father gives me 50 francs a month, at least he told me that's all he was going to give me next year, and to get me used to the regime he sent me, on 14 August, a hundred francs, saying that was all he *could* give me this year. When I got this letter, I realized what he had in mind, namely to reduce my allowance bit by bit until he's giving me nothing. So I immediately had enquiries made of the Brazilian Consul to find out whether there were any prospects in South America. He sent word that a French artist could earn enormous amounts of money in the republic of Buenos Aires,[3] and if I wanted to go there he would pay my passage as well as that of the young man who was my intermediary and who would sail with me. He refused to enter into a contract or to give me

1 On 5 June 1826.
2 The opera was *Les francs-juges*, but the Odéon was not permitted to mount new works by French composers, of which the Opéra and the Opéra-Comique had the monopoly.
3 Perhaps he meant Rio de Janeiro?

anything in advance. That's partly what has delayed me. In any case, I didn't have a penny to get to Le Havre, I don't know any Portuguese and it takes at least four months to learn it. Charles and Charbonnel[1] made me see the force of all these arguments; but the most powerful ones from my point of view were the terrible emotional effect such a departure would have on my parents and the severe damage the journey would have on my career. First of all I should have to pass up the Prix de Rome, for which I'm the current favourite now that Pâris and Simon are no longer in the running. At least M. Le Sueur thinks I should win the first prize in the next couple of years, if justice is done. My rivals are mere blockheads, except for this year's second prizewinner who stands the best chance of winning the first one, according to the excellent habit established for what they call the 'Concours' of the Institut. Then again, if I went to Buenos Aires both the opera I've finished and those yet to be started would run a dreadful risk of never being performed in Europe. So I'm staying. I've no pupils left; they've all gone off to the country.[2] The little money left over from my lessons will keep me going until I get a job or my father sends me some money. I wanted to find a job in the Théâtre des Nouveautés which they're building at the moment; they were giving 600 francs and a fee to cover October without having to do anything. It was a job singing in the chorus; but when I saw what it was like, I decided I really couldn't prostitute myself like that.[3] I'm trying to get into the Opéra chorus. It's very hard. M. Le Sueur doesn't want me to join; he says it would do me a lot of harm, even from the musical point of view, and that people would look askance at my works when they found out I was in the Opéra chorus. He has several times offered me money, but I can't accept it without knowing when I might be able to pay him back and I don't want to be in debt to anyone, not even him. Pending a decision I'm getting fat on pears and plums and plenty of water. I've changed my lodgings and am now at no 58, Rue de la Harpe, Hôtel de Bourges. Charbonnel is a neighbour of mine, we have adjoining doors. I'm learning Italian.[4] I really do need a piano so that I can learn to accompany my singers,[5] but I can't hire one or buy one. Ye Gods

1 Charles Bert and Antoine Charbonnel, friends from La Côte who were studying in Paris. Berlioz shared lodgings with Charbonnel.
2 Berlioz was teaching the guitar, perhaps also the flute and harmony.
3 Berlioz auditioned for the Théâtre des Nouveautés but did not start work there in the chorus until March 1827.
4 In the hope of winning the Prix de Rome.
5 For Les francs-juges.

above! But then it's all *for my own good*. Adieu, send me a reply and put a stamp on the letter.

    Your friend for life,
    H. Berlioz

In the autumn of 1826 Berlioz enrolled at the Conservatoire, studying composition with Le Sueur and counterpoint with Antoine Reicha.

23 *To his sister Nanci Berlioz*   Paris, 28 September 1826

My dear sister,

    I'm even more puzzled than usual as to what can have prompted you to write to me in such an unduly harsh manner. The reason for my incomprehension, especially at this moment, is the reply Alphonse recently received from papa; far from matching the style of your letter, his is full of expressions of tenderness and goodwill. There's not a shadow of the indignant tone that pervades yours, and which is totally without justification. First of all you seem to regard as a crime the fact that I have not left Paris over the holidays, when I told you more than once that I couldn't and explained the several reasons why not. You obviously don't regard these reasons as relevant and think the considerations behind them the last I should be concerning myself with. My own view, on the other hand, is that they are of the greatest importance; you regard my predominant interests as nothing, I regard them as something. So our opinions on the subject are diametrically opposed. I won't attempt to counter yours as you don't like arguments and, even though I'm not so set against them as you are, I've not the slightest desire to stir up a controversy which has been going on for the last four or five years.

    You say papa has firmly made up his mind not to send me any more money. On the contrary, he wrote to me several months ago saying, 'I will pay for your journey if you come down from Paris, for your return there, for furnishing your apartment and I will give you 600 francs a year.' Has he perhaps changed his mind because I did not come down from Paris? No, because that would have been tantamount to saying 'If next year you want to stay in Paris to pursue the career you have begun, you must agree to jeopardize, if not destroy, the fruits of your labours over the past year.' That would be treating me like a child, knocking down my card house so that I can be made to build it up again. Anyway it's quite clear from the letter he wrote to Alphonse that

[33]

there's no question of this and that he intends to give me 50 francs a month as he promised.

You go even further and say that my father won't even pay for my *journey* if I do consent to come down; you say he's afraid I'll contract debts but that he won't pay them.

The upshot of that is that I must in either case *not stay, not leave, not borrow money*! Please tell me in your next letter how I should proceed ... You see, my dear Nanci, what a maze of inconsistencies you've got yourself into and my father too, by your own account! You must have had a giddy spell and now you can't help but agree with me on the following point: I had either to *leave* or to *stay* and, whether I *left* or *stayed*, in the unforeseen circumstances I had either to borrow money or die of hunger. I defy you to find your way round that one.

As for papa's fears about my debts, I haven't contracted any, not even for the slightest amount. I've sorted out my finances as I explained in my last letter. As mama was kind enough to send me 100 francs I've bought myself some kitchen utensils, which are quite cheap in Paris, and for less than 20 centimes a day I eat almost as well as in a restaurant. As I'm in no doubt about papa's goodwill I'm taking the initiative of asking him to let me have my allowance at regular intervals, like most of the young men I know; if, for example, I could collect my 50 francs from M. Bourget on the first day of every month, a regular, reliable payment like this would make me organize my finances and I wouldn't get into a muddle working out fractions of weeks and months as in the past. In any case don't worry about me, I'm quite certain to have a number of harmony pupils after the holidays and that will make a big difference to my income. Adieu, my dear Nanci, don't hold it against me if I speak frankly, I love you as much as ever and embrace you as your brother and friend.

H. Berlioz

24 *To Léon Compaignon*   Paris, 14 October 1826

My dear Compaignon,

I've had a thousand things to do and my head is in a whirl; my opera for the Odéon is finished but I'm still touching it up. The necessary permission hasn't come through; all the young composers signed a petition which we sent to Sosthène; we've had no reply so far.

Added to this, as my father sends me only 50 francs a month I have to spend the whole day rushing around giving lessons, correcting proofs,[1] etc, etc. That's why I haven't written to you till now. Over the matter you mentioned in your last letter, I suggested to a writer I know that he might collaborate with you on the work in question; to my great surprise he refused, saying that 'he didn't go in for collaborations. And anyway he already had so many librettos in his bottom drawer, none of which have seen the stage, that there was no point in adding to their number.'

There's really only one thing for it, you must come and spend a fortnight in Paris. There's no other way we're going to make any progress. Even though we could offer the work as it stands, I haven't got the time to organize things.

Come to a decision, please.

Adieu. Yours ever,

H. Berlioz

25 To his sister Nanci Berlioz   Paris, 20 January 1827

My dear sister,

[...] I gather, from the news Marc's mother sent him, that mama is quite recovered and that everyone in the family is fairly well. Now to reply to papa's question about what I'm doing at present. I'm so busy, from 7 o'clock in the morning, that I haven't really a free moment until the evening. As the Odéon theatre is just about to obtain permission to put on new operas, I want to seize the advantage and hold myself ready to be one of the first composers played. My opera was finished two months ago and at the moment I'm working hard copying out parts for the sections of the work which I want to be performed when the time comes for the opera to be considered; it's an immense labour and, with my harmony pupils, takes up my whole day. I've bought an alarm clock and I get up regularly at seven o'clock, sometimes six. I'm having a hard time getting used to it and without the clock's infernal din I'd never manage to get out of bed and work in daylight. I tell you this reluctantly, because I know perfectly well the difficulties I have to overcome, and I don't want to be told: 'you see, you see, you're killing yourself with work, and all for nothing, you'll never make it, etc, etc.' But I also know perfectly well that these difficulties are the initial ones common to all young men, in all careers and in all periods of history, at least for those who don't wish to remain in the foothills.

1 Berlioz was earning extra money as a music publisher's proof-reader.

Papa should have received several days ago the fourth volume of Andras and *Le bon jardinier*. Poor Croullebois has just lost his wife.[1]

Adieu, dear Nanci, and when you write try to water your remonstrances down a little.

I embrace you.

H. B.

In March 1827 the Théâtre des Nouveautés opened its doors, with Berlioz singing in the chorus. Anxious to keep the news from his parents he concealed his nightly employment even from his neighbour Charbonnel. He remained in the job for about five months.

26 *To his sister Nanci Berlioz*   Paris, 4 June 1827

My dear sister,

[...] You never tell me what you're reading. I have a high enough opinion of you to suppose that you have a thorough knowledge of Walter Scott, that giant of English literature; but Cooper, do you know Cooper, the American Walter Scott? Even if he doesn't equal his model or even come near him as far as depiction of character and dialogue are concerned, one can't help admiring his description of nature in all its savagery and the interest he gives to his protagonists. Among others there's one who appears in three works, the famous hunter Natty Bumpo; a unique character, a European whose love of solitude has led him to turn native, or very nearly; a philosopher of the desert. He appears first in *The Last of the Mohicans*, then in *The Pioneers* and finally in *The Prairie*. That's the order in which the three books should be read. As you go on, you get more and more attached to the hunter, and his death, expected as it is at the age of ninety, affects the reader to an extent I can't possibly describe. *The Prairie* came out only a month ago and I devoured it without stopping; I reached the dénouement at seven o'clock in the evening and at 11 I was still weeping all over the pedestal of one of the columns of the Panthéon. I urge you to read all three of them, you'd certainly like them in spite of various fairly obvious weaknesses.

I could also tell you a number of things to do with my art, and with a success I had recently with an instrumental composition, but as this is

1 Andras was the publisher of a medical textbook; *Le bon jardinier* was an agricultural journal; Croullebois had published Dr Berlioz's book on chronic diseases in 1810.

[36]

unknown territory for you, you wouldn't understand me and so wouldn't be interested.[1] Ah! If only I could teach you about music, what strong, new sensations you would experience, of whose existence you are now unaware.

Adieu, dear Nanci, embrace Adèle and Prosper[2] for me, and give me news of papa and mama; I worry about her getting tired, working at her silkworms, but she's lucky to have your valuable help and support.

H. Berlioz

27 *To his sister Nanci Berlioz*   Paris, 28 July 1827

I write a few lines in haste, dear Nanci, to tell you that your letter has arrived as well as the note it contained. It all arrived just in time because I've just received it and in an hour and a half's time I shall be in the Institut.[3]

The preliminary round took place the day before yesterday, to decide which candidates should go through into the main examination. We were asked to write a 'fugue in severe style', a kind of musical problem with practically no point to it but very difficult to solve. There were only four of us and out of this number I was the only one to give the correct 'answer', as it's called, which is the main object of the fugue. One of the others, who won the second prize last year and is expected to win the first prize this year, therefore got the 'answer' wrong but redeemed the error to some extent by merit of another kind which was to be found at various points in his piece. It was possible to let him through at a pinch, so by rights there should be only two of us; in fact there are four. The other two are pupils of Berton and were allowed through despite vigorous opposition from MM. Cherubini and Le Sueur.

That gives you a glimpse already of the way things are judged at the Institut. I'm resigned to it; I'm told I should get the second prize, and if they give it to me I shall take it, but there won't be much glory in defeating my rivals. Only they're a long way from suspecting the true nature of dramatic music.

Alphonse will shortly be sitting his third examination; he won't be

---

1 If Berlioz had the overture to *Les francs-juges* played at this time, no record of the event has survived. He might simply be referring to the composition of the *Waverley* overture, based on Scott, which falls at about this period.
2 Berlioz's younger brother, then aged six.
3 Berlioz had passed the preliminary round of the Prix de Rome and was therefore about to enter 'en loge' to compose the required cantata, *La mort d'Orphée*.

going down to La Côte this year but is putting the journey off until we can make it together.

Adieu, my dear Nanci.

Until I get out of prison.

Your brother,

H. B.

P.S. Every evening we have a reception in the great courtyard of the Institut, when friends and acquaintances can come and see us from six until nine o'clock. There's a supervisor who makes sure no one brings us anything in from outside which could have any bearing on the examination.

At the formal hearing of the four cantatas on 25 August 1827 Berlioz's cantata was declared unperformable since it proved beyond the abilities of the Institut's pianist to read at sight. Berlioz withdrew his cantata in disgust.

The following month Charles Kemble's company opened a season of Shakespeare in English at the Odéon Theatre. Berlioz saw Hamlet *on 11 September and* Romeo and Juliet *on 15 September and was overwhelmed both by the impact of Shakespeare and by adoration of the leading actress Harriet Smithson, who played Ophelia and Juliet. His account of these experiences in his* Mémoires *recalled those days with great vividness, but there are few references to them in the little correspondence that survives from the autumn of 1827.*

28 *To Ferdinand Laforest*[1]   Paris, 12 October 1827

My dear Laforest,

You did promise to write to me first, but day after day has gone past and I've had no news of you. No doubt you're out hunting with your friends and every day will find you guilty of assassinating hares and partridges, you laugh, you sing, you drink, at times you sigh for someone who is dear to you; but let me tell you, you are not acquainted with love, although you say you feel it strongly. That's not the rage, the fury, the delirium which takes possession of all our faculties and makes us capable of anything; you're not the sort of man to ruin yourself willingly for the person you love. You're lucky in that respect and I

1 Laforest was a medical student with Berlioz and had just moved back to his native Maine-et-Loire to practise.

would not wish on you the intolerable sufferings to which I have been subjected since your departure. You left Paris at the moment when the explosion was imminent. I'll tell you about it when you get back, but for the moment I'm not capable of giving you an outline of my sad story. It's only a few days since I've been able to write again. It's not my fault that you haven't seen me at all, but never mind. I'm putting all my efforts into preparing the parts for my Mass which will be performed *for certain* on 22 November.[1] I'd like you to be there. After the performance we'll get thirty or so close friends together for a meal in honour of St Cecilia. It's up to you to be there, I'll bring Valentino and M. Le Sueur. Come, come . . .

They gave *La vestale*[2] three days ago and Adolphe Nourrit played Licinius very badly. As his voice isn't strong enough at the bottom he took the liberty of completely altering the recitative passages which he found awkward, and in the third act he gave us

et vi - van - te des - cend dans la nuit des tom-beaux

instead of

et vi - van - te des - cend dans la nuit des tom-beaux

Impious blasphemer, daring to mutilate a role like this and lay a hand on the tabernacle of genius! . . .

Unbearable anxiety, I have a fever, my heartbeat's irregular, but still everything has to be finished! I digress and tell you things you can't understand.

I can't go on. I intended to write you a long letter, but I can't go on.

Ah! I can't say to myself as Cortez said to Amazily 'every moment of your life is a blessing from the gods';[3] it is very far from being a blessing.

Adieu, give me your news and tell me you're coming back soon. I'm

1 The second performance of the *Messe solennelle*, this time in the church of St-Eustache. The Mass was subsequently 'destroyed', according to Berlioz, but was rediscovered in Antwerp in 1991 and performed for the third time in 1993.
2 By Spontini.
3 In Spontini's opera *Fernand Cortez*.

not very demonstrative about such things but you don't know how much your friendship means to me; you have one of those open, straightforward characters which are very agreeable.

H. Berlioz

29 To Quatremère de Quincy[1]   Paris, 22 October 1827

Monsieur,

I take the liberty of asking your help in obtaining the payment of the small allowance normally given, after the examination, to the candidates who have presented themselves at the Institut. As M. Guiraud[2] has been paid, I felt I had reason to hope that my request would not be unsuccessful; at the moment I have an urgent need of the sum due to us from the Institut; without it I cannot pursue a rather important musical project that I'm engaged on,[3] and I count on your goodwill to obtain it for me.

I am ashamed at bothering you with such a small matter; please accept the excuses and respects of your humble servant,

Hector Berlioz
pupil of M. Le Sueur

30 To Humbert Ferrand   Paris, 29 November 1827

My dear Ferrand,

You have maintained an inexplicable silence towards me, as well as towards Berlioz[4] and Gounet. I know you've been ill a second time, several people have told us; but couldn't you make use of your brother's pen to let us know how your convalescence is going? Why leave us full of anxiety like this? We thought for a long time you'd gone off to Switzerland, but I kept saying, if that's so I don't see any reason not to write to us: there's a post in Switzerland as elsewhere. So I think your silence must be regarded as the result not of forgetfulness but of casual unconcern allied to an idleness with which you are amply provided. But I hope you'll recover enough energy to send me a reply.

My Mass was performed on St Cecilia's day with twice the success it

1 Permanent Secretary of the Institut.
2 Jean-Baptiste-Louis Guiraud, winner of the Prix de Rome in 1827. He later emigrated to New Orleans where his more famous son Ernest Guiraud, Bizet's friend and Debussy's teacher, was born.
3 The performance of the Messe solennelle.
4 See p. 12.

had the first time; the slight corrections I've made to it have been real improvements. The movement *Et iterum venturus* especially,[1] which didn't come off the first time, was performed now in overwhelming fashion by six trumpets, four horns, three trombones and two ophicleides. The choral melody that follows, which I had sung by all voices in octaves,

with an outburst of brass in the middle, produced a tremendous effect on everybody. As for me, I'd managed to stay calm until that point and it was important that my equilibrium shouldn't be disturbed. I was conducting the orchestra, but when I saw the scene of the Last Judgment, that proclamation sung by six basses in unison, the terrible *clangor tubarum*, the cries of fear from the crowd represented by the choir, and all of it performed exactly as I'd conceived it, I was seized by a convulsive trembling which I was hardly able to control until the end of the piece. It forced me to sit down and give the orchestra several minutes' rest; I couldn't stand up any more and I was afraid the baton would leap out of my hands. Ah, if only you'd been there! I had a magnificent orchestra. I'd invited forty-five violins, of whom thirty-two turned up, eight violas, ten cellos, eleven double basses; unfortunately the chorus wasn't large enough, especially for a huge church like St-Eustache. The *Corsaire* and the *Pandore* were complimentary, but without going into details: banalities aimed, as they say, at the general reader. I'm waiting for the verdicts of Castil-Blaze, who promised me he'd come, of Fétis and of *L'observateur*;[2] those were the only newspapers I invited, the others being too concerned with politics. I chose a very bad moment for the concert. Many of the people I'd invited, including the Le Sueur ladies, didn't come because of the fearful rioting which went on in the St-Denis area for several days [...] Even so, I succeeded beyond my expectations; I have supporters at the Odéon,

---

1 The *Resurrexit*.
2 Castil-Blaze was notorious, in Berlioz's opinion, for his free adaptations of Weber and others, and for his uninhibited admiration for Rossini. Fétis, historian and lexicographer, had just founded the *Revue musicale*.

the Bouffes, the Conservatoire and the Gymnase. Congratulations reached me from all around. The very evening of the performance I received a complimentary letter from a man I do not know, full of charming phrases. I sent invitations to all the members of the Institut in the hope that they would hear performed music which they call unperformable; because my Mass is thirty times more difficult than my prize cantata, and you know that I had to withdraw it because M. Rifaut couldn't play my music on the piano, and that M. Berton[1] was quick to say my music was unperformable, even on the orchestra.

My great crime, in the eyes of this old, cold classicist (at the moment, anyway) is that I'm trying to do something new.

'It's a chimera, my dear boy,' he said to me a month ago, 'there's nothing new in music; the great masters complied with certain musical forms which you won't adopt. Why try and do better than the great masters? Now I know you have a great admiration for a man who is, undoubtedly, not without talent ... not without genius ... I mean Spontini.'

'Oh yes, monsieur, I have a great admiration for him, and always will have.'

'Ah well, dear boy, Spontini ..., in the eyes of true connoisseurs he doesn't enjoy ... great *respect*.'

Upon which, as you can imagine, I bowed and left. Ah, the gouty old fool! If that's my crime then it's certainly a major one, because never was admiration so great nor so well deserved; nothing can equal it, unless it's the contempt I feel for the academician's petty jealousy.

Must I demean myself and go in for the Prix de Rome again? ... Yes I must; my father wants me to. He attaches great importance to this prize. For his sake I'll enter again; I'll use a little bourgeois orchestration in two or three parts which will be as effective on the piano as on the mightiest orchestra; I'll fill it full of repetitions, since *those are the forms with which the great masters complied, and one must not do better than the great masters*, and, if I get the prize, I swear to you that I'll tear up my *scena* in the presence of those gentlemen as soon as the prize has been awarded.

I express myself, dear Ferrand, with some passion on the subject, but you can't imagine how little importance I attach to it. For three months I've been prey to an insurmountable affliction and I'm disillusioned with life to the utmost degree; even the success I've achieved could only momentarily alleviate the painful burden which weighs on me, and

1 Berton was a sixty-year-old composer who taught at the Conservatoire.

now it returns more heavily than before. I can't give you here the key to the enigma; it would take too long and in any case I don't think I could manage to form the letters to tell you about it. When I see you again, you shall learn everything. I conclude with this phrase which the King of Denmark's ghost addresses to his son Hamlet:

ferwel ferwel remember my[1]

The following spring Berlioz decided to give a concert of his own works in order to attract the attention of Harriet Smithson and advance his career.

31 *To the Directeur des Beaux-Arts,*
Vicomte Sosthène de la Rochefoucauld　　　　　Paris, 3 May 1828

Monsieur le Vicomte,

Following the generous reply you were kind enough to make to M. Chenevaz, deputy of the Isère, last Thursday, I beg to hope that it will be possible for you to let me have the Salle des Menus-Plaisirs for my concert. But since you were not certain that the hall would be free on Sunday 18 May, you were not able to give him a definite answer. My renewed request in this matter will perhaps strike you as importunate; but, Monsieur le Vicomte, I am forced to make it by my situation, and I beg you to excuse me if I do not await your decision with more patience. A concert of the nature of the one I wish to give demands infinitely careful preparations; I have to arrange dates with my singers and chorus for preliminary rehearsals, and it is impossible to obtain a definite promise from the instrumentalists unless I inform them of the date and time of the final rehearsal. As I do not yet have your permission to use the hall, I can neither do nor arrange anything; and I fear that time is short for me to overcome the innumerable difficulties which lie before me. The intention of this concert is to make my name known and it is, for me, of the utmost importance; my whole musical existence is at stake. If I obtain from you permission to use the hall of the Ecole Royale it will be very much to my advantage in all respects; if on the other hand you are unable to grant me that permission, it is urgent that I take steps to secure another hall.

I therefore take the liberty, Monsieur le Vicomte, of asking you to let

1 Berlioz quotes Shakespeare in garbled English, as he heard it at the Odéon, but the line is in fact 'Adieu, adieu, remember me'.

me know your decision in the matter as soon as possible.

The final concert of the Ecole Royale is firmly fixed for Sunday 11 May. That of the Société des Enfants d'Apollon always takes place on Ascension Day, 15 May, so that unless some request was made before mine the hall should be free on the 18th. If nonetheless it were not available and it were possible for you to let me have it for 25 or 26 May, the feast of Pentecost, I would wait until then.

I would ask you, Monsieur le Vicomte, to take into consideration the difficult position in which I find myself and to continue to give me the kindly support which I have always had from you when I asked for it. The career of a composer becomes more thorny day by day, and if a powerful hand does not come to my aid, despite my invincible determination, I am afraid I shall use up my strength in abortive efforts and never reach the goal upon which my heart is so passionately set.

I have the honour to be, Monsieur le Vicomte, with the most profound respect, your humble servant,

Hector Berlioz

32 *To the Editor-in-chief of the Revue musicale*[1]   Paris, 16 May 1828

Dear Monsieur,

Allow me to trespass upon your goodwill and ask for the assistance of your journal in justifying myself in the eyes of the public with regard to certain rather serious charges.

The rumour has spread in musical circles that I was going to give a concert composed entirely of my music, and already a movement of censure has risen against me. I am accused of presumption and temerity and held responsible for the most ridiculous claims.

My answer to all that is that I simply want to make myself known so as to inspire, if I can, some confidence in the writers and directors of our opera houses. Is this desire to be disapproved of in a young man? I think not. And if such an end is not reprehensible, how can the means be which I use to attain it?

Because concerts have been given made up entirely of the works of Mozart and Beethoven, does it follow that in doing the same I entertain the absurd pretensions which have been attributed to me? I repeat, my approach is simply the easiest way to make known my attempts in the field of dramatic music.

As for the temerity which prompts me to reveal myself to the public

1 Fétis. The same letter was sent to other journals.

in a concert, it is quite natural and here is my excuse. For four years I have been banging on every door; not one has been opened to me. I am unable either to obtain an opera libretto or to have performed the one that I have set.[1] I have tried every means of getting a hearing without success, there is only one left and I am employing it, and I think I may fittingly take as my motto this line of Virgil:

Una salus victis nullam sperare salutem.[2]

I remain, Monsieur, etc,
Hector Berlioz
Pupil of M. Le Sueur

After many administrative difficulties Berlioz finally obtained the hall of the Conservatoire (known as the Ecole Royale de Musique) for Monday 26 May. The programme consisted entirely of his own works, all except the Resurrexit *receiving first performances: overture* Waverley, Mélodie pastorale *(from* Les francs-juges), Marche religieuse des mages *(now lost),* Resurrexit *(from the* Messe solennelle), *overture* Les francs-juges, *cantata* La révolution grecque. *The conductor was Nathan Bloc.*

33 *To Humbert Ferrand*   Paris, 6 June 1828

My dear friend,

You are no doubt consumed with impatience to know the result of my concert; if I didn't write to you earlier, it was because I was waiting to see what the papers said. All those that mentioned me, apart from the *Revue musicale* and the *Quotidienne* which I haven't yet managed to get hold of, should reach you at the same time as my letter.

Great, great success! A success that left the public astonished and aroused the enthusiasm of those who took part.

There'd been so much applause at the final rehearsals on Friday and Saturday that I wasn't in the least worried about what effect my music would have on a paying audience. The *Waverley* overture, which you don't know, opened the concert in the best possible way, being greeted with three bursts of applause. After that came our favourite *Mélodie pastorale*. It was shoddily sung by the soloists, and the chorus at the

1 *Les francs-juges.*
2 'Salvation for the defeated lies only in not hoping for any salvation', the line from the *Aeneid* Berlioz used many years later in *Les Troyens.*

[45]

end was way off the mark. The chorus singers didn't count their bars' rests; instead they were waiting for a sign from the conductor which he never gave, and they realized they hadn't come in when the piece was nearly over. It didn't produce a quarter of the effect it should.

The *Marche religieuse des mages*, which you don't know either, was loudly applauded. But when it came to the *Resurrexit* of my Mass, which you haven't heard since I touched it up and which was sung for the first time by 14 female voices and 30 men, the hall of the Ecole Royale de Musique witnessed for the first time the sight of orchestral players putting down their instruments right after the last chord and clapping louder than the audience. The sound of bows tapping on cellos and basses was like hail: all the men and women of the chorus were applauding, and when one burst was over, another would begin. There were shouts and people jumping up and down! ... Finally I couldn't stand it any more from my position on the edge of the orchestra and I stretched myself out on top of the timpani and started to weep.

Ah, if only you'd been there, dear Ferrand! You would have seen the triumph of the cause you've been defending so vigorously against the narrow-minded and the short-sighted. Truth be told, at the very height of my emotion I was thinking of you and could not suppress a groan at the thought that you were not there.

The second part of the concert began with the *Francs-juges* overture. I must tell you what happened at the first rehearsal of this piece. Hardly had the orchestra heard that astounding solo for trombones and ophicleide to which you set words for Olmerick in the third act,

when one of the violinists stops and shouts out: 'Ah! Ah! the rainbow is the bow of your violin, the winds are playing the organ, the weather's beating time.' Thereupon the whole orchestra went wild, applauding an idea whose import they couldn't even grasp; they stopped playing in order to applaud. The day of the concert, this introduction produced an effect of stupefaction and terror that's hard to describe. I found myself next to the timpanist who held on to one of my arms, shook it with all his might, and was moved to shout convulsively from time to time, 'It's superb! It's sublime, my dear fellow! It's terrifying! It's enough to drive one mad! ...'

With my other arm I was holding on to a lock of my hair and pulling it in a frenzy; I wanted to be able to cry out, forgetting that I was the composer, 'It's monstrous, colossal, horrible!'

Now you know our *Scène héroïque grecque*; the line 'Le monde entier . . .' wasn't half as effective as this astounding passage. In fact, it was very badly performed; Bloc, who was conducting, got the tempo wrong at the start of 'Des sommets de l'Olympe . . .'. And in bringing the orchestra back to the right speed he caused a momentary confusion in the violins which nearly wrecked everything. Even so the effect is as great as you can imagine, perhaps greater. That urgent march of the Greek auxiliaries and that exclamation 'Ils s'avancent!' are astonishingly dramatic. I'm not displeased with you, as you can see, and I say frankly what I think about my music.

One of the singers from the Opéra was saying to one of his colleagues, the evening of the rehearsal, that this effect in *Les francs-juges* was the most extraordinary thing he'd heard in his life.

'Oh, after Beethoven, that is?' said his friend.

'After nothing', he replied; 'I defy anybody to find a more terrifying idea than that.'

All the Opéra personnel came to my concert. Afterwards I thought the embraces would never stop. Those who enjoyed it most were: Habeneck, Dérivis, Adolphe Nourrit, Dabadie, Prévost, Mlle Mori, Alexis Dupont, Schneitzoeffer, Hérold, Rigel, etc. There were no constraints on my success, not even the criticism of MM. Panseron and Bruguière,[1] who considered my style to be new but bad and that it is a mistake to encourage this sort of writing.

Ah, my dear Ferrand, send me an opera![2] *Robin Hood*! . . . What can I do without a libretto? I beg you, finish something.

Adieu, my dear Ferrand. I send you some weapons to use against the detractors; Castil-Blaze couldn't come to my concert as he was not in Paris. I've seen him since and he's promised to mention it even so. He never hurries; luckily I can do without him, and easily.

Only yesterday I discovered that the article in the journal *Le voleur*, which is the most enthusiastic on my behalf, was written by Despréaux, who was a fellow candidate of mine for the Institut. I find this support from a rival very flattering.

H. Berlioz

1 Minor composers known for their *romances*.
2 A libretto, he means.

*In July 1828 Berlioz again entered for the Prix de Rome and won a
Second Prix with his cantata* Herminie. *It was probably at this time
that he first read Goethe's* Faust *in Gérard de Nerval's translation. In
August he visited his family at La Côte-St-André, his first return home
in three years. From there he visited his relations in Grenoble.*

34 *To Humbert Ferrand*   Grenoble, 16 September 1828

My dear Ferrand,

I leave tomorrow morning for La Côte – I've been away since the day
your letter arrived. It's impossible for me to come and see you;[1] as I
leave on the 27th of this month, I simply cannot suggest to my parents
that I break my stay before then. I had already talked to my family
about you; everyone was looking forward to seeing you and the
general impatience was redoubled by your letter. This wish to see you
on the part of my sisters and the young ladies of the area does perhaps
have a slight ulterior motive; it's a matter of balls and tea-parties in the
countryside. They're looking for agreeable escorts, in rather short
supply round here, and although this turning the house upside down
may be to some small extent in my honour, I am the last person in the
world to be dispensing high spirits and gaiety. I saw Casimir Faure[2]
recently at my father's; he's staying in the country with his own father
and we're only two hours' journey away from each other. Robert[3]
came with me; the ladies treat him as their adored minstrel. Please
come as soon as you can; your music awaits you.

WE'LL READ *HAMLET* AND *FAUST* TOGETHER. Shakespeare and
Goethe! The silent confidants of my torments, the elucidators of my
life. Come, do come! No one here understands this frenzy of genius.
The sun blinds them. They just find it bizarre. The day before yester-
day, travelling in a carriage, I wrote the ballad of the King of Thule in
Gothic style;[4] I'll give it to you to put into your *Faust*, if you have one.
Adieu; time and space are separating us. Let's be together again before
the separation goes on any longer.

> But enough of that.
> Horatio, thou art e'en as just a man
> As e'er my conversation cop'd withal.

1 Ferrand then lived at Belley, 35 miles from La Côte.
2 A childhood friend.
3 Alphonse Robert.
4 The first of eight settings from *Faust*, published in 1829.

I'm suffering deeply. If you didn't come, it would be a cruel blow. But no, you'll come.

Adieu.

Tomorrow I'll be at La Côte. The day after, Wednesday, I shall have to help my family entertain M. de Ranville, the Procuror-General, who's coming with my uncle to spend two days with us. On the 27th I leave; the week after that there's a large party at the house of Hippolyte Rocher's cousin, the lovely Mlle Veyron.

Imagine!

Hector Berlioz

35 *To his sister Nanci Berlioz*   Paris, 1 November 1828

My dear sister,

[. . .] Recently, after the Odéon theatre had reopened, the orchestral players wanted to thank their conductor, M. Bloc, for the energetic way in which he had defended their interests during the period of administrative chaos, so they arranged a banquet for him and invited me too. After the appropriate toasts, M. Bloc got up and said: 'Gentlemen, I drink to the success of an artist who does not belong to the administration of the Odéon, but whom we should be proud to have among us, M. Berlioz.' The motion was received with applause, shouts and embraces, so that I was quite overcome. I was hardly expecting, indeed I was so far from expecting any such expression of esteem and support that I was extremely moved. Immediately afterwards, I proposed a toast to the memory of Weber and Beethoven;[1] you can imagine the reception it had. And to crown the occasion they chose that moment to give M. Bloc the collected works of Beethoven as a present from the orchestra; the applause went on and on.

Talking of this poor immortal, I've sent you a little work by Weber which is the most charming and delightful thing you can think of. I don't know whether you'll manage to learn the *Walze au chalet*, because it's very difficult; there's only one way to go about it and that's to learn each bar by heart and above all not to be surprised by the strange things you find in it. The G sharps in the key of D and the C sharps in the key of G are there only to give local colour to the tune. As you know, the instruments Swiss shepherds play have their fourth note sounding too high, an effect which Weber copies by using a sharp and

1 The performances of Beethoven's Third and Fifth Symphonies at the Conservatoire under Habeneck earlier in the year had been another revelation for Berlioz.

which one gets used to very quickly. The tempo is very fast and the tone one of open, unsophisticated gaiety. Imagine a Swiss mountain, the setting sun, dancing in the open air, the smell of wild thyme, a beautiful, calm evening. O Weber, Weber! . . . To die at thirty-five, alone, in London, far from his wife and two children, a man whose only desire was to live!

I've made friends with a young German who knew Weber well;[1] recently we spent five hours at a stretch playing extracts from *Der Freischütz*, *Oberon* and *Euryanthe* to M. Le Sueur, who had never heard them before; we played them all from memory, Schlösser playing and singing the passages in German, I singing the ones that had been translated into French. M. Le Sueur was over the moon; he reacted strongly to these new and unfamiliar forms.

My friendship with this young man came about in a rather curious way. I was at M. Le Sueur's the day he made himself known to him for the first time, with a letter of recommendation; this letter was from his elder brother who had been in Paris five years earlier and had had several composition lessons from M. Le Sueur – I had got to know him too then. Finding ourselves together some days later, the conversation turned to modern composers; I saw that he was beating about the bush over Rossini because he thought, for no reason whatever, that I was an ardent admirer. As for me, because he didn't come clean about what he really felt I thought he didn't dare to admit he was a Rossiniste, so for half an hour we went on using periphrases to hide an opinion which we both felt it would have been rude to give straight out. Finally I said to him, 'What do you think of *Le comte Ory*?'

'Good heavens, it's not . . .'

'Splendid, surely?'

'On the contrary, it's appalling.'

'So you're not a Rossiniste, then?'

'Heaven preserve me! How could an admirer of Weber, Beethoven and Spontini be a Rossiniste? I must say, this is what I find amazing about you.'

'Well', I said, 'if Rossini had no other supporters but me . . . where did you get that from?'

Whereupon gales of laughter at our rhetorical circumlocutions. Then the conversation livened up. He knows English, admires Shakespeare, has seen Goethe while staying in Weimar, detests the absurdities of the Italian School, loathes all that is mediocre in music and literature, so

1 Louis Schlösser.

there was ten times as much as was needed to bring us together. He's very witty and well-read into the bargain, he's been a brilliant student in more than one discipline and speaks French like a native. Nothing makes me so impatient as seeing foreigners speak our language so well when we can't speak a word of theirs. I bitterly regret not being able to learn English more quickly; it's not much, going three times a week to a public course where you take an hour to learn what would take you fifteen minutes in a private lesson. But I haven't got the money for a teacher all to myself.

Schlösser told me some charming things about Goethe: the old man is as vigorous as a thirty-year-old! He receives strangers with a cordiality and simplicity which are delightful coming from such a person. Generally his mood is of a gentle gaiety which comes close to melancholy. He survives the loss of his two famous friends, Schiller and Beethoven, with more courage than you would think possible.

They've profaned his *Faust* by turning it into a low melodrama at the Porte St-Martin. Even if it was any good, audiences like the one at this theatre wouldn't understand it, although the other audiences pretty well match it when it comes to rude common sense, sensitivity and imagination. Rossini and Franconi's horses,[1] that's what they like: showy dances, bouts of clowning, nothing goes down better.

Adieu, dear Nanci, I must leave you to go and have dinner at M. Le Sueur's where they're having a big get-together today. Embrace Prosper and Adèle for me and tell her that I'll reply to her at the same time as I write to mama.

Your brother and friend,
H. Berlioz

36 *To the Directeur des Beaux-Arts,
Vicomte Sosthène de la Rochefoucauld*   Paris, 12 November 1828

Monsieur le Vicomte,

Two months ago the committee of the Opéra received a ballet on the subject of *Faust*. The author, M. Bohain, wanting to provide me with the opportunity to have one of my works produced on the stage of the Opéra, confided to me the task of writing the music on the condition that my being entrusted with this would not be frowned on by the administration. M. Auber has been kind enough to recommend me

1 Franconi managed a circus.

warmly to M. Lubbert[1] and dispose him in my favour in the matter, but as I have not yet received the scenario of the ballet and as I am afraid of direct competition from within the Opéra, I am writing to you, Monsieur le Vicomte, and I take the liberty of looking to that kindness which you have so often shown me in the past to give me the support that I need in this present situation.

I have set to music most of the poetic texts in Goethe's drama, my head is full of *Faust*, and if nature has endowed me with a certain imagination I do not believe I could possibly find a subject on which it could play to greater advantage.

A single word from you will solve all difficulties and put an end to all hesitations. I beg you, Monsieur le Vicomte, to be good enough to utter it and thereby decide my very future.

I have the honour, Monsieur le Vicomte, to be, with the deepest respect, your most humble and obedient servant,

Hector Berlioz

Berlioz soon gave up his English lessons for lack of money. He discovered Thomas Moore's poems at this time, in a French translation, and began to set some of them to music. His passion for Harriet Smithson had not in the least diminished, in fact it was beginning to be the cause of grave unhappiness.

37 *To Edouard Rocher*   Paris, 11 January 1829

[...] Your letter for M. de Fillière[2] was not without effect; his uncle spoke to the Opéra on my behalf and I had been so warmly recommended by Auber that M. Lubbert made no difficulties about entrusting me with the *Faust* ballet music. I was just about to start on it when the success of the *Faust* at the Porte St-Martin came along to spoil everything. They decided at the Opéra not to put on the ballet as the subject was now hackneyed, and I was advised not to compose the score. I've finished the music for the separate items in Goethe's drama, the original *Faust*.[3] I think it's my best work so far.

It seems that the brain, like the fingers, acquires a skill which it retains, because when I wrote all that I was a long way from being

1 Director of the Opéra.
2 Evidently a gentleman from Dauphiné with a family contact at the Opéra.
3 The *Huit scènes de Faust*, which Berlioz published at his own expense as Opus 1 a few months later.

overcome by the feelings of joy, calm, naivety, etc, which I had to depict. Oh, if only I didn't suffer so much! . . . What musical ideas there are fermenting inside me . . . Now that I have shaken off the bridle of routine, I see stretching before me a vast field which academic rules had prevented me from entering. Hearing that fearful giant Beethoven has shown me the point that the art of music has reached, it is a question of seizing it at that point and taking it further . . . No, not further, that's impossible, he has reached the limits of the art, but equally far along another path. There are new things to be done and many of them, I feel it with the utmost intensity, and you may be sure I shall do them, if I live. Oh, must my whole destiny be drowned by this desperate passion? If, on the other hand, it turned out well, everything I've suffered would serve to feed my musical ideas, I should work like . . . My powers would be tripled, a whole musical world would come bursting fully armed out of my head, or rather out of my heart, to gain what is most precious for an artist, the approval of those capable of appreciating him.

Time lies ahead of me, and I'm still alive; with life and time many things can happen.

Adieu, continue to love me. I continue to be your faithful friend,
H. Berlioz

38 *To his sister Nanci Berlioz*   Paris, 29 March 1829

[. . .] Ah! You talk to me of the *beautiful*, the *great*, the *sublime* . . . There's a collection . . . and all gloomy! But the sublime is not sublime for everybody. What sends some people into transports is unintelligible, even ridiculous to others. And then there is the prejudice of education and the varieties in human nature. As Geniuses take wing, they distance themselves from the level of those to whom, by their own account, such Geniuses are answerable. This happens in music especially and in dramatic literature. The other day I heard one of Beethoven's last quartets.[1] M. Baillot included it in one of his evening programmes. I rushed to attend in order to see what effect this incredible work would have on the audience. There were nearly 300 people there, and the six of us who found ourselves half-dead at the truth of the emotion we felt were the only ones who did not find this composition absurd, incomprehensible and barbarous . . . It reached such

1 On 24 March 1829 the Baillot Quartet performed op. 131 in C sharp minor and op. 135 in F.

heights that one could hardly breathe . . . He was deaf when he wrote this quartet; and for him, as for Homer, 'the universe was enclosed in the depths of his soul'. It is music for the composer himself or for those who have followed the unfathomable course of his genius. There is another who takes wing in very nearly the same region, and that is Weber. Spontini is not far behind, but he has the misfortune to have been born in Italy, even though he has completely abjured the trivial style. I think his first impressions have left their mark on the development of his ideas; and then he has written only for the stage. Oh, *La vestale*! . . . As for you, you don't understand Shakespeare and Moore does not send you into ecstasies. Perhaps it's better that way. What is certain is that you force yourself to say 'I am happy' when you're not. Whereas I can say to myself quite easily 'I am unhappy' and I am. You have to laugh, it's so curious. But there, I'm only joking.

Have you read *Le dernier jour d'un condamné*?[1] It's full of weeping and gnashing of teeth. And Jean Paul, there's a thinker![2] He's not coldly pedantic like so many others I know and detest.

You mention my uncle: I saw him here last week. He left the day before yesterday. I could talk to you about him at some length.

Adieu; what a cloud of confused ideas! But the one thing they all have in common is my friendship for you.

H. Berlioz

39 *To Johann Wolfgang von Goethe* Paris, 10 April 1829

Monseigneur,

For some years *Faust* has been my constant reading. As a result of my study of this astonishing work (even though I was able to view it only through the fog of a translation) it ended by exercising on my spirit a kind of enchantment; musical ideas formed themselves in my head around your poetic ones and, although I was firmly determined never to join my feeble chords to your sublime words, little by little the seduction worked so powerfully on me, the enchantment was so violent, that the music for several scenes was composed almost without my knowledge.

I have just had my score published and, however unworthy it is of being offered to you, I take the liberty today of sending you a copy. I am quite convinced that you must already have received a very large

---

1 By Victor Hugo, recently published.
2 A volume of Jean Paul Richter's works had just been published in French.

number of compositions of all sorts inspired by your stupendous poem; I am afraid therefore that in following in the footsteps of so many others I am merely being importunate. But if, in the atmosphere of glory in which you live, you remain untouched by the approval of the humble, I trust at least that you will pardon a young composer who, with his heart swollen and his imagination inflamed by your genius, has been unable to stifle a cry of admiration.[1]

I have the honour to be, Monseigneur, with the deepest respect,
Your most humble and obedient servant,
Hector Berlioz

40 *To Edouard Rocher*   Paris, 25 June 1829

My dearest friend,

Forgive me, I'm a wretch. I've gone a whole year without writing to you and you don't reproach me for it! . . .[2] But it would hardly have been to your advantage to have to look at the picture of my anguish. I haven't the courage to describe the temporary dénouement of my tragedy. I will merely say that having been lulled all winter by the most intoxicating hopes, I've seen them all vanish and am now left alone with the most terrible despair. A mystery which I have not yet managed to unravel leads her obstinately to refuse even to listen to talk of any sort of liaison. It can't be that she has no intention ever of marrying. She refuses to explain herself over this. As for me, she absolutely will not reply to me in writing. She has merely sent word that 'she was considerably annoyed that I could not control myself, that she had already refused several times to hold out the slightest hope, that she couldn't understand why I should be so persistent'; but that 'there is nothing more impossible'.

There we are . . . And I haven't been able to find her for a single moment to talk to her; she was afraid of me and fled at my approach!

Now she's left! . . . London! . . . Enormous success! . . . While I am alone . . . wandering through the streets at night, with a poignant misery which obsesses me like a red-hot iron on my chest. I feel like rolling on the ground to try and alleviate it! . . . Going out into society doesn't help; I keep myself busy all day long but I can't take my mind

---

1 Goethe passed the score of the *Huit scènes de Faust* to Zelter, the composer with whom he most regularly discussed musical matters. Zelter judged the work to be an abomination, so Berlioz heard nothing from Goethe in response. Soon afterwards Berlioz withdrew the work, only to rework it many years later into *La damnation de Faust*.
2 Not in fact true: letters survive written five months before and eleven days before.

off her. I haven't seen her for four months now. She won't be coming back this year, even though the English Theatre begins again in a month or two. You talk to me of my parents, all I can do for them is to stay alive; and I'm the only person in the world who knows the courage I need in order to do this. My musical future becomes more promising every day. We shall have to see what transpires ... There are a thousand possibilities; maybe she is bound by some promise. Maybe she loves someone else and wants to remain faithful to him. No one knows who her Paris acquaintances are.

I can't really explain to you everything that's happened.

I've come back from the country! Gazing at the woods and the solitude is more than I can stand.

Adieu.

H. B.

41 *To Humbert Ferrand*   Paris, 21 August 1829

My dear friend,

Here's the music you've been waiting for for so long.[1] I and my printer are both to blame. In my case, the Prix de Rome examination is some slight excuse and all my recent perturbations, the new 'pangs of my dispriz'd love' unfortunately give me every justification for not thinking about anything. Yes, my poor dear Humbert, my heart is the seat of a raging fire; it's a virgin forest that has been struck by lightning. From time to time the blaze seems to have been dampened, then a puff of wind or a new outbreak or the roar of trees engulfed in flames reveals the overwhelming power of the devastating scourge.

There is no point going into detail about the new shocks that I have recently undergone, but everything has happened at once. That absurd, shameful Prix de Rome examination has just let me down severely in my parents' eyes.[2] The judges, who are not the Francs-juges,[3] are determined, they say, not to encourage me to follow a mistaken path. Boieldieu said to me: 'My dear Berlioz, you had the prize in your hand and you've thrown it to the ground. I came with the firm conviction that you would have it; but when I heard your work! ... How do you

---

1 The *Huit scènes de Faust*.
2 Berlioz's cantata for the Prix de Rome that year was *Cléopâtre*.
3 In Berlioz's opera of that name, the Francs-juges act with pitiless cruelty in condemning their victims.

expect me to give the prize to something about which *I have no idea. I do not understand* the half of Beethoven, and you want to go beyond Beethoven! How do you imagine I could understand? You throw off modulations and make light of harmonic difficulties; and there am I *who have never studied harmony and have no experience of this branch of the art*!' (It's my fault, perhaps!) 'I like only music which consoles me.'

'But, Monsieur, if you want me to write gentle music, you shouldn't give us a subject like Cleopatra: a queen in despair, who makes an asp bite her and dies in convulsions!'

'Oh, my dear Berlioz, there are always ways of being graceful about anything. I'm not by any means saying that your work is bad; I'm only saying that I don't yet understand it, I should have to hear it several times with orchestra.' (Did I refuse to allow it?) 'And then, when I saw all these bizarre forms, this hatred for everything conventional, I couldn't help saying to my colleagues at the Institut that a young man with ideas like that, who writes in such a manner, MUST DESPISE US FROM THE BOTTOM OF HIS HEART. You are a volcanic being, my dear Berlioz, and you must not write just for yourself; not everyone is made of the same metal. But come and see me, give me that pleasure, we'll talk, *I want to study you*.'

Meanwhile, Auber took me aside at the Opéra and, after saying much the same sort of thing, but with the rider that one had to write cantatas 'as one writes a symphony', without troubling over the expression of the words, he added:

'You shun the commonplace, but there's no need to force yourself never to write platitudes. The best advice I can give you is to try and write in a dull way and, when you've written something that seems to you to be horribly dull, that will be just what's needed. And consider the fact that, if you wrote music as you imagine it, the public would never understand you and music publishers would never buy your scores.'

But, I repeat, when I write for bakers and seamstresses I shall not be tempted to choose as my text the passions of a queen of Egypt and her meditations upon death. My dear Ferrand, I wish I could let you hear the scene where Cleopatra muses on the welcome that her ghost will receive from the Pharaohs buried in the pyramids. It's terrifying, frightening. It's the scene where Juliet reflects on her burial in the vaults of the Capulets, her living body surrounded by the bones of her ancestors and the corpse of Tybalt; fear which grows and grows ... reflections which end in cries of terror accompanied by a host of

[57]

double basses plucking out this rhythm:[1]

In the middle of all that, my father is getting tired of giving me an allowance, which I can't do without; I shall go back to La Côte where, no doubt, various new irritations await me. But I live only for music, it's the only thing that carries me over this abyss of miseries of every kind. Never mind, I must go there and you *must* come and see me; after all, we hardly ever see each other, my life is so fragile and we'll be so near to each other! I'll write to you as soon as I arrive.

Guillaume Tell?[2] In my opinion all the newspapers have gone completely crazy; it's a work with some good pieces in it, it's not stupidly written, there are no *crescendos* and a little less of the bass drum, that's all. Otherwise, no real feeling, but the usual mixture of art, habit, experience and audience manipulation. It goes on and on; there are yawns all round and the administration is being prodigal with free tickets. Adolphe Nourrit, as the young Melchtal, is sublime; Mlle Taglioni is not a dancer, she's an airy spirit, Ariel in person, a daughter of the skies. And they dare to rate it higher than Spontini! I was discussing this in the theatre the day before yesterday with M. de Jouy.[3] They were playing *Fernand Cortez*, and although Jouy wrote the libretto of *Tell*, he spoke of Spontini as we do, with nothing but admiration. Spontini keeps coming back to Paris all the time; he's quarrelled with the King of Prussia, his ambition has been his undoing. He's just put on a German opera which has fallen flat.[4] Rossini's successes are driving him mad, which is no surprise. But he ought to be above worrying about the public's infatuations. The composer of *La vestale* and *Cortez* writing for the public! ... To think that people who applaud *Le siège de Corinthe*[5] come and tell me they *like* Spontini, and that he actually values such support! ... He's very unhappy; the non-success of his last opera is killing him.

---

1 It is possible that Berlioz had drafted this music for a work based on *Romeo and Juliet* before using it in *Cléopâtre*. It was later incorporated in *Lélio* as the *Chœur d'ombres*.
2 Rossini's last opera was staged at the Opéra on 3 August 1829.
3 One of the librettists of *Guillaume Tell*.
4 *Agnes von Hohenstaufen*.
5 Rossini's opera played at the Opéra in 1826.

I'm setting some of Moore's Irish songs, which Gounet is translating for me; I wrote one several days ago which I'm delighted with.[1] A libretto destined for me is to be offered to the Feydeau shortly, I'm very glad to say; let's hope it's accepted.

You keep on promising me something and you don't deliver; even so, we're on the brink of a theatrical revolution which should work in our favour, so bear it in mind. The Porte St-Martin is bankrupt, the Nouveautés likewise, and the directors of these two theatres are keen to have music. It's likely that the Minister will authorize a new opera theatre; I say this because I know it's true.

Adieu.

H. Berlioz

42 To Humbert Ferrand   Paris, 3 October 1829

My dear Ferrand,

Just two words in haste. Hostilities have recommenced. I'm giving a concert on 1 November, All Saints' Day.

I've already got permission to use the Salle des Menus-Plaisirs;[2] this time Cherubini, instead of putting obstacles in my way, is merely being unfriendly. I'm going to include *two* grand overtures, also the *Concert de sylphes* and Conrad's big aria (I've added an obbligato recitative and retouched the scoring). Dabadie promised yesterday to sing it for me. Hiller is going to play for me a Beethoven piano concerto which has never been heard in Paris. Sublime! Immense!

You will have seen from the newspapers the success Mlle Heinefetter has had at the Théâtre Italien; she's going to sing a scene from *Der Freischütz* in German. In fact there's nothing she'd rather do; all we need is permission from M. Laurent, the director. Habeneck's conducting my orchestra which, as you can imagine, will be fulminating. Shall it be said that you are never to hear me? Come to Paris, even if only for a week.[3]

I wasn't able to get down to La Côte. I've so much running around and copying to do, I must bring this letter to an end. But write to me as

1 Berlioz's *Neuf mélodies*, settings of Thomas Moore's poems, were published the following February.
2 The hall later known as the Salle du Conservatoire in the Rue Bergère.
3 The programme was: overture *Waverley*, *Concert de sylphes* (from the *Huit scènes de Faust*), Conrad's aria (from *Les francs-juges*), overture *Les francs-juges*, Beethoven's Fifth Piano Concerto, Agathe's aria (from *Der Freischütz*), *Le dernier jugement* (i.e. the *Resurrexit* from the *Messe solennelle*).

soon as you can, please. Above all, assure me you'll find some pretext to give your father as to why you must spend All Saints' Day here.

Adieu.

Meyerbeer recently arrived from Vienna; the day after he left again he passed on via Schlesinger some complimentary remarks about *Faust*.

A musical journal has devoted a three-column article to me.[1] If I can get hold of a copy, I'll send it to you.

Farewell, wee may meet again, I trust, come, come then; t'is not so long.[2]

H. Berlioz

43 *To his father Dr Louis Berlioz*   Paris, 3 November 1829

My dear papa,

First of all, to calm your anxiety, I can tell you that I've had a great success with both performers and public and that I've covered the costs of the concert and even made 150 francs profit. I thought it better not to mention this concert to you beforehand, it would only have increased your anxiety. Although it gave me far less trouble than the first one,[3] I was still unable to stand up after the last rehearsal. I was prostrate with fatigue, but I've almost completely recovered now. Cherubini contented himself this time with not putting too many obstacles in my way. Whatever I asked him for he first of all refused and then agreed to a moment later. So the concert took place and my orchestra of a hundred players was conducted by Habeneck. Apart from a few mistakes, which were the result of too few rehearsals, the main pieces in the programme were performed with terrific panache. The sextet from *Faust*[4] was the only piece that the players and the public could not get the measure of, due to lack of time.

I was put to a terrifying test, which I hadn't expected; Hiller, the young German I mentioned to you, was playing in my concert a piano concerto by Beethoven, a really marvellous piece. It was immediately followed by my overture to *Les francs-juges*; seeing the effect of the sublime concerto, all my friends thought that I was lost, crushed, done for, and I admit I had a moment of mortal terror. But as soon as the overture began and I saw the impact it was having on the people in the stalls, I was completely reassured. The effect was terrific, fearful,

1 The *Revue musicale*.
2 Berlioz's salutation in English is half borrowed from Moore, half invented.
3 On 28 May 1828.
4 The *Concert de sylphes*.

volcanic, the applause went on for nearly five minutes, with shouting and stamping. After calm had been to some extent restored, I needed to edge my way between the music stands to collect a bundle of music which was on one of the theatre seats (the orchestra was on the stage). The audience caught sight of me and then the shouts and bravos began all over again, and the orchestra joined in with a hail of bows tapping on violins and double basses and on the stands; it almost made me ill. I was overwhelmed by this unexpected outburst; I was trembling, as you can imagine. But you weren't with me. I was the only one of the family there at such a moment; everyone was embracing me except my father, my mother, my sisters! . . .

The concert ended with my chorus *Le dernier jugement*, which made almost as great an impression as the *Francs-juges* overture; there weren't enough voices, the orchestra drowned them.

When it was all over and I thought the exits were clear, I left, but the players were waiting for me in the Conservatoire courtyard, and when I appeared the shouting began again in earnest; when I arrived in the orchestra pit last night at the Opéra, the players all came to congratulate me and made me the centre of attention. So there, I've had a great success and I'm completely satisfied; today's copy of *Le Figaro* contains a notice of the concert; I'll send it to you with the other papers.

I've been feeling desperately sad since yesterday; I keep wanting to cry, I wish I could die; I feel depression is going to descend on me more heavily than ever. I think I need some sleep. I can't string my thoughts together.

Adieu, dear papa, I embrace you all tenderly, mama, you, and my sisters and brother.

H. Berlioz

44 *To his sister Nanci Berlioz*   Paris, 28 December 1829

My dear sister,

Your letter hasn't been lost. Hippolyte[1] has faithfully delivered it to me. I've found three romances for two voices which I thought would suit you. There's one by Onslow[2] which is charming; they're with the bookseller, who's waiting to send them with the parcel of books until

---

1 Hippolyte Rocher, cousin of Edouard.
2 A French composer of English descent, successful particularly in the field of chamber music and song.

papa's last order but one is paid for. Everything's ready, there won't be any delay.

I should say to mama that I've just ordered a complete set of clothes at a cost of 160 francs, which leaves me rather low in funds, as you may suppose. But I couldn't do without it any longer, my whole wardrobe is very much the worse for wear. I'm having to dress up much more often, as I'm spending more time in society this winter. I've bought several folded cravats and a few dozen detachable collars.

A dedicated and well-known music-lover, the Baron de Trémont, holds splendid musical occasions at two o'clock every Sunday. I dined with him a fortnight ago at Kalkbrenner's[1] and he invited me to attend them. I spend Sunday evenings with M. Leo, a rich German amateur who's very fond of me. Sometimes we swallow Blangini's[2] insipid nocturnes, but not often; more usually there's good music and delicious tea; there's a good gathering, it's all very informal. Occasionally I spend Tuesday evenings with M. Mazel, another amateur who has friendly get-togethers; there are plenty of musicians there, but sometimes young ladies as well who regale us with Pleyel's sonata. In the mornings I sometimes go and see M. De Latouche, the Mephistopheles of modern literature.[3] My publisher Schlesinger also organizes Beethoven quartets on Fridays, played sometimes well, sometimes badly. To begin with only men used to attend, but now the ladies are starting to infiltrate; and they're all totally ugly! Do you know anything worse than ugly women who beat time with their heads and would like to be drooping lilies, but in fact look like poppies, smiling with pleasure, as if they could understand compositions of that sort?

And then the rest of the time I work, reading new books at odd moments. I very much enjoyed Hoffmann and his *Contes fantastiques*. I was deeply moved by *The Borderers*.[4] I'm waiting for Thomas Moore's life of Byron. Talking of Moore, I'm dedicating my Irish melodies to him.

And then for ninety-hundredths of the time I'm depressed about everything. My engravers don't keep their word, the lithographer makes stupid mistakes, my boots leak, my teeth hurt, my nose hurts, I'm furious with everything, I bang the piano with my fist, I want to

---

1 A composer of German birth who spent his career in London and Paris and enjoyed an immense reputation as a virtuoso pianist.
2 A minor composer of *romances* from Turin.
3 De Latouche was a fashionable writer, a friend of Stendhal and Balzac. His recent *Fragoletta* caused a scandal with its tale of androgyny.
4 By Fenimore Cooper.

smash and destroy everything. I go out, I feel cold, I climb the heights of Montmartre, I end up feeling hot, I see a great waterless plain, I think of La Côte, of you, I come home again, I see the cemetery of Montmartre, Hamlet, Shakespeare, life, misery, death, fruitless activity, the effort that leads to inertia, the possibility of brief but immense happiness, the rarity of that substance, then I hate everything totally, then I think of philosophy, I burst out laughing, I grind my teeth, I think of music and then I blush, I become serious once again, I stop, I ponder, I plan, I hear my heart beating, I'm alive.

Go and drink a glass of water.

Hiller usually comes to collect me at 11 o'clock and we have lunch together. When I've written something new, or he has, then we find a good piano and he plays the new music, when it's playable on a piano, and we give each other advice. Only he's very fond of Bach fugues, but when he sees me coming in he shuts the book, because he knows quite well that if he went on I should make my escape. I loathe those scribblings; it sounds to me like the music a kitten might make playing around on the piano keys, or like the noise of a dozen bottles of water being emptied all at once. Then Hiller moves on to a Beethoven Adagio, which he plays to perfection. When it's finished, if one of us is not in tears we look at each other for a moment without saying anything . . . A deep sigh . . . A long silence . . . and we go our separate ways. We descend from the palace of the clouds, to scrabble about in the great, filthy bazaar that is Paris with fools and knaves, music salesmen who call themselves artists, poor devils who talk seriously of Mozart, Beethoven, Spontini and Weber, and venture opinions on these men . . . And I think of those capons who sometimes, from their dung heap, turn a haggard eye upon the sun and cluck stupidly as though greeting the morning star.[1]

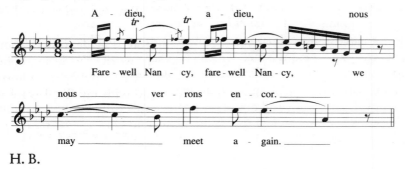

H. B.

1 The music is adapted from Berlioz's Moore setting *Adieu, Bessy* which was published with the English text awkwardly fitted to the music as well as Gounet's French translation.

My dear papa,

I discovered a few days ago from your bookseller that you have discontinued your subscription; the reason you gave was your failing sight. Was this affliction really the cause? I hope not. I have been waiting for news of you these last few days, and I am surprised not to have received any. What can lie behind this unaccustomed silence? Nanci owes me a reply; I beg her not to keep me in suspense any longer. Is she still troubled by nerves? Mama is neglecting me too, and I should really have liked one of her letters last week, which I had to spend almost entirely alone in my room suffering from an inflammation.

My right eye tooth was rotten inside and very painful. It was too late to fill in and if I had had it taken out I should have been considerably disfigured. Hoping against hope, and with no great confidence in this well-known remedy, I tried some Paraguay-Roux and the tooth was better almost at once.[1] The pain stopped almost immediately. A few days later the rotten bits of tooth fell out and now I'm no longer bothered by it. I wish I could also find a remedy to calm the feverish fury which so often torments me; not that I shall ever find one, it's the way I am. What's more, the habit I have of continually observing myself means that no sensation escapes me and reflection renders it double, so that I see myself in a mirror. I often have the most extraordinary feelings which I cannot possibly describe, caused, it would seem, by nervous exaltation and comparable with the sensations brought on by opium. But the surprising thing is that I remember quite well feeling exactly the same thing when I was twelve; I can recall those miserable days I spent gripped by emotion with no subject or object. I can see myself now, on Sundays especially, during the period when you were explaining Virgil's *Aeneid* to me, in the congregation at Vespers. The influence of the calm, monotonous chanting, together with some of the words like 'In exitu Israel' which conjured up the past, was so great that I was seized by an affliction that drove me almost to despair. My imagination surrounded me with all my Trojan and Latin heroes; the unhappy Turnus above all broke my heart; noble King Latinus, Lavinia resigned to her fate, and all that brilliant armour which I saw reflecting the Italian sunlight through clouds of dust, those customs so different

1 Paraguay-Roux was a patent medicine for toothache recently produced by the pharmacists Roux and Chaix.

from our own, all blended and mixed with ideas from the Bible and memories of Egypt and Moses, brought me to such a pitch of indefinable suffering that I should have liked to be able to weep a hundred times as bitterly.[1]

Well, that fantastic world has remained within me and has grown with all the new ideas I have come across as I have progressed in life; it's become a veritable sickness.[2]

Sometimes I feel I can hardly bear this suffering (moral or physical – I cannot tell the difference), especially on fine summer days, finding myself alone in an open space like the garden of the Tuileries. How right M. Azaïs is![3] I can easily believe that there resides in me an 'expansive force' which acts violently. I see the whole of this horizon, this sun, and I suffer so much that if I did not contain myself I should be shouting and rolling on the ground. I have found only one way of completely satisfying this immense appetite for emotion, and that's music. Without it I could certainly not survive. Chiefly it is the compositions of the great *free* geniuses that from time to time inspire me to live with an incalculable energy, but my own compositions do too. And there's something quite extraordinary in all this; sometimes, when I'm looking forward to the effect a piece of music will have, it's played badly and I find it extremely painful. But if on the other hand it's played splendidly, then the imagination, carried beyond the poetic thoughts of the composer and finding the music more beautiful and more powerful than it was expecting, becomes drunk with a violent pleasure which is absolutely at one with my nature. But enough of this, perhaps this letter may arrive at an inconvenient moment, so, silence. [...]

I ought to have written to Adèle today, but I forgot, so I'll be in touch with her another time.

Adieu, dear papa, let me have your news soon.

Your affectionate son,

H. Berlioz

1 The association of Book XII of the *Aeneid* with the chanting of *In exitu Israel* at Sunday Vespers remained with Berlioz all his life; he recalled it again thirty years later: see p. 379.
2 Berlioz speaks of a 'fantastic' world at the very moment when he is about to begin the *Symphonie fantastique*.
3 A French philosopher of the previous generation.

My dear Ferdinand,

I must write to you again this evening, not that this letter will, perhaps, be any more cheerful than the others, but never mind. Can you explain to me what it is, this power of emotion, this ability to *suffer* which is destroying me? Ask your angel ... that seraph who has opened for you the gate of heaven![2] Let us not complain ... the fire is going out, wait a moment ... I must tell you, dear Ferdinand ... To light it, I've burnt the manuscript of my *Elégie en prose*![3] Tears as always, tears of sympathy; I see Ophelia shedding them, I hear her tragic voice, the light from her sublime eyes consumes me.[4] Is this true misery, dear Ferdinand? I cannot express it!

I've spent a long time drying the tears that fall from my eyes ... In the meantime, I seem to see Beethoven looking at me severely, Spontini, who has himself known my troubles and been cured of them, considering me with an air of indulgent pity, and Weber, who seems to be whispering in my ear like a familiar spirit, living in a happy land where he is waiting to console me.

All this is crazy, completely crazy, for a man who plays dominoes in the Café de la Régence or for a member of the Institut ... No, I want to live ... once more ... Music is a celestial art, nothing surpasses it, except true love. One will perhaps make me as unhappy as the other, but at least I shall have lived ... with suffering, it is true, with rage and cries and tears, but I shall have ... nothing ... My dear Ferdinand! ... I have found in you all the signs of true friendship, and the friendship I have for you is also absolutely true; but I'm afraid it will never provide you with that calm contentment that one finds away from volcanoes ... I'm beside myself, quite incapable of saying anything ... reasonable ... It's a year ago today since I saw HER for the last time ... Oh, poor girl! How I loved you! I *love* you, and I'm shaking as I write the words! ...

If there is an afterlife, shall we meet? Shall I one day see Shakespeare? Will she know me? ... Will she understand the poetry of my love? Oh, Juliet, Ophelia, Belvidera, Jane Shore, names which Hell repeats unceasingly ...[5]

1 A young German pianist and composer who came to Paris in 1828 aged seventeen. He played Beethoven's Fifth Piano Concerto in Berlioz's concert the previous November.
2 Camille Moke, a pianist, attached then to Hiller but soon to become Berlioz's fiancée.
3 The autograph of the *Neuf mélodies*, of which the *Elégie* is the last, has not survived.
4 Still Harriet Smithson.
5 Belvidera, in Otway's *Venice Preserv'd*, and Jane Shore, in Nicholas Rowe's play of the same name, were parts Harriet Smithson had played in France.

Back to reality!

I am a miserably unhappy man, a being almost isolated from the world, an animal burdened with an imagination that he cannot endure, devoured by a boundless love which is rewarded only by indifference and contempt. Yes! But I've come to know several musical geniuses, I've laughed in their glittering light and even to remember the fact makes me grind my teeth!

Oh, sublime beings! Destroy me! Summon me to your gilded clouds and deliver me! . . .

REASON.

'Be calm, you fool, in a few years the only sufferings of yours that will survive will be what you call the genius of Beethoven, the passionate emotion of Spontini, the fantastic imagination of Weber, the colossal power of Shakespeare! . . .

'Beyond all doubt, Harriet Smithson and Hector Berlioz will be reunited in the oblivion of the tomb, which will not prevent other wretches from suffering and dying! . . .'

The Symphonie fantastique *was completed in April 1830, but Berlioz's plan to perform it on Ascension Day (May 30) had to be abandoned because of too many other musical events taking place on the same day. The Théâtre des Nouveautés, where he planned to give it, was also inadequate for the purpose. During this period Berlioz fell in love with Camille Moke, having concluded that Harriet Smithson was an unworthy object of his love.*

47 To Edouard Rocher   Paris, 5 June 1830

My dear Edouard,

Forgive me if I write no more than a few lines, I can hardly hold my pen, I'm dying. I wrote to my father today, asking his permission for me to marry. You know that charming young person we met together one day, the one I said had told me of all Mlle Smithson's infamous behaviour. Well, my dear fellow, it's her. I've loved her ever since I was cured, but she loved me even before the hydra abandoned my heart; she loved me even while everyone thought her affections were settled on another. She told me so herself, before I said anything. I didn't mention it to you out of prudence. I was consumed with anxiety. Today we took the important step. She has just made a complete declaration to her mother, and I on my side have written to my father giving him all the preliminary information about her family, her education, her talents and her financial means, which are in a much happier state than mine as she earns ten or twelve thousand francs a year with her piano lessons and recitals. Her mother intended a brilliant match for her and is furious; she wanted to separate us, but finally agreed to let me into the house so as not to reduce us to despair.

I was there yesterday evening; she is ill and anxious. I can hardly drag myself along and can't enjoy a minute's peace until my father replies or arrives in person. I've begged him to come. If he speaks to you, urge him to make the journey, I've a thousand reasons for wanting him here. Tell him that you have heard talk in Paris of Mlle Moke's prodigious talent as a pianist; tell him that I pointed her out to you one day but without letting you into any secrets, and that that is all you know. But don't let my father find out anything about my cruel emotional involvement with H. Smithson; there's no point.

Adieu, write to me at once if you have any news. I feel as though I'm going to die. Yesterday evening I fainted in front of her, hearing her mother spell out all her fears; she still thinks my father will give me nothing, and refuses to make up her mind as to what she thinks about her daughter's love for me. When I recovered consciousness, to see her holding me and covering me with tears ... Oh my dear Edouard, what if my father decides to oppose it! Not that he would have the slightest justification for doing so. It would be terrible to die at this moment.

Adieu, adieu.

H. Berlioz

In July 1830 Berlioz entered for the Prix de Rome for the fifth time. His cantata Sardanapale *was finally judged the winner, a success which guaranteed him a generous scholarship for five years and required him to study in Italy and Germany. His confinement in the Institut to sit the examination finished just as three days of revolution broke out in the streets of Paris, toppling the monarchy of Charles X and bringing in the citizen-king Louis-Philippe.*

48 *To his father Dr Louis Berlioz*   Paris, 2 August 1830

My dear papa,

I was the first to leave the Institut, last Thursday at 5 o'clock, at the moment the Louvre was being captured. This depressingly important competition was the only thing that could keep me barricaded and immured in this fort for two days, while there was a massacre taking place under our eyes. The bullets and cannon balls were aimed directly at us, from a battery in the Louvre raking the Pont des Arts and reaching the doors of the Institut, which were riddled with them. As soon as I'd written the last note, you can imagine that my first impulse was to follow where mortal anxiety led me, through the last of the cannon balls, the screams, the dead, the wounded, etc. Luckily I found everything as I had hoped. When I left Mme Moke's house, the first task was to run and arm myself and to attempt to be useful – but not the easiest to accomplish. After running around for three hours, all I could find was a pair of long cavalry pistols without any ammunition.

The national guard sent me to the Hôtel de Ville; I rushed there, no cartridges. Finally, by badgering passers-by I ended up completely equipped. I got a ball from one, powder from another, a knife to cut the lead from another. And then, of course, I had no fuse. On the Friday evening there was rumour of an impending clash at St-Cloud. A crowd of us left for the barrier at the Etoile, but we arrived separately and once more nothing happened. The guards camping in the Bois de Boulogne dispersed and everyone turned back towards Paris.

The thought that so many brave people bought our liberty with their blood while I was one of those who were of no use whatever does not leave me a moment's peace. It's a new tribulation, to add to so many others . . .

I am very impatient to have your news. What is happening at Grenoble? Here everything is calm, and the admirable sense of order which has prevailed during the three days of this fantastic revolution continues ever more insistently; not one theft or crime of any kind. The masses are sublime!

Adieu, my dear father.

Your affectionate son,

H. Berlioz

49 *To Gaspare Spontini*   Paris, 15 September 1830

Monsieur,

For a long time I have been burning with the desire to see you and to express to you in person my unbounded admiration for your genius. M. Le Sueur, whose pupil I am, has promised several times to introduce me to you, but my impatience does not allow me to wait any longer. In any case, these introductions have something cold and dull about them which would assort ill with the intimate, profound and considered love inspired in me by your compositions. I hope, Monsieur, you will do me the honour of receiving me. If knowing, understanding and being moved by your works are entitlements to your benevolence, I swear to you that I deserve it as much as anyone.

I have the honour to be, Monsieur, your devoted servant,

Hector Berlioz

50 *To Humbert Ferrand*   Paris, October 1830

Oh my dear, inexpressibly dear friend!

I'm writing to you from the Champs-Elysées, in a corner of an outdoor tavern, bathed in the glow of the setting sun; I see its golden rays playing on the dead and dying leaves of the young trees which surround my retreat. I've spent the whole day talking about you to someone who understands, or rather guesses at, your feelings. I can't help writing to you. What are you doing, my dear, dear fellow? I expect you're eating your heart out because of miseries that affect you only in your imagination. There are so many which beset us at close quarters, I'm sad to see you succumb under the weight of cares that are alien or very far removed. Why, oh why? I understand it better than you think: it's your way of life, your poetry, your *Chateaubriandism.*

Not seeing you causes me a strange suffering; chained up as I am, I can't cross the miles that separate us. But I'd have so much to say to you ... If my good luck has any power to distract you from your gloomy thoughts, then I can tell you that my music's going to be performed at the Opéra in the course of this month. Once again it's to my beloved Camille that I owe this good fortune.

This is how it all came about: in her slim figure, her flighty caprices, her intoxicating grace and her musical genius I saw Shakespeare's Ariel. My poetic ideas turned towards the drama of *The Tempest* and inspired me to write a gigantic overture of an entirely new kind for orchestra, chorus, four players at two pianos, and *harmonica.*[1] I offered it to the director of the Opéra, who agreed to put it on as part of a large, spectacular event. My dear Ferrand, it's much larger than the *Francs-juges* overture. It's entirely *new.* My adoring thanks go to my blessed Camille for having inspired this composition! I told her just recently that the work was going to be performed;

1 The harmonica was a type of glockenspiel, with steel bars struck by hammers. Berlioz's overture on *The Tempest* was later (in 1831) incorporated in *Le retour à la vie (Lélio).*

she was beside herself with joy. I whispered *confidentially*, in her *ear*, after two eager kisses and an impassioned embrace, telling her of *great, poetical love* as we conceive it. I'm going to see her this evening. Her mother does not know that my music is to be heard very soon at the Opéra. We'll keep it a secret until the last moment. Being a man dominated by his imagination, you are a man in utter misery – as I am. We are a wonderfully well-assorted pair.

My friend, at least write to me, as we never see each other.

Prize-giving at the Institut takes place on the thirtieth of this month. Ariel is as proud as the proverbial peacock of my crown, but he (or she) attaches no more importance to it than does public opinion; Camille is too musical to be misled by it. But the overture to *The Tempest, Faust,* my songs, the *Francs-juges*, they're different; they're full of fire and tears.

My dear Ferrand, if I die, please don't become a monk (as you've threatened); live as prosaically as you can; it's the way to be ... prosaic. I saw Germain recently and we talked a lot about you. What is there to do, or say, or write from such a distance? When shall I be able to communicate my thoughts to yours? I'm surrounded by people singing that dreadful *Parisienne*.[1] Semi-intoxicated national guards-men bellow it out in all its mediocrity.

Adieu; the marble I'm writing on is freezing my arm. I think of the wretched Ophelia: *ice, cold, moist earth*, Polonius dead, HAMLET ALIVE ... She is indeed wretched! Through the Opéra-Comique going bankrupt she has lost more than 6000 francs.[2] She's still here; I met her just recently. She recognized me with the utmost composure. I suffered the whole evening, then went to confide in the *delicate Ariel*, who said with a smile, 'You weren't taken ill? You didn't fall over backwards? ...'

No, no, no, my angel, my genius, my art, my thought, my heart, my inspiration! I suffered without a groan, thinking of you; I adored your strength; I blessed my recovery; from my isle of delights I braved the savage waves that broke upon its shore; I saw my ship smashed and, with a glance at my leafy cabin, I blessed the bed of roses upon which I was to lie. Ariel, Ariel, Camille, I adore you, I bless you, in a word *I love you*, more than the poor French language can say; give me an

1 A popular song of the 1830 Revolution.
2 Harriet Smithson appeared in May at the Opéra-Comique in *L'auberge d'Auray*, a comic opera by Hérold and Carafa. Her role was in English while the rest of the cast spoke (and sang) in French. In June the directors of the theatre absconded, so she was never paid.

orchestra of a hundred players and a choir of a hundred and fifty voices, and I'll tell you.

My dear Ferrand, adieu; the sun has set, I can no longer see, adieu; no more thoughts, adieu; far too many feelings, adieu. It's six o'clock, it will take me an hour to get to Camille's, adieu!

H. Berlioz

51 *To his father Dr Louis Berlioz*   Paris, 31 October 1830

My dear papa,

The prizes at the Institut were given out yesterday.[1] I received mine in the most complete isolation. M. Le Sueur was ill in bed and could not attend. Mme Moke was as good as her word and did not appear. I had no father, no mother, no master, no mistress, nothing . . . except a crowd of curiosity-mongers, following the stir made by the final rehearsal of my piece. Here are the facts. As I had already been awarded the prize, I added a long piece of descriptive music for the burning of Sardanapalus' palace; I no longer had anything to fear from the members of the Academy and I allowed my imagination free play. In the middle of the blazing tumult I brought back all the musical ideas of the scene, piled up one upon the other; the song of the dancing girls in the first part now changed (by means of some melodic modifications) into cries of female terror, and with it the proud passage in which Sardanapalus refuses to give up the crown; and then all the terrifying amalgam of sounds of misery, cries of despair, outbursts of pride which even death cannot stifle, the roaring of the flames, leading to the crumbling of the palace in which every anguished voice is silenced and the flames extinguished.

I HAD A STAGGERING SUCCESS. I cannot describe it any other way.

The final rehearsal took place on Friday at the Institut. For the first time since the prize has been awarded, the hall was full, as on the days of public sessions; but full of artists, which was the audience I needed. They played two other scenes as well: the one by Montfort who won the second prize, and an Italian piece by a past winner who had come back from Rome. Both of them were *sunk*, that's the term that's used for well-bred whistling. At the end of the rehearsal we came at last to my piece. I had arranged with the orchestra not to stop and to go right through without a hitch; everything went well and at the end the

1 The cantata *Sardanapale* was performed on 30 October 1830 at the Prix de Rome award ceremony. Only a fragment of the work has survived.

audience were flabbergasted by the conflagration. I was crushed by applause, embraced by I don't know how many people, *carried*, so to speak, as far as the courtyard of the Institut, in short *plunged* into success. And then when I arrived at the Opéra that evening, the same thing all over again ... What really touched me was the emotion shown by those old veterans in the orchestra pit, who are not normally moved by anything and sit at their desks like insensate machines. Some of them broke with habit to the point of taking my hand and congratulating me at great length; and I heard others saying to each other in that marvellously objective tone of voice with which they describe everything, 'Heavens above ... I've heard some damned odd music in the last twenty-five years, but that beats everything, I've never heard anything like it.' – 'It's what you might call an astonishing conception!' Oh, father, if only you'd been there!

Well, anyway, yesterday, when the prizes were given out, here too I had a huge success, both when the names were read out, and afterwards and during the performance of my scene (because they interrupted the orchestra in the middle with applause). Would you believe that, as ill-luck would have it, the huge impact of the burning of the palace was lost? Where it crumbles at the end, the crowning glory of my firework display, something immense, new, original, my personal discovery, it all went for nothing. The instruments who should have been responsible for this effect have bars' rest to count beforehand and then enter like thunder. Well, no, they didn't enter! An unbelievable lapse of concentration, followed by terror and panic! I was in the orchestra pit, signalling to them to start playing, but they thought I was wrong and didn't come in; then the moment for the entry went past and it was too late. Oh, of all things! I was so angry I nearly died, I couldn't restrain myself from throwing my score *across the orchestra*, I knocked over the desk next to me, I would have exterminated everything if I could. They still applauded three separate times at the end (because the orchestra went on playing), but what an effect compared with what it might have been! Imagine a rocket or a luminous bomb which soars into the air with a huge din and then doesn't explode. And then there were all the people who had been brought along by those who'd heard it the day before, all telling them (as I heard): 'Just you wait, you're going to hear something extraordinary; it's an incredible effect, as though you're watching the leap from the Kremlin.'[1] M. Rocher was there, and on his way out did his

1 Perhaps an allusion to the officers of Peter the Great, who would leap on horseback from the Kremlin's ramparts if ordered to do so.

best to console me, assuring me the whole work had been felt and appreciated. But, good Lord, you can't feel and appreciate what you don't hear. All the enthusiasts from the day before came up to me, not to embrace me but to join me in cursing the performers' incompetence. It was a concert of imprecations addressed by the remainder of the orchestra to the poor devils who, without meaning to, had played this abominable trick on me; they were abject in apologizing for their inattentiveness, but what good was that! It's all over. And to think that Spontini was there and that he had come especially for this piece! Dear God, and this was the mighty novelty I was offering him the first time he was to hear my music! [...]

Adieu, my dear papa. Your affectionate son,
H. Berlioz

52 *To François-Joseph Fétis*   Paris, 6 November 1830

Monsieur,

May I venture to invite you to attend the final dress rehearsal this evening of my overture *The Tempest*?[1] As the forms that I have employed in this score are not widely used in our musical world, I should be much obliged if you would be good enough to hear it twice before passing judgment on it.[2] In the event of your wishing to attend the revival of *Otello*[3] which also takes place this evening, I have the honour to inform you that we shall begin at the Opéra at half-past six precisely and be finished by half-past seven. Your name is on the list of theatre passes; please give your name to the attendant as you come in. Despite the relatively small number of singers and the lack of string players, I have reason to hope that the performance will be, if not poetic, at least accurate and satisfying.

I have the honour to be, Monsieur,
Your devoted servant,
Hector Berlioz

Before departing for Italy Berlioz was determined to give a concert to include the first performance of the Symphonie fantastique. *This took place on 5 December 1830 at the Conservatoire, conducted by*

1 The overture on *The Tempest* was given at the Opéra on 7 November 1830.
2 Fétis reviewed the work warmly in the *Revue musicale*.
3 By Rossini.

Habeneck. The programme also included the Francs-juges *overture, two choral pieces from the* Neuf mélodies, *and* Sardanapale. *The concert was attended by Fétis, Spontini, Meyerbeer and the young Liszt, and was clearly a sensation and a success. Berlioz tried in vain to plan a repeat performance a week later.*

53 *To Humbert Ferrand*   Paris, 12 December 1830

My dear Ferrand,

For various reasons I can't give my second concert. I'll be leaving Paris at the beginning of January. My marriage is fixed for Eastertide 1832, provided I don't lose my scholarship and that I spend a year in Italy. It's my music that has wrung an agreement out of Camille's mother! My beloved symphony is the reason, then, that she is mine.

I'll be at La Côte around 15 January. We must definitely meet; see that we don't miss each other. You'll come to La Côte; you'll accompany me to Mont Cenis or at least as far as Grenoble, surely, won't you?

Yesterday Spontini sent me a wonderful present: a score of his *Olympie*, costing 120 francs, with his autograph inscription on the title page: 'My dear Berlioz, when you read through this score, think occasionally of your good friend Spontini.'

I'm drunk with happiness. Now that Camille has heard my *Sabbath*,[1] she refers to me all the time as 'her dear Lucifer, her handsome Satan'.

Adieu, my dear Ferrand; write me a long letter at once, I implore you.

Your constant and devoted friend,
H. Berlioz

54 *To Stephen de la Madelaine*[2]   Paris, 30 December 1830

My dear Stephen,

I couldn't find a moment to come and say goodbye to you. As all my evenings have been occupied (you can guess who by) I haven't been able to attend the Opéra, so I'm having to make my farewells to you in writing. I'm leaving, but without anxiety, I'm glad to say. My Ariel, my

1 The finale of the *Symphonie fantastique*.
2 A Conservatoire friend of Berlioz's whose career was to be in government administration. But he also wrote novels and treatises on singing and was active as a music critic.

angel, can no longer be torn away from me; such are the ties that bind us, we can be separated only by our own will. I still have one misery to undergo, that of leaving her . . . Wretched routine! How much longer will you rule over us? . . . However much I belabour it, it still rears its stupid, ridiculous head. But one day, I hope, I shall beat it down low enough to place my foot on it and crush it.

During my exile I'll try and write something important; I shall attempt to realize an immense project I have in mind and when I get back we'll shake up the musical world in a curious fashion.[1] Meanwhile, keep battering away at what's left of the tumbledown academic hovel as a further proof of your friendship towards

Your devoted

Hector Berlioz

P.S. I leave in six hours' time ALONE. Adieu.

Berlioz left Paris at the very end of 1830 for a period of twenty-two months. He stayed with his family at La Côte-St-André for a month, and then took the boat down the Rhône from Lyon to Marseille, then another boat from Marseille to Livorno. At the end of February he arrived in Florence.

55 *To his father Dr Louis Berlioz*   Florence, 2 March 1831

I can't wait for the end of my journey, my dear papa, to let you know how it has been progressing. As I feared, our captain didn't leave Marseille until two days after he'd promised. When we did finally set sail, the Sardinian boat, on which I found myself with ten or so French-speaking Italians, spent a whole day out of action for lack of wind; then we moved on very slowly for eight or nine hours before the flat calm returned to plague us, for which we were to receive forceful amends. Be that as it may, the crossing from Marseille to Livorno should take four or five days with the most mediocre weather and it took us eleven, partly because of the calm and partly because of the contrary wind. When we reached the gulf of Genoa, we were assailed by a furious wind coming down off the snowy mountains on the coast and we began to die of cold. At all events, with the wind catching it

---

1 Berlioz mentioned various large-scale projects in the following years which were not to be realized. This one was probably *Le dernier jour du monde*, an oratorio planned to incorporate the *Resurrexit* from the 1824 Mass.

beam on, the ship was scudding along quite fast enough to satisfy our impatience: the captain, a good fellow but no expert at his job, had ordered full sail and this gave the wind such a purchase that the ship began to list horribly and we were all in some desperation. We had a young Venetian corsair captain on board who knew the ropes; seeing the storm worsen, he kept on saying to us: 'That imbecile is going to take us to the bottom with all those sails.' As it was, the worst we suffered was seeing the waves break over the bridge, flood it and then withdraw.

But the next night the storm increased and as I was entertaining myself in the cabin watching the contortions of passengers trying to get up on deck to vomit and bumping into each other (I'm not sea-sick), I heard the corsair shouting to the sailors in Italian: 'Take courage, by God, it's nothing.' I realized at once that it was a lot, and I confess my heart started to beat fearfully, seeing the fury of the cross-wind filling the fourteen sails. A moment later the sailors in despair started to mutter 'Ah, Holy Madonna, all is lost!' Our old captain still didn't move or say anything, and the corsair shouted out in Italian, 'Never mind the Madonna, for the love of God, take in the sails or we're done for any minute!' Then some of the other passengers with me on the bridge, clinging as best we could to the rigging (it was impossible to stand up straight, the deck was at such an angle), all shouted out together: 'Captain Jermann, take command, you can see this old fool's lost his head.'—'Quick, quick, all hands to the topgallant!' Not before time all the sailors, young and old, hurled themselves at the mainmast, and while they were climbing a final gust of wind gave us such a buffeting that all the furniture, utensils, trunks, etc, down below were hurled about with a terrific crash. On the bridge the barrels toppled over and rolled about banging into each other; all over the boat water was pouring into hatchways and with the ship creaking like an old nutshell we all thought our last moment was at hand. But in the meantime the ship had rolled, and while it was coming upright our intrepid sailors had managed to fold the largest sail, and as the wind paused for breath at that moment we were allowed some respite. Finally, in the space of two minutes, twelve sails were taken in and we were no longer terrified by the wind whistling in the rigging. Then the water to pump out of the inside! . . . a fire in a bale of wool! . . . Hell cannot be worse than a moment like that.

As for me, I took precautions against any needless suffering; to prevent myself swimming I twisted my arms up in my cloak so that I would sink to the bottom like a sack of lead. Now I'm glad to have been through this trial and seen for myself that death is uglier from a distance than close to. The truth is that when this storm started in the night, I could not have stopped myself trembling, but when I thought we were done for and saw the furious sea turning us white with its spray, like the boa constrictors in America that slobber over their victim before devouring it, then I began to look at everything with a strange indifference; I began to look ahead to the morrow, and it seemed to me that the white valleys I saw foaming in front of me were going to rock me into a painless sleep.

When we reached Livorno, six of us found lodgings in the same hotel. The next morning we had a visit from our brave sailors who came to join in the rejoicing at having escaped from the sea and to wish us a safe journey; we tried to give them money but they refused, saying they 'didn't want us to think their visit had an ulterior motive'.

Poor humanity; what a living! To spend your life in a prison made of planks, to have to climb up in the darkness through the furious elements on slippery masts and hang on to ropes above the abyss like spiders on their webs, and all so as to eat biscuits as hard as wood, seasoned with raw cod and a little wine. When I talked to them about it (they all spoke French) they said: 'What are we to do? It's better than being a brigand in Calabria, or dying of hunger.'

Since I landed, I have been – indeed *we* have been – harassed by the police.[1] We are searched by them both on the way in and on the way out and there are dozens of formalities to be gone through to be able to stay in a town. As soon as we arrived here, my travelling companions left me. I was in a state of considerable indecision. The Italian revolution is spreading like a torrent and the papal nuncio refused to visa my passport for Rome. I wrote at once to the French Academy and Vernet[2] replied that he had taken steps to ensure that I would be allowed in, sending me a draft for 175 francs to cash in Florence for the month of February. Meanwhile all the French are escaping from Rome, and I have to go and bury myself in that wasps' nest because forty old dodderers, high priests of routine, have decided I won't know my job unless I pass through that musical sewer.

I've seen a new opera here by the young Bellini on *Romeo and Juliet*;[3] wretched, ridiculous, feeble, null; the little idiot isn't worried that the ghost of Shakespeare might come and haunt him in his sleep;

---

1 Italy was then seized with insurrections and the French were widely assumed to be assisting the rebels.
2 Horace Vernet, the painter, was Director of the French Institut's school in Rome.
3 *I Capuleti e i Montecchi.*

he would thoroughly deserve it. And the posters say: *Il celebre Maëstro Bellini!* But one must be fair to the Florentines: it was the first perform-ance and their coldness was admirable, not a single burst of applause. The grand duke was there; he seems to be very well liked, for they greeted him with several extremely vigorous acclamations.

I've renewed my acquaintance here with a young Danish architect I knew in Paris; a Dane! . . . There's a Shakespearean idea; we've talked about Elsinore and Hamlet's castle . . . Oh! A Roman *Hamlet*! Even though I'm in Italy, my thoughts are dark and clouded; my life is in Paris and my sufferings are inexpressible; there is not a moment, not one, night or day, when I can put my hand on my heart and say: 'I'm glad you're still beating'. I miss the salt water.

I cannot leave for Rome until three days' time; I'm dying to know how long Vernet intends to keep me away from Paris. And no letter from Camille! . . . If there had been any in Rome they would have been forwarded, as I asked.

My address is:

Pensionnaire de l'Académie de France, Villa Medici, Roma.

I think you have to stamp letters as far as the frontier.

Adieu, dear papa, send me news as soon as you can; I embrace you all.

H. B.

Berlioz reached Rome in early March 1831 and took up his lodgings at the Villa Medici. His greatest anxiety was the lack of news from his fiancée Camille, so within a month he decided, contrary to the regula-tions, to return to Paris and give up his scholarship rather than be separated from her. He waited in Florence in case a letter should reach him there.

56 To Humbert Ferrand   Florence, 12 April 1831

My sublime friend! You're the first Frenchman to let me have any sign of life since I've been in this garden full of monkeys called Italy 'the beautiful'. I've just received your letter, sent on from Rome from where it took seven days instead of two to reach Florence. Oh, all is well! Curses! Yes, all is well, since all is ill! What can I say? I left Rome to return to France, forfeiting the whole of my scholarship, because I was getting no letters from Camille. An infernal sore throat has kept me holed up here. I wrote to Rome asking them to forward my letters here, otherwise yours would have been lost, and that would have been a pity. Who knows whether I shall receive any others?

Don't write again, I shouldn't know where to tell you to send your letters. I'm like a floating balloon, destined to burst in the air, fall into the sea or come to rest like Noah's ark. If I reach Mount Ararat safe and sound, I'll let you know at once.

Believe me, I'm at least as anxious for us to meet again as you are; it took me a whole day of conflict and hesitation before I could put the idea aside.

I understand perfectly how angry you must be, seeing what's going on in Europe. Even I, who take not the slightest interest in it all, sometimes surprise myself by giving vent to a curse! Ah yes, liberty! Where is it? Where has it been? Where can it be? In this world of *worms*? No, my dear Ferrand, the human race is too base and stupid for the beautiful goddess to let fall a divine ray from her eyes upon it. You speak to me of music and of love! What do you mean? I don't understand ... Is there something on earth called music and love? I thought I'd heard these two ill-omened words in a dream. You are doomed to misery if you believe in them. AS FOR ME, I NO LONGER BELIEVE IN ANYTHING.

I wanted to travel to Calabria or Sicily and join the band of some robber chieftain, even as a simple brigand.[1] Then at least I should have witnessed some magnificent crimes, thefts, assassinations, rapes and burnings, instead of all these petty, shameful crimes, these acts of feeble treachery which are a sickness to one's soul. Yes, that's the world for me: a volcano, rocks, rich booty piled high in caves, a concert of terrified screams accompanied by an orchestra of pistols and carbines, blood and Lacryma Christi, a bed of lava rocked by earthquakes; now there's a real sort of life! But there aren't even any brigands any more. O Napoleon, Napoleon, genius, strength, energy, willpower! Why did your iron hand not crush another handful of this human vermin! Like some brazen-footed colossus, your slightest movement would overturn all their fine edifices of patriotism, philanthropy and philosophy! Absurd rabble!

And they talk of art, of thought, of imagination, of impartiality, of *poetry* indeed! As if they had any part in all that!

For such pygmies to speak of Shakespeare, Beethoven, Weber! But dumb animal that I am, why should it worry me? What is the whole

---

1 This paragraph reappears almost unchanged in one of the monologues in *Lélio*, which Berlioz was soon to write.

world to me, apart from some three or four individuals? Let them wallow as much as they like: it's not for me to pull them out of the mud. In any case, all that is perhaps no more than a web of illusions. Nothing is real except life and death. I met that old witch out at sea. After a wonderful storm lasting two days our ship began to sink in the Gulf of Genoa; a gust of wind blew us over on our side. I had already wrapped my arms and legs in my cloak to stop myself swimming: everything was cracking and splitting, inside and out. I was smiling as I saw those great white valleys of water coming to cradle me in my last sleep; the *grim reaper*, with a sneer on his face, was advancing on me, thinking to frighten me and, as I was preparing to spit in his face, the ship righted itself; he disappeared.

What else can I tell you? About Rome? Well, nobody was killed; only the brave Trasteverini[1] wanted to slit all our throats and set fire to the Académie on the grounds that we were in league with the revolutionaries to expel the Pope. We had no such ideas. The Pope was quite safe from us! He looks too good a man for anyone to want to upset him. Even so, Horace Vernet armed us all, and if the Trasteverini had come they'd have had a warm reception. They didn't even try and set fire to the old academic barracks! Imbeciles! Who knows, perhaps I might have given them a hand? . . .

What else?

Ah yes! Here, in Florence, during my first visit I saw an opera on *Romeo and Juliet* by a little good-for-nothing called Bellini; I 'saw' it; what they call 'seeing' . . . , and Shakespeare's ghost did not arrive to exterminate this whipper-snapper! The dead don't return!

Then there was a miserable eunuch called Pacini who'd written a *Vestale* . . .[2] Licinius was played by a woman . . . I had enough strength left, after Act I, to escape; I pinched myself on the way out to see if it was really me . . . and it was . . . O Spontini!

While I was in Rome, I wanted to buy a piece by Weber; I go into a music shop and ask for it . . .

'*Weber, che cosa è? Non conosco. Maestro italiano, francese, ossia tedesco?*'

I reply solemnly:

'*Tedesco.*'

The fellow had a good search; then with an air of satisfaction:

---

1 Inhabitants of the more populous part of Rome.
2 Pacini's *La vestale* (1823) was unacceptable to Berlioz as an admirer of Spontini's French opera of the same name.

'*Niente di Weber, niente di questa musica, caro signore, eh! eh! eh!*'
'Toad!'
'*Ma ecco Il pirata, La straniera, I Montecchi, Capuleti dal celeber-rimo maestro signor Vincenzo Bellini; ecco La vestale, I arabi del maestro Pacini.*'
'*Basta, basta, non avete dunque vergogna, corpo di Dio? . . .*'
What can one do? Sigh? That's childish. Grind one's teeth? That's trivial. Be patient? That's worse still. One must concentrate the poison, letting some evaporate so that the rest is stronger, and shut it up in one's heart until it spews it forth.

No one writes to me, of either sex. I'm alone here; I know nobody. This morning I attended the burial of the young Napoleon Bonaparte, the son of Louis, who has died at the age of twenty-five while his other brother has fled to America with his mother, poor Hortense.[1] She came from the Antilles, the daughter of Joséphine de Beauharnais, a merry Creole who gave an exhibition of negro dances on the bridge of the ship to entertain the sailors. Now she's on her way back an orphan, a mother who has lost a son, a wife who has lost a husband, a queen who has lost her country, desolate, forgotten, abandoned, barely managing to snatch her youngest son from the murderous hands of the counter-revolutionaries. Those young fools who believed in liberty and dreamt of power! There was some singing and an organ; two unskilled labourers were tormenting the colossal instrument, one pumping air into the bellows, the other activating the pipes by putting his fingers on the keyboard. He, inspired no doubt by the occasion, had pulled out the piccolo stop and was playing *jolly little tunes* which sounded like wrens twittering. You want some music; very well, I'll send you some. It's nothing like birdsong, even though I'm as happy as a finch.

1 Louis Bonaparte, the Emperor's brother, settled in Florence. One of his sons, Napoleon-Louis, died there aged twenty-seven in 1831; the other son later became Napoleon III, although the rumour that he had fled to America was false.

'Mix grave and gentle, jesting and severe.'
O Monsieur Despréaux!¹
Adieu, I've got red before the eyes.
I'll wait a few days for a letter I'm expecting, then I'll leave.
H. Berlioz

In Florence Berlioz heard news not from Camille but from her mother informing him that her daughter was soon to marry the piano maker Pleyel and had broken off her relationship with Berlioz. Seizing the pistols he had been issued at the Villa Medici and equipped with a chambermaid's disguise Berlioz set off for Paris determined to murder Camille, her fiancé, her mother and then to kill himself. By the time he reached Nice in mid-April his fury had cooled and he decided to stay awhile there and seek Vernet's pardon for abandoning his duties in Rome. He stayed three weeks and there composed the overture Le roi Lear *and part of another, on Walter Scott's* Rob Roy.

57 *To Edouard Rocher*   Nice, 30 May 1831

Dear Edouard,
   So you're getting married! A good thing, because you'll be happy; not as much as I should like, but (I hope) as much as our sad, civilized society will allow. From what I've heard, you've made the best possible choice. Make use of it, don't misuse it. Marriage is a *sturdy* bond, since it can't be broken. From it stems a whole lifetime of happiness or misery; and often the happiness and misery depend to some extent on ourselves. If you're willing to listen to me, even though you may think I have little experience in the matter, I say to you that once the first moments of delirium are past, nothing on earth can bring them back; and if you love your wife and if her mind is a little above the common run, you can clip the wings of pleasure and keep it close to you for longer than it had intended. First, the woman you have chosen must really believe that you are devoted to her, body and soul, that you will never deceive her and that you have the most complete confidence in her. If she deceives you, kill her without hesitation. But if ever you are unfaithful to her, never look me in the face again, because you would

1 The first passage of music is the 'Dies irae' theme from the finale of the *Symphonie fantastique* (Berlioz in fact quotes a further 58 bars) and the second is the concluding phrase of the popular song 'J'ai du bon tabac'. 'Mix grave and gentle, jesting and severe' is a quotation from Boileau-Despréaux's *L'art poétique* (1674).

be unable to without blushing. I know these principles are not those of the 'beau monde'; but I take satisfaction from that and I have too high an opinion of you to think that you have ever shared the beliefs of that world which is called 'beau', and which I find so ugly.

From the physical point of view, I recommend you always to observe the greatest delicacy in your marital relations. *Try to have an apartment separate from your wife's*, never get dressed in front of her, and never treat her thoughtlessly. Puerile as these points may seem, I can assure you that they have the most serious consequences. Never be weak; it is for the elm to support the vine. But do not be lacking in consideration either; marriage, like government, needs Napoleon's iron hand in the velvet glove. As far as possible keep your wife away from those brainless, heartless people who abound in society; you can do so easily enough and it's of the greatest importance.

To turn to my own affairs, I expect you know that Camille is married! She's married Pleyel! From what you know and what you *don't* know you can judge the extent of such a crime and the depravity of her character. Her mother is a thousand times more despicable than she is. I'm beginning to recover. It's because of her treacherous behaviour that I'm now in Nice. Good luck saw to it that a thousand miles stood between us. You know me well enough to imagine what I did and what I should have liked to do. I ought to have started back for Rome yesterday, but I'm not going until tomorrow. It'll be the third time I've crossed Italy *entirely alone*. But this time I'm totally devoted to my art and to my friends, restored to life,[1] friendship and music. It'll be marvellous to see you again and I'll tell you all the things I daren't write. Write to me in *Rome, Académie de France*, with news of yourself especially. I'll discuss money next time.

Adieu, your sincere friend,

H. Berlioz

58 *To his family*   Rome, 24 June 1831

Adèle[2] says in her last letter, which I found here on my arrival, 'Nanci will write to you in a couple of days', and this letter hasn't come. I wrote back to Adèle on 6 June, and since then every postal delivery has been a disappointment. So don't promise me letters if you're not going

1 *Le retour à la vie*, the 'return of life', later titled *Lélio*, was the work Berlioz began to draft on his return from Nice to Rome, a journey which occupied the second half of May 1831, taking him through Genoa, Lucca, Pisa and Florence again.
2 Berlioz's younger sister, now aged seventeen.

to write them; it's a torment to have one's expectations consistently dashed.

I trust everything goes well at home and that Nanci has at least received news of my return to the Prison. What an accursed place! But I'll be out of it soon. In a week at the most I'll be off to stay in Tivoli. I went there on foot last Saturday at two in the afternoon in a cloud of burning dust; there were two of us; three quarters of the way there we couldn't do any more and climbed aboard a passing carriage. It's fifteen miles from Rome to Tivoli. We arrived at half-past eight in the evening and at four o'clock the next morning we were up and away. I've never seen anything so beautiful and delightful. The waterfalls, the clouds of vapour, the smoking chasms, the limpid stream, the caves, the countless rainbows, the olive groves, the mountains, the rustic houses, the village, it's all breathtaking and original. The people round there are very good-looking, but even more inclined to beg than in Rome. At least their begging habits are not as grossly distasteful as those of the Romans. They're quite open about it, so that it ends up by being funny; they name the sum they would like and laugh as though it were a joke. Young men and women in their twenties would see us go past as they were harvesting the crops and would shout out, 'Hey there, gentlemen, give us five sous, give us a sou, what's that to you?'

I also saw Hadrian's villa and those sublime ruins aroused so many thoughts and sensations in me, I feel they wanted to make up to me for the non-impression of all the ones in Rome. Imagine a country property four miles in circumference in which the Emperor Hadrian had brought his dreams to life. At the entrance is a Greek theatre; there are only two columns and some arches of the amphitheatre left, and the middle is a mass of cabbages. But to do justice to the proprietor, that's the only part that's cultivated; all the rest is in the most magnificent state of abandonment. The imperial palace, the baths, the library, the leisure rooms and the courtyards are, for ruins, quite well preserved; in the rooms belonging to the Emperor's guards sparrow-hawks and kites are building their nests; the Vale of Tempe (an imitation of the one in Greece)[1] is today a forest of reeds; I wasn't able to see Tartarus or the Elysian Fields or a host of other things whose names escape me, one gets confused. There are walls six metres thick, of prodigious height, covered in stucco with frescoes painted on them, towers, vaulted roofs, columns everywhere; but no statues, because some Pope, I don't know

1 The Vale of Tempe in Thessaly, between Mounts Olympus and Ossa, was held to be one of the most beautiful sites in Greece.

which one, had them taken away to make lime with. My entry into this monument brought me face to face for the first time with the grandeur that was Rome. I was overwhelmed, disturbed, obliterated. If only I had been alone! But patience, it's only half an hour to Tivoli and when I'm settled in there I'll go and spend the day there sometimes.

I'm delaying my departure from here until I've finished the music for a 'Mélologue' in six movements[1] which I composed on the way from Florence to Rome. The words were completed a long time ago, so I've only got to put the finishing touches to two orchestral sections. It's a work of a new kind with no model behind it; the idea for it came from a little sketch by Thomas Moore at the end of his melodies.[2] Luckily I had everything finished in my head and in my notebook before setting foot in the Académie's portals, because once there I had not a single idea or sensation; boredom has established its dominion and its leaden sceptre seems to me a hundred times heavier there than elsewhere. Sometimes I try going down into Rome, but I'm even more bored there. There are no theatres, not a trace of any music, no literary meetings, and cafés that are dirty and dark with poor service and no newspapers. In this city of *marble* you're served on nasty little *wooden* pedestals like the one we have in the kitchen to put the lamp on. Everything here is a hundred and fifty years behind the civilized world and behind the rest of Italy in general. The people are so slipshod, soft and idle; nature provides them with everything and they don't know what to do with it. If only this lovely place was populated by the English, what a difference there'd be!

Two evenings ago I felt some real emotion in our monastery for the first time. There were four or five of us sitting in the moonlight around the fountain by the steps in the garden; we drew lots to see who should go and fetch my guitar, and as the company was composed of the small number of students whom I can tolerate, I began to sing without waiting to be asked. As I was starting an aria from *Iphigénie en Tauride* M. Carle Vernet[3] arrives; after two minutes he starts to weep, with loud sobs, and unable to control himself he runs into his son's drawing-room, crying in a stifled voice, 'Horace! Horace! Come here!'

'What is it, what is it?'

'We're all in tears!'

'Why, what's happened?'

1 *Le retour à la vie.*
2 The alternation of dramatic monologue and six musical numbers was indeed novel. The subtitle 'mélologue' (which he later changed to 'monodrama') came from Moore.
3 Horace Vernet's father, also a distinguished painter.

'It's M. Berlioz singing Gluck. Yes, monsieur,' he says to me, 'it's enough to lay one flat; you have a melancholy character, *I* understand you, but there are people who . . .'

He can't finish his speech, but no one is laughing. The fact is that we were all too deeply moved. I was in the right mood, it was dark, there was nothing to unsettle me under that echoing portico, and I was letting myself go as if I were alone. M. Horace is always saying it's superb and that he's 'crazy about music' but he doesn't feel anything; I notice that all the people who speak of their great love of music are precisely the ones who understand it least. He's the most contented man one can imagine; at forty-two he still has the same tastes he had at eighteen. Recently he had the honour of going to a masked ball at the Princess de Wolkonski's house; his daughter went as a girl from Naples and he as a hussar captain, and they danced the tarantella and the mazurka together with terrific success. Every week he holds a large party, with dancing. I nearly always go, but if I miss one, Mme Horace never fails to ask what I was doing and why I didn't come. This evening it's the director's birthday party, there'll be a big ball, and father Carle will buttonhole me to talk about Gluck; he's so happy that I'm not like my predecessor[1] who found all that 'rococo'! He's a remarkable man, who spends half the day on horseback (as he no longer paints) and the rest of his time making up puns and worrying about the health of his son, whom he loves to an extent uncharacteristic of old men. Anyway, that'll see me through the evening with the help of half a dozen cups of tea, provided that Mlle Horace doesn't regale us with some fashionable air;[2] I'd rather listen to Le Sueur's daughters or to the squeaks of a bat than to her singing. And then the *celeberrimo maestro Bellini*, a little good-for-nothing who has taken it into his head to write a *Romeo and Juliet*! This clown is the favourite of the moment. Rossini is not particularly to the Romans' taste, they find him TOO SERIOUS, he sends them to sleep, he's TOO MUCH FOR THEM. Wretched apes! Soon Bellini himself will be *too sad*, they'll have to find another *celeberrimo maestro* who's more entertaining. The men on the moon have as much idea of music as these people.

    H. Berlioz

1 One of the previous Prix de Rome composers.
2 It was for Louise Vernet, Horace's daughter, that Berlioz wrote the song *La captive* the following year.

At last it's raining! I can see clouds! Ah! Blessed be the sky of Subiaco and cursed the leaden sky of Rome which burns unceasingly and has neither thunder nor lightning! The countryside here is the most picturesque I've seen in my life. It doesn't have Tivoli's waterfalls, but a furious torrent almost as wide as the Anio which comes roaring down in two or three places as noisily, if not as majestically, as the great waterfall at Tivoli.

And then the mountains! Ah, the mountains! An hour ago I was among them. This morning I climbed a lofty mass which the landscape painters call the Whale, because in fact it looks like a huge whale coming up out of the sea to take a breath. At one o'clock in the afternoon I reached the topmost point, I built a little pyramid with lumps of rock and finished it off with a flat stone in the form of a druidic altar. Oh, how I breathed, how I gazed, how I lived! Not a cloud! I'd been climbing on hands and knees for half an hour, then I lay down on some clumps of boxwood with a soothing wind gently rocking me. Before reaching the upper heights I found a little uninhabited house, crossed a garden filled with vines and maize and beyond the boundary hedge found myself in a charming flat meadow planted with olive-trees ... Immediately I seemed to hear mama, fifteen years ago, singing this couplet:

> A little cottage I desire,
> A shady orchard set above,
> Wherein to spend Spring's lovely hour
> And be with her, my muse and love.

Higher up, where the vegetation ended, I came across peasants harvesting thinly sown corn. They seemed anxious at seeing me climbing all on my own and with no apparent purpose (I'd left my gun behind at Subiaco); there's a superstition in these parts about *jettatori* (people who cast spells). I think they took me for a *jettatore*; they asked me cheerfully where I was going and what I wanted to do up there. Luckily I had a good idea: I told them I had made a vow to the *madona* and it was to fulfil that that I was climbing. At which they went back to their harvesting without bothering about me. When I reached the top, I could see at my feet the monastery of St Benedict where I'd been the day before. This monastery reminded me of our old priest Durand who often used to tell us of St Benedict hiding under a thorn bush to escape the temptations of the devil. I saw the cave where the saint fought the demon. A chapel has been built so that this cave is behind the altar. To the side is a little thicket of rose bushes; in a corner there's a pile of rose leaves which the Benedictine monks give to those afflicted people who have visions; the leaves make them disappear. In the church are hung up the remains of two carbines, palpable proof of two major miracles: some hunters had overloaded their weapon, but they prayed to St Benedict as it went off and they weren't hurt at all. These Benedictines are not like the Carthusians, as they didn't even offer me a glass of water, even though I could have done with one. Subiaco is a dirty village dedicated to St Andrew (a second point of resemblance with La Côte) and built round a sugar loaf with a little fort on the top. Down below runs the roaring torrent which would make the fortune of any other people, but which here serves only for washing.

To eat, there are no potatoes, no cows' milk, no figs, no oranges, but quantities of goats and nuts; every day it's the same food. There are several French landscape painters in the building with me, who have come to Subiaco to copy the beauties of nature; we dine together, one of them is a comrade of mine at the Académie. The other inn is full of Swiss, Irish and French painters; we all know each other already.

Yesterday evening the children of the house were dancing the saltarello to the sound of a tambourine played by a little girl from nearby. I came to watch them. Then the eldest girl, who is twelve, began to plead gently: *Signore, oh! signore; pigliate la chitarra francese*. I picked up the *chitarra francese* and *lo ballo* began again with renewed vigour. Our painter friends heard our *ballo* and came to join in; all the little peasant girls were mad with excitement and danced with delightful abandon while their neighbour shook her tambourine and I took the skin off my fingers improvising saltarellos on the *chitarra francese!*

The whole area knows now about the existence of a *maestro dell' Accademia di Francia*; overtures were made through the painter I know, who is well up in the high society of Subiaco, to get me to take part in the local musical get-togethers. Yesterday, during lunch, the chorus master arrived with one of the local gentry to sound me out, but Gibert (that's the name of my academician friend) tried to make them understand that I was a savage and that it would be very difficult to tame me; they didn't dare approach me directly and I hope they'll refrain from doing so. There are some pretty women singing in the chorus, but I've seen them out walking. It's not enough to compensate for the pain their music would cause me, and I shouldn't be any use to them ... [...]

   H. Berlioz

Berlioz spent the summer of 1831 mostly in Rome, where he became friendly with Mendelssohn. In October he visited Naples.

60 *To his family*   Naples, 2 October 1831 (Mount Posilippo)

I arrived yesterday evening in Naples and today I write to you from Mount Posilippo on Virgil's tomb. It's the first thing I've come to visit. An old woman took me to see the owner of the vineyard in the middle of which the tomb lies, and here I am. As I eat yellow grapes, I look out over the lightly rippling sea. Through the mist that envelops it I can make out the island of Capri, which I intend to visit soon, and in my reverie I recall the poetic impressions made on me in my childhood by the author of the *Aeneid*. I had an extremely interesting journey. I saw the ruins of the famous Capua, so fatal to Hannibal's army; I climbed Monte Cassino and admired the celebrated Benedictine monastery. This building is larger than the Chartreuse and more richly decorated than any other religious monument. The church, with the remains of St Benedict and St Scholastica in the same tomb, is even more magnificent than St Peter's in Rome. You're walking on agate and porphyry and there's marble of the rarest and most precious kind, gold, alabaster, copper and frescos. All this luxury brought together on an arid mountain-top proclaims the devotion of the Italians to these twin saints and the immense influence of the Catholic church in the Middle Ages. I'd already been to the houses in Subiaco where the brother and sister had founded their order, and I was glad to find them asleep on their monuments. In Caserta I also saw the huge, magnificent palace of the King of Naples, but nothing can efface or even equal this gulf down below me here, with Vesuvius smoking, the sea covered with boats, and in the middle of them the frigate that guards the port crossing to intercept anyone with cholera, the motley crowd rushing through the streets, the hosts of soldiers in their red and gold uniforms, brilliant military music on one hand and firing practice on the other. On the mountainside splendid poplars covered with luxuriant vines, which would break under the weight of their masses of grapes without the support of the tree beneath them; thickets of acacia, pomegranate, fig-trees, orange-trees; the peasants from the islands with their green jackets trimmed with gilded copper and red handkerchiefs on their heads; armies of fishermen pulling in their nets, and naked children running about in the water and on the sand, throwing shells at each other. What life! What movement! What sparkling activity! How different it all is from Rome and its sleepy inhabitants, its naked, sparse, uncultivated, deserted soil! The fields of Rome, with their sombre, melancholy air, are to the plains of Naples what the past is to the present, what death is to life, or silence to a loud, harmonious noise.

5 October

'Eh! Eh! Eccellenza! Eccellenza! *Quatro* carlini.'
'No.'
'*Tre* carlini; è un bono somaro, vedete, bianco e polito.'
'No, no.'
'Oh! celenza, *due* carlini, lo mio somaro è piu forte.'
'No, ancora una volta, andaro a piede.'
'Alora celenza, per *uno* carlino.'
'Per niente, corpo di Baco, andate al diavolo!'
'Buon viaggio, celenza!'

So I went up Vesuvius, on foot in spite of the shouts of the Resina peasants who were determined that his *excellence* should take a donkey (*somaro*). I got back this evening, aching all over but not regretting the effort. I was with two Frenchmen, a Prussian and a Russian, who had travelled from Rome with me. When we reached the hermit's cottage the Russian and I drank some delicious water and some strong Lacryma Christi, which revived us somewhat; the others were riding donkeys and weren't at all tired. From there we sallied forth on to the sea of lava which surrounds the foot of the great cone. It's terrifying; the paths of Hell could not be more awful. As we were patiently climbing, turning round now and again to look at the sunset, we heard shrill female voices ringing out from one of the valleys; it was some Frenchwomen singing the *Marseillaise*. Thoughts of politics and patriotism seem so bizarre in such a situation and clash so violently with such scenery that I suffered a kind of giddiness from the jumble of a thousand jarring thoughts. Finally, in pitch darkness, we reached the main crater; today it's full of lava almost up to the edge, while two months ago it was five hundred feet deep. You walk on burning crusts, crossing crevasses in which you can see the lava, red and immobile, six inches from your feet. We reached a rather large stream of lava, which exhales such a strong smell of sulphur that you can hardly breathe.

Even so we stayed there some time and scooped up some pieces of the burning liquid on the ends of our walking-sticks, turning our heads away because of the heat. From time to time the glare from the eruptions in the middle of the crater enabled us to see the magnificent tableau in its totality. Nothing could be finer than the rain of red molten rocks, falling back from an immense height after the explosion and rolling to the very outside of the cone, where they then remain fixed and unextinguished, like a burning necklace round the gigantic neck of the volcano. To our right as we left the main crater we saw the lights of the fishermen, a vast number that lit up the sea there like glow-worms in a field. In the middle of the slope a sort of abscess had formed some days before, from which a veritable river of lava flows in four diverging streams; these fiery torrents are on the side facing Pompeii. Vesuvius seems to be waiting for the ancient city to be completely excavated before engulfing it a second time.[1] It really is the scene of the Blocksberg from *Faust*: a ballet of sparks, fiery serpents, infernal rattlings, blinding flashes against total blackness, screams from top to bottom, in the depths of the valleys, on the peaks, far and near; trembling torches, stars in the sky, fire on the water, fire on the land, fire in the air. The scene even had witches; our Frenchwomen, with their peals of laughter, their screechy voices, their shouted conversations and their shopgirls' manners (to go no further) could fill the role perfectly.

As soon as I've recovered from my extreme exhaustion after this, I shall set out for Pompeii where I'm going to meet some French artists I know.

They were saying in the café this morning that the new volcano which appeared two or three months ago off the coast of Sicily, not far from Stromboli, has just been extinguished and swallowed up by the sea from which it arose. What a terrifying struggle that must have been! A volcano and the sea at grips with each other.

7 October

We're not going to Pompeii until Monday, but I couldn't bear to spend today in Naples. I said goodbye this morning to my travelling companions and went out to the island of Nisida. What a day! I got up in a melancholy frame of mind, full of that romantic sadness you feel at the age of fourteen, when you still believe in happiness, when you see life through a poetical prism, when you weep at Florian's novels and an old

1 The systematic excavation of Pompeii did not begin until 1806, when the French annexed the kingdom of Naples.

tower on a black rock makes your head spin. I was rather tired when I reached the bay of Baiae; it's there that Nero prepared a *pleasure-trip* for his mother Agrippina, from which she escaped by swimming, much to her illustrious son's disappointment. It's there too that Virgil had Aeneas land with his tattered fleet. From the seashore I took a little boat with four rowers, who brought me swiftly to Nisida, a charming little island covered with fruit trees, bearing olives, oranges, figs and vines; it's high, of a strange shape, verdant, red and golden. Seeing it from a distance, I thought of my Irish song, *Le coucher du soleil*: 'à ces îles heureuses que dérobent des voiles d'or'. I was prepared even so to be cruelly disenchanted. So I wasn't unduly surprised, when I reached the summit, to find a prison full of convicts and to hear, instead of pastoral songs, the sound of chains and the shouts of the inmates. On my way from Naples to Baiae I'd begun a composition whose principal idea, inspired by my insular excursion, was rather to my liking, and although the prison and the convicts have cooled my imagination a little, I hope I can recover and return to finish my little musical poem on the lines I had in mind originally.[1] As the wind was freshening, one of my oarsmen came to collect me and I got on board again. The waves were already large and our nutshell, with no sails or rigging, felt like a dead leaf balanced on the water; at all events we arrived without mishap. I invited my four Tritons to come and eat some macaroni, an invitation they accepted with cries of joy. They took me straight away to a hut a mile from the sea, in the middle of a poplar wood, and there under a tent of reeds and straw they sank not a plate but a cauldron of macaroni, washed down with four jugs of wine. I held my own as best I could while we discussed the island of Elba, where one of them had been, Napoleon, their unfortunate King Joachim Murat, the projects he had put in hand for the beautification of Naples, his bravery, his sad end, etc, etc.[2] After many farewells, and the same number of *celenzas*, I left them to climb Posilippo a second time. When I reached the peak my feelings were such as I cannot describe, as I looked at the sun going down behind Cape Misenum. The incomparable view, overwhelmingly sublime, the murmuring of the sea below me, the sight of my charming island, its graceful name, all plunged me into a whirlpool of

1 It is hard to know what, if anything, came of this composition.
2 Joachim Murat, Napoleon's most brilliant cavalry commander, was made King of Naples in 1808. Having courted the favour of the allies in 1814 he was repudiated by Napoleon in 1815. After Waterloo he attempted to win back his kingdom, but was captured and executed.

memories made stronger still by my isolation. Timbrio, Nisida, Fabian, Blanche, Galatea, Michel Cervantes;[1] Aeneas, Misenum, Palinurus, the young Iulus, Dido, Lavinia, Amanda, the kindly King Latinus, Turnus so proud and unlucky, Nisus and Euryalus; Mezentius;[2] Virgil, whose fame, like all fame, like the brightness of the star that rules our captive planet, is slowly fading, finally to disappear and fall into oblivion ... Those thoughts had not come to me for so long ... Oh, the power of genius! ... Across so many centuries, the sight of those places sung by the Latin poet, a fortuitous resemblance between the name of an island and that of one of Cervantes' heroines, made me shed torrents of tears. [...]

  H. B.

                   8 October

I have to finish this letter without telling you about Pompeii; that must be for another time. I will write from Rome where I hope to find news of you. I had written to my grandfather ten days before I left. I fear I'll have to go back to the papal city before long, since all these trips are expensive and I'll have to leave without seeing Paestum, Salerno and Amalfi, perhaps even Ischia and Procida. At Pompeii they've just discovered a magnificent new house; the King of Naples went there yesterday. This morning in the museum I saw the ancient musical instruments found in the ashes of Vesuvius at Herculaneum. I tried out two pairs of little cymbals;[3] the wind instruments are all in fragments. I'll write to you about all this when I get back to Rome.

  H. B.

61 *To his family*   San Germano, 17, 18, 19, 20 or 21 October
                    (I'm not sure) 1831

[...] Since my last letter I've been to see the famous ruins of Pompeii; I don't want to bore you with a description of this skeleton of a city, but it is for certain the sort of thing one can imagine for oneself in advance. My four travelling companions and the guide did much to spoil my little ancient world, I must admit; I didn't really feel the impact of Pompeii. I railed inwardly against the circumstances that prevented me

1 These are all characters in Cervantes' *La Galatea* in Florian's French adaptation.
2 These are all (except Misenum) characters in the *Aeneid* (although Amanda should correctly be Amata); Iulus is another name for Ascanius.
3 These little cymbals, still housed in the Naples Museum, were the inspiration for the 'antique cymbals' used in the *Reine Mab* scherzo in *Roméo et Juliette* in 1839.

from being alone, wandering at night between columns and the shadows of columns, seen only by moonlight, and free to abandon myself to all the caprices of my impressionability (not necessarily to say *imagination*). It must be wonderful to be able to indulge in silent reverie, walking on those great polished slabs, along those long echoing streets, through temples and palaces; to go and sit in the great theatre where tragedies were performed, and think of Sophocles and Euripides; to look with a shudder behind the cloud of the past and see the gladiators in the middle of the immense amphitheatre, the lions, the tigers and, more frightening still, the crowd thirsty for blood, their eyes fixed on the heart of the victim lacerated by the hooves of some desperate animal and cheering to its final throb. I should like to have slept in one of those beautiful rooms paved with mosaics, which one imagines inhabited by beautiful women in Greek robes, with proud, imperious glances, surrounded by ravishing slave-girls playing the lyre and singing of love. But none of that is possible. There are attendants everywhere, keeping a close eye on you; I couldn't even steal a tiny little bit of debris from a fresco or a mosaic for papa. [...]

H. Berlioz

62 *To Victor Hugo* Rome, 10 December 1831

Oh! You are a genius, a man of power, a colossus who is both tender, pitiless, elegant, monstrous, raucous, melodious, volcanic, affectionate and *scornful*. This last constituent of genius is certainly the rarest, neither Shakespeare nor Molière had it. Beethoven alone among the *great* gauged correctly the size of the human insects that surrounded him and on his level I see none but you.

Know then, if I am writing to you, if I ramble, if I exaggerate, if I force you to turn your head for a moment with importunate cries of admiration, know that I am in Rome, exiled for two years from the musical world by an academic ruling reinforced by the need for the Prix de Rome scholarship, that I am dying for lack of air like a bird under a vacuum-jar, deprived of music, of poetry, of theatres, of excitement, of everything, then consider that after a wait of six months I finally managed to get hold of *Notre-dame de Paris*, that I have just read it amid weeping and gnashing of teeth, and you will understand why I am writing to you, I whose name you don't even know, I who am asking for nothing from you, not even for an opera libretto.

Is it my fault or yours? Who has inflamed my heart? Who has turned my head into a still from which, these two days past, corrosive tears have run unceasingly? Who has magnified my disdain and hatred for the whole of our stupid, idiotic world? Who has made me blaspheme for nights on end? Who, if not you? So who else can you blame for my ridiculous outburst?

I am not a toady, no; may I turn into a Pacini or a Coccia[1] if I have ever said the opposite of what I think! I would say it to you too, to your face, in spite of your eagle's eyes. During the end of my stay in Paris I would have delivered my soul up to the devil for a year if that had been the price of seeing you and talking to you *frankly* for an hour. I could have been introduced to you or have introduced myself on the off-chance, but the fear of looking like a hanger-on has always held me back. Then, who knows? Perhaps we should not have hit it off. Poets and men of letters have such strange ideas about music; their feeling for this beautiful art is often like that of the smart young ladies of the Rue Vivienne for the vaudeville singers whom . . . but hush, I'm nervous . . . they say you have reworked *Notre-dame* as an opera and that the Jolly Jumbo is writing the music . . .[2] He's certainly jolly, the large man . . . It's true that Weber is dead.

There, that's the end of my broadside. I'm feeling better. I'll go back to thinking about my Esmeralda and to cursing the disposition they all have towards falling in love with Baudets, as Titania did with Bottom.

That poor, dear monster Quasimodo! Enough.

Addio, signore, mille grazie, I was starting to dry out and shrivel here like a plum in the sun. Now my skin is beginning to swell and glisten again, my blood is coursing, my life as an artist takes hold of me once more. *Viva l'ingenio tuo!*

Hector Berlioz

63 *To his father Dr Louis Berlioz*   Rome, 18 February 1832

I was going to write to you, my dear papa, when your letter arrived. It set off a storm of tumultuous and painful thoughts in my mind. [. . .]

I think I can admit without fear of offending you that my ideas on education are quite different from yours. Education in the French provinces is completely absurd for many children. Parents only ever have two careers in mind, medicine and the law, and even when they don't have a fixed goal for their sons they still insist on making them

---

1 Coccia, like Pacini, was a minor Italian opera composer.
2 The 'gros homme gai' was Rossini, who did not set *Notre-dame de Paris* as an opera. Louise Bertin's opera on the subject, with a libretto by Hugo himself, was played at the Opéra in 1836.

lose (I say 'lose' advisedly) the ten best years of their youth in dreadful colleges learning a dead language they never get to know. What's the use of knowing Latin even very well? Just for enrolling in those two Faculties! A young man who knows English and German and who from an early age is familiar with what goes on around him without worrying what the Greeks and Romans did, a young man who from an early age sets himself the task of seeing the world in which he has to live and not a dead world which means nothing to him, such a man has a thousand advantages in getting on in life and getting as far as his merits can take him. In politics, diplomacy, travel, shipping, the arts, literature, commerce and the exact sciences even, it is clear that we have to start by communicating freely with the great centres of civilization that adjoin our own.[1] [...]

After I had sent my last letter I feared that my reply to mama on the subject of money might have upset you and I regretted having allowed it to go. But since you brought it up it's better to discuss it frankly. I truly believed that the thousand francs allowance which you had promised me in the event of my marrying would still be available to me if I remained a bachelor, especially since you had not said it wouldn't. I made my plans accordingly without thinking for a moment that you would need the money. When mama sent me the money and made a few comments – kindly and indulgent, I admit – I thought I detected the same old rules which have always plagued me horribly: being kept on a leash. I confess I was appalled. I say so plainly since it's best to call a spade a spade. Any bond of obligation, any apparent restriction, anything that interferes in the least with my liberty, is quite unacceptable to me. I have suffered terribly in the last eight years; the last period of my life is a sad story of which you know only certain incidental episodes and out of which my character today is formed. I feel like a skinned animal: every part of my being has developed such painful sensitivity that I turn red at the slightest contact. This makes me prefer a thousand times to do without money than to have it at that price. Five hundred francs guaranteed, which I would not have to ask for, would be more precious to me, I assure you, than five thousand which I would have to get in small irregular sums with conditions, and so on. Besides, now that I know you would have to make economies on my behalf, I don't want to hear any more about it. I'll make my own

---

1 Berlioz may have regretted that he never developed an aptitude for foreign languages and felt at some disadvantage in England and Germany, perhaps even in Italy. But he surely never regretted his command of Latin, of Virgil in particular.

arrangements. My personal expenses are quite small, and with my scholarship I would have needed nothing but for the recent trip to Naples. The only privations which I suffer because of lack of money are concerned with my art; it's only in this area that I need a great deal in order to be able to exercise my musical powers more quickly and on a larger scale.

You mention marriage. I have ideas on that subject which would take us far, too far to go into in a letter. Suffice it to say that I have not the least inclination of that kind at present. I am all too aware that an ordinary marriage, what's known as a marriage of 'convenience', a 'nice, suitable' marriage, would be death.[1]

Berlioz remained in Rome until May 1832, making occasional excursions to the outlying countryside. He composed little, it seems. He witnessed the Carnival and accumulated impressions that would contribute to many later works set in Italy: Harold en Italie, Benvenuto Cellini, Roméo et Juliette *and* Béatrice et Bénédict. *He returned home via Florence, Perugia, Milan and Turin, crossing the Alps on his way back to his family at La Côte-St-André. There he spent five months, completing* Le retour à la vie *and preparing orchestral material for his planned concerts in Paris.*

64 To Ferdinand Hiller   La Côte, 7 August 1832

What an odd, prickly, irritating, coquettish fellow this Hiller is! If we were both women, given the feelings we have, I should detest *her*; if he alone were the woman, I should be wincing with hatred for *her*, loathing coquettes as I do. So Providence has ordered all things for the best, to use idiots' language, by planting us both on this globe in masculine guise.

No, my dear practical joker, you *had no choice* but to keep me waiting two months for your reply; but I too *have no choice* but to hold this against you and to *abandon utterly* my confidence in any promises you may make of this sort. As I'm not seriously angry, or at least not suffering from wounded pride, I wrote you a second letter from Grenoble; but six hours later, thinking of what was in it, I burnt it. 'There are some things,' Napoleon used to say, 'you must never utter; even more decidedly, you must never write them down.' Oh

---

1 The remainder of the letter is missing.

Napoleon, Napoleon! Now *there's* a cup of enthusiasm that's near to running over ... To prevent any such mishap, instead of telling you about him, what he achieved in Lombardy and the sublime vestiges he left behind him, which I could trace as far as the Alps on my way back to France, I shall tell you about three serious mistakes in the French of your letter!! OH!!! ... As you're learning Latin, I shall play the pedagogue. 1: There's no accent on 'negre';[1] 2: you say that here I'm finding 'des grands amusements': it has to be '*de* grands amusements'; 3: 'Il est possible que Mendelssohn l'*aura*': ... que Mendelssohn l'*aie*.

Remember these points in future.

Ouf!

I am in fact with my family, but there's only my younger sister who adores me, which I allow her to do in a highly edifying manner ...

Nanci has married a judge in the law courts of Grenoble.[2] I've just spent a fortnight with her; her husband and brother-in-law are good sorts, excellent and cultured, but I find them unbearable. I begged them once never to talk to me about music, or art, or anything truly poetic; they haven't been able to manage it. Their opinions are detestable and after conversation with them I emerge feeling cross and edgy. That's when I'm dangerous. When I see attacks being mounted on the objects of my admiration, my one and only gods whom I treasure in my heart of hearts, then I truly realize that my hatred and contempt for the riff-raff of mankind are no mere high-falutin fantasy and that from words I could pass to deeds quite easily.

Oh, when I get back to Italy!!! Seriously, my dear fellow, I have to have *liberty*, *love* and *money*. We shall find it in due course, together with a small luxury, one of those superfluities which certain characters find necessary, namely Vengeance, general and particular. One lives and dies only once.

While I'm here in the provinces, cut off from my usual excitements, alone with my thoughts, which go round and round like a hedgehog pricking me with its sharp spines, my ideas are becoming firmer and more solid through studying the profound works of Locke, Cabanis, Gall and others;[3] not that they teach me anything except technical details, because I generally find that I've gone further than they have and that they don't dare to pursue the consequences of their principles

1 In modern French 'nègre' does have an accent.
2 Nanci married Camille Pal on 16 January 1832.
3 Locke, seventeenth-century English philosopher; Cabanis, eighteenth-century French medical materialist; Gall, eighteenth-century German doctor, inventor of phrenology. These books were evidently to be found in Dr Berlioz's library.

for fear of public opinion. Public opinion, the queen of the earth! But there are no kings and queens left, there has been a 'trembling of thrones' (as Lamartine says) which has overthrown them all; why then respect this other old, stupid authority?

I'm spending all my time copying out the parts of my *Mélologue*; I've been doing nothing else for the last two months and I've still got enough left for another sixty-two days; you can see how patient I am. One needs patience for everything, not for putting up with one's troubles, but in order to *act*. The need for music often makes me ill; it makes my nerves tremble. Then there's the influence of cholera which has kept me in bed for several days;[1] I'm free of it today and ready to start again. I'm going to see Ferrand; we haven't seen each other for five years. Extremes meet, as you see. He's more religious and fanatical than ever; he's married a woman who adores him and he adores her too. It's a curious match, and she is lively and sincere.

65 To Thomas Gounet   Belley,[2] 25 August 1832

My dear Gounet,

[. . .] What can I tell you about my time in the Dauphiné? I copy out parts, I take my little brother out hunting with a net, I read M. de Balzac, Saintine, Michel Raimond, then I get bored; I play a game of *boules*, then I get bored; I travel around the neighbouring countryside, then I get bored; I think of my Italian mountains where I was free to be bored; then I miss them and get bored even more; in short, life is charming. [. . .]

Your devoted,
H. Berlioz

66 To Thomas Gounet   Paris, 7 November 1832

I've just arrived. I'm staying at 1, Rue Neuve-St-Marc, where H. Sm . . . used to live. It's strange! I'm dying to embrace you; until this evening, eight o'clock at the Café Feydeau.

H. Berlioz

---

1 France was then suffering a cholera epidemic, which was one reason why Berlioz stayed so long at La Côte before returning to Paris.
2 Berlioz was visiting Ferrand at Belley.

To his sister Nanci Pal   Paris, 26 November 1832

Dear Nanci,

I seize a passing moment to write to you. I received mama's letter the day before yesterday, and the note that came with it; let her know as soon as possible.

My concert is fixed and advertised for Sunday 9 December, in twelve days' time.[1] Everything's going so smoothly that I'm terrified. When I arrived, the players greeted me with the greatest affection and enthusiasm; they're enthusiastic to the point of rivalry over playing in my orchestra. It'll be a gigantic occasion from the instrumental point of view. There won't be enough voices; I can't have more than fifteen women and twenty men. Cherubini has behaved charmingly towards me, going as far as to say he was '*delighted* to see me again'. M. Véron, the director of the Opéra, wouldn't let me have A. Nourrit[2] and gave me someone else, Dupont, and when I went to see him at home he overwhelmed me with elaborate compliments; I'm curious to see the results of his honeyed words. He's coming to the concert.

Notice of it has produced enormous interest. Everyone's talking about it. I've never had so much time in hand before. Everything's ready today and the concert isn't for twelve days. I've made the acquaintance of Eugène Sue;[3] we were brought together by a certain M. Legouvé (a charming young man with an income of thirty thousand livres who wrote to me recently *asking to meet me*).[4] [. . .]

Adieu, dear sister, I embrace you.

H. B.

At the concert on 9 December Berlioz was formally introduced to Harriet Smithson, who recognized herself as the subject of the Symphonie fantastique *and its sequel. Her relationship with Berlioz then developed rapidly. The following letter seems to belong to their stormy courtship:*

1 On his return to Paris Berlioz's first concern was to arrange a concert in which to present his new works. Like his previous concert in Paris it was given in the Salle du Conservatoire, was conducted by Habeneck, and included the *Symphonie fantastique*. Its sequel, *Le retour à la vie*, was heard for the first time.
2 For the tenor solo in *Le retour à la vie*.
3 Author of highly successful novels, including *Les mystères de Paris*.
4 Legouvé became a close and generous friend and left some valuable memories of Berlioz in his *Soixante ans de souvenirs* (1886).

If you do not desire my death, in the name of pity (I dare not say of love) let me know when I can see you. I cry mercy, pardon on my knees, between my sobs!!!

Oh, wretch that I am, I did not think I deserved all that I suffer, but I bless the blows that come from your hand.

I await your reply like the sentence of my judge.

H. Berlioz

69 *To his father Dr Louis Berlioz*   Paris, 14 December 1832

Dear papa,

I'm sending you today ten copies of the *Mélologue*[1] with various newspapers. I would have sent you all those that mentioned me, but as several of them weren't stamped I couldn't post them. I'll get hold of others which I'll send you with those that haven't yet said anything. Fétis received full in the face the blow I aimed at him in the *Mélologue* in the tirade about *arrangers* and *correcters*, and he had his revenge today in a virulent article in *Le temps* in which fury exudes from every word.[2] Never mind, the success is enormous; every day I receive a heap of letters from people I don't know, showering me with compliments. M. d'Argout wrote a charming one the day before yesterday. There are demands for a repeat performance from all sides and I intend to give one; I'm certain to make a large profit. Hats are doffed to me in the street and in the theatre by people I've never seen before. Wherever there's a buzz of conversation, in the salons, at the Opéra, in the foyer, in the corridors, everywhere my concert is the sole topic. Bocage, playing the role of the artist,[3] was superb in his verve, sensitivity, inspiration and malice. In the tirade about arrangers and in the one about brigands he was interrupted by endless applause. When it came to: 'Oh, why can I not find her, the Juliet, the Ophelia that my heart desires!' the handkerchiefs started to appear.

The orchestra, made up of the same performers, will be firm and secure next time; confidence was all it lacked. One more careful, paid

---

1 The printed text (libretto) of *Le retour à la vie*.
2 Berlioz's public attack on Fétis for his effrontery in re-writing Beethoven and Mozart earned him the hostility of a powerful figure in French music. They became respectful friends many years later.
3 A spoken role.

rehearsal will take care of all the details and nuances. [. . .]

Adieu, dear father, I embrace you tenderly together with mama, Prosper and dear Adèle.

H. Berlioz

70 *To Franz Liszt*   Paris, 19 December 1832

My dear Liszt,

You showed yourself a true friend yesterday morning, but it would have been better for me if it had been over some other matter.[1] After I left, I had a meeting with H. S. which, but for you, would have plunged me into unmitigated happiness, into a fever that no tongue could express; this joy, this passionate love has been poisoned, but I drink the draught whole, even if I am to die thereafter.

Everything about her delights and enthrals me; when she avowed her feelings openly, I was alarmed and driven nearly mad. I ask you, in the name of our friendship, never again to speak *either to me or to anyone else* about what you said to me. There is no question of our marrying at the moment.

I shall never leave her. It is my destiny. She understands me. If it is a mistake, I must be allowed to make it; she will brighten the last moments of my life which, I hope, will not be a long one. It's impossible to put up a continued resistance to emotions of this kind. Stifle, I beg you, all discussion of the subject with Dumas, and with Hiller when he arrives; even say the opposite of what you think; you must, I beg you on my knees.

Yes, I love her! I love her! And my love is returned. She *told* me so yesterday in front of her sister; yes, she loves me, but you're the only person I'm telling. I want to bury my happiness, if that's possible. So, *silence*! Nothing now can separate us. She knows about the business with Mlle Moke, I had to tell her everything. She, she, H. S. was the one I needed; my existence is complete, hers is the heart which answers to mine. Don't be moved to pity by what I'm writing to you; one must respect love and enthusiasm when they are as profound and sincere as mine.

Adieu, dear friend, you know what my heart expects from yours.

Hector Berlioz

P.S. Our concert has been postponed until Sunday 30 December.[2]

1 It is hard to guess what Liszt's annoying behaviour might have been.
2 A repeat of the concert of 9 December.

71 *To Albert Du Boys*[1]   Paris, 5 January 1833

My dear Albert,

[. . .] What an incredible novel my life is!

Harriet Smithson was brought to my concert, not knowing it was to be given by me; *she* heard the work of which *she* is the subject and prime cause, *she* wept at it, *she* witnessed my wild success; it all went straight to her heart; *she* expressed all her enthusiasm to me after the concert, *she* agreed to let me be introduced; *she* listened to me, in tears, as I told her like Othello of the vicissitudes of my life from the day I fell in love with her; *she* asked my pardon for the torments she had unwittingly made me suffer (she knew practically nothing of it all) and finally on 18 December, in her sister's presence, I heard these words: 'Berlioz, I love you.' Since then all my efforts have been confined to quelling the volcano in my head, I've felt I was going mad. Yes, she loves me, she has a heart like Juliet's, here indeed is my Ophelia. When I'm unable to see her, we write each other as many as three letters a day, she in English, I in French. Oh, my dear fellow, there is justice in heaven after all! I used not to believe it. It is to my art, to my brain that I owe her love! My beloved symphony! I should like to burn it on an altar and release its perfumes. What love, Albert, what idolatry! *Quanti palpiti!* You have witnessed my anguish; can you imagine what I'm feeling? This is not a love of the senses, no, it is the heart alone and the head which are scented with this sublime feeling. But she is going through a time of trouble and cruel suffering which all my efforts are powerless to allay. It drives me to despair; with every drop of blood in my veins, I wish to spare her a moment's pain and I am unable to. Don't suppose, Albert, that our love, our meetings are other than what an honourable woman would allow herself; if you did, you would be wrong. On the contrary, she conducts our tête-à-têtes with a reserve that makes me desperate. My Ophelia!!! Sometimes I spend hours on my knees before her, holding her hands in mine, watching her eyes slowly fill with tears, until a kiss is planted on my forehead. I get up, I roar, I crush her in my arms, we walk furiously round the room, exclaiming about the strange destiny which, *from the opposite ends of Europe*, led us *to rush to Paris at the same moment* and be together.[2] She's going to take part soon in an important production of

---

1 A lawyer friend from Grenoble whose poetry Berlioz had occasionally set.
2 While Berlioz was in Italy Harriet had been acting in England. She returned to Paris at the same time as Berlioz to open a season of English theatre at the Théâtre-Italien; the venture was a disaster.

Shakespeare's *Romeo* and it's been agreed that I shall be there (for all her other performances, she's asked me not to come as my presence could upset her). Yes, I shall be there, and when the tragedy is over, the real *Romeo* created by Shakespeare, then at last I, yes I shall be at the feet of my Juliet, ready to die, ready even to *live* if she so wishes. I am mad, dearest I am dead!! Sweetest Juliet! my life, my soul, my heart, all, all, t'is the heaven oh!!!!! . . .¹ speak then, my orchestra . . . [. . .]

   H. Berlioz

On 3 February 1833 Berlioz wrote to his father seeking permission to marry, but received a refusal. Relations with his father now entered a phase of prolonged bitterness.

72 *To his father Dr Louis Berlioz*   Paris, 16 February 1833

I would not have believed, dear father, that considerations arising from social prejudice could have the power to dictate to you the reply that you sent me. It is a very great misfortune for us all that it should be so. My inner life, the life of my heart, has so far experienced nothing but being wounded and broken, and it is not my fault if nature and my own character lead me irresistibly to accept the one unique chance of *complete* happiness which has yet presented itself to me. I would do *anything* to grasp it.

As I see it, I am forced to employ legal means instead of the gentler and more seemly ones I had hoped for.² This may lead to unhappiness for which you would bitterly reproach yourself. And in the end what will be the advantage of torturing me for a further three months? Haven't I been tortured enough?

It is borne in upon me that my share of suffering, sorrow and frustration is larger than that of most men. I am a victim of cruelty and a cruelty made worse by the fact that it is pointless. If Harriet or I were to die during these interminable three months, I feel it would be terrible for you to think that you had prevented me from knowing a moment's happiness. But if, after all, such is my destiny, then let it be fulfilled!!!

   Your affectionate son,

   Hector Berlioz

1 From 'I am mad' Berlioz writes in English.
2 On 14 February Berlioz set in motion a 'respectful summons' in order to seek a decision from the courts. Edouard Rocher assisted in this process.

73 *To Edouard Rocher*   Paris, 12 March 1833

Dear Edouard,

Thank you for this new proof of your friendship; give Simian[1] too my sincere thanks. This business has shown me that I could count on you and what I could expect from my father's so-called determined common sense. I'm only twenty-nine and a half and I realize that at such an age I must still be classed as a child. My father is the stronger, therefore he is right. My father treats me as every father treats every son; whereas I, I'm an exception. Yes, an exception by my character, by the life I've led so far, by my lofty sensibilities, by my disdain for life and death, by my ideas about everything. My father has never understood me and never will; I've always felt that I had no father.

For the moment, don't go on with the summonses; I no longer need to get married straight away. If Harriet insists later on, then I think the first efforts you have made will still count for something.

I expect you read in the newspapers about the accident that has happened to my poor Ophelia; she broke her shinbone getting out of a gig. Luckily it looks much less serious than we originally feared.

Adieu, my dear Edouard, from your true and devoted friend,

Hector Berlioz

74 *To his sister Adèle Berlioz*   Paris, 3 April 1833

Dear Adèle, excellent sister,

[...] I won't say anything to you about the way my parents are treating me. If their despotic will is unshakeable, mine is a thousand times more so. They take pleasure in torturing me to no purpose; after all that they've inflicted on me since the age of twenty there was hope that they might finally leave me in peace, but I was wrong; I hope their conscience is clear.

Harriet Smithson will be my wife sooner or later; I hope it will be after the end of the legal proceedings that I am being obliged to take. We shall probably get married in France, but it could possibly be in England or Germany. I'll go on writing to you from time to time, wherever I happen to be. We were both talking about you recently and she was envying my luck in having a sister like you; hers brings the difference sharply home to her. [...]

---

1 A notary at La Côte.

Adieu, my dear sweet sister, adieu, nothing will ever alter the affection of your brother and friend,

H. Berlioz

75   *To his sister Adèle Berlioz*   Paris, 30 May 1833

My dear Adèle,

Has my silence upset you? Oh, don't let it, please. If you knew how continually taken up I am by the strangeness and outlandishness of my position and by worries about Harriet's health, you would forgive me. It's three months now since she broke her leg and she's still having trouble walking, even with crutches. She takes exercise for several hours a day by walking across her room and staying sitting up; all the rest of the time she spends miserably in bed listening, when I'm not with her, to the infernal concert of her sister's conversation – she insists on tormenting her about me with a truly diabolical perseverance. There are no ridiculous slanders she won't invent to try and separate Harriet from me. Luckily none of it has any effect; but can you imagine what patience I have to bring to bear not to exterminate this blasted little hunchback who pursues her own egotistical interests towards and against everybody and has just told me to my face that if she was strong enough she would *throw me out of the window*? Most of the time we can laugh at it, but there are days when my patience nearly runs out and, but for a glance from my dear, beautiful, beloved Harriet I think the accursed *dwarf* might pass an uncomfortable minute or two. But I know that in many situations 'patience and the passage of time accomplish more than violence or anger'¹ and I contain myself. One day, dear Adèle, I'll write you a long letter telling you every possible detail about Mlle Smithson, about her truly incredible character and the delightful discoveries I continue to make in that respect. To tell you now would be premature and, as you are still under the influence of a host of *terribly unjust* prejudices, you wouldn't believe me. [. . .]

Your brother,

H. Berlioz

---

1 A reference to La Fontaine's fable *The Lion and the Rat*.

My dear Humbert,

[. . .] Would you like to know what I'm doing? During the day, if I'm feeling well I read or sleep on my sofa (at the moment I'm in excellent lodgings) or I throw together a few pages for *Europe littéraire*, who pay me very well for them. In the evening, from six o'clock, I'm with Harriet; she's still unwell and in pain, which I find distressing. I'll tell you about her at length some other time. Only you must know that any opinion you may have formed of her is as mistaken as could be. Her life, like mine, is a novel, and her manner of seeing, feeling and thinking is not the least interesting part of it. Her behaviour, in the situation she has been in since childhood, is quite incredible and it took me a long time to believe it. But enough on that subject.

I'm working on the big operatic project I wrote to you about from Rome eighteen months ago, and, as you haven't managed to conquer your idleness and get down to it since then, I've given up on you and gone to Emile Deschamps and Saint-Félix, who are working away busily. You won't hold it against me, I hope, as I've been fairly patient.[1]

I have to go now for that very reason. I'll write again soon.

Adieu. Your sincere friend,

H. Berlioz

Dear, good and faithful friend,

[. . .] My life is as frayed and disordered as ever. This evening I shall perhaps see Harriet for the *last time*; she is so unhappy, my heart bleeds for her, and her irresolute, timid character prevents her from making the smallest decision. But it must finish; I can't live like this. The whole business is sad and bathed in tears, but I hope it won't go further than tears. I've done everything that the most devoted heart could do. If she is not happier or in regular employment, that's her fault.[2]

Adieu, my friend. You mustn't doubt my friendship; that would be a grave mistake.

---

1 Even with new collaborators this project, probably a new version of *Le dernier jour du monde*, came to nothing in that form.
2 Her attempts to get into theatrical ventures were mostly unsuccessful and her broken leg made her chances more remote.

It was in fact your *Chœur héroïque* which was to be performed at the Tuileries.[1] But it wasn't, because there were no *candles*; the players were unable to see anything when my piece's turn came and they ended the concert by repeating the *Marseillaise* and the vulgar *Parisienne* which they knew by heart.

The first rehearsal of this enormous orchestra took place indoors, in Cicéri's painting studio in the Menus-Plaisirs, and the effect of the *Monde entier*[2] was enormous, even though half the singers were non-musicians who couldn't read music or sing. I had to go out for a moment, my chest was pounding so. In the chorus from *Guillaume Tell*, 'Si parmi nous il est des traîtres', I felt almost ill. In the open air ... *nothing* ... no effect! Music is decidedly not made to be heard in the street, however it's done.

Adieu; write and tell me the ending of that cheeky plot involving the false Benedict.

Please don't forget to remember me to your brother and your parents.

Yours as ever,
H. Berlioz

78 *To Humbert Ferrand*   Paris, 30 August 1833

[...] She wants to wait a few months ... Months! Good God! I don't want to wait any longer, I've suffered too much. I wrote to her yesterday to say that, if she wasn't willing for me to come and collect her next Saturday to take her to the registry office, then I was leaving *next Thursday* for Berlin.[3] She doesn't believe I'm serious and has sent word that she would let me have an answer today. There'll be more fine speeches, entreaties to go and see her, claims that she's ill, etc. But I shall be firm and she will see that even if I have spent such a long time weak and wilting at her feet, I can still rouse myself, escape from her and live for those who love and understand me. I've done everything for her, there's no more I can do. I'm sacrificing everything for her and she doesn't dare take risks for me. She's too weak and *reasonable*. So I'll leave, and to help me survive this fearful separation, an

1 On 28 July 1833 the statue of Napoleon in the Place Vendôme was inaugurated with a concert which was to include a new arrangement of the *Scène héroïque* on a text by Ferrand, composed in 1826.
2 The closing section of the *Scène héroïque*.
3 The terms of the Prix de Rome required a period of study in Germany, after Italy, and Berlioz was still expecting to go there.

extraordinary chance has thrown into my arms a poor young girl of eighteen, charming and high spirited, who four days ago ran away from a wretch who had bought her as a child and kept her shut up like a slave for four years; she's in mortal terror of falling into the monster's hands again and declares she will drown herself rather than become his property once more. I was told about her the day before yesterday; she's determined to leave France; I had the idea of taking her; she was told about me, she wanted to see me, I saw her, I reassured and consoled her a little; I suggested to her she should come with me to Berlin and I could find a job for her in the chorus, with Spontini's help;[1] she has agreed. She is beautiful, alone in the world, desperate and trusting, I shall protect her and do all I can to stay close to her. If she loves me, I shall squeeze my heart to try and extract a drop of affection. At any rate I shall pretend that I love her. I've just seen her, she's very well brought up, plays the piano quite well, sings a little, talks well and knows how to manage her strange situation with dignity. What an absurd story!

My passport's ready, I've got one or two things to settle, then I'm off. We've got to put an end to this business. I'm leaving poor Harriet in great misery and in a dreadful position; but I've nothing to reproach myself with and there's nothing more I can do for her. I would still, now, give my life to spend a *month* with her and be loved as I should be. She'll weep and be despairing, but it'll be too late. She'll suffer the consequences of her unfortunate character, which is weak and incapable of deep feeling or decisive action ... Then she'll recover and start to find fault with me. That's how it always is. As for me, I must leave before all that without listening to the cries of my conscience, which is always telling me I am too unhappy and that life is an abomination. I shall be deaf. I promise you seriously, dear Humbert, not to belie your oracle. [...]

I shall write to you from Berlin.

H. Berlioz

79 To Humbert Ferrand   Tuesday, 3 September 1833

Harriet came and I'm staying. We've announced our engagement. In a fortnight it will all be settled, if the laws of mankind are good enough to allow it. It's only their slowness that frightens me. At last!!! Oh, it had to happen, believe me. It was no good.

1 Spontini was the King of Prussia's Generalmusikdirektor in Berlin.

Several of us drew lots as to who should look after the poor fugitive. Jules Janin has taken charge of her departure.

H. Berlioz

Scorning the objections of his parents Berlioz and Harriet were married at the British Embassy on 3 October 1833. Liszt was one of the witnesses. Their honeymoon was spent at Vincennes, just east of Paris.

80 *To his sister Adèle Berlioz*   Vincennes, 6 October 1833

My dear, good little sister,

It's a very long time since I last wrote to you and you must be thinking me ungrateful as well as forgetful, but after so many uncertainties I didn't want to put pen to paper until I could announce that I was at last married. Yes, my dear Adèle, it's done. The ceremony took place last Thursday according to the French and English forms of service. Harriet was afraid I would be emotional and had given me strict instructions to contain myself as far as possible in front of so many witnesses, and I followed her advice so well that my calm was superb and it was she on the contrary who shed tears. I'm with her at Vincennes in a pretty little country cottage far away from all those busybodies. The day of our marriage her sister left us together and we had the most comical wedding feast you can imagine; there were no servants to wait on us so we had our dinner sent over from the restaurant in Vincennes. We picked the dessert in the garden and the weather was wonderfully warm, gentle and refreshing. In short, a moment of extraordinary happiness. I go to Paris from time to time to see what's going on there and to pursue the thread of my usual occupations. Now I've got to redouble my activities and my creative work. When I think that I've wasted an hour that I could have devoted to my beloved's happiness, I reproach myself for it all day long. My wife is so delightfully *pure* and good; it's almost unbelievable to find all that I have found in an actress of her age. Down with the calumnies, I say, may they rebound upon the wretches who uttered them! She can withstand them; I have every confidence in her. Oh, how right I was to listen to the voice of my heart! So often it deceives me, but this time it told only the truth. I'm going to put on a little concert which won't cost anything, so that the proceeds will all be profit. In a month or two I may put on an enormous one in Lyon, and Harriet will come with me. This winter we'll both go to Prussia, which I have to visit under the terms of my scholarship. My wife has just had a rather lucrative offer from there to go and play in English tragedy. I'm no longer counting on any help from our parents, even though my finances are very difficult at the moment, but my father has written me such a terrible letter, quite without provocation, that really it would be crazy to try and disarm his prejudices. Perhaps one day he will realize how unfounded they are. As for you, you are goodness itself and I know that you share intimately in my happiness and in my anxieties.

Adieu, dear sister, adieu.

I'll write to you again and Harriet will add a few lines in her own hand.

Write to me at the same address in Paris.

Your affectionate brother,

H. Berlioz

On 24 November 1833 Berlioz attempted to promote his own and his wife's careers by putting on a concert at the Théâtre-Italien, which he conducted himself. Scenes from Hamlet *and other plays were followed by some musical items:* Sardanapale, Les francs-juges *overture, and Weber's* Konzertstück, *played by Liszt.*

81 *To his sister Adèle Berlioz*   Paris, 28 November 1833

Dear Adèle,

I should have written to you in the last few days to let you know that we have finally got through our benefit performance. I thought I was going to die of fatigue and boredom. But the necessity was there to force me through to the end. Despite her fear and the weakness in her right leg, Harriet made a reappearance as Ophelia and was, as you might expect, heartrending, sublime and overwhelmed with applause. But the evening was too long; we miscalculated the length of each piece and of the entractes, with the result that my concert didn't start till a quarter to midnight. The players were surly and uncooperative, and some had even left. Also, apart from an overture and one other piece, what they played was dreadful. Finally, at half past midnight, the orchestra began to leave one by one *in full view of the audience*! The people in the stalls stood up and asked for the *Symphonie fantastique* and I was forced to make a speech pointing out the empty desks and the impossibility of performing such a work with the players I had left, so then they had pity on the general abandoned by his soldiers and began to shout: 'At the Conservatoire! Some other time!'

The receipts came to 5000 francs which will get us out of difficulty *for the moment*; expenses came to 2500 francs. Anyway, we live to fight another day; all I ask for is time and tranquillity. I'd love to see you, dear Adèle; write to me at least. I think love for my sublime darling will drive me mad. Oh, how I wish you could meet her!

Nanci has not done me the honour of answering my letter. I'd never have believed it of her. Adieu, you at least have remained true to me and I thank you for it.

Adieu, adieu, dear sister.

Although Harriet hasn't met you, she too loves you with all her heart.

Hector Berlioz

Determined to do better, Berlioz put on his next concert in the Salle du Conservatoire on 22 December, with Girard conducting. It included the Symphonie fantastique *and three new works: the overture* Le roi Lear, *the song* Le paysan breton, *and a song from Hugo's* Marie Tudor *(now lost).*

82 *To Thomas Gounet*   Paris, between 15 and 20 December 1833

My dear Gounet,

I hope you'll come next Sunday and hear my *Roi Lear* overture which is *something* ... This something was a wild success at the rehearsal this morning and I hope it'll be the same on the day.[1]

Adieu, you are as special as good music.

H. Berlioz

83 *To Frédéric Chopin*   Paris, ?1834

My dear Chopin,

Make my apologies to Liszt and those gentlemen, I shan't be able to come to dinner with you this evening, I've too much work to do.

I'll see you, I hope, the day after tomorrow, as well as Liszt, in the morning.

Yours,

H. Berlioz

1 The concert was indeed a success.

My dear friend,

Thank you for your article, as much on my own behalf as on that of my wife, to whom it gave the greatest pleasure.[2] I've sent it to Ferrand who asked me for it. Come and see us one evening. What happened to that article I gave you for the *Dictionnaire de la conversation* on the *Armides* of Gluck and Rossini?[3] I do need it for various details that I want to put into the life of Gluck. J. David is starting up a huge newspaper called *Le publiciste* which will appear every five days and he's asked me to contribute this biography to it.[4] Write me a word on the subject, please.

Could you come to the Conservatoire tomorrow morning to the rehearsal of Beethoven's Cyclopean Symphony?[5] I'll be there at nine o'clock precisely. It's prodigious, astounding . . .

You know I'm writing a work for chorus, orchestra and solo viola for Paganini?[6] He came and asked me in person a few days ago. Could you put a four-line announcement of this into the column of *La revue de Paris*? It's been announced in *Le rénovateur* and I've today been to ask the same favour of M. de Briant on *La quotidienne*; he wasn't in.

When on earth will your work appear?

Addio, addiosissimo, tutto tuo for ever.

H. Berlioz

1 D'Ortigue was a music critic who consistently supported Berlioz throughout his career despite differences of opinion on the matter of church music. He was one of the very few people outside his family whom Berlioz addressed in the familiar 'tu' form (Liszt was another).

2 D'Ortigue's notice of the concert on 22 December appeared in *La quotidienne* of 17 January.

3 The *Dictionnaire*, with d'Ortigue's article on *Armide* inspired by Berlioz, had appeared in 1832. Rossini's *Armida* was first heard in Naples in 1817 but never played in Paris.

4 Berlioz's study of Gluck appeared in two parts in the *Gazette musicale* in June 1834. It was in 1834 that Berlioz's work as a critic began to absorb most of his time and provide most of his income.

5 The Ninth, about to receive its second Paris performance, Berlioz's first hearing of it since he had been in Italy when it was first played there.

6 Destined eventually to be *Harold en Italie*, the work was originally entitled *Les derniers instants de Marie Stuart*.

To Emile Deschamps[1]   Paris, 6 March 1834

If the rehearsal of *Don Giovanni* doesn't go on beyond midnight, it would be kind of M. Deschamps to call in at my house on his way back from the opera. I'm slaving too hard this evening to come to the *prova prima*, but there's a lot I should like to discuss with the poet on the subject of Mozart. We must make this masterpiece sparkle, so as to induce giddiness in lovers of the bass drum ... You will come, won't you?

With my compliments,
Hector Berlioz

86 *To his sister Adèle Berlioz*   Paris, 20 March 1834

Dear sister,

Yes, it's very bad of me, I know, and I've been reproaching myself daily, not to have written to you for so long, but really for two months now I've been so taken up with my work, under such a burden from several pressing compositions, that I sometimes find myself with a pen in my hand for twelve or thirteen hours at a time. I'm on the point of completing a large instrumental composition for Paganini. He's going to play it in London this year and I'm devoting all the time to it my newspaper scribbling leaves me. Requests come from all sides for articles on music and on Italy, and as they pay promptly I say yes to everyone;[2] I look forward to the time when I can earn more money with less time and trouble.

Harriet is depressed, seeing me working like this without being able to help me at all. As the director of the English theatre in Germany wasn't able to give satisfactory guarantees of his solvency, I refused to accept the engagement he was offering her, which would have entailed travelling to no good purpose – painful for her and a nuisance for me. In a week's time we're moving to Montmartre, on the heights of Paris; we have a little apartment with four rooms, a garden and a view over the plain of St-Denis for 70 francs a month. It's much cheaper than here and in half an hour you're in Paris. I'll have more peace to work, here we're worn out with visitors.

So you've turned down an uncouth suitor! ... You did the right thing

1 Poet and translator and close friend of Berlioz's. He had collaborated on the French translation of *Don Giovanni*, played at the Opéra on 10 March 1834 and one of the most successful productions of the period. In 1839 he supplied the vocal text for *Roméo et Juliette*.
2 Articles on his Italian trip appeared in *Le rénovateur* in April and May.

a thousand times over if you didn't like him, and I'm sure you'll have the courage, in such matters, to fend off insinuations accompanied by arguments couched in terms of the more precious metals. You have a strong character; you're a good sister who doesn't give in to absurd prejudices; you don't play the stupid prude, like our noble sister Nanci who hasn't deigned to reply to the letter I was silly enough to send her at the time of my marriage. I'm not writing to my father, although I'm quite certain that now my letter would not be ill received; my father's heart and mind are of too elevated a stamp to remain for long under the influence of the notions which separated him from his son. But I'm afraid he might attribute this quite natural step to an ulterior motive and I'll refrain from taking it until circumstances are more propitious. You ask whether I'd rather have a girl or a boy;[1] I'd far rather have a nice little girl who looks like her mother and whom we shall name after my dear sister (Harriet's already agreed on this) than a little scamp who would perhaps make me send him to the devil, like Prosper. But we haven't reached that point yet; and the problem won't be resolved until August. We're a little worried about that period, as you can imagine, and neither of us is used to the domestic difficulties which are then bound to increase. [...]

Adieu, love me always as I love you.

H. B.

87 *To his sister Adèle Berlioz*   Montmartre, 29 April 1834

Dear sister,

There's no need for you to be worried; I've no more sympathy with all this stupid political commotion than I'd have with a gang of schoolboys fighting over some stolen apples.[2] It's merely a question of strength and success. Even so, simple interested onlookers like myself have been victims of it all, as have the participants in these bloody pranks; and to that extent your fears could be justified. It was only when Harriet and I heard the call to arms under our garden wall at one o'clock in the morning that we realized the curtain had gone up in Paris as well. I went to see it all next morning, but it was over; *power remained with the law*, as the political jargon has it, which is to say *power remained with the power*. I've no news of Ferrand or of A.

1 Harriet was now four months pregnant.
2 Riots in Paris on 13 April, following serious disturbances in Lyon, were harshly put down.

Berlioz, I'm afraid they may have been somewhat spattered with the mess in Lyon. As the republicans are obviously only out to get what doesn't belong to them, they ought to organize themselves into vast bands of brigands, stopping on the main roads and ransacking villages. It would at least be more productive and much more amusing.

Thank you for the good news about my father's health; Harriet on the other hand is suffering considerably. We hoped that when the vomiting stopped she would regain her strength, but she's tormented by all sorts of pains that come and go unpredictably.

She sends you her warmest good wishes in return for the interest and affection you have shown her.

I'm working too hard; we're very peaceful here in our hermitage. The only things that tire me are the nightingales singing day and night under our windows.

I'll send you shortly a biography of Gluck which I've been commissioned to write and which will appear in a few weeks' time.[1] You'll only read it because it's by your brother, as this piece of prose can be of no interest to you otherwise. I'm about to finish a new symphony, in an entirely different form from the other one.[2] It'll be for my concerts in November. There's talk of my writing a large work in five acts; we're in negotiation with the Opéra over this important project on which the outcome of my life as an artist would depend, no less.[3] I hope it will come to something. I've got steady, powerful support . . .

Adieu. Yours as ever,

[unsigned]

88 *To his sister Adèle Berlioz*   Paris, 12 May 1834

Dear Adèle,

[. . .] Last Monday we had a sort of picnic. My friends came to spend half a day with me. They were celebrities in the worlds of music and poetry, Alfred de Vigny, Antoni Deschamps, Liszt, Hiller and Chopin. We chatted, discussed art, poetry, ideas, music, theatre, in short what goes to make up life, surrounded by the beauties of nature and under this Italian sun we've had for several days now.[4] My poor sister,

1 The biography was divided into two long articles in the *Gazette musicale*, published in June.
2 *Harold en Italie* is a symphony with a prominent part for solo viola.
3 There was a possibility of a libretto on *Hamlet* to be set by Berlioz for the Opéra.
4 One of the ideas discussed at the picnic was evidently an *opéra comique* on Benvenuto Cellini's autobiography, probably proposed by de Vigny.

Harriet so often wants to meet you! When shall we find ourselves together? My father is well, from what the ladies of the Rocher family tell me; I hope the same is true of everybody. [...]

Hector Berlioz

Harriet gave birth to a son, their only child, on 14 August 1834. He was named Louis, after his grandfather.

89 *To Humbert Ferrand*   Montmartre, 31 August 1834

My dear Humbert,

I'm not forgetting you in the least, but you don't realize the extent to which indispensable labours hold me in thrall. I'd have written to you twenty times over without these damned newspaper articles I'm forced to write for the few wretched hundred-sou pieces they bring in. I had just read in the press of the sad event which has come to put your courage to the test, and was preparing to write to you when your letter arrived. I wouldn't offer you any of the kind of banal condolences that are ineffective and irrelevant at a time like this. But if anything can soften the blow you have just received, it would be knowing that your father's end was as calm and peaceful as anyone could wish. You mention mine; he wrote to me recently, in reply to a letter in which I informed him that Harriet had given birth to our son. His reply was as kind as I was hoping it would be and arrived in good time. She had an extremely painful labour; for some moments I was even worried she might not survive. But all ended happily after forty hours of terrible suffering. She sends you her sincere thanks for the messages you've sent in each of your letters; she has long recognized, as I have, that our friendship was of a special, indeed spiritual nature. Why must we be so far away from each other? [...]

I think I told you that my symphony with solo viola, *Harold*, was finished two months ago. I expect Paganini will find that the viola is not treated enough as a concerto soloist; it's a new kind of symphony and not a composition written to show off a unique talent like his.[1] I shall always be in his debt for having commissioned it from me. It's being copied out at the moment and it'll be performed next November at the first concert I'm giving at the Conservatoire. I'm hoping to give

1 Paganini did indeed find the solo part too undemonstrative, as Berlioz anticipated, and he never played it.

three in a row. With these in mind I've just finished several pieces for voice and orchestra which will, I think, fit well into the programme. The first symphony, in Liszt's arrangement, has been engraved, but it won't be printed and published until October, so I shan't be able to send it to you till then.[1] I'm going to have *Le paysan breton* engraved and you can have it straight away. Tomorrow I'll ask at M. Schlesinger's for you to be sent my articles in the *Gazette musicale* on Gluck and *La vestale*.

Do I know Barbier indeed![2] To the extent that I've just been responsible for his suffering a rather unhappy disappointment. I had suggested to Léon de Wailly, who's a very talented young poet and a close friend of his, that he should write me a libretto in two acts based on the memoirs of Benvenuto Cellini. He chose Auguste Barbier to help him and the two of them wrote me the most delightful *opéra comique* you can imagine. The three of us presented ourselves, like fools, to M. Crosnier;[3] the libretto was read out in front of us and *turned down*. Despite Crosnier's protestations, we think I am the reason behind the rejection. At the Opéra-Comique I'm looked on as a *sapper, an overthrower of the national style*, and they don't want to have anything to do with me. As a result, they turned down the words so as not to have to accept the music of a *madman*.

Even so I've written the first scene, the song of the Florentine goldsmiths, which they all found utterly overwhelming. It'll be heard in my concerts.[4] I read out to Léon de Wailly this morning the passage in your letter concerning Barbier; as for him, he's travelling round Belgium and Germany at the moment. As he was about to leave, Brizeux arrived from Italy, more besotted than ever with his beloved Florence. He's brought back some new verses; I hope for his sake they're as ravishing as those in *Marie*. Have you read *Marie*?[5] Have you read Barbier's most recent work on Italy,

Divine Juliet stretched out on her bier,

as he calls her? It's called *Il pianto*. It too contains some beautiful things. I confess I was absolutely astonished not to find you sharing my enthusiasm for *Les iambes*, when I recited some fragments to you. Ah!

1 Liszt's transcription of the *Symphonie fantastique* for piano solo was the first version of the work to be published.
2 The poet Auguste Barbier.
3 Director of the Opéra-Comique.
4 It was announced for Berlioz's concerts that winter but evidently not performed. It was probably the basis of the *Chant des ciseleurs* in the opera.
5 Berlioz had set Auguste Brizeux's poem *Le jeune pâtre breton* on a text from *Marie*.

yes, it's wild and fine. Send me your *Grutli*.[1] I'll make sure I show it to him, and to Brizeux, Wailly, Antoni Deschamps and Alfred de Vigny, who are the ones I see most often. I see Hugo only rarely, he lords it too much. As for Dumas, he's a scatterbrain with no conviction and no artistic conscience. He's leaving with Baron Taylor to explore the Mediterranean coast. The minister has provided a ship for this expedition. So for a year at least our theatres will have a break from all that adultery. De Wailly is not discouraged; with the help of the *young* Castil-Blaze (who's not like his father) he's just finished the outline for me of a grand, three-act opera on a historical subject which has never been treated before, in accordance with Véron's request; we'll see shortly whether this one has any more luck. It must succeed, it must! I'm not anxious; if only I had something to live on ... I'd set my hand to many other things apart from operas. Music has broad wings which the walls of a theatre don't allow it to spread completely.

> Patience and the passage of time
> Accomplish more than violence or anger.[2]

I'd go on writing to you all through the night, but as I have to row my galley all day tomorrow, I must go to sleep. Harriet thanks you most warmly for your 'good friendship'.[3] Remember me in turn to your wife and family.

Adieu; you have my affection as surely as I have yours.

H. Berlioz

90 *To his Royal Highness the Duc d'Orléans*[4]   34, Rue de Londres,
Paris
17 October 1834

Monseigneur,

Would it be ill-considered for an artist, whose career is impeded by difficulties without number but whose determination remains proof against their attacks, to seek the support of a highly placed patron? Your Royal Highness has too often shown what the young might expect from his kindly sympathy for me not to be encouraged in the approach I am making herewith. It is highly probable, Monseigneur, that

---

1 Poems by Ferrand that were evidently never published.
2 La Fontaine, already quoted on p. 107.
3 Which Berlioz writes in English.
4 The Duc d'Orléans was the eldest son of King Louis-Philippe. The *Grande symphonie funèbre et triomphale* was dedicated to him in 1843.

my name has reached Your Highness accompanied by such epithets as 'mad' and 'eccentric'. Even though I am assured by my friends, and by the tiny section of the public known as my fanatics, that these charges of madness and eccentricity have always been levelled at artists who deviated however slightly from the central path trodden by the masses, it is nonetheless the case that I am barred from practically every avenue by a constant and unwearying opposition. I am therefore asking, Monseigneur, whether Your Royal Highness would be kind enough to attend the concert I am about to give at the Conservatoire, the programme of which I enclose herewith. Perhaps, when he has heard my music played by a hundred and thirty young musicians who are more or less unmoved by the faults I am reproached with, Your Highness will agree with my friends that a place at Charenton is not my most urgent requirement.[1] Opinionated as I am, and determined to work with the utmost perseverance to reach my goal even if I have to clear a way with teeth and nails through the door that refuses to open, I am certain that I shall one day succeed.

Unfortunately it could be that that day will not arrive until I have lost both teeth and nails — a daunting prospect for an artist who feels himself to be at the height of his powers and is afraid that from here on his progress may only be downhill . . .

May I hope, Monseigneur, that Your Highness will grant me a moment of his time and come to judge *for himself* whether or not I am worthy of his noble protection?

I am, with profound respect, Monseigneur,
Your Royal Highness's
most humble and obedient servant,
Hector Berlioz

The concert took place on 9 November 1834, conducted by Girard. With the Symphonie fantastique *were* Sara la baigneuse *and* La belle voyageuse, *both being heard for the first time. In the second concert, on 23 November, also conducted by Girard,* Harold en Italie *was played for the first time, with Urhan playing the viola solo.*

1 Charenton was the location of Paris's madhouse.

My dearest friend,

I was almost expecting a letter from you. I'm taking advantage of a free half-hour this evening to reply to it. I'm crushed by fatigue and there's still a lot to do. My second concert has been given and your *Harold*[1] had the reception I was hoping for, even though the performance was still insecure. The *Marche des pèlerins*[2] was encored; it's now taken on the role of a pendant (religious and gentle) to the *Marche au supplice*.[3] Next Sunday at my third concert, *Harold* will reappear in full force, I hope, and in a perfect performance. The *Orgie de brigands* which concludes it is a piece of some violence; I wish I could let you hear it! Your poetry figures in it largely; I'm sure I owe you more than the odd idea. [. . .]

The *Symphonie fantastique* has been published. But since poor Liszt has spent such terrible amounts of money to achieve this, we agreed with Schlesinger[4] that he should not give away a single copy, so even I haven't had one. They cost twenty francs; would you like me to buy you one? I wish I could send it to you without all these explanations, but, as you know, for some time now our financial position has been rather difficult. Still, after the receipts of the last concert, which were 2400 francs (double that of the first one), I've reason to hope I may make a profit on the third. All the copying is now paid for; it was an enormous task. [. . .]

Harriet thanks you very much for what you said about her and especially about her little Louis, who's the sweetest, prettiest child I've ever seen. My wife and I are as united and happy as it's possible to be, in spite of our material problems. I think they only make us love each other more. The other day, during the performance of the *Scène aux champs* in the *Symphonie fantastique* she was almost ill with emotion. The memory of it was still making her cry the next day.

Adieu, adieu; all good wishes and remember me to your wife and family.

H. Berlioz

1 'Your' *Harold*, because the work was dedicated to Ferrand.
2 The second movement of *Harold en Italie*.
3 The fourth movement of the *Symphonie fantastique*.
4 The publisher.

The third concert that season, with the second performance of Harold en Italie, *took place on 14 December.*

92 *To Edmond Cavé*[1]   Paris, 18 December 1834

Monsieur,

I have just sent to the Minister the request for payment of my scholarship from the Académie des Beaux Arts.[2] As the director of the Théâtre Nautique has not paid my wife a single penny of her salary,[3] we are forced by financial straits to ask you to expedite as far as possible the payment for my first term.

Trusting in your goodwill, I am

Your devoted servant,

Hector Berlioz

93 *To his sister Adèle Berlioz*   Paris, 10 January 1835

My dear little Adèle,

We received your charming bonnet for Louis the day before yesterday. It's admirable, superb, transcendent; Harriet is more delighted than I can tell you; you have made her as happy as a queen (or as they used to be) and she joins me in thanking you. I haven't written to you for a long time, it's true, but you know how many things I have to do. Four concerts in one and a half months, and several new works to produce, which doubles the difficulties; then endless articles to write for my wretched *Rénovateur* and for the *Gazette musicale*.[4] Without those I don't really know what we should have lived on while I was putting on my concerts, as that damned Théâtre Ventadour[5] has gone bankrupt; I haven't managed to extract a penny of my wife's salary. This leaves us without nearly two thousand francs which we were counting on. It's true I've earned almost that from my concerts, despite the enormous costs. But I had to spend a lot in advance on our wretched furniture and you can imagine the money didn't stay in the house long. But I don't know why I'm telling you all that.

---

1 Director of the Département des Beaux-Arts.
2 Even after his return from Italy Berlioz was still entitled to his scholarship until 1835.
3 In November 1834 Harriet had played in a mime *La dernière heure d'un condamné* at the Théâtre-Nautique. Berlioz had to institute legal proceedings to secure her payment.
4 Berlioz wrote frequently for *Le rénovateur* throughout 1834 and 1835, and he started a regular column for the *Journal des débats* in 1835. He wrote for the *Gazette musicale* (later the *Revue et gazette musicale*) until 1863.
5 The Théâtre-Nautique.

Our little boy is as delightful as ever, you have no idea what a beautiful child he is. He never cries, but bursts out laughing when you take the trouble to play with him. Harriet becomes prouder of him every day. Mme Rocher came by to see us; I was in bed with a severe cold, and my wife, not being dressed or prepared to undergo an examination, remained out of sight. Since then I've called on Mme Rocher three times, leaving my card each time as she and Hippolyte were out; I haven't seen them again. [. . .]

Adieu, your brother and friend,

H. Berlioz

94 *To Humbert Ferrand*   Paris, 15 April 1835

It's true, my dear Humbert, I've been owing you a reply for a long time; but it's also very true, in the most rigorous sense of that word, that I haven't had a moment's leisure in which to write to you. Even today, I'm still afraid I shan't be able to tell you the half of what's on my mind. I'm in the same situation with my sister; for three months now I haven't been able to write her a line.

I'm having to work terribly hard for all these newspapers who pay me for my prose. You know I'm at present producing music notices (concerts only) in the *Débats*; they're signed H***. It's an important business for me; I get a hundred francs for each article; the effect they have on the musical world is truly extraordinary. It's something in the nature of an event for the artists of Paris. Despite M. Bertin's[1] invitation, I refused to write an account of *I puritani* or of that miserable *Juive*;[2] I had too many rude things to say about them; people would have thought I was jealous. I still keep on with *Le rénovateur*, where I only half contain my ill humour in the face of all these delights. Then there's *Italie pittoresque*, which has just extracted another contribution from me.[3] On top of which the *Gazette musicale* harasses me every Sunday for some concert notice or the review of some idiocy that's just appeared in print. And then there are the thousand attempts I've been making for two months to give another concert; I've tried all the halls in Paris, as the one in the Conservatoire is closed to me thanks to the monopoly held by members of the Société des Concerts. I've come to

1 Armand Bertin was the proprietor of the *Journal des débats*.
2 *I puritani*, by Bellini, first performed at the Théâtre-Italien on 25 January 1835, and Halévy's *La juive*, first performed at the Opéra on 23 February 1835.
3 This was a collection of essays which appeared in 1836. Berlioz's contribution was the basis for chapters later incorporated in his *Mémoires*.

the firm conclusion that this is the only hall in Paris where my works can be heard properly. I hope to give a final concert on 3 May, by which time the Conservatoire concerts will have come to an end.¹ I've just rewritten or rather written the music for your scene in the *Francs-juges*, 'Noble amitié'. I've composed it in such a way that it can be sung either by a tenor or by a soprano and, although it's a male role, I had Mlle Falcon in mind when I was writing it; she could make a real impact in it; I'll take her the score some day soon. [. . .]

I leave you to go to the *Débats* with my article on Beethoven's Fifth Symphony, which contains the phrases you mention. Meyerbeer is due to arrive to begin rehearsals for his major work, *Saint-Barthélémy*.² I'm very curious to get to know this new score. Meyerbeer is the only established composer to have shown any real interest in me. Onslow, who was at Liszt's recent concert, overwhelmed me with his inflated compliments on the *Marche des pèlerins*. I like to think he didn't mean a word of them. I'd rather have honest hatred from those people.

Liszt has written a wonderful fantasy for full orchestra on the *Ballade du pêcheur* and the *Chanson des brigands*.³

Adieu. With all best wishes,

Yours heart and soul,

H. Berlioz

95 *To his sister Adèle Berlioz*   Paris, 17 April 1835

[. . .] You see that I have barely time to breathe. This need to keep working is not what irritates me most, since it prevents me from developing feelings about any number of things which, if I reflected on them, would cause me pain. But Harriet is depressed to see me alone doing the work and not to be able to do anything herself, accustomed as she has been all her life to supporting her whole family. Sometimes she's nearly mad with frustration. The consolations I can offer her are not very effective; one can't argue with facts. I took her to see Hugo recently to ask him for a role suitable to her talent, in which her inability to speak French properly might be capitalized upon. Hugo is happy to look for one, but a number of bungled attempts have spoilt the market for dramatic opportunities of this sort. But we are not

1 Berlioz did give a concert on 3 May 1835, conducted by Girard, which included both the *Symphonie fantastique* and *Le retour à la vie*.
2 Eventually entitled *Les Huguenots* and first performed at the Opéra on 29 February 1836.
3 Two movements from *Le retour à la vie*.

giving up hope. Hugo is due to come any day now and tell us whether he's been able to overcome or circumvent the problem. He offered me a libretto last month. Scribe has done so too, but these offers don't amount to anything because of the opposition of the directors of the Opéra and the Opéra-Comique. I shall have to spend several more years composing outside the theatre before I can place my foot on the neck of these stupid industrialists.

Meanwhile my artistic life is one of considerable pain and suffering. To be obliged to see the best years of my life lost to opera for the simple reason that three scoundrels have the misfortune to be imbeciles simultaneously. Véron,[1] for example, had to be forced by Meyerbeer through legal action to put on *Robert le diable*, which has made his fortune against his own wishes; since when he has produced nothing but platitudinous rubbish, culminating in *La juive*. It's the same elsewhere. One must be patient. Everything will come right. [. . .]

H. Berlioz

96 To his sister Adèle Berlioz   Montmartre, 2 August 1835

Dear sister,

I did indeed receive your first letter, but the truth is, without any exaggeration, I've had no time in which to reply. You know I've had a violent sore throat, but not that it lasted more than a fortnight. Although there were times when I could work in bed, this indisposition has lost me a lot of time even so. For me these days time is money; and the money I earn is the whole family's livelihood. I can find absolutely no way of continuing work on a vast musical composition which I've begun and of which I have high hopes.[2] I have to write for the papers all, all the time, with the prospect of being without a penny any day after I've failed to do so. You can have no idea what it's like to be spurred on by need and to escape it only by work, patience and courage. I earn money, it's true, but we need a lot of it; the nurse is very expensive. I lost a lot when a theatre went bankrupt. When I got married, neither Harriet nor I possessed anything and there are still many things we're short of. My scholarship has come to an end and I have nothing now but my pen. But the really appalling thing about this

---

1 Director of the Opéra.
2 Berlioz was working on a vast project in seven movements entitled *Fête musicale funèbre à la mémoire des hommes illustres de la France*. The work was never completed, but it was probably refashioned as *Le cinq mai* and parts of the *Grande messe des morts*, the *Grande symphonie funèbre et triomphale* and the *Te Deum*.

situation is that my newspaper work brings me less than a quarter or a sixth of what I would get from my concerts if I could compose; and as I told you, I can't compose because my work is a long one and wouldn't earn anything for six months. So in order to finish it I shall have to wait until I've put enough aside to keep me for several months *without doing anything*. Harriet is devastated to see my state of slavery, all the more so because she can't do anything herself. For a moment we were on the point of leaving for North America, but uncertainty as to her future over there and the fact that Louis was too young prevented us. She is really the one who needs courage, because after all I am busy, I'm creating things, I'm active, I can try and forget, whereas she's tormented all day long by the servants who steal from us, she works herself into a terrible state of anxiety at the least sign our son is not well, she's surrounded by a world she was not brought up to where people do not even speak her language, and she's inactive while feeling herself to have an immense talent which could make us rich if circumstances were different. One has to admit that her despairing moods are well justified. In a few years' time there will be no, or almost no theatres left in France (except the boulevard theatres). There are none left in England; all the actors with any talent for serious drama are going off to America. The art has been killed by politics, Methodism, and the old age of our civilization. Music on the other hand is invading everywhere, but it's the wild enthusiasm of a child who seizes something shiny without thinking what he's going to do with it. They're putting on various sorts of concert everywhere, but the *contredanse* rules and the bass drum and the flageolet bring in all the money. In six or seven years, nonetheless, it's likely that the French will begin to understand real music. In my own case, I have my public which is increasing daily but which daily is becoming hungrier. 'Are you working? When will we have a new symphony? When's the next concert?' Those are the questions I'm bombarded with when I go down into Paris. And I can't compose . . . [. . .]

You ask for details of my standing with the Opéra (I'm not talking of the Opéra-Comique, which is a theatre for grocers), so here they are: I shan't make any progress there while M. Véron is in office; well, he's leaving and handing over the job to his associate, M. Duponchel, the costume designer, who imagines he likes my music, though his understanding is on precisely the same lines as M. Véron's. Six months ago Duponchel committed himself to Meyerbeer and M. Bertin, in the presence of myself and Barbier, to the effect that if, as was probable, he became director of the Opéra, his first action would be to arrange for me to write a work. Ministerial intrigues are blocking his nomination for the moment. The event which is putting the whole of Paris into disarray, and with good reason, is causing further delays;[1] and we wait. But I know so well what sort of animals directors are, so I'd exchange Duponchel's promise for a few shillings. I'll not forget that the only way Meyerbeer could get a production of *Robert le diable*, which has been wholly responsible for the theatre's prosperity for the last four years, was to pay the Opéra administration sixty thousand francs of his own money because they refused to pay for it. To get any sympathy from those good-for-nothings you simply have to be as mediocre a human being as they are.

Those are my positive thoughts on this subject.

Harriet thanks you for your kind wishes and especially for your words about Louis. He's charming, his teeth are still hurting him, he's got five of them, he can almost walk by himself; we're going to wean him shortly. Adieu, my dear sister, a model of sisterhood. I embrace you tenderly.

Your affectionate brother,
H. Berlioz

Duponchel did succeed Véron as director of the Opéra and was as good as his word in promising to mount an opera by Berlioz. The librettists set to work to adapt Benvenuto Cellini *for the Opéra. On 22 November and 13 December 1835 Berlioz gave two concerts in the Conservatoire, the second of which he conducted himself. The new work,* Le cinq mai, *was heard at both.*

97 *To Victor Hugo*   Montmartre, 9 December 1835

I have received your wonderful poetry.[2] It was extremely good of you to think of me and, even more, to say that I may count you among my true friends. Words like those strike sparks, giving the weary soldier strength to pick up his weapon and hurl himself like a lion into the fray. Thank you! If I were a great poet like you, perhaps I would find words to express what I felt on reading your latest work, but in my

---

1 On 28 July 1835 a violent attempt on the life of Louis-Philippe was made in the Boulevard du Temple by Fieschi.
2 *Les chants du crépuscule.*

impotence I could do no more than cry 'Oh!!!' like savages before the rising sun.

H. Berlioz

P.S. Would you have a free moment next Sunday to come and hear me?

98 *To Humbert Ferrand* Montmartre, 16 December 1835

My dear Ferrand,

I'm not to blame for not writing to you for so long; you can have no real idea of all I have to do in a day and how little leisure I have, *when I have any*. But there's no point giving me a going over about it: I'm sure you're in no doubt how much I enjoy writing to you. [. . .]

I'd like to send you my score of *Harold*, which is dedicated to you. It's had twice as much success this year as it did last and without a doubt this symphony buries the *Symphonie fantastique*. I'm very happy to have offered it to you before you've had a chance to hear it; that'll be a further pleasure for me when the occasion arises. Frankly, nothing I've written could be more to your taste.

An opera of mine has been accepted by the Opéra; Duponchel looks favourably on the idea; the libretto, which will be in verse this time, is by Alfred de Vigny and Auguste Barbier. It's painted in delightfully vivid colours. I can't start work on the music yet, I'm *short of metal* like my protagonist (perhaps you already know it's Benvenuto Cellini). I'll try and find time in the next few days to send you notes for the article you have in mind, and especially for *Harold*.

I've had a great success in Germany, thanks to Liszt's piano arrangement of my *Symphonie fantastique*. I've been sent a great wad of newspapers from Leipzig and Berlin in which Fétis has been given a good thrashing for his attitude to me.[1] Liszt is not here. In any case, we're too close to each other for his name to detract from the article rather than helping it.

Thank you for all you have to say about my wife and son; it's true, I love them more every day. Harriet is touched by all the interest you are taking in her. But what delights her still more is that you mention our little Louis. [. . .]

Adieu, adieu.

Yours as ever,

H. Berlioz

---

1 These articles included Schumann's very extensive study of the *Symphonie fantastique* published in the *Neue Zeitschrift für Musik* in July and August 1835.

P.S. The two movements of *Harold* can't be separated from the rest without turning into nonsense. It's as though I were to send you the second act of an opera.

99 *To his mother Madame Berlioz*   Montmartre, 4 January 1836

Dear mama,

My last letter crossed with the one from Adèle. I was very slow in thanking you for all the kindness and affection yours contained. I've explained why to Adèle. I can assure you that when I get back from all the things I have to do in Paris I'm so tired as to be incapable of writing two lines of common sense; and on the other hand, when I stay at home my time is taken up with urgent tasks of a different sort. In her last letter Adèle repeats the offers you made me previously, adding one of various items of linen I might be glad of. As for the cloak, I never wear one. But some shirts FOR ME, a pair of sheets and some napkins would be very useful. The cold is frightful this year, but it's especially bad in Montmartre. What's more, country houses like the one we are in are not built to withstand the winter and we can't find a way of keeping the rooms warm. Apart from that we're all reasonably well, except for me – I've been feeling rather out of sorts for some time. Louis is growing and getting stronger, but he's still not talking. [. . .]

We're living very much on our own this winter, not being able to accept all the invitations we receive because we're so far away and because it's almost impossible to reach the heights of Montmartre by coach. In any case, all these visits are costly and for that reason my poor wife always refuses them. And then it's quite a business separating her from her son for an entire evening, and the servants are so unreliable! Servants in Paris are a plague! You have no idea how dishonest and lazy and insolent they are! It's astonishing. Harriet thinks they've got worse since the July Revolution and I believe she's right. You're very lucky to have Monique! And then they're very expensive, they have to have *coffee* etc, etc. We've changed them several times, but it's always the same. We're tired of struggling with the problem and are keeping the ones we have.

Adieu, dear mama, that's enough talk of our troubles, I embrace you tenderly and my father too. Harriet thanks dear Adèle again for the pretty dress she sent for Louis.

H. Berlioz

If you could find some reliable woman at La Côte who would suit us, perhaps our best plan would be to bring her here. Write me a note on the subject. No one could be better than you, dear mama, to find the right person for us.

100 *To Franz Liszt*   Montmartre, 25 January 1836

My dear friend,

I have received your letter and reply forthwith. I'd already seen M. Bartholini, and before doing so had written an article on your Conservatoire, based on a printed prospectus he sent me.[1] The few lines were necessarily far from complete, but they'll serve to prepare the way for a second article which will be worthier of its subject and for which information sent by you will prove invaluable.

I'll see M. Levy one day soon.

You catch me in one of those moments of profound dejection which always follow after those intense rages that eat inwardly at the heart without being able to explode ... You have the misfortune to be as familiar with them as I am. The subject of this *unerupted heartquake* is as follows: I'd been appointed general manager of the Gymnase-Musical with a salary of 6000 francs a year, plus two benefit concerts with all expenses paid and royalty payments for each of my compositions. Thiers[2] has absolutely refused to allow singing at the Gymnase and so has lost me the job. I was intending to add a choral school to the establishment like the one set up by Choron, but now it's gone bankrupt and closed. THEY USE IT AS A BALLROOM ...

What's more, the Commission de l'Opéra asked the same M. Thiers to authorize Duponchel to sign a contract with me for my opera – the libretto is by de Vigny, Barbier and Léon de Wailly. M. Thiers refuses, saying that as it is not certain that M. Duponchel will be the director of the Opéra at the time when my work is put on, he has no right to saddle any future successor with a piece he might not approve of. At the moment I'm suggesting to Duponchel that he draws up a conditional contract; he's hesitating, claiming he's uncertain whether this will suit Rossini and his banker Aguado. This fellow hurled himself headlong into the arms of Rossini some time ago, and you can imagine the consequences. The arms of Rossini!! ... Meyerbeer and Bertin are now encouraging me to write my opera even so, feeling

1 Liszt was then in Geneva assisting the foundation of the Conservatoire.
2 Minister of the Interior.

[131]

that when the time comes to produce it some way will surely be found round all the difficulties; that's what I'm going to do.

As for the Napoleonic piece of mine which you mention,[1] I too think it's good; it's grand and tragic. Unfortunately I had to have it sung by twenty basses, for want of a single good one, and you know how expressive choral singers are.

Richault[2] asked me a month ago to arrange the *Francs-juges* overture for piano duet; I've done so with Chopin's help and it's being engraved at the moment together with the full score. I'll send it all to you. *Harold* has had an enormous success this year, thanks to the magnificent performance I was able to give of it, for the first time. I'm conducting my own concerts nowadays and it shows in the performances; in the past the speeds were always wrong. I don't know how to get the two scores you wanted to you; I have an unreasoning fear of seeing them lost on the way. If it would not be too much of a disturbance for you to come and see us and warm us by your presence, if only for three weeks and even if you had to hide in the dome of the Panthéon, I confess it would make me very happy.[3]

You are in the best possible situation for writing great things, so make use of it. Go to Switzerland and Italy on foot, that's the only way to see and understand the beauties they have to offer. You don't say anything about your private life in Geneva or of the host of things which touch you most nearly. Do you feel there's a demarcation line between us, beyond which friendship and confidences are not permitted? This wasn't my feeling. Never mind, I am nonetheless yours as ever,

H. Berlioz

Give Bloc[4] my kindest regards and assure him I'll do whatever I can on his behalf.

101 *To Friedrich Hofmeister*[5]   Paris, 8 May 1836

Monsieur,

You have recently published an overture, in a piano duet reduction, under the title *Ouverture des francs-juges*, to which you attach my name

1 *Le cinq mai.*
2 The Paris music publisher.
3 Liszt had gone with Marie d'Agoult to Switzerland, where their first child was born in December 1835. The risk of scandal made a return to Paris at this time an impossibility.
4 Bloc, who had conducted Berlioz's music in 1828, was the first director of the Geneva Conservatoire.
5 Music publisher in Leipzig.

not only as composer but as arranger. It is painful for me to have to protest that I am a complete stranger to this publication which has been brought out without my consent and without even my knowledge. The piano arrangement which you have just produced IS NOT BY ME and indeed I should have difficulty recognizing my work in what is left of the overture. Your arranger has cut, trimmed, pruned and reconstituted my score in such way that in many places there is nothing left but a ridiculous monstrosity, and I would ask him to keep all the credit for it to himself. If a similar liberty had been taken towards me by a Beethoven or a Weber, I should have submitted uncomplainingly to what would nonetheless have certainly seemed to me a cruel humiliation. But neither Weber nor Beethoven would have imposed this submission on me: if the work is bad, they would not have gone to the trouble of revising it; if they thought it was good, they would have respected its form, its ideas, its details, even its faults. But then, as men of their calibre are no more common in Germany than elsewhere, I have reason to suppose that my overture has not fallen into the hands of any very extraordinary musician. A simple inspection of his work provides ample proof of this. I am not speaking of the pianistic style which he has substituted for the orchestral one, and which frequently looks as though it has been taken from sonatas written for eight-year-olds; I shall say nothing either of the total lack of intelligence he demonstrates from one end of the work to the other, whether in reproducing in the most tame and niggardly fashion passages the orchestral effect of which could be got over only by using the full resources of the piano, or in often mistaking the subsidiary idea for the main one, and vice versa; in all that, the arranger is not at fault; I am convinced he was not acting out of malice. But what strikes me as truly deplorable is that you should have instructed such a surgeon to perform such serious amputations on me. One does not normally cut off a part of the body without knowing its overall importance, its special functions, its relationship with other parts and its internal and external anatomy. It is only the executioner who can cut off a malefactor's hand without troubling himself over joints, ligaments, nerves and blood vessels; so he goes about it with a single brutal chop of his hatchet and the patient's head comes off soon after. It is the punishment for parricides. That, sir, is what your arranger has inflicted on me. [. . .]

My dear friend,

What's become of you? Not so much as a line from you! . . .

You must take up your pen even so, to tell me who you've given my scores to; they still haven't arrived here and I'm worried, I'm going to need them for a concert. Put me out of my misery as soon as possible. Have you finished working on them? Are you pleased?

Meanwhile, I'm going on with my opera, in the middle of daily rehearsals for the one by Mlle Bertin.[1] It's going on for ever, it'll make me ill. What a hellish world that is! What an icy, hellish conspiracy! They all sing out of tune, shout out of tune, rasp out of tune, moo and hum out of tune, without any assurance, vigour or intelligence. It's horrible; what'll happen to me when it's my own music? It's only when there's an audience that all this hubbub calms down and becomes musical; until then, I defy you to have an idea of the chaos. The string rehearsals in particular are of a painfulness beyond all imagining.

Adieu, I don't know why I'm telling you all this, but I'm in a rage about it. I'd like to rip my score into little pieces, it seems to me to contain nothing but effects like those I'm hearing down at the Opéra every day. A concert of bats.

You will write soon, won't you?

Have you seen my articles about you?[2] I couldn't get them put in any earlier.

Please present my best respects to Mme d'Agoult.

And to your daughter!

The echoes of your last success in Paris are still to be heard and when you return you will find that in the opinion of that capricious band of children called the public you are ten times greater than before.

Adieu.

My warmest best wishes.

If you go to Italy, go to Subiaco. If you go to Subiaco, make enquiries about the pyramid I built on the large rock on the left bank

1 Berlioz composed the bulk of *Benvenuto Cellini* in 1836, although he had to break off repeatedly to assist with rehearsals of Louise Bertin's *Esmeralda* at the Opéra. This was a favour both to the Opéra management and to the composer's father, Armand Bertin, proprietor of the *Journal des débats*.
2 Berlioz's report on the Geneva Conservatoire appeared in the *Débats* on 26 August 1836, and an article on Liszt also appeared in the *Revue et gazette musicale* on 12 June.

of the Anio and pay it a visit for me. I'm told the shepherds haven't entirely demolished it.

H. Berlioz

103 *To Auguste Bottée de Toulmon*[1]   Montmartre, 11 November 1836

My dear Bottée,

I ask you, being as you are the pearl of musical booklovers, if you would help me out of an embarrassing situation. I trust in your erudition no less than in your kindness and come to ask assistance of them both. This is the position. I have been obliged to promise a newspaper some biographies of Italian composers and (with the exception of Marcello) I don't really know where to find notes for these macaronic illustrations. Give me a little help. Have you some information in Italian that I can translate? Is there anything in Choron? In Michaud's biography?[2] If you have discovered some indispensable book of this kind, send me word, I should be eternally grateful. I'm so crushed by work of every kind, with my articles, my endless rehearsals of *Notre-dame*[3] and the completion of my opera that I don't know how to find time to come and see you. I shall come even so, if you'd be kind enough to see me at the library or at your house, perhaps during the morning of one of my rehearsal days, Tuesdays, Thursdays, Saturdays and Sundays, whichever you like.[4]

Adieu, pardon this new obsession of mine!

Yours devotedly,

H. Berlioz

104 *To his sister Adèle Berlioz*   Paris, 22 December 1836

It's true, dear Adèle, our letters cross, but the worst thing is I can't make them cross more often. You have no idea of the slavery to which my thousand and one projects subject me. I won't go on about it, having told you this story often enough. So to answer your questions as directly as possible, I'll launch out on the facts straight away.

1 Librarian at the Paris Conservatoire.
2 Choron published a *Dictionnaire des musiciens* in 1810–11 and Michaud's *Biographie universelle* had been appearing in separate volumes since 1811.
3 Louise Bertin's *Esmeralda*.
4 Between April and August 1837 Berlioz published a number of articles on Italian composers such as Buononcini and Marcello.

I've just given two concerts;[1] in terms of artistic success I've never had anything like it, thanks to the vastly superior performance I obtained by conducting the orchestra myself. In terms of financial success, the cost of each of the two concerts was 1800 francs and the receipts from the second one were divided between Liszt and myself, so my share comes to 1600 francs net, plus 160 francs I'm owed for tickets distributed round Paris and 64 francs for the box from the Minister of the Interior who came to my first concert but who, I'm sure, will never pay. If we assume this to be more than likely, then in a fortnight I shall have earned 1700 francs, which I was desperately in need of to pay the man who supplies my furniture and various other debts which will be due shortly.

You can imagine I had a moment of complete panic when I began to think that I had nothing new to offer the public and that I might not cover the costs. Luckily Harriet was more confident than I was and urged me to persist. So I announced a programme of my two large symphonies,[2] which had never been given together in their entirety, and the crowds came. Unfortunately I was again, as always, assassinated by demands for tickets from the forty or fifty newspapers, large and small, which prattle away in Paris. To avoid the avalanche of insults for which these gentlemen can be relied upon when their requests are refused, I was obliged to give them everything they were asking for. Hence a considerable loss in receipts. I don't normally take much notice of these mean little acts of revenge, but the theatre directors are set trembling by the smallest word in print, and my position with Duponchel, who is not among the bravest in this respect, forced me to bow my head and pay the levy. The press treated me very well, it's a concert of praise in every key. Even *Le courrier*, the leader of the opposition against me, was very kind this year. I'm annoyed that you haven't seen either *Le journal du commerce*, or *Le monde*, or *La loi*, or *L'entracte*, or *Le contemporain*, or *La presse*, or *Le carrousel*. I didn't think to collect them and send them to you. I've even received some verses from an unknown poet who seems to have a very pronounced passion for my music. Enough on that subject.

Esmeralda, as you know, was buried under the weight of a systematic opposition in which politics played a large part.[3] At the last performance, which had to be abandoned before the end, the stalls

---

1 On 4 and 18 December 1836 in the Conservatoire, both conducted by Berlioz, the second shared with Liszt.
2 The *Symphonie fantastique* and *Harold en Italie*.
3 *Esmeralda* was performed at the Opéra on 14 November.

were shouting: 'Down with the Bertins! Down with the *Journal des débats*!' Only Quasimodo's 'bell' aria found any real favour with this hostile faction; they absolutely refuse, too, to let Mlle Bertin take the credit for it and insist, despite all my denials, in attributing it to me. This piece shows really a very remarkable musical invention; it won the favour of an encore at the first three performances, and at the première Alexandre Dumas, who is no lover of the Bertins, began to shout with the full force of his mulatto lungs: 'It's Berlioz! It's Berlioz!' So much for justice! If I did contribute to the effect this aria made, it's in a very small way. It really is by Mlle Bertin, but (between ourselves) it ended badly, that's to say it ended in such a way as to nullify the effect of the fine things there are in it. My collaboration was limited to suggesting to the composer a conclusion worthier of the opening; that's all and I've never admitted it to anybody.

As for *my* opera, the situation is that I've finished; I have only the scene of the dénouement left to write and the orchestration of a large part of the score. [. . .]

So much for *external affairs*. Let's turn to the *ministry of the interior*.

Harriet and I have been through an agonizing time because of Louis. A wretched servant took him to Paris without our permission and contrived to arrange a fearful accident. Going into a café (God knows why) she pinched his finger in the door. The poor boy had the nail torn off and the doctor had to tidy up the wound by cutting off the bit of flesh that was left. Luckily the bone wasn't damaged and the nail has already begun to grow back. But the pain he suffered! I thought his mother would go mad. Each change of the dressing was a new drama. Now at last all is well and the new servant we've entrusted ourselves to seems more reliable in every respect. His mother too has been in pain from a bruise on her left side, which she got from the corner of a piece of furniture. Louis has become as affectionate towards Harriet as he used to be towards me. An infernal creature we had as a servant in Montmartre taught the child to reject his mother and grumble at her every time he saw her. This miserable young woman loathed my wife because she was obliged to supervise her constantly and she thought up this horrible means of revenge. Since we got rid of her, Louis is showing his mother affection again. His feelings for me at the moment are more like passion than anything else. He calls out to me in his dreams, he refuses to eat or lie down when I'm out of the house, and when I come back he shouts with joy and jumps about endlessly. He kisses my hand most tenderly, and elegantly too. At dinner he has to be on my knee; he gives me everything he has, he comes into my study to collect me for meals, and in the evening he recounts, verbally and in very expressive pantomime, all the things he's seen in the street during the day (he never leaves the window panes). Yesterday it was a troupe of itinerant musicians; he imitated the clarinet for me, the side drum and the barrel-organ in the most original manner, singing and gesticulating till we nearly died of laughter. [. . .]

Your affectionate brother,

H. Berlioz

105 *To Robert Schumann*   Paris, 19 February 1837

I am, Monsieur, considerably in your debt for the interest you have been kind enough to show in some of my compositions.[1] I am told that, thanks to your efforts, the *Francs-juges* overture has recently been heard in Leipzig and that the generous acclaim it received from the public was in no small measure due to the superiority of the performance. Please will you pass on my gratitude to the gentlemen of the orchestra. I set all the more value on their patience in studying this difficult work since I have had no reason so far to congratulate myself on the same quality being shown by several music societies who have wanted to undertake the same enterprise. Apart from the societies in Douai and Dijon, the others have given up after a preliminary rehearsal, and after the work has been torn apart in a thousand different ways, it has had to return to the library shadows, as being worthy to figure at best in a collection of monstrosities. Apparently a test of this kind provided the London Philharmonic Society with considerable amusement; some Parisian players who knew the work perfectly, having played it in Paris, had been graciously allowed by the English virtuosos to join them on this occasion and they told me frankly that they had partaken of the British hilarity; only the subject was quite different. Imagine speeds twice too fast in the Adagio and twice too slow in the Allegro, producing that featureless *mezzo termine* which is intolerable to anyone who possesses the slightest musical feeling; imagine violins sight-reading passages which are still difficult despite the *tempo confortabile* at which the Allegro was taken, the trombones coming in ten or twelve bars early, the timpanist losing his head in the

1 In 1835 Schumann published a long analytical essay on the *Symphonie fantastique* in his own journal, the *Neue Zeitschrift für Musik*, on the basis of Liszt's piano transcription, and in 1836 he wrote favourably about the *Francs-juges* overture, which was performed in Leipzig later that year. Berlioz was wrong in thinking that Schumann was responsible for that performance.

triple-time passage, and you'll get some idea of the jolly rumpus that ensued. I am not denying the skill of the Philharmonic gentlemen of the Argyle Rooms, God forbid! I'm just drawing attention to the extra-ordinary system which obtains for conducting them at rehearsals. Certainly, we in Paris often produce dreadful music when we first try out a new piece; but as we do not believe anyone has innate know-ledge, not even English players, nor that there is any disgrace in applying one's attention and courage to the study of something one cannot understand straight away, we have been in the habit of going over it three, four, ten times if necessary, and several days in a row. As a result, we have achieved performances that were almost always correct and sometimes startling. No doubt this is what you did in Leipzig and, I repeat, in the absence of the composer who was thus unable to support his work, such perseverance both honours the per-formers and flatters the composer, who returns his profound gratitude. It is so rare, however, that I have repented a thousand times of having been crazy enough to allow the overture in question to be published. [...] One has to be a rare genius to create those things which both artists and public can respond to immediately and whose simplicity is in direct ratio to their mass, like the pyramids of Djizeh. Unfortunately, I am not one of those people; I need large resources to produce any effect, and I should be afraid of permanently forfeiting my friends in the world of music if I brought my symphonies out in print too soon and exposed them, too young as they are to travel without me, to still more cruel mutilations than the ones suffered by my ancient overture. And, except in two or three hospitable and cultured cities like your own, this without a doubt would be their fate in every case.

And then, I confess to you, I love these poor children of mine with a paternal love that has nothing Spartan about it, and I infinitely prefer seeing them obscure but intact rather than sending them far from home to find glory or fearful wounds and death.

I must admit, at the risk of seeming ridiculous, that I've never understood how rich painters could separate themselves without a rending of entrails from their finest pictures for a few pounds, and send them off to the four corners of the world, as happens every day. That has always seemed to me like the greed of the celebrated anatomist Ruysch[1] who, when his daughter died aged sixteen, found a way of using an ingenious process of injection which he had invented to give

---

1 The Dutch anatomist Frederick Ruysch (1638–1731), whose specimens were purchased by Peter the Great.

the beloved corpse the eternal appearance of life and health, but then could not resist the lure of a sovereign's gold and handed over the masterpiece of a new art, namely the body of his own daughter. [...]

I feel that to gain a following in Germany, that homeland of music, is the highest prize of all and, I'm afraid, too difficult to win (if ever I do) without looking forward to the moment when I shall be able to make my pilgrimage there and lay my modest offering at its feet. Then once more, to make sure it is accepted, I shall certainly need the support of your friendship and of your noble and elevated talents.

Until then, I venture to hope that my reserve will be seen as no more than a perfectly natural diffidence which has so far been fully justified by events. So, like a prudent navigator, I will content myself for the moment with tacking round our shores without risking shipwreck on a long voyage.

Those are my reasons which, I hope, you will appreciate.

I would not like to end my letter without telling you what delightful hours I have spent recently reading your wonderful piano pieces;[1] I find people were not exaggerating when they assured me that they were the logical continuation of the works of Weber, Beethoven and Schubert. This was Liszt's description of them and his incomparable playing will shortly be able to give me a more complete idea and a more intimate knowledge of them. He intends to play your sonata called *Clara*[2] at one of the magnificent soirées where he surrounds himself with the élite of our musical public. After that I shall be able to speak to you with more assurance about the overall form and the details of these essentially new and progressive compositions.

Your devoted
H. Berlioz

106 *To Auguste Barbier*[3]   Paris, 24 February 1837

My dear Barbier,

I'm having to write to you as I'm unable to come and see you. Your new poem is superb and in every respect worthy of its predecessors. I'm particularly enthusiastic about the ode to Shakespeare and about

1 The works which Liszt may have played for Berlioz were the *Paganini Studies* op. 3, the *Impromptus* op. 5, the Sonata in F sharp minor op. 11, and the *Concert sans orchestre* op. 14.
2 The Sonata op. 11 was dedicated to Clara Wieck, later Schumann's wife.
3 One of the librettists of *Benvenuto Cellini*.

'Les défricheurs'.[1] You are a great poet. It'll make me swell with pride to have you as a collaborator.*

Adieu.

Yours ever,

H. Berlioz

* and as a friend!!

107 *To his father Dr Louis Berlioz*   Paris, 8 March 1837

Dear papa,

[...] I'm still working hard on several fronts; my position on the *Journal des débats* is becoming more important and secure; I'm besieged by a host of other newspapers wanting me to write for them. I think I'll accept the offers of the *Chronique de Paris* and *L'encyclopédie du xixe siècle*, because of the support these papers can give to the powerful influence of the *Débats*. But all that takes an enormous amount of time and if I wrote a decent symphony it would bring in, to be realistic, ten times more than all my articles earn in a year. But one has to make one's name at the Opéra, and writing articles is my engine of war for battering down the door of this immense theatre. *Stradella*[2] is irredeemably dead; it's the last word in mediocrity, or rather it's execrably dull, whatever I may have said in my articles in the *Débats* and the *Gazette musicale* last Sunday. At the moment there are only two works to be produced ahead of mine. Halévy and Auber are not halfway through finishing their scores[3] but they are refusing to yield their rightful position and make way for mine, which is finished. So be it. Meanwhile, I've been to see the Minister of the Interior who wants to commission a large work from me for the anniversary of the death of Maréchal Mortier, etc, at the Invalides.[4] I went to see him about something else; he came out with this news unexpectedly. I asked for a certain freedom over the forces to be employed and he seems willing to oblige. In any case, the affair will soon be settled, as it must be if I'm to have time to write the work between now and 28 July. Only I'm afraid of the fever this project is going to put me in, with the five or six

1 In April 1837 Barbier published *Lazare*, a new collection of poems, some of which appeared in advance in journals.
2 By Niedermeyer, first performed at the Opéra on 3 March 1837.
3 Halévy's *Guido et Ginevra*, first performed on 5 March 1838, and Auber's *Le lac des fées*, first performed on 1 April 1839 (after *Benvenuto Cellini*).
4 Maréchal Mortier was killed in Fieschi's attempt on the life of the King in July 1835. For this commission Berlioz composed the *Grande messe des morts* (the *Requiem*).

hundred performers I shall have at my disposal. What a *Dies irae*!!! [. . .]

Harriet and Louis are well, my uncle comes to see us from time to time; I give him tickets for the Opéra whenever I can, that's a regular thing; otherwise, I haven't any news of him.

Adieu, dear papa, write to me when you can, and at slightly greater length, it's a long time since we had a real talk together.

Your affectionate son,

H. B.

108 *To his sister Adèle Berlioz*   Paris, 17 April 1837

[. . .] The Minister asked me if I was willing to accept 4000 francs;[1] I didn't think this was an occasion for haggling, even though the payment is fairly niggardly, because the performing costs will be enormous; I asked for 500 performers and I'll have 430.

The ministerial decree was finally signed three weeks ago and I have it on my desk; there are no problems from that quarter. I'll have finished it in two months, I hope. I found it hard to get on top of my subject; to begin with, I was so wildly intoxicated by the poetry of the *Prose des morts* that my brain could form no clear ideas, my head was boiling and I was giddy. Today the eruption is under control, the lava has formed its bed and, with God's help, all will be well. It's a grand affair. No doubt I shall once more bring upon myself the reproach of *innovation*, because it has been my wish to recall this area of the art to a *truth* from which Mozart and Cherubini seem to me too often to have strayed. Then there are some startling combinations which, I'm glad to say, have never been tried before and which, I think, I'm the first to consider.

Adieu, adieu.

Your affectionate brother,

H. Berlioz

109 *To Marie d'Agoult*   Paris, 15 June 1837

Madame,

My wife and I are most grateful for your kind interest in the project which we have in hand;[2] not that we lack confidence in Mme Sand's kindness and artistic sympathy, but the support of an intermediary such

---

1 The commission for the *Requiem* was signed by M. de Gasparin on 22 March.
2 Harriet had recently had some success at a private performance of part of *Jane Shore*, which encouraged Berlioz to approach George Sand to write a play with a role for Harriet. Liszt and Marie d'Agoult, then guests of George Sand at Nohant, acted as intermediaries.

as yourself was exactly what was required, I admit, to persuade me to make such a request of her. Since she does not regard our idea as inadmissible and since even in the midst of her labours she has already found a few moments in which to think about it, I intend to thank her and discuss the matter with her directly.

The journey to Italy greatly appeals to you, Madame, and yet it will, I believe, be your first visit to that beautiful country.[1] If this were to be your second, your joy at returning would far exceed the enthusiasm you show for getting to know it. Only may God protect you from *ciceroni*, customs officers, Austrians, English tourists, Roman conversations, translations of Scribe and operas by Vaccai.

I cannot hold it against Liszt that he will not be coming to Paris in July, as he led me to hope; the attractions which draw him to the other side of the Alps are too strong and I rejoice in his good fortune. When you are in Naples, and when Liszt feels the need for one of those grand emotions which both of us have exhausted ourselves pursuing and which Italian art can never provide, let him climb Posilippo one evening and from the summit of that hill which Virgil loved let him listen to the infinite arpeggios of the sea while the sun, that resplendent sun so different from our own, descends slowly behind Cape Misenum, its last rays gilding the pale olive-trees of Nisita ... that is a concert worthy of you and him, and the only one I recommend to you.

You are right, Madame, to regard life in Paris as a desperate struggle, but a few peaceful hours spent in Capri or Amalfi will soon make you forget both the Great City and the poor galley-slaves you have left behind there.

Their wishes for your journey are nonetheless sincere.

I have the honour to be, Madame,

your humble servant,

H. Berlioz

P.S. I would ask Liszt not to forget my manuscript of *Roi Lear* when he sends me his.[2] I look forward impatiently to his article on Schumann.

110 *To George Sand*   Paris, 20 June 1837

I cannot thank you enough, Madame, for the kindly response you have made to an idea in which I take a lively interest. Harriet asks me to tell you that, in writing for her, you allow her to breathe and live once

1 She and Liszt were about to set off for Italy for a stay of over two years.
2 Liszt was arranging *Le roi Lear* overture for solo piano.

more. In actuality her position is extremely distressing.

She is prevented from working because of the impossibility of finding an English theatre that is concerned with *literature*, either in Paris or in London, where the art of drama has been obliterated for good. This enforced inaction is all the more painful for her because, modesty aside, she feels that she has an exceptionally powerful talent and because, by an ironic quirk of fate, she sees her own original ideas now being used to make the fortunes of a crowd of actors and actresses of the second rank.

I do not believe, Madame, that you ever saw her in her heyday, or that you know her Juliet or her Ophelia or her Jane Shore; but I am sure you must have guessed at all that is new and poetical in her artistic feeling, in which a modern truthfulness and passion are always combined with an antique beauty. A play of yours, performed by her, would certainly be something most remarkable and of irresistible interest. Mme d'Agoult gives me hope that you may be thinking of it for this winter.

The outline is a new one: to find room in a French play for an Englishwoman who speaks French with difficulty and with an accent for which justification must be found, or who does not know enough French to express certain ideas and so speaks in her native language, even resorting occasionally to gestures. There must surely be a plot to be discovered which hangs on a lack of understanding or on the false interpretation of language or of a single word; you will find it, I am sure, and the result will be a fine and beautiful work for which all lovers of the theatre will be eternally grateful to you. You will, what is more, be offering a helping hand to a great artist who has all too many reasons for despair and whose suffering is profoundly worthy of your sympathy.

As for finding a theatre that will produce the play, I fancy there will be an embarrassment of riches to choose from.

Please accept once again, Madame, my wife's warmest gratitude, as well as that of

your humble servant,
Hect. Berlioz

George Sand never did write a play with a role for Harriet, who was destined never to appear again on the stage. Berlioz meanwhile completed the Grande messe des morts *on 29 June 1837.*

My dear friend,

I delivered your message to M. Bertin. Armand will see that your mother has the 500 francs.

Give Mme Sand very many thanks from Harriet and myself for her kind promise, until the time when we can speak to her face to face. Will she be coming to Paris soon?

I dare say you already know about the hammer blow I've just received! Luckily I have a strong skull and it'd need a really sharp tomahawk to split it. The Council of Ministers has decided, after three days of indecision, to cancel the funeral ceremony at the Invalides. Let's have no more talk about the heroes of July! Woe betide the conquered! And woe betide the conquerors! As a result, I'd already taken three sectional rehearsals for the singers when I found out *by accident* (nobody actually told me) that the ceremony was not going to take place and that consequently my *Requiem* would not be performed. Tell me if that's not enough to make one spout like a whale! Everything was going as planned, I had it all under control, the 420 performers were organized and tuned like one of your excellent Erard pianos, nothing was missing, and I think there were things that were going to be heard *for the first time*.

Politics has intervened to set all that straight. It's left me still feeling rather ill. That's the sort of thing art is exposed to when one accepts the help of a government as unstable as ours. But, capricious as this support may be, one has to accept it for want of any other. So much for elected governments; they're cheap to come by, but what a stupid nonsense.

I say no more on the subject, as I don't imagine we're in agreement. Happily we see eye to eye on all other matters.

Adieu! adieu! All my best wishes and my respects to the ladies.

H. Berlioz

I look forward to the music and your article on Schumann.[1]

112 *To his mother Madame Berlioz*   Paris, 12 October 1837

Don't be angry, dear mama, that it's been so long since I wrote to you; being as far away as you are, you can have no real idea of what my life

---

1 The music was *Le roi Lear* arranged for piano and the article on Schumann appeared in the *Revue et gazette musicale* on 12 November 1837.

is like since that *gentleman* de Montalivet[1] has been keeping me waiting for my 4000 francs. So far I haven't succeeded in getting either what's owing to me or what's owing to the copyist and to the singers in the chorus who had started rehearsing. It's true that the same goes for the other expenses incurred last July; no payment has so far been made to the architects or the masons or the construction engineers, etc, but it's still shocking behaviour nonetheless and the 4000 francs are leaving a very unpleasant hole in my finances. So I've had to work to make up as far as possible for lost time over the four months I spent composing the *Requiem*. Apart from that, the director of the *Gazette musicale* has been away in Prussia for seven weeks and, as usually happens on such occasions, I've been acting as director and editor-in-chief during his absence. Then there are the endless visits to the Minister's secretaries and friends, my work for the *Journal des débats* and the *Chronique de Paris*, performances that I have to attend, the final scenes of my opera to orchestrate, moving house, Louis being slightly ill (he's quite better now), so you can understand how little free time I have.

But I must thank you for the most recent fruits of your affection. M. Joseph Rocher came yesterday bringing the preserves you so kindly sent for Louis. They're really splendid, the sort one never sees any more. Adèle will forgive me if I don't reply this time to her charming letter, which I enjoyed very much; I hope to do so soon. I hear good news of all of you; it seems that even my father is feeling better than ever. I can understand, dear mama, how lonely you must be during his long absences. Harriet too complains about mine, because whether I'm out or in my study, she's still on her own for a large part of the day. Louis serves as some sort of distraction; he's so kind and intelligent. But his almost exclusive predilection for me often reduces his mother to tears. He's beginning now to show a more equal affection for each of us.

You saw in the papers that my poor teacher Le Sueur had died. We buried him yesterday with full honours. It was a very sad ceremony for those of us who were his pupils and who were there in large numbers. Most of the members of the Institut and artists of all kinds went with him to the cemetery. I was asked to hold a corner of the pall with Halévy and two other members of the Institut. I've already been to several occasions of this kind, but the poor man had been so unfailingly

---

1 The Minister of the Interior.

kind to me, it was hard this time to retain my bearing and my sang-froid.

My uncle will be leaving us in a few days. He intends to come and see you as his regiment leaves and will give you my news at greater length.

Adieu, dear mama.[1]

I embrace you tenderly, and papa too; all best wishes to Prosper and Nanci; as for Adèle, let her wait for my next letter.

Your affectionate son,

H. B.

On 17 October 1837 General Damrémont was killed at the siege of Constantine in North Africa. Berlioz proposed to the Minister of War that his Requiem, *ordered by the government and then countermanded, should be performed at the ceremony in General Damrémont's memory. The first performance of the* Requiem *thus took place at the Invalides on 5 December 1837, conducted by Habeneck and with Duprez singing the tenor solo.*

113 *To his father Dr Louis Berlioz*   Paris, 7 December 1837

Dear father,

We too captured Constantine the day before yesterday, the Constantine of music! I couldn't find a minute yesterday to write to you. I'd been very worried about the performance two days before the ceremony, but in fact it was perfect. I can assure you without self-deception that it was an immense and widespread success with the artists as well as with the public. The Duc d'Orléans sent word to me that he had found my work extremely beautiful and that he's never been so moved by music. The most vicious elements of the opposition are silent, while those that were less so have been annihilated and are joining the ranks of my supporters. Out of all the papers I read yesterday there are thirteen for and two against (*Le corsaire* and *Le constitutionnel*), but *Le corsaire* wasn't at the ceremony, as is proved by a number of errors it makes, and *Le constitutionnel* wanted to exact revenge for an article I wrote two years ago on Hérold. Those are the inevitable rewards one reaps for being a critic. Since yesterday I've received I don't know how many letters of congratulation; I can't possibly describe to you how excited all my friends are. There's no question but that it made an

1 This is one of Berlioz's last letters to his mother; she died four months later.

extraordinary impact. In the movement describing the Last Judgment, one of the chorus had a nervous seizure and the curé burst into tears at the altar. The good fellow was still crying in the sacristy a quarter of an hour after the performance. The current topic of conversation in all the places where music is discussed is whether my *Requiem* is or is not superior to all those that are generally known; it seems that out of every hundred artists there are nearly ninety who come down on the side of the affirmative.

As for comparing the effect produced the day before yesterday with that of any similar occasion in the past, it's really not possible. I feel sad that neither you nor any of the family could be in Paris. I'm not looking forward to an article in *Le national* by that boor Mainzer, because I didn't use his workers' chorus; he was very annoyed and won't miss the chance to get his own back, as he did on Duprez, writing an unflattering article on him *without having heard him* because he hadn't been given tickets for his first performance. That's how the business of criticism is carried on!!!

Le corsaire mentions Mlle Falcon's solo in my Mass and *there is no female solo*, and Mlle Falcon *wasn't even there*; *Le constitutionnel*, or *Le journal de Paris*, mentions one for Lablache; Lablache wasn't there either and there was no bass solo.

Never mind, these are the inevitable problems one comes across when one is much in the public eye and when furthermore one has the bad, or good, fortune to write for the *Journal des débats*. You can be happy, papa, and mama and my sisters too, because it's the greatest and most hard-won success I've ever had. I'll send you all the newspapers tomorrow. I'm sorry I can't send you the letters as well; I've just had a charming one from Rubini, and another from the Marquis de Custine and one from Legouvé. Adieu, dear papa, everything is going well in every way. Harriet wept a lot yesterday, but tears of joy don't do much harm. Louis is enthusiastic about *his father's big trumpets* . . .

I reopen this letter to tell you that the Minister of War has just written me a congratulatory letter containing some most warmly expressed compliments.

[unsigned]

114 *To Maurice Schlesinger*[1]   Paris, 7 January 1838

My dear Maurice,

I absolutely *must* be protected and sheltered from albums. I've been trying in vain for a fortnight now to find three hours in which to think in peace about the overture for my opera; not to be able to find them is a torture beyond your imagination and one that is absolutely *unbearable* for me. So I give you notice that even if I have to live on bread and water until my score is finished, I don't want to know about critical activity of any kind. Meyerbeer, Liszt, Chopin and Kalkbrenner don't need any praises from me. Your albums, I know, also contain several charming pieces which you don't refer to and whose composers you don't even mention. But I'm at the end of my tether, I want some time to myself to finish my opera; in short I want to be an artist. I'll return to being a galley-slave afterwards. Until that time, let no one talk to me of any kind of critical enterprise; I am beset, engulfed, exterminated. So be careful about driving me back into my lair, it'd be an act of foul inhumanity. I've never been a supporter of suicide, but I do have a pair of loaded pistols and if you go too far in exasperating me I could well blow your head off.

Your devoted friend,
Hector Berlioz

115 *To Franz Liszt*   Paris, 8 February 1838

I was really delighted, dear friend, to have your letter; all the more so because I was hardly expecting it. The inhabitants of Paris are accused of forgetting the rest of the world, but I think the rest of the world has a slight tendency to attribute to Paris its own indifference and forgetfulness. I remember the time when I, like you, was travelling through Italy; nothing then seemed more exhausting than to have to pick up my pen and direct my thoughts towards this large, muddy, disdainful city, so different from the peaceful capital of the Roman states where my favourite occupation was sleeping, and from my beloved villages among the Abruzzi and in Sabinum where I spent so much time hunting, fishing, dancing, singing and playing the guitar. So I understand perfectly why you have been out of touch for so long, and why it needed the sound of gunfire from the Invalides to remind you of me. I've never seen Como or its lakes, but I imagine they must be ravishing

1 Music publisher and proprietor of the *Revue et gazette musicale*.

and you must be happy there. Other people have told me of the sensation you produced in Milan; I said a few words about it in the *Débats* and elsewhere; I'd have liked to have some details, without which I didn't dare spread myself. Our friend Heine recently mentioned us both in the *Gazette musicale*, showing both wit and irreverence, but not a hint of unkindness; on the other hand, he's woven a splendid garland for Chopin, who has deserved it, as we know, for a long time.

It would have made me very happy, I promise you, to have you there for the performance of the *Requiem*. I think you would have felt that the mighty musical machine ran quite well; there was real weeping and gnashing of teeth; the weeping was *for* the work, the gnashing was against. [. . .]

Yours ever,

H. Berlioz

116 *To Queen Victoria*
Her Majesty the Queen of England   Paris, 17 March 1838

Madam,

I intend to publish next May the full score of the *Requiem* which was performed at the Hôtel Royal des Invalides for the funeral service of General Damrémont, and of which I am the composer. The noble protection which the Queen of England affords to the fine arts and to music in particular emboldens me to beg Your Majesty to be kind enough to honour me with her subscription.

I am, Madam, with the profoundest respect,

Your Majesty's most humble and obedient servant,

Hector Berlioz

117 *To Ludwig Rellstab*[1]   Paris, 31 March 1838

I am, Monsieur, most grateful for the kind intentions which have led you to write to me. I enclose with my letter an extract from a book on music (by M. d'Ortigue) in which you will find some *accurate* details about my life.[2] (Please take whatever you wish from it. The biography

---

1 German poet and music critic, the Berlin correspondent of the *Revue et gazette musicale*. His poems were set to music by Schubert and Liszt, among others.
2 The book was d'Ortigue's *Le balcon de l'opéra* (Paris, 1833).

by M. Fétis[1] was in fact written out of open hostility, and many of the facts it contains are *absolutely wrong*.

Here are one or two notes to add to M. d'Ortigue's contribution:

I compose without an instrument, as I don't play the piano at all.

My opinions on harmony, melody, rhythm and orchestration are, I think, the same as everyone else's, prejudices aside. These prejudices are so ingrained here in France, and in our Paris Conservatoire especially, that a man who refuses to share them passes for an extravagant innovator. My most active sympathies are engaged by Gluck and Beethoven first of all, and after that by Weber. I am a profound admirer of Mozart, but he *moves* me less than the three composers I have just mentioned, except for *Die Zauberflöte*, which I regard as his masterpiece.

I hate the modern Italian school, from Rossini on, except in comic opera; as for their attempts at what is called *opera seria*, if one passes over some more or less brilliant effects in the realm of real music, I can find nothing in it but an insolent parody of dramatic convention and of the art's expressive and poetic capabilities. I believe there is still much to be done in the fields of rhythm and orchestration; I am not imbued, as rumour in Paris has it, with exaggerated ideas as to the expressive power of instrumental music; I merely believe that it is capable of rendering certain *feelings* and certain *poetical ideas*. Nowhere in the world has anyone ever wanted to deprive the musical domain of these, but they have often been the pretext for works that were ridiculously ambitious.

The overture *Rob Roy*, mentioned by M. d'Ortigue, is no longer extant, I burnt it after hearing it at the Conservatoire.[2] Several years ago I wrote a *Messe solennelle* which merited and underwent the same fate. Here is the list of the works I have composed since M. d'Ortigue's biography was published:

1   *Harold*, symphony with a solo viola.

2   *Le cinq mai, ou la mort de Napoléon*, cantata to words by Béranger, for solo bass, chorus and orchestra.

3   *Sara la baigneuse*, to one of Victor Hugo's *Orientales*, for four male soloists, chorus and orchestra.

4   A *Requiem Mass*, for a very large body of voices and instruments; it was performed recently at the funeral of General Damrémont

---

1 In Fétis's *Biographie universelle des musiciens*, whose second volume, containing the article on Berlioz, appeared in 1837.
2 In 1833.

after the capture of Constantine. It will be published by subscription, in full score, next May.

5   And finally a large *opera semi-seria* in two acts, currently in rehearsal at the Opéra.[1]

My unfortunate position as a music critic not only makes me a host of enemies here, because of the praise I do not dispense (even though I'm wildly prodigal with it), but also means that because of the praise I do dispense people in Germany attribute to me opinions about music which are not mine at all. There are very few living composers about whom I can express my views more or less frankly; this is accepted, and the result is that when I do happen to say what I really think, many people then believe I am not being sincere.

I should like to thank you, sir, for your friendly offer to perform my instrumental music in Berlin; the only work I have allowed to be engraved is the overture to the *Francs-juges* (composed fifteen years ago),[2] in the hope of escaping public exhibitions in those *unsavoury haunts* to which certain speculators drag composers in spite of themselves when their works become public property. This overture has already been performed in Weimar, in Leipzig, in Aix-la-Chapelle and in Vienna, and I should be very flattered if it were to be given in Berlin. It is extremely difficult, but Prussian orchestras are so capable that, with your hand to guide them, I am sure it would receive a good performance. I am, Monsieur, delighted that this affair has secured me the advantage of your acquaintance, which, if you so desire, may in time become yet closer, an outcome which, I assure you, would be for me both flattering and agreeable.

I have, Monsieur, the honour to be
your devoted servant,
Hector Berlioz

118 *To Ernest Legouvé*[3]   [Paris,] 3 July 1838

My dear Legouvé,

At the end of this month I shall be in a terribly awkward situation; tell me *frankly* whether you can help me escape from it. Nearly a year ago I borrowed a thousand francs; it's due to be repaid on 1 August

---

1 Rehearsals for *Benvenuto Cellini* began in March in the expectation of an opening night in June.
2 Twelve, in fact.
3 See p. 101.

and I cannot possibly do so. My opera is going to be staged around 12 or 15 August; a month after the first performance, then, at the latest, I could repay you both the thousand francs I already owe you and whatever you are kind enough to lend me in addition to get me out of this difficulty.

Despite all the ways in which you have shown yourself to be my friend, it has been painful for me to make this confession to you, but you'll admit you would not have found it less difficult yourself if the roles had been reversed.

Adieu, write to me briefly in any case; I have only the rest of this month in which to straighten myself out. I'm fatally depressed and I have two rehearsals a day. Musically speaking, all is going well, both at the Opéra and elsewhere.

Have you heard about my success at the Festival in Lille?...[1]

H. Berlioz

119 *To his sister Adèle Berlioz*   Paris, 12 July 1838

Dear Adèle,

I'm only writing to say I've had your letter and the note that was in it. I'm spending my life at the Opéra. At the moment we're having two rehearsals a day; I'm off there straight away. In several days' time the orchestral rehearsals begin; the dénouement approaches. But one of the actors is ill, which I find very worrying. Otherwise, everything is going splendidly. Duprez-Cellini[2] is superb, the energy and beauty of his singing are incredible. The censors have deprived us of the Pope, we've had to replace him with a Cardinal-cum-minister. It would have been intriguing, though, to see Clement VII coming to grips with that bandit-genius of a Cellini. The other actors are putting a lot of effort into doing their jobs, with one or two exceptions. The choruses are going wonderfully!

You know (because I've told you) about my success at the Festival in Lille. My music was performed by *six hundred* musicians in front of an audience of *five thousand*. You've read the northern newspapers, the Paris ones copied them. I've seen a lot of people who were at this musical event; during the coda to my *Lacrymosa* there were tears and even, according to several letters, two or three real faintings! I am of

1 On 25 June 1838 the *Lacrymosa* from the *Requiem* was performed in Lille with Habeneck conducting. Legouvé responded generously to this letter and made Berlioz a further loan. The overture to *Benvenuto Cellini* was dedicated to Legouvé in thanks.
2 Gilbert Duprez, singing the title role.

course most grateful to these ladies for so kindly being taken ill in my honour.

Habeneck, the conductor of the Opéra, was in Lille and conducted it all; he's told me details which made me sorry not to have been there. He wrote to me after the first concert (my piece was requested again for the second one) and on his return to Paris Cherubini, who had had a *Credo* of his performed, had some sharp words to say to him about the letter I had from him.

We've still got one bridge to cross before *Cellini* is performed, namely the orchestral rehearsals, after which comes the fusillade from the newspapers and from the well-known enemies hidden in the corners of the stalls. But I'm armed against them from head to toe.

Adieu, dear sister.

We're all well.

Embrace Nanci and Mathilde[1] for me.

Please God, my father is well? . . .

Say to Camille that he's an excellent brother-in-law and that I love him sincerely.

H. B.

Benvenuto Cellini was performed at the Opéra on 10 September 1838 after several postponements. It was not well received and two further performances, on 12 and 14 September, were poorly attended. Duprez then withdrew from the role of Cellini, and since no singer was covering the part a long wait intervened before a further performance could be given.

120 *To his father Dr Louis Berlioz*   Paris, 20 September 1838

Dear father,

I ought to have written to you ten days ago; it's a question of finding the time amid the sort of storm I've just been through. You've seen the newspapers, at least the bad ones, because those are always the ones you come across in situations like this. The good ones are *La quotidienne, Le messager, Le journal de Paris, La France musicale, La gazette musicale, L'artiste, La presse.* The truth is that the second and third performances went wonderfully thanks to the suppression of the

---

1 Mathilde Pal, his sister Nanci's daughter. Adèle was staying with her sister's family in Grenoble.

scenes which had upset the public most. If I run into any obstacles this week, it'll be Duprez's giant *amour-propre* which is the reason. Success did not centre on him; on the contrary the two female singers took the honours of the singing and the acting. As a result he has refused to sing this role again and A. Dupont is going to replace him. But as he wasn't expecting this any more than I was, he has to learn all this music, and we have to bide our time until he knows it. This will mean a break of eight or ten days. After that, because of the way the repertory is organized, I'll have *more* performances than I would have done if Duprez had kept on with his role.

It's impossible to describe all the underhand manoeuvres, intrigues, conspiracies, disputes, battles and insults my work has given rise to. It's a miracle I've managed to stay on top of it all; the fury of certain newspapers against what they call my *system* can give you only a very feeble idea of the bitterness of the struggle. It's even got to the point of pamphlets being written for and against. In the uproar my defenders talk almost as much nonsense as my detractors. One must simply let things take their course; all this disturbance will pass in time. The French have a mania for arguing about music without having the first idea about it, or any feeling for it. It was like this in the last century, is so now and will be again. The important thing is for my music to be heard often, *very* often. I rely on my score to pull me through more than on all the things that might be said in its favour. The two performances that followed the première show me that this is a reasonable expectation.

The changes made to the opera meant so much reworking that I'm completely exhausted. But the worst is over. I hope that neither you nor my sisters will be unnecessarily worried by this storm. You must have seen it coming as I did. It was inevitable. We just had to remain masters of the field, and we did so more easily than I expected with respect to the furious enemies I've made over many years because of my pamphlets, the protection afforded me by the *Débats*, the sort of music I write and the jealousies of the critical profession. And they were all there at the Opéra that day.

Adieu, dear father, I embrace you tenderly; I look forward to your news.

H. Berlioz

Dear Adèle,

Just a couple of words so that you're not worried by the mention of my illness in Janin's article.[1] I'm much better, I hope to be out of the house the day after tomorrow and to be conducting the rehearsals for my second concert next week. The first one was a huge success, you may have seen the letter from a German in the *Gazette musicale*, in which he expresses his astonishment and the strong emotions it aroused in him.[2] Yesterday Lord Burgersh, the president of the London Philharmonic Society, who was at the first concert, sent word asking if I would spend two months in London to conduct my symphonies and what my terms would be ... it may come off; I'm confident about the money, but I have my fears about the performers, because the English are execrable musicians who refuse to rehearse and, like the Italians, think they're the world's greatest virtuosos.

Harriet has been ill with a cold like mine, Louis too. But we're all improving.

There have been no more performances of *Benvenuto* so far, but they say it will return on Monday, this new delay being due to De Candia's[3] first appearances at the Opéra. One must just be patient.

I repeat, Prosper needs blankets;[4] of course, the directors of the boarding school do their duty, but this does not stop these poor children arguing every evening over whose turn it is to have the mattress to cover himself with.

Adieu, adieu.

H. Berlioz

Dear sister,

I've received your letter and its enclosures.

Shakespeare says that troubles always come in pairs, it's the same with pieces of good fortune. After my letter to my father, you must

---

1 Falling ill in November, Berlioz was unable to conduct the concert which he gave on the 25th. Habeneck stood in for him.
2 The author was Stephen Heller, actually of Hungarian origin, who was later to become one of Berlioz's close friends.
3 Mario de Candia, an Italian tenor.
4 Berlioz's younger brother Prosper, aged eighteen, had recently arrived in Paris to attend a preparatory school.

have seen dozens of newspapers talking about Paganini's noble action.[1] Now I've been told that I've been appointed sub-librarian at the Conservatoire. The librarian, one of my best friends,[2] doesn't draw a salary, whereas I on the other hand will have 2000 francs a year, without having any duties or work to do. It's a sinecure I've been given and the salary could rise to 3000 francs next year. I haven't yet received my official nomination, but I'm assured that it's settled. [...]

Adieu, dear Adèle, I hope that keeps you happy for several days!

H. Berlioz

123 To Humbert Ferrand   Paris, 2 January 1839

Dear friend,

I've been waiting for days for this letter of yours, but I thought you were in France.[3] Yes, it's all true, the exact truth; you say you've seen Janin's pamphlet, and several others no doubt.

Paganini declared himself a long time ago as one of my most ardent supporters; he made his enthusiasm public again at the first performance of *Benvenuto*. Finally after my second concert, which I conducted, he came up to me, took me by the arm, led me on to the stage of the Conservatoire just as the players were leaving, and there *went down on his knees in front of me*; I thought I was dreaming . . . As you know, the poor man has completely lost his voice, so it was his charming little boy (who understands him better than anybody) who told me what he wanted to say. It was the first time Paganini had heard my symphony *Harold*, which is dedicated to you. That's what provoked this explosion of feeling. Two days later, on Tuesday morning, I had to go back to bed because of my bronchitis; young Achille came into my bedroom and gave me a letter from his father which 'did not call for a reply', he said, and then ran off. Thinking this was a letter of congratulation, I opened it. Imagine what I felt when I read this first sentence: '*Beethoven spento non c'era che Berlioz che potesse farlo rivivere*' ('With Beethoven dead, it was only Berlioz who could bring him back to life') – and with it the note for twenty thousand francs offered in such a way . . . Harriet comes in at this moment and seeing me in tears thinks it's some bad news: 'What is it? What's happened? . . . Be brave.'

---

1 After Berlioz's concert on 16 December 1838, at which *Harold en Italie* was played, Paganini sent Berlioz a gift of 20,000 francs.
2 Bottée de Toulmon.
3 Ferrand was in Turin.

'No, nothing of the sort, it's a letter from Paganini, and do you know what he's sent me? Twenty thousand francs . . .'

'Good God! Is it possible?'

And she translates the letter to herself; then running to my little boy she cries, 'Louis, come here, come and thank the good Lord with me for what he has done for your father', and mother and child both knelt down by my bed.

You can appreciate the scene . . .

Four days later, when I was able to leave the house, another scene of the same kind was waiting for me at Paganini's. I rushed over to Néothermes where he was living and I found him alone, walking round the billiard room. As the room is remote and peaceful, I could actually hear his voice. First of all there was silence for about five minutes during which we both embraced each other and wept hot tears. Then, as I tried to speak, Paganini stopped me: 'Not a word. I'm too happy, it's the most satisfying occasion of my life. You have introduced me to new sensations and I could do no less for a man such as you.' Then wiping his eyes and laughingly giving the billiard table a blow with his fist, he said, 'Ah! I am so, so happy to think that those wretches who have been writing and speaking against you won't be so brazen from now on. Because I have a reputation for knowing what I'm about and for not being easily won over.'

Paganini left last week for Marseille and his last words to me were 'Adieu . . . love me!' I shall write to him shortly, I'm composing a new symphony for him.[1]

I can't describe the impact made by this astonishing demonstration of approval. My friends are triumphant, the uncommitted are coming over to my side and my enemies are furious and are trying, in vain, to devalue the fine action of a great artist whom they will not or cannot understand. The English newspapers are excellent, London is in a hellish uproar.

As for my opera, it was billed twice while I was ill and twice, because two of the actors really were indisposed, they had to change the programme. It's been announced for next Monday, we had a rehearsal the day before yesterday.[2] [. . .]

H. Berlioz

1 Paganini's gift enabled Berlioz to compose his symphony *Roméo et Juliette*, later dedicated to Paganini.
2 The fourth and last complete performance of *Benvenuto Cellini* was given on 11 January 1839.

My dear Edouard,

As we agreed, I've handed over the amount I owed you to M. Bourget; you will therefore find the receipt in with this letter. It remains for me to thank you for having waited so long for this repayment. I would have written to you yesterday, if I'd not been kept at the Opéra all day. There were two rehearsals of *Benvenuto* (morning and evening) and it should be given again on Friday, if there are no more accidents. I suppose this revival will be the signal for further pandemonium. If it were not forbidden to bring canes into the stalls, there'd be some heads broken perhaps. The Paganini affair and the startling success of my last concert have delighted my supporters and friends, but have exasperated my enemies still further. People write me anonymous letters full of insults; I've been particularly amused by one lately which invited me to blow my brains out. I'm sure if I lived in Spain or Italy I'd already have been assassinated twenty times over.

All that's of no importance. This life of violent vicissitudes suits me so well, I couldn't stand any other. My only requirements are time and good health; as for patience, that I have, to rival the drip of water that hollows out rocks or builds stalactites.

Since Duprez has left the cast, all my actors and particularly my two actresses[1] are working for my opera as energetically as they know how. I'm worried for Alexis Dupont;[2] in the powerful scenes the part overwhelms him, although he's full of charm in the slow, quiet passages. As for the chorus, their sloppiness and apathy would drive a saint to despair. I've given up trying to breathe life into this troupe of corpses. The orchestra's not bad. The only problem will be the lack of several key players who are ill. In short, poor *Benvenuto* has had an unlucky time, it is indeed *malvenuto*, as the *Charivari* says. Adieu, I must leave you to go and see my brother who is still ill.[3] All best wishes to Charles Bert and all my friends.

H. Berlioz

---

1 Mme Dorus-Gras, singing Teresa, and Mme Rosina Stoltz, singing Ascanio.
2 Dupont replaced Duprez as Cellini in the fourth performance.
3 Prosper Berlioz in fact died a few days later, aged eighteen.

Dear friend,

[...] At the moment I'm pondering a new symphony.[1] I should dearly like to come and finish it beside you, in Sorrento or Amalfi (go to Amalfi!), but impossible, I'm in the breach and must stay there.[2] I've never led such a hectic life; the musical battle which I've just provoked has been an unusually lively and violent one. I've received numbers of letters in prose and verse from my supporters, but also *anonymous* invective from my opponents; one of them was even stupid enough to invite me to blow my brains out ... Charming, don't you think? When Paganini wrote me his famous letter and when people saw his excitement after hearing *Harold* for the first time at the Conservatoire, there was grinding of teeth on one side and furious applause on the other. I'm sure that if I'd been living in Italy and the theatre of war had been, for example, Rome, then certain individuals would gladly have assassinated me, at least if I hadn't taken steps to prevent them.

Bah! I like the life; I like swimming in the sea, just as you do. And by dint of being rolled over and over in the waves we shall end by taming them and no longer allow them to wash over our heads. [...]

Your friend,
H. Berlioz

126 *To his sister Adèle Berlioz*   Paris, 1 March 1839

My dear Adèle,

[...] It's unfair of you to reproach me with not replying about the journey you want me to make to La Côte. You're quite right in thinking I do not need to be asked to come and see my father and the rest of you, and that I would have come often, during the seven years since I've seen you, if it had been at all possible. I'm hurt by your insistence.

I do not leave Paris because it would be crazy to do so. I'm to make a long journey to Germany next year and I'm busy making all sorts of preparations for it, composing and organizing events to strengthen my position in France before I leave.[3] I am not alone, I have a wife and a

---

1 *Roméo et Juliette.*
2 Liszt was then en route from Florence to Rome.
3 It was more than three years before his plan to give concerts in Germany could be realized.

son, and *you don't know what it is* to have to battle every day with the necessities of life for oneself and one's family.

Paganini has just written to me, inviting me most warmly to come to Marseille where he's organized two concerts for me. I've had to tell him I'm not coming. It would be utterly extravagant. You are ignorant, and cannot be otherwise, of the thousand difficulties and dangers of my position.

Your last letter made me extremely angry and that is why I have not replied until today. As usual on these occasions, I've allowed a day or two to go by so as to regain my sang-froid; I do hope you will never write to me like that again. [. . .]

Adieu, dear sister, I embrace you warmly in spite of everything. But don't make me preach; it's so ridiculous.

H. Berlioz

127 *To Director of the Opéra, Edmond Duponchel*   Paris,
                                                 after 17 March 1839

Monsieur,

I have the honour to inform you that I withdraw my opera *Benvenuto*.[1] I am in no doubt that you will be pleased by the news.

I have, Monsieur, the honour to be
your devoted servant,
H. Berlioz

128 *To Faurie de Vienne*[2]   Paris, 1 April 1839

I thank you a thousand times, Monsieur, for your kind letter which I read with pleasure. I do not often come across intelligent sympathy of the sort you have been good enough to honour me with. Yes, Gluck for me is a passionate cult (though I hope reason too plays its part) and you have delighted me by saying that you also share this cult. But I have seen productions of all his works, I have seen them all on the stage (with the one exception of *Echo et Narcisse*[3]) fifteen or twenty times each. I have lived in Paris for nineteen years and I have never missed a

---

1 Three performances of Act I of *Benvenuto Cellini* were given on 20 February, 8 March and 17 March, coupled on each occasion with a ballet.
2 Faurie de Vienne was a retired tax-collector from Besançon whom Berlioz evidently did not know. He had doubtless been prompted to write by Berlioz's remarks about Gluck's *Orphée* in the *Débats* of 17 March.
3 The pastorale *Echo et Narcisse* had not been played in Paris since 1780.

performance of them; so I have not resorted to guesswork, as you suppose. I sincerely hope no one intends to put on one of his master-pieces at the Opéra; the performing conditions in that bazaar which calls itself a theatre would turn any such project into an impertinence and a profanation. You can have no idea of the outrageous tinkering that goes on there. Music and drama are dragged through the mire.

I was very interested to read your paraphrase of the Lord's Prayer and the *Ave Maria* which seem to me conceived in a most poetic manner. I dare not accept your offer to send me extracts of the music; if it were engraved, then well and good, but in manuscript it is too dangerous. I should be afraid of it going astray.

My wife too was touched by your appreciation of her talent. Unfor-tunately, she has never been able to learn French well enough to speak it on stage. Talma, who lived in England and knew English like an Englishman, never dared act in London because of his accent. It's an insurmountable difficulty. As for the English theatres, they have all gone to rack and ruin.

In offering you sincerest thanks, I have the honour to be, Monsieur, your devoted servant,

    H. Berlioz

129 *To his sister Adèle Suat*[1]   Paris, 9 April 1839

Dearest sister,

[...] Your idea of sending Louis to my father was accepted by his mother in an initial burst of pride at sending my father such a sweet boy; then there were tears at the extravagant notion of being separated from him, then finally, as it's still a long way off and he'll be bigger by then, she has more or less agreed. But you will have to come and fetch him. He's the most charming and the most fearfully badly brought up child I know. He threatens everyone with his sabre and says all sorts of nasty things when he's crossed, and swears like . . . his father. The day before yesterday he ran my bed through with his bayonet wearing my national guard uniform. And with it all he's charming. He's enchanted by the idea of going to pick strawberries and peaches with his grand-father, but I'm not sure how he'll take his parents' absence, as he can't be separated from us for an evening without tears. Anyway, you'll see that for yourself when you come to Paris.

---

1 Adèle married Marc Suat, a notary from St-Chamond, near Lyon, on 2 April 1839.

I'm unwell, I can't put up with the cold any longer and it's been freezing for three days.

I can't manage to stay peacefully at home and work; I have to be out all the time, first performances, concerts, rehearsals.

Adieu, dear sister, all my best wishes to your husband.

I embrace you both.

H. Berlioz

130 *To his father Dr Louis Berlioz*   Paris, 11 May 1839

Dear father

[...] I loathe the profession of critic, having to marshal a heap of platitudes which sicken the heart. I'm approached about the unlikeliest beginner, whether singer or pianist, about the most tawdry *opéra comique* which is not worth an old cigar-end, about all the most shameful sores of the musical world, giving me a terrifying notion of the power of the *Journal des débats* and increasing, if that's possible, my contempt for all this cretinous behaviour. Every now and then my patience comes to an end and I pulverize two or three mediocrities with a clench of my fist. This is followed by despair, tears, missions to sue for peace, letters from the humble bowed down to the ground, or anonymous invective or visits from women with recommendations from my best friends. Then acts of revenge (always anonymous) in the less important papers. Then invitations to dinner, soirées given in order to persuade. For example, there's the new young singer, Mlle Nathan, on whose behalf M. Crémieux, the well-known lawyer, and his wife have practically fallen over backwards with their toadying attentions. I refused to go to their dinner; nothing daunted, they arranged an immense soirée at M. Custine's attended by Lamartine, Balzac, Hugo, Gautier, Chateaubriand, Mme Girardin; all the fashionable names in Parisian literature, painting and music had been invited. This time I accepted because the Bertin family were going as well and I realized I had to give in. And all that because Duprez is Mlle Nathan's teacher and he is crass enough to be afraid I'll visit my revenge on his pupil for the wrongs he's done me. This young person makes her debut next Wednesday, she's Jewish, all Jewry will be there to support her, she'll have a terrific success and she's very mediocre. Harriet agrees with me and even Meyerbeer himself, despite being a Jew, cannot deny it when asked for the real truth. I shall be an object of lifelong hatred if I say even half of what I think. Maybe I'll say the whole of it. What a profession! [...]

It all eats up my time, which I feel I could be making better use of. My head is full to bursting with projects, plans and ideas which I can't realize. The fever of my choral symphony, on Shakespeare's *Romeo*, has passed; everything's so firmly fixed in my head now that I'm working coolly, like a copyist, which is why imagination, flying ever in advance, summons me to fresh compositions. But I still have plenty to do on *Roméo*; the final reconciliation scene between Capulets and Montagues, which has never been set by any of the composers who've written operas on this subject, will be one of immense grandeur. Please God I don't fall down on it! If, dear father, you come in November, you'll hear it *conducted by me*. Conducting the orchestra myself is really the only way not to have my music distorted more or less. There's a huge difference when anyone else takes over the job, however devoted and intelligent he may be. If only you could come!

Adieu, dear father,

I embrace you tenderly.

Your affectionate son,

H. Berlioz

131 *To Eugène Scribe*[1]   Paris, 31 August 1839

My dear collaborator,

[...] I shall not take the liberty of indicating to you the kind of dramatic ideas that would suit me best, as you are aware of them well enough. But in our search for a subject which can lend itself to broad, impassioned musical development and to effects of surprise, it is, I'm sure, right to tell you even so that I have an antipathy to certain nations, as I do to certain individuals. Luther, for example; the Christians of the Early Empire and those loutish Druids. I should be delighted by an *antique*[2] subject but I'm afraid of the costumes the actors would need, and also of the firmly prosaic attitude of our audience. Perhaps a simple love story, but a violent love, studded with scenes of terror involving the masses and set either in the Middle Ages or in the last century, that would be the most suitable sort of thing for

1 The most successful playwright and librettist of the day, Scribe collaborated with Meyerbeer, Auber, Halévy and many other composers. Duponchel, the director of the Opéra, evidently took the view that Berlioz might be more successful a second time if he had the right libretto, so a proposal to set a Scribe text was extremely promising for Berlioz. The collaboration led to *La nonne sanglante*, eventually abandoned after many years' desultory work.

2 That is, from ancient Greece or Rome. Was he thinking of Virgil perhaps?

me. Of course one would not have to keep to the heroic or dithyrambic style throughout; on the contrary, I'm very fond of contrasts. There you have my full confession. Duponchel has also been sermonizing me about writing music that's less difficult to play and easier to understand for mixed operatic audiences. I agree entirely with him over this.

Your devoted

H. Berlioz

132 *To his sister Nanci Pal*   Paris, 16 September 1839

My dear Nanci,

[...] I've finished with my grand symphony as far as composition is concerned,[1] but now I have to come to grips with copyists, lithographers, etc. I'm snowed under with reviews; every week some new platitudes to record.[2]

What a profession! And my rehearsals will soon be upon me, and my good friend Cherubini will be plaguing me as usual![3]

The director of the Théâtre de la Renaissance has asked me for an opera, but I don't dare to accept; the organization is too precarious. In any case I'm working on a large work for the Opéra in which Scribe is involved. I don't like having so many things on the stocks at the same time. They're dropping like flies in that damned great theatre, and in any case the male singers there bellow like bullocks and the orchestra destroys itself daily. What a prospect! And not to be able to shake any sense into it all. It's only in my concerts that I can more or less do what I want; there I get obedience without any argument and even with confidence and alacrity.

Adieu, adieu! It was well worth writing to tell you this good news!

My sincere best wishes to Camille and to yourself and the little lass.

H. Berlioz

133 *To Louis Viardot*[4]   Paris, 11 October 1839

A thousand thanks, Monsieur, for your gracious offer.

My attendance at the Théâtre-Italien will be all the more valuable in my eyes in that today it will afford me the opportunity of studying the

1 *Roméo et Juliette* was completed on 17 September 1839.
2 Operas reviewed by Berlioz that month were Donizetti's *Lucia di Lammermoor*, Halévy's *Le shérif*, Ruolz's *La vendetta* and Adam's *La reine d'un jour*.
3 Berlioz depended on Cherubini's goodwill in obtaining the Conservatoire hall for his concerts.
4 Journalist and translator, director of the Théâtre-Italien.

development of a marvellous talent in which all true friends of the art of music take an interest, and because the crowds who will be drawn to the Odéon by a performance unrivalled throughout the world will make this study daily more difficult.[1]

Please accept my congratulations on this new success, to whose acclaim I should be happy to lend my support.

Your devoted

H. Berlioz

134 *To his father Dr Louis Berlioz*   Paris, 26 November 1839

Dear father,

I write just half a dozen lines to let you know of a great success![2] *Roméo et Juliette* has been received with acclamation, as my uncle Auguste will be able to confirm, since he was at the concert with my cousins. The exhaustion of rehearsing almost did for me, but success has put me back on my feet again. And if it weren't for a bath I unwisely took this morning, which has given me a cold, I would be free of coughs or any other infirmity. How sad that you can never be in Paris on these occasions! This first concert, apart from its immense importance musically speaking (as the art form which it contained was totally new) has reassured me of the real interest a new composition of mine can now excite in the true music-loving public.

There was such a crowd that 1500 francs' worth of listeners were turned away at the box office. Despite the enormous number of tickets snatched from me by those incredibly grasping members of the press, the receipts came to 4559 francs.

At ordinary prices the capacity of the hall is only 5000 francs. The Queen sent word at midday that she would be coming, all arrangements were made to receive her and I don't know what kept her at the Tuileries. The two young princes, the Duc d'Aumale and the Duc de Montpensier were the only ones to appear in the royal box. I imagine the arrival of the Duc d'Orléans, who was expected that day, will have been the reason for this contretemps.

I've had any number of complimentary letters today. The gutter

---

1 On 8 October Pauline Garcia made her debut at the Théâtre Italien (then housed in the Odéon) in Rossini's *Otello*. She was rapidly judged to be no less fine a singer than her sister Maria Malibran. The following year she married Viardot and became known as Pauline Viardot.

2 *Roméo et Juliette* was first performed on 24 November 1839 at the Conservatoire with Berlioz conducting. There were two further performances in the following weeks.

press apart, I think from what I've heard that the reviews will be extremely favourable. It's probably the greatest success I've had so far.

I embrace you in the hope that this news will provide you with some moments of happiness.

Balzac said to me this morning, 'That was a *brainy* audience you had.' And indeed the cream of the intelligentsia was there. A number of enemies who arrived with sinister intentions had to put a good face on things and look as though they were in raptures. They'll get their own back with anonymous insults in the smaller newspapers.

The second performance will be even more satisfactory, I hope; it'll take place next Sunday. But the first has been a *tour de force* that could only have been brought about by my system of sectional rehearsals; the performers themselves are amazed at what they did.[1]

Adieu, dear father, embrace my sisters for me, I must leave you and turn to some slight changes I want to make in my score.

H. Berlioz

135 *To his father Dr Louis Berlioz*　　　　　Paris, 1 December 1839

Dear father,

I felt, in spite of my fatigue, my complete extermination, that I must send you a few lines; the second performance of *Roméo et Juliette* has been a stupendous, overwhelming success![2] I was greeted with torrents of applause, shouts, tears, everything.

At the end of the concert, at the moment where the Capulets and Montagues are reconciled, the whole orchestra and chorus stood up hurrahing loudly enough to bring down the roof of the hall, while the audience, in the stalls and in the boxes, began to applaud as noisily as they could; for a moment I was afraid of losing my sang-froid, something I dread above all else, but I held out!

Adieu for this evening.

H. Berlioz

1 Berlioz applied for the first time the method of rehearsing each section of his choir and orchestra separately, a method previously used only by choral ensembles.
2 The second performance took place earlier that day.

My dear Humbert,

Today I have a little free time and am less blown about than over the last ten days, so I can answer you in not too depressed a mood. I needed your congratulations, full as they were of warmth and true friendship; I'd been looking forward to them all the time. Now I'm happy, my success is complete. *Roméo et Juliette* again gave rise to tears (there was much weeping, I promise you). It would take too long here to tell you all the ups and downs of these three concerts. Enough for you to know that the new score has stirred up unbelievable passions and has even caused some startling conversions. Of course, the nucleus of *enemies-come-what-may* remains tougher than ever. An Englishman bought the little pine baton, which I used for conducting the orchestra, from Schlesinger's manservant for 120 francs. The London press, too, have treated me splendidly.

For these three concerts the performers cost 12,100 francs and the receipts reached 13,200 francs; so of these 13,200 francs, I receive only 1100 as profit!!! It's sad to think that such a splendid result, once you've taken into account the tiny capacity of the hall and the habits of the audience, is a wretched one when it comes to my trying to live off it. Serious art certainly cannot support its devotees and the situation will remain the same until the time a government realizes that it's unjust and unkind. [. . .]

Yours ever,

H. Berlioz

You must be good enough to allow me two more days for my article;[1] I've spent the day in bed, trembling like someone with a fever. These infernal nervous attacks have come on worse than ever and, feeling as I do, it's really extremely difficult to write anything that makes sense. So don't expect anything from me before five o'clock on Saturday. It's the safest course.

I send you our overture *Le roi Lear* which is published at last, together with the manuscript which I beg you to keep.[2]

The dedication of a piece of music is a banal homage whose only

---

1 On Donizetti's *La fille du régiment* for the *Journal des débats*.
2 *Le roi Lear* was dedicated to Bertin.

value lies in the merit of the work, but I hope you will accept this one as the expression of the gratitude and friendship that I have felt towards you for so long.

H. Berlioz

138 *To his father Dr Louis Berlioz*   Paris, 30 July 1840

Dear father,

I'm sorry not to have written before to tell you about the new success I've just had.[1] But the service I've seen in this musical army has been so rough that I'm still prostrated by it, and yesterday I could hardly form my letters, the muscles of my hand were so tired from waving my arm and holding the baton.

Everything went splendidly; the greatest success came with the dress rehearsal in front of the most intelligent audience Paris can provide.[2] It wasn't only the women who wept. After this test, which settled the fate of the work itself, there remained that of the performance *on the stage*. Our stage was Paris, its embankments and its boulevards. And the old know-alls of military music were claiming that I'd never manage to have the *Marche funèbre*[3] performed *on the march* and that my 210 musicians wouldn't stay together for twenty bars. In the event these experienced prophets were proved wrong. I placed the trumpets and drums in front so that I could give them the beat while walking *backwards* and (as I had intended from the start) because in the opening bars these instruments play by themselves, they could be heard by the rest of the band. So that not only the *March funèbre* but also the *Apothéose*[4] was played six times, on the march, with an ensemble and an effect that were truly extraordinary. The Minister sent one of his heads of department to congratulate me in the warmest fashion after the second performance of the triumphal march, which had made a tremendous impression on all the mob around and above us. Yesterday he had Cavé, the director of the Department of Fine Arts, write me a letter full of the most high-flown compliments.

This time I wrote my piece in such large letters, even the

---

1 For the tenth anniversary of the July Revolution of 1830 and for the inauguration of the column in the Place de la Bastille which commemorated it, Berlioz was commissioned by de Rémusat, Minister of the Interior, to write a symphony for large military band, the *Grande symphonie funèbre et triomphale*. It was first performed at the ceremonies on 28 July 1840.
2 The final rehearsal was held two days earlier in the Salle Vivienne.
3 The first movement.
4 The last movement.

short-sighted could read them. Also, extraordinarily enough, there was *not one detractor*. Even Mainzer, my well-known enemy from *Le national*, went so far as to praise my composition in his article yesterday. Not that that in any sense proves this work's superiority over the ones that have preceded it.

But it's a banner, a colossal inscription, and the whole world has seen it. *All* the artists are manifesting an enthusiasm which, towards me, could be taken for respect. (I tell you that in the hope that you won't show my letter to anyone except my sisters.) I'm receiving congratulations in verse and prose. So far I've seen only three newspapers that discuss my music in detail. *Galignani's Messenger* (enthusiastic), *Le national* (the conversion of Mainzer) and *L'univers* (enthusiastic). If I can send you these articles, I will.

Now I'm going to the Ministry where M. de Rémusat, I'm told, has 'many things to say to me'. Which does not mean that two years ago they didn't commission Rossini to write a *Requiem* for the Emperor! A Rossini *Requiem* would be curious!! If he writes it. In that case I should most probably be given some triumphal, heroic song to compose for the processional entry into Paris.[1] It would need large forces and large amounts of money and rather more time in which to make the preparations, and one would have to resist being crushed by such an emotional subject ... I mean Napoleon ... I'm really annoyed to have written this triumphal march for our petty July Heroes, it would almost have done for the great Hero. I embrace you, dear father, with all my heart, in the hope that my letter will give you some pleasure.

H. Berlioz

P.S.   Apparently I shall receive three or four thousand francs for this score which I wrote in less than forty hours.[2] In that case I ought to have had fifty thousand for the *Requiem* ... It's always like that. Compositions, like men, have to take the rough with the smooth.

In August 1840 Berlioz gave two further performances of the Grande symphonie funèbre et triomphale *in the Salle Vivienne, and then paid a short visit to La Côte-St-André to see his father, their first meeting for eight years.*

1 Napoleon's ashes were laid to rest in the Invalides on 15 December 1840. Berlioz was asked to write music for the ceremony but was given only two weeks' notice, so he declined on the grounds that he needed more time for such an important commission.
2 This lends support to the supposition that at least some of the music had existed already, perhaps as part of the *Fête musicale funèbre* (see p. 126).

Dear father,

How are you? Is it already cold at La Côte? I fear so, to judge by the uncomfortable temperature here. Nancy or Adèle will send me news of you soon; I'll insist, as you find writing so tiring.

I arrived home aching and exhausted at four o'clock in the morning. Impossible to describe how overjoyed Harriet and Louis were; you'd think I was coming back from New Holland at least. We talked a lot about La Côte and especially about you, dear father. Harriet is deeply touched by your wish to get to know her; be assured that we shall seize with the utmost eagerness the opportunity for *all three of us* to spend a month with you, when it comes round.

The presents I brought for Louis made him jump for joy; but I must confess that, despite the pleasure he got from Mathilde's letter and the slippers, Monique's brioches and pots of jam were incomparably more successful.

I arrived to find that I had been condemned to two days in prison for missing my guard duty on 30 July. When I went to see the 'competent authority' who had condemned me in my absence and put it to him that my guard duty of 29 July and my direction of two hundred musicians for five hours in the hot sun surely constituted an exemption for the next day, he exclaimed, 'What, you're the etc, Berlioz who etc?'

'Yes, by your leave!'

'Oh, it's that imbecile of a sergeant-major who didn't realize, etc, etc.'

Eventually, thanks to etc, etc I think my prison sentence will be reduced to nothing.[1]

Nothing new in my dealings with the Opéra; Frédéric Soulié is at work and I wait.[2] Meanwhile I'm preparing for my concerts in November. Adieu, dear father, all my best wishes to my sisters and their husbands, if they're all still with you. I embrace you tenderly.

H. Berlioz

---

1 It was not. Berlioz had to serve his two days' confinement three weeks later.
2 Soulié was at this time proposed as a collaborator with Scribe on the libretto of *La nonne sanglante*.

Dear sister,

I haven't replied to you because I was preparing for a great battle which we won yesterday evening. Don't you read anything at La Côte? I've just put on a festival at the Opéra;[1] I conducted 450 players and singers in fragments of my *Requiem*, of my symphonies, an act of *Iphigénie en Tauride*, a portion of Handel's *Athalia* and a madrigal by the old Italian master Palestrina. A fortnight before, there were conspiracies to prevent the Opéra orchestra playing for me, insults in the smaller newspapers, threats, etc, etc. The rehearsal the day before yesterday was terribly tiring and confused, so you can imagine the anxiety I felt. But when I made my entrance yesterday evening on that immense Opéra stage, made more immense still by a ramp sloping down into the audience, when I saw my attentive army and the full auditorium bathed in light, when I heard the audience shudder at the first chorus sung by the priestesses of Diana (during the storm) and the applause after the chorus of Scythians,[2] I realized all was going well. So I began my *Dies irae* confidently, in spite of the two or three scoundrels I knew to be in the stalls. The effect of this mass of sound was terrifying; the house was shaking with the impact of the voices and the thunderclaps and the trumpets. This depiction of the Last Judgment overwhelmed them and three times in the middle of the piece applause and shouts from the audience drowned the noise of my crowd of singers. At the end of the piece some kind opponent was stupid enough to let fly with a whistle, which I would willingly have spent a thousand francs to buy for him; instantly the entire audience stood up with cries of fury and my players added their applause to that from the stalls and the boxes. The women were applauding with their music, the violins and double basses with their bows, the timpanists with their sticks, so it was, one might say, a *furious* success.

The rest followed naturally from there; the scoundrel in question was thrown out and the *Lacrymosa*, the *Fête chez Capulet* and the whole of the *Symphonie militaire*[3] were received with an enthusiasm that's very rare at the Opéra, especially from an audience that's had to pay more for its tickets than usual. The *Apothéose* was interrupted by applause five times, and at the final return of the theme of triumph the

1 The day before, 1 November 1840.
2 From *Iphigénie en Tauride*.
3 The *Grande symphonie funèbre et triomphale*.

whole stalls stood up waving their arms and shouting; it was superb. I'm worn out, but less so than two days ago.

Harriet is weeping tears of happiness.

For me it's an occasion which will have incalculable consequences.

Adieu, embrace my father for me.

H. B.

141 *To François Buloz*[1]   Paris, between 15 and 20 November 1840

Monsieur,

In the notice appearing in the *Revue des deux mondes* of the festival I gave at the Opéra there were errors of fact which I think I may ask you to rectify.[2]

The author of the article wishes to make me guilty of the crime of *lèse-majesté* with respect to Gluck and Palestrina: 'Poor Gluck', he writes, 'you little thought, when all those years ago you used trombones to evoke the spirits of hate and anger, that the day would come when M. Berlioz would make you the free gift of several ophicleides; nor did Palestrina, who has been torn from the Sistine Chapel where a few sopranos suffice to perform his polyphonic lines, expect to have his peaceful, smooth, religious inspiration crushed beneath the pomp of voices and instruments.'

In fact, the act of *Iphigénie* was performed exactly as the composer wrote it; there were therefore no ophicleides. As for Palestrina, so little did a few sopranos suffice that his madrigal 'Alla riva del Tebro', which by the way being a secular piece could never have been heard in the Sistine Chapel, is in four parts (SOPRANOS, CONTRALTOS, TENORS and BASSES); it suggests a curious abstractedness indeed to find crushed beneath the pomp of instruments a chorus sung according to the composer's text, UNACCOMPANIED.

These errors, which impugn my role as an interpreter of masters whom I admire, are the only ones I think it necessary to mention.

I am, etc,

H. Berlioz

1 Editor of the *Revue des deux mondes*.
2 On 15 November the *Revue* printed a notice of Berlioz's concert by Scudo, one of his most virulent opponents. The notice was a scathing attack on Berlioz both as conductor and as composer.

Dear sister,

I write to you at long intervals, it's true, and this time it's again on business!! Your husband wrote to me some years ago to say that my mother had left me the sum of six thousand francs, deposited I don't know where in Grenoble. This is to say that in two months' time at the latest I shall be in desperate need of it and to beg you to forward it to me even *earlier* if that is possible. I shall deposit it with Rothschild, as I've done with my money so far, at 4 per cent. The truth is I can't make ends meet and I'm gradually spending my modest capital. And in two months the said capital won't exist any more.

Perhaps you saw in the papers that I was replacing Habeneck at the Opéra.[1] It's a job worth 10,000 francs a year. It has in essence been offered, promised and confirmed. But before I can have it, old Cherubini has to hand over his job to Habeneck in one way or another. The other day he was believed to have died, that's what started the rumour of my nomination. But the illustrious old gentleman returned from the grave fiercer than ever and furious with me, not that I covet his position. He says he's going to *stick a knife* in me. He thinks his wife wants to poison him, he's practically in his second childhood, and the Minister doesn't dare retire him! And he's the director of the Conservatoire![2]

Something else.

You know that my opera[3] is on the stocks. It's by Scribe, with Germaine and Casimir Delavigne as collaborators. While waiting for the libretto to be finished (the contract is duly signed and sealed) I've been asked by the Opéra to write recitatives for Weber's *Freischütz*, which they're putting on at the moment. I've agreed on the express condition that there'll be no tinkering, no Castilblazery[4] with this German masterpiece. I am the composer's shield and I will defend him against all the mutilations which they were already preparing for him to undergo; and in the course of the rehearsals I hope to breathe a little life into those worthless, lymphatic creatures, the singers. The unfortunate thing is that Duprez is demanding the main role and can't be refused, but he won't be able to sing two notes of it. He has no voice

---

1 Having been conductor at the Opéra since 1821, it was rumoured that Habeneck was to replace Cherubini as director of the Conservatoire.
2 Cherubini died shortly after retiring the following year, aged eighty-one.
3 *La nonne sanglante*.
4 See p. 41.

left either at the top or at the bottom. Duprez no longer exists! Audiences put up with him and laugh in his face every so often. *Sic transit gloria* of singers.[1] This project will be quite lucrative for me, but it won't be put on for three and a half months or longer. So I have to spend a certain time in frustration before I take up these posts which I'm bound to get both at the Opéra and at the Institut.[2]

I turned down a third proposition from London a fortnight ago, with an eye to the future as always and, more than that, so as not to leave Paris for an instant. Everyone agrees that I'm right.

Tell my father about all this, as soon as you can.

We're all well here.

My best wishes to your husband; I'm in such a hurry I write this standing on one foot and beating my wings.

Yours,

H. Berlioz

143 *To his brother-in-law Marc Suat*   Paris, *c.* 27 April 1841

[...] My dear Suat, I hope this hasn't caused you worries or embarrassments of any kind![3] I agree with you, tangible rewards for my position are taking their time to reach me! Everyone thinks I'm on the way to being rich or at least quite comfortably off, yet apart from after Paganini's present I've never had a single moment's respite from financial difficulties. All the avenues and jobs are occupied by or are earmarked for *stupid old men* and the feebleness with which the arts are controlled allows them to be so. The heads of the administration complain about it but the situation continues even so! Everything is going to rack and ruin as a result, and I suffer fearfully from the consequences. Music as I conceive it is a calamitous art for anyone who practises it, and will remain so until the time it receives worthy recompense from a monarch or at least a minister. If Napoleon were alive...

I've refused to accept offers from publishers wanting to buy my symphonies, so as not to ruin myself completely; by keeping them in manuscript and in my own exclusive possession I've at least ensured for myself a visit to Germany which could be fruitful. But I don't dare

1 The part of Max was sung in fact by Marié, not Duprez.
2 Berlioz never became conductor of the Opéra and he did not become a member of the Institut until 1856.
3 Berlioz acknowledged receipt of 6000 francs from his mother's estate.

leave Paris without having one of the jobs which must of necessity fall
vacant one day. [. . .]
    H. B.

144 *To his father Dr Louis Berlioz*   Paris, 8 or 9 June 1841

Dear father,

    I have just put on *Der Freischütz*, this evening is the second perform-
ance. Everything points to its being a financial success. Weber's masterpiece is being given as well as is possible in the present state of singing
at the Opéra. At any rate the chorus and orchestra are good. I didn't
want to receive a credit for my recitatives, even though, by the performers' admission, they've been completely successful.[1] I tried as best I
could to reproduce Weber's style, without striving for effect. It appears
I succeeded, because I keep finding performers who attribute to Weber
recitatives which were written by me, for example the one during the
casting of the bullets in the second act, which all the Opéra orchestra
attributed to him during rehearsals.

    For this work the director intends to allot me author's rights for each
performance which will, I think, be satisfactory.

    I almost had to conduct the performance of this masterpiece, as
Habeneck had fallen seriously ill and his assistant wasn't very reliable.
I refused, having no official position entitling me to a place on the
rostrum. The director wants Habeneck to stand down so that he can
offer me his job. But the latter won't agree as yet.

    My thanks, dear father, for your recent support; Suat has been most
helpful in the matter.

    But when will I stop being a burden to you? I'm tortured by this
problem day and night. And everyone thinks I'm rich! Borrowers write
to me asking for 4000 francs!

    Apparently you're keeping fairly well, thanks to the fine weather! If
it would not be too tiring for you to write me ten lines, I should be very
happy to receive them!

    Adieu, dear father, I embrace you tenderly. Louis and Harriet are
well.

    H. Berlioz

1 Since spoken dialogue was not permitted at the Opéra, Berlioz was engaged to compose
recitatives for the production. He also orchestrated Weber's *Invitation à la valse* as ballet
music.

145 *To his sister Nanci Pal*   Paris, between 23 and 25 August 1841

Dear sister,

[...] No doubt you saw in the papers that the composition of mine which excites the greatest curiosity (the *Requiem*) has recently been performed in St Petersburg with enormous success. I heard the details just the other day from a musician who'd arrived from Russia. They'd brought together the singers of the Imperial Chapel (the foremost choir in the world), the choruses of the two opera houses and those of a regiment of the guard (excellent), together with all the orchestras of St Petersburg. Henri Romberg[1] was not deterred by the huge costs of such an undertaking and made a clear profit of 5000 francs. Here in Paris I wouldn't cover a third of the costs. Apparently the *Lacrymosa* and the *Dies irae* made a powerful impression on the audience, and it seems that if I were to go to Russia I'd be well received.[2]

Before thinking about putting into practice this ever-present idea of travelling, I must finish the score of *La nonne*. I've almost finished the first act, but I've had to stop for a few days, I couldn't do any more. The Opéra is in tatters; apart from a few moments when Duprez seems to come to life, as a singer he's finished, dead and buried. It looks as though they're counting on me to replace the Meyerbeer opera which he still hasn't delivered,[3] but even if I'd finished it now, I'd never risk putting it on with the forces available. What can one do? ... That's what's bound to happen when authority is vested in people who know nothing about music or in moribund, ill-natured dotards. [...][4]

Adieu, dear sister,

H. B.

146 *To Gaspare Spontini*   Paris, 27 August 1841

Dear maître,

[...] Yesterday *Cortez*[5] was given at the Opéra. Still rent asunder by the terrible impact of the revolution scene, I come to you crying: Glory,

1 Conductor of the Imperial Opera at St Petersburg.
2 An idea which became reality six years later.
3 *Le prophète* was eventually staged at the Opéra in 1849 after many promises and many delays.
4 Nowhere in his correspondence did Berlioz mention an important work which he had composed in the previous eighteen months and which was published at this time: *Les nuits d'été*, six songs on poems by Gautier for mezzo-soprano or tenor and piano. They were all later orchestrated.
5 Spontini's *Fernand Cortez*, first played at the Opéra in 1809.

glory, glory and respect to the man whose mighty imagination, warmed by his heart, created this immortal scene!! Has indignation, in any musical drama, ever before been able to borrow such a style from nature? Has warlike enthusiasm ever been more burning and more poetic? Have daring and will-power, those proud daughters of genius, anywhere been shown in such a light, painted with such colours? No, and everyone knows it. It is real, it is strong, it is beautiful, it is new, it is sublime!

If music were not abandoned to public charity, we should have in Europe a theatre, an operatic Pantheon, exclusively devoted to the performance of monumental masterpieces, in which they would be produced at long intervals, with a care and a magnificence worthy of them, by ARTISTS, and heard, as part of solemn musical festivals, by audiences of feeling and intelligence.

But music has nearly everywhere been disinherited from the honour of its noble origins and is no more than a foundling whom, it seems, they are trying to turn into a fallen woman.

Adieu, dear maître. There is a religion of beauty; I belong to it. And if it is a duty to admire great things and to honour great men, I am conscious, as I shake your hand, that it is also a pleasure.

H. Berlioz

147 *To his sister Adèle Suat*   Paris, 6 October 1841

Dear little sister,

[. . .] My father has notions from time to time about travelling which lead me to hope I might see him here; just fancies perhaps . . . I can't think of any motive apart from his presence that would lead me to put on concerts this winter. I'm absorbed now and for some time to come by the composition of this great devil of an opera. Scribe has been here, exhausted by work and as thin as a consumptive. He's keeping me waiting for the second act; he asked me to allow him a fortnight's rest after his hard labour for the Théâtre-Français; I gave him only a week which he's gone off to spend at Chartres, after which he'll pick up his pen once more and keep on then until my opera's finished.

Unfortunately, vocal standards at our great opera house are not improving, quite the reverse; and I don't really know what line I'll take once I've finished. [. . .]

Adieu.

H. Berlioz

148 *To Richard Wagner*[1]   Paris, 12 October 1841

Monsieur,

I have passed on Mme de Weber's letter to M. Pillet;[2] he had already received a similar one. What M. Pillet wants is to put on a benefit performance for the composer of *Der Freischütz*, but he feels there are great difficulties to overcome before he can accomplish this. I can assure you that I am doing everything in my power to assist him in his aims. The problems are unfortunately ones of financial administration, about which I understandably know nothing and against which all the noblest sentiments expressed by artists battle in vain.

I will speak to M. Pillet again on the subject.[3]

Yours most sincerely,

H. Berlioz

149 *To A. Raoux*[4]   Paris, 11 January 1842

I thank you, Monsieur, for the information you have been kind enough to send me about the valve horn; I shall make every effort to learn of the improvements that you have brought about in the manufacture of this instrument and shall soon have the opportunity of acknowledging your efforts. If you would care to call on me next Friday at eleven o'clock in the morning, I shall be at home to receive you.

Your devoted servant,

H. Berlioz

150 *To his sister Nanci Pal*   Paris, 5 February 1842

This evening I've got a dreadful article to write on a large operetta by Auber;[5] it's music for milliners sung by smart young ladies-about-town and commercial travellers; I'll say it's *quite nice*, without adding 'for

1 Berlioz and Wagner first met at the time of *Roméo et Juliette* in November 1839. In October 1841 Wagner was still in Paris, seriously short of funds.
2 Léon Pillet succeeded Duponchel as director of the Opéra in 1841.
3 The idea of a benefit performance for Weber's widow came to nothing.
4 A Paris maker of brass instruments. In the winter of 1841–2 Berlioz's chief preoccupation, after *La nonne sanglante*, was a series of sixteen articles on instrumentation, the basis of his *Grand traité d'instrumentation et d'orchestration modernes* published in 1844. The article of 9 January 1842, dealing with the horn, clung to the view that the application of valves to the horn could be of only limited use, notably for low notes. Raoux's response was one factor that converted Berlioz to a more sympathetic attitude to valves.
5 *Le duc d'Olonne*, performed at the Opéra-Comique on 4 February 1842. Auber became director of the Conservatoire four days later.

salesgirls'. What drudgery!! I'm putting the article off till tomorrow and allowing myself the pleasure of writing to you, all of you who dance in Grenoble and don't particularly care about what they sing in Paris. It's been a long time in fact since we've been in touch, even briefly ... I've had so much to write this last month, in the *Gazette musicale*, in the *Débats* and elsewhere ... I can't tell you anything about balls in Paris, you know I don't even go to the ones at the Opéra; and invitations come raining down on us. Harriet never goes out, and she complains bitterly because I go out all the time.[1] But I do have to attend to my affairs and see people; a further inconvenience of this continual rushing around is that I spend a fortune on cabs. Spontini, who was here recently, was saying to me: 'Good Lord, what a life people lead in Paris nowadays! No one has a moment's rest; it's a living hell!' Before he left he did his best to smooth my path to the Institut, always supposing a place becomes vacant soon. You see how we sell the skins of academicians before laying them in their graves.[2] At the moment it's de Vigny's turn, he's in competition with the Baron Pasquier; it seems certain M. Pasquier will be elected. What has he produced? God himself doesn't know. Halévy will be solidly behind me too, when the bear etc. At my peril I've given his opera *La reine de Chypre* a good send-off in an article which has had a very powerful impact on the Parisian public.[3] Halévy couldn't be happier or more grateful for it. The director is not quite so pleased, because I had some words to say about *his* queen whose despotism was holding up performances of *Der Freischütz*.[4] I won, the queen had to give up her role to Mme Nathan, and *Der Freischütz* is going to reappear from time to time. (It's being given tomorrow.) With regard to *Der Freischütz* Mme Weber wrote to me recently to try and get the Opéra to put on a benefit performance for her; I was unable to arrange it. The widow and children of this sublime composer are extremely poor, as you can imagine! So much for being a poet! Auber has his horses, his town houses, his country houses, a superabundance of luxury; he won't die of a broken heart ... he won't write *Oberon* either. He'll die without having lived. He sees nothing, hears nothing. He doesn't like music, but it pays him well.

1 Berlioz's liaison with the singer Marie Recio seems to have begun in 1841.
2 'Never sell the bear's skin until it's brought down' (La Fontaine). Cherubini had little over a month to live, but his Institut chair was filled by Onslow; in the election Spontini voted for Onslow, not Berlioz.
3 In the *Journal des débats* on 26 December 1841.
4 Rosina Stoltz, who sang the role of Agathe in 1841, was the mistress of Pillet, director of the Opéra.

I met Hugo this afternoon and while we discussed his recent book *Le Rhin* he walked me up and down the bank of the Seine by the Champs-Elysées for so long, I'm exhausted.

You know I gave a huge concert last Tuesday.[1] Neither you nor my father nor my uncle nor my sisters nor my brothers-in-law will ever be here to witness another occasion of such happiness; that's certain! You can't imagine the shouts, the tears, the outpouring of emotions of every kind that greeted the *Apothéose* of my *Symphonie militaire*, which I've just re-scored for two orchestras. At the moment when the second (string) orchestra burst in, part of the audience got to their feet in wild excitement and the two hundred players couldn't make themselves heard through the interminable din of hurrahs. Since then I've been told any number of curious details about this climax of nervous intensity. If my father had been there, with all of you and my uncle, and memories of the empire, and the even more potent thought (arising from the work itself) of those three days when people were killing themselves with such gusto in the streets of Paris, it would without doubt have been an experience such as he has never had before. The auditorium was a fine sight, full right up to the top of the steps leading to the door. In spite of the costs of two orchestras and of the copying, I still made a profit. The copying costs won't have to be deducted at the next concert; it'll take place on Tuesday 15 February.[2]

Out of the letters I had, I've chosen one to send you from a young cabinet-maker who had the unusual and charming idea of writing to Harriet and not to me. He asked our cook to pass on these two pages to us but apart from two spelling mistakes they don't smell of the workshop at all. The common people of Paris are making progress in strange directions, one has to admit. I was told there were about twenty blind men in the audience, including the traveller Arago[3] (brother of the astronomer), who were responsible for the most bizarre demonstrations. As for me, my throat was on fire, I had cramp in my right arm (so that I had to conduct with my left) and a sort of buzzing inside my head which prevented me from hearing anything. It was similar to what I imagine it must be like being a naval gunner between decks on a frigate during a battle, only there were no deaths.

Harriet and Louis were thrilled, as you can imagine. Will the

1 In the Salle Vivienne on 1 February 1842. Besides the *Apothéose*, the concert included Berlioz's *Rêverie et caprice* for violin and orchestra and Beethoven's Triple Concerto.
2 The second concert included the *Symphonie fantastique* and part of *Harold en Italie*.
3 Jacques Arago, whose successful book *Promenade autour du monde* was published in 1822.

reception be as warm at the second concert? One must hope so, but in this situation I'm always afraid it won't be. Twice in succession is too much to hope for.

I've had a request from Bordeaux to organize and conduct a festival there in September. They're going to build a hall specially, there'll be six hundred performers and the city will donate thirty thousand francs. So far I've only had an informal communication and I'm waiting for the official letter. It will probably come off, so here's to the *Lacrymosa* and the great earthquake in the *Requiem*, and the finale of *Roméo et Juliette*! With four hundred voices one can produce quite a good account of those *ditties*.[1]

I'm leaving *La nonne* on one side, the oil in her lamp has run out. Scribe has still not given me the third act and in any case there's no immediate hurry; the Opéra is not overflowing with singers. Duprez has only six or seven notes left and the rest have too many.

H. Berlioz

151 *To his brother-in-law Marc Suat* Paris, 10 August 1842

My dear Suat,

Thankyou for the good news about Adèle, I hope by now she is more or less recovered.[2] But there's no need to look for reasons to console yourself for having two daughters. Pretty girls are not that common, and all those who appear are welcome!!! Louis is already of this opinion.

You ask me, my dear Suat, what I'm doing. Truth be told, I'm working hard. At the moment I'm putting the finishing touches to a *Grand traité d'instrumentation* which, I hope, will earn me a reasonable amount of money. It's a work which doesn't figure in the teaching literature and which I've been encouraged to undertake on all sides. My articles on the subject in the *Gazette musicale* were no more than the surface, the flower, and now I have to give substance to it all and busy myself with the smallest technical details.

Scribe still hasn't handed over the last two acts of my opera. But now at least he's married and the honeymoon is over; I don't know what he has in mind.[3]

1 The Bordeaux visit did not come off.
2 In July 1842 Adèle gave birth to her second daughter Nanci.
3 Scribe never sent Berlioz a complete libretto for *La nonne sanglante*, so he was unable to compose more than the first two acts, of which parts of the second survive. Berlioz retained little hope for the project after 1842.

I shall soon be publishing all my symphonies one after the other, it's time this was done. The first to appear will be the last I wrote, the *Grande symphonie funèbre* composed for the re-interment of the July victims, the work for which the poor Duc d'Orléans had just accepted the dedication when death struck him down so cruelly.[1] I can't tell you how sad I was at this appalling accident. I seem indeed to be surrounded by burials and catastrophes; it was not long ago that I was watching the funeral procession of the d'Urville family, killed so terribly in the railway fire at Versailles . . .[2]

We're all well here; Harriet sends you her very best wishes and embraces Adèle tenderly.

Does that mean your ideas of coming to Paris have had to be put aside?

Adieu, my dear Suat, from your sincerely devoted friend

H. Berlioz

On 20 September 1842 Berlioz left Paris for his first concert tour abroad, the first of a long series that continued until the end of his life. He had been planning the tour for a long time, as a means of making his music better known abroad. The money he received from his mother's estate (6000 francs) and the advance for the Grand traité d'instrumentation *(2500 francs) made the tour possible, since in his absence he forfeited his income from journalism, although he later published a lengthy account of his travels first as articles and later in the* Mémoires. *The first tour was really two tours, first to Brussels in September and October 1842, and then a longer tour to Belgium followed by many cities in Germany between December 1842 and May 1843.*

Berlioz was also either escaping from, or creating, a tense situation at home: Marie Recio accompanied him on both tours amid a certain degree of secrecy.

1 The Duc d'Orléans died on 13 July after jumping from his carriage when the horses bolted.
2 On 8 May a disastrous fire killed many victims in one of the earliest rail disasters.

152 *To Leopold I, King of the Belgians*   Brussels, 21 September 1842

Sire,

Allow me to place before Your Majesty the programme of a concert I am giving next Monday at one o'clock in the hall of La Grande Harmonie.[1]

It would be a powerful encouragement for me if, on the first occasion that I play my compositions in Belgium, I were to be granted the great favour of the King's presence.

I am, Sire, with the profoundest respect, Your Majesty's most humble and obedient servant

Hector Berlioz

153 *To Joseph-François Snel*[2]   Brussels, 12 October 1842

My dear Monsieur Snel,

We missed each other by a few minutes yesterday evening, so I was deprived of the opportunity of spending a couple of hours with you before my departure. I had, nevertheless, so much to say to you after all you have done for me here. It seems straightforward to you and you have gone about it all so naturally that you're surprised at my reacting so strongly. But that's not how I see it; I am as touched and grateful as I could possibly be for your kind and cordial friendship. Among artists, and great artists especially, it is rare to find such a warm welcome as you extended to me. I am now set thinking as to how I shall find the opportunity to give worthy expression to my gratitude. Perhaps one day you will come to Paris to organize a performance of one of your great works, and then no doubt I shall have the satisfaction of helping to do justice to it, as is only right and proper for the products of such an elevated mind as your own.

In the meantime I shake your hand and offer you my most sincere and steadfast friendship and esteem, quite independent of the admiration which your superiority as an artist inspired in me from the very first.

Yours ever, with all best wishes,

H. Berlioz

1 Berlioz's first concert in Brussels, on 26 September, included movements from *Harold en Italie*, *Roméo et Juliette* and the *Grand symphonie funèbre et triomphale*. The second concert, on 9 October, in a different hall, the Temple des Augustins, included the *Symphonie fantastique*.
2 Conductor of the Grande Harmonie and of the Grand Théâtre, Brussels, and a fertile composer.

P.S. As soon as my *Traité d'instrumentation* appears you shall have a copy. I'll send you first the *Francs-juges* and the *Symphonie funèbre* which perhaps you'll be able to put on somewhere in the open air.[1]

154 *To his sister Nanci Pal*   Paris, 23 October 1842

My dear sister,

I've arrived from Frankfurt after giving two successful and profitable concerts in Brussels. My arrival in Germany was to have been heralded by two letters from Meyerbeer which were lost, so that I turned up in Frankfurt out of the blue to find that no preparations had been made for my concerts. But the theatre director insisted on making up for this contretemps and has put a large-scale organization into effect to produce two splendid evening occasions in which large extracts will be heard from my *Requiem* together with my first two symphonies. As a result, and to give him a month to get everything ready, I left all my music there and returned by diligence to reassure Harriet who was really ill and *desperate* because of my absence, and particularly because of the way I'd left her. I'd departed without warning and had merely left her a letter to tell her I'd gone, otherwise I should never have got away from Paris. This ordeal has hardened her in respect of my forthcoming travels and I shan't have to hide them from her any more.

My visit to Belgium was a brilliant success. I had an audience with the King and the members of the artistic world vied with each other to fête me.

In Frankfurt, as soon as people heard my name I received the warmest, I might even say the most respectful of welcomes. I also found several old Paris friends there. The journey down the Rhine is wonderful and all those old castles, those ruins and gloomy mountains sent me into a waking dream, lulled by memories of Goethe's poems and Hoffmann's tales. It's one of the most beautiful travel impressions I've ever had. I was also amused to hear long dissertations at table about *me*, held in English between some sons of Albion who were on their way from Brussels where they'd heard me and who didn't recognize me. So I'm going back to Germany and from there I'll go to Prussia in a few weeks. I'll write to you before I leave the second time.

My best wishes to Camille, who abandons you without fear or remorse. *I've received the money.*

Let me know as soon as you can about poor Adèle. Her health seems

---

1 Marie Recio added a thankyou message of her own to this letter.

to have been bad for some time. My uncle and my father must be harvesting the grapes if not pressing them by now. Embrace both of them for me.

This is an utterly empty letter . . . I'm still in a whirl from the speed of events during my travels.

H. B.

155 *To his sister Adèle Suat* Paris, 24 November 1842

Dear, good little sister,

It's been a long time since I personally gave you any news from us. I'm glad to say yours reaches me regularly, but it doesn't seem to me it's been very good for some months . . . How are you now? Are you a little better? Your children cause you delight and are the death of you at the same time. Luckily your husband treats you, I'm sure, with the greatest care and tenderness and on your own behalf I thank him most warmly. Harriet sends you her love and her affectionate best wishes.

I've just made a short musical journey to Belgium and Frankfurt, and now I'm all set to go back there. But this time it will be for longer. I have to make the grand tour including Vienna and Berlin. Two concerts are being organized for me in Frankfurt for Christmastide. I shall give a third concert in Brussels on my way through; and as a farewell to Paris last week, I put on at the Opéra my *Grande symphonie funèbre*, the one I wrote for the July celebrations, with an additional chorus.[1] The performance was marvellous and a resounding success. I was recalled twice and had to walk out on to the fore-stage after the *Apothéose* which had been interrupted by applause long before the end. Even the boxes, which at the Opéra never harbour applause, were in an uproar. In short, success was complete.

As usual I was on my own, as Harriet was feeling too unwell that evening to attend.

Adieu, dear good sister, my best wishes to your excellent husband. On behalf of us all I embrace your pretty little daughters.

Your affectionate brother,

H. Berlioz

1 On 7 November at the Opéra, with Habeneck conducting. A choral entry was added at the end of the last movement, with words by Antoni Deschamps.

Paris, between 1
and 10 December 1842

You wish to know what is happening in what is called 'the musical
world'; on any count, I am the least well-qualified person to give you
this information. To know that world you have, first of all, to live in it,
and I have to admit that for some months I've escaped from it, just as
Bertrand, Robert's trusty Pylades, escaped not long ago from the
prisons of Lyon.[2] What little I do know on the subject I have 'picked up
in society', the sort of thing one could wholeheartedly confide only to
readers of certain newspapers which are no longer read and never have
been. So I ask you, in all good faith, even if your journal no longer has
thirty thousand subscribers, as one of your devotees assured me the
other day, could there be anything more indiscreet than a young
sylphide like yours, elegant, smart, radiant, smiling, perfumed, winged
and armed with a golden lyre at least as sonorous as the brazen
trumpet of her old grandmother, the dotard Fame? . . . Come on, do me
the justice of doing me justice! Admit that I can't tell you anything
about what I don't know and very little about what I do. What could I
discuss in my article? Concerts, singing courses at the Opéra-Comique
and the other opera theatres, the music section of the Institut and
composers, child prodigies, musical news-sheets, strings of virtuosos
and shooting stars!

Now, mark me well.

As to concerts, there aren't any, it's such a bad season for them that
even Musard[3] has disappeared. And whatever the experts may say,
Musard is not, alas, like the mountains Victor Hugo tells us of,
'mountains whose summits are so high that the last rays of centuries
long since vanished below the horizon shine upon them still'![4]

No, no, and once again alas, no, one may lift up one's eyes but
nothing shining is to be seen, not even Musard . . . 'Is he king upon
some island?'[5] In any case, where concerts are concerned, you know
the language we are allowed to use, both we who pay for them and you
who *give* them! It's always: 'M. So-and-So played a fantasy on the
clarinet which delighted the audience. M. So-and-So possesses a

---

1 Editor of *La sylphide*. This letter was clearly written for publication, and it appeared in
the second December issue of that journal.
2 An allusion to *Robert Macaire*, the popular boulevard play.
3 Conductor of highly successful promenade concerts.
4 A phrase applied by Hugo to Dante and Shakespeare.
5 Also Victor Hugo, from *Les rayons et l'ombre*.

marvellous talent. Mlle So-and-So played an air and variations on the piano which was unanimously applauded; the talent of this young person is highly remarkable. Every day the art of singing makes extraordinary progress, as we can see from the manner, both skilful and graceful, in which Mlle ***, one of M. ***'s best pupils, sang the famous cavatina "Au clair de la lune" with solo bassoon accompaniment. The bassoon part was excellently (or admirably, or magnificently, or sublimely, or any other adverb which lies) *sung* by M. ***, the father of the interesting singer. M. ***'s place in the Institut awaits him. We are told that this great artist has finally decided to publish his complete works for the bassoon. That will surely be an epoch-making concert!!!' [. . .]

The other day I saw a child prodigy who really astonished me; and I swear to you no deceit was required to persuade us of his qualities. He's only seven years old, dear sir. When he was placed before the piano to IMPROVISE, he struck two or three wrong chords. Then, turning to his father, he repeated on the spur of the moment the famous phrase uttered by Kalkbrenner's son: 'Papa, I've forgotten the rest.' This child will go far! [. . .]

Liszt is in Germany, Ernst is in Germany, Artôt is in Germany, the little Millanollo girls are in Germany, Hauman is in Germany, Rubini is in Germany, Doehler is in Germany, I am going to Germany; we'll all stay there until the spring; what a fine winter for dilettanti . . . in Paris!!! . . .

Yours ever,
H. Berlioz

Berlioz left Paris on 12 December 1842 with Marie Recio and went first to Brussels, where no concert was given. From there he went to Mainz and Frankfurt, but despite his plans no concerts were given there either. The first concert was on 29 December in Stuttgart, the second on 2 January 1843 in Hechingen, the seat of the Prince of Hohenzollern, and the third on 13 January in Mannheim. Thence they returned to Frankfurt.

157 *To Auguste Morel*[1]   Frankfurt, 16 January 1843

Feel for me, my dear Morel; Marie wanted to sing at Mannheim and at Stuttgart and at Hechingen. The first two times it was bearable, but the last! . . . and the very thought of another singer made her indignant.

From Frankfurt Berlioz left for Weimar on 17 January without inform-
ing Marie, but she discovered his whereabouts and followed him there.
There was a concert in Weimar on 25 January, and then they pro-
ceeded to Leipzig, where Mendelssohn, whom Berlioz had known in
Italy, was conductor of the Gewandhaus orchestra.

158 *To Felix Mendelssohn*   Weimar, 23 January 1843

My dear Mendelssohn,
    It's a long time since we last saw each other and we have probably, in our search for beauty, followed different paths, whether parallel or divergent. I have nonetheless no compunction in asking you for your help in getting a public hearing for some of my compositions in Leipzig.
    Would that be possible? When and how and on what conditions?
    Please write me a couple of lines on this subject as soon as you can, because I'm giving a concert here the day after tomorrow and depend-ing on your reply I will either leave for Leipzig immediately or remain in Weimar until matters are arranged in Dresden, where I'm also going.
    All best wishes
    in a modern version . . . of the ancient Roman.
    H. Berlioz

159 *To Jean-Baptiste Chelard*[2]   Leipzig, 2 February 1843

My dear Chelard,
    Would you be kind enough to go to the Erbprinz Hotel and rescue a rather nice waistcoat which I must have left there, as it wasn't in my trunk when I arrived here. It's the one I was wearing the day of the

1 One of Berlioz's close friends, Morel was a composer who left Paris in 1850 to direct the Conservatoire in his home town of Marseille. The following fragment is all that survives of the letter.
2 Chelard was a French composer whom Berlioz had known in the 1820s. In 1830 he moved to Munich and then in 1836 to Weimar, where he conducted the court orchestra.

concert, it's a dark reddish colour. It must have been found in my room. Then send it on to me by the quickest means you can (Leipzig, Hotel Bavaria). I've been in Dresden where everything is ready. I'm giving a concert here on Saturday. I've already had one rehearsal, the orchestra is admirable, excellent, and so is Mendelssohn.

I'm dreadfully tired after travelling 175 miles today on a train.[1]

All the best.

I'll write to you less hurriedly after the concert.

Remember me to Mme Chelard and all your family.

Yours,

H. Berlioz

P.S. The black eyes[2] send their regards.

160 *To Felix Mendelssohn*   Leipzig, 2 February 1843

To the chief Mendelssohn

Great chief,

We promised to exchange our tomahawks; here's mine! It is rough, yours is simple. Only squaws and palefaces like ornamented weapons. Be my brother! and when the great Spirit has sent us hunting in the land of souls, may our warriors hang our tomahawks together over the door of the meeting-house.[3]

H. Berlioz

161 *To Auguste Morel*   Dresden, 18 February 1843

My dear Morel,

I'm extremely worried; I wrote to my wife from Weimar, sending her a 200-franc note, on the 27th of last month and I've had no reply to that letter. I'm writing to her again today sending her a 500-franc note. When you get this letter, will you please go to my house and find out whether the two notes have reached her and why no one has written to me. I had a letter from her in Leipzig but before my first letter could

---

1 To Dresden and back. The railway network was expanding at precisely the moment when Berlioz stood to benefit greatly from it.

2 Marie.

3 One of Berlioz's most celebrated letters, this note accompanied his baton as a gift to Mendelssohn in exchange for the one with which Mendelssohn had been rehearsing his *Walpurgisnacht* in Berlioz's presence. Berlioz told the story in his *Mémoires* and reprinted the letter there, remarking on its allusion to Fenimore Cooper's *The Last of the Mohicans*.

have reached Paris. I should be most grateful if you would write and let me know at once what is happening at home, *poste-restante* at Leipzig.

I've just given two magnificent and financially productive concerts in the large theatre in Dresden. The greatest stir was caused by two movements from the *Requiem* (the *Offertoire* with the choir singing on two notes) and the *Sanctus*, in which the solo tenor part was sung by the famous German tenor Tichatschek, by the *Symphonie funèbre* with two orchestras and choir, and by the cantata *Le cinq mai* on the death of the Emperor. This was splendidly sung by Wächter, the bass from the theatre, an excellent singer and a man of refined musical feeling. *Harold*, in which Lipinski played the viola solo, and the *Symphonie fantastique* also made quite an impression on the public and the performers.

The day after my first concert Dresden's military bands came and woke me up with an aubade which led, as you can imagine, to the serious consumption of glasses of punch. They're all full of the wildest enthusiasm which they can only express by shaking hands and by bowings and embracings, since I don't know a word of German.

I also gave a fine, if unproductive concert in Leipzig. I'm going back there to conduct the last scene of *Roméo et Juliette*, for which Mendelssohn is training the chorus in my absence.[1] Then I'll be going to Berlin where Meyerbeer is expecting me.

Write and tell George Hainl[2] that if the festival takes place in May I shall be there, provided he offers terms I can accept, because I have to say I've no desire to spend my own money getting to Lyon. I'd also like to have something else played other than the *Symphonie funèbre* and to conduct my music and to know what the orchestral forces are.

Don't say a word in your reply about M, because she came after me and rejoined me at Weimar; I'll tell you all about it. Write to me as though I hadn't written you this letter. All your news will be thought of as coming spontaneously from you.

Adieu, all my best wishes. We shall have a lot to talk about on my return.

Yours ever,
H. Berlioz

---

1 At the second Leipzig concert, on 23 February, the *Offertoire* from the *Requiem* made a profound impression on Schumann, with whom Berlioz spent a good deal of time during his visit.
2 Conductor of the Grand Théâtre, Lyon.

My dear Morel,

Thank you for your letter and the details it contains. Do write to me when you have time, I should be delighted to hear from you. I've arrived here from Hamburg where I didn't know a soul. I gave a large concert there which was an enormous success.[1] I was recalled twice at the end of the evening. The performances (and really excellent they were, carried off with quite unusual polish and aplomb) were of *Harold*, *Le cinq mai* in German, the overture to the *Francs-juges*, *L'invitation à la valse*, the *Romance* for violin which I wrote for Artôt[2] and which was gracefully and elegantly played by M. Lindenau if not with outstanding artistry, the *Offertoire* and *Quaerens me* from the *Requiem*, the cavatina from *Benvenuto*[3] and two *Romances*, including *L'absence*[4] which I have orchestrated in the key of F sharp and which is ten times more effective like that than it is on the piano. Mme Cornet, the wife of the theatre director, sang the cavatina; for *Le cinq mai* I had Reichel, a prodigious bass who goes down to low B:

M sang the two *Romances* and the one in F sharp very well. This letter is for you alone, naturally. If you mention the Hamburg concert, make it very laconic because I'm afraid the Parisian public must be beginning to tire of my dispatches from the front.

Let me have news of my *Traité d'instrumentation*, which you can get from Schonenberger when you can.[5] Tell him, if it's not too late, not to engrave the full score example taken from my *Reine Mab* scherzo, because the violin harmonics have been wrongly copied. At the very least ask him to leave the bars where these notes come blank. I'll straighten them out when I get back.

It looks as though the Opéra's *ultimo giorno* is on the way. It's imminent for all theatres of this kind because they're all equally bad. A

---

1 On 22 March 1843. On the way to Hamburg he also gave a concert in Brunswick on 9 March.
2 The *Rêverie et caprice*.
3 Teresa's Cavatina in Act I, 'Entre l'amour et le devoir'.
4 The fourth song of *Les nuits d'été*.
5 Berlioz had left the *Traité* in the hands of the publisher Schonenberger to be printed while he was away.

thousand good evenings to Desmarest to compensate him for the bad ones he spends at the opera.[1] Schlesinger is still threatened with financial disaster and his brother here is in despair about his involvement with Halévy.[2]

Adieu.

All best wishes to Delord and to the friends of Le Divan.

H. Berlioz

163 *To the musicians of the Royal Chapel in Berlin*[3] Berlin,
24 April 1843

Messieurs,

I cannot leave without expressing to you my gratitude for the manner in which you have welcomed me. Despite your heavy burden of work, you have brought to my compositions all the energy and all the patience imaginable, and you have performed them with an intelligence and a verve that are beyond praise. Please believe, gentlemen, that I shall never forget what I owe you and that I carry away with me the liveliest admiration for your talents.

I remain, Messieurs,

Yours sincerely and gratefully,

Hector Berlioz

Berlioz left Berlin on 26 April. He gave a concert in Hanover and another in Darmstadt and arrived back in Paris at the end of May after an absence of five and a half months.

164 *To his sister Adèle Suat* Paris, 8 June 1843

Dear little sister,

Will you forgive me for being so slow in replying to your charming letter which reached me in Berlin? I hope so. I've been so busy, so preoccupied, so absent-minded, so overworked, so fêted and so ill during this long and difficult journey!!! But now I'm back again and all my friends are delighted at what they're kind enough to call my brilliant tour of Germany. I also know that many people are furious

1 Desmarest was a cellist in the Opéra orchestra.
2 The Berlin music publisher Heinrich Schlesinger was the brother of Berlioz's Paris publisher Maurice Schlesinger.
3 Berlioz gave two concerts in Berlin, both highly successful.

about it. But I gave my father some details the other day which I'm sure he'll have passed on to you.

I was very happy to get your letter; your style of writing, dear little sister, makes my own letters seem stupid beside yours which are so straightforward and full of feeling! ... Harriet has often said to me how sorry she is not to be able to write to you in French. She was extremely touched by your offer to have her to stay with you in St-Chamond while I was away, and I thank you sincerely on my own behalf. Now I have to return to my Parisian activities, my boring articles, my half-criticisms, correcting the proofs of the works of mine that are being published,[1] etc, until the concert season is upon us.

My uncle[2] was still here when I returned, and I saw him over a period of four or five days; he's looking younger.

I believe Dufeuillant[3] is in Paris. He's angry with me for not replying to one of his letters. I can't go and see him as I don't know his address. I'm counting on your husband to persuade him to accept the continued activity of my travels and an understandably concomitant absent-mindedness as an excuse for my silence.

Your children are well, I hope; Harriet often talks to me of your peaceful, happy family; she's envious of it. Louis is really grown-up and intends to write you a nice letter so that you can judge his progress for yourself. Harriet is looking sad again because I've had two invitations from the Philharmonic Society of London to go and conduct a concert there. But that journey isn't definitely fixed; I haven't had a reply to my letter stating my musical and financial conditions.[4]

We both send our best wishes to your good husband and send quite *inordinate* embraces to your little girls and yourself.

Adieu, dear sister,

Your most affectionate brother,

H. Berlioz

165 *To his sister Nanci Pal*   Paris, 12 July 1843

Dear sister,

Thank you for your complaints; they prove that you attach some importance to my letters. But you must know that I always see my

---

1 Currently in press were the *Grand traité d'instrumentation*, the *Symphonie fantastique* and the *Grande symphonie funèbre et triomphale*.
2 Félix Marmion.
3 A childhood friend from La Côte.
4 Berlioz did not arrange a visit to London until 1847.

correspondence with all of you as being collective and, as I'd written to my father and to Adèle since I came back to Paris, my conscience as regards you was clear. Even so, I confess my guilt and *I shall not do it again*.

You're in the country, at the foot of your wall of rock, warmed by a heat that has claims to being sultry; even though the sun here this year is rather cool, I don't imagine your domain is exactly refreshing. You must be bored; and why should you not be bored when everything in the world is bored? I should like to go on my travels all over again; I should like to see again all those German orchestras which here I feel the lack of daily. I should like to earn some money, which again I shall always feel a terrible lack of, and it's only outside Paris that I've *won* it (for money represents victory) until now.

What can I tell you? I'm being pulled in all directions ... The director of the Opéra wants me to write an opera in two or three acts, while he waits for the everlasting *Nonne* which Scribe won't finish, because small operas don't have their own fixed place and can be put on whenever the director likes. I've agreed;[1] but Armand Bertin and my serious friends are against it, saying I must *on no account* write a small work, because they never succeed, witness the most charming of them all, Rossini's *Le comte Ory*[2] which has never made money, etc ... They're right. One must be patient. But, as Hamlet says: while the grass grows, the horse grows too![3]

And then the Opéra is at bay, Halévy's last success (*Charles VI*)[4] has killed it.

You can see that music is not at present in a rosy state in Paris, and that even so it's full of very sharp thorns ... that's not just a figure of speech. Camille would have been delighted last week, there was a revival of *Oedipe à Colonne*,[5] his favourite masterpiece. No one went ... Now I'm ill! If anyone were to make me consul in Tahiti or in Nouka-Hiva I'd be away under full sail.

The Duchesse d'Orléans has just sent me a rather valuable bronze piece. It's a present in return for the symphony I dedicated to the Duc d'Orléans.[6]

---

1 The project of a two- or three-act opera never came to anything.
2 Composed for the Opéra in 1828.
3 Berlioz cites *Hamlet* as it was given by the English company in 1827, but Shakespeare's text is: 'Ay, sir, but "while the grass grows", – the proverb is something musty.'
4 First performed on 15 March 1843 while Berlioz was away, *Charles VI* had over a hundred performances in its first production.
5 By Sacchini, first played in 1786.
6 The *Grande symphonie funèbre et triomphale*.

Adieu, dear sister, forgive me for writing you such a sad letter. As soon as I feel cheerful I'll write you one full of nonsense.

H. B.

166 *To his sister Nanci Pal* Paris, 12 August 1843

What it is to arrive *on time*! Herewith my immediate reply. I was stirred, troubled, moved by your letter! You are a good sister, I love you; you have feeling and intelligence! I wish I could write to you *as you expect me to*, I'd have a thousand things to say to you! But a thousand is too much! One would need volumes for that and 'I'm fearful of large works', as was the excellent La Fontaine.[1] I'm in the middle of writing a series of letters in the *Débats* on my visit to Germany; the first of these letters will be published tomorrow.[2] You wouldn't believe the trouble I have writing these *partial* accounts (because one can't tell the general public everything), these souvenirs which ... enough, enough, let's not pursue that subject. More to the point, in Stuttgart I had to go and see a lady (because I was ill-bred enough not to have replied to her very friendly letter) called Ducrest who gave concerts like those you hear in musical snuffboxes; this doughty singer of *Romances* wrote to say that she had had the honour of making your acquaintance, but even so I did not set about making hers. [...]

This morning I met an architect who has been to the South Sea Islands and he assured me that I wouldn't find nature in the tropics beautiful for longer than a fortnight; he says it's three times as boring as Paris. In that case I refuse the post of consul in Tahiti. I now know that Tahitian women are Protestants! The horror of it! If they were Roman Catholics at least!! ... And what's more, they've got into the habit of dressing themselves, which is highly indecent when one dresses oneself as they do. In Nouka-Hiva, the same silly habits apply, more or less. So, all things considered, I'm staying in Paris; people dress themselves and protest about it more.

The Opéra is tottering, it's giddy! I only wish it could regain its strength and balance, because Pillet is truly on my side and I shall never find a director who's better disposed towards me. One of these evenings Duprez will spit his lungs out. In *Guillaume Tell* he's frightening!

1 La Fontaine in fact wrote: 'I am fearful of long works.'
2 These articles eventually formed the section in the *Mémoires* entitled 'Travels in Germany, I'.

Adieu, dear sister. Harriet, who declares you to be a superior kind of woman (forgive me for not beating about the bush), greets you and is more than ever sorry not to be able to write to you.

My best wishes to Camille and to my niece,

H. Berlioz

167 *To his sister Nanci Pal*   Paris, 6 or 7 September 1843

Dear sister,

[...] I'm putting on a festival on the 14th in aid of a musicians' society I belong to.[1] I've asked Spontini for the second act of *La vestale* and have begged him to conduct the performance himself. This poor, great man has gone appallingly mad. He sees himself surrounded by conspiracies; he claims that a cabal is being organized for the day of the concert. He knows for certain that the fire at the Berlin opera house is a punishment from God, brought on by the injustices that have been done to him[2] . . . Two days ago I walked with him as far as the foyer of the Opéra reasoning with him as one would with a child, urging him to be calm, proving to him that he was being *absurd*, that on the contrary all the musicians in Paris are devoted to him and that even if they weren't they would still do what I wanted. Where on earth has his genius run off to? . . . How was this man able, as he did, to set to music the two most intense and noble passions of the human heart: love and enthusiasm? Never mind, he wrote *La vestale* and *Cortez*, he was sublime, he has a right to our respect, to our most devoted homage. The beautiful is so beautiful! And despite the rapid progress of the art of music in some areas, the longer I live the more I admire Spontini's masterpieces.

Mention the good Donizetti in the same breath as him! . . . Rossini is still here, sulking, because he wasn't given a hero's welcome when he arrived. He's going to leave and go back to eat and sleep in Bologna. I haven't seen him. The Opéra is in disarray, Duprez and the money-lenders will soon have brought it to its knees. [. . .]

Adieu, dear sister, I have to give an account of Dresden for Sunday, so I leave you.

H. Berlioz

1 This was postponed and then cancelled (see p. 199).
2 The royal opera house in Berlin burned down on 18 April 1843.

168 *To Théophile Gautier*   Paris, between 7 and 12 November 1843

My dear Thé (other people say Théo; I take off the 'o' and only keep the 'thé') – first piece of folly![1] I'm giving a concert – second folly! Now commit the third folly of announcing it so as to get the public to commit the fourth and largest, that of coming to it.[2]

In your column you can go on at length about my visit to Germany, then say that on Sunday the 19th at the Conservatoire Duprez, Massol and Mme Gras-Dorus will sing a grand trio of my devising;[3] Duprez will sing *Absence* by M. Th. Gautier, a highly promising poet (with orchestra). I orchestrated this piece in Dresden, it hasn't yet been heard in Paris.

There'll be a violin solo[4] played by Alard. Then the overture to *Le roi Lear*, the symphony *Harold*, the *Reine Mab* scherzo and the finale of the *Symphonie funèbre* (the *Apothéose*) with the two orchestras.

I must also ask the young, highly promising poet to come to the rehearsal on Saturday if he has time, such is my impatience to have him hear the song *Absence* rendered thus by the orchestra and Duprez.

Adieu,
All best wishes,
H. Berlioz

169 *To Queen Marie-Amélie*
To Her Majesty the Queen of the French   Paris, 14 November 1843

Madame,

Permit me to bring to Your Majesty's notice the concert that I am giving next Sunday in the Salle du Garde-meuble. I should be very happy if it were of sufficient interest for the Queen of the French to deign to do me the honour which was accorded me recently by almost all the sovereigns of Germany, that of coming to hear my works.

I am with the deepest respect, Madame,
Your Majesty's
very humble servant and subject,
Hector Berlioz

1 Berlioz puns on o = eau = water and thé = tea.
2 Gautier wrote a regular column in *La presse*, but he was away in London and did not get Berlioz's letter in time to announce the concert.
3 These three singers were reunited to sing the Trio from Act I of *Benvenuto Cellini*, all singing their original roles.
4 The *Rêverie et caprice*.

Dear sister,

This time I haven't a moment to spare for writing rubbish (forgive me). I reply to you purely out of politeness. I send you a letter from Louis telling you in his own fashion about my concert. A staggering, breathtaking success, with a small profit despite the enormous expenses. I've had a letter from Spontini who has nothing good to say of anything and who had never paid me a compliment in his life; here's the beginning, half in Latin, a quarter in Italian and a quarter in French:

'Vivat! terque quaterque vivat!! You first of all, my very dear Berlioz, for your gigantic, fantastic, astounding compositions, quite in keeping with your genius, and your brave and exceedingly stout-hearted army for their perfect and utterly admirable performance in the ultimate sense of those words!' What a sentence! but it would be hateful and wrong of me to pass comment on the strangeness of the style when the opinion Spontini wanted to express makes me so happy.

Yes, as I said to him yesterday, it was one of my life's dreams to move the composer of *La vestale* and I've succeeded in doing it.

What's more, in several weeks' time I shall have the good fortune to conduct the second act of this masterpiece at the Opéra, at the Festival of the Musicians' Association.[1] I had originally asked Spontini to take my place for this part of the programme and he had agreed, but now he's relying on me to conduct *La vestale* because his bad relations with Léon Pillet don't allow him to appear in public at the Opéra. There'll be *five hundred* of us at least; it'll be superb. The committee has just sent a letter to all the singing actors and actresses in Paris, inviting them to take part in the choruses; we'll see if they have the courage to accept ... I doubt it.

To return to the concert last Sunday, I've never seen a concert hall in such an uproar; hats in the air, the orchestra interrupted, encores, etc ...

You mention Duffeuillant's marriage, I don't know anything about it. Much good may it do him!

Give all my love to father; is he going to Grenoble this winter? I haven't seen M. Rocher, I don't know any details of your life at La Côte. [. . .]

Forgive me, dear sister, for this disorganized letter. I'm thrown into a

---

1 This concert never took place.

turmoil by I know not what, nothing and everything. It's in the air! It's what I did yesterday, what I'm doing today, what I shall have to do tomorrow that's pressing on me and making me agitated in this way.

Adieu, another time I'll make more sense.

Yours,

H. Berlioz

Greetings to Camille!

171 *To Georges-Henri Vernoy de St-Georges*[1]   Paris, ?early 1844

My dear St-Georges,

I wrote a note addressed to you at home about the role of Griselda which M. Crosnier mentioned to Mlle Recio as suiting her perfectly; I am now asking for it on her behalf. See if it's possible for you to give it to her.[2]

I'll see you this evening very probably.

Yours ever,

H. Berlioz

172 *To Louis Schlösser*[3]   Paris, 28 January 1844

My dear Schlösser,

I have to admit this is a rather late reply to your kind letter! But what can one do? Life in Paris is organized in such a way that none of us can ever do what we most want to and troubles, worries, labours, projects and ventures take up our attention, our time and everything. Twenty times I've said to myself: 'Tomorrow I must write to Schlösser' and this tomorrow has not come until today ... and even now I'm not sure about it. But I will at least try.

The musician you sent to me didn't leave his name or the place where he's staying; he's been back several times without finding me in and I haven't seen him again. I hope he's found a position that suits him, even though the Paris orchestras are overflowing with players and hangers-on.

---

1 After Scribe, St-Georges was the most sought-after librettist of the day.
2 This letter shows Berlioz attempting to promote the career of Marie Recio, now almost at its end. In December 1843 the Opéra-Comique, of which Crosnier was the director, staged Flotow's *L'esclave de Camoëns* on a libretto by St-Georges. It was rumoured that one of the singers was leaving the production.
3 After his studies in Paris with Kreutzer and Le Sueur, when he and Berlioz met, Schlösser returned to Darmstadt, where Berlioz had seen him again the previous May.

I've given my first concert at the Conservatoire and I'm organizing another for next week in a concert hall you don't know (Herz's). I've written a new overture for it, a scena with chorus and two other pieces.[1] I've got my usual orchestra but I'm anxious even so, as we have to play the programme on a single rehearsal ... I wish I could obtain the patience and concentration in Paris which the orchestral players in Darmstadt proved themselves so capable of. We should work better and produce some amazing performances. At the first concert we had two rehearsals and everything went with a tremendous swing. Perhaps we shall be lucky enough to steer clear of danger this time, but the risk is considerable, you'll agree.

What's happening in Darmstadt? Have you read my last letter in the *Débats* in which I described my visit to you? It's all being published now in book form and I'm endlessly correcting proofs.[2] At the moment Richault is engraving the score of *Le cinq mai* in German and French. I must send it to you as you have Reichel to sing it. Mlle Recio has been engaged by the Opéra-Comique, she sang twice with great success last week in another theatre in charity performances; but she's going to write you a few lines to tell you about it. [. . .]

Adieu, my dear Schlösser, write to me from time to time, please. I'm capable of replying by return of post despite appearances. It's not impossible I may see you this summer, there are plans here for a large musical enterprise which could well bring me to Baden ... and then ... we could go and drink some more milk on your mountain. I hope so.[3]

Meanwhile I shake you by the hand and send you 132 most sincere best wishes.

H. Berlioz

---

1 The concert in the Salle Herz took place on 3 February 1844. The new overture was *Le carnaval romain*, constructed out of themes from *Benvenuto Cellini*. The concert was remarkable also for two other features. Marguerite's *Romance*, from the *Huit scènes de Faust*, was announced but cancelled when Mme Nathan, the singer, was taken ill. Reviving this piece may have been the first step toward the composition of *La damnation de Faust*, begun the following year. It was also the first concert at which a saxophone was heard. Berlioz had arranged his *Chant sacré* for six Sax instruments and orchestra, including two new saxhorns (described as 'cylinder bugles') and a saxophone, at that time a very large bass instrument akin to the ophicleide.
2 The *Voyage musical en Allemagne et en Italie* was published in two volumes in 1844.
3 This proposal came to nothing.

To the Minister of the Interior[1]   Paris, 26 February 1844

Dear Minister,

Pardon me for thus appealing directly to your goodwill on my own behalf, but I am forced to do so by the excessive difficulty of my position which, strange and exceptional as it is, and very different from what it is generally believed to be, had already attracted the attention and interest of one of your predecessors. M. le Comte de Montalivet, learning that I was very far from being able to exploit the faculties and experience which he was kind enough to credit me with, and being informed of my inability to set myself to any large-scale composition since I had no steady income even for as little as a few months, had promised to help me out of my difficulties. M. Armand Bertin and M. Cavé in turn came on his behalf to inform me of his intentions and of the means he had in mind to fulfil them. It was a question of appointing me to a post at the Conservatoire with a salary which would have permitted me to work in peace of mind and in a manner truly useful to art. But as M. de Montalivet left the Ministry of the Interior shortly afterwards, the only result of his promises was my appointment as Librarian of the Conservatoire, with a salary of 118 francs a month. That is all the fixed income that I have.

I have therefore to keep writing pointless articles in various newspapers and devoting my energies, against my will, to empty critical endeavours which have no value or effect since I cannot write freely, but which are my only means of livelihood. I am a composer and I do not have the time to compose! To the extent that I cannot continue with the large work I began for the Opéra two years ago and, when its turn to be performed comes shortly, I shall not know how to find the time to finish it and arrange for its production.

Both in France and in Germany I have gained wide experience of conducting large numbers of performers, and I have no choir or orchestra to conduct.

I do not think it is gross conceit on my part to consider myself capable of teaching harmony, instrumentation and composition in general, far more than certain unknown professors at the Conservatoire; and I have never been able, in that establishment, to obtain so much as a class in *solfège*!

When, very occasionally, I do manage to write some medium-sized musical work, it is normally enough to assure that, when performed, it

1 Count Duchâtel.

is financially successful despite the enormous costs involved; this is because of the interest aroused in the general public by my compositions. But as I am continually interrupted and continually distracted by occupations hateful to art and artist alike, I sometimes have to spend a year writing something which in happier and more normal circumstances I would finish in two months. It is harsh to be forced to admit that *I have no time to work* and that I am producing almost nothing of what it is in my power to produce!

Pardon me, Minister, for inflicting the bizarre difficulties of my life upon you and for asking your help in overcoming them; they are difficulties all the more cruel for being generally disbelieved, since everywhere in Europe where my name is known people imagine me to have financial resources which I am very far from possessing.

You will perhaps regard it as right and just to accomplish what M. de Montalivet began, by allowing me to exercise my energies in their proper sphere instead of diverting them from their course dishonourably and to no good artistic purpose.

The creation for me of an instrumentation class at the Conservatoire would help me to attain this end. Is it presumptuous of me to hope for such a thing?[1]

I am, Minister, with profound respect,
Your most humble and obedient servant,
Hector Berlioz

174 *To Franz Liszt*   Paris, 16 March 1844

My dear Liszt,

You have so frequently offered to assist me in giving my concerts that this time I accept. I'm told you're due to arrive on the 22nd of this month, and for 6 April next, a day when the Royal Theatres are closed, I've hired the theatre of the Opéra-Comique for a splendid evening occasion with 180 performers. If, without interfering with your other plans, you can play at least one item at this, you will assure the success of the enterprise. I'm expecting to have two Italian singers, Salvi and la Brambilla together with some others. Alard will play the Beethoven Violin Concerto, the rest of the programme belongs to me. Reply to this as soon as you receive it; so far I've announced only the date and place of the concert and I'm anxious to

---

1 It was. Berlioz never obtained a teaching post at the Conservatoire.

be able to publish the programme. Prices are double.[1]

All best wishes,
Hector Berlioz

175 *To his sister Nanci Pal*   Paris, 19 May 1844

Dear sister,

I have no idea now when I last wrote to you; but anyway, as you say, it doesn't do to hold it against me too seriously. My life is unbelievable. It's one long act of somnambulism. Torments all day and all night, bouts of rage and pity simultaneously; then a cessation of feeling and complete indifference.[2] I hear nothing, feel nothing; and through it all I'm engaged in more artistic endeavours than ever before, apart from composition, which has been put to one side. I've just given my fourth concert, which everyone says was the best in Paris for ten years.[3] I was amazed by the performance; my great devil of an orchestra was sublime! No question but it leaves most German orchestras desperately far behind; Liszt was marvellous and the proceeds (12,000 francs) sensational; my profit altogether was 6000 francs, expenses and the poor tax[4] took the rest.

I've been asked to go to Baden this summer to conduct the festival which is going to take place there; I've had a request from Milan to go there as well and give some concerts in September, when they're holding the North Italian Scientific Congress, but everyone tells me the Milan players have as much chance of playing eight bars of my music as I have of playing a Liszt fantasy on the piano. I've had approaches from Lyon too;[5] and as well as all that I've got to finish my book on Italy,[6] correct proofs of my symphonies and organize a huge project which I'll tell you about if it comes to anything and which, on its own, will cause more uproar than everything I've done so far.[7]

1 Liszt was on tour in Germany, entangled – it was said – with the celebrated 'Spanish dancer' Lola Montes. He did not get back to Paris until 5 April and could not play in this concert. In the event the singers and the programme were considerably changed.
2 However long relations with Harriet may have been deteriorating (for at least two years, one may suppose), things came to a head in 1844. Berlioz's sister Nanci was his closest confidante.
3 On 4 May 1844 in the Théâtre-Italien, with Liszt playing.
4 A tax was levied on theatre and concert receipts for the benefit of the poor, an imposition which Berlioz, being poor himself, greatly resented.
5 He did not go to Baden that year, nor to Milan, but he did get to Lyon in July 1845.
6 The *Voyage musical en Allemagne et en Italie*.
7 The enormous concert given on 1 August 1844 in the Palais de l'Industrie with a thousand musicians performing. Berlioz composed his *Hymne à la France* for the occasion.

The King of Prussia has written to me. I had his letter yesterday in which he says he is sending me a gold snuffbox and the grand gold medal of scientific merit; this is his way of thanking me for dedicating my *Traité d'instrumentation* to him.

My uncle has left; he came to my two concerts at the Opéra-Comique and the Théâtre-Italien. M. Burdet[1] was there too. He is, by his own account, a passionate admirer of great music.

What can I say about the business with uncle Victor? It's my father I'm worried about in all this. Adèle must be cross with me; but she's been out of touch for quite some time anyway.

All best wishes to Camille and my niece,

Adieu,

Your exhausted brother,

H. Berlioz

176 To Auguste Barbier   Paris, 14 June 1844

My dear poet,

I've at last found[2] the music for your magnificent hymn to France, and as of yesterday your name is posted on all the walls of Paris. I think it will be large enough and simple enough in form to support reasonably well the crushing weight of the parallel which is bound to be made between your words and my music. I've done my best. As to the performance, it will be on a fairly grand scale; there'll be (for the *Hymne à la France*) five or six hundred voices and four hundred instruments.

The last verse especially is orchestrated monumentally.

Come and see me one morning before ten o'clock and we'll talk.

All best wishes,

H. Berlioz

177 To Adolphe Dumas[3]   Paris, 14 June 1844

My dear Dumas,

Don't be too angry with me! I've made vain efforts to find something worthy of your poetry; I've had to give up. My inventions (if what I came

---

1 Husband of Berlioz's cousin Odile.

2 Berlioz often referred to the process of composition as 'finding' the music (see the next letter).

3 A minor poet and playwright, no relation of Alexandre Dumas. His *Chant des industriels*, having failed to inspire Berlioz, was set by Dumas's brother-in-law Amédée Méreaux and performed at the 1 August concert.

up with can be so described) were not worth a cuss, and the occasion is too important to risk failing, especially when it involves your fine lines.

All best wishes,
H. Berlioz

178 *To his sister Nanci Pal*   Paris, 23 June 1844

Dear sister,

Thank you for your kind letter, you mustn't mind that I'm slow replying, you have a fairly good idea why. The large festival I'm organizing for the end of July is a monstrously difficult undertaking; even so I hope to bring it off; my only real worry is about the receipts which will also have to be monstrous if I'm to make a profit. Anyway it's a battle that has to be joined. But my domestic life is more dreadful than ever; now there's not a moment's respite. I rented an apartment in the country; she stayed there a fortnight and on her return my torture began all over again. It's an impossible existence, with shouts and insults and curses and imprecations and recriminations, all so revolting and absurd that it would be enough to send me mad if I didn't know what was causing this insane behaviour. The cause is, since you must know the whole story, her now confirmed habit of drinking brandy. I regard the whole subject with unmitigated disgust, as you can imagine ... If you could see how disorganized she is, how she dresses and how she has abandoned all care over her appearance! She can't even manage to keep our accounts. She gets up in the middle of the night when she knows I'm asleep, comes into my bedroom, shuts the doors and begins to hurl invective at me for three hours at a stretch, sometimes until dawn; then next day she asks me to forgive her, swears that she loves me, that I could trample her underfoot without changing her affection for me; and in the evening it all starts again. It's truly intolerable. On his last visit to Paris, my uncle came to the house once. She refused to see him and he did not come back. I have to ask all my friends not to come either. If I'm lucky enough to make a profit out of the festival, I'll leave as soon as possible.

When Louis comes home from school, he says he needs his sleep, but it doesn't do any good. This fury has to take its course. The poor boy is becoming more affectionate than ever, and in spite of it all his mother loves him dearly, devotedly even ... This infernal habit is too strong for her; she has even got to the point where I have hardly been able to believe the servants when I've questioned them on the subject. Not that she denies the facts, but she claims that I am the cause of it all and that she needs this 'consolation'.

Pity me; I don't know how it will all end, but end it must.

Don't tell father anything, there's no point worrying him with such unhappy news. My life is in turmoil. Write me a few lines when you can.

Yours,
H. Berlioz

179 *To Robert Griepenkerl*[1]   Paris, 26 July 1844

My dear Mr Griepenkerl,

I am writing you these few lines in the middle of a musical storm, a storm of which I, however, am master and which, one must hope, will not wreck my ship. I have just organized the first Paris Festival; I have to conduct and rehearse 500 chorus singers and 480 instrumentalists. You can imagine the fever that is coursing through my bloodstream ... but the papers will give you the details. Allow me simply to shake your hand and thank you from the bottom of my heart for your warm sympathy. Nothing in the world is better able to give me patience, strength and courage than this parallelism between my thoughts and those of a mind as distinguished as your own. Thank you a thousand times for everything you have been kind enough to say and write about me. I cannot send out my symphony *Harold* at the moment, it is the property of Schlesinger who is going to publish it soon. The *Symphonie fantastique* is engraved and would appear within a month if I had time to correct the proofs. I will try and send you my new overture *Carnaval romain* soon; it's a wonderfully *wild* piece which had a *wild* success in Paris this winter.

Please thank M. Leibrock for me for his piano duet arrangement of the overture *Le roi Lear*, it is an admirable piano reduction.[2]

At the moment I am also publishing two volumes concerning my visits to Germany and Italy with various odd bits and stories. I will send them to you as soon as possible if you will tell me an *infallible* means of getting them to you.

Forgive this disorganized letter, I haven't slept for several nights. I

1 A writer and critic whom Berlioz met in Brunswick in 1843. In his admiration for Berlioz Griepenkerl wrote a small book, *Ritter Berlioz in Braunschweig*, the same year.
2 J. A. Leibrock, cellist and harpist from Brunswick, published a German translation of Berlioz's articles on instrumentation as well as his four-hand arrangement of *Le roi Lear*.

have already taken seven sectional rehearsals and I have a dozen or so more before the main dress rehearsal.

May I assure you, dear Griepenkerl, of the warm friendship I have had for you since our first meeting. I shall retain it always.

Your devoted,

H. Berlioz

Please write to me when you can, I do not need to tell you how happy I shall be to hear from you.

180 *To his father Dr Louis Berlioz*   Paris, 19 August 1844

Dear father,

You must be wondering about my silence since the great occasion of the festival ... I've written only six lines to my uncle, while I was taking a bath after escaping from the battle. It was an immense success for me, not that you would have realized it probably because of the papers you take, the *Siècle* and the *Revue des deux mondes*; if you would like to take the trouble to read the other, non-hostile ones, I'll send them to you. I also thought I had had a magnificent financial success, since my concert on the first day produced 37,000 francs! We were expecting the dance-concert at reduced prices, conducted by Strauss[1] on the second day, to attract a large audience of the middle and lower classes. It didn't turn out like that ... I had the satisfaction (a rather disagreeable one, even so) of seeing that music for the populace no longer commands an audience. Strauss's takings were only 2600 francs, and, as we were jointly responsible, the costs of the second concert had to be paid out of the takings of the first. Then, since artists (in France) are veritable serfs, liable for duty both in body and pocket, the administration of the Hospices came to exact from us a levy of 5000 francs and M. Delessert, the Prefect of Police, having sent me a veritable army of municipal guards, policemen, etc, to keep order, had me allocate to these gentlemen the modest sum of 1231 francs. So after paying this whole mob of performers, printers, copyists, engravers, carpenters, suppliers of wood, zinc, curtains, furniture, etc, my own net profit out of these monstrously large receipts was 860 francs.

The government ministers came to the rehearsals and to the concert, wrote me nice letters and paid for their seats like simple members of the

---

1 Berlioz's partner in the venture was Isaac Strauss, no relation of the Viennese Strausses, a violinist and conductor who provided dance music at salons and spas.

bourgeoisie; one paid 40 francs for four seats, the other 150 francs for fifteen. But ministers aren't rich, any more than the city of Paris, which is unable itself to pay its officers and imposes them on us in exorbitant numbers.

So you see why I say that musicians, in France, are serfs. We pay tithes. For my five concerts this year, I have been taxed to the extent of nearly 9500 francs. That is the freedom we enjoy. That is the fine recompense from the government for having gambled my livelihood and given Paris the longest festival of music that has ever taken place in Europe. But it was something to allow me to do it; I had my fears up to the last moment.

It was, I must say, a curious spectacle, quite apart from the musical interest!! The enthusiasm from an audience of 8000, the total silence during the pieces, the shouts and hurrahs afterwards, all the men standing up, throwing their hats in the air, asking for an encore of the last verse of my *Hymne à la France*. There was a terrible (politico-musical) moment when in Halévy's piece the refrain struck up 'Never in France, never shall the Englishman rule'; it sounded like a rebellion, a war cry, the first grumblings of a European revolution.[1]

When the concert was over I was, as you can imagine, half dead. They brought me linen and flannel, then on the stage, in the middle of the orchestra, they built a little room *out of harps with their covers on* and I managed a complete change of clothes before leaving. [. . .]

Your affectionate son,
H. Berlioz

181 *To his sister Nanci Pal*   Paris, 24 August 1844

Dear sister,

You'll have had some of my news from my father who will, no doubt, have passed on the contents of the letter he has had from me. I couldn't give you a precise reason for my long silence; there are any number of them, the main one being the permanent disarray of my domestic situation. Things came finally to such a pass, even during the fearful rehearsals for the festival which sent me back home half dead, that because I could no longer stand sleepless nights spent with my eyes open and my ears besieged by cries and insults I had to take a room elsewhere, in which I sleep every evening. I appear in the house as little as possible. Next Wednesday I shall most probably leave for Germany.

1 This was a chorus from Halévy's opera *Charles VI*.

She has finally agreed to return to the country while I'm away and I've given up my apartment in Paris. Her address is: 4, Rue des Imbergères in Sceaux near Paris. As Louis is on holiday, he'll stay there for a time.[1]

Don't send the quarterly instalment of my allowance for October until you've had a letter from me. I should be afraid some accident might befall the bank-note; I'll leave her enough money for her not to go short of anything.

All this wouldn't matter if she were not really suffering; but it is absolutely impossible for me to change my way of life as completely as I should have to to keep her calm, and equally impossible, despite all her good qualities and her tender feelings for me, to live with this dreadful addiction and the consequences it brings.

What an extraordinary life I lead! . . . These are no more than asides, I've no right to complain, especially to you.

Adieu, dear sister, I embrace you lovingly. All best wishes to Camille.
H. Berlioz

Berlioz did not go to Germany (he hoped for an engagement in Baden-Baden), but spent the whole of September 1844 in Nice, recuperating from his concerts and escaping from conflict at home. There he composed the overture Le corsaire.

182 *To his sister Nanci Pal*   Paris, 5 November 1844

Thank you, dear Nanci, both for your letter and for your strictures which I always appear to deserve to some small degree, but which never wound me because I myself know that regarding the charge of indifference you lay against me I'm wholly innocent.

I haven't been able to reply to you these last few days, not having had a moment really to call my own. I've had articles to write, a host of pieces of music to write and I'm a long way from finishing them. I've composed a grand overture for my next series of concerts[2] and I'm writing music for the places indicated by Shakespeare in *Hamlet*, which is going to be put on at the Odéon in a verse translation by Léon de Wailly.[3] Within the next fortnight I have to complete a little volume of

1 Louis was in boarding school near Rouen but was at home for the summer holiday.
2 *Le corsaire*, first performed on 19 January 1845.
3 This project did not come off, but it probably prompted the composition of the *Marche funèbre pour la dernière scène d'Hamlet*.

pieces for the 'orgue-mélodium' which I've been asked to write by the instrument's manufacturer.[1] You can see I have plenty to do. At the same time I've had to run round looking for an apartment and gradually get together the performers for my concerts at the Cirque etc.

Many thanks for your kind letter to Harriet. Please go on sending her now and then all the tokens of interest and affection you can. She will unfortunately never be cured, that's certain; everyone says such a change is impossible. Armand Bertin mentioned to me the other day the wives of Louis XVII and Charles X, two princesses of the house of Savoy who both died of this addiction and who were driven to corrupting members of their bodyguard in order to obtain this damned poison.

Adèle is wrong, we're not going back to the Rue de Londres, but Harriet is determined to move back in with me and I've given up arguing about it so as not to distress her. As I haven't moved in yet, write to me at the Rue de Londres; I'm in a hotel on the Rue Richelieu which I'm leaving soon.[2] Louis is turning out very interestingly; he's working and M. Bertin is trying to get him a half-scholarship in a college at Versailles.

Adieu, adieu, how will it all end?

Love me always and never doubt my heartfelt affection.

All best wishes to Camille,

H. Berlioz

183 *To his sister Nanci Pal*   Paris, 30 November 1844

Dear sister,

Thank you for your letter and all the kind thoughts it contains. Your enthusiasm is wonderful; 'I am happy with you' (as the great Emperor used to say, or rather *the* Emperor, as there's only one), and I promise you I'm very anxious to hear the sublime evangelist,[3] but I don't know where or when he's going to speak, I hear no more news about him than about the King of the Congo (so much for fame!). I'm writing to you on the run before getting back into my carriage. I'm

1 Jacob Alexandre, inventor of the 'orgue-mélodium', a variety of harmonium. His son Edouard became one of Berlioz's close friends.
2 The disorder of Berlioz's domestic life can well be imagined. Eventually, by the end of the year, Harriet moved to a new apartment in the Rue Blanche while Berlioz moved to Marie Recio's address in the Rue de Provence.
3 Père Lacordaire, a celebrated clairvoyant.

putting on my first musical occasion at the Cirque.[1] I don't know where to turn next, there are so many things to be done all at once. I've just obtained a half-scholarship for Louis at the Royal College in Rouen and, what's more, a fine speech from the minister who granted my request straight away. M. Villemain[2] is very unctuous! Even so, I take his support and his compliments for what they're worth. Harriet is still at Sceaux; I'm free to walk the streets of Paris and I'm working ten times harder than usual.

I had a real disappointment this morning (not a rare occurrence, but this one really set me back). *Hamlet* is to be played on 6 December by the English troupe which has just arrived and that day I shall be FORCED to be at the Opéra to hear and condemn a pale opera by Niedermeyer (who needs a Mayer?) which I have to review the next day.[3] I'd give five hundred francs to be free that evening. That's how mediocrities are preferred above . . . *Shakespeare*!!! at least as far as the article is concerned (there's fame again for you!!)

I shall have (when I go to it) a fearful stirring of the heart, seeing this prodigious masterpiece again after fourteen years. This morning I wept, 'went on my way weeping' (going about my business), thinking of Hamlet, Ophelia and *all that is no more*, all that has become as poor Yorick, or very nearly. But please forgive me.

Adieu, my heart is full; if I have caused others to suffer, I too have had my share and it's not over yet.

Adieu, adieu, my dear, it is only sisters who remain always the same and for whom one's own self does not change.

H. B.

184 *To Gustave Boutry-Boissonade*[4]   Paris, 1 February 1845

Monsieur,

Please accept my warm and sincere thanks for the verses you sent me. They were responsible for the only moment of tranquil pleasure I have enjoyed for a long time. You cannot imagine how valuable such frank and spontaneous sympathy as yours is to me, because you do not know the weight of the rock I am rolling in my Tartarus, or that it consists of sorrows which cannot be described or explained to others,

1 The new Cirque Olympique, an enclosed hippodrome off the Champs-Elysées. Berlioz gave four large-scale concerts there between January and April 1845.
2 Minister of Education.
3 Niedermeyer's *Marie Stuart*, reviewed by Berlioz on 10 December.
4 An unknown poet.

not even to poets. If I manage to obtain a moment's respite, I will write to see if I can arrange to shake you by the hand, thank you once more and assure you that I understand the feelings which prompted your epistle.

I live at the moment like a wounded, bleeding wolf, alone in the depths of a wood; the hard labour of my concerts can barely wrench me out of my gloomy inertia and I behave like a sleepwalker.

Forgive me, pity me, and let us hope I can soon write to you asking you to come here, or rather if I can come and see you; on that occasion you will no doubt pardon me for the necessary reserve which is all I can offer for the moment. Most convicts are freer and happier than I am.

Adieu, Monsieur, with all my gratitude.

Hector Berlioz

185 *To his uncle Félix Marmion*   Paris, 20 February 1845

Dear uncle,

I should have replied to you earlier, but you will no doubt be aware that these monstrous concerts give me plenty to keep me occupied. The second, which took place last Sunday, was a stunningly brilliant affair, the performance, the compositions, the layout of the orchestra and the auditorium, etc, all that was applauded by five or six thousand hands. The receipts were all the more flattering because the Champs-Elysées was under six inches of snow and slush. So when the sun shines, we can expect the hall to be full on every occasion. If so, I shall have initiated an excellent institution. Most of the costs are now covered. I took only a thousand francs profit, but the remaining concerts will cost half as much and bring in more.

You can't imagine the terrifying effect produced in this vast hall by the *Dies irae* from my *Requiem*; I have just performed it a second time and am about to do so a third time. I have a little orchestra consisting of fifty violins, twenty violas, twenty cellos and fifteen double basses with double and triple woodwind, and in addition a chorus of 300 voices.

All these forces came together wonderfully on Sunday; and we presented Félicien David's symphony *Le désert* in a manner designed to bury irretrievably the Théâtre-Italien, which has put it on several times.[1]

---

1 David's *Le désert*, an 'ode-symphonie' for chorus and orchestra, was a runaway success following its first performance the previous December.

Louis is in Rouen and writes to me often. His mother is still the same, I spend very little time at home ... There's nothing one can do except resign oneself and keep quiet.

It's not my fault if I didn't see our elderly cousin Mme de Maistre. I went to her house three times without finding her and I simply don't have the time to go visiting.

I don't know if my bookseller sent you my *Voyage musical en Allemagne et Italie* as I asked him to. You might find these two volumes entertaining, especially the one on Italy.

Adieu dear uncle, I hope to see you soon.

H. Berlioz

186 *To Mikhail Ivanovich Glinka*[1]   Paris, 25 March 1845

My dear Monsieur Glinka,

It is not enough to perform your music and to *tell* everyone that it is fresh, lively, charming in its verve and originality, I must allow myself the pleasure of *writing* several columns on the subject, all the more so as it's my duty. Is it not my job to inform the public of the most remarkable things of this kind that are taking place in Paris? So please would you let me have some notes on yourself, on your initial studies, on musical institutions in Russia, on your works, and if I can study your score with you to get to know it better, I shall be able to write something passable and give the readers of the *Débats* an approximate idea of your decidedly superior talents.

I am horribly tormented by these damned concerts, with the players' pretensions etc, but I shall certainly find the time to write an article on a subject of this nature; I do not usually have anything so interesting.

With my sincerest best wishes,

Hector Berlioz

187 *To Alfred de Vigny*   Paris, 10 May 1845

My dear de Vigny,

I know one doesn't usually give away tickets for benefit performances, but if you had two seats at your disposal, please send them to me

---

1 Glinka was spending nearly a year in Paris following the poor reception of his opera *Ruslan and Lyudmila* in St Petersburg in 1842. His friendship with Berlioz affected him profoundly. Some extracts from *A Life for the Tsar* and *Ruslan and Lyudmila* were included in Berlioz's concert on 15 March, and on 16 April Berlioz wrote an extensive appreciation of Glinka's music in the *Débats*.

at 41, Rue de Provence. I should be very grateful and, as there is a musical pretext involved – since they are going to sing, I shall be able to mention the performance in one of my articles. This indiscretion stems purely from our desire to see *Chatterton* again.[1]

Adieu, my very best wishes.

H. Berlioz

188 *To his sister Adèle Suat* Paris, 6 June 1845

My dear Adèle,

I should have written to you these last few days and I haven't done so because of any number of problems mixed up with all sorts of things to do in a hurry, articles, pieces to orchestrate, proofs to correct, etc, etc, etc. I expect you are well and truly installed in Vienne,[2] if you prefer staying amid that gloomy Roman antiquity to your dark factory in St-Chamond, so much the better; but I fancy that, deep down, the alternative is not worth a pin to you.

Nanci sends me good news of father, but she adds that he's increasingly buried and countrified. He's happy, though, as long as he can more or less escape the depression which weighed on him so heavily during the early days of his bereavement. Nanci was completely bowled over by Liszt's playing and is sorry that when he came to Grenoble he didn't play any of my compositions. I, on the other hand, am delighted; nothing upsets me more than those travesties of the orchestra reproduced on the piano. And if I have to appear before my compatriots, let it be in my natural state and with *all my charms*. Unfortunately I feel that will only happen if the Dauphiné emigrates to Paris. Liszt has asked me to go to Bonn for the inauguration of the Beethoven monument, a great musical celebration which is to take place in August. But the financial arrangements so far are not acceptable, and I am obliged to admit that *gold is not a chimera*, whatever Scribe may say on the subject.[3]

I'm going to give some concerts in Bordeaux while waiting for something better. I'm led to hope for a good result from the curiosity of the people in those parts. I'm absolutely terrified of their orchestras and, in the present heatwave, of the way they'll make me sweat. I find

---

1 De Vigny's play *Chatterton* was revived on 13 May with Marie Dorval. The two singers involved turned out to be so bad that Berlioz felt unable to say anything about the play.
2 The Suats had moved to Vienne, a Roman town just south of Lyon.
3 'L'or est une chimère' is a line from *Robert le diable*.

bad music more and more intolerable. I shan't be away for more than a month at the most.[1]

Adieu, dear little sister, I embrace you with all my heart; pass on to your husband all my best wishes.

Your devoted

H. Berlioz

189 *To his sister Nanci Pal*   Lyon, 7 July 1845

Dear sister,

I'm taking advantage of a day when there are no rehearsals that absolutely demand my presence to go and embrace father. So do come to La Côte that day. I've told Adèle. The coach will drop me at La Frète[2] on Wednesday, the day after tomorrow, at eleven o'clock in the morning and will pick me up again an hour after midnight.

The festival will take place here on the 20th and I'm already exhausted thanks to the delicious equatorial temperatures we're enjoying.

Yours ever,

H. Berlioz

If Camille could send a vehicle of some kind to take me from La Frète to La Côte that would be very kind of him, otherwise I'll walk in spite of the sun.

190 *To his sister Nanci Pal*   Lyon, 16 July 1845

My dear Nanci,

It never occurred to me that you would not make the journey to Lyon; but I'd written to you so that the three of us could be together with father on the day I was able to get to La Côte. Anyway I saw Adèle and you'll have seen her too by the time my letter arrives, so she'll have told you all the details.[3]

The Hôtel du Parc is full so I've booked two double rooms for Adèle and yourself in the Hôtel du Nord next to the theatre for Saturday night.

I never stop rehearsing with one group or another, either at the

1 Berlioz left not for Bordeaux but for Marseille and Lyon, where he gave two concerts in each city.
2 The coach-stop on the main Lyon–Grenoble road, forty miles from Lyon and five miles from La Côte.
3 Berlioz sent this letter to Adèle's house in Vienne.

Cercle or the theatre, and also in the barracks of a regiment of the line. It will go well, provided the outsiders from Dijon and Châlons don't do anything silly. Everybody's putting a lot of enthusiasm and hard work into it, but I'm prepared for one or two mistakes which the audience won't notice. Adèle wanted to come to the final rehearsal, but I'd rather you didn't see me messing about in my musical kitchen, so I ask you not to come and hear me until everything's ready.

I think the programme's well chosen for the occasion, for the audience and for the artists at my disposal. So far the pieces that have made the biggest impression have been the *Scène aux champs* from the *Symphonie fantastique*, the *Carnaval* overture and *Le cinq mai*. Unfortunately Alizard isn't here to sing this last item, the local man's voice is uneven and he's not musical; every time it comes to one of his entries I'm terrified. I'm going to make him rehearse it again shortly to reassure myself. I shall be spending the whole of next Saturday with the technicians in charge of the staging and with the performers, but between two of these stints I'll find a moment to come and embrace you if you arrive in good time. In any case, send a message to me in the theatre once you're at the hotel. The box has been reserved for you for a long time, so that reproach was no more justified than the other. So Camille has not been able to get away. My father has never at any point considered making the journey. As for my uncle, I doubt whether he'll come; 'but since I have you I am well contented'.[1]

Rachel[2] opened her run of performances yesterday to a half-empty house; she must be absolutely furious. The inhabitants of Lyon are wildly opposed to rises in seat prices. Even so, I hope we'll have a good audience.

Adieu, until we meet, my affection to Adèle and to Suat, and my respects to Mlle Mathilde.

H. Berlioz

191 *To his sister Nanci Pal*   Lyon, 26 July 1845

Dear sister,

I only have time to write you a couple of lines.

The second concert[3] was much less well attended than the first, as you forecast when you heard that Rachel was playing *Andromaque* the

---

1 A near-quotation from Boileau's *Satires*.
2 The stage-name of the great tragic actress Elisabeth Félix, then performing in Lyon.
3 The first concert (which his sisters attended) was on the 20th, the second on the 24th.

night before and *Virginie* the night after. Luckily the audience was much more appreciative than on the first evening and their applause made up for the lack of receipts.

I'm leaving this evening for Paris. Your letter is full of warmth, and of reserve and good sense as well, but it would take too long and serve no purpose to reply. There's a whole story there of which I'm powerless to alter the details ... My destiny is to be constantly off the route generally followed by others, and that despite myself; the impossibility of my domestic life and Harriet's *monomania* or *illness* have brought all that about; nothing could survive such a miserable situation, not even the deep affection I still have for her. As for the person you speak of, she is not called by the name I mentioned in front of you. That lady is associated with Méry[1] and not with me.

Adieu, don't talk to me about all that, there's no point; my main desire is that my father shouldn't be troubled by it, and I hope no one in this dumb country of ours will be so stupid as to mention it to him.

Adieu, yours ever,
All best wishes to Suat and to Adèle.[2]
H. Berlioz

I shan't write to you from Paris except to acknowledge receipt of my allowance. I'll be there on Monday.

Soon after his return to Paris Berlioz was on the road again, this time to the Beethoven celebrations in Bonn, organized by Liszt. The object of the festival was to erect a statue of Beethoven in his birthplace. Berlioz's two articles about the celebrations appeared in the Débats *on 22 August and 3 September and were later reprinted in* Les soirées de l'orchestre. *Berlioz stayed in Frankfurt on his return.*

192 *To his sister Nanci Pal*   Frankfurt, 26 August 1845

My dear Nanci,

I received your letter and enclosures; I should have replied to you earlier, but first I had to write three important articles, two for the *Débats* and another almost as long as the first two put together for a new journal (*Le monde*) which is due to be published in Paris in a few

---

1 Joseph Méry, poet and librettist, who had been with Berlioz in Marseille earlier that month.
2 Nanci was staying with Adèle on her way back to Grenoble.

weeks' time and has asked me for a complete account of the celebrations in Bonn, Cologne, Brühl, Stolzenfels, Koblenz, etc.

I expect you've read my two letters on the subject in the *Débats*, so I won't go over again what you know from so many other sources. The King of Prussia was very nice to me, he recognized me among the crowd of guests at the castle in Brühl. The Princess of Prussia chatted with me too for a few moments, but without recognizing me, which is not very flattering to my external charms because we'd had a very long conversation in Berlin.[1] And the amusing part is that at the end of the evening she upbraided Meyerbeer for not introducing me to her. Her disgruntled majesty was not aware of the good fortune she had enjoyed in speaking to me personally.

The meeting of musicians and men of letters in Bonn was extremely interesting; I didn't know where to put *my head* (that's an accurate way of describing it) because every minute there was a new embrace or a new introduction. Whatever people may have said of it, the ceremony was made fine by its aim and by the feelings of those involved. Liszt was perfect in his devotion and generosity and in his understanding of his position; he played Beethoven's sublime concerto[2] like an assembly of gods. Now *there's* something which might reasonably give you nervous spasms, it's real music, inspired, grand and poetical! His cantata is very beautiful too and, I think, deserves all the compliments I've paid it.[3] He was surrounded by a crowd of little cliques, as envious as they were obscure, who gave him plenty to think about.

Bonn is a provincial city and therefore full of petty, mean, stupid ideas whenever the pride of the race or the natives is at stake. Unfortunately Liszt had to conduct one of the concerts and it's something totally alien to him; he conducts like Musard!!![4] That's to say, not only does he not conduct, but from time to time he prevents the orchestra from doing their job. This leads to opposition from the players and quite serious opposition too because it's based on something real and rational.

The Viennese who were there made so much of me, begging me to visit them in their own city, that I've decided to do so and to go to

1 In March 1843.
2 No. 5 in E flat major.
3 Liszt conducted his *Festkantate zur Enthüllung des Beethoven-Denkmals in Bonn* twice, since the party of English and Prussian royalty took their seats too late for the first performance.
4 The Parisian ballroom conductor.

Vienna before travelling on to Russia once I've finished what I've taken on here.

I've had news of Louis from the headmaster who is very happy with him and tells me that he's won two prizes.

Adieu, dear sister.

All my best wishes to Camille and to Adèle,

Your devoted,

H. Berlioz

193 *To Almire Gandonnière*[1]   Paris, 3 October 1845

Monsieur,

I should be very much obliged if, when you are in Paris, you would be kind enough to call on me around eleven o'clock or midday; we'll talk about our project which, I see, is in good shape. It's simply a question of shortening the recitatives as far as possible.[2]

Hasty best wishes,

Your devoted

H. Berlioz

On 22 October 1845 Berlioz set out with Marie on a tour of over six months, taking in Vienna, Prague, Budapest, Breslau and Brunswick. As on the 1842–3 tour he wrote a detailed account of his travels which is found in the Mémoires. *He gave his first three concerts in Vienna in November, with great success.*

194 *To Maurice Schlesinger*   Vienna, 12 December 1845

My dear Maurice,

I'm sending you news entirely about music, which interests me enormously and which, I hope, you will consider to be of some slight interest to your readers.[3] The news I'm about to give you would be best published first in the *Gazette musicale de Paris*. My success here grows

---

1 Editor of *La chronique*.

2 The project was *La damnation de Faust*, which was to occupy Berlioz for the next twelve months. On his return from Bonn he had begun to plan the work, incorporating his *Huit scènes de Faust* of 1829. He chose Gandonnière to write his text, although in the end he wrote much of it himself.

3 An account of Berlioz's Viennese exploits appeared in Schlesinger's *Revue et gazette musicale* on 21 December, evidently written by Berlioz himself.

in an astonishing fashion and the occasion yesterday evening[1] can only increase it further. Your brother[2] must have sold plenty of copies of the *Carnaval romain* since they're all being ordered from Berlin instead of from you, because Paris is so far away. I'm going to give a fourth concert in a few days, for which we're putting on *Roméo et Juliette*, with the prices of the boxes quadrupled. M. Hoven (Vesque de Puttlingen)[3] has insisted on arranging *Harold* for piano duet; he'll write to you about publishing it. I can assure you it's a very good arrangement. [. . .]

Yours ever,
Hector Berlioz

195 *To Jean-Emile Desmarest*[4]   Fischofstadt, Vienna, Austria, 5.15
16 December 1845

My dearest Desmarest,
    The good news first; probably, very probably, you know it already. Enormous success here! Calls to be taken, encores (even double encores). There was one piece, the *Carnaval* overture, in a concert I was not conducting, which the audience wanted to hear three times in a row. Banquets, speeches, portraits, wreaths, a conductor's baton in silver gilt offered by the forty principal professionals and amateurs of Vienna, in fact a breathtaking success! And all that is due almost entirely to our poor *Symphonie fantastique*: the *Scène aux champs* and the *Marche au supplice* have turned the Austrians inside out; as for the *Carnaval* and the *Marche des pèlerins*,[5] they are popular pieces. They're now even making a pâté here named after me. I've got some excellent players; a young orchestra, half Bohemian and half Viennese, which I've formed, because they've only been playing together for two months, and which is now roaring ahead like a lion.
    This morning for the first time I conducted the orchestra of the Kärntnerthor (the leading orchestra in Germany), who are very put out because things have been so arranged that I'm giving my concerts in another theatre than theirs.[6] It was at the rehearsal of a concert of Dreyschock's,[7] who asked me for two pieces. Thunderous applause! . . .

1 A banquet in honour of Berlioz's birthday.
2 The Berlin music publisher Heinrich Schlesinger.
3 Viennese civil servant and composer under the name 'Hoven'.
4 A cellist in the Opéra orchestra and a long-standing friend of Berlioz's.
5 The second movement of *Harold en Italie*.
6 Berlioz's concerts were given in the Theater an der Wien.
7 Alexander Dreyschock, celebrated Bohemian virtuoso pianist.

I'm now hoping for a big success tomorrow in the hall of the Conservatoire.

On the 30th of this month I'm giving my fourth concert in the Theater an der Wien with orchestra and chorus almost doubled for a performance of *Roméo et Juliette* complete. Ah! I have a good, solid bass for Friar Laurence: Staudigl. What a musician! What a voice! After that, there are other projects in the air.

But enough news for today. [. . .]

Your ever devoted and sincere friend,

H. Berlioz

196 *To Joseph d'Ortigue*   Prague, 26 January 1846

My dear d'Ortigue,

I should have written to you long ago but you are no doubt aware of the events which made my journey to Vienna such a happy one for me and my friends. I'll tell you all about it in more detail when I get back as it would take me at least twenty columns of the *Journal des débats* to write it all down for you.

I'll tell you simply about my visit to Prague.[1] I arrived expecting to fall among a lot of antiquarian pedants refusing to accept anything but Mozart and ready to spit on every modern composer. Instead of which I found musicians who were sympathetic, attentive and unusually intelligent, who rehearsed for four hours without complaint and at the end of the second rehearsal were more enthusiastic about my music than I could have dared to hope. As for the general public, it's gone up like a barrel of powder; I'm now treated here as a Fetish, a Lama, a Manitou. At the concert yesterday FIVE pieces were encored, and I thought they'd all gone mad at the end of the *Reine Mab* scherzo, performed, I have to admit, with a verve and at a speed that were extraordinary. I've made an important correction to this piece: it was too long, and by shortening it I've greatly increased its impact. But the piece that moved the connoisseurs and made the deepest impression was the *Scène d'amour* (the Adagio) from *Roméo et Juliette*.

I'm going back to Vienna after my third concert which takes place tomorrow in the theatre; a sixth one is advertised in Vienna and I'll arrive just in time for the rehearsal, if the carriages of the train don't jump off the rails.

In Vienna there are mutterings in one little hostile corner, but here

1 Berlioz gave three concerts in Prague, on 19, 25 and 27 January 1846.

nothing of the sort, there's adoration (ridiculous word but true). And it manifests itself in the most original manner and in terms that I would not for the world want to be read by our cynical Parisians.[1] If you see Pixis tell him that I'm more than happy with his compatriots;[2] the day before yesterday I listened to his nephew at the Conservatoire, he's a young violinist of fourteen, already very talented and due to bring honour to his name. When I've again taken my leave of my dear Viennese I'm going to visit Heller's compatriots[3] (please would you go and see him for me and show him my letter; it will save me writing. I know I ought, considering the kindness he's shown me on so many occasions, to write to him at length and I will do so one day before I leave Pest). After Pest I'm going to Breslau[4] where three concerts have been arranged for me, then on to Brunswick to see our friends from 1843 who were also so enthusiastic, and to let them hear the *Fantastique* which they don't know.

See if you can find a way of inflicting a few words about this Prague success on one of the more important newspapers. You can write a notice of some six or seven lines and mention Vienna as well. But if it means walking more than a hundred yards, never mind. The business with the baton must have made quite a stir in Paris;[5] the preparations for the occasion had been kept secret so successfully that it was a complete surprise for me. Send me twenty-two lines, *poste-restante* to Pest (Hungary). Adieu, all best wishes, please greet Mme d'Ortigue on my behalf and embrace your big son for me.

    Your devoted
    H. Berlioz

P.S. Would you be good enough to hand the enclosed letter to the concierge at 41, Rue de Provence on your way past?[6] Adieu once again. [. . .]

After his triumphs in Prague Berlioz returned to Vienna to give one more concert on 1 February 1846 and then moved on to Budapest. His two concerts there (15 and 20 February) were a further triumph, with

1 One of Berlioz's admirers in Prague was Hanslick, later to turn sharply against Berlioz's music.
2 The pianist Pixis, though born in Mannheim, was Bohemian.
3 Stephen Heller was Hungarian.
4 Now Wrocław in Poland, then the capital of Silesia.
5 The presentation of a silver-gilt baton at Berlioz's birthday banquet.
6 Doubtless a letter from Marie to her mother.

an especially noisy welcome for his arrangement of the Rákóczy March, *done specially for the occasion.*

197 *To Joseph d'Ortigue*   Breslau, 13 March 1846

Many thanks, dear friend, for your letter. It reached me this morning and in it I found news of Paris which I've been deprived of for a very long time. Desmarest has sent me no more than a few lines.

I appreciate the reasons you state as to why I should return to Paris, but I still have four concerts to give: one here (next Friday), two in Prague which I'm going back to and where at this moment *Roméo et Juliette* is being put on without me, and one in Brunswick where I've been invited to go back and visit those excellent musicians who welcomed me so warmly three years ago. So I shan't be back in Paris until around the end of April. There's been serious talk in Vienna of appointing me not to Donizetti's post, which is not vacant as he's still alive, but to Weigl's (the director of the Imperial Chapel), who has just died.[1] Someone of considerable influence in the Austrian capital asked me if I would accept this position and I replied that I needed to think about it for twenty-four hours. The post entailed remaining indefinitely in Vienna without the briefest leave in which to come back once a year to Paris. On this point I made a curious discovery, namely that my heart is so closely wedded to Paris (by Paris I mean friends like yourself, the intelligent people who live there and the hubbub of ideas by which one is surrounded) that at the mere thought of being excluded from it I literally felt my heart fail me and realized the torment of being deported. So my reply was a peremptory negative and I asked not to be considered as Weigl's successor. Donizetti's post is not so bad as it would give me six months' leave; but there's no question of it.

Thank Dietsch for me for the interest he's showing on my behalf and tell him that I'm setting up some hard work for him with my grand opera *Faust* (concert opera in four acts) which I'm working at furiously and which will soon be finished.[2] It has some choruses that will have to be studied and polished carefully. I have high hopes of this work which is preoccupying me to the point of forgetting the concert I'm organizing (or rather which is being organized) here. I've not been very impressed

1 Donizetti was Kapellmeister to the Austrian court, but already mortally ill. Weigl (who had just died at the age of eighty) was director of the Imperial Chapel.
2 Much of the composition of *La damnation de Faust* was achieved on this tour. He still called it a 'grand opera' or 'concert opera', but ultimately titled it 'dramatic legend'.

by the example the Breslau musicians have shown me of their *savoir-faire*. Still, they're very enthusiastic and treat me as well as they are able. There's even a poster this morning with the words 'Grand Concert given by M. Kapellmeister Schoen[1] in honour of M. le chevalier Berlioz from Paris'. So tomorrow evening I shall have to go and exhibit myself in a box in all my finery. They're sending a cab to collect me; because of the Polish war[2] there'll be no firing of cannons, but smoking in the hall is forbidden.

Adieu with my affection to all.

If you see Perrot remember me to him.

Your devoted

H. Berlioz

198 *To Felix Mendelssohn*   Prague, 14 April 1846

My dear Mendelssohn,

I'm afraid I shall not be able to shake you by the hand on my way through Leipzig. I am really sorry about it. May I say that in Breslau I heard your *Midsummer Night's Dream* and that I have never heard anything so profoundly Shakespearean as your music. On my way out of the theatre I would willingly have given three years of my life to be able to embrace you.

Adieu, adieu.

My love for you equals my admiration, and that is a great deal.

Yours heart and soul,

Hector Berlioz

199 *To Joseph d'Ortigue*   Prague, 16 April 1846

My dear d'Ortigue,

I didn't reply to your last letter because I didn't have anything interesting to tell you. I gave an excellent concert in Breslau and hurried back here where I was expected and where I found that the Academy of Singing had learnt *Roméo et Juliette* perfectly. I breathed a sigh when I heard my music performed for the first time by an amateur chorus, so different from those theatre bawlers. A large audience came to the final dress rehearsal which we had yesterday and

---

1 Moritz Schoen, violinist and conductor in Breslau.
2 The beginnings of the 1848 Revolution were already manifest in parts of Prussian Poland.

which Liszt helped me to manage by acting as interpreter.

I was glad to see that he was often amazed and moved by this work, which until now was absolutely unknown to him. I think you'd be happy with the large changes I've made to it. There's now only a single prologue (the first),[1] much modified and shortened, and there are very significant corrections in the scherzo, in the grand finale, and in Friar Laurence's measured recitative. At last it all works well, and I'm suppressing entirely the tomb scene which you didn't care for and which other people will always react to as you did.[2] But the Adagio, everyone agrees, here as in Vienna, is the best piece I've written so far. At the rehearsal yesterday this and the *Fête chez Capulet* were wildly applauded, breaking the local habit of never saying a word during rehearsals.

I have a very good Friar Laurence (Strackaty), a Bohemian, who has a fine voice and true musical feeling. After the rehearsal all these gentlemen surprised me by inviting me to a grand supper at which I was presented with a silver-gilt cup on behalf of the principal musicians of Prague, with any number of vivats, wreaths, applause and speeches. Liszt made a wonderfully warm and enthusiastic one in terms too glowing for me to repeat here, then our compatriot the Prince de Rohan,[3] Dreyschock, the Director of the Conservatoire,[4] the two Kapellmeisters from the theatre and the cathedral, the city's leading music critics, etc. I (in my toasts) drank to the health of those among the latter whom I had not yet met, as I had not made a single visit to the press, thanking them for their goodwill, which I hardly deserved since they must have found my behaviour impolite at the very least. But I thought that 'my rudeness to them was a compliment'. This phrase made them laugh uproariously and flattered them deeply, when they understood it. The Viennese critics prefer a different treatment. They also had to go without it even so, but there are two Charles Maurices[5] among them who will continue to hold this against me.

They made me promise yesterday to come back and put on *La damnation de Faust* here once it's been given in Paris; I've still got four large sections to write before it's finished.

H. Berlioz

---

1 In the original version of *Roméo et Juliette* a Second Prologue followed the *Reine Mab* scherzo.
2 Berlioz in fact retained the movement *Roméo au tombeau des Capulets*.
3 A French nobleman who lived most of his life in Prague.
4 Johann Friedrich Kittl.
5 Maurice was a notoriously rancorous Parisian theatre critic.

*The two Prague visits were among the greatest triumphs of Berlioz's
career. On his way home he gave a concert in Brunswick on 24 April
and reached Paris at the beginning of May.*

200 *To Johann Friedrich Kittl*[1]   Paris, 6 May 1846

My dear M. Kittl,

I have only been back in Paris a few days and send you greetings
since I have a few free moments. My last concert in Germany, the one
in Brunswick, was extremely brilliant and productive. The performance was admirable from the point of view of ensemble and nuance
and left nothing to be desired. But how I love Prague audiences! They
seem to me far above all others. I should dearly love to see them again
next year and it will be none of my doing if I do not pay you a second
visit. Your generous welcome, all the flattering attention I was paid by
the musicians and music-lovers of Prague have made an immense
impression here; I'm besieged with questions about you personally,
about the Conservatoire, the principal artists, etc, etc, and you can
imagine what sort of answer I give ... All my friends are deeply
grateful for what you have done for me.

A few days before I left, Count Nostiz[2] asked me to buy two Vuillaume violins (imitations of Guarnerius) for the Conservatoire. I went
to see this violin maker; he said that he hadn't any of these violins in
stock at the moment and that it would take him two months to make
them. He also set a price of 300 francs each instead of the 250 francs
that Count Nostiz had in mind. Please would you go and see the Count
and tell me what I should do about this. I think Vuillaume will agree to
reduce the price a certain amount, and I'll inform you when he has
decided to start on them, which he does not seem disposed to do
without positive assurance that he can sell them. [. . .]

Yours heart and soul and do not forget us.

H. Berlioz

201 *To his sister Nanci Pal*   Paris, 29 June 1846

My dear Nanci,

Again I've been running around a little to keep my legs in trim. First
of all I spent eight days as an inhabitant of Lille, perhaps the busiest

1 Director of the Prague Conservatoire.
2 President of the Society of Fine Arts in Prague.

and certainly the most serenaded person there, since I had to weather *four* serenades, three instrumental and one vocal.[1] The inhabitants of the large square where I was staying must have found my presence more than somewhat inconvenient. Overall the *Apothéose* went well and the 250 military bandsmen did their duty *pluckily*; the cantata was sung with unusual verve and with the sort of fresh voices we can't find in Paris for our choirs. But while I was talking with the Duc de Nemours and the Duc de Montpensier[2] in the next-door salon someone stole first of all my hat, then all the music for the cantata, orchestral parts, choral parts and a score. So there's a work lost, and I don't feel up to starting it all over again. That's the only result of this ear-splitting festival supported by M. Rothschild[3] for which I was summoned from Paris and for which I had to spend three nights composing the cantata.

Still, yesterday the Mayor of Lille sent me on behalf of his city a very fine gold medal with the inscription: 'Inauguration of the Northern Railway, the city of Lille to M. Berlioz'. The chaos there was unbelievable. At the ball Jules Janin lost his Turkish decoration inlaid with diamonds, valued at 800 francs. Everyone was dying of thirst, there were no rooms for the Parisians and Belgians who all arrived on the same day, the members of the municipal council were arguing and fighting among themselves, fire broke out to set the seal on the whole uproar, etc, etc.

Hardly had I got back when I set off for Rouen, where I went to see Louis who has just taken his first communion; he's sturdy and sensible, the headmaster is extremely pleased with him and sang his praises at some length, even though he's not a very fast learner. We had dinner together and I brought him some little presents from Paris and Prague which he was delighted by. From there I went to spend four days at the Château de Montville (you know the village with the notorious trumpet last year) to which M. de Montville had invited me;[4] I worked there despite the obvious distractions of the beautiful scenery.[5] *La damnation de Faust* is progressing, but it's a huge score and I'll finish it only just in time for the first performance in November. It's not what you think, there's only one scene in Hell at the end; the dénouement on the

---

1 In June 1846 Berlioz was commissioned at short notice to compose a cantata for the opening of the railway line from Paris to Lille. The words were by Jules Janin. On 14 June the *Apothéose* was given in the city square, followed by the inaugural cantata, the *Chant des chemins de fer*, in the Town Hall.
2 Two of Louis-Philippe's sons.
3 Chairman of the Compagnie du Chemin de Fer du Nord.
4 It is not known how Berlioz made the acquaintance of the Baron de Montville.
5 It was there that Berlioz composed the duet 'Ange adoré' for *La damnation de Faust*.

other hand takes place in Heaven. If you don't believe me I can recite the final chorus to you. It'll be an opportunity to get you to admire my poetry which you've never been lucky enough to see so much as a sketch of and which it is high time you got to know:

Chorus of angels:

But no, I'll keep my poetry for another time. I'll have great trouble finding the singers I need; Pillet and I are daggers drawn because of my articles on the Opéra.[1] My patience finally gave out; there was no way I could help it; it's a disgraceful theatre. Adieu, give me news of father in your next letter and pass on all my best wishes to Camille and Mathilde. Your devoted brother,

H. Berlioz

My address is now 10, Rue Neuve St-Georges.[2]

202 *To August Wilhelm Ambros*[3] Paris, 21 August 1846

My dear Ambros,
[. . .] I'm still quite exhausted by our great occasion yesterday. I mean my *Requiem* which we performed in the church of St-Eustache for a memorial ceremony in honour of Gluck, organized by the Association of Paris Musicians.[4] There were nearly five hundred performers and everything went magnificently, apart from a few small slips, and we'd had only one orchestral rehearsal. The effect was, I must say, tremendous. There was a reasonable amount of weeping and trembling. I would love to have seen you there, my dear Ambros, you and our friends from Prague. When shall I be able to let you hear this score in the Spanish Room of the Archduke's Palace and with the help of the excellent Kittl? . . .

I shall finish *La damnation de Faust* shortly. Write and tell me if for the translation I can still count on your friend and compatriot, Nolte, who was kind enough to offer me his pen for this difficult and tiring task. As for you, I have too much experience of your kindness not to hope that you will help him, for which I thank you in advance. Please send me his name and address so that I can write to him about it.

1 Berlioz's feuilleton in the *Débats* on 24 May, soon after his return from Germany, was an extensive attack on the mediocrity of the Opéra, of which Pillet was the director.
2 This was the address of Adolphe Sax's atelier, which Berlioz used as a forwarding address.
3 A young lawyer and composer who was among Berlioz's most enthusiastic admirers in Prague. He wrote a four-volume history of music (1862–81).
4 The work's second complete performance. Louis, aged twelve, was present.

mors —— stu-pe - bit   et —— na-tu - ra

pp

I keep coming back to the *Requiem;*[1] all those sinister harmonies are groaning in my head, I feel as though yesterday I witnessed an apocalyptic scene, I hear nothing but cries of terror, rolls of thunder, the sound of worlds crumbling to the *clangor tubarum.*[2] Forgive this preoccupation of mine.

Adieu, my dear Ambros, I shake you by the hand and beg you humbly to write me a few lines *at once* to tell me what you are going to do with my score of *Roméo* and to give me your news.

Your devoted
Hector Berlioz

203 *To his father Dr Louis Berlioz*   Paris, 16 September 1846

Dear father,

I interrupt you in the middle of your grape harvest to send you some of my news in person. I've heard some of yours from my sisters, even if our correspondence is not as frequent as it might be. I know you have benefited from the warm, settled weather this year. It looks as though the autumn is going to be equally fine and I have reason to think that your end-of-year labours may be more pleasant than tiring for you.

I too am working hard at a very large composition which I'm just about to complete and which I want to put on here in Paris towards the end of November. I've been forced to be librettist as well as composer because I began the score on my travels through Bavaria, Austria, Hungary, Bohemia and Silesia, and it progressed too fast for my suppliers of verse in Paris to keep up with it and so I've had to do without their help. I've been quite surprised at how easy it was to write what was needed. I won't tell you about my long journey which, as you know, was a great success in all respects; I'll be writing some more letters about this in the *Débats* in a few months' time and you'll be able to read various details which I can't tell you now. All I can say is that I

1 The musical extract is from the *Dies irae.*
2 'The clamour of trumpets' (Virgil, *Aeneid*, Book II).

conquered most of Vienna and the whole of Prague, from where I receive daily requests asking me to return. I was even asked to remain in Vienna and replace the choirmaster of the Imperial Chapel who died while I was in Austria.[1] But this would have meant abandoning France completely and I have to admit that for all the Viennese amiability and the kindness of their Emperor such a step would have been impossible for me. Paris is the only place in the world; it's an electric city which alternately attracts and repels, but to which in the end you always have to return when once you've lived there and especially when you're a Frenchman.

You will have heard about the performance of my *Requiem* at an occasion in honour of Gluck, organized last month by the Association of Paris Musicians. It was incomparably more effective this time than at its first performance in the Invalides. There were 500 performers, I conducted, the church of St-Eustache is excellent for sound, everyone was enthusiastic and there was a huge audience. The impact of the *Dies irae* was truly extraordinary, especially the verse 'Judex ergo cum sedebit'. Baron Taylor, the president of the musicians' association, was a tireless helper in overcoming the difficulties that two or three of my loyal enemies were intent on putting in our way to prevent the performance. Thanks to the hatred stirred up daily by my articles in the *Débats* and to the smouldering anger of some petty, envious natures, I am obliged (in Paris) to proceed on my way like a red-hot bullet, whistling, smashing and burning. I note that this hostile attitude has increased since my travels to Germany, as my resounding success has produced exasperation.

We're supposed to have a Department of Fine Arts ... we really need another Paul-Louis Courier[2] to breathe some importance into it.

Louis is here on holiday, the headmaster of the college in Rouen is very pleased with him; but despite all the good reports I have of him I haven't been able to secure more than a half-scholarship. The Minister of Education has fallen out with Armand Bertin over some argument the *Journal des débats* picked with him and I'm in a poor position for asking favours.

Adieu, dear father, I don't dare to hope for a reply from you; but I trust one of my sisters will step in for you as soon as possible! I embrace you with all my heart.

H. Berlioz

1 Weigl.
2 Noted for his petitions on behalf of the underprivileged under the Empire.

204 *To King Louis-Philippe*   Paris, 17 November 1846

To His Majesty Louis-Philippe King of the French

Sire,

Allow me to present to Your Majesty the libretto of my new work *La damnation de Faust*, opera-legend in four acts. I shall be very happy if it is of sufficient interest to Your Majesty for you to deign to honour with your presence the performance of it to be given under my direction at the theatre of the Opéra-Comique on Sunday 29 November at 1.45.

The choice of the principal performers, the size of the forces employed and the total effect that I hope to obtain will perhaps provide some excuse in Your Majesty's eyes for the temerity of this request.[1]

I am with the profoundest respect

Sire

Your Majesty's

most humble and most obedient servant,

Hector Berlioz

205 *To Hermann-Léon*[2]   Paris, between 22 and 31 December 1846

My dear Hermann,

In spite of all my efforts there's no possibility of putting on the third concert. So I must abandon the idea until circumstances change. Please accept the enclosed note which I'm sorry I cannot replace with something worthier of your talent.

My sincere thanks.

Yours ever,

H. Berlioz

P.S. Please send me back your part.

Berlioz's response to this disappointment was to embark on yet another trip abroad, this time to Russia, encouraged by a generous invitation. His domestic affairs were still making life in Paris difficult

1 The first performance of *La damnation de Faust* was postponed until 6 December, with a second performance on the 20th. Berlioz was bitterly disappointed by the small numbers who attended despite the rapturous response of his more discerning friends. The King did not attend.
2 The bass who sang Mephistopheles in *La damnation de Faust*.

for him, and he may also have been troubled by his liaison with Marie Recio, as the following letter suggests. He went to Russia without her.

206 *To Rocquemont*[1]   Paris, January or early February 1847

My dear Rocquemont,

Diligence and mystery! I intend to leave for Russia *alone*. To do this I need your help. So tomorrow please go to Sax's and make up a parcel of works I want to take with me. [. . .] Have the rest delivered to 43, Rue Blanche. [. . .]

Make up a parcel wrapped in waxed cloth with this address: M. H. Berlioz, via Cologne, and leave it with Desmarest's concierge, 13, Rue Joubert, telling her I'll come and collect it. But don't come to the house. I'll arrange a meeting to pay you what I owe you. Remember that you mustn't mention all this to a living soul and that you know nothing about it either. [. . .]

207 *To his sister Nanci Pal*   Paris, 21 January 1847

I haven't sent you news of all I've been doing these last two months, my dear Nanci, because it would probably not have borne much resemblance to the accounts with which your beloved paper *Le siècle* has favoured you ... Between ourselves I'm very sad that this is the only paper father sees, as it has been biased against me for the last ten years. But if you've read any of the others you'll have seen that *Faust* was a very great success and that at the second performance, for the first time in my life, I had *three* pieces encored, which has never happened in Paris before. I was given an official dinner and with the help of a subscription from both professionals and amateurs I was deemed worthy of a gold medal which is being struck at the moment and which, I'm told, will be very valuable. But now that the work has been heard, now that everyone is talking about it and thirty news-papers have heaped praise upon it, I am unable for lack of a theatre or a concert hall to put it on again. There would be no need for further rehearsals, my performers know their parts perfectly, the expenses would be reduced by half and the takings would be more, but I can't have the Opéra-Comique because of two new pieces which are occupy-ing it every evening. There are too many disadvantages about giving concerts in the daytime, and I can't have the Théâtre-Italien because of

1 Berlioz's copyist and librarian.

a ruling obtained from the Minister by Léon Pillet which forbids it to be open on days when there are performances at the Opéra. As for the Opéra, I wouldn't want to use it even if Pillet and I were not at daggers drawn, and the Conservatoire is reserved by special decree for the Société des Concerts to the exclusion of all other concerts until May. As a result I've spent a vast amount of money putting on this work, with the takings not entirely covering the costs, and now that it could bring me in a large profit for certain, I'm held up for lack of a hall. THERE IS NO CONCERT HALL IN PARIS.

And then the niggardly attitude in high places is not what it was five years ago; the Minister of the Interior, who has responsibility for the arts, cares as little about them as he does about the grocery trade.

There's nothing one can do in this appalling country, and my only desire is to leave it as soon as possible. I'm waiting for the German translation of *Faust* to be finished before leaving for cities that are more welcoming than our wretched Paris. Like a bird of prey, I'm obliged to seek my livelihood at a distance; only the birds of the farmyard are happy living on their dungheap. Despite the rigours of the weather I've made up my mind and I'll be travelling overland to St Petersburg next month. I need to be there at the beginning of Lent. It will be hard going but I'm not inclined to hesitate. After that I'll probably travel to England by sea when the ice allows navigation to proceed. As you see, I'm not satisfied with things, forced as I am to exile myself in order to make a living because I'm surrounded by cretins who have accumulated as many as three highly remunerative positions, like Carafa, for example, a composer from Pacotille whose only recommendation is that he's not French.[1]

I'll write to my father before I leave.

Adieu, I embrace you.

All best wishes to Camille.

H. Berlioz

208 *To Honoré de Balzac*   Paris, 1 or 8 February 1847

My dear Balzac,

You were kind enough to offer me your fur-lined cloak. Would you be good enough to send it to me tomorrow at 41, Rue de Provence? I'll

---

1 Carafa, a Neapolitan, was highly successful and entirely without talent. He was professor of counterpoint and fugue at the Conservatoire, director of the Gymnase for military music, and a member of the Institut.

take care of it and I'll return it faithfully to you in four months' time. The one I was counting on seems to me much too short and I'm particularly worried about my legs being cold.

All best wishes,
Your devoted
Hector Berlioz

The trip to Russia is described in detail in Chapters 55 and 56 of the Mémoires. *Berlioz left on the 14 February 1847 and arrived in St Petersburg two weeks later after an excruciating journey. He was warmly welcomed by Russian musicians thirsty for a chance to hear his music. He gave two highly successful and profitable concerts in the Dvoryansky Hall in March and then travelled on to Moscow where he gave the first two parts of* La damnation de Faust. *He then returned to St Petersburg to conduct two complete performances of* Roméo et Juliette *on 5 and 12 May.*

209 *To his sister Adèle Suat*   St Petersburg, 7 May 1847

Dear little sister,

I've just received Nanci's very brief letter; not realizing that I was still in St Petersburg, our sister has economized on the lines, but even so I'll be here for another fortnight. On my return here from Moscow, where matters also went extremely well, I've just put on my symphony *Roméo et Juliette* in the large theatre; the auditorium was full and I had such a success that we're repeating it next Wednesday. That will nevertheless be my farewell concert. The sun is now so fine and warm that everyone will soon be off to the country; after this interminable winter it's something of a necessity. Both audiences and performers treat me with the greatest sympathy, I'm surrounded by kindnesses and marks of affection. Yesterday the Grand Duchess[1] did me the honour of commanding a Mass in her chapel for me alone so that I could see and hear in their liturgical context her wonderful court choir, who leave the wretches of the Sistine Chapel in Rome so far behind them. I'm still nervous and trembling from the inexpressible emotion I felt. They are truly celestial choirs, and infinity opens up before the listener at the sound of their strange, sublime harmonies. I would not recommend anyone endowed with any sensitivity or suffering from any

1 Maria Nicolayevna, Tsar Nicolas I's daughter.

profound grief to expose himself to such an experience, it's enough to break one's heart and tear out one's soul. And then what majesty there is in this Greek ritual, what simple, dignified ceremonial ... It's immensely beautiful.

They would like to keep me here, indeed everyone says they will do so. The truth is that my name has been mentioned in high places and a number of people are busy trying to arrange matters; but it's a very large question (it involves giving me overall control of music in Russia: theatres, churches, military bands, conservatoires, everything in fact). There are any number of posts which can't be got rid of instantly, this man has to be pensioned off, that one dismissed, etc, etc. The Tsar on his own could settle everything with a word, but he says that his musical budget is not very abundant at the moment. His sons don't have much power and don't dare to speak out too openly. I hope things will sort themselves out in my absence. The Tsarina is very kind and gracious to me, as are her entourage; she's expected to come again to my last concert. [...]

Dear God, how sad I am! I find myself in one of my nervous states, thanks to the performance of *Roméo* and the Greek Mass and the springtime. It came over me the day before yesterday during the concert, at the scene in Capulet's garden; then at the moment of the *Serment de réconciliation* when the choir launched into the final display of my musical fireworks, instead of the joy I should have experienced at the work's crowning glory, I felt only a terrible tightening round my heart, and with a kind of anxiety I followed each bar of my score which, as the end drew near, brought me ever nearer to silence and darkness. The audience called for me I don't know how many times, and I had to go up on the stage, acknowledge their applause and look happy, when I would rather have lain down in the corridor and wept copiously ... I had to come to Russia, it seems, to hear a truly noble performance of this favourite work of mine which has always been mutilated to some extent everywhere else. But I was also in the right mood the day before yesterday, quite ill, as one has to be to capture its spirit. And how well I conducted, how well I played the orchestra! Only the *composer* can know how well the *conductor* served him. It's such a difficult job with this score, a moment's loss of concentration and one is done for, a breath of coldness and it falls flat and the nightingale is only a blackbird, the orange blossom smells of elderberries and Romeo turns into a student ... Laugh at me! Adieu.

H. Berlioz

The Russian concert season over, Berlioz headed home on 22 May. In Riga he gave a concert and then continued via Tilsit to Berlin.

210 *To Count Michal Yurevich Wielgorsky*[1]   Tilsit, 1 June 1847

My dear Count,

[...] There are at the moment eleven hundred boats on the river at Riga and everyone is busy buying or selling corn from eight in the morning to eleven in the evening, with the result that the audience was entirely composed of ladies, except for a very small number of men.[2] Even so I don't regret the exhaustion this concert caused me nor the time it made me lose, thanks to the demonstrations of enthusiasm from this orchestra whom I did not know and whom I now feel I can count as being loyal friends. And then there was the stroke of good luck in store for me in Riga. *Hamlet,* the real *Hamlet* of Shakespeare, was being played there, and very well played too, by an actor called Baumeister whose name I had never heard. As always, I was overwhelmed by this masterpiece from the greatest human genius; the English are right when they say that the most prolific creator after God was Shakespeare ... It ought not to be allowed to present his masterpieces before such a motley collection of idlers, idiots, semi-idiots, semi-literates, grammarians, schoolteachers, soldiers, nannies, flirts, busybodies, toothless lionesses, wet nurses, dandies, corn merchants, horse dealers and commercial travellers.

If I were enormously rich, what performances I would put on for myself and my friends. And I would expel all those people sent here by God to bring artists to humility and to clip the wings of their ambition!

Luckily he has also put here several lofty spirits supported and inspired by fine hearts, to restore the courage of these same artists when they fall asphyxiated amid the mob of cretins. You know these hearts, my dear Count, and these rare spirits, and you must know the respect and the gratitude they inspire. [...]

Adieu, my dear Count, with all my devoted and respectful affection,

Hector Berlioz

1 An amateur composer, one of Berlioz's St Petersburg admirers.
2 In the *Mémoires* Berlioz records an audience of 132 women and seven men.

My dear Morel,

[. . .] I gave *Faust* yesterday. The performance was marvellous from both the orchestra and the chorus, the chorus especially. Boetticher is an excellent Mephistopheles but the Faust and the Marguerite were extremely feeble. The chorus in Pandemonium and the one in Heaven are quite different when performed with this sort of verve and these fresh, agile voices from what they must have seemed in Paris; the *Chœur de sylphes* when sung like this has a sound which even the St Petersburg performance had not brought home to me. An encore was asked for as always, but because I didn't pick up the phrase 'da capo', which is what they shout here, instead of the word 'bis' which you can hear above the bravos, I didn't play it again; I'm told the Berliners were shocked by this. Some of the orchestra were hostile because of various criticisms they claim I made of them in my letters about my first visit to Germany. For this the Intendant, who on this occasion did his duty, ordered some of them to make a full apology and gave them all a thorough dressing-down. Nothing of all this affected the performance; on the contrary the orchestra was marvellous (keep this incident to yourself). The King invited me to dinner at Sans-Souci and afterwards we had a long talk walking in the garden; I was the only musician in the party. [. . .]

Yesterday I saw *La vestale* done here *complete*, that's to say as it was published, without any cuts, and even though the Julia and the Licinius were weak, the rehearsal especially made a tremendous impression on me. The final aria, which is never sung in Paris, is sublime! What a work!! What a libretto! And in addition, I saw *Hamlet* in Riga!!!!! . . .

Every evening in Paris you have twenty vaudevilles and music for *porters* . . .

Yours ever,

H. B.

212 *To Joseph-Esprit Duchesne*[1]   Paris, ?July 1847

My dear M. Duchesne,

Would you be good enough to slip into your article a few words about Mlle Charton, a charming person with real talent whose voice is

---

1 Head of personnel at the Ministry of the Interior and an occasional music critic for the *Journal des débats*. From 1852 to 1870 he was mayor of Vervins, near the Belgian border.

as fresh as her face and who sings in tune and vocalizes with considerable facility. This recommendation is not sent just to be obliging, since I don't know her. She's recently sung in *Ne touchez pas à la reine* with great success.[1]

Yours ever,
With all best wishes,
H. Berlioz

---

213 *To his sister Nanci Pal*   Paris, 25 August 1847

My dear Nanci,

Since my last letter, I had to abandon the idea of going to La Côte completely. I'd been given a *verbal* promise at the Opéra of a fairly important post and I was to begin it on 1 September.[2] But while this business was dragging on, thanks to all kinds of conflicting intrigues and the meanness of the directors over the matter of my salary, the director of the Drury Lane Theatre came from London and offered me the post of conductor of the English Grand Opera, which will occupy me for only three months in the year and will bring me in 10,000 francs. In addition he is asking me to give four concerts in London consisting entirely of my own works and is guaranteeing me a further 10,000 francs for those. Besides all that he wants me to write a three-act opera which will be staged in a year or fifteen months from now. As a result, I have decided to release our poor Parisian directors politely from their promise and have renounced fair France for perfidious Albion. So, since I don't intend to be in England until November, as soon as I've completed one or two arrangements here and an article I have to write for the *Débats*, I'll leave for La Côte. As you see, everything is fitting in splendidly with your plans. Even so, I don't see how we can all stay with father. It'll be a veritable caravanserai.[3]

I urge you to bring your husband, it's vital that he comes. We must go hunting together, or at least have a long talk over hill and dale while

---

1 Anne-Arsène Charton was to become, under the name Mme Charton-Demeur, the creator of two great Berlioz roles, Beatrice in *Béatrice et Bénédict* in 1862, and Dido in *Les Troyens à Carthage* in 1863. On returning from Russia he was probably hearing her for the first time, aged twenty-three, singing in Boisselot's opera at the Opéra-Comique.
2 Duponchel and Rocqueplan, successors to Pillet as joint directors of the Opéra, promised Berlioz a position, first musical director, then chorus master, in return for Bertin's political support. Their bad faith soon became clear and Berlioz withdrew from the negotiations.
3 Berlioz visited his father at La Côte in mid-September and took Louis, aged thirteen, with him. It was the last time he was to see his father.

we pretend to hunt. Still, this murderous pastime does have its attractions for me. I went to stay last winter with my dentist, who has a charming property near Beauvais, and killed a number of rabbits and partridges. I blew the cobwebs off myself.

My uncle will be returning, no doubt?

Adieu.

All my best wishes,

H. Berlioz

214 *To Humbert Ferrand*   Paris, 1 November 1847

My dear Ferrand,

I leave for London the day after tomorrow; I've been asked to go there, on excellent financial terms, to conduct the orchestra of the English Grand Opera and to give four concerts. God knows now when we shall see each other, as my tenure is for six years and for the four months of the year during which there is the possibility of meeting you occasionally in Paris.

You've heard how well my Russian visit went; I was given an imperial welcome. Huge successes, huge takings, huge performances, etc, etc.

And now to England. France is becoming more and more unresponsive to music; and 'the more I see of foreign lands, the less I love my own'. Pardon the blasphemy!¹

But art, in France, is dead; it's putrefying . . . So one must go to other places where it still exists. It seems there's been a remarkable revolution in England over the last ten years in the nation's musical understanding.

We'll see. [. . .]

Your devoted

H. Berlioz

215 *To his father Dr Louis Berlioz*   London, 7 November 1847

Dear father,

I'm writing you a few rather hasty lines to let you know that I've arrived in London and to give you my address. I'm staying at the house of M. Jullien (a French musician married to an Englishwoman) who is

1 Berlioz deforms a line from P.-L. de Belloy's tragedy *Le siège de Calais* (1765): 'The more I see of foreign lands the more I love my own.'

the director of the Drury Lane Theatre, the orchestra of which has been entrusted to my care.[1] I've known him for a long time and I'm entirely at my ease with him in every respect. The crossing was delightful, the sea was calm and the boat glided as though it was on a lake. I was accompanied by an English man of letters, M. Gruneisen,[2] who, when we arrived at Folkestone, insisted on jumping on to land before me so that he could hold out his hand with a cordial 'Welcome to British soil!' That's one of those nice English ideas suggested by national pride, which would never occur to a continental. London is terrifyingly large. It takes three quarters of an hour to get from Jullien's house to Drury Lane, and they call that a 'few steps'. We're going to spend the rest of this month and some days of the next in preparation and rehearsals; the English Grand Opera can't open till around 10 December. I've already seen my orchestra at work and it's one of the most excellent I could wish for; I find it contains quite a number of French and German players whom I know, who welcomed me with open arms. I have every reason to believe that things in my department will go splendidly. I'm now going to settle down to write a piece on the theme of *God Save the Queen* for the opening of the theatre. I hadn't thought of doing so, but Jullien, whose eyes and ears are everywhere, would like me to repeat here the scene with the Hungarians in Pest by plucking the English national heartstrings in the same way. It's the custom in any case for this well-known tune to be played at important occasions of this kind.[3]

My concerts won't begin until the middle of January; the English translator of my works will have had time to finish his task, I'll know my soloists better, we shall have moved in. So this delay suits me, indeed it is only sensible. I'm quite surprised at knowing so much English; I can say more or less everything I want to and without too much of an accent, but I don't understand near half of what's said to me. It's something I shall have to get down to seriously.

Adieu, dear father, I embrace you tenderly and ask you to have news of you sent to me as soon as possible.

H. Berlioz, c/o M. Jullien, 76, Harley Street.

---

1 Louis Jullien was a French violinist and conductor who went to London in 1838 and had much success conducting promenade concerts, balls, outdoor concerts, 'monster' concerts and provincial tours. He was one of the great showmen of his time. This was his first venture into opera.
2 Charles Lewis Gruneisen was music critic for the *Illustrated London News*.
3 Whether or not Berlioz ever arranged the British national anthem, such a thing has never come to light.

My dear Rogé,

[...] I've come to London alone; you can guess the reasons why. Apart from any other considerations I had a profound need of the liberty which has been denied me at all times and in all places until now. It needed, not a *coup d'état*, but a succession of *coups d'état* to succeed in regaining it. Even so, until the main rehearsals begin, the isolation I'm living in most of the time is going to seem strange.

Since I've broached confidential matters, would you believe that in Petersburg I fell in love, truly and grotesquely, with one of your chorus? ... (At this point I allow you a laugh on full orchestra and in the major! ... Come on now, don't be upset ...) I continue. – In love poetically, fatally and absolutely *innocently* (in whichever way you care to interpret the term) with a young girl (not all that young) who said to me: 'I'll *wrote* to you', and who, speaking of her mother's obsession with marrying her off, added: 'It's a bore!'

How many walks we took together in the outskirts of Petersburg and out into the countryside, between nine and eleven o'clock at night! ... What bitter tears I shed when, like Marguerite in *Faust*, she said: 'Heavens, I can't understand what you see in me ... I'm only a poor young girl far below your level ... it's not possible that you can love me like this, etc, etc.' But it's so possible, it's true, and I thought I would die of despair when I went past the Grand Theatre on the coach out of Petersburg. And finding no letter from her in Berlin made me really ill. She was so adamant that she would *wrote* to me! ... And in Paris too, no news. I've written; but no reply. There's a *bore*! It's so undignified! I know you have a kind heart, so enough laughing, I'm weeping real tears as I write this ... Be so good as to pass on to her the enclosed note, and tell her too, if you can, how unhappy her silence is making me. I expect she's married by now. Her fiancé left for Sweden the evening of my first concert and must have been back for some time. She damages her fingers making corsets – her sister runs a business selling them – but not to the extent that she can't write to me. She can write and she knows how, since she knows five languages, Russian, French (given some *tiny* mistakes like the ones I've mentioned), German, Danish and Swedish.

---

1 A French cellist whom Berlioz had known at the Paris Conservatoire. A Saint-Simonian and ardent traveller, he was playing in the Imperial Opera in St Petersburg when Berlioz visited.

O God! I see us still on the banks of the Neva, in the evening, at sunset ... What a burst of passion! I crushed her arm against my chest ... I sang her the beautiful phrase from the Adagio of *Roméo et Juliette* – You can tell how I love her!

I promised her, I offered her all that I could promise or offer ... and I've not had so much as two lines since my departure. I'm not even sure that it was she who waved goodbye to me as I climbed into the coach! Adieu, adieu. You at least, you will *wrote* to me.

H. Berlioz

P.S. As it could well be that by now she's married in one way or another, see that no one is aware of your message, so as not to compromise her. And when you reply, don't laugh at me too much.

---

217 *To Henry Fothergill Chorley*[1]   London, 14 November 1847

My dear M. Chorley,

I share your sorrow, I assure you.[2] Even if I was not so close to Mendelssohn as you were, I still knew him well; and even if we had never met I should mourn him as a great artist and a man of eminently superior mind.

It is a harsh blow that death has delivered to the cause of worthy and serious music and we must all feel it deeply.

I shall be with you before five o'clock on Wednesday with the scores, if they haven't already reached you by then.

My hasty best wishes,
Your devoted
H. Berlioz

1 Music critic for the *Athenaeum* and a much travelled writer on music.
2 Mendelssohn died in Leipzig on 4 November 1847 aged thirty-eight.

My dear Morel,

Jullien asks me to write to you in confidence to find out the truth about the success of Verdi's opera.[1] Never mind the merits of the work, he wants to hear about it from the director's point of view.

We shan't open for another week; *La fiancée de Lammermoor* with Mme Gras and M. Reeves must, in my opinion, do well.[2] Reeves has an attractive, natural voice and sings as well as this frightful English language allows him to.

The baritone Whitworth is not so good; we're expecting Staudigl daily. We're putting on the opera by Balfe[3] in the meantime. The orchestra is superb and, apart from some imperfect intonation in the woodwind, one couldn't find a better. We have a chorus of 120 which is also good. All of them gave me a very warm welcome the day Jullien played *L'invitation à la valse* in one of his concerts. The orchestra gave me an ovation and the audience demanded an encore of the piece by . . . Weber! And then there are large numbers of French, German and Italian musicians who knew me already and are utterly devoted to me. They include Tolbecque, Rousselot, Sainton, Piatti, Eisenbaum, Baumann, etc, etc. I don't begin my concerts until January. [. . .]

I'm terribly bored in the fine flat which Jullien has given me. But I've had any number of invitations since I've been here, and your friend M. Grimblot is good enough to come and see me regularly. He took me to his club, though God knows what entertainment is to be found in an English club! A week ago Macready[4] gave a magnificent dinner in my honour; he's a charming man and not in the least pretentious in his own home. He's terrifying at rehearsals, and has reason to be. I saw him the other day in a new tragedy, *Philip van Artevelde*;[5] he's superb in it and he produced the play in a truly extraordinary manner: no one here understands as he does the art of

---

1 *Jérusalem*, a new French version of *I lombardi*, was played at the Opéra on 22 November 1847.
2 Donizetti's *Lucia di Lammermoor*, given as *The Bride of Lammermoor*, with Berlioz conducting. Mme Gras had sung Teresa in *Benvenuto Cellini* in 1838; Sims Reeves was the leading English tenor of his time who had already sung the role of Edgardo at La Scala, Milan. The opera opened on 6 December.
3 *The Maid of Honour.*
4 The actor Macready had known Harriet Smithson since 1824 and had appeared with her many times.
5 By Henry Taylor, first staged in 1834.

managing crowds and of getting them to act. It's admirable.

Yours as ever,

H. Berlioz

219 *To Auguste Morel*   London, 14 January 1848

My dear Morel,

[...] I'm working here like a horse tied to a mill-wheel, rehearsing every day from midday to four o'clock and conducting at the opera every evening from seven o'clock until ten. Only two days ago did rehearsals cease and I'm beginning to recover from an attack of influenza which was troubling me, being treated as it was by fatigue and cold draughts in the theatre. You've already heard no doubt of the frightful situation Jullien has got himself into, taking us all with him. But as one must do as little as possible to spoil his reputation in Paris, don't pass on to anyone what I'm about to tell you. It's not the Drury Lane enterprise which has dissipated his fortune; that was already gone before the opening and he had no doubt counted on enormous receipts to restore it. Jullien is still the same madman you remember, he hasn't the least idea of the requirements of an opera theatre, nor of the most obvious requirements for a good musical performance. He opened his theatre without having a *single* score of his own, with the exception of Balfe's opera, which he then had to have copied, and until now we've been relying on the goodwill of Lumley's employees,¹ who are lending us the orchestral parts of the Italian operas we're putting on.² Jullien is at the moment making his tour of the provinces, earning a lot of money with his promenade concerts; the theatre here brings in highly respectable receipts every evening and, to cut a long story short, having agreed to have our salaries cut by a third *we're not being paid at all*. The only payments being paid are weekly ones to the chorus, the orchestra and the workmen, so the theatre can keep going. And yet Jullien sold his music shop in Regent Street a fortnight ago for nearly two hundred thousand francs ... and I can't get paid, and the principal actors, the scene painter, the chorus and ballet masters, the producer, everyone is in the same position. Can you imagine it? [...]

If Jullien doesn't pay me when he gets back I shall try to arrange things with Lumley and give my concerts in Her Majesty's Theatre. There's now a good position here that I can have, left vacant by the

1 Lumley was director of Her Majesty's Theatre.
2 Donizetti's *Linda di Chamounix* was also in the repertory.

death of poor Mendelssohn.[1] Everyone is talking to me about it from morning until night, the press and musicians are very well disposed towards me, and already the two rehearsals I've held of *Harold*, *Le carnaval romain* and two parts of *Faust* have made them open their eyes and ears wide. I have reason to believe that *this* is where I can find a good post. As for France, I've given up thinking about it and God preserve me from succumbing to temptations like the one you held out to me in your last letter of coming and giving a concert in Paris in April. If ever I have enough money to GIVE concerts to my Parisian friends I shall do so, but don't imagine I'm so simple as to rely on the public to cover the costs. I will not make new appeals for its attention, to be met only with indifference and to lose the money which I make with much difficulty by travelling. I shall be extremely sorry about it, because the sympathy of my friends in France remains the dearest to me of all. But the evidence is there; when I compare the impressions my music has made on all the European audiences who have heard it, I am forced to conclude that the Parisian audience is the one that understands it least. Have I, at my Paris concerts, ever seen *society people*, men and women, *moved* as I've done in Germany and Russia? Have I seen princes of the blood taking an interest in my compositions to the point of getting up at eight o'clock in the morning to go into a cold, dark hall and hear them being rehearsed, as the Princess of Prussia did in Berlin? Have I ever been invited to play the smallest part in concerts at court? Is not the Société du Conservatoire, or at least those who run it, hostile to me? Is it not grotesque that concerts are given of works by everyone who has any sort of musical reputation, except mine? Is it not wounding for me to see the Opéra continually having recourse to musical bunglers and its directors continually armed with prejudices against me which I should blush to have to fight against, if their hand were forced? Does not the press become daily ever more corrupt and do we see anything in it nowadays (with a few rare exceptions) except intrigue, underhand dealings and cretinism?

Even the people I've helped and supported so many times in my articles, have they ever shown the least real gratitude? And do you imagine that I'm taken in by a mass of furiously smiling people who only hide their nails and teeth because they know that I have *claws* and *tusks*? To see nothing on all sides but imbecility, indifference, ingratitude or terror, that's my lot in Paris. If only my friends were happy there! But far from it, you're nearly all slaves in constricting,

1 Mendelssohn had no official position in London, but he had conducted there frequently.

badly paid jobs; I can do nothing for you and your efforts on my behalf are impotent. So France has been wiped off my musical map and I've made my decision to turn my eyes and thoughts away from it as far as I can. I'm not in a melancholy mood today, I'm not suffering from spleen; I write to you with the utmost sang-froid, the most complete lucidity of mind. I see the facts as they are.

A real regret for me in these increasingly frequent absences from Paris is not seeing you; and I'm sure you didn't think otherwise. You know how much I appreciate the rightness of judgment, the goodness of spirit and the love of art which you have shown me so often. So forgive me for being so frank in making you my profession of nationalistic faith.

Adieu, I shake you by the hand and assure you, as ever, of my warm and sincere friendship.

H. Berlioz

220 *To Alexey Fyodorovich Lvov*[1]   London, 29 January 1848

My dear General,

[. . .] We used to have a superb orchestra, but the director has taken the flower of it off with him on his tour of the provinces where he's giving popular concerts, so we have to content ourselves with what he didn't want and keep going all the same.

I hear arguments about music, about audiences, about performers which would make the four strings of your violin break in fury if they could listen to them; I put up with English female singers who would snap and twist the hairs of your bow . . .

I've also been asked to put on four concerts; I'll give the first in a week's time, 7 February. We haven't so far been able to have the whole orchestra together even once for rehearsal. These gentlemen appear when they please and disappear about their private business, some in the middle of rehearsals, some a quarter of the way through. The first day I had no horns at all; the second I had three; the third I had two who left after the fourth piece. So much for discipline in this country. Only the chorus singers are devoted to me, almost as much as the ones in St Petersburg . . . Oh, for Russia and its cordial hospitality, its literary and artistic habits, and the organization of its theatres and chapel, so precise, clear and inflexible, without which, in music as in

---

1 Infant prodigy on the violin and then simultaneously composer and general, Lvov was a leading figure in St Petersburg musical life and a keen admirer of Berlioz's music.

many other things, nothing fine or beautiful can be achieved! Who will restore them to me? Why are you so far away?

Now I've been ill in bed for five days with violent bronchitis; it's the result of anger, disgust and vexation. Still, there's plenty to do here, because of the public, which is attentive, intelligent and really appreciates serious music.

I've heard poor Mendelssohn's last oratorio (*Elijah*). It's wonderfully grand and of an indescribable harmonic sumptuousness. [. . .]

221 *To Alfred de Vigny*   London, 10 February 1848

My dear de Vigny,
    [. . .] My music has caught these English audiences like fire on a trail of gunpowder.¹ I had the very devil of a reception, I was recalled, I had to repeat two of the scenes from *Faust,* and all the press notices are favourable. Only the *Morning Chronicle* has reservations because (says this old simpleton of a critic) I make mistakes of *counterpoint* and *rhythm . . . Sancta simplicitas*! I wish you could hear the *Concert de sylphes*, which had such an effect on them. Truly, I think you'd like it. Macready is away in the provinces. The theatre drags itself along, there's only a fortnight left until it expires, it's due to close on the 25th.
    Adieu, adieu, *remember me! I am very happy to be able to call myself your friend.*²
    H. Berlioz

222 *To Auguste Morel*   London, 6 March 1848

My dear Morel,
    [. . .] May the fires of Heaven and Hell combine to burn up that damned city of Paris . . .³ I hope at least we shall be relieved of the *droit des hospices* for concerts,⁴ I hope there'll be no more subsidies for our stupid opera houses, I hope the directors of these places will go back whence they came and at top speed, I hope there'll be no more

1 Berlioz gave his first London concert on 7 February 1848 in the Theatre Royal, Drury Lane. It was an enormous success.
2 'Remember me!' are the words of the Ghost in *Hamlet*: the rest is Berlioz's own English.
3 In February 1848 the streets of Paris erupted in violence and Louis-Philippe abdicated. The Second Republic was proclaimed on 26 February.
4 The tax on concerts, also known as the *droit des pauvres*, was reduced from 12.5 per cent to 1 per cent on 24 February.

censorship of sung material, I hope in fact we shall be free to be free. If not, then there's further mystification for us to undergo.

What's become of M. Bertin? The rumour is that he's in hiding ... What's become of all our 'precious villains', as Shakespeare calls them?

Please write to me.

I'm giving a concert at Exeter Hall in a few weeks.

Adieu, adieu,

H. Berlioz

223 *To Joseph d'Ortigue*   76, Harley Street
                                                      London, 15 March 1848

My dear d'Ortigue,

I've been wanting to write to you for a long time and today is the first moment I've had. Life in London is even more absorbing than in Paris; everything is in proportion to the immensity of the city. I get up at midday and at one o'clock visitors arrive: friends, new acquaintances and musicians who've come to introduce themselves whether I like it or not; that's three hours lost. From four to six I work. If I don't have any invitations, I go out for dinner some way away from here, I read the papers, after which it's time for theatres and concerts: I stay and listen to whatever music there is until 11.30, then at last three or four of us musicians go off together to have supper in some tavern and smoke till two in the morning. So much for the external details of my life here. [. . .]

All in all, I'll stay here as long as I can, because it takes time to get oneself known and to acquire a post. Luckily circumstances are favourable and sooner or later this post will come up and will, I'm told, be one worth having. My only hopes for a musical career are centred now on England or Russia. My period of mourning for France was over long ago; this last revolution has made my decision all the firmer and more insistent. Under the old government I had to combat the hatred engendered by my articles against the ineptitude of those who governed our theatres and against the public's indifference. Now I should have to deal with the mass of great composers whom the republic has discovered, and with music calling itself popular, philanthropic, national and economic. The arts in France are now dead and music in particular is already beginning to putrefy, I hope they give it a quick burial, I can smell its miasma from here ...[1]

1 In London Berlioz began to compile his *Mémoires*, whose Preface, dated 21 March 1848, expresses sentiments similar to these.

It's true, I always feel a certain automatic response turning me towards France whenever I've had some success in my career, but it's an old habit I shall grow out of in time, a prejudice decidedly. From the musical point of view France is merely a land of cretins and ne'er-do-wells, you have to be an outright chauvinist not to recognize the fact. [. . .]

Your devoted
H. Berlioz

224 *To his sister Nanci Pal*   London, 16 March 1848

Dear Nanci,

How are you all getting on in the middle of this infernal hullabaloo? Has this affected your husband or my father financially? Let me know. As for me, this means that France is finally closed to me. Art there is now buried, it was merely moribund before, now it's dead and it smells like a corpse. My friends are pressing me to return to Paris, saying that there are developments in my favour . . . I know the men and the materials of our damned country too well not to believe precisely the opposite. This is the moment when cretinism can and will raise its head; after the art of the antichamber we shall have the art of the gutter. What's more, while the republic leaves artists entirely free to die of hunger, it's still imposing the burden of taxes which was weighing on them; I read this in yesterday's papers. So I'm staying here where I still have things I can do, where I am liked and respected; to go to Paris would be to abandon my prey for a shadow. But Jullien still won't pay me and, whatever happens, this year will be disastrous for me. [. . .]

Adieu, dear sister, write to me as soon as you can.

I embrace you, Camille and Mathilde too.

H. Berlioz

P.S. The riots here are over;[1] they don't know how to go about these things. They know how to go about stealing jewellery, though. In the commotion in Trafalgar Square I lost a nice tie-pin which someone snatched off my cravat. That's how things are.

---

1 There were disturbances too in London in response to similar events on the Continent, but much less violent. The Chartist demonstration on 10 April was a fiasco.

225 *To James William Davison*[1]   London, 17 March 1848

My dear Davison,

   [...]

P.S. I looked out for you the other evening at Exeter Hall, like hunting for a diamond in the sand. I wanted to say to you, something you know as well as I do, that Mendelssohn's symphony is a masterpiece struck in a single instant, like a gold medal.[2] I know of nothing so new, so alive, so noble and so expertly crafted in the freedom of its inspiration. Only the Paris Conservatoire is unaware of this magnificent composition; it'll discover it in ten years' time.

226 *To Charles Hallé*[3]   London, end of March 1848

My dear Hallé,

   I'm truly *sorry* to have the pleasure of seeing you; my thanks nonetheless for coming to the house immediately after your shipwreck on the English coast. If you're around this evening we can grieve together over a cigar. I'll come by about ten o'clock.

   Yours ever,

   H. Berlioz

227 *To his sister Nanci Pal*   London, 5 April 1848

Dear sister,

   [...] The news from Paris gets more and more upsetting every day. I won't say alarming, there can be no alarms when hope has vanished. They're all going to massacre each other before two months are out. Here everything is in preparation. Next Monday we shall have a hundred and fifty thousand Chartists roaming through the streets of London. The clubs are busy making long lances to arm those who haven't got guns. The Irish are seething in their corner. But the haughty English aristocracy won't budge an inch; they find it quite natural that they should have everything and other poor wretches

---

1 Editor of the *Musical World* and music critic of *The Times*. The overture *Le corsaire* was dedicated to him.
2 The 'Italian' Symphony, performed in Exeter Hall on 13 March.
3 Originally Karl Halle from Hagen, Germany, Hallé had been in Paris since 1836 and had played a Beethoven concerto in one of Berlioz's 1845 concerts. He was a refugee from the disorders in France, little knowing that he would stay in England for the rest of his life and found Manchester's famous orchestra.

nothing. What's worth taking is worth holding on to.[1]

I've lost nearly four thousand francs in Paris, or at least I consider them as being lost.[2] For me, that's a lot of money. [. . .]

Adieu, I embrace you, your brother,

H. Berlioz

228 *To Edouard Monnais*[3]   London, 1 May 1848

My dear Monnais,

[. . .] My God, how I should like to travel in earnest, that's to say go for three or four thousand leagues without stopping and see something new and less ugly than what is before me now!

Years are like days, they follow each other but have few features in common. Last year at this season I was in Russia, very happy, making excellent music on the grand scale, earning a lot of money, but today there are only irritations of every kind . . .

Adieu, I shake your hand and thank you sincerely for your true friendship.

H. Berlioz

26, Osnaburgh Street, Regent's Park[4]

229 *To Louis-Joseph Duc*[5]   London, 26 May 1848

My dear Duc,

[. . .] For the last seven years I've lived entirely from what my works and concerts have brought me in from abroad. Without Germany, Bohemia, Hungary and above all Russia, I should have been dead in France a hundred times over. People talk of a 'position' to be gained and 'posts' that can be canvassed for. What position, what posts? There are none vacant. Isn't Auber at the Conservatoire, Carafa at the Gymnase, Girard at the Opéra? Apart from that, what is there? Nothing, and has love of mediocrities been banished from the French character by the Revolution? It's possible, but in that case it will have

1 A quotation from Beaumarchais's *Barbier de Séville*.
2 Berlioz was reckoning on the loss of his two regular sources of income: the librarianship of the Conservatoire and his writing for the *Journal des débats*.
3 Theatre and music critic who wrote for the *Revue et gazette musicale* under the name Paul Smith.
4 Berlioz moved from Harley Street when Jullien's creditors called. Marie Recio had just joined him from Paris.
5 Distinguished architect and friend of Berlioz's in Rome. He designed the column in the Place de la Bastille.

been replaced by love of men and things that are worse still (if there is anything worse than mediocrity). No, there's nothing I can do in France except cultivate the friendships I hold dear. As for my career, I've done enough trying, suffering and waiting; France is not the place to pursue it. All I've ever found there were insults, more or less well disguised, and stupid opposition, because the national mentality is stupid when it comes to higher questions of art and literature; and I have an unalterable and ever-increasing contempt for those French ideas which other peoples are simply ignorant of. I found nothing but indifference and disdain under the last government, and now I would find these supplemented by serious causes of anxiety. I wrote to Louis-Philippe three times, when he was King, requesting an audience, and I never received so much as an answer. I wrote to Ledru-Rollin[1] recently and he was just as polite as the King. There's only one opera house in Paris, the Opéra, and it's run by a cretin and its doors are closed to me. Do you think they'll dismiss Duponchel and, if he's dismissed, that they won't find twenty others? Yes, perhaps they'll come to me one day, when I'm very old and tired and no longer good for anything; but by that time I shall still perhaps have some of my memory left and this belated confidence of theirs, if it ever happens, will be all the more painful for me as a result. So there's nothing better for me to do than what I'm doing. I'm a savage, I protect my liberty, I keep going as long as the earth will carry me and as long as there are deer and moose in the forest, and if I often have to suffer exhaustion, insomnia, cold, famine and the insults of the palefaces, I can at least dream as I wish by the side of cataracts and in the silence of the forest, adore the grandeur of nature and thank God for leaving me the power to appreciate his beauties.

I saw *Hamlet* a few days ago; Marie and I came out of it literally shattered, trembling and drunk with relief and admiration. [. . .]

Yours very sincerely,
H. Berlioz

230 *To his sister Nanci Pal*   London, 11 July 1848

[. . .] Harriet was walking (on the 27th) in the garden in Montmartre around seven o'clock in the evening. Someone fired at her and one of the bullets lodged in a tree a few inches from her left side. It was a miracle she escaped. I don't know what's going to become of us, I

1 Minister of the Interior in the provisional government.

return the day after tomorrow to the hell of Paris. I don't know yet where I shall stay.[1] I can't go to Montmartre. I'll take a student's lodgings and live for twenty sous a day ... [...]

Berlioz gave a second concert on 29 June in Hanover Square Rooms. Many refugees from European turmoil took part, and the audience gave him a great ovation. For all the opportunities London offered, Berlioz was now extremely short of funds and he felt he had to return to Paris, however much he scorned the state of musical affairs there. He and Marie left on 13 July and took an apartment in the Rue de la Rochefoucauld.

Two weeks later, on 28 July, his father, Dr Berlioz, died at La Côte-St-André, aged seventy-two. Berlioz was not called to the dying man's bedside and he did not attend the funeral, but went a month later to confer with his two brothers-in-law, both lawyers, over the settlement of the estate.

231 *To his sister Adèle Suat*   Paris, 21 August 1848

My dear Adèle,

I shall leave next Monday, the 28th, and go straight to Vienne to spend several hours or days with you before our sad, sad family reunion. Nanci has been told and replied yesterday. She is offering to advance me some money for the journey. If you write to her before I arrive, thank her for her offer, which I do not accept, not being quite in that state of financial deprivation.

I quite understand that it might have been less painful for all of us (though I'm not sure) to postpone our return to the melancholy atmosphere of poor father's house by some months. But as you know I have very little time at my disposal and I must take what the demands of my situation leave me. The details you recount in your letter tear at my heart; from the few lines Suat wrote me, I thought that father had at least been spared the sufferings of a long agony. Oh, why was I not at least there to share your misery, if not to alleviate his! . . . I can't believe he would not have recognized me . . .

I'm now in a state of complete despondency. I feel as though my life no longer has any purpose. Instinctively, in everything I did, there was

---

1 Marie had evidently given up her apartment in the Rue de Provence. Harriet was living in the Rue Blanche, Montmartre.

always an inclination towards my father, a desire to see him approve them, a hope that he would be proud of them . . . And now . . .

Adieu, dear sister, at least there will always be between all of us who are left in this sad world a reciprocal communion of strong and unchanging affections.

All best wishes to your good husband.

I'm delighted to know that, thanks to your initiative, the clouds which had formed between Nanci and yourself have been permanently dispersed.

I embrace you warmly,

H. Berlioz

While he was at La Côte, Berlioz had an urge to revisit Meylan, the scene of his childhood passion for Estelle Dubeuf. His nostalgic pilgrimage there is recounted in Chapter 58 of the Mémoires. *He discovered that Estelle was living nearby, a widow aged fifty-one, and he wrote to her, though he had no reply.*

In Paris he resumed his work for the Débats, *and his sinecure at the Conservatoire was not after all taken away. Louis, aged fourteen, was still in school in Rouen.*

232 *To his son Louis Berlioz*   Paris, 21 October 1848

My dear Louis,

Your mother is a little better, but she still has to stay in bed and refrain from talking. And the slightest access of emotion would be fatal to her. So don't write her a letter like the last one you sent me. Nothing is so upsetting as seeing you abandon yourself to inactivity and depression; you'll reach the age of eighteen without being able to start on any career. I've no money, you'll have no position, what shall we live on? You're always talking of becoming a sailor, so it looks as though you really want to leave me! . . . Because once you're at sea, God knows when I should see you again. If I were free and entirely independent, I would leave with you and we could go and try our luck in the Indies or elsewhere, but travelling demands a certain financial stability, and the little I have forces me to remain in France. In any case my composing career keeps me in Europe, and I should have to give it up completely if I left the old world for the new. I'm talking to you here like a grown-up young man. When you think about it, you'll understand. But whatever happens, I shall always be your best friend and the *only* one entirely devoted to you and full of an unchanging affection for you.

I know you love me, which makes up for everything. Even so it will be very sad if, at twenty, you are still no good to yourself or to society.

I'm sending you some envelopes so you can write to your aunts. My sister Nanci mentions you, so I enclose her letter. There's no need for black wax;[1] anyway there's no way I can send you any as one can't put wax sticks in the post.

Tell me about your teeth: has someone cleaned them properly?

Adieu my dear boy, I embrace you with all my heart.

H. Berlioz

233 *To his sister Adèle Suat*   Paris, 1 November 1848

My dear Adèle,

I've just spent three violently agitated weeks and I'm numb with every kind of exhaustion. Sixteen or seventeen days ago Harriet had an attack of apoplexy which left her paralysed all down her right side and she's lost the use of speech. I had to go to Montmartre twice a day and the doctor did his best to do the same; he bled her regularly, applied mustard plasters and gave her the rest of the treatment indicated by her condition, without the slightest effect. Finally, since the day before yesterday, she has begun to be able to pronounce a few words of English but she can't say even two in French. The paralysis seems to be letting up slightly, but even the imperceptible sensation she has just in her feet is hard to observe. At that very moment the committee of the Association of Paris Musicians had just entrusted me with the organizing and conducting of an immense musical celebration which took place in the palace of Versailles. You can imagine how busy I've been! The concert took place last Sunday, in the dazzling theatre to which the public until now had only been admitted once by Louis-Philippe. The takings were enormous and we turned away more than five hundred people. I had a tremendous success with my own compositions. But this pomp and circumstance has totally exhausted me, wasted any amount of my time and brought me in nothing, because the takings go to the funds of the society. A party from the government came, including M. Marrast[2] who *demanded* the royal seat. So the chair in the middle of the amphitheatre has now been occupied by five sovereigns: Louis XV, Louis XVI, Louis-Philippe I, Napoleon I, and Marrast O!!!! [. . .]

1 A token of mourning.
2 President of the Assemblée Nationale.

All best wishes to Suat, and to you whatever is left over and above those.

H. Berlioz

234 *To his sister Nanci Pal*   Paris, 24 February 1849

Dear sister,

I wrote to Camille two or three weeks ago and asked for news of you; he did not reply. Is your illness worse? Let me know how you are.

Harriet had a second attack last week; she remained unconscious for two days, groaning all the time. The doctor again bled her thoroughly but without much hope. Against all expectation she now seems better. The doctor says it was a single cerebral congestion, but you can imagine how serious that is in her present state. Still, yesterday she began to eat a little and to say a few intelligible words. She's quite conscious now, but without any memory of her last seizure, of the last bleeding, or anything. She was almost cheerful yesterday; you know as well as I do how terribly heart-rending that can be.

I've never had so many things to do, so many demands on my time, and with this sad preoccupation I have hardly any to spare. I've also had to deal with one of my London friends (Wallace)[1] who had no sooner arrived in Paris than he was struck down by ophthalmia, which is keeping him in his room in total darkness. I'm sorry for the poor young man and go to keep him company when I can. All the time there are musical events which I have to attend, then my articles to write and I can't do any work on my *Te Deum*.[2] Last Sunday some fragments of *La vestale* bowled over the Conservatoire audience. Spontini was applauded and called back, the enthusiasm was at fever pitch. But the poor man didn't really enjoy it. The sole idea he has in his head is that he is dying and every moment of the day he says that his last hour has come. He has his wife read out to him the prayer for the dying and asks for his Bible. He invited me to dinner the night before last; I spent the evening reasoning with him, proving to him that he was in good health. It was no good. He seized me in his arms with a sort of frenzy, saying, 'Ah, my dear Berlioz, I'm so frightened of death! Dying is such a terrible thing!!! My hour has come, I know it. You will take my place

---

1 Vincent Wallace, composer of *Maritana*, whom Berlioz met in London. His adventures are told in *Les soirées de l'orchestre*.
2 Berlioz had been planning a *Te Deum* for two or three years, using music which he had composed many years before. The main task of composition was undertaken in 1849.

at the Institut. Make sure there's no music at my funeral, I don't want any . . .'

As you can see, dear sister, I'm surrounded by the sick. Today's ceremony[1] was certainly funereal into the bargain. There are four pieces of wood draped with flags in the Place de la Concorde, four altars on which resin will be burnt this evening and that's all. A fine anniversary and well worthy of the inauguration of their confounded Republic.

Adieu, I look forward to news of you in the next week.

Your brother,

H. Berlioz

235 *To Franz Liszt*   Paris, *c.*25 March 1849

My dear Liszt,

I saw Belloni[2] the day before yesterday; he told me of the problems and serious worries you're having.[3] I can assure you I feel for you deeply. Happily I know of your energy and decisiveness in emergencies. Belloni tells me of your idea of going on tour in North America.[4] That strikes me as a *violent* idea. Crossing the Atlantic to play to the Yankees, who at the moment are interested only in the mines of California . . . You alone can judge how useful such a tour might be. As for what might be done here before then, I have absolutely no idea. It varies from day to day depending on whether the temperature of revolutionary feeling is up or down, whether socialism is set to Storm, Flat Calm or Continuously Dull.

The Théâtre-Italien's wings have given up beating.[5] The Opéra has never had any (wings) unfortunately; *Le prophète*, they say, is going to give it some.[6] Concerts (apart from the Conservatoire ones) don't produce anything. When the mob of provincials attracted by the Universal Exhibition have filled Paris, when the new Chamber is elected and sitting, when the emotion of the first performances of *Le prophète* has died down, perhaps then some enterprise may be worth considering. We all await you with impatience. [. . .]

1 The anniversary of the revolution of February 1848.
2 Liszt's agent in Paris.
3 Liszt moved to Weimar in 1848, but revolutionary events in central Europe and internal difficulties in Weimar hampered his plans.
4 Liszt never went to America.
5 The theatre closed in 1848 but reopened soon after under new management.
6 Meyerbeer's long-awaited *Le prophète* opened at the Opéra on 16 April 1849.

I persist in my intention not to go to the mountain ever again; perhaps in the end the mountain will start coming towards me. It's a question of time and sang-froid. As for time, I don't know how much I have left, but I do have some sang-froid, despite the repressed anger which is bubbling away inside and which I have difficulty controlling. Our delightful country of France is certainly the most ... But enough; you can see I know how to keep the steam in and shut off the valve.

Adieu, I do need to talk to you. Please tell the Princess[1] that I kneel before her.

Your devoted

H. Berlioz

236 *To his sister Nanci Pal*   Paris, 25 April 1849

My dear Nanci,

[...] I was lucky enough to have a success ten days ago at a Conservatoire concert in front of that terrible audience who acknowledge no one but Beethoven and Mozart. I was confronting it for the first time;[2] Habeneck was opposed till the day he died to the smallest fragment of my works being performed at these concerts. At the committee's somewhat tardy request I gave two scenes from *Faust*. The chorus and ballet of sylphs especially made a tremendous impression. I'll admit to you that I was as nervous as a beginner; during the performance I was alone backstage with the *firemen*. It's more than fifteen years since I offered the public any of my works without conducting it in person, and in putting myself into the hands of Girard (who in fact acquitted himself well) I felt rather like a hen who has hatched some duck eggs and is for the first time watching her brood launch themselves on the water, into which she dare not follow them. The performers were even happier about it than I was, because of their anxiety about this prejudiced and pig-headed audience and because similar attempts by Onslow, Halévy, Félicien David, Prudent and others had been so disastrous. That's one barrier down, one more prejudice conquered. And now along comes Fétis himself asking my permission to play my symphonies in his Brussels Conservatory! After

1 Liszt was joined in Weimar by the Princess Carolyne Sayn-Wittgenstein, whom Berlioz had met in Russia in 1847.
2 On 15 April the Société des Concerts played two numbers from *La damnation de Faust*. The only previous work of Berlioz heard in their concerts was the *Rob Roy* overture, played in 1833.

writing at length to prove that they aren't music ... What clowns!¹

Louis has gone back to Rouen. His mother is better but she's still paralysed down her right side. Louis found nothing to complain of in *Le prophète* ... the skating scene, the one in the church in Münster, the electric sun and the burning-down of the palace seemed to him the best parts of the *score*.²

Adieu, let me know how you are.

H. B.

237 *To his sister Nanci Pal*   Paris, 1 June 1849

Dear sister,

[...] The day before yesterday we had a kind of riot at the Poissonière gate. It began at a socialist banquet in which a crowd of uninvited brothers thought it fitting to take part; once their bellies were full the said brothers ran off without paying. That's practical communism if ever there was. We've had two red deputies from the Haut Rhin in 1793 costume, bonnets on heads and sabres at sides. These vile nincompoops imagined they would cause a great sensation in Paris. Everyone who met them dressed up like that laughed in their faces ... and there wasn't a single clap of thunder in the heavens. If only one could give socialism another little push in this direction, it would soon be dead of ridicule and all the dogs of France and Navarre would lift their legs on it! Adieu, I've run out of space.

All best wishes to Camille and Mathilde, I embrace you warmly.

H. Berlioz

238 *To Theodor von Doehler*³   Paris, between 10 June and 14 July
                                                                          1849

My dear Doehler,

[...] How lucky you are to be in Florence! In this idiotic city of Paris one doesn't know what to do on the days when there isn't a riot; one swells up with boredom ... That's my sole distraction: I settle myself comfortably at my window and spend hours watching the hearses taking the erstwhile angry brigade to the cemetery in Montmartre.

The other day we buried that poor devil Kalkbrenner, luckily for

1 Fétis had been particularly critical of *Lélio* in 1832 and *Harold en Italie* in 1834.
2 Spectacular staging was part of the secret of Meyerbeer's success.
3 Austrian composer and pianist who had occasionally played in Berlioz's concerts.

him. . .[1] He was going mad enough to count as an original. Judge for yourself the degree and intensity of this negative faculty in his brain. Two days before his death he stopped me in the Rue des Trois Frères to ask how you had to organize the *sharps* so as to play the piano in E flat . . . I replied that you needed seven sharps and two double sharps.

'Ah', he said with a protective air, 'that's good; do you know Cherubini was embarrassed by that question and couldn't answer it!'

'Good heavens,' I said, 'thanks to you, music's come on a long way since Cherubini!'

Adieu, all best wishes,

Hector Berlioz

239 *To his sister Nanci Pal*   Paris, 20 July 1849

Dear sister,

[. . .] I'm in a fairly good mood today because there's been a considerable lessening in the problems weighing on my spirit. Four days ago Harriet had a third attack, more violent than the others, during which I thought I was going to watch her die. The convulsions caused by compression of the brain, the rattle in the throat, the black colouring in the face are more dreadful than anything I've seen . . . Fortunately she was heavily bled in time and this dissipated the most violent symptoms almost immediately; she gave a deep sigh and the convulsions ceased. But for two days the poor invalid knew nobody, she looked me full in the face but her eyes were dull and lifeless. She's been better since yesterday, she recognizes me perfectly, but she can't remember anything about this terrible crisis; she only realized she'd been bled when she looked at her arm. I've just left her, she's almost cheerful; she managed to explain to me that she wanted to have news of you and I gave her what had just reached me.[2] It's a fearfully mysterious thing that can cover up pain so that the patient doesn't remember it . . .

Paris is no more agreeable than usual; you're lucky living on a rock in the open air. The Opéra is closed, all the other theatres will shortly follow suit and lock their doors. In this time of liberty, fraternity, equality, obscenity, dishonesty and stupidity people now are interested only in what fills their stomachs. The arts and artists are so irrelevant in

1 Kalkbrenner, virtuoso pianist, who had spent most of his life in Paris and London, died aged sixty-three on 10 June 1849.
2 Nanci had been suffering from breast cancer since the beginning of the year.

such a disordered society, I'm surprised they're not being driven out, as happens to useless mouths in cities which are under siege and suffering from famine. God may be great, but certainly these socialists of ours aren't prophets. The whole thing fills one with horror and pity.

Oh, for the sea! Oh, for the sea, a good ship and a following wind, to escape the old continent and go and live among naive and primitive savages and never again to hear about our own savages, with their hidebound, wild and rotten ways!

Is there a reading-room in your fortress? With books one can live anywhere. Adieu, write to me more often, as you see I reply promptly and I like having your letters so much.

Adieu again, all my best wishes,

H. Berlioz

240 *To Armand de Pontmartin*[1]   Paris, 9 August 1849

My dear Monsieur de Pontmartin,

[...] How miserable your kind invitation has made me! It would have been so delightful to be able to accept it! I see myself sailing down the Rhône, making ten leagues an hour, arriving in Avignon at Mme Pierron's, who offers such a marvellous spread, dining in luxury, introducing myself to your nice donkey and asking her to take me to M. de Pontmartin's country residence ... then the charming chats, every kind of reverie, jokes, smokes, in short all the delights of Horace's villa at Tibur (plus the cigar, of course. Horace wouldn't allow smoking in his house as Virgil didn't like the smell. I was told this in Tibur itself by a pageboy in the Hotel della Regina, so it must be true.)

But I shall console myself this winter when I join you by the fireside in d'Ortigue's house, or mine, or even yours if you will allow me, and I shall say: do you remember those five delightful days we might have spent at your villa? And the larks we might have netted? Do you remember how we might have bathed in the Rhône? (I'm sure the Rhône is polite enough to run past your door!) Do you remember that superb ham? And that marvellous melon from Cavaillon which you were going to offer us? It will be a treat; the pleasures of the mind and the imagination are the best, aren't they? You're reduced now to plain reality; I'm truly sorry for you.

But if you would like, one evening, to tell your slave to bring up from

---

1 For many years literary critic of the *Gazette de France*, de Pontmartin lived on his family estate near Avignon. Berlioz had visited him there in 1845 and 1847.

the cellar an amphora of that famous Falernian which a well-bred Horace must surely possess, and to drink from it half a dozen cups in my honour, then the anxieties on your behalf will lose much of their immediacy and I'll return your toast with modern wine the first chance I get.

All best wishes to d'Ortigue – I thought he was still living comfortably in his square off the Rue St-Lazare.

Ever your devoted and disappointed

Hector Berlioz

241 *To his sister Adèle Suat* Paris, 25 August 1849

My dear Adèle,

[. . .] There's no need for me to insist on the deep sympathy which unites all three of us in everything which pertains to the memory of our admirable and excellent father. This memory will never leave me; the arrival of that bitter anniversary had already revived it most painfully ... I have his book, as you know, annotated in the margin with his own hand.[1] I read it recently; the marks of his pen brought before me the vision of him meditating on the book and carefully correcting it, and reminded me of the total honesty there was in his manner of practising medicine and of the wisdom enshrined in his talents, which were made to shine in a broader sphere of activity. But his utter kindness and the care with which he surrounded us when we were children are for us further causes of grief. I find that at the period of life I have reached time seems now, as it ushers us into the age of decline, to give us clearer sight, so that from a distance we have a better view of the objects of our earliest affections, and to make us weep for them more bitterly.

I should like to see both you and Nanci again. At least let me have reliable news of Nanci at once, from her herself. I'll write to her soon.

I've recently returned to (musical) work. I'm concluding, finishing, completing my piece.[2] I'm full of a kind of feverish impatience to have still more musical *projects*. And I want to be done with them as soon as possible.

What's more, this burning preoccupation is the only thing that can help me fight off a travel sickness which has me ever more tightly in its grasp. Shall I tell you about it? I dream of nothing but boats, the sea,

1 *Mémoires sur les maladies chroniques* (Paris, 1816).
2 The *Te Deum*.

far-flung islands and adventurous exploration. My musical tours in Europe have only served to develop these instincts which have lain more or less dormant in me for as long as I can remember. I realize how empty and puerile they are but cannot escape from them. If I can't go to South America, New Zealand or the Pacific Islands, without the things that keep me here I should go back to exploring the *terra firma* of this ancient Europe of ours and take a chance on giving financially rewarding concerts in the northern countries I've not yet visited, Sweden and Denmark, and return to Russia where I was welcomed so warmly. Perhaps I'll be able to go to Holland this winter; it's only a step away now, thanks to the railways. Journeys on land are so easy nowadays and so cheap! [...]

Adieu dear sister, I embrace you tenderly and your nice little daughters as well; all best wishes to your husband, if he's back at home.

H. Berlioz

242 *To his sister Nanci Pal*   Paris, 1 September 1849
                                               19, Rue de Boursault[1]

I have to tell you, dear sister, that I've recently been taken over by the very devil of a finale, a double chorus (call it what you will) which was preventing me from sleeping and from paying any attention whatever to anything else.[2] That's why I haven't written to you. Now that the finale is in hand, that's to say sketched out so that it can't now escape from me, here I am back in the real world. What's more I wrote Adèle a letter which perhaps she's told you about; I was asking her for news of you. You don't say anything about your health, but I don't need to tell you that I want to know what kind of state you're in, especially since the unsatisfactory business of the douches or baths at Lamothe. Make good this omission as soon as you can.

You will no doubt be amazed at this revival of my musical passion. But I must tell you that it springs from a keen desire to put an end to my involvement with the art for some considerable time; it's like the last chapter of a novel which you are all the happier writing because you swear to yourself you won't start another one.[3] Music here is lost, for a long time to come, and my only thought is to prevent myself

1 Berlioz's and Marie's home for the next seven years.
2 The *Judex crederis* in the *Te Deum*.
3 Apart from *La fuite en Egypte*, written in 1850, Berlioz composed almost nothing for the next five years.

feeling the pain that the sight of its agony arouses in me, or at least to resist heartbreak as best I can.

From another point of view, I was rather glad to have this powerful source of distraction to drag me away from the dreams of travel which obsess me more and more. I have a sickness for far-off lands. If I were free, I should no doubt disappear for several years and escape to the other hemisphere, leaving this old, mad, profligate, crazy, stupid Europe, which I so cordially detest. But, as you know, I can't even leave Paris. [. . .]

H. Berlioz

243 *To his sister Nanci Pal*   Paris, 29 October 1849

Dear sister,

I've just received your second letter and the note it contained. I didn't reply to the first, as I should have done, because I was sure a second one would follow it before long. In any case I've been so weighed down by sad events lately, there seemed no point, to say the least, in involving you as well. I wrote to one of my oldest friends (of twenty years' standing) in London to ask him for information about a bitterly sad episode in Irish history, on which I'm publishing a composition. I've used verses by Moore, but he leaves the central event shrouded in mystery. I received simultaneously from Mme Strich (my poor friend's wife) the details I'd asked her husband for and the news of his recent death. This combination of circumstances and melancholy tales made me really ill . . .[1]

I'm no more cheerful today; I've just been to the church of the Madeleine to the funeral service for poor Chopin who has died at the age of thirty-nine.[2] This time, at least, the service was a seemly one; the whole of artistic and aristocratic Paris was there. The pall-bearers were Meyerbeer, Paul de Laroche, Eugène Delacroix and Prince Czartoriski. They performed Mozart's *Requiem* accurately but to no effect. And a few notes on the organ and the *De profundis* sung in fauxbourdon touched the congregation more deeply than that great composer's famous but unfinished score. Luckily I finished my article on Chopin last Saturday and shan't have to rewrite it; it would be too embarrassing to have to mention Mozart's *Requiem*. I no longer have the

1 If Strich was the name of Berlioz's friend of twenty years, nothing is known about him. The composition in question was the *Elégie*, last in the collection of Thomas Moore settings composed in 1829.
2 Chopin died on 17 October.

courage to go on as I should with this everlasting play-acting, producing admiration to order.

To come back to my Irish story, it was Leigh Hunt, the English poet and friend and companion of Byron, who was kind enough to do the research for my enquiry and to pass on to Mme Strich the details she sent me.[1] [. . .]

Adieu, I'm very sorry you can't read music, otherwise I'd send you my latest published works and I think my *Elégie* on the English poem 'When he who adores thee' would move your heart and soul . . . Mme Viardot played it for me on the piano the other evening (without singing it). It needs a man's voice for this desperate farewell to the beloved and the fatherland; there are only two or three singers in Europe capable of performing this piece well. And Pischek, who's the best of them, doesn't know either English or French.[2] I'll have it translated into German for him.

I should have mentioned that my *Te Deum* is finished. I wonder whether there'll be anyone in the Ministry willing to help me have it performed. I doubt it. Adieu.

Farewell.

H. B.

244 *To Franz Liszt*   Paris, 8 January 1850

My dear Liszt,

I've just started a Philharmonic Society of 200 members (110 singers, 90 instrumentalists).[3] We're giving our first concert on 19 February. We shall meet on the second Tuesday of each month at eight o'clock in the evening in the St-Cécile hall on the Rue du Montblanc. It looks promising, from all points of view. Would you allow us to put your name at the head of our list of honorary members? The society would hope to perform some of your new works when you next come to Paris.

1 There is no evidence that Berlioz met Leigh Hunt in London, as is usually supposed. Berlioz was preparing a new edition of the Moore songs, in which the story of Emmet was included.
2 Berlioz first heard the great Bohemian baritone Pischek in *Fidelio* in Frankfurt in 1842 and came to admire him above all other singers. Of the *Elégie* Berlioz said in the *Mémoires* that Pischek accompanying himself would realize his ideal of how the song should be performed.
3 The Société Philharmonique de Paris was Berlioz's chief preoccupation in 1850–51. In an attempt to spread the expense and labour of concert-giving he assembled a committee of management. He himself conducted and included many works by other composers in the society's twelve concerts, the last of which was given in April 1851.

These are just a few lines written in haste; we have committee upon committee and discussions about everything. I have the greatest difficulty conforming to those procedures of representative government which force us to spend a week doing what I could do in an hour.

I'll write to you at greater length some other time; but let me have an answer as soon as you can, so that we can put your name on the first poster together with those of Meyerbeer, Ernst and Spontini.

All best wishes,
Your devoted
H. Berlioz

245 *To his sister Nanci Pal*   Paris, 3 April 1850

Dear sister,

[. . .] Hugo's salon is really not in the least entertaining, for all Mme Hugo's grace and kindness and her daughter's considerable charm. Her sons are two extremely conceited young men and extremely concerned with seeing that their father gets his share of glory, not to mention their own merits. As for him, he is, as he's always been with me, very cordial, but serious; but it's not possible for us to talk in his house as we do when we happen to meet in the street or in the Champs-Elysées. Added to which, his evening receptions bring with them a collection of abominable old ladies, ugly enough to make a dog bark and malicious and pretentious in the highest degree: old mother Gay and Mme Hamelin[1] especially like to queen it there, accompanied by other less monumental horrors. Two evenings ago, if Mme Janin hadn't arrived to prove otherwise, I should have thought I'd stumbled on a witches' coven. The best thing about these people is that no one plays any music.

I was, however, victimized a few weeks ago in the brilliant salon run by Gudin, the seascape painter, by airs and variations and all manner of possible platitudes with piano accompaniment. Alexandre Dumas, who detests even *bad* music, amused himself inventing asides which he dropped to right and left as he made his way through the throng. He had his daughter on his arm; she's a young person of nineteen, looking too much like her father to be pretty, but giving the rather attractive false impression of being a quadroon, with a physiognomy whose originality was further accentuated that evening by a coiffure of gold sequins which made her look like a Madagascan odalisque.

1 Sophie Gay and Mme Hamelin, both seventy-three years old, held literary salons.

Adieu, my poor sister, I hope you've read my letter to the end and that it's made you forget your troubles for a couple of minutes.[1]

I shake poor Camille by the hand.

Adieu once more, I embrace you.

H. Berlioz

246 To his sister Adèle Suat   Paris, 29 April 1850

Dear little sister,

I should have written to you two days ago to acknowledge receipt of the 500 francs enclosed with your letter; but I simply forgot three times to do so. I'm in the middle of organizing the performance of my *Requiem* for the victims of Angers.[2] The ceremony will take place in St-Eustache next Friday and I don't know what my legs or my head are doing. I've got to conduct three rehearsals with 400 people, find patronesses to organize a collection, write hundreds of letters, etc.

Also Harriet has recently had another attack, which I'm glad to say was alleviated by further bleeding . . .

Is Nanci's improvement continuing? I'm not asking her to write to me, I realize only too well she's not up to it. But I thank you for staying with her as much as you can, I'm quite sure your care is the most valuable thing of all for her.

Adieu, I have time only to embrace you and ask you to embrace our poor invalid for me.

All best wishes,

H. Berlioz

247 To Honoré de Balzac   Paris, 12 June 1850

Dear and revered maître,

News reached me simultaneously of your marriage and your return.[3] I haven't seen you since just before my departure for Russia, that's three long years.

Have you ever thought of the torment suffered by certain passionate souls at seeing the features of their idols only in the reflection of the reflection of the reflection of a mirror set up right next to them, when,

1 Nanci, terminally ill, died on 4 May 1850. This is Berlioz's last known letter to her.
2 On 16 April a bridge at Angers collapsed when a regiment of soldiers failed to break step, and 219 men were killed. The Société Philharmonique put on the *Requiem* on 3 May in their memory.
3 Balzac married Mme Hanska in Russia on 14 March and came back to Paris in May.

by a simple turning motion, the living idol could appear before them in the flesh? This torment is what I feel in your case: turn the mirror and allow your real self to be seen. In less nonsensical language, tell me when I can come and shake you by the hand and ask you to introduce to Mme de Balzac one of her most humble servants,

Hector Berlioz

248 *To his sister Adèle Suat*   Paris, 24 September 1850

Dear sister,

I was going to reply to your first letter this very day, when the second reached me. After my return from Le Havre I didn't feel capable of describing to you this melancholy journey. Louis wrote to tell you that he was leaving and in fact we left in a hurry because I was suddenly told that the ship on which I was hoping to find Louis a place was about to go to sea. The owner said we had to be in Le Havre on Thursday 12 September at the latest. There was no time for havering. Even so, when we arrived, the loading of the vessel wasn't finished and as two of the passengers had been allowed to delay their embarkation we had to wait six days in the hotel. During all this time the poor boy was cheerful and full of enthusiasm. At the dinner table he was listening avidly to the conversations of travellers arriving from New Orleans or Mexico and leaving for Valparaiso or California. One day he heard a naval officer say to me: 'Out of every ten young men who take up our career, at least eight of them abandon it after their first voyage.' That evening when we were alone Louis said to me: 'He thinks I'll be disillusioned with sailing; well you'll see, in spite of the seasickness which everyone says is unpleasant, in spite of exhaustion and everything else, I shall persist.'

We met several of my friends in Le Havre. Louis even came across two of his fellow-pupils from the lycée in Rouen. They all congratulated him on taking up such a fine career. I pray God they may be right. Finally on the Tuesday at six o'clock in the morning I took him to the ship, and at seven, in splendid weather and with a light westerly wind (the best), the ship, the *Félix*, set sail. Despite all our efforts and our mutual promises to bear this separation calmly, you can imagine what we were both feeling ... I for my part headed towards the train for Paris and, after I'd embraced Louis, I wasn't even able to follow him as far as the lighthouse from where I could have seen the *Félix* broaching the open sea. What breaks my heart is not so much thinking of the dangers of sailing as of those of manoeuvring. I'm continually afraid of accidents on board, of depression brought on by isolation, of seasickness, fever in the Antilles, I don't know what . . . [. . .]

Now, as far as my financial situation is concerned, I'm not hurt, dear sister, by the question you ask, it's too delicately expressed for me to be offended by it. All I can say to you is that my personal outgoings *would be exactly the same and perhaps greater if I lived in Paris alone.* I cannot, in my position, in the company I keep, live in a room twenty foot square like a first-year student. In that case I should do better leaving Paris, giving up my career and everything and going to live in the provinces. Until now I have not spent more than my income, except last year, because of the copying costs of my last three works for which I was expecting something from the Minister of the Interior, something which never came.[1] Louis also increased my expenses when he left the boarding school, and now his career at sea is increasing them by a good deal more.

You talk of my posts, but I have only one, in the Conservatoire Library, where I now have the title of Head Librarian but without a penny more in salary.[2] It brings in 118 francs a month. I write about one article a month in the *Journal des débats*; if it fills as much as ten broad columns I get 100 francs; if not, I get 75 francs and often only 50 francs. That's all. My share in the profits of the Société Philharmonique last winter, which were shared between two hundred of us, was 84 francs. This musical institution also took up an enormous amount of my time both as conductor and composer and as president of the committees. But it will improve in due course; in any case it's something that I founded and I cannot, indeed must not, now abandon it. It seems to me you're worried by the idea that I have large debts, but this is what they all come to:

> 900 fr borrowed for Louis's departure
> 300 fr or thereabouts to the doctor in Montmartre
> 350 fr to my tailor
> 180 fr due to my copyist
> <u> 32 fr to my hatter</u>
> <u>1762 fr</u>

You ask for these details and I give them to show you that your questions on this subject have been taken kindly; I shall also need something with which to pay Louis's allowance and his shore expenses

1 He had *Tristia* and perhaps the *Te Deum* copied in the hope of performances.
2 Bottée de Toulmon, the librarian, died on 22 March 1850, to be succeeded by Berlioz.

when he comes back, at least 2500 francs, but that can be found more easily as there is time ahead of us. I may also have some unexpected income or receive an offer of an engagement in London in 1851 for the Great Exhibition.

So, dear sister, see what you, your husband and Camille can do to get me out of the difficult spot I'm temporarily in. And try and find an opportunity to make a good sale of a small part of the possessions my father left me.

Adieu, with many embraces,
Your devoted
Hector Berlioz

P.S. Remember me to everyone and especially to my uncle and aunt Marmion.

249 *To Pauline Viardot*   Paris, 30 September 1850

I am truly sorry, my dear Madame Viardot, not to be able to accept your invitation.[1] A host of worries, a host of anxieties, a host of unpostponable tasks, a host of idiocies, a host of occupations absolutely prevent me from doing so.

So when are you coming back to Paris? May hail, cold, wind, neighbours and games of whist plague you in the country! May local poets come to read you their verses! May the priest try to convert you! May you be invited on daunting picnics! In short may the provinces unleash themselves upon you, those are my wishes on your behalf. Perhaps then you might return to the civilized world.

If M. Viardot found wolves and bears to hunt, all well and good; but I'm willing to bet there's nothing in your woods except titmice . . . if that.

With affectionate best wishes,
Your devoted
Hector Berlioz

250 *To Auguste Morel*[2]   Paris, 15 November 1850

My dear Morel,

[. . .] Our concerts continue; the second one[3] took place the day before yesterday and exhausted me to such an extent that I've just got up for the

1 The Viardots invited Berlioz to their country estate, Courtavenel, in Brie.
2 Morel had recently left Paris to become director of the Marseille Conservatoire.
3 The second of the autumn season.

first time since Tuesday evening. We had seven rehearsals for the *Symphonie fantastique* and twice I got as far as saying to the orchestra that I was giving up trying to put it on. I wanted to postpone the concert for a fortnight. But they'd put so much work into it that when they promised me an extra, CAREFUL rehearsal on the Tuesday of the concert, I agreed to let the publicity go ahead; and I'm very glad to say that this rehearsal was enough to reassure me. The performance was in fact excellent and full of qualities which our orchestra had not yet demonstrated. The audience was inordinately enthusiastic; they wanted us to play *Le bal* again (which I refused to do), the Adagio had three or four bursts of applause, and as for the *Marche au supplice*, there was so much shouting that I did have to repeat it. After the finale the ladies of the chorus played a joke by presenting me with a huge, *fantastic* wreath of oak, laurel and privet (Virgil's *albaque ligustra*), something I was quick to hide from the *Parisian* gentlemen in the hall, who found it far too amusing. Tell Lecourt[1] that his Ballade *Sara* has been a great success at the two concerts which have just been given. Even so, the critics are still blaming me for turning such words into a choral piece; they say I should have used only a solo voice. I must say I wasn't in the least prepared for this sort of recrimination. [. . .]

All best wishes,

H. Berlioz

251 *To his sister Adèle Suat*   Paris, 25 November 1850

Dear little sister,

First of all, some good news: I had a letter from Louis the day before yesterday from La Pointe-à-Pitre (Guadeloupe). He's enthusiastic about the sea and his sailor's life, luckily he was seasick only once, the day after he sailed; his only complaint is that he has to *wash the bridge* every morning. Not exactly a heroic task, it's true, but one which all beginners have to perform along with many others of the same sort. He finds the heat in the roads rather trying, as the captain won't let him go ashore. Which doesn't prevent him stuffing himself with coconuts, avocados, bananas, oranges, sweet limes, sugar cane and other fruit from the Antilles. By now he'll be in Port-au-Prince (Haiti) where he'll find a letter from me. Harriet has been asking me regularly over the past few days when we would have a letter from Louis and I had to

---

1 A Marseille lawyer and cellist to whom Berlioz dedicated *Sara la baigneuse* when it was published in 1851.

keep on giving her the same answer, because she's partly lost her memory. She's not talking any better than before and her condition is still the same. [. . .]

The weather here is terrible; for two days a furious storm has been raging; tiles and chimneypots are falling into the streets like hail. It makes me detest Paris and all the links that bind me to it. Oh, if I were free, I should escape to Tenerife or the Ile-de-Fer or Madeira to find sunshine, peace, the beauties of nature and kind people, and forget the feverish agitations of the Parisian world! It's barely a ten-day voyage, and once on one of these happy isles (the Canary islands) you can believe yourself in the antipodes. And one can live there on nothing and for nothing; and there are people there who haven't yet heard that France is now a Republic! . . .

Adieu, dear sister, I embrace you with all my heart as well as your girls; all best wishes to Suat.

H. Berlioz

252 *To Alexey Fyodorovich Lvov*   Paris, 1 February 1851

My dear Monsieur Lvov,

Many, many thanks for your parcel and for the kind letter that came with it. I will indeed, and as soon as possible, write the piece you suggest for the *Journal des débats*.[1] I would in fact have started on it this week if an obituary article had not, sadly, had a prior claim. Spontini has just died and I have to write a long article about him. Even though I had been expecting it for a long time, his death has affected me profoundly. He was not a likeable man, but I liked him from having admired him. Indeed the very asperities of his character attracted me to him, no doubt because they latched on to the asperities of my own. [. . .]

My warmest thanks for the fine pieces of yours which you have sent me; we shall certainly perform them at the Société Philharmonique when the schedule of works that the chorus have to learn allows it. Bortnyansky's biography will also, I'm sure, be welcomed. We gave his *Pater* (in Latin) at the concert last Tuesday: it was very well sung and even better received.[2]

Be kind enough to greet the artists of the Imperial Chapel on my

1 Berlioz wrote about Lvov and the Imperial Chapel in the *Débats*, but not until 13 December 1851.
2 The Société Philharmonique had also sung *Le chant des chérubins* by Bortnyansky in their concert on 22 October 1850.

behalf, and tell them that I retain the most affectionate and sincerely admiring memories of them. I have finally succeeded in getting their name known in Paris and in getting them appreciated, *by my word alone*, at almost their true value.[1] People no longer believe that the miserable castrati of the Sistine Chapel in Rome are the one and only religious choir worthy of the name.

What's happening about *Ondine*?[2]

Yours sincerely,

H. Berlioz

P.S. Remember me, please, to the Counts Wielgorsky and the other friends I left behind me in Petersburg.

253 To Pierre Erard[3]   Paris, 10 February 1851

My dear Erard,

I've finished my article based – and profitably so I think – on everything you've told me face to face and in writing.[4] It'll take up about fifteen columns of the *Journal des débats*. As a result it's too long to appear tomorrow, the session of the Assembly will take up too much space, but it will undoubtedly appear the day after tomorrow.

Now I must tell you how surprised, I may even say distressed, I was by the present you sent yesterday. I have never in my life dreamed of anything of the sort as a return first of all for doing my duty and then for expressing in the case of a great man like Spontini all the admiration I feel for him. What can have possessed you to offer me such a magnificent present?[5] I don't know. In any case I can accept it only on condition that you give me the opportunity to be of serious use to you in the important enterprises you are conducting, either in London or in Paris. And I beg you to see that I am offered this opportunity very soon.[6]

Adieu, I shake you by the hand.

Yours sincerely,

H. Berlioz

1 Berlioz had devoted an article to them in the *Débats* on 19 October 1850.
2 Lvov's opera, performed in St Petersburg in 1848.
3 Head of the firm of Erard, makers of pianos and harps.
4 The article was an appreciation of Spontini, whose wife Céleste was Erard's sister.
5 The present was either a piano or a harp, both of which Berlioz possessed in later life.
6 Berlioz was indeed of serious use to Erard, who might have guessed that Berlioz was about to be nominated for the jury on musical instruments at the Great Exhibition in London. Erard's instruments were commonly reported in Berlioz's articles at that time, always favourably.

My dear Hiller,

You don't lunch at home, you don't dine at home, you don't sleep at home; how the devil can I get hold of you?[1] But I agree with you; we must talk and have lunch together. I shall therefore expect you on Wednesday at midday at the Café du Cardinal on the corner of the Rue de Richelieu.[2] I can't get there at eleven o'clock because of a chorus rehearsal that day.

I'm still at work on an article which is a torture for me, and in which my only pleasure will be writing something about you. You'll say that's not to be undervalued, but all the rest is fairly hard going.[3]

Adieu until Wednesday
since it is impossible
to see you
before
then,
H.B.
V[4]

255 *To his sister Adèle Suat*   Paris, 17 March 1851

Dear little sister,

I am taking advantage of the delightful occasion of a severe inflammation and accompanying fever, which have kept me in bed for the last three days, to write to you. As I can't find a minute to myself when I'm well, I'm somewhat consoled by this indisposition which gives me a chance to talk to you briefly. You have no idea of the ever-increasing whirlwind of activity I live in. It's a veritable hurricane, especially at the moment, with musical business of every kind, preparations, plans, projects, for France, for England, goings, comings, people wanting favours, intriguers, bores and plain imbeciles, all of whom make claims on my time.

You know that, under protest, I put myself down as a candidate for the place at the Institut left vacant by the death of Spontini; I learnt

---

1 Hiller, who had recently become Kapellmeister at Cologne, was visiting Paris.
2 Where it is still in business.
3 Berlioz's article of 23 February devoted two columns to Hiller and the difficulties he had trying to give a concert in Paris.
4 V = vale = farewell.

from a newspaper yesterday, to my great astonishment, that the Music Section had put me forward as their third candidate, even though that section is totally hostile to me. I wasn't expecting them to put me forward at all. The sly fellows didn't dare ... It doesn't matter, we know from an unimpeachable source that Thomas will be chosen. Do you know of M. Thomas?[1] ...

The foreigners living in Paris aren't slow to laugh at such a choice. But it's always like that at the Institut ... You've heard about the ovation I had to go through at our last concert, the superb golden crown presented by two beautiful ladies in the middle of the performance of *Roméo et Juliette*, the fearful applause from public and performers, etc, etc? I'm told the crown is worth two thousand francs. Now there are plans for a festival in Lille at the end of June in which all the northern provinces are going to take part. I'm going to be invited to conduct two of my works. It'll be a brilliant occasion.[2] Then there's talk of various things for the Universal Exhibition in London, and if only one of them comes to anything I'll be going to England in May.

At the moment my main preoccupation is with Louis's imminent arrival. I'm now finding it almost impossible to contain my impatience. He's due to disembark at Le Havre towards the end of this month; I'll go and meet him and get on with making the necessary arrangements for his second journey. Harriet is still in the same condition and is waiting for her son with considerable anxiety. [...]

Your devoted
H. Berlioz

256 *To Johann Vesque von Puttlingen*   Paris, 31 March 1851

My dear friend,

Many thanks for thinking of me and for your excellent notion of sending me your latest work.[3] I've already read it avidly and enjoyed it as a purely musical composition. Unfortunately my ignorance of the German language prevents me from appreciating the expressive merit that also resides, I'm sure, in your songs and from grasping the close links between them and the poetry they set. I'll go and see poor Heine one of these days. I'm sure he'll be delighted to know you've published a collection of this kind and have not, unlike so many others, omitted to

1 Ambroise Thomas, eight years younger than Berlioz, and at that time the composer of *opéra comique*, was duly elected.
2 This did not take place.
3 Vesque had recently published a collection of eighty-eight settings of Heine.

mention his name. He's still at death's door, but still alive mentally. He gives the impression of standing at the window of his tomb so that he can continue to look out at this world of which he is no longer a part, and jeer at it.[1]

On one of my last visits, when he heard my name announced, he greeted me from his bed with this sad, charming epigram: 'What! Berlioz! You haven't forgotten me, then? *Original as always*!!'

Yes, alas, it is a sign of great originality in this fearful city of Paris not to forget those elsewhere, the half-dead and the dead! That at least, my dear de Vesque, is one thing I do possess, I promise you. I think of you often and all the marks of affection you lavished on me during my stay in Vienna are as close and dear to me as if I had received them yesterday. But what a life it is I'm leading here! An unending whirlwind, with never a moment's peace for calm contemplation; always on the run or working at top speed; always vibrating, always buzzing; always having to suppress attacks of boiling indignation; every morning, after a few hours of more or less restless sleep, to go back into this cold, disordered world, hissing like a red-hot iron plunged into water; and, as I go, always stumbling over snakes and toads! . . .

Oh, if I were free, free with a tiny private income, how happily I should set sail tomorrow for Palma or Tenerife and lie there sleeping in the warm sunshine of those blessed isles among the good people who inhabit them, untouched by the fever of art! . . . Oh, the sea, the sea! The open spaces! The dazzling light! The heat! The luxuriant tropical vegetation! The silence! . . . The life of the instincts! . . .

Forgive me, dear friend, for letting go with these ridiculous exclamations, I'm really ill, as you see.

Remember me to your charming family, to Mme de Vesque and your brother, and believe me to be always

Yours most sincerely and affectionately,

Hector Berlioz

The Société Philharmonique gave its last concert on 4 May 1851, at which point its dire financial circumstances put an end to any further ventures. On 9 May Berlioz left for London with Marie to take up his duties as a French representative on the international jury on musical

1 Heine had lived in Paris for nearly twenty years. He lived until 1856.

instruments at the Great Exhibition in Hyde Park. They were accom-
modated at 27, Queen Anne Street, near Cavendish Square.

257 *To his sister Adèle Suat*   London, *c.*20 June 1851

My dear Adèle,

I am taking advantage of a moment's respite we're being allowed today to let you have some news. I've been busy in London for six weeks with the ridiculous job of examining the musical instruments sent to the Exhibition. There are days when despair overwhelms me and when I'm on the point of going back to Paris. No one can imagine the appalling drudgery of my particular task. I have to *listen* to the wind instruments, both wood and brass. My head is bursting from hearing hundreds of these foul machines, each more out of tune than the last, with three or four exceptions.

Apart from this tribulation, my stay in London is very enjoyable, with invitations arriving from every quarter; from the Lord Mayor, from the Mayor of Birmingham, and from my compatriots, not to mention the hospitality which the English offer in abundance. Then there are the theatre directors and concert promoters whom one has to satisfy as far as possible, and the exhibitors who have explanations to give me. Sunday is the only time I can breathe and go for walks in the countryside. In the middle of all that I have to find time to write long articles for the *Journal des débats*; I've already done three of them, only one of which has appeared. So you won't be surprised that I missed our uncle when he came to spend just three days here. When he wrote, he addressed the letter to no. 19 in my street instead of no. 27; that meant his note was a day late in reaching me and when I got to his hotel he'd just left. As for meeting in the Crystal Palace, there was not much chance of that, it's far too big and holds too many people.

The Minister of Commerce is paying me quite well for my time here, even though they showed extraordinary stinginess in leaving us to cover our own travelling expenses; so please ask Camille not to send his usual two-monthly instalment[1] either here or to Paris. I'll let him know when I'm back in France.

The warm weather has arrived today for the first time; I was afraid I wasn't going to see a summer this year. The London parks and squares are now charming. As for the countryside round about, it's delightful and the vegetation is richer than we ever see on the Continent. I say

1 A regular annuity from the proceeds of his father's estate.

nothing to you about the strange and interesting things I've seen here, you can find out about them by reading my letters in the *Journal des débats*. The first one appeared on 31 May, I think. I recommend you to look out for the second one which (unless it appeared in Paris today) is not published yet. You're certain to find it of interest. It has my account of the extraordinary ceremony I went to in St Paul's Cathedral and the amazing effect of a choir of *six and a half thousand* children which I heard there. I've never *seen* or *heard* anything so moving in its immense grandeur as this mass of poor children singing, arranged in colossal tiers. Read it.[1]

I'm waiting daily for a letter from Louis who is now in Guadeloupe.

I've good news of Harriet: that's to say she's in the same condition as usual.

Adieu, dear sister,

All best wishes to your husband and the children.

Your devoted

H. Berlioz

P.S. I'll be here for another fortnight, at the very least.

258 *To Joseph d'Ortigue*   London, 21 June 1851

My dear d'Ortigue,

[...] Try and read my second article in the *Débats*; if it hasn't appeared in Paris today, you must keep a daily watch for it. It contains my account of the *unparalleled* impression made on me recently in St Paul's Cathedral when I heard *six and a half thousand* children from charity schools, who come together there once a year. It was incomparably the most imposing, the most Babylonian ceremony which it has so far been my lot to attend. The emotion is still with me as I write. It was the realization of a part of my dreams and proof that the power of massed musicians is still totally unrecognized. On the Continent at least, they have no more conception of it than the Chinese have of our music.

On this subject, see also my article of 31 May; you'll find a description of my visit to the Chinese Singer and her music teacher. You'll see the truth about these crazy ideas that various *scholarly* theoreticians have on so-called quarter-tone music. There's nothing so stupid as a *scholar*.

1 Berlioz wrote five long articles on his experiences in London; they were assembled the following year in *Les soirées de l'orchestre*.

Tell M. Arnaud that I shall be happy to set to music a series of his poems on Joan of Arc, if for me too *a voice from on high* makes itself heard. He should try and keep the verses short; long verses and long lines are fatal to song-writing. It would need to be possible to turn it into a popular legend, quite *simple*, but *dignified*, made up of a multitude of parts or songs.[1]

Adieu, I'm besieged by musical instruments and still more by their manufacturers.

France wins, without any possible rivals, over the remainder of Europe. Erard, Sax and Vuillaume. All the rest belong more or less to the company of cauldrons, whistles and toy fiddles.

Best wishes to our friends.

My respects to Mme d'Ortigue.

Greet Jacquot for me.

I'm very fond of him.

H. Berlioz

259 *To his brother-in-law Camille Pal* London, 26 July 1851

My dear Camille,

I'm leaving here the day after tomorrow, so if you will be kind enough to send the payment to me in Paris, I shall be there to receive it. I was beginning to tire of this whole business, all the more so since the excellent M. Buffet, Minister of Commerce, finding that our stay in London was being prolonged unduly, declared that as from 15 July he would cease to pay us. I had no intention, despite this strange way of going on, of leaving my post on the jury before my job was done. It doesn't finish until tomorrow. And if I had allowed myself to abandon it, I can now see that the result would have been a considerable blow for the French exhibitors, to whom, in the event, I have been able to do signal justice. The Minister therefore will bankrupt those members of the jury who have done their duty the most thoroughly; last week there were only twelve of us left, today I am alone. This musical task has been the hardest and longest of all.

Adieu, I continue to wait for news of you.

All best wishes to Mathilde. I don't know if we shall see each other this autumn. I hope so.

Yours ever,

H. Berlioz

1 Berlioz never composed these songs.

My dear Liszt,

I have just arrived from London. Belloni tells me that you want to put on *Benvenuto* in Weimar. I'm deeply grateful to you for thinking of it. It would be a great pleasure for me to see this poor work reborn, or rather born, under your direction. I've put the score in the hands of my copyist who is correcting it and making some changes which I think are necessary. Everything will be ready in a few days and Belloni will send you the parcel. Don't forget to let me know when it arrives, because I haven't got another copy of this work. Then, when the Weimar copyist has finished with it, remove it from circulation in the theatre; I know what happens to manuscripts in those madhouses.

I'll send you at the same time a printed libretto which tallies with the score and which is indispensable for the translator.

Adieu, I've time only for a handshake. The Anglo-French whirlwind which is now bestirring Paris is taking up all my time. My *Te Deum* is to be performed in Notre-Dame next month with large forces.[1]

All best wishes,
H. Berlioz

261 *To his sister Adèle Suat* Paris, 1 October 1851

Dear sister,

[...] And now the Minister of Commerce is depriving me of 420 francs owed to the jury of the Exhibition in London; he says the funds are 'exhausted'; meanwhile the Minister of the Interior has had my salary from the Conservatoire stopped for the three months of my stay in England. It seems he wants to punish me for having done my job so conscientiously. By these means he loses me another 355 francs. Isn't it enough to make one mad? Has anyone ever seen a government acting in such a manner?

On another front, the Prefect of the Seine is offering me a post at 4000 francs which I see I shall be forced to accept, whatever repugnance I may feel at the musical duties I shall have to take on. I'll give you details when everything is settled. It's two months now since

1 Vain hope: there was no performance of the *Te Deum* until 1855.

they've been setting it up in the most complete secrecy. [. . .]

Adieu, I embrace you with all my heart.

H. Berlioz

262 *To his sister Adèle Suat*   Paris, 9 December 1851

Thank you, dear little sister, for your solicitude. And I'm happy to see that you share my view of the serious events which have just come to pass.[1] Yes, I exclaimed with joy and admiration when they read out the edicts of our admirable President. He has not only annihilated those ambitious wretches called representatives, but he has made them *ridiculous*; so that's the end of them. This *coup d'état* is a masterstroke, an outright masterpiece. The day before yesterday I went to take my card to the President, and when I was handed a book in which the *non-tremblers* could sign their names, I wrote mine in large letters, saying to the usher: 'it's to offer him my compliments and my thanks.'

You see, dear sister, that your husband, you and I are all in total agreement.

Now to reply to your questions about my position and my resources; you shall know what I think, I shan't try and hide it and I wager that here too you will agree with me.

Yes, of course, poor Harriet's house in Montmartre causes me serious problems but, in all honesty, should not this expense be met before all others? Louis has written to you saying things which are perhaps sensible from the economic point of view, but it was extremely wrong of him to mention them to his mother without warning me, and I have had the greatest difficulty in removing the impression which his ill-considered words had made upon her in her poor state of health. No doubt she would resign herself to going into a nursing home, but the very thought of leaving her house, her garden, her flowers, her sunshine, her grassy path, her view over the plain of St-Denis, the open air and her two servants who are honest, I'm sure, all that sets her spirit in a total ferment; she would not last two months shut away behind the cold walls of those gloomy places they call 'houses of health'. She would be dead almost as soon as she was through the door. I finally succeeded in persuading her that I had no part in the proposal Louis made to her on this subject. And that's

1 On 2 December 1851 Louis-Napoleon dissolved the Assembly and seized power in a *coup d'état*. Two hundred and eighteen Deputies were arrested.

the truth. I shall resign myself to anything, to living in a student's lodging, to eating dry bread, rather than deal Harriet such a mortal blow. [...]

The post I mentioned to you has not yet been given me, and all the indications make me fear that it won't. The proposal was to give me control of the teaching of music in the schools in Paris and to be Director General of the Orphéon.[1] The idea came from M. Berger, the Prefect of the Seine. He OFFERED me this position, which I had never dreamt of, and for nearly six months now the business has been dragging on with no decision being made. It's no longer possible to give concerts. There's nothing one can do in this damned country of ours. I had a letter recently from St Petersburg asking me to go and direct a festival there in March, but the sum offered for such a journey was paltry and, bearing in mind the dangers of being absent in such circumstances, I have had to refuse. They try and take away my post as Librarian of the Conservatoire every time I leave Paris. I almost lost it recently during my stay in London. [...]

Adieu,

H. Berlioz

263 *To his sister Adèle Suat*   Paris, 16 January 1852

My dear Adèle,

[...] The business with the Prefect of the Seine seems to have fallen into oblivion; I've heard no more about it. It's not entirely certain that M. Berger is remaining as Prefect. He's very well disposed, even so. I don't know what the reasons are that tell against him. The President goes from strength to strength, he is realizing all my dreams about the government. He is sublime in his reasoning, his logic, his steadfastness and his decisiveness. Last night he was at the Théâtre-Français where his entrance and his departure were both greeted by vivats and interminable applause. My admiration is wholly disinterested, because I'm certain that for all official ceremonies, like the one that's just taken place at Notre-Dame, he will always choose men of the establishment, old men and old works.[2] [...]

Your devoted

H. Berlioz

1 The Orphéon was a large and very active organization of choral societies. The post of director went in May 1852 to Gounod with a salary of 6000 francs.
2 For a service of thanksgiving on 1 January 1852 Louis-Napoleon chose music which had been played at Napoleon I's coronation, and some pieces by Adam.

[...] Nothing is possible in Paris any more, and I think next month I shall return to England where the *desire to love* music is at least real and persistent.[1] Here all the posts are filled; mediocrities devour each other and one watches the squabbles and the feasting of these dogs with almost as much anger as disgust.

The opinions of the press and the public are of a stupidity and a frivolity unmatched in any other nation. With us, beauty resides not in ugliness but in dullness; we don't favour the bad over the good, we prefer the mediocre. The feeling for truth in art is as dim as that for justice in the moral domain, and without the energy of the President of the Republic we should now be finding ourselves assassinated in our own homes. Thanks to him and the army, we are out of danger at the moment; but we artists, we *live dead* (pardon the antithesis). [...]

My dear Camille,

[...] I shall have other matters in hand in a few days' time in London. I hope to acquit myself honourably, but I'm very concerned about my performers and the new repertoire I have to teach them, given the meanness with *time* practised not only by the English but by the foreigners who have settled in England. The question of success in my case depends entirely on the number of rehearsals I shall be able to have. I'm certainly not going to Weimar. The Leipzig papers say that my opera won't be performed until the 27th of this month.[2] If I went, it would not leave me time to be in London when my business there demands it. Liszt will keep me abreast of things, and I'll let you know what happens. The press and the public in England are very well disposed towards me. The only hostility will be from the supporters of Costa,[3] the Habeneck of that country, who don't look upon my arrival in England with much favour. But then life is a battle; *vae victis*![4]

As ever, with all best wishes to Mathilde.

H. Berlioz

1 Berlioz was invited by the New Philharmonic Society, which had just been formed, to conduct six concerts in Exeter Hall, London, between March and June.
2 *Benvenuto Cellini* was played in Weimar on 20 March, with two more performances shortly after.
3 Sir Michael Costa, of whom Berlioz had no very high opinion, conducted the (old) Philharmonic Society as well as the Royal Italian Opera at Covent Garden.
4 'Woe to the losers!'

Monsieur,

I think I owe it to you to offer some explanations about the perform-ance of your fine work at the Second Concert of the New Philharmonic Society.[2] You were absent, but I can assure you that I spared no pains to secure a good reading of it. Some mistakes, though not many, were remarked upon in the performance of the final section. We might well have had more serious accidents to complain about, since Mr and Mrs Reeves, who had been entrusted with the parts of Telemachus and Eucharis, were not present at any of the orchestral rehearsals. At the first (with the wind instruments and the double quartet) I had to sing the arias and recitatives as best I could, while conducting the orchestra at the same time. At the second, with eighty players, only Miss Dolby and Mr Weiss were in attendance. At the third in the Blagrove Rooms, with half the orchestra, I was again obliged to sing the parts of Eucharis and Telemachus, Mr and Mrs Reeves having again failed to put in an appearance. These two artists rehearsed only once, with me at the piano, on the very day of the concert, and the orchestra was therefore obliged to accompany them without having heard them. So you will understand why the brass were at times lacking in confidence in the recitatives.

All the same, the only serious error to be regretted was not commit-ted by the orchestra. I was on the point of refusing to conduct the performance of such an important work under such strange conditions. I was restrained by the fear of seeing my conduct misconstrued. It is the first time in my life I have ever been placed in such a position. As you see, I was forced to go through with it, and it is I alone, I assure you, who have been compromised.

Please accept, Monsieur, the assurance of my highest esteem for your merits as a musician together with my personal best wishes.

Yours very sincerely,

Hector Berlioz

1 A reputable Victorian composer then living in Manchester.
2 Berlioz's first concert, on 24 March, included parts of *Roméo et Juliette*, Mozart's 'Jupiter' Symphony and Beethoven's Triple Concerto. The second concert, on 14 April, included Loder's *The Island of Calypso*, which was unsatisfactorily performed, according to some of the critics.

You tell me you've gone mad! You have.

You must be mad or half-witted to write me letters like that; it was all I needed in the middle of my labours night and day. In your last letter from Havana you told me you would arrive with a hundred francs and now you owe forty!!! Who told you to pay fifteen francs to bring in a packet of cigars? Couldn't you have thrown them in the sea?

Here is half a banknote for a hundred francs; you'll have the other half when you have acknowledged receipt of this one. You can then stick them together and get money from a money-changer. It's a usual precaution when one puts money in the post. I'm writing now to M. Cor and M. Fouret to find out the facts about your next sailing. You are right in thinking I'm not prepared to ignore the stupidities and idiocies you speak of. You have begun on a career chosen by yourself; it is very hard, I know, but the hardest part is behind you. You have only a five-month voyage to complete, after that you will spend six months doing your hydrography course in a French port and after that you will be able to earn your living.

I am working to put aside the necessary funds for your expenses during those six months. I have no other means of solving your difficulties.

What is this you say about your torn clothes? In just six weeks in Havana have you destroyed your belongings? Your shirts are rotten? Do you have to have dozens of shirts every five months? Are you making fun of me?

I would ask you to weigh your words when you write to me; that style does not meet with my approval. If you thought that life was a bed of roses, it's time you began to realize the contrary. In any case, to put the matter briefly, I have no intention of providing you with a life other than the one that you have *chosen*. It is too late. At your age one should have enough knowledge of the world to conduct oneself differently from the way you appear to be doing.

When you send me a reasonable letter in acknowledgment of the half-note, you will receive the other half and my instructions. Until then, stay in Le Havre.

Adieu.

H. Berlioz

My dear d'Ortigue,

I'm sending you just three lines to tell you that our last concert took place last Wednesday with extraordinary success, a huge crowd and large takings.[1] I was recalled four or five times. Two movements from *Faust* were encored with shouts and stamping, and the English papers are saying that a musical success of this violence is unknown in London. In short, it's amazing. After the *Chœur de sylphes* someone threw me a garland; this success has therefore been crowned, as the military men would say, with laurels, oak-leaves and all St John's herbs. I intended leaving yesterday and again tomorrow. But I'm staying a few days longer even so, unless I can use more dispatch than I expect in getting through last-minute business, visits, dinners, letters of thanks, etc.

Still, this prolonged stay causes me anxiety from the financial point of view. I have so much rent to pay in Paris, plus the expenses of my son who is there at the moment, etc, that the luxury of living in London when I no longer have things to do here would be the end of me. In fact it's not entirely a luxury because it is really and truly to my disadvantage to leave England at the moment when I have so many things about to come to fruition here.

A naive music-lover from Birmingham recently deplored the fact that he had not engaged me *this year* to conduct the festival in his part of the world, saying, 'It's very unfortunate for us, because it seems Mr Berlioz is even better than Mr Costa.'

I shall really miss my magnificent orchestra and the chorus. What beautiful women's voices! I wish you could have heard Beethoven's Choral Symphony which we gave for the second time last Wednesday. Truly, the combined forces in the huge concert room of Exeter Hall were wonderfully impressive.

In Paris I shall soon have forgotten all these musical delights as I return to my stupid job as a critic, the only one left to me in our beloved country.

I think in London tomorrow I shall finish making arrangements to publish my book in English.[2] Mitchell is going to be in charge of it.

1 The climax of Berlioz's concert series was his performance of Beethoven's Ninth Symphony, played in both the fourth and sixth concerts on 12 May and 9 June.
2 In London Berlioz compiled a collection of his essays and articles into a book entitled *Les soirées de l'orchestre*, published in Paris at the end of the year. But there was no English edition at that time.

Adieu. I shake you by the hand and I believe that you will take more pleasure than any of my other friends in what I have just told you.

Adieu again.

Greet Mme d'Ortigue for me.

Your devoted

H. Berlioz

269 *To Franz Liszt*   Paris, 2 July 1852

My dear and excellent friend,

[...] I shall try to pay you a short visit towards the end of November, if that seems to you a suitable time. I should be very happy to hear a performance of our opera.

I must say that your remarks about *Benvenuto* are absolutely to the point, and that the whole section you suggest cutting has always seemed to me frigid and unbearable.[1] But no one had ever pointed me in the direction of the very simple way in which this cut can be made; this you have done. It is merely a matter of not having the Cardinal leave the stage after the scene with the statue and of going straight on to the dénouement. But I *have* found a way of keeping the foundrymen's chorus 'Bienheureux les matelots', which can begin the last act, by giving the solos to Francesco and Bernardino; also Ascanio's aria (with a change of words) and Cellini's aria 'Sur les monts'. Despite the rather popular style of the second of these, I think they deserve to be kept. If your tenor were to find Cellini's aria unsingable (something I should fail to understand) it would always be possible to cut it in accordance with the scenario I'm going to send you. [...]

Yesterday I had a proposition from America, to go and give a series of concerts in New York. I didn't accept. But if I ever do accept, seduced by more generous offers, it will be entirely in the hope that when I return I shall be able to resign my post as a music critic, which is my shame and despair. If you knew what I've listened to here on my return from London ... and what people want me to praise and what I shall not praise ...

1 After the three performances of *Benvenuto Cellini* in the spring, Liszt and Hans von Bülow proposed rewriting the second act quite radically by cutting a large part of the final tableau and combining it with the third tableau, thus making an opera in three tableaux. This was the basis of the 'Weimar' version of the opera, which was heard later that year in Weimar.

Adieu, I hope to see you soon.
Your devoted
H. Berlioz

270 *To Madame Le Sueur*   Paris, 29 July 1852

My dear Madame Le Sueur,

[. . .] Both intellectually and physically I am unable to write anything
worthy of the ceremony which is being prepared or of the illustrious
composer whom it is designed to honour.[1]

I have no experience of this kind of work and the prostrate condition
in which I find myself renders me unfit for the honoured task that you
wish to entrust to me.

I shall do my utmost to spread the word of this ceremony, which I
am not even sure I shall be able to attend. In the event that I cannot
come to Abbeville I would ask you to let me have the necessary details.

You know how urgently I have always seized every opportunity to
show my respect and admiration for my teacher's standing as an artist.
I hope therefore that my inevitable reserve in these circumstances will
not bring you to doubt either the feelings I shall always retain for his
memory or those that I beg you to accept herewith.

Your devoted
H. Berlioz

271 *To his sister Adèle Suat*   Paris, 17 August 1852

Dear sister,

[. . .] I have been desperately anxious recently about the violent
storms that have ravaged the whole of the north coast of France.
Thinking of these squalls has kept me awake at night, but luckily Louis
had already been at sea for nine days when these storms burst and so a
long way from the coasts where they were so terrifying . . . Harriet is
still in the same condition, and less unhappy perhaps than we think.
During the summer months she stays there calmly looking at her
garden and out over the plain of St-Denis and the hills of Mont-
morency. She has two attentive servants who are familiar with all her
ways, tactful friends who come and see her from time to time, her

---

1 Mme Le Sueur invited Berlioz to compose a cantata for the inauguration of the statue of
Le Sueur in Abbeville on 10 August 1852. But composition of any kind was far from his
thoughts in the years 1851–4 and the cantata was provided instead by Ambroise Thomas,
another of Le Sueur's pupils.

newspaper which she reads two or three times of a morning, my visits and . . . hope.

As for me, I'm publishing various works, correcting proofs and no longer getting enthusiastic about anything. I let the mountain come to me nowadays and have stopped taking steps towards it. Did I tell you that someone came offering me 25,000 francs to go and spend five months in New York and to put on some of my works there? The impresario who made this proposition had been at my last triumph in London; he was quite worked up about it and was absolutely determined to have me. He intends to return next year bringing me new offers from a Philharmonic Society in the United States; if they're acceptable and firmly *backed*, we'll see. But I'm tired of all these wanderings! Crossing the Atlantic to make bad music . . . they'd have to pay me a large sum.

Liszt has made me promise to go and spend a week in Weimar next November to hear my opera *Benvenuto* which is still being played there. The intendant of the theatre will pay my travelling and living expenses. I shall find several of my German friends who are looking forward to seeing me there. There's some idea of fêting me . . .

How is my uncle? Was he happy with his visit to take the waters? Give me his news in detail when you write. I shall say nothing about the celebrations on 15 August.[1] I didn't see anything, I was in bed. Its impact reached me only in the form of the fabulous number of cannon shots that were fired, preventing me from sleeping all day long. Last Tuesday evening the grotesque ball of the Women of La Halle took place at the Innocents' market.[2] All those women selling poultry will have beautified themselves with breathtaking results; it must have been a curiosity on a grand scale. But I didn't feel strong enough to take part in this fishwives' romp. Adieu, my head is spinning.

H. Berlioz

Embrace your daughters and husband for me.

This letter doesn't make any sense . . . it's the work of someone unhinged . . . but my head feels like a balloon that's about to burst. Adieu again, dear sister.

I'm going to bed.

1 15 August, the Feast of the Assumption, was celebrated as a national holiday by the new régime.
2 The church of the Holy Innocents used to stand at the corner of Les Halles, Paris's central market at that time.

Dear sister,

[...] You don't know, and indeed never will, what my life in Paris is like; I *do not have the time* to enjoy the pleasure of seeing my friends just in order to see them. I always have so many things in hand. At the moment there's a book I'm publishing,[1] there's my *Requiem* which has just been performed at St-Eustache,[2] there are proofs to correct, committees to preside over, intrigues to defend myself against, rehearsals to take. I'm leaving for Weimar on the 12th of next month. Liszt is expecting me there to let me hear a performance of my opera *Benvenuto Cellini* which has been in the repertoire of the Ducal theatre for six months. I also have to give a concert there, and I shall come back as soon as I can to Paris. I've been a little uneasy since Friday; the reason is the emotions produced by the *Requiem*. You have never missed such an opportunity of hearing this work. It was colossal! There were nearly six hundred of us, I'd built a set of tiers in the choir to raise the chorus up and the effect was much better as a result. All the smart world of Paris was there. There was the Institut, well-known artists in every field and a closely packed crowd. I had the pleasure of seeing many people in tears. The director of the Opéra[3] wanted, *the day before* this ceremony, to prevent all the personnel of his theatre from taking part; Baron Taylor, our president, tried in vain to get him to go back on his decision, which was directed solely at me. So I then explained the situation to the Minister of the Interior who immediately sent the order to the noble Roqueplan to put up a notice at the Opéra saying the ban was lifted. This blow at the said gentleman made my success the next day all the more piquant. In fact, all the performers were determined to come despite the ban. It's made a considerable stir. This funeral Mass was celebrated for the repose of the soul of Baron de Trémont, who has just left his whole fortune to musicians.

I am sorry that none of you was present; it was one of those artistic celebrations that one sees only two or three times in one's life.

Adieu, dear little sister, all best wishes to your husband and to your *young ladies*.

H. Berlioz

P.S. There are moves afoot to get my new *Te Deum* performed at the

1 *Les soirées de l'orchestre.*
2 On 22 October in memory of the Baron de Trémont.
3 Roqueplan.

ceremony which is to take place on 4 December.[1] But I doubt they will succeed. The President doesn't like music, and my work would demand an outlay of some thirty thousand francs. If it came off nonetheless, then I should not go to Weimar.

273 *To Auguste Barbier*   Weimar, 19 November 1852

My dear Barbier,

I am taking advantage of a quarter-of-an-hour's respite amid rehearsals to tell you that the first performance of the revival of *Benvenuto* took place the day before yesterday with monumental success, under Liszt's baton. I was forced to appear after the last act and cheered in a highly agreeable fashion.

Really, my word of honour, *Benvenuto* in his present state is a nice lad. The grand finale of the Carnival, the *Serment des ciseleurs*, the arias for Ascanio and Teresa, the *Prière* for two voices with the litanies, and especially the scene with the Cardinal made an impression out of the common run. We have two talented ladies, a very good Fieramosca and a Cellini who passes muster in the energetic scenes. Even so he manages the Romance quite well; as for the aria 'Sur les monts', he never dared sing it ... The production is excellent, the *Pantomime* of Harlequin and Pierrot very well done. All in all, it's charming.

To describe to you the *melancholy* joy I felt, on comparing this well-intentioned performance with the foul cabal we had to put up with at the Opéra, would be difficult for me. It made my heart contract. I leave you now to go to the final rehearsal of the concert I'm giving tomorrow, which includes *Roméo et Juliette complete* and the first two acts of *Faust*. I have a chorus of a hundred and a good orchestra. All the hotels in Weimar are full of music-lovers who have come from Hanover, Brunswick, Jena, Eisenach and Leipzig to be at this concert and at the second performance of *Cellini* which takes place on Sunday, the day after tomorrow.

I'll give you the details when I get back to Paris. I leave next Tuesday. Adieu, adieu, I shake your hand and finish by relaying the remark of a critic from Brunswick who embraced me with this single compliment:

E pur si muove![2]

H. Berlioz

1 The coronation of Louis-Napoleon as Napoleon III.
2 'But nevertheless it moves!', words attributed to Galileo after the retraction of his ideas on the rotation of the earth.

My dear M. Duchesne,

Don't blame me; I wanted, when I wrote, to have some good news to tell you. But I'm like Sister Anne,[1] I see nothing on the horizon. The Emperor won't make any decision concerning the ceremonies for his marriage[2] or in the matter of founding an Imperial Chapel. So the *Te Deum* remains a myth.

I may say it's a charming idea of yours to have got me into the way of writing to you from time to time. I shall take advantage of your permission, if you will do the same with me.

I've just been to a fearful concert in the hall of Ste-Cécile, in which I heard some very bad works and an estimable symphony by the estimable Gade, a disciple and imitator of Mendelssohn. This Gade, whose name is written in music as follows

INSERT MUSIC EXAMPLE 11

was born in Denmark; you can tell that from the nebulous sadness of his music. It would seem he has not often felt the sunshine. 'Everything by a Danish author has a Danish atmosphere'.

Still, there's unquestionably talent there. It would be better if one could say the contrary.

Auber produced a delightful opera[3] recently. The third opera house[4] is giving birth to some atrocious ones; which is all it's good for.

We had some trios at my house the other evening, with Vieuxtemps, Mlle Clauss and Cossmann.[5] That's all! you'll say. Yes, that's all! They played us some trios by Schubert, in which there are some new and admirable things. And what a performance! Vieuxtemps's most recent concerto is a masterpiece and a masterpiece of orchestral writing. His talent as a performer is greater than ever it was; he's causing a sensation, such a sensation that in spite of the costs of his little orchestra of

1 Sister Anne is a character from Perrault's Bluebeard story. Bluebeard's wife, under mortal threat, keeps calling out to ask if her sister Anne can see help arriving. But she always replies, 'I can see nothing.'
2 To the Spanish countess Eugénie de Montijo, announced for 30 January 1853.
3 *Marco Spada*, played at the Opéra-Comique on 21 December
4 The Théâtre-Lyrique, the recently renamed Théâtre de l'Opéra National.
5 Vieuxtemps, the Belgian violinist, and Cossmann, the Weimar cellist, were well-known instrumentalists. Mlle Clauss, a pianist from Bohemia, was only eighteen years old and had made her debut in Paris the previous year.

fifty players, I believe he made fifty francs on his first concert and will make a hundred on the second . . . thanks to the Russians, the Germans and the English who are in Paris.

I'm going to see *la colonne* tomorrow, so I can be proud of being French.[1]

As for making music myself in Paris, that's something that won't happen again. I am content with London where I have good friends and a splendid orchestra and an admirable audience. They are busy at the moment trying to arrange three concerts for me in April. I don't know whether it will be possible to remove certain obstacles which have just presented themselves owing to a Dr Wylde, a professor at the Conservatoire,[2] the friend of a millionaire and an imitator of Handel. I'll let you know the end of this little intrigue, which is worthy of Paris.

All best wishes,

I've moved to 19, Rue de Boursault.

H. Berlioz

275 *To his brother-in-law Camille Pal*   Paris, 29 December 1852

My dear Camille,

[. . .] I have a number of things on the go, but nothing definite. The success of my opera *Benvenuto* at Weimar has received an extraordinary amount of publicity. There is now talk of putting the work on in London and Karlsruhe. I'm busy on the Italian translation for London; it's a difficult and delicate task. As for Karlsruhe, the theatre there will use the translation already used at Weimar. It's possible that nothing will come of all this, but I'm being prepared.[3] My *Te Deum* has also been announced as forming part of the musical manifestations at the Imperial wedding.[4] But the Emperor has no chapel as yet and is postponing all decisions in the matter for several months. The book I've just published[5] is a success and is *selling*, to the great satisfaction of the publisher, as he admits.

All in all, the past two months have been very successful ones for me. The performance of the *Requiem* in Paris, those of *Benvenuto*, *Roméo et Juliette* and *Faust* in Weimar, the celebrations in my honour

1 Berlioz frequently referred (ironically) to the pride a Frenchman feels when he looks at 'the column' (in the Place Vendôme).
2 The Royal Academy of Music.
3 The Karlsruhe proposal came to nothing, but the London one came to pass in July 1853.
4 This was not to happen.
5 *Les soirées de l'orchestre*.

organized in that charming and artistic city, the decoration of the White Falcon bestowed by the Grand Duke, the success of the book, the propositions made to me from London – all that is quite reassuring for the future. But I could do with a grand enterprise that would bring me in some money *smartly* (to use a military expression). If the *Te Deum* is performed, that will be an opportunity to make some. It cost me enough to *copy*.

Adieu, my dear Camille, Adèle often sends me news of you, and ends by telling me how well my niece Mathilde is doing.

I shake both of you by the hand.

H. Berlioz

276 *To the Emperor Napoleon III* Paris, 7 January 1853

To His Majesty Napoleon III
Emperor of the French

Sire,

Permit me to place before you a volume that I have just published which contains, together with literary fantasies of varying kinds, a sufficiently faithful picture of the present state of music in Europe. Perhaps thanks to the calm which France enjoys at the present time and which she owes to you, the author of such a book may be forgiven for hoping that Your Majesty might, if he so wishes, find the time to look through it.

Books about art, in general, infect the air around them with boredom, they are manchineel trees to which it is dangerous to come too close.[1] This one, if one may trust its recent reception by the public, appears to be reasonably inoffensive. Whence my presumption in presenting it to Your Majesty.

I am with the most profound respect
Sire,
Your Majesty's most humble
and obedient servant and subject,
Hector Berlioz

---

1 The tree's leaves exude a deadly poison, a fact dramatized in the last act of Meyerbeer's *L'africaine*.

My dear Chorley,

[...] Once again I have been thrown into it, or rather left out of it, by the agents of *officialdom* over the Emperor's wedding. I had been asked to call on Colonel Fleury, His Majesty's secretary, and he gave me almost official notice of the performance of my *Te Deum*. But twenty-four hours earlier the Minister of the Interior had made different arrangements for the musical portion of the ceremony; he had summoned his head of the Imperial Chapel (M. Auber) who summoned his orchestral conductor (M. Girard) who summoned his chief copyist (M. Leborne) and shamelessly they disinterred all the oldest stuff from the Opéra library to be performed *with one rehearsal* at the ceremony in Notre-Dame. Three movements of an oratorio by Le Sueur, two movements of a Mass by Cherubini, one movement of a Mass by Adam (all *fathers of the Church*), plus a march from the BALLET *Les filets de Vulcain* by Schneitzoeffer, and some plainsong orchestrated with violin etc by Auber! ... What do you think of this omelette, this *olla podrida*? ... That's how the business was organized. Now they're saying in the government offices that I'll be amply recompensed and that my *Te Deum* will be performed for the coronation. I don't believe a word of it. That'll be a second piece of mystification. They'll get someone to arrange a quadrille by Musard, if they can't find anything worse. [...]

Yours most sincerely,

H. Berlioz

278 *To Joseph-Esprit Duchesne*   Paris, 10 February 1853

My dear Monsieur Duchesne,

Forgive me for not having thanked you yet for the splendid basket of game which you were kind enough to send me. Your partridges, your hare, your rabbits were much admired by various friends, people of taste, whom I invited in to welcome them. [...]

Meanwhile everything here is shut against me, the Opéra, the Conservatoire and the Church. As for the Opéra-Comique, it does no more than give me a rather silly smile while the third theatre, the so-called Théâtre Lyrique, is no more than a musical drain in which all the donkeys of Paris go to have a piss. I've no desire to swell their numbers.[1]

Nothing is settled as regards England; I wait. And what of you, hunting and administration aside? You dream! For what is there to do at Vervins if not dream? What sort of countryside is it? Do they play whist? Do they go to bed at nine o'clock? Are there lanterns to guide the whist-players back home? Do they have a high opinion of Voltaire's tragedies? Do they believe firmly and steadfastly in the republic? In liberty? In equality? Do they admire the socialists' daydreams? Do they treat art and artists with a healthy suspicion? Do they believe that the newspapers tell the truth, the whole truth and nothing but the truth? That newspaper hacks earn 40,000 francs a year? That Mme Sand always wears men's clothes? That Dumas is in exile? That Gueymard is a singer? That Adam is a . . . etc.

If they don't do all those things, believe all those things, say all those things, then what the devil do they believe, do and say? After all, you're not in the provinces; Vervins must be some little-known capital, like San Marino or Monaco . . . or Paris.

But enough of this rambling, let me have your news and write me one of those charming letters of yours in the hand of a *maire* (only the 't' is missing, it's a new kind of pun).

All best wishes,

Yours most sincerely,

H. Berlioz

279 *To George Hogarth*[2]   Paris, 23 February 1853

My dear Hogarth,

[. . .] If you reply straight away I shall have your letter on Friday, the day after tomorrow; and if I send the music the same day you will receive the parcel next Monday.[3] [. . .]

Yours most sincerely,

H. Berlioz

1 Recent repertoire at the Théâtre-Lyrique included operas by Adam, Girard, Sarmiento, Bousquet and Jean-François Gautier. Ironically, in 1863 the Théâtre-Lyrique was to be the only French theatre bold enough to mount *Les Troyens*.
2 Secretary of the Philharmonic Society, London.
3 Letter-writers enjoyed a rapid mail service in 1853.

My dear Liszt,

[. . .] I find your desire to see me write a solemn Mass very flattering, even though I'm not in the least sure that I could produce anything new on such a well-worn text.[1] But a solemn Mass is the worst sort of large composition to embark on, if you take account of its chances of being well and frequently performed. The only thing that can put such an enterprise on the right road is a royal commission, as you say. But Kings and Emperors have other projects to commission these days.

You can see from what happened over my *Te Deum* what opportunities I would have to put on such a work in France. In England, in Prussia and everywhere that's dominated by those terrible schisms, those scrofulous bastards of rationalism called Protestantism, Lutheranism or any other of those 'isms', in those places the Mass is an object of horror.[2] Requiem Masses at least have a protectress in France, the most powerful of all, unwearying and always at her task, namely death . . . As for songs of gratitude, exultation or faith, one must put those out of one's mind. [. . .]

Adieu.

Your devoted

H. Berlioz

My dear Ernst,

[. . .] We were almost hoping to see you in Paris for the end of the concert season, though it's true that, as the concerts haven't finished yet, you're free to come any time you like in the certainty that you will always find yourself in the midst of a crowd of small and middling virtuosos who clutter up the place with their universal scraping and strumming. This year especially the number of pianists has been exorbitant; a cloud of grasshoppers has descended upon Paris. So much so that Zimmermann[4] said the other day: 'It's terrifying! Everybody these days plays the piano and everybody plays it well.' To

---

1 Liszt may have been unaware that Berlioz had composed a *Messe solennelle* in 1824.
2 These lines are clearly intended for Liszt the devout Catholic.
3 Virtuoso violinist, born in Moravia, trained in Vienna, and regarded by some as Paganini's successor.
4 Zimmermann retired as professor of piano at the Conservatoire in 1848.

which I replied: 'Indeed, my poor Zimmermann, we're the only two left who don't play it.' [. . .]

I shall probably be going to London; the director of Covent Garden[1] would like to put on my opera *Benvenuto Cellini*; and if the conditions I've just sent him are accepted I shall have to start again on the painful business of rehearsing singers.

I think I shall after all be engaged by Bénazet for a large concert in Baden-Baden in August. Might you be in that part of the world by any chance? [. . .]

Yours most sincerely,
H. Berlioz

Berlioz and Marie left for London on 14 May. In addition to preparing Benvenuto Cellini *at Covent Garden Berlioz had also been engaged by the (old) Philharmonic Society to conduct the first half of their concert on 30 May.*

282 *To Gemmy Brandus*[2] 17, Old Cavendish Street, 1 June 1853

My dear Brandus,

I made my first reappearance before an English audience the day before yesterday at the fourth concert of the Philharmonic Society in Hanover Square. It was a risky venture. The supporters of the classics were out in force.

The performance of *Harold* was wonderfully spirited and precise and I can say the same for that of the *Carnaval romain*. The applause for me was enormous in spite of the rage of four or five personal enemies, who were apparently bunched together in a corner. Gardoni's delightful singing of my new piece in the ancient style, *Le repos de la sainte famille*, made a tremendous effect and it had to be repeated.[3] I'd never heard it before, not even with piano; I can assure you it's very nice.

Davison[4] came, full of good humour, to embrace me after the concert, but hasn't written anything yet. Yesterday's *Morning Herald*

1 Frederick Gye.
2 Parisian music publisher who purchased Schlesinger's business, including the *Revue et gazette musicale*, in 1846.
3 The third movement of *La fuite en Egypte*, composed in 1850 and later incorporated in *L'enfance du Christ*.
4 Music critic of *The Times*.

contains a splendid article, the writer of which is so far unknown to me. Put a few lines into Sunday's *Gazette* if possible. Mention Sainton, the leader of the Covent Garden orchestra, who played the viola solo in *Harold* superbly.

Bottesini too had a great success, playing with his usual extraordinary dexterity a new double bass concerto of his own, very remarkable, *pleasant to listen to* and well orchestrated. All my friends here say that this success with the *old* Philharmonic Society was something extremely hard to achieve. The hall was packed and I had the pleasure of seeing that a large part of the audience came just for me, since a third of them left after my last piece ended. [. . .]

Yours most sincerely,

H. Berlioz

283 *To Auguste Barbier*   London, 10 June 1853
                                          17, Old Cavendish Street,
                                                   Oxford Street.

My dear Barbier,

Won't you come and see our *Benvenuto* at Covent Garden? The production will be splendid and the performance, under my direction, something exceptional! I have the most marvellous tenor you could ask for (Tamberlick), who sings and understands his role admirably, an excellent Teresa,[1] a ravishing Ascanio[2] and the two best workaday singers one could have for Francesco and Bernardino.[3] A superb orchestra, an excellent chorus, and a *passable* conductor (I'm conducting).

Everyone is absolutely devoted to me; the producer[4] has promised me a brilliant carnival scene. The impatience with which London operagoers are awaiting the work has been further increased by my recent success at the Philharmonic Society. I have every reason to hope that we shall earn ourselves a dazzling retribution.

Do come, my dear, great poet. Such emotions are not frequent visitors in one's life . . . And London is so near to Paris. *Benvenuto* will be given around the 22nd of this month. Make no mistake about the

1 Mme Julienne.
2 Mme Nantier-Didiée.
3 Stigelli and Polonini.
4 Augustus Harris *père*.

difference there'll be between the *Malvenuto* of Paris and the *Benvenuto* of London. [. . .]

Yours,

H. Berlioz

Despite Berlioz's keen anticipation of success and despite the high quality of the performance – with which Berlioz was delighted – the first performance of Benvenuto Cellini *on 25 June was a disaster, overthrown by a faction that resented the intrusion of non-Italians in a house wedded to Italian opera. The performance was also the victim of rivalry between Covent Garden and the supporters of Her Majesty's Theatre. Berlioz withdrew the work and returned to Paris soon after.*

284 *To Frederick Gye*[1]   London, 26 June 1853

Monsieur,

May I thank you for the care you have taken in putting on my opera *Benvenuto Cellini*. Unfortunately I must at the same time ask you to agree not to give my work again, as I cannot expose myself a second time to such acts of hostility as we had to face last night, to the great amazement of an impartial audience, acts which surely have barely been equalled in the history of the civilized theatre. I am more sorry than I can say to have exposed you in this way, as well as the distinguished artists who were kind enough to take part in the performance, to so much trouble and unpleasantness simply by accepting your offer to put on my work.

Please accept, etc.

Hector Berlioz

285 *To Franz Liszt*   Paris, 10 July 1853

My very dear Liszt,

A most unfortunate misunderstanding has led to your letter of 3 May staying in Paris where I have now found it on my return from London. It is affectionate and charming and has given me all the more pleasure because I was still somewhat depressed by the rebuffs I have had to endure at Covent Garden. You will already have heard that a determined, wild and angry group of Italians got together to put a stop

1 Director of Covent Garden.

to the performances of *Cellini*. These clowns, with the help of some
Frenchmen who came over from Paris, made hissing noises from the
first scene through to the last and even whistled *during* the performance of the *Carnaval romain* overture,[1] which had been applauded a
fortnight earlier at Hanover Square. They were absolutely implacable;
the presence of the Queen and of the royal family of Hanover, who
were at the performance, and the applause of the great majority of the
audience did nothing to restrain them. They would have continued
throughout the following evenings, so I withdrew my score next day.
There were Italians hissing even *in the wings*. I didn't lose my temper
for a moment even so, and conducted without the slightest mistake,
which doesn't happen with me often. With only one exception, the
actors were excellent and the performance of the chorus and orchestra
must be reckoned as one of the best ever. The work has benefited
greatly from this production. A number of details in the score have
been improved, small cuts made and stage effects added. [. . .]

Adieu from your devoted and be-whistled

H. Berlioz

*In August Berlioz paid his first visit to Baden-Baden, where he was
later to be a regular visitor for many years. He gave one concert there
and then went on to give two concerts in Frankfurt on 20 and 24
August. He was composing nothing at this time, although the idea of a
large-scale opera on the* Aeneid *was already lodged in his mind. In
October he set off on yet another concert tour, to Brunswick, Hanover,
Bremen and Leipzig, returning in the middle of December.*

286 To Humbert Ferrand   Hanover, 13 November 1853

My dear Humbert,

I write to you somewhat at random, not knowing if you are in Belley,
in Lyon, in Sardinia, or *in Europe*. But I hope my letter will find
you. [. . .]

After my return from London I went in August to Baden-Baden,
where I'd been engaged by M. Bénazet, the director of the casino.
There I organized and conducted a fine festival in which we played the
first two acts of *Faust*, etc. From there I went to Frankfurt, where I gave
two more concerts in the theatre, again including *Faust*.

---

1 The overture was played as an entracte.

There wasn't the huge crowd one found in Baden-Baden, but I was fêted in a way quite exceptional in 'free' cities, that's to say cities that are the slaves of mercantile values, of *business*, like Frankfurt. From there I went back to Paris. Hardly had I returned, when I received a double proposition from Brunswick and Hanover, and I left once more. To describe to you the delirium of the audience and the performers in Brunswick after the performance of *Faust* would take too long: a gold baton and money presented by the orchestra; supper for a hundred guests, including all the notables of the city (you can imagine the menu), the Duke's ministers and the musicians of the chapel; a charitable institution founded in my name (*sub invocatione sancti*, etc); an ovation from the crowd one Sunday when they were playing *Le carnaval romain* at an open-air concert; women kissing my hand in the middle of the street on their way out of the theatre; anonymous wreaths arriving at my house of an evening, etc, etc.

Here it's a different story. When I arrived for my first rehearsal, the orchestra greeted me with trumpet fanfares and applause and I found my scores covered with laurel wreaths the size of good large hams. For the last rehearsal the King and Queen[1] arrived at nine o'clock in the morning and stayed until we'd finished work, that's to say at one o'clock in the afternoon. At the concert, enormous hurrahs and demands for encores, etc. The following day the King sent for me and asked for a second concert, which will take place the day after tomorrow.

'I did not think', he said to me, 'that one could still find new beauties in music, but you have proved me wrong. And what a conductor you are! I cannot *see* you (the King is blind), but I feel it.'

And when I began to exclaim how lucky I was to have such a *musician* listening to me:

'Yes', he said, 'I am much indebted to Providence, which has granted me a feeling for music as a compensation for what I have lost!'

These simple words, this allusion to the double misfortune which the young King suffered fifteen years ago touched me deeply.

You were much in my thoughts three weeks ago, during a walking tour I made in the Harz mountains (where the sabbath scene in *Faust* takes place). I have never seen anything so beautiful. What forests! What torrents! What rocks! They are the ruins of a world . . . I looked

---

1 King Georg V and Queen Maria of Hanover had been present at the performance of *Benvenuto Cellini* in London. The King was Queen Victoria's cousin and an ardent musician.

for you, I missed you on those poetic heights. I confess I was suffocated by emotion.

Adieu; write to me *poste-restante* at Leipzig until the 11th.

Warmest wishes.

Your devoted

H. Berlioz

This morning I had a visit from Mme von Arnim, Goethe's Bettina, who had come, she said, not to *see* me but to *look at* me. She's seventy-two and has a lively wit.[1]

287 *To Baron Wilhelm von Donop*[2]   Hanover, 16 November 1853

My dear Baron,

Captain Nieper was kind enough to translate for me the various letters in which you express such a warm sympathy for my compositions. May I thank you and assure you that nothing can give me greater courage, in struggling against the innumerable difficulties of my life as a Pioneer,[3] than support such as yours. To be sure, men whose passion for art is intelligent, free of prejudice and absolutely pure are very rare! And you are one of those. Please God, however, that I do not think too often about the existence of such people in the world, because that would be enough yet again to make me undertake some new work which would bring me more sorrow than I can bear. Of the last two works I have written (the *Te Deum* and the *Tristia*) I have not yet had the chance to hear a note. In Paris *Faust* ruined me, *Roméo et Juliette* brought down upon me all the most absurd attacks from the French newspapers, and an English newspaper (*Galignani's Messenger*) criticized the *Scène d'amour*, claiming that this movement was absolutely empty of ideas and that I didn't understand Shakespeare. It's true the English audience in Exeter Hall didn't agree on the matter, which consoled me for this inept observation.

But the things that hold me back and will, I hope, continue to hold me back are material difficulties; I'm no longer capable of embarking once more on the harrowing efforts I made in Paris ten or fifteen years ago. Little by little there has formed itself in the city a crystallization of

1 Bettina von Arnim, née Brentano, had known both Goethe and Beethoven and was given to elaborating details of her relationship with both. She was sixty-eight, not seventy-two.

2 One of Berlioz's most fervent admirers, Baron Donop lived in Detmold and had heard Berlioz's concert in Brunswick on 22 October.

3 An image from Fenimore Cooper.

mediocrities which bars avenues, blocks up all doors, whispers in the ear of all the powers that be and makes it impossible for me to get my music played, just like those ocean insects around the lovely Polynesian islands, coral and madrepores, building rocks on which ships come to grief. If I allow myself to mention details that are of no interest to anyone except me, it's by way of replying to the implicit reproach in some of the things you said when I had the honour of meeting you in Brunswick. You spoke to me of new works which I *ought to undertake*.¹ Alas, my dear Baron, I think it far more useful to spend what energy I have in making sure my existing scores are as well and widely known as possible, rather than abandon them to the hazards of musical life and produce sister works whose early steps I should be powerless to protect. I am all too well aware of what happens to music that to some degree goes its own way, at the hands of the incompetent and the uncaring. [. . .]

Adieu, my dear Monsieur, may I thank you once again, shake your hand and sign myself

Your devoted Pioneer,
Hector Berlioz

288 *To Johann Christian Lobe*²   Leipzig, 28 November 1853

Monsieur,

You ask me to write for your paper a summary of my opinions on the art of music, on its present state and on its future, absolving me from the task of discussing its past. I thank you for that consideration. But the summary you ask for would fill a large doctoral volume, and your *Fliegende Blätter*, if loaded with it, would be so weighed down that they could no longer fly.

What you ask me to give you is quite simply a profession of true faith.

This is the line taken by virtuous voters with candidates canvassing to be national representatives. I, however, have not the least ambition to *represent* anybody; I don't want to be a deputy or a senator or a consul or even a burgomaster. And even if I did aspire to the heights of being a consul I could not, I feel, do better towards gaining the votes, not of the people, but of the practitioners of art, than to imitate Marcus

---

1 According to the *Mémoires* the Baron suggested an opera on *Romeo and Juliet*, while Berlioz must have hinted that a much larger project was already simmering in his mind.
2 A composer and copious writer on music, Lobe began publishing a series of *Fliegende Blätter* in Leipzig in 1853, in which this letter appeared.

Coriolanus by betaking myself to the Forum, baring my chest and displaying the wounds I have received in the defence of my country.

Is not my profession of faith to be found in everything I have had the misfortune to write, in what I have done and in what I have not done?

As to the present state of the art of music, you know what it is and you cannot believe I do not know too. What it will become, neither you nor I can have the slightest idea.

So what can I say on the subject?

As a composer I shall, I hope, be forgiven much because I have loved much. As a critic I have been, I am being and I shall continue to be viciously punished because I have had, because I have now and shall continue to have, all my life, vicious hates and immeasurable feelings of contempt. It is true, but these loves, hates and feelings of contempt are no doubt the same as yours; what need for me to detail the objects of them?

Music is the most poetic, the most powerful, the most living of all the arts we have. It should also be the freest of them; but this, as yet, is not the case, which is the reason for the sorrows we artists feel, our obscure enthusiasms, our feelings of lassitude and despair, and our longings for death.

Modern music, *Music* (I am not speaking here of the courtesan of that name who is to be found everywhere) is in several respects like the Andromeda of ancient legend, divinely beautiful and naked, the looks from whose blazing eyes are fragmented into many-coloured rays as they pass through the prism of her tears. Chained to a rock by the shore of a vast sea, whose waves break incessantly over her lovely feet and cover them with mud, she awaits Perseus the conqueror who will break her chains and smash in pieces the chimera called Routine, whose jaws menace her with effusions of foulest smoke.

And yet, I believe, the monster is growing old. Its gestures no longer display the energy they once had, its teeth are rotten, its claws blunt, its heavy paws slip as they grasp at the edges of Andromeda's rock, it is beginning to recognize the futility of its efforts to climb it, it is fated to fall back into the abyss and already from time to time one can hear its death rattle.

And when the beast is well and truly dead, what will there be for the devoted lover of the sublime captive to do but swim out to her, untie her chains and carry the bewildered maiden over the waves to Greece, even at the risk of seeing Andromeda repay such passion with coldness and indifference? In vain the satyrs in the nearby caves will laugh at his eagerness to deliver her, in vain they will cry out to him in their goatish voices: 'Leave her in chains! Can you be sure that when she is free she will want to give herself to you? While she is naked and in chains, the majesty of her sorrow is all the more vulnerable.' The lover who is in love is appalled by the thought of such a crime; he wants to receive, not take by force. Not only will he behave chastely in his rescue of Andromeda but, after gently holding her wounded feet and bathing them in the tears of love, he would, if it were possible, give her wings as well to make her freedom more complete.

That, Monsieur, is all the profession of faith I can make you, and I make it only to show that I do have a faith. So many professors lack one! Unfortunately, yes, I have one, for too long I have proclaimed it from the rooftops, in pious obedience to the precept of the Gospels. How wrong the proverb is that says 'Faith alone can save.' On the contrary, faith alone can destroy; it is faith that will destroy me. That is my conclusion. I will add merely the words that my friend Griepenkerl, an admirer of Galileo, puts at the bottom of all his letters: *E pur si muove!* – Do not denounce me to the Holy Inquisition![1]

Hector Berlioz

289 *To Joseph Joachim*[2]   Leipzig, 9 December 1853

My dear Joachim,

[...] I'm staying here until next Tuesday. My concert is tomorrow. All's going well. Even if the Leipzigers seem cold, they're getting the idea gradually. *All* the newspapers have treated me admirably. The opposition is furious and we don't care a fig. Liszt is coming back again from Weimar tomorrow.

I've arranged one or two concerts with Dresden for next spring and I've had an offer from Oldenburg for the same period. Wouldn't it be better to make the Eberfeld venture coincide with the other two?[3]

Please let me have some details by return of post.

Brahms is a success here.[4] He impressed me very much the other day

---

1 See p. 292.
2 Still only twenty-two, Joachim was already known as an international violin virtuoso and had played under Berlioz in Paris and London. After a spell with Liszt in Weimar he was now in charge of the orchestra in Hanover, where he had been Berlioz's host a few weeks before.
3 The Dresden concerts did take place; in fact there were four, not two. But the Oldenburg and Eberfeld visits did not take place.
4 Brahms and Berlioz were together in both Hanover and Leipzig and seem to have admired each other. Following Schumann's proclamation of his genius in September, the twenty-year-old Brahms was being lionized everywhere.

at Brendel's[1] with his Scherzo and his Adagio. Thank you for introducing me to this young adventurer with timid manners who is taking it into his head to write new music. He will suffer grievously ...

As for my admiration for you, it has been growing since I left you. And when I consider your musical *worth*, the completeness, the brilliance and the purity of it, I surprise myself sometimes by crying out (all on my own, for no reason): 'Ah, it's enormous, prodigious!'

Adieu, greet our friends in the Hanover orchestra for me; I remember them with affection. Best wishes to Müller in particular.

Yours very sincerely,
Hector Berlioz

290 *To Joseph d'Ortigue*   Paris, 17 January 1854

Yes, my dear d'Ortigue, you're right, it is my unconquerable passion for what I know of art that provides me so readily with reasons for bitterness, for misery even.[2] Forgive me for having allowed you to read my thoughts so easily; I felt they were bound to cause you pain and it was impossible for me to restrain the words which were burning my lips. It is quite natural that your religious convictions should have led you to similar opinions in your theories about art. I should have thought of that and held my peace. When it's a question of criticisms aimed at what concerns me directly, my compositions for example, my extreme habit of contradiction leads me to bear them as I should, that's to say in silence and even with resignation. But as soon as the contradiction strikes at my idols (obviously I'm a fanatic), my blood boils and my heart leaps and beats so fiercely that its seizures give the impression of anger and are likely to cause offence to the people I'm talking to.

I have a love of the beautiful and the true, you are right about that, but I have another love of a quite other fury and immensity: I have a love of love. So when some idea aims to deprive the objects of my affections of the qualities which make me love them, and when someone in this way wants to prevent me loving them or to get me to love them less, then something inside me is torn in two and I cry like a child

---

1 Brendel was editor of the *Neue Zeitschrift für Musik*.
2 Despite their close friendship Berlioz and d'Ortigue agreed to differ on the subject of religious music, Berlioz believing that it should not be exempt from the expressive resources of modern art, while d'Ortigue studied plainchant in admiration for its purity and otherworldliness. Berlioz's review of d'Ortigue's *Dictionnaire liturgique* appeared three days later.

who has had one of his toys broken. The comparison is a just one: such behaviour is certainly puerile. I feel it and I will make every effort to mend my ways. In any case you have punished me in a Christian fashion, rendering good for evil, because your letter made me happy. Let me shake your hand and thank you.

Your notes are excellent, I think I shall manage. But I never felt less like writing. This article is one of the many that I don't know how to begin. And I'm so sad within. Life is passing . . . I should so much like to *work*, and I'm obliged to *labour* in order to live . . .

But what does it all matter . . .

Adieu, adieu.

Your devoted

H. Berlioz

---

291 *To Gemmy Brandus*   Paris, January 1854

My dear Brandus,[1]

Several Paris newspapers are announcing my impending departure for a city in Germany where, if they are to be believed, I have recently been appointed conductor.[2] I realize what a bitter blow my final departure from France must be for many people, and how unhappy it must make them to have to bring themselves to accept this grave piece of news and to noise it abroad.

I should therefore be delighted to be able to deny it quite simply by saying, like the hero of a well-known drama: 'I remain with you, beloved France, fear not!' My respect for the truth obliges me to make just one rectification. The fact is that I am due to leave France, one day, in a few years' time, but the orchestra whose direction has been entrusted to me is not in fact in Germany. And since everything becomes known sooner or later in this benighted city, I may as well tell you now the location of my future residence: I am director general of the private concerts of the Queen of the Ovas in Madagascar. The orchestra of Her Majesty Ova is made up of highly distinguished Malaysian players and some Madagascans of supreme talent. They don't like whites, it's true, and as a result I should find my early days on foreign soil extremely difficult if so many people in Europe had not taken it upon themselves to blacken me. I expect therefore to arrive among them hardened against their ill-will. Meanwhile, please inform

---

1 This letter appeared in Brandus's *Revue et gazette musicale* on 22 January 1854.
2 The city was identified in the press as Dresden.

your readers that I shall continue to live in Paris for as much of the time as possible and go to theatres as little as possible, but go to them nonetheless and fulfil my functions as a critic as before, indeed more so. I intend during these last days to enjoy myself to the full, especially as there are no newspapers in Madagascar.

I am, etc.

Hector Berlioz

292 *To his sister Adèle Suat*   Montmartre, 6 March 1854

Dear sister,

Harriet died last Friday, 3 March. Louis had been to spend four days with us and had gone back to Calais the previous Wednesday. Happily she saw him once again. I had just left her a few hours before her death and I came back ten minutes after she had breathed her last, painlessly and without moving.

Yesterday the final rites were performed. I had to organize everything myself, town hall, cemetery . . . Today I am suffering dreadfully.

Her condition was appalling. Paralysis was complicated by erysipelas and she could breathe only with the greatest difficulty. She had become a formless mass of flesh . . . and beside her the radiant portrait I had given her last year in which you can see her as she once was, with her large, wonderful eyes. No more.

My friends supported me, a large number of men of letters and musicians with Baron Taylor at their head conducted her to the Montmartre cemetery near to the house.

And the sparkling sun, the panorama over the plain of St-Denis . . .

I couldn't follow the procession, I stayed in the garden. I had suffered too much the day before on my way to find Pastor Hosemann, who lives in the Faubourg St-Germain. One of those brutal coincidences that happen saw to it that the carriage I was in went past the Odéon theatre where I saw her for the first time *twenty-seven years ago*, when the élite of the intelligentsia of Paris, that's to say of the world, was at her feet. The Odéon where I suffered so deeply . . .

We were unable to live either together or apart and we came to realize this terrible fact over the last ten years. We inflicted so much suffering on each other. I have just been again to the cemetery, I am quite alone. She lies on the slope of the hill with her face turned towards the north, towards the England to which she never wanted to return.

I wrote to poor Louis yesterday. I shall write to him again.

What a fearful thing life is! ... Everything comes back to me all at once, happy and bitter memories alike! Her fine qualities, her cruel demands, her injustices, but also her genius and her unhappiness. Horrible, dreadful! I can't give vent to what I feel. She brought me to an understanding of Shakespeare and great dramatic art, she suffered poverty with me, she never hesitated when it was a matter of risking our livelihood for a musical enterprise ... But then the reverse side of this courage was that she was always opposed to my leaving Paris, she didn't want to let me travel. If I hadn't taken extreme measures I should still today be almost unknown in Europe. And her *unjustified* jealousy, which in the end was the cause of everything that has changed my life. My dear sister, I wish I could see you. It's impossible. And in a month's time I'm leaving for Germany; I have an engagement in Dresden; the King of Saxony's Intendant wrote to me yesterday, they're expecting me. I've no taste for anything, I have as much interest in music and the rest as ... I've kept her hair. I'm alone in the large salon next to her empty bedroom. The garden is beginning to blossom. Oh, oblivion, oblivion! Who will take my memory from me? Who will blot out so many pages of the book of my heart ... We live such a long time! And then there is Louis, so grown-up, he no longer looks anything like the dear little boy I used to see running up and down these garden paths. Over there is his daguerrotype portrait taken at the age of twelve. It seems to me I have lost that child; the tall one I was embracing six days ago cannot console me for the loss of the other.

Don't be surprised at such a curious thought, I could give you plenty of others of the same kind. What a fatal ability it is to remember the past, which is why I have been so wretchedly successful in some of my works in evoking similar feelings.

Still, everyone says we should be glad to see an end to her suffering; it was a fearful existence. I could only be grateful to the three women who looked after her.

Adieu, dear sister, I congratulate you on being able to save Mathilde.[1] I embrace you; be careful what you write to me, your letter can either help me to remain calm or distress me further.

Adieu.

Luckily, there is always TIME which marches onward, crushing and destroying everything, sorrows as well as the rest.

H. Berlioz

1 Adèle's niece, Mathilde Pal, had recovered from a serious illness, perhaps typhoid.

Three weeks later Berlioz set off for Germany again, stopping in Hanover and Brunswick on his way to Dresden, where he was engaged for four concerts.

293 *To Baron Wilhelm von Donop*   Hanover, 31 March 1854

My dear Baron,

[...] We've just finished the last rehearsal for the subscription concert in which I had been invited to take part. The King wanted the programme to be made up exclusively of my music. As a result we performed the overture *Le roi Lear* (asked for by the King), a romance (*Le pâtre breton*) for tenor, the violin solo called *Tendresse et caprice*, divinely executed by Joachim, a song (*Absence*) the words of which had been kindly translated by M. Nieper and which Mme Nottès sang incomparably, the *Reine Mab* scherzo and the *Scène d'amour* from *Roméo et Juliette* (asked for by the Queen) and my *Symphonie fantastique* which had never before been played in Hanover. I cannot describe to you the miraculous perfection with which it was all given by the orchestra ... In the *Symphonie fantastique* there's an Adagio (the *Scène aux champs*) which is the elder brother of the Adagio in *Roméo et Juliette*. It's the first time I've had the opportunity to hear these two movements in the same concert. In one (the one from *Roméo*) there is the expansive love of the Midi, the Italian sky, the starry night ... In the other you would recognize, I think, the desolation of the suffering love of the north, the sombre menace of a stormy horizon during a summer evening with clouds giving forth silent flashes of lightning. In one it is love in the *presence* of the loved one, in the other it is love in the *absence* of the being whom he asks all nature to restore to him.

It's naive of me to tell you all this. But this morning I was devastated by this contrast and I feel the need to confess it to you who, I'm sure, will not make fun of my emotions. How sorry I am not to have you in the audience tomorrow! The Queen was at the rehearsal and after our Shakespearean scene Her Majesty was kind enough to say things that would have made you happy.

My God, what an orchestra! How it understands things! What nuances! What colouring! I can do what I like with it; I feel it is I who am singing with its voice ...

I leave on Sunday for Brunswick. Karl Müller has begged me to give a few pieces at a concert he has fixed for next Tuesday.

Another city full of friends ... Dear Germany, how grateful I am to her, and how passionately I want to prove myself worthy to some small extent of her charming hospitality; and how her pure and noble love of art inspires me with respect!

Enough exclamations or I'll make you laugh.

A thousand apologies for showing myself to you like this in a state of undress. Another time I'll have a morning suit buttoned up to the chin.

Yours very sincerely,
Hector Berlioz

294 *To James William Davison*   Dresden, after 8 April 1854

[. . .] In Brunswick we performed *your* overture *Le corsaire* for the first time.[1] It went very well and made a great impact. With a large orchestra and a conductor with an arm of steel this piece comes over with a certain swagger. [. . .]

295 *To Franz Liszt*   Dresden, 14 April 1854

Dear friend,

[. . .] I often see M. von Bülow who is a dignified and charming gentleman. He's already found such a large number of engraving mistakes in the score of *Faust* I brought for you that I'll take it back to Paris to have them corrected.[2] On the other hand I'll leave you and Cornelius as well copies of the Kistner edition of *La fuite en Egypte*.[3] He's just sent them to me with a stupid mistake in the prosody of two of the lines of German, and it's been taken over into the full score as well as the vocal score.

I should be happy if M. Cornelius was also willing to take on the translation of *L'arrivée à Saïs*, which I'm finishing the orchestration of here.[4] But as no German publisher has so far had the courage to acquire the new work (Kistner refused it, triple rat! . . .), I wouldn't

1 The *Corsaire* overture had been played in Paris in January 1845 in its original version, as *La tour de Nice*. In Brunswick, on 1 April, the new version was first heard. The work was dedicated to Davison.
2 The full score of *La damnation de Faust* had just been published, with a dedication to Liszt. The arrival of the score may have prompted Liszt to compose his *Faust Symphony*, dedicated in turn to Berlioz.
3 Peter Cornelius, another Liszt disciple, was a poet and composer deeply devoted to Berlioz and his music. Kistner, the Leipzig publisher, was putting out *La fuite en Egypte*.
4 Prompted by the success of *La fuite en Egypte* in Leipzig, Berlioz decided to extend it with a sequel, *L'arrivée à Saïs*; he then added an introductory part called here *Le massacre des innocents*, later changed to *Le songe d'Hérode*. The full work had not yet acquired its title *L'enfance du Christ*.

know what arrangement to come to with M. Cornelius, who has already written too much *for love*. Later on I'll write to him about it and beg him to tell me frankly what I can do to compensate him for his work. It's three times longer than *La fuite en Egypte* and more difficult to fit to the music. Beale will no doubt publish it in English, but only when I've written a third part to this little Biblical trilogy. This third part, which he came to Paris to ask me for, would be in fact the first and would have as its subject the slaughter of the innocents. The whole work would therefore run in historical order, at concerts of sacred music:

1 *Le massacre des innocents*
2 *La fuite en Egypte*
3 *L'arrivée à Saïs*,

and it would last an hour and a half.

The plan of *Le massacre* is beginning to come clear in my mind – Chorley too gave me a few ideas for it. [. . .]

Your devoted
H. Berlioz

296 To Karol Lipinski[1]   Dresden, 18 April 1854

My dear Lipinski,

I was promised the twelve boys, they aren't here. The solos in the choruses still weren't sorted out today; the chorus is a long way from knowing some of the pieces; the solo singers *still haven't looked at their parts*. And they want *Faust* to be performed on Saturday . . . It's impossible unless we have a chorus rehearsal tomorrow, Wednesday, one for the soloists on Thursday morning, a full rehearsal on Thursday at 3 o'clock, and another full rehearsal on Friday or Saturday morning. It would be the ultimate folly to risk a performance of *Faust* like this. As for *Roméo et Juliette*, no one has looked at it and it's much more difficult than *Faust*; it's no use imagining the chorus will learn that in four days, or five, or six. It's madness. I wish I was in the antipodes. I thought people knew things which they don't. I've been misled, I'm devastated. I appeal to your friendship to get me out of this terrible and embarrassing situation; I've just written to M. de Lüttichau.[2]

All best wishes,
H. Berlioz

1 Conductor of the Dresden opera orchestra.
2 Intendant of the Dresden opera.

297 To Franz Liszt
Dresden, 23 April 1854

Dear friend,

I'm very happy to be able to tell you that our *Faust* had a great success yesterday. I can honestly say that it was the most magnificent performance this difficult work has ever received. I'm very sorry you couldn't have heard the last two acts, which you don't know. The *Course à l'abîme*, the *Pandaemonium* and the *Scène des follets* made an extraordinary impact. [. . .]

    Your devoted
    H. Berlioz

298 To Robert Griepenkerl
Dresden, 26 April 1854

My dear Griepenkerl,

[. . .] I'm sending you a libretto of *Faust* with the preface I've been unwise enough to write in reply to the unbelievable nonsense put about by certain newspapers on the subject.[1]

Several people in Dresden felt I was so undeniably right that it wasn't worth the trouble of replying. What! Can I not do what every other composer does and use a famous poem as a source of musical situations and arrange them according to my own designs, without putting German men of letters into a rage? It's utter imbecility. Have the English ever taken it into their heads to reproach me for mutilating Shakespeare by making a libretto out of *Romeo and Juliet*? Is Shakespeare less worthy of respect than Goethe?

I think there's animosity against me brewing in the minds of certain German critics, which will increase with my growing popularity in Germany. Well they needn't hold back, I shall enjoy watching their indignation wax.

But to attack me as a *librettist*, it's too stupid.

Adieu, dear Griepenkerl. I'm looking forward to a magnificent performance on Saturday.[2] I tell you in confidence that I've never seen an orchestra like the Dresden one, consisting entirely of young players and virtuosos. What a change over the last eleven years!

    Yours most sincerely,
    H. Berlioz

---

1 Karl Banck, critic of the *Dresdner Journal*, (and others) attacked Berlioz for infidelity to Goethe's *Faust*. Berlioz added a Preface to the printed score justifying his own work, but he later regretted doing so.
2 Berlioz's third Dresden concert, including movements from *Roméo et Juliette*.

My very dear friend,

[...] I have a meeting tomorrow about the performance of the *Te Deum* in the church of St-Eustache next year on the eve of the opening of the Exhibition; several friends are getting together to cover the costs of the performance.[1] One is donating 3000 francs, another 2000 francs and they're on the way to collecting the rest. It's Ducroquet, the builder of the new organ in St-Eustache, who has been the moving force behind the idea. What a pity you won't play the organ; you would have done a splendid job for us during and after the *Te Deum*. Because Ducroquet, reasonably enough, wants to show off his instrument and as the organ part in my work is rather modest I suggested the idea of an organ solo to be played after the *Te Deum* by whoever the organist is to be, either Hesse, or Lemmens, or that delightful little organist with his rings, brooches and gold-headed walking stick who *prettifies* the tunes he plays and goes under the name Lefébure-Wély[2] ... We're also counting on support from the Empress because of a children's institution that she's patron of, from which I shall use seven or eight hundred of them for the Chorale of the *Te Deum*.[3] The gentlemen in question are expecting receipts in the church that day of 15,000 francs. I'm trying to calm the effervescence of these hopes; I know my Paris all too well. [...]

Your devoted
H. Berlioz

300 *To his sister Adèle Suat*   Paris, 27 August 1854

Dear sister,

I've been desperately anxious these last few days about Louis, as you can imagine.[4] Happily, he's just written to me; nothing has happened to him. His letter is in two parts, one written before and one after the bombardment of the fort. He doesn't say anything about his im-

---

1 This project was ultimately successful in bringing the *Te Deum* to performance.
2 Hesse (from Breslau), Lemmens (from Brussels) and Lefébure-Wély *fils* (organist of St-Roch, Paris) were three of the best-known organists of the day.
3 After his experience in St Paul's in 1851 (see p. 279) Berlioz added a part for massed children's voices to his *Te Deum*, modelled partly on the opening chorus of Bach's *St Matthew Passion*.
4 An Anglo-French force was sent to capture Bomarsund, in the Baltic, as a pre-emptive strike against Russia in the Crimean War. The attack on 16 August was successful and the fort was destroyed.

pressions, but I can imagine what the poor boy must have felt, never having seen so much as a skirmish before and now finding himself for the first time in the middle of the hell of a naval battle. I'd been to spend a week at St-Valéry-en-Caux by the sea,[1] to recover from the effects of the cholera which I was feeling like everyone else, when I saw in a local newspaper that the Phlégéthon was to be included in the force attacking Bomarsund. I came back to Paris at once, in the hope of receiving news more quickly there, and by good luck Louis's letter had just arrived. You're thinking I've come back from Germany. I had to cancel the journey to Munich I was going to make when I heard there was a place vacant at the Académie des Beaux-Arts.[2] I was besieged with advice: 'You must put your pride in your pocket' – 'you must make your visits like the other candidates' – 'you must keep on applying' – etc, etc. Finally I gave in and rushed round Paris day and night for a week making my visits, in the certain knowledge that the decision would go in favour of a man called Clapisson who got sixteen votes last year while I was in Germany. In fact he was at the head of the list yesterday with twenty-one votes.[3] Now I have to wait for a new vacancy and, since I've begun, I'm in duty bound to persist.

The appointment is worth 1500 francs, that's all, but for me it's a lot. I say nothing about the *honour* involved, which is a fiction given the people they let in and have always let in to the Académie. I've only applied twice. Hugo had to bang on the door five times, de Vigny four times; Eugène Delacroix has not yet been admitted after six successive attempts and Balzac was never elected. And it's full of cretins . . .

One has to resign oneself to considering it as no more than a question of money, a lottery, and to wait patiently for one's number to come up. I'm a member of all the Academies of the Arts in Europe except the Académie de France.

You mention our next meeting. I've already told Camille last month that I shouldn't be able to get down to La Côte until the beginning of November, but I shall certainly be there then.[4] I very much doubt whether Louis will be able to accompany me. It will be wonderful to see you again, dear sister! I feel we have millions of things to say to each other, and I shall find pleasure even in our painful recollections of the past. I was re-reading two letters only lately, one from you, the other from Nanci, telling me of our father's death. This inexorable

1 On the Normandy coast.
2 Made vacant by the elevation of Halévy to the post of permanent secretary of the Institut.
3 Clapisson was a successful composer of light operas.
4 Berlioz paid a visit to La Côte, Vienne and Grenoble in September.

accuracy of the memory is one of the scourges of my life ... I have spent two days in anguish ... in heart convulsions caused by these two letters ... Tears come to my eyes again as I write to you. I am beginning to live only in the past. And to add to my misery, my sensitivity and imagination and all the feverish activity of my heart and mind are continually on the increase.

My passion for music, or rather for *art*, is taking on outlandish proportions. I feel my abilities to be greater than ever, but material obstacles prevent me from giving them rein. At this moment I am truly ill from this lack of fulfilment of my love for art. But then! In France? Nothing, absolutely nothing! Indifference and idiocy, base industrialism, the savagery of the governing classes, ignorance, the brutality of the rich, the vulgar preoccupations of everybody ... Snakes, hedgehogs, toads, geese, guinea-fowl, crows, bugs and vermin of every kind: that is the delightful population of Paris, our Paradise on earth.

And then my damned column, for which I have to busy myself with so many small, mean-minded actions and often to speak of them with a kind of deference! ...

Oh, how I breathed the heady air a week ago, stretched out on the high cliffs of St-Valéry, with the calm sea murmuring gently three hundred feet below my grassy couch! What marvellous sunsets! What peace up on those heights! What purity there in the atmosphere!

It is only through such passionate conversations with Nature that I can for a moment forget the pain caused by my wounded love of art. But they serve only to revive it more keenly; it all remains as it was. Shakespeare and Beethoven are perhaps the two greatest landscape artists who ever lived, and Christopher Columbus was, I'm sure, one of those mighty poets who have written nothing, like Cortez and Napoleon.

And then I feel myself torn in the opposite direction by the mania for analysis which the, so-to-speak, chemical philosophy of our age encourages in us. We no longer say, 'What do I know?', like Montaigne, but 'What for?' I am obsessed by plans for compositions, vast, bold ones which I feel certain of being able to realize. I make a start and then I stop: 'Why undertake such a work', I say to myself, 'and fall passionately under its spell?' ... only to store up for myself more bitter disappointments when it's finished, if I think it's beautiful. To see it entrusted to children or to brutes, or buried alive ... The most colossal productions of the human spirit can find neither hearth nor home in the modern world. The English talk of raising a statue to Shakespeare four hundred feet high and they *don't have a single theatre* where the masterpieces of this demigod can be decently staged. It's a belated expression of national vanity on their part, but the feeling of admiration is neither widespread nor real.

I've just finished my 'trilogie sacrée' *L'enfance du Christ*; I don't know when I'll be able to hear it, nor if I shall be able to introduce it to those men of intelligence in Paris who are on my side. It is overall so naively gentle in its colour and its forms that I don't really see how to find singers here capable of doing it justice. They're all infected to a greater or lesser degree with the false and trivial taste that reigns over our theatres. Can you imagine, the role of the Virgin Mary sung by an exponent of roulades whose larynx is continually itching, or by a prima donna in all her finery whose chief concern is for cavatinas that make an 'effect', in which she can 'let go' with her voice and show off her nice arms and shake out her hair? . . .

Luckily I can find what I want in Germany.

Adieu, dear sister, forgive me for going on so about my own private concerns and continue loving me as I love you.

All best wishes to your husband and to your dear little daughters.

Your devoted

H. Berlioz

301 *To his son Louis Berlioz*   Paris, 26 October 1854

My dear Louis,

[. . .] I have some news to tell you which will probably not cause you any surprise and which I imparted *in advance* to my sister and my uncle during my last visit to La Côte. I have remarried.[1] This liaison had, as you can imagine, gone on so long as to be unbreakable; I could neither live alone nor abandon the person who had been living with me for fourteen years. My uncle was of this opinion when he last came to see me in Paris and was the first to raise the subject. All my friends agreed. Of course, your interests have been safeguarded. If I die first, my wife inherits no more than a quarter of my tiny fortune, and I know that she intends to leave this quarter to you in her will. She brought her furniture with her as a dowry; it's more valuable than we thought, but it is to be returned to her if I die first. Everything has been arranged in accordance with my brother-in-law's suggestions. My life is more

---

1 Berlioz's marriage to Marie Recio took place on 19 October, six months after Harriet's death. The day before, he completed his *Mémoires*, which he kept hidden from his new wife (who is not mentioned therein). He later added three more chapters, and the book was published in 1870 after his death.

regular and comfortable like this. I'm sure that if you harbour any painful memories of Mlle Recio or have any uncharitable feelings towards her, you will bury them deeply inside you for love of me.[1] The marriage took place informally, without publicity or secrecy. If you write to me about it, don't say anything I can't show to my wife, as I'm determined to have no dark corners in my domestic life; but I leave it to your heart to tell you how to respond. [. . .]

Adieu, dear son and friend, dear Louis! Love me as I love you.

H. Berlioz

302 *To Hippolyte Lecourt*   Paris, 1 November 1854

My dear Lecourt,

If you hadn't become a sensible person you would commit the folly of coming to Paris on 7 or 9 December next to hear my oratorio *L'enfance du Christ*. I shall be putting it on for the first time on the 10th, the day before my birthday, which was celebrated in the same way last year in Leipzig, and which we shall be celebrating for once in Paris. But please don't go to these extravagant lengths; I should hate to be the cause of such a disruption.[2]

303 *To Princess Carolyne Sayn-Wittgenstein*   Paris, 16 December
                                                                   1854

Madame,

I thank you most warmly for the interest you have been kind enough to take in my little oratorio.[3] It is currently enjoying a success in Paris quite sickening for its elder brothers. It's been received like a Messiah, and we've all but had the Magi offering it incense and myrrh. That's what the French public are like. They're saying I've turned over a new leaf, I've changed my *style* . . . and other rubbish. It reminds me of the following story. In 1830 I was sent to Rome as a student subsidized by the Académie des Beaux-Arts. The rules stated that I had to compose in Rome a piece of religious music which, at the end of my first year in exile, would be judged at a public session in the Institut de Paris. Well, as I was unable to compose in Italy (I don't know why), I simply copied

1 Louis seems never to have established good relations with his stepmother; he and his father became much closer after her death in 1862.
2 Lecourt did not travel from Marseille to Paris to hear *L'enfance du Christ*, but he did make the journey for the *Te Deum* in April 1855.
3 *L'enfance du Christ* was first performed in the Salle Herz on 10 December.

out the *Credo* of a Mass of mine that had already been performed twice in Paris before I left for Rome and sent it to the judges.[1] They declared that this piece already showed 'the beneficial influence of my stay in Italy', and that there was no mistaking the 'complete abandonment of my unfortunate musical tendencies' . . . How many academicians there are in the world! . . . Even so, I hope you will like my little *piety*, and I shall be very happy to arrange a hearing for you. [. . .]

I remain, Madame, yours most sincerely,
H. Berlioz

304 *To his sister Adèle Suat*   Paris, 5 February 1855

Dear sister,

I have just re-read your letter . . . I am alone by my fireside, bearing the shock of my son's lamentable behaviour. He didn't even let me know he was at Toulon; I told you in my letter the day before yesterday. This wretched child is undisciplined, outrageously undisciplined, and now he *hates* me because I'm irritated by his absurd conduct. He *hates* his benefactor, Admiral Cécille, because this excellent man has asked for him to be punished for missing his ship's sailing; he *believes* that this request from the admiral absolves him, Louis, from all gratitude towards his benefactor![2] It's appalling! Unbelievably stupid! I wrote to him as gently and calmly as possible when he was about to leave Toulon, and you've now read the letter he sent back forty days later!

I'm overwhelmed with a dull misery which I can neither dispel nor endure. It's a new sensation for me, I've never felt it before.

My God! What can I do? Nothing! I've no reason to reproach myself, except for being too indulgent perhaps . . . But I can't change my nature either and vicious stupidity revolts me a thousand times more today than ever it did.

I'm leaving at ten o'clock on Wednesday, the day after tomorrow, for Germany. Reply to me *poste-restante* at Weimar.

Would your husband please subtract the money you sent to Louis from my instalment for March? I shall be back between 10 and 12 March, he can send me my share to Paris.

I'm having discussions with a publisher here who wants to exploit

1 It was the *Resurrexit* from the 1824 *Messe solennelle*; it had been played four times before in Paris, not twice.
2 Admiral Cécille had helped Louis with his entry into the navy in 1850.

me; this chicanery over money makes me furious and I shall not submit to it. Another publisher came yesterday to make me a still worse proposition, I very nearly showed him the door.[1] It would take too long to explain to you. I tell you, today, if the world was a bomb of powder, I'd put a match to it!

Adieu, adieu, I have barely enough kind feelings left to embrace you with all my heart.

H. Berlioz

305 *To his uncle Félix Marmion*   Weimar, 25 February 1855

Dear uncle,

[. . .] I was invited here by the Grand Dowager Duchess, the sister of the Tsar of Russia, to organize a concert made up almost exclusively of my music and to conduct it at court on the 17th of this month, her Imperial Highness's birthday. Liszt welcomed me by playing, for once, a concerto for piano and orchestra of his own.[2] Four days later I gave another enormous musical evening at the theatre, including *L'enfance du Christ*, my *Symphonie fantastique* and a 'monodrame lyrique' for which I wrote the words and the music, called *Le retour à la vie*.[3] This had never before been performed on the stage. The theatre had to be turned upside down somewhat to enable the performance to take place, that's to say the apron of the stage had to be extended; the orchestra, the choir and the solo singers were positioned behind the lowered curtain so that they were invisible while the hero of the *Monodrame* speaks and acts on the proscenium. It would be difficult for me to give you an idea of how successful the evening was. I was acclaimed, recalled and applauded like a fashionable tenor. The Duchesses summoned me to their box, sweating and puffing as I was, to compliment me with the warmth of thoroughbred dilettanti. Then the young people of Weimar gave a supper for me at which toasts were all the rage. One of them, not knowing enough French and in consideration of my profound ignorance of German, made me a fine speech in Latin, and the poet Hoffmann[4] improvised a song also in Latin which was immediately set to music by a young composer[5] and sung in chorus at sight by the guests. [. . .] The Neo-Weimarians mentioned in

1 The two publishers were evidently Richault and Brandus, Berlioz's principal publishers.
2 The Concerto no. 1 in E flat, receiving its first performance.
3 This work had not been performed since 1835. It was not renamed *Lélio* until June 1855.
4 Hoffmann von Fallersleben, the Weimar court poet.
5 Joachim Raff.

the song make up a club of young, so-called *progressive* artists, and I am appointed their standard-bearer. [. . .]

We have 22 degrees of frost here and 18 inches of snow. My wife's health has been deteriorating for the last two months, and she is suffering badly from it all. She asks to be remembered to you and assures you of her affection.

Adieu, dear uncle, please pass on my greetings to my aunt. I embrace you *laeto corde*, but I'm absolutely exhausted.

H. Berlioz

306 *To Gaetano Belloni*   Gotha, 28 February 1855

My dear Belloni,

Despite the length of the concert on the 21st in the theatre at Weimar, it was simply one long crescendo. [. . .] Interest centred on the strange, poetical composition *Le retour à la vie*, a lyric drama with one real character; the singers who appear with him are only figments of his exalted imagination, so they are not visible to the audience and are heard, as are the chorus and orchestra, from behind the curtain. An extended apron had been built over the place where the theatre musicians normally sit and this allowed the character put on stage by the composer to act without restrictions. A young actor from the drama troupe, M. Grans, showed considerable talent in performing his difficult task, and a dangerous one because of being so novel. He was particularly good in the scene where he fancies himself to be at his mistress's feet, singing a hymn of love. This piece, delightfully sung by M. Caspari, seems to have been the one the audience liked best. Personally, the one I think is the best, the most characterful and stylistically the most impressive is the *Chœur d'ombres*, 'Grauen des Tod's, Nacht ohne Sterne!', which is unlike any other page in my output. The course of the drama dictates that the finale, based on Shakespeare's *The Tempest*, be played with the curtain raised. After this I was recalled four times by the entire audience and Mlle Genast, who had sung the role of the Virgin Mary in the *Trilogie* with admirable charm and modesty, came on stage as a representative of the Ducal Chapel and offered me a wreath, at the appearance of which the acclamations from the hall doubled. [. . .]

*To Pier Angelo Fiorentino*¹   Gotha, 28 February 1855

My dear Fiorentino,
    [. . .]

P.S. – I'm being pushed, urged, goaded even, into writing a large theatrical machine.² I must consult you on the subject and we can go on with the conversation we began on the Rue St-Georges about the material impossibilities of such an undertaking, thanks to the habits of the Paris Opéra.

Although Berlioz stopped a few days in Gotha, he did not give a concert there. He returned to Paris on 2 March and left ten days later for a return visit to Brussels. There he gave three performances of L'enfance du Christ.

308 *To Augustin Vizentini*³   Brussels, 15 March 1855

Monsieur,
    Would you be kind enough to call the cornets and trumpets to tomorrow's rehearsal (as well as the instruments I mentioned to you this morning). I've had to make a small addition to *L'enfance du Christ* which they will have to rehearse because, I now see, the horns will never make themselves heard.⁴
    Yours ever,
    H. Berlioz

309 *To Gaetano Belloni*   Brussels, 19 March 1855

My dear Belloni,
    [. . .] I've found here (you might say) a very ingenious inventor who has made for me an electric metronome with which I can conduct

---

1 Italian-born music critic with a regular column in the *Constitutionnel* and the *Moniteur universel*.
2 In Weimar Berlioz was urged, contrary to his better judgment, to compose the Virgilian grand opera he had been thinking about for four years. Princess Carolyne Sayn-Wittgenstein, following Baron von Donop's similar urgings, was to take up the cause – finally with success – a year later in February 1856.
3 Director of the Théâtre du Cirque, Brussels, where the performances of *L'enfance du Christ* were given.
4 The cornets and trumpets have very little to play in the work. Although Berlioz added them to reinforce the horns in Brussels, he did not remove them later.

choruses placed a long way behind the stage without there being the slightest delay in the vocal entries.[1] In this way I've been able to control the orchestra in front of the stage and the invisible choir of angels backstage with amazing precision, conducting one with my right hand and the other with a finger of my left, pressing a brass button fitted to my desk which is attached to electric wires. I'd been calling for this for ten years and pointed the way in my novel *Euphonia*, in *Les soirées de l'orchestre*[2] – it's of the greatest importance to composers.

If Verdi uses offstage choirs or orchestras in his opera[3] I shall tell him, when I get back, what will have to be done to obtain similar equipment for the Opéra. If that great imbecile of a theatre weren't so slack and sleepy it would long ago have provided itself with all the performing aids modern science has to offer. But it prefers a regime of din and discord.[4]

Adieu. With sincere best wishes,

H. Berlioz

310 *To Franz Liszt*   Brussels, 23 March 1855

My very dear Liszt,

Here are just a few lines written in haste between my second and third concerts. I'm having a gigantic success here and making hardly any money, as always. They say this is because it's Lent, and the Devout of Brussels won't go into the theatre during this period. Next time the weather will be too good or too bad, or there'll be too many balls, or . . . etc.

Fétis is very well disposed, but he admits to 'understanding nothing' of all that.[5]

The enthusiasm he sees all around him makes him think that all his 'young folk' at the Conservatoire have gone mad. The performance yesterday was quite good, but the first one was terrible. Those singing

1 The inventor was named Verbrugghen, whose 'electric metronome' Berlioz adopted with enthusiasm.
2 In *Euphonia*, first published in 1844, Berlioz imagined 'an ingenious mechanism which would have been discovered five or six centuries earlier if anyone had troubled to think about it. It picks up the conductor's movements and conveys them directly *before the very eyes* of each player. It gives the beats of the bar and the various degrees of loud and soft with great precision.'
3 *Les vêpres siciliennes*, then in rehearsal at the Opéra.
4 Three other Parisian theatres equipped themselves with electric metronomes immediately, but the Opéra did not do so until 1861 when Berlioz, supervising performances of *Alceste*, persuaded them to.
5 Fétis had been director of the Brussels Conservatoire since 1833.

animals who can't tell A from B in music (with perhaps a couple of exceptions) didn't know their parts and sang all over the place. Then fear completely destroyed their presence of mind; there was even a moment when I thought the Père de famille was going to sing the *Marseillaise* rather than stop altogether.[1] Only the chorus did well, thanks to my electric metronome which is an invaluable help in conducting unseen choirs. The orchestra has a passion for emphasizing the downbeats. What's more it suffers from gout, and to get it to run you have to singe its calves with a red-hot iron. [. . .]

I had a long conversation about you recently with a woman who, in her way, is a great enthusiast for the great in art.

'O Liszt,' she said, 'I'm so fond of Liszt; I really think if I had to decide between a good Italian opera and a recital by Liszt, I shouldn't hesitate, I'd choose Liszt!'

Which reminds me of a farce in Paris in which Bouffé was playing the part of a hunchback condemned to death, who was allowed to choose anything he wanted before he was executed. 'Let me have a melon,' said the little hunchback.

'But there aren't any melons in winter.'

'No melons? Very well then, bring me Walter Scott. Yes, all things considered, I'd prefer Walter Scott!' [. . .]

'Your name, sir?' said the people of Rome to a poor fellow they'd just seized after Caesar's murder.

'My name's Cinna.'

'Cinna! One of the great Caesar's assassins! Away with him, tear him to pieces!'

'Stop! Mercy! I'm not who you think, I'm Cinna, Cinna the poet!'

'Ah! So you're Cinna the poet! All the better, death to Cinna the poet! *Tear him for his bad verses!*' (Shakespeare).[2] I don't know what made me think of that.

Don't forget to pass on my good wishes to the homonym of the Great Fantastical, M. Hoffmann.[3]

Adieu, I remain at the princess's feet and, in your guise as Prospero, I beg you to convey my respects to the fair young Miranda.[4]

H. Berlioz

---

1 At the first concert Berlioz, with his back to the audience, sang the Père de famille's part in *L'enfance du Christ* when the singer, Barielle, lost his place.
2 *Julius Caesar*, Act III scene 3.
3 Hoffmann von Fallersleben, no relation of E. T. A. Hoffmann.
4 The Princess's daughter Marie.

Berlioz returned to Paris on 29 March and set about organizing the first performance of the Te Deum, *intended to coincide with the opening of the Exposition Universelle. It took place in St-Eustache on 30 April.*

311 *To Franz Liszt*   Paris, 30 April 1855

Dear friend,

I send you three lines to say that today the *Te Deum* was given the most magnificently accurate performance. It was colossal, Babylonian, Ninevite.[1] The large church was full. The children sang as one soloist, and the soloists as ... I was hoping for and as I had the right to expect of them, given the scrupulous care with which they'd been chosen. Not one mistake, not one hesitation. I had a young man from Brussels conducting the organist in the loft at a distance and he kept him in time despite the space between us.

Belloni is furious; we have been 'robbed as if in a wood'. But who cares ...

Heavens, if only you'd been there! I promise you, it's a formidable work, the *Judex* goes beyond any of the enormities I've been guilty of so far. You are the first person I'm writing to, harassed as I am, because I know that nobody in Europe is as interested in this *arrival* as you are. Yes, the *Requiem* has a brother, a brother who has come into the world with teeth, like Richard III (minus the hump);[2] and I tell you, today he bit the audience to the heart. And what a huge audience it was! There were 950 performers. And not a single mistake! I can't get over it.

Friends of mine came from Marseille (Lecourt, Rémusat, etc) Lecourt was in a state; he was streaming, it was a flood! Adieu, I'm off to bed. How unfortunate that I should be the one responsible for that! I should make a curious article of it. We shall see what sort of *song* it draws from our colleagues. It's not a question of *piccoli paesi* this time, it's a scene from the Apocalypse.[3]

Laugh, make fun of me! Nothing affects me today. But with your

1 Berlioz echoes Heine's recent description of his music as recalling 'Babylon, the Hanging Gardens of Semiramis and the wonders of Nineveh'.
2 'O, Jesus bless us, he is born with teeth!'
  And so I was; which plainly signified
  That I should snarl and bite and play the dog.
  I have no brother, I am like no brother.
  (*Henry VI*, Part III, Act V scene 6.)
3 'Sempre piccoli paesi' ('always the little landscapes'), a remark attributed to Salvator Rosa when only his small paintings were admired.

hand, *colla tua possente mano*, shake those of Cornelius, Raff, Pohl and all our friends.

I won't add anything for the Princess, I have a long letter I'm sending in reply to hers.

Adieu, adieu, adieu,

H. Berlioz

312 *To Franz Liszt* Paris, 10 May 1855

Dearest friend,

[...] Yesterday I sent you a parcel containing three manuscript volumes bound together, as I promised you.¹ As you know, M. Pohl is being good enough to take care of the translation. He has agreed not to publish it in my lifetime and I'm handing over to him all the rights in Germany. It'll contain a whole mass of words, allusions and phrases which he will find quite unintelligible, but I'm asking you please to explain them to him.

I'm giving him a year to make his translation. After that time please would you send the original back to me if I haven't been to collect it myself. I am counting on his honour as a translator not to make any changes or any concessions to ideas which are not mine, in short purely and simply to translate with the most scrupulous fidelity.

If I die before receiving my manuscript back from you, please keep it and make arrangements for an equally *accurate* edition with Michel Lévy (Rue Vivienne), who has already suggested the idea to me. You should then send the proceeds of this sale, whatever they may be, half to my wife and half to my son.

Forgive me for writing to you in this testamentary tone, but, as the old wives say, we shan't die of it.

Acknowledge receipt just of the *parcel* (I'll know what you mean).²

Yours ever,

H. Berlioz

313 *To Joseph-Esprit Duchesne* Paris, 8 June 1855

My dear Monsieur Duchesne,

[...] I'm up to my eyes in proofs: proofs of *L'enfance du Christ*, proofs of the *Te Deum* which I'm publishing by subscription, proofs of

1 The manuscript of the *Mémoires*.
2 So that Marie should not know about it.

Lélio (Le retour à la vie). Not to mention the trials I have to go through with my articles. I've just written my last one before my departure for London. It will appear tomorrow (I leave then too). About the one on Halévy you mention, I'll say . . . no, I shan't say anything. Some things are too obvious to need expressing.[1]

I'm going to conduct the last two concerts of the New Philharmonic Society, for which I've been asked to include *Roméo et Juliette* and *Harold*. In the first one I have to conduct the Symphony in G minor by Mozart, the Piano Concerto in E flat by Beethoven, the overture to *Die Zauberflöte* and another overture by an English amateur called Mr Leslie who met me walking along Regent Street one day and said: 'I'm delighted to meet you, Mr Berlioz, I was wanting to come and see you to discover why I find your music absolutely incomprehensible.'

Yours very sincerely,
H. Berlioz

314 *To his sister Adèle Suat*   London, 22 June 1855
                                        13, Margaret Street (Portland Place)

Dear sister,

I've been here ten or twelve days without finding a moment to write to you. I was hoping to hear some news from you and from Louis. I'm beginning to worry that nothing has arrived. Tell me why this long silence. I shall be here until 7 July because of a third concert I've been asked to conduct on the 6th at Covent Garden.

Right from the first day I had an enormous success with the New Philharmonic Society concert. The huge auditorium of Exeter Hall was boiling over. They encored the movement called the *Fête* in *Roméo et Juliette*, the first time this has happened in the work's history.

Very probably, to judge by the growth of my influence here, by the various offers people are making me and by the friends I'm making every day, I shall end up by settling in London where I'm gradually making a place for myself.[2]

Marie and I are literally overwhelmed with invitations. We shan't be dining at home a single day this week, and on Sunday we're going to spend a day in the country with an English family who know very little

---

1 Berlioz's review of Halévy's new *opéra comique, Jaguarita l'indienne*, appeared on 19 May.
2 Berlioz was offered the post of conductor of the Crystal Palace concerts, but he refused it. It was taken by August Manns instead.

French. Keeping up a conversation for that length of time will put my knowledge of English to a stiff test.[1]

In general, though, the mood is sombre, especially after the latest news from Sebastopol.[2] The lists of the dead posted in the streets and the levies of troops and money announced in France are not designed to be reassuring. I really am anxious at not having had a word either from Louis or from you. Please write without delay.

I recently spent part of the day at the Crystal Palace in Sydenham;[3] it's one of the wonders of the world. It was like seeing the palace of Aladdin or the gardens of Semiramis. It's unearthly. [...]

Adieu, dear sister, I embrace you with all my heart. My best wishes to your husband and daughters.

H. Berlioz

315 *To Franz Liszt*   London, 25 June 1855
                                          13, Margaret Street, Cavendish Square

Dearest friend,

The London whirlwind has been spinning so fast for me this year, I haven't so far had two minutes to write to you. Today, being Sunday, I'm being left in relative peace and I'm taking advantage of it. Wagner and I have talked a lot about you these last few days and you can imagine how affectionately because, I swear to you, I believe his feelings for you are as strong as mine.[4]

No doubt he'll tell you all about his stay in London and what he has had to suffer from a hostility born of prejudice. His passion, warmth and enthusiasm are superb and I confess I am even won over by his outbursts of violence. It seems I'm prevented by some fate from hearing anything of his latest compositions! The day he conducted his *Tannhäuser* overture at the Hanover Square Rooms at Prince Albert's request I was at that same moment obliged to attend an appalling chorus rehearsal for the New Philharmonic concert I had to conduct two days later. It was for the choral passages in the first four parts of *Roméo*, and it was so prodigiously awful that despite the opinion of

---

1 Their hosts were Mr and Mrs Alfred Benecke, of Champion Hill, Camberwell, both more German than English. Mrs Benecke was a relative of Mendelssohn.
2 The French attack on Malakoff on 18 June was a failure, as was the English attack the same day on the Redan.
3 Whither it had been removed from Hyde Park after the 1851 Great Exhibition. It burned down in 1936.
4 Wagner was in London conducting the rival organization, the Old Philharmonic.

Dr Wylde, who thought it was all very well sung, I had to cut these horrors short and suppress the sung parts entirely. Despite some missed entries in the orchestra, the first two movements of *Roméo* went well. The *Fête* was even played with such verve that for the first time in the work's history it was encored with loud hurrahs by the whole of the vast audience in Exeter Hall. There were a lot of mistakes in the scherzo.

I'm staying in London several days longer because of a concert I've been asked to conduct at Covent Garden after our last one with the Philharmonic.

Wagner finishes his Hanover Square concerts tomorrow, Monday, and is leaving immediately the day after. We're having dinner together before his concert. There's something singularly attractive about him and even if we both have our sharp corners, at least they match:

　　　　　　　　　explain this
　　　　　　　　　　　　　　　　　　to Cornelius

[. . .] Monday morning. I'm back from my excursion to the country. That's to say, I came back yesterday evening. Klindworth was there. He played a delightful, melancholy piece by you; then he, the two young ladies of the house, a young German painter and I all sang some pieces for five voices by Purcell which these ladies apparently know as well as their Bible and which both Klindworth and I found only moderately charming. The others lapped them up like sweetened milk. These English get-togethers do possess some fundamental feeling for music, but it's conservative, primarily religious and anti-passionate. Wagner got across the London public by appearing not to take Mendelssohn seriously. And Mendelssohn is, for many of them, a Handel and a half . . .!! Apart from which, if I weren't guilty of the same mistake myself with regard to other masters whom I loathe with the violence of a giant cannon, I'd say Wagner is wrong not to consider the puritan Mendelssohn as a fine and powerful individual voice.

When a master is a master, and when that master has at all times and in all places treated art with honour and respect, he too should be honoured and respected, whatever the divergence between the path he followed and our own. Wagner could turn the argument against me if he knew the composers I abominate so heartily. But I'll be careful not to tell him. When I hear or read certain pieces by that gross master,[1] I content myself with a vigorous grinding of teeth until I'm back home and can heap curses upon his head in private.

Nobody is perfect.

Adieu, adieu, lay all these imperfections at the Princess's feet, and I hope she will be kind enough to honour them with a pitying glance.

Yours,

H. Berlioz

On his return to Paris Berlioz's main preoccupations were the Exposition Universelle, for which he had to serve on the jury judging musical instruments, and the revision of his Grand traité d'instrumentation. *The London publisher Novello had commissioned an essay on conducting,* Le chef d'orchestre, *to be added to the second edition of the* Traité.

316 *To Heinrich Heine*   Paris, 16 August 1855

My very dear Heine,

Forgive me for not yet having been to thank you for your delightful, wonderful poems;[2] I have the dubious honour to be a member of the musical instrument jury for the Exhibition and from nine o'clock in the morning to five o'clock every day I am obliged, instead of hearing a great poet, to listen to dreadful pianos and still more dreadful manufacturers. But despite everything I shall come and see you, perhaps even today if our quota is limited to around *fifty* instruments.

Adieu, with all best wishes,

Yours sincerely,

H. Berlioz

317 *To Jean-Baptiste Vuillaume*   Paris, 21 August 1855

My dear Monsieur Vuillaume,

Would you be good enough to send me the upper limit of your octobass and some details about the mechanism of the movable nuts

---

1 Berlioz seems to be referring to Handel, whose *Samson* he was then studying.
2 *Poèmes et légendes*, recently published.

operated by the left hand.[1]
Yours ever,
H. Berlioz

318 *To Tito Ricordi*[2]   Paris, 1 September 1855

Monsieur,

My duties as a member of the jury set up to judge the musical instruments at the Exposition Universelle have left me in a position to make some important observations on this subject. I think that an essay on new instruments and on improvements to old ones could be a useful addition to my *Traité d'orchestration et d'instrumentation*, for which you hold the publishing rights in Milan.

I should also like to add to this work a special final chapter entitled 'The Conductor's Art'. Would you be interested in acquiring the rights over these new chapters so as to add them (with a mass of corrections) to your edition of the *Traité d'instrumentation*? It would necessitate the engraving of twenty or thirty new plates of text and perhaps five or six music examples. I should be asking you for 600 francs for the rights over the manuscript (in Italy and Austria).

Please let me know if this proposition appeals to you.[3]

I have the honour to be, Monsieur,

Your devoted servant,

H. Berlioz

1 Vuillaume introduced his octobass, much larger and lower than a double bass, in 1849. The player stood on a platform and stopped the strings with levers. Berlioz described it with enthusiasm in the second edition of the *Grand traité*.
2 The leading Italian music publisher, whose firm had published the *Grand traité* in Italian in 1844 and the second edition of the *Requiem* in 1853.
3 Ricordi did not take up Berlioz's offer.

Universal
Exhibition
1855
Mixed Jury
International
Class
Panorama
Room Staircase

Paris, 5 September 1855

Dear sister,

I have just received your letter; it doesn't surprise me, but it made me angry. It is truly impossible to get this poor child to understand the necessity of *anything*. He's never accepted that the world contains anything except what he likes to see there. It's a want of intelligence ... I learn from you that he set sail yesterday and, I must admit, the pain and anxiety caused by this news overwhelm all the other feelings his behaviour might inspire in me.[1] It's a hard, hateful task, being a father who loves his son! If one were without heart or compassion, it would be just about tolerable. But neither is everything roses in the life of a young man who needs to spread his wings and who, at the age of twenty, feels only the harsh constraints that society lays on those not born under a lucky star. One could write at length on this subject ... The world is horrible and abominably organized ...

But as each of us is bound to take it as it is, it's clearly wrong to behave as though there existed a different one ... Forgive me, dear sister, for telling you my secret thoughts. I shall play my role of traditional father as I *must* ...

The world's a stage (Shakespeare and Cervantes have said so) but it's a tragic theatre rather than a comic one. [...]

I bid you adieu.

H. Berlioz

---

1 Louis had written to tell his father that he was to sail for the Crimea, but he confided the letter to an intermediary, not the post, so Berlioz did not receive it. In fact Sebastopol fell on 9 September, so Louis's ship arrived too late to be in danger.

320 *To the Grand Duchess Maria Pavlovna of Saxe-Weimar*   Paris,
10 September 1855

[. . .] My *Benvenuto Cellini*, who was assassinated in France several
years ago, has regained some spark of life, thanks to the offices of a
famous doctor, your Kapellmeister at Weimar. A German publisher[1]
has come forward who is willing to get him to breathe the open air of
publicity, and I take the liberty of asking Your Imperial Highness to
continue your patronage of the convalescent by accepting the dedication of this work [. . .]

321 *To Richard Wagner*   Paris, 10 September 1855

My dear Wagner,
    I was delighted to have your letter. You're quite right to deplore my
ignorance of the German language and as for your remarks on the
impossibility of my understanding your works, I have taxed myself
with this many a time. The flower of meaning almost always fades
beneath the weight of a translation, however delicately that translation
is done. There are accents, in *true* music, which demand their particular word, and words which demand their particular accent. To
separate one from the other, or to deal in approximations, is to put a
puppy to suck at a she-goat and vice versa. But what's the answer? I
find it devilishly difficult to learn languages; I barely know any words
of English or Italian. [. . .]
    So you're melting glaciers with your work on the *Niebelungen*![2] It
must be marvellous to write like that in the presence of mighty nature!
Another pleasure which is denied me! Beautiful countryside, lofty
peaks, the wide sweep of a seascape, they absorb me completely instead
of provoking thought. I feel, but am unable to express. I can only draw
the moon by looking at its reflection in the bottom of a well. [. . .]

322 *To Camille-Marie Stamaty*[3]   Paris, end of September 1855

My dear Stamaty,
    [. . .] So you're at Dieppe? Are there fine cliffs there? So I'm told, but
I've never been tempted to go and admire them because of the bathers,

1 Litolff of Brunswick.
2 Wagner was in Switzerland at work on *Die Walküre*.
3 Pianist and composer of French-Greek birth, a pupil of Kalkbrenner.

male and female, cluttering up the streets, ruining the countryside, disturbing the sea and the peace of decent folk. I've contented myself so far with going to meditate at St-Valéry-en-Caux, a charming little town which is hardly known and where you can stroll from morning till night without bumping into a celebrity or wearing a black coat or even shaving.

I'd be there at this moment if the Exhibition jury hadn't reduced me to slavery. We've heard 387 pianos, at least 400 brass instruments, not counting packets of flutes, faggots of oboes and other 'faggots' generally known as bassoons, and bleating flocks of melodiums, harmoniums, etc; now we're being exposed to the wind of organs and to that of calumny. We'll have suffered martyrdom for two months and that's all the reward we'll get for it.

I've finished my new edition of the *Traité d'instrumentation* and *L'art du chef d'orchestre* which is to be added to it. The volume is being engraved at the moment in Paris and London. Otherwise I have my compositional ideas[1] which I'm keeping in check and which, I hope, won't force my hand. I've no illusions, I know the world we're in; and I have no intention of giving the rogues and idiots who swarm all over Paris the satisfaction of laying up bitter disappointments for me. I've had enough of them. If I do settle down to work, they shan't know about it.

That's all my news.

Adieu, my dear Stamaty, I was going to burden you with some philosophizing but I'm being called to go and *jurify* with Halévy.[2]

Yours ever,

H. Berlioz

323 *To Franz Liszt*   Paris, 17 November 1855

Dear friend,

Just a few lines to tell you that the two mighty battles of yesterday and the day before have been won.[3] The giant orchestra played like a string quartet. Yesterday particularly, we moved the orchestra down into the main nave and the sound was doubled, producing a tremendous effect. There was an apocalyptic audience. I thought I was in the

1 *Les Troyens* again.
2 Halévy was chairman of the jury.
3 On 15 and 16 November Berlioz conducted two colossal concerts in the Palais de l'Industrie to mark the closing of the Exposition Universelle. The programme included the first performances of his cantata in honour of Napoleon III, *L'impériale*.

valley of Jehosaphat. The takings were sixty thousand and some hundred francs!

I won't attempt to describe to you the Babylonian splendour of the official ceremony, but on that occasion the orchestra caused a scandal. After my piece, the *Apothéose*, ignoring etiquette, my lads raised a storm of hurrahs and applause and threw their hats in the air, as though they were at a rehearsal.

I wish you could hear the cantata (*L'impériale*) with its final tremor when the theme returns:

> Then shook the souls triumphant of the mob
> Entire, as at the cry of destiny,
> When sounded forth the cannons' mighty voice
> T'announce the final dawning of this present day.

And underneath this tidal wave the drums beat the general salute as for the entrance of the Emperor at religious ceremonies. I assure you, this polka would make you want to dance.

Adieu, I have two or three more tasks and a third and final grand concert to get through to fulfil my contract, then I shall breathe again.

Your devoted, but aching and exhausted
H. Berlioz

324 *To Auguste Morel*   Paris, 9 January 1856

My dear Morel,

[. . .] I'm beginning to recover from the dreadful fatigue brought on by the concerts for the Exhibition; I'm going to give *L'enfance du Christ* here on the 25th of this month. On the 28th I'm leaving for Gotha where the Duke has invited me to put on the same work. On 8 February I'll be at Weimar where again I've been invited by the Grand Duke to go and put on *Faust complete*, and on the 16th, the Grand Duchess's birthday, there'll be a revival (a gala performance) of *Benvenuto Cellini* in a new production. The score of this work, dedicated to Her Imperial Highness the Grand Duchess, has just been published by Meyer[1] in Brunswick

Perhaps I shall go on from there to Holland.

The score of *L'enfance du Christ* has been on sale for some time, as well as the vocal score of *Lélio* (a lyric monodrama) and the new edition of the *Traité d'instrumentation* with the addition of *L'art du*

---

1 Actually Litolff, Meyer's successor.

chef d'orchestre. My cantata *L'impériale* is due to appear in a fort-night's time; I'll send it to you. [. . .]

Prince Napoleon[1] is being very gracious towards me; he's amazed by the paltry position I hold in Paris and is unable to do anything to change it. The Emperor is inaccessible and loathes music like ten Turks. [. . .]

I can't attempt any musical undertaking of the slightest importance in Paris; obstacles on every front. No concert hall and no performers (or not those I should like)! There's not even a free Sunday I can have to give my little concert. Some are taken by the Société des Concerts, the rest by the Société Pasdeloup which has booked the Salle Herz for the whole season.

I'm forced to content myself with a Friday. Pasdeloup is our one-time timpanist, now turned conductor. He's collected under him a band of lads from the Conservatoire and, by dint of some wriggling, has managed to secure the patronage of M. de Nieuwerkerke and the Princess Mathilde to conduct the concerts in the Hôtel de Ville; he'll end up (you'll see) by being the Emperor's *maître de chapelle*. Apart from young Bennet, Théodore Ritter, an admirable boy in whose future I have sincere confidence, Camille Saint-Saëns, another great musician nineteen years of age, and Gounod, who has just produced a very fine Mass,[2] I see nothing but flies hovering above this stinking bog called Paris.

Adieu, that's enough of that, too much in fact. What's the point of recrimination? Cholera exists, as we know, so why shouldn't Parisian music exist?

I shake you by the hand and ask you to give my affectionate best wishes to Lecourt.

Yours very sincerely,

H. Berlioz

325 *To Hans von Bülow*   Weimar, 12 February 1856
                                              Hôtel du Prince Héréditaire

My dear Monsieur von Bülow,

[. . .] Yesterday we rehearsed *Le corsaire* at length for the forth-coming concert at court. I am grateful to you for kindly agreeing to make an arrangement of this overture, and if you don't possess it I'll

---

1 The Emperor's cousin, in charge of the Exposition Universelle.
2 The *Messe de Ste-Cécile*.

send it to you; but I think it will reduce to piano solo, which is much better. When two pianists play a piece for four hands, whether on one piano or two, they are never together (at least to my ears) and the final result of the performance is always (again in my opinion) more or less of a muddle. What's more, piano duet arrangements have the drawback of accumulating a mass of notes in the bass register of the piano, the sound of which is out of proportion to that of the right hand of the *primo* player, and the result is a harmonic paste which is more noisy than harmonious and horribly indigestible. So it's better to entrust the transcription of a symphonic work to the two hands of a single intelligent pianist, where possible. Then the composer can at least count on not being pulled by two horses in opposite directions ... Forgive these blasphemies against pianists ... They are certainly not aimed at you, I may say: you are a *musician*. [...]

Looking forward to your reply, I shake you by the hand, with my affectionate wishes to you and my admiration for your outstanding talents.

H. Berlioz

326 To his sister Adèle Suat   Paris, 3 March 1856

Dear sister,

[...] I've returned with a head full of projects which will occupy me, or rather absorb me, all year.[1]

I was welcomed as usual in Germany. My opera *Cellini* is going splendidly; *L'enfance du Christ* was given a first-class performance in Gotha. The Duke gave me his cross[2] and overwhelmed me with invitations and marks of politeness. The Duchess, who is a virtuoso, has also been very kind to my wife. We were both invited to the court ball (on Shrove Tuesday) and to the supper afterwards. The Weimar court showed unexceptionable goodwill, as always. I conducted the concert which takes place annually in the palace on the Grand Dowager Duchess's birthday; also on Saturday, the DAY BEFORE YESTERDAY (such is the speed of travelling that I can write this in Paris today, Monday), I conducted a large-scale performance of my dramatic legend *La damnation de Faust*. The ladies and young amateurs of the Weimar Singing Academy joined the theatre chorus; I had a choir of

1 It was during this visit to Weimar that the Princess Sayn-Wittgenstein finally persuaded Berlioz to set everything else aside and compose *Les Troyens*, no matter what obstacles the work might face.
2 The Ritterkreuz des Ernestinischen Hausordens.

150 voices, a charming Marguerite and an excellent Mephistopheles; only Faust turned out to be weak and cold. Several pieces were encored, I was recalled three times, and the Grand Duke had me come to his box to congratulate me and to ask me to come back as soon as possible.

Two hours later I was on the railway platform, where players and audience were waiting for me. My departure was marked by vivats and hurrahs, and before that they welcomed me with a chorus from *Benvenuto Cellini* and a long burst of applause. At one o'clock in the morning (on Sunday) the train set off, and at five in the morning (on Monday) I arrived in Paris.

Liszt is as always an excellent friend and his friends are my friends. I only wish he would let me *once* conduct my opera. But his devotion doesn't extend as far as that.[1]

Adieu, all best wishes to your husband and children. Marie sends you hers.

I embrace you all.

Where is my uncle?

Write to me soon.

Hector Berlioz

327 *To Franz Liszt* Paris, 12 April 1856

Dear friend,

I realize I'm guilty of a crime against you which I tax many other people with, namely of keeping you waiting for a reply.

Very many thanks for your warm and charming letter and for the details it contained about the last performance of *Cellini*. I've spent my time since my return from Weimar orchestrating the six pieces of *Nuits d'été*[2] and having a look over all my music so as to correct mistakes in the engraving. This boring but important task is still not finished.

Then I've begun to rough out the plan of the great dramatic machine in which the Princess is being kind enough to take an interest. It's beginning to come clear, but it's enormous and therefore dangerous. I need extreme calmness of mind, which is exactly what I possess least of. Perhaps it'll come. Meanwhile I'm ruminating, *collecting myself*, as cats do when about to make a desperate leap. I'm trying above all to

---

1 Berlioz was never happy with Liszt's conducting and found his tempos too slow.
2 These songs, composed in 1840–41, were orchestrated in 1856 (except *Absence*) and published by Rieter-Biedermann of Winterthur.

resign myself to the miseries this work cannot fail to cause me ...
Anyway, whether I succeed or not, I shan't tell you any more about it
from now on until it's finished. And God knows when that will be: I
haven't imposed on myself the obligation to work fast.

I've no news to give you about the state of musical life in Paris. It's
still the same petty story. [...]

Adieu.

H. Berlioz

328 *To his brother-in-law Marc Suat*   Paris, 12 April 1856

My dear Suat,

I wrote recently to Camille to ask him to find me a buyer for the Le
Jacques property.[1] I've decided to sell it. Prices are rising in a frightening manner and my income doesn't. I've had to leave the apartment
where I've been for eight years because the owner wanted to increase
my rent by *two thirds*. After looking around for a fortnight we've had
to rent an apartment for July on the Rue Vintimille near the toll-gate.
It's *smaller* than ours, on the *fifth* storey, and it costs 400 francs more
than we're paying here in the Rue de Boursault (that's to say 1300
francs).

There are threats of still further price rises. Houses are selling at
enormous prices; if I had the necessary funds I'd be very tempted to
buy the one I'm going to live in, which they've just finished building.
Even if I only put my money into government stocks and not into a
house, which would bring in much more, I'd still have 4½ per cent
instead of the 2½ per cent I get from my property. It's diabolical to be
as worried as we are, living modestly, and in a financial position which
should ensure us a comfortable life.[2] So, my dear Suat, do what you
can to help this sale and indeed that of my other properties. Camille
writes to say that you will be better able to speed this transaction on its
way than he is.

I talked about it the day before yesterday to M. Beaufeu, my notary,
who will look after his side of things. I'm always being promised the
earth and nothing happens: 'You'll be director of the Opéra, you'll be
conductor at the Opéra at least, you're going to be a member of the
Institut, you can be director of the Conservatoire,' etc ... Meanwhile

1 Part of Berlioz's inheritance from his father.
2 In the later part of his life Berlioz kept careful monthly and annual accounts of his income
and expenditure.

the living are still in good health, jobs don't become vacant, and I have nothing and have to redouble my efforts to make both ends meet. [. . .]

Yours very sincerely,

H. Berlioz

329 *To his brother-in-law Marc Suat*   Paris, 1 May 1856

My dear Suat,

I was very depressed by your letter. All the sensible, serious men of business I know here are unanimous about the enormous advantage of my investing the money from my land instead of receiving the tiny revenue, and it seems to be impossible to sell it! [. . .]

Paris is growing,[1] houses and rents are rising in price, and the longer one waits the more likely one is to lose this present opportunity of investing capital profitably. Meanwhile here I am living in a *hovel* on the fifth storey with no room to turn round or entertain anyone and it's costing me 400 francs more than the apartment you saw, and which I had to leave.

I'm not in need of money at the moment, but I'm worried about the future; I shan't have the Industrial Concerts[2] to conduct every year, nor engagements in Germany, and I shan't regularly be composing scores like *L'enfance du Christ* etc, etc. [. . .]

Yours very sincerely,

H. Berlioz

330 *To his sister Adèle Suat*   Paris, 11 May 1856
17, Rue Vintimille

Dear sister,

[. . .] Your ideas about where I might live are partly true and partly false. I've spent some time looking everywhere except in the faubourg St-Germain, where I wouldn't want to be. It would be like living outside Paris. If I'd wanted to add another 200 francs to my rent I could have had the fourth floor of the house where I am (for 1500 francs) and it's perfectly good enough. But it seemed to me an enormous sum.

You ask how I've managed before now. I've been terribly pressed

1 The transformation of Paris masterminded by Haussmann, Préfet de la Seine, was under way.
2 Concerts for the Exposition Universelle.

and often in debt and have only been saved by my long tours. These days I am, it's true, incomparably better off; only it seems to me stupid not to be entirely free from such worries, just by rearranging my financial affairs. What you say is true, with respect to the position in which I have always found myself. All one can do is recognize this misfortune and resign oneself to it. I'm not anxious to have a large fortune, but the irritations of the little things in life exasperate me.

And then I'm always looking towards the moment when I can free myself from this journalistic ball-and-chain that I drag around trembling. If I had another 2000 francs a year I could send it to the devil. My articles have done me more harm than good; someone was saying to me again yesterday that without them I should have been elected to the Institut eight or ten years ago. All my enemies to a man come from there.

I'm taking considerable trouble over this candidacy;[1] they say I have a chance. I'm not expecting anything. We'll see. The most likely rival is Neidermeyer who has the support of a group of priests and officials at Court. And then he's so decently mediocre! That poor devil Adam! We were at the Opéra together at 11.30 in the evening; he went home at one o'clock, went to sleep, and at three o'clock he was dead.

I'm working hard on my large work. That's possible in my hovel because I'm only writing the words; when it comes to composing the music I'll be in torment, not having space to myself, nor being able to turn round or have a large table or make any sort of noise without being heard, etc.

It's rather curious to think that never in my life have I been able to have a room to work in, on its own and convenient, a studio, that's to say. I've always more or less written on my knee, on pedestal tables, on the ends of things so to speak, in cafés, in the street, in railway carriages or on steamboats, and I've always hankered after the sort of studio that painters and sculptors have, untidy but large, echoing and isolated.

The good thing about where I am now is that I have a balcony, fresh air and a splendid view over the whole of Paris and Montmartre. [. . .]

Adieu, dear sister,

I embrace you all.

H. Berlioz

1 A vacancy in the music section of the Institut was created by the death of Adolphe Adam on 3 May.

Dear Princess,

I owe you many apologies; I'm ashamed at not having replied to your nice, encouraging letter. I wanted to be able to announce something positive on the subject of the great enterprise of which you are the *cause*.[1] It was only the day before yesterday that I finished versifying the first act. This will be the longest of all and I spent ten days writing it, from 5 to 15 May; these were the only days I had completely free since my return from Weimar. I won't describe to you the phases of discouragement, joy, disgust, pleasure and fury I passed through successively during those ten days. Twenty times I was on the point of throwing everything on the fire and devoting myself for ever to the contemplative life. Now I'm certain I shall have the courage to go on to the end; the work has me in its grip. I also re-read your letter every now and then to spur me on. In general I was disheartened in the evening and returned to the charge in the morning, while the day was yet young. Now I barely sleep, I dream about it constantly; and if I had the time to work, in two months this whole mosaic would be finished. [. . .]

The music will take a full year and a half, I *reckon* (an American term), to construct. It will be a mighty construction: may it be built of fired bricks and not of unfired ones like the palaces of Nineveh. Without firing, bricks very soon turn to mud and dust. [. . .]

Adieu, Princess, you too will one night have to be *accountable* to Virgil's ghost for the crimes I'm committing against his beautiful poetry, especially if my palace is built of unfired bricks and if my hanging gardens are only painted with willows and wild plum trees.

H. Berlioz

332 *To Toussaint Bennet*[2]   Paris, 11 June 1856

My dear Bennet,

[. . .] I've just finished the third act of my libretto and what's more yesterday I completed the words *and the music* of the duet in the fourth act, a scene stolen from Shakespeare and Virgilianized, which sends me into ridiculous transports. I had only to *edit* those immortal lovers'

1 *Les Troyens.*
2 A shipbuilder and enthusiastic musician whose son, Théodore Ritter, showed stupendous promise as a pianist, never fulfilled.

ramblings which make the last act of *The Merchant of Venice* the worthy pendant of the sublime hymns of *Romeo and Juliet*. It's Shakespeare who is the real author of the words and the music. It's curious that he, the poet of the north, should intervene in the Roman poet's masterpiece. Virgil forgot this scene. What singers those two were!!!![1] [...]

    H. Berlioz

333 *To his uncle Félix Marmion*   Paris, 24 June 1856

Dear uncle,
    Even if the news has not reached you through the press, Adèle will have told you of the success of my candidature for the Institut.[2]
    Despite various petty coteries which were hostile, or at least favourable to my rivals, and to their great annoyance, everything went well. You will have seen that the other candidates were always eight votes behind me, and finally fourteen. It's a *coup d'état* in the empire of the arts. Whence incredible rejoicing among the young generation of musicians and among those old musicians with young ideas. Horace Vernet, who seconded me energetically, is triumphant. The musical section (Auber, Halévy, Thomas, Reber, Clapisson) have behaved with the utmost cordiality. Only Carafa covered himself with ridicule by his spiteful opposition – which failed, what's more. [...]
    Letters of congratulation are reaching me from all quarters and this rejoicing by unknown friends all over the world gives my election a value I was not expecting. I would almost wager that you, dear uncle, are happier about it than I am. Until now I have always passed, in the eyes of the bourgeois of Paris, as a kind of gypsy; now, suddenly, I've become civilized. I was sitting on a bayonet, now here I am in a chair. My musical worth has been generally agreed upon for the last three days ... Poor Adam had to die to bring about this miracle. What a sad comedy!
    I'm in the middle of writing an immense work, an opera in five acts, both the words and the music. [...]
    Adieu, dear uncle, I embrace you with all my heart.
    H. Berlioz

1 The love duet in Act IV is based on the scene for Jessica and Lorenzo in Act V of *The Merchant of Venice*, 'In such a night as this ...'.
2 Berlioz was elected to the Institut on 21 June.

My dear Baron,

[...] I have followed your advice; I am at the moment busy on the composition of an opera in five acts on a subject very close to my heart. I've just finished the libretto; I shall polish it, file it down and correct it as best I can for another month and after that I shall immediately settle down to writing the score. It's a sea of music; God grant that I don't drown. [...]

Yours very sincerely,
Hector Berlioz

While composing Les Troyens *Berlioz gave up all concert tours except his summer visits to Baden-Baden which took place every year from 1856 to 1863. This summer, 1856, he also visited the spa Plombières, in the Vosges.*

Thank you, Princess, for your great kindness in writing me such a valued letter! What an analysis! That's what's called 'entering into the spirit of things'!

You intended to encourage me ... I do not misjudge the value of fine words: you go so far as to give me credit for the beauties of Virgil's poetry and to praise me for my thefts from Shakespeare. My courage will take me to the end, fear not. It was not necessary to try and trap me with praise diverted from its rightful object. It is beautiful because it's Virgil; it is striking because it's Shakespeare; I am well aware of that. I'm nothing but a marauder; I've been foraging in the garden of these two geniuses, I've stolen a bunch of flowers to make a bed for music, and pray God it is not asphyxiated by the perfumes. [...]

My thanks then for all the encouragement that you, in your goodness, have given me. On my return to Paris I shall try and free myself as far as possible from all other occupations and begin my musical task. It will be hard; may all Virgil's gods come to my aid, or I'm lost. What is immensely difficult about it is to find the musical *form*, that form without which music does not exist, or is no more than the downtrodden slave of the word. That is Wagner's crime; he wants to dethrone it, to reduce it to 'expressive accents' by exaggerating the system of Gluck (who, I am very glad to say, did *not* succeed himself in obeying his unholy theory). I am on the side of music that you yourself call *free*.

Yes, free and proud and sovereign and all-conquering; I want it to take everything, to assimilate everything, so that neither Alps nor Pyrenees bar its way. But to make its conquests it must fight in person and not through its lieutenants. By all means let it have, if possible, good verses lined up in order of battle, but it must be in the thick of things like Napoleon and march in the front rank of the phalanx like Alexander. It's so powerful that it can conquer by itself in certain cases and it has the right a thousand times over to say, like Medea: 'Myself! That is enough'. To want to restore it to the old recitation of the ancient *choros* is the most unbelievable and happily the most unproductive folly that could be found in the whole history of music.

To discover the means of being *expressive* and *true*, without ceasing to be a musician, and on the other hand to give music new means of organization, that is the problem. [. . .]

Your most devoted and grateful Iopas,[1]

H. Berlioz

336 *To Xavier Raymond*[2]   Paris, 19 September 1856

My dear Raymond,

In case M. Bertin should ask why I am silent about all the wonders offered for admiration in the opera houses, please tell him that I am making incredible efforts to extract a long article from my wretched brain. In this article, justice will more or less be done to the gods of the Opéra, of the Opéra-Comique, of the Théâtre-Lyrique, of the concert of the Philharmonic Society of Boulogne-sur-mer (I went to it), to Thalberg, to all and sundry and their relations. I shall send you this verdict next Tuesday.

Adieu.

H. Berlioz

337 *To his sister Adèle Suat*   Paris, 26 October 1856

Dear sister,

[. . .] Today I needed to write to you. I'm trembling from head to foot, from my heart to my head, with impatience, misery, enthusiasm, overabundance of life . . . I can't write my score fast enough; I need an enormous, disastrous length of time. I'm worried about its future.

1 Iopas is Dido's court poet in *Les Troyens*.
2 Editor of the *Journal des débats*.

There are no singers. The Opéra is in the hands of the greatest enemies of *my art*. The Emperor knows nothing, understands nothing. Nothing is done or rehearsed in this little world except stupidities and platitudes . . . The cretins and clowns live on. And time passes. And then a mass of little pinpricks which irritate me, as though I had a nail in my shoe . . . My London publisher sends me the English score of *L'enfance du Christ* and there I find fearful passages in the translation. For example:

Original: 'Jésus! quel nom charmant!'
Translation: 'Jesus! the name is good'

Isn't it enough to make you throw yourself down a well? [. . .]

And I had the misfortune to open a volume yesterday . . . I have three editions of Shakespeare, two in English and one in French, a TRANSLA-TION! I came to *Hamlet* and couldn't put it down. I read it from beginning to end. It has made me ill; I seem to feel my heart successively contracting and dilating in my chest . . . this prodigious, tragic picture of human life . . . the terror caused by contemplating such a gigantic genius . . . the knowledge of the causes which still prevent so many people from understanding him . . . the crimes of his interpreters, of his translators . . . And the poet's indifference towards the effect he may make! Like the sun that sheds its light on the earth, without worrying whether the clouds of this puny planet may interpose themselves. [. . .]

338 *To Princess Carolyne Sayn-Wittgenstein*   Paris,
14 November 1856
4, Rue de Calais[1]

Dear Princess,

[. . .] I have not rested a single day from my Phrygian task, despite the wretched moments of disgust brought on by my illness. I found everything I'd written cold, flat, stupid and dull: I wanted to burn it all . . .

The human mechanism is quite bizarre and quite incomprehensible. Now that I'm better I re-read my score and it seems to me it's not as stupid as I thought. I am still on the large ensemble number

Châtiment effroyable!
mystérieuse horreur!

---

1 Berlioz and Marie moved to their final home, a fourth-floor apartment in the Rue de Calais, in September.

after Aeneas has narrated the terrible fate of Laocoon. I'm writing a number in two days and sometimes in one, and I then spend three weeks ruminating on it, polishing it and orchestrating it. [. . .]

An article, finished today, has interrupted me; another will interrupt me the day after tomorrow. And so it will go on to the end.

How good you are to take the interest you do in the crystallization of this long work! I thank you again. That gives me patience and courage. But when I have the misfortune to go to the Opéra, patience and courage fly away together. They recently put on a *Rose de Florence* by M. de St-Georges, with music by one Biletta ... When an audience listens to such a conception without a murmur, it's worthy of the society of bushmen and Hottentots on the Cape of Good Hope.

All best wishes to Liszt.

Yours very sincerely,

H. Berlioz

339 *To his brother-in-law Camille Pal*   Paris, 5 December 1856

My dear Camille,

[. . .] For several months I've been suffering from a neurosis which has attacked my intestines and leads every day to the most curious and painful nervous attacks. The only way I can forget this strange disease is through the distraction that comes from intense, prolonged work. And the doctors want to stop me working.[1]

But for the last two days I've been drawing breath a little. I'm absorbed in the immense operatic score my uncle spoke to you about. It's going ahead quite smoothly, but as the music progresses I make changes and corrections in the libretto. I keep filing away. I'm following Boileau's precept to the letter: 'sometimes to add and often to erase'.

I shall need a long time, more than another year, to finish it all. There's no hurry. So as not to be disturbed, I shan't be giving concerts in Paris this winter, I shan't be going to Germany and I'll content myself with a visit to London in May. I've promised to go and inaugurate a new concert hall with the first performance (in England) of my oratorio *L'enfance du Christ*. Again, I'd give a lot to be free of this journey.[2]

---

1 This malady got progressively worse for three years and remained with him for the rest of his life.
2 He was freed of it; it never took place.

Adieu, all best wishes to my niece and to you.
Yours very sincerely,
H. Berlioz

340 *To Toussaint Bennet*   Paris, 26 or 27 January 1857

[...] I've completely finished the duet and finale of the fourth act. See
how easily you persuade me to talk about my work ... Ah, I have no
illusions and you make me laugh with that old phrase about a 'mission
to accomplish'. Some missionary! ... But there is an inexplicable
mechanism inside me which functions aside from all the promptings of
reason, and I let it do so since I can't prevent it.

What upsets me most is my conviction that beauty doesn't exist for
the vast majority of these human monkeys! ...

Mme Viardot, who came to see me the day before yesterday,
admitted naively and sadly that she had never seen or read Spontini's
La vestale.

That such an artist, who has spent her life in the musical and
theatrical world, should have found herself, as luck would have it,
everywhere except where this light of genius was shining! Isn't it
enough to make one cry out against the fate of masterpieces! It's true
she was brought up in the middle of the Italian grocers' shop, but this
colonial education did not prevent her later from getting to know
Mozart, Haydn, Beethoven and Gluck and even waxing enthusiastic
about the solid, *bewigged* face of that barrel of pork and beer called
Handel!

So here I am with an act and a half of my score *finished*. In time the
rest of the stalactite will perhaps take shape, if the roof of the cave
doesn't crumble. [...]

Adieu to all.
H. Berlioz

341 *To Princess Carolyne Sayn-Wittgenstein* Paris, 13 February 1857

Dear Princess,

[...] You reproach me for not telling you about *Les Troyens*. I'm on
the way to finishing the fourth act which comes to me in waves, but
disordered waves. The end and the middle are written, I'm going to
begin on the beginning.

The first act is entirely complete, it's the longest; it lasts one hour and
ten minutes. Each of the other acts will therefore have to be condensed

as far as possible to keep the whole work within reasonable proportions. The second and the fourth will be short. As for my impressions of this music, they vary according to my mood, depending on whether it's sunny or raining and whether I have a headache or not. The same piece which sent me into transports of joy when I read it through the day before, today leaves me cold and dissatisfied. My only consolation for these changes of mood is that they have occurred all my life with every piece I've ever written.

The other day I was putting the finishing touches to the instrumental passage with chorus for Andromache's mime;[1] in comes the cornet player Arban, who has a very good feeling for a melodic line. He begins to play the clarinet solo extremely well and I'm in seventeenth heaven. Two days later I send for the clarinettist of the Opéra (Leroy), a virtuoso of the first order, but cold. He tries his solo. My piano was slightly low in pitch, it was impossible to get the two instruments in tune, the virtuoso phrased only *more or less*, he found it very *pretty* . . . and I was in a rage, out of temper with Andromache and Astyanax, ready to throw the whole thing on the fire. What a monstrous thing *more or less* is in a musical performance!

Still, I think this young man will understand his solo in the end if I make him study it bar by bar. But there's no point in doing this for the moment.

The last thing I've written — and which, I hope, you will like — is the ensemble which precedes the love duet in the fourth act:[2]

> Tout n'est que paix et charme autour de nous,
> La nuit étend son voile et la mer endormie
> Murmure en sommeillant les accords les plus doux.

It seems to me there is something new in thus expressing the pleasure of *seeing* the darkness and *hearing* the silence and in giving sublime music to the sleeping sea. What's more, this ensemble leads into the duet in a quite unexpected manner and one which came about by chance, because I wrote the two pieces separately without thinking about how to join them together. [. . .]

Yours very sincerely,
H. Berlioz

---

1 A long and deeply expressive clarinet solo, the *Pantomime*, no. 6.
2 The *Septuor*, no. 36.

342 *To his sister Adèle Suat*   Paris, 12 March 1857

I was delighted to have your letter this morning, dear Adèle. I'm so ill; I needed that to make me feel a little better. I'm suffering more than ever from neuralgic pains. The reason, I think, is the turmoil I've been in for eleven days because of not being able to work on my score. I'm in a real wasps' nest with people putting on concerts; they want to get me out of bed when I'm asleep so I can hear their masterpieces *in my own apartment*. Others come to take me to *theirs*, and they all insist that I must attend their musical undertakings, publicize them and mention them in my articles; it's enough to drive one mad. Added to which we just had the first performance of the *real* masterpiece of poor, inspired Weber (*Oberon*) at the Théâtre Lyrique; I saw it three times and had to help at the dress rehearsal to give some guidance to the conductor, who didn't know whether he was on his head or his heels. It was a magnificent success. The whole of Paris is absorbed with *Oberon*, this marvellous opera which has been the subject of contemptuous remarks for thirty-two years. Read my article about it.[1] [. . .]

All best wishes to your husband and to our two virtuosos. I'll write again in a few days.

H. Berlioz

343 *To Princess Carolyne Sayn-Wittgenstein*   Paris, 24 March 1857

Good heavens, Princess, how your letters rustle with ideas! I hardly dare reply. I do so nonetheless and leave Ascanius and the Tyrians running around in the African forest, with trumpets sounding and thunder rolling,[2] to give myself the pleasure of writing to you. [. . .]

It would take too long to mention all the numerous little changes I've made here and there. When the score is finished, and only then, will I be certain of having finished the libretto. I'm now trying every possible way of saving time. It's too long. I must find at least twenty-five minutes for the ballet.

I spent yesterday evening at the Tuileries and was able to speak with the Empress at length about *Les Troyens*. I did not forget to ask her permission to read her the libretto on some later occasion, which she seemed pleased to grant. The Empress, to my great surprise, showed herself very familiar with the poets of antiquity; she knows the *Aeneid*

1 In the *Débats* of 6 March, later reprinted in *A travers chants*.
2 Berlioz was composing the *Chasse royale et orage*, no. 29, at that moment.

down to the smallest details. Heavens, how beautiful she is! Ah, if only I had a Dido like that! The piece would fail ... The audience would throw apples at an Aeneas capable of entertaining even for a moment the idea of abandoning her.

If I succeed in obtaining this reading, whenever it may be, it will be a good opportunity to tell the Emperor the truth about *His Opéra* and the people who run it. It must be done calmly and coolly ...

We should support Carvalho and the Théâtre-Lyrique, you say![1] Yes, that's what I'm doing, just to give this director the idea of being what we should like him to be. At heart he isn't ... It's the same as with thirty thousand other things. There's nothing real in his so-called feeling for music that has style. 'All is vanity, lies and frailty', says the song; to which I would add 'and stupidity'. Carvalho is merely a little less stupid than his colleagues.

I've heard talk about this plan to build a new boulevard which would mean the demolition of the Théâtre-Lyrique, but I don't know where or when they'll construct the building to replace it.[2] [...]

Yours sincerely,
H. Berlioz

344 *To his sister Adèle Suat*   Paris, 9 April 1857

Dear sister,

[...] I've recently received a very important proposition from America. It consists of going next October and spending five months in New York, Philadelphia and Boston, to introduce my works. I was being offered twenty thousand dollars (105,000 francs) together with travelling expenses. The money would be paid to me in Paris. After serious thought I've refused for this year but offered to accept for 1858. For me, the most vital thing is to finish my opera. The organizers will be in Paris in six weeks' time and we'll continue our negotiations.[3]

The friends I trust approve my staying in Paris. In any case this neurosis has made me so weak, I wouldn't have the strength to carry out such an arduous expedition. [...]

Adieu, dear sister, if you know where my flighty, impalpable butter-

---

1 Léon Carvalho had begun an illustrious career as an opera manager with his first term (1856–60) as director of the Théâtre-Lyrique. He mixed older works (Mozart and Weber) with a wide range of new pieces.
2 In 1862 the theatre in the Boulevard du Temple was demolished and a new Théâtre-Lyrique opened in the Place du Châtelet.
3 This proposal never worked out.

fly of an uncle is, send him my very best wishes and remember me to
your aunt.

H. Berlioz

345 *To his sister Adèle Suat*   Paris, 7 May 1857

Dear little sister,

[...] We came back home, Marie and I, at two o'clock this morning.
There'd been a grand reception at the Hôtel de Ville for the young
Prince Constantine.[1] The Prefect put on a good show for our Imperial
guest. Unfortunately he had deemed it necessary to regale him with an
immense staged concert in which various portions of operas were
acted, complete with costumes and décor. And our singers did not
distinguish themselves. The Duke is an educated music-lover and his
rapture must have been considerably modified. But as for the rest ...
Mountains of flowers, waterfalls, fountains in the reception rooms,
scintillating illuminations, supper, cold buffet, and finally the *earthquake*! All Russia's snowdrops were there; and what diamonds on
their heads and shoulders! Uniforms of every country: Hungarians,
Greeks, Turks, Persians, Englishmen (even), Russians (of course),
Austrians, Americans, Albanians ... and Frenchmen. All the women
were placed in the middle of this immense room and the men in a circle
round them, like the trimmings on a basket of fruit. There was no sight
of any tail coats, none of that gloomy black attire. It was splendid! I
doubt whether Louis saw anything as brilliant at his party in Bombay
with a Parsee. (He wrote me a second letter before he left.)

At one o'clock we made an energetic assault on the tables; we were
then lucky enough to find our wraps and a carriage straight away. As
well as everything else, it was a magnificent moonlit night. [...]

Adieu, dear sister, I'm going to bed, without supper this evening but
also without third-rate music.

H. Berlioz

346 *To his sister Adèle Suat*   Paris, 26 June 1857

Dear forgetful one,

At last I have news of you! How can you leave me almost two
months without a reply when you know what anxiety and impatience
these silences cause me? [...]

At the moment I'm finishing the music of the second act (I finished

1 Brother of Tsar Alexander II of Russia.

that of acts I and IV a long time ago). It is, I think, the hardest part of my task; the scene with Cassandra and the Trojan women was particularly difficult, but I hope I have achieved my aim and succeeded in expressing that ever-growing enthusiasm, that love of death which the inspired virgin communicates to the Trojan women and which finally draws from the Greek soldiery a cry of horrified admiration.

I've also done the Carthaginian National Anthem for the third act, which greets Dido several times over on her entrance. It's Carthage's God save the Queen.

As you see, I'm making progress and by this time next year it will definitely all be complete. [. . .]

Adieu, naughty sister; I don't embrace you, hard feelings have returned.

H. Berlioz

Berlioz's only travels in 1857 were to Plombières in July, followed by another stay in Baden-Baden with a concert there on 18 August. The rest of the year was almost entirely devoted to Les Troyens *with, of course, regular feuilletons to write for the* Journal des débats.

347 *To his sister Adèle Suat*   Plombières, 4 August 1857

Dear sister,

[. . .] We'll be leaving for Baden-Baden, Marie and I, next Monday. The waters do both of us a great deal of good and we like this heat that you complain about so much. This weather suits me admirably; it's a tropical climate so I go looking in the woods to see if there are any pineapples yet like the ones that grow in Guyana and the Antilles. You can't imagine how beautiful our woods are at daybreak and when the moon rises. Three days ago, while Marie was taking her bath, I went early in the morning all alone to the Stanislas fountain; I'd taken my manuscript of *Les Troyens*, some music paper and a pencil; the owner of the little house arranged a table for me in the shade, together with a jug of milk, some kirsch and sugar, and I worked in peace looking out over this beautiful countryside until nine o'clock. I was in fact composing a chorus, the words of which seemed rather appropriate:

> 'Vit-on jamais un jour pareil?'
> 'Has ever such a day been seen? . . .'[1]

1 The opening chorus of Act III, no. 17.

Adieu, dear little sister, I embrace you with all my heart. Marie sends you best wishes and asks to be remembered to your husband. The lovely little carrying bag embroidered by my nieces has seen use for the first time; we're delighted with it.

H. Berlioz

348 *To Hugo von Senger*[1]   Baden-Baden, August 1857

Monsieur,

I am very touched by the confidence you have in me and I sympathize deeply with your feelings of artistic disappointment,. You obviously have a remarkable talent, which will rapidly develop. But you are greatly mistaken if you think I can be of any help to you in Paris; I do not possess the kind of influence there that would be necessary in order to find you a position. There I am myself surrounded by enemies who paralyse my efforts, prevent me from putting on my works and force me to leave France to get them known.

Paris is the capital of musical barbarism, don't forget that. Everything there is in the hands of barbarians.

It would therefore be far better for you to remain in Germany, where your merit as a composer will be recognized sooner or later. Trust my unfortunate experiences in the matter, and believe me when I say how sorry I am to be able to offer you no more than this depressing advice.

I shake your hand.

H. Berlioz

349 *To Auguste Morel*   Paris, 7 September 1857

My dear Morel,

[...] I've gone back to working on my score and if I wasn't constantly interrupted every third day, I should be progressing at a good speed. In six or seven months the work will finally be finished; and to get a better idea of its faults I shall then settle down to write the piano score. That's the most useful occupation of all in such cases; anyway the vocal score is valuable on its own account, especially for rehearsal.

Our concert in Baden-Baden was splendid, everything went well. The Karlsruhe choirs are admirable and they sang the *Judex* of my *Te Deum* admirably. It's a really terrifying movement from every point of view.

---

1 A young German composer whose career left little mark.

I'm very sad about the bad impression created by the recent performance of *Euryanthe*.[1] Despite the changes they very sensibly made to the libretto, it doesn't work. You'll be able to read any day now the analysis I've made of the German drama in the *Journal des débats*. I don't think anyone has ever been crass enough before to put such nonsense on a stage. We all agree that the music is good, with some wonderful moments, but in my opinion it can't be compared with *Oberon* or *Freischütz*. [. . .]

Adieu, I shake your hand.

Yours very sincerely,

H. Berlioz

350 *To Emile Deschamps*   Saint-Germain, 31 October 1857

I'm almost tempted, my dear Deschamps, to be grateful for the impossible musical obstacles we have both come up against, since they were responsible for the cordial, charming letter you've just sent me.

May I shake you by the hand; nothing gives me greater pleasure than proofs of affection from a man of intelligence. Prickly trees so rarely produce sweet and succulent fruit . . . Very well, if that's what you want, let's lament together. Yes, perhaps it would have been a good idea. But perhaps also the music might have seemed indiscreet in taking up such a large part of the performance of your poem. There's no imperative need for it and, I must confess, I was afraid that my long orchestral pieces might have the same effect on the audience as long stretches of verse recited in a concert between movements of a symphony.

The arts are brothers, it's true, but they're jealous brothers. You may say I malign them. But you have to admit that Paris is a curious place for creative artists who have the slightest inclination to do something different. I am less sensitive than you to the various sorts of difficulty we're destined to labour under; experience has hardened me. And I've seen so many instances of the kind of absurdity which is distressing you that I can now guarantee a project to be unrealizable simply because it is excellent.

Thank you for the most enjoyable evening I spent with your two entertaining friends. Why do we see each other so rarely? Let me know

1 Weber's *Euryanthe* was revived at the Théâtre-Lyrique on 1 September; Berlioz's notice, which appeared a week later, was reprinted in *A travers chants*.

[357]

at least whenever you come to Paris and remember the way to the Rue de Calais from time to time.

At the moment I'm staying with friends in St-Germain. I've been given the use of a salon that gets the sun, leading out into a garden with a view over the Marly valley, the aqueduct, woods, vineyards and the Seine. The house is on its own; silence and peace all round; and I'm working on my score in a mood of inexpressible happiness, without thinking for a moment about the miseries it's sure to cause me later. The view over the countryside seems only to add to the intensity of my Virgilian passion. I feel as though I knew Virgil; I feel as though he knows how much I love him. Don't you too have this pleasant illusion? ... Yesterday I was finishing an aria for Dido, nothing other than a paraphrase of the famous line:

Haud ignara mali miseris succurrere disco.[1]

After singing it once, I was naive enough to say out loud. 'That's right, isn't it, dear Master? *Sunt lacrymae rerum*?', as though Virgil were there.

Adieu, a thousand best wishes for an early performance of your *Roméo*, for which your poetry provides quite enough music.

Yours very sincerely,
Hector Berlioz

351 *To Princess Carolyne Sayn-Wittgenstein*   Paris,
                                                     30 November 1857

Many thanks, Princess, for your charming but far too flattering letter. I'm not entirely as much to blame as I appeared to be. The truth is, I didn't dare write to you. I was afraid my letter might be inopportune and perhaps importunate. I was afraid I might from now on have become in your mind a composer of the past, with old ideas and violent convictions, who expresses his opinions, what's more, in an extremely brutal manner. Perhaps it's true – but then it's so easy to abstain from certain topics of dispute and there are so many other things about which I have the pleasure to agree with you, that I hope in future not to have the misfortune to be led into wounding discussions. I am very sorry to hear that you have been seriously ill and for some time. But since you were able to travel to Dresden, I trust that now you are almost entirely recovered.

---

1 'Not unfamiliar with evil, I have learnt to help the unfortunate', rendered by Berlioz as 'Qui connut la souffrance ne pourrait voir en vain souffrir', at the arrival of Aeneas and his men in Act III, no. 25.

I, too, am still in rather poor health. Nonetheless I don't have the interesting pallor you are kind enough to credit me with, I'm simply tired and suffer at times from suppressed exasperation.

There was no great merit in my refusing the American engagement you mention. I needed to stick at my task, didn't I? And it would be supremely silly, wouldn't it, to interrupt it for another one in which art was not greatly involved? True, money is highly necessary in order to make music, but on the condition that the music exists in the first place. I should be in a poor way now if I'd accepted.

The talk in America is all of bankruptcies, and the theatres and concert societies are heading for the Niagara Falls. Ours don't run this danger. There are no cataracts with us because there's no current. We sail along on a totally calm pond, full of frogs and toads and enlivened by the flight and quacking of the occasional duck; there's no fear of shipwreck except when the ships are utterly rotten.

But I'm living in my score like La Fontaine's rat in his cheese, if you'll pardon the comparison.

I'm about to begin the fifth act and in a few months it will all be finished. The libretto has again been considerably changed since we last talked about it. There's a new, longer ending;[1] I've cut a good deal and added somewhat. I haven't read it to the Empress. The Marquis de Belmont, who was in charge of arranging an evening at St-Cloud for me, died while I was at Baden-Baden and I haven't yet got round to finding anyone else to introduce me to her *gracious* Majesty. I'm thinking of nothing but finishing the work. These last few months the opera houses have granted me some respite; I've only occasionally been interrupted in my work. I'm doing it with a concentrated passion which seems to grow as it's satisfied. What will be the value of the result? God alone knows. In any case it makes me really happy to be Robinson Crusoe hollowing out, equipping and fitting a mast on this large canoe, not that I shall be able to launch it unless the sea itself comes to claim it. And I shall never forget, Princess, that it is to you and you alone that I owe my indulgence in this luxury of composition. Certainly, without your encouragement and your indulgent reproaches I should never have undertaken anything of the kind; may I thank you for both of these, whatever the miseries this work may cause me later.

Please tell the Princess Marie that I kneel at her feet and give my

---

1 This longer ending, with the appearance of Clio, Muse of History, and a procession of Roman notables, was to be replaced in 1859.

affectionate best wishes to Liszt. I saw M. and Mme von Bülow for a moment at Baden-Baden.[1]

Yours very sincerely,
Hector Berlioz

352 *To his sister Adèle Suat*   Paris, 15 January 1858

Dear sister,

These are just a few lines to thank you for your last letter. I'm ill once again and spending most of my time in bed. We're all overwhelmed too by the attempt on the lives of the Emperor and Empress yesterday evening, which nearly succeeded.[2] A large number were injured. We still don't know any precise details. It's extraordinarily lucky that there wasn't a worse disaster; those brigands had left or thrown several other explosive devices in the Rue Le Peletier which didn't go off. Only two men have been arrested, apparently with pistols and daggers in their possession. Where should we be today if these wretches had succeeded? The Emperor went to the Opéra nonetheless and stayed there till the end of the performance. When he left, you can imagine the reception awaiting him out on the boulevard!

One is disgusted to be living in this country of assassins! But the rest of the world's no better.

The performance was a benefit for Massol[3] and, if he'd invited us, Marie and I might have gone. In all probability I should have got up and had myself driven there, and we might have been killed or wounded like so many others. [. . .]

Your devoted
H. Berlioz

353 *To Hans von Bülow*   Paris, 20 January 1858

Thank you for your charming letter, charming in its style, in the warmth of feeling that prompted it, in the good news it contains, charming from every point of view. I read it with the contentment of a cat drinking milk.

---

1 Von Bülow and Cosima Liszt were married in Berlin on 18 August; they spent a few days of their honeymoon as guests of the Pohls in Baden-Baden.
2 On 14 January Orsini and some accomplices threw three bombs at the Emperor's carriage as he and the Empress arrived at the Opéra. There were several killed and over a hundred injured.
3 The tenor who had sung Fieramosca in *Benvenuto Cellini* in 1838.

So here, without delay, is my answer. I got up this morning with the intention of working exclusively on my score. The fire was lit, the door closed; no possibility of interruptions from fools or importunates, and then your letter arrives to upset all my fine plans for working and I succumb to the pleasure of writing to you, saying like the Roman: 'Serious matters can wait till tomorrow!' Not that I imagine you'll find anything of interest in my reply, but it gives me extreme pleasure to send it. It's pure, concentrated, unadulterated egoism, an *elemental* egoism (as the chemists would say).

I'm delighted by your faith, your enthusiasm, even by your hatreds. Like you, I still have fearful hatreds and volcanic enthusiasms. But as to faith, I firmly believe there is nothing true, nothing false, nothing beautiful, nothing ugly . . . Don't believe a word of it, I malign myself. No. I adore what I find beautiful more than ever and the cruellest drawback about death, to my way of thinking, is that it puts an end to love and admiration. It's true, one wouldn't know one wasn't loving any more. Or to put it another way, no philosophizing, no nonsense. [. . .]

You ask what I'm doing. I'm finishing *Les Troyens*. I haven't been able to work on it for a fortnight. I've reached the final catastrophe. Aeneas has sailed away. Dido doesn't know it as yet, she's about to learn the news and she has a presentiment of his departure . . .

Quis fallere possit amantem?[1]

The task of expressing this heart-rending anguish and of finding notes for these cries of misery appals me. How am I to go about it? I'm particularly anxious about finding a way to set the following passage, spoken by Anna and Narbal in the middle of the religious ceremony of Pluto's priests:

> S'il faut enfin qu'Enée aborde en Italie,
> Qu'il y trouve un obscur trépas!
> Que le peuple Latin à l'Ombrien s'allie,
> Pour arrêter ses pas!
> Percé d'un trait vulgaire en la mêlée ardente,
> Qu'il reste abandonné sur l'arène sanglante
> Pour servir de pâture aux dévorants oiseaux!
> Entendez-vous, Hécate, Erèbe, et toi, Chaos?[2]

---

1 'Who can deceive a lover?', *Aeneid*, Book IV, 296. The scene Berlioz describes is the beginning of Act V, Tableau 2, of the opera.
2 The beginning of Act V, Tableau 3.

Is this a violent imprecation? Does it have the force of a concentrated, unheeding fury? If poor Rachel weren't dead, I should go and ask her that question. I'm sure you'll be thinking it's very good of me to be troubling myself to such an extent about expressive truth and that it'll always be *true* enough for the general public. Yes, but for us? ... Anyway, perhaps I shall succeed.

You can have no conception, my dear Bülow, of the ebb and flow of contrary feelings to which my heart has been subjected since I began on this work. Sometimes I feel a passion, a joy and a warmth worthy of a man of twenty. At other times I'm terrified by the disgust, the coldness, the repulsion with which it inspires me. I'm never in doubt; first I believe, then I no longer believe, then I believe once again ... and, when all is said and done, I go on rolling my stone. One more mighty effort and we shall be at the top of the mountain, one carrying the other.

The one fatal blow for Sisyphus at this juncture would be a discouraging word from the world outside. But no one is in a position to discourage me, no one hears a note of my score, so there's no possibility of my being depressed by anyone else's opinions. If you were here, I shouldn't show anything even to you. I'm too afraid of being afraid. [. . .]

H. Berlioz

354 *To his son Louis Berlioz*   Paris, 24 January 1858

Dear Louis,

[. . .] This month I've again been rather ill and in bed; I'm up again now and renewing work on my score. The day before yesterday I read out the libretto of *Les Troyens* at the house of a fellow member of the Institut, M. Hittorf.[1] A large number of painters, sculptors and architects from the Institut were there, also M. Blanche, secretary to the Minister of State, M. de Mercey, director of the Beaux-Arts, etc, etc. It was extremely successful; they found it imposing and fine, and I was interrupted several times by applause. All in all, it restored my courage a little for finishing this huge score. [. . .]

---

1 Ignace Hittorf, architect of the Gare du Nord and the surroundings of the Etoile, which Haussmann declared to be so bad that he had to mask the buildings with trees.

Dear Louis,

[...] I'm working as best I can to finish my score and making headway slowly. At this moment I'm on Dido's final monologue: 'Je vais mourir dans ma douleur immense submergée.' I'm happier with what I've just written than with everything I've done before. I feel the music for these terrible scenes in the fifth act will be heart-rendingly truthful.

But I've made further changes to this act. I've cut a long section of it and added a character number, designed to contrast with the epic, high-flown style of the rest. It's a sailor's song; I was thinking of you, Louis, when I wrote it and I send you the words.[1] Night has fallen and you can see the Trojan ships in the port: Hylas, a young Phrygian sailor, sings perched on the top of one of the masts.

                    Vallon sonore, [etc] [...]

Adieu. I embrace you, dear Indian,[2] with all my heart; come back to me well, wise and rich and all will go splendidly.

356   *To Adolphe Samuel*[3]   Paris, 26 February 1858

My dear Samuel,

[...] Yes, *Les Troyens* is almost done; I've nothing left to write except the final scene. Tomorrow I've got to read the libretto in front of a score of people. I read it last month to a gathering of fellow-members of the Institut and it made a considerable impact. It's said to be very fine. I wish there was a way of your getting to know it. I've worked at this libretto with inordinate patience, and now I'm not going to change anything. But how should I not be patient? I was reading yesterday in a life of Virgil that he spent *eleven* years writing the *Aeneid*; and this poetic miracle seemed to him even then to be so incomplete that, before he died, he gave his heirs orders to burn it.

Shakespeare made three versions of *Hamlet*. This is the only way to work if one wants to produce great things, things that will last.

I think you will be happy with my score for *Les Troyens*. You can imagine easily enough what the scenes of passion are like, also the love

1 The beginning of Act V, Tableau 1, no. 38.
2 Louis's ship was in Indian waters.
3 Young Belgian composer and critic, a pupil of Fétis. He had assisted Berlioz with his Brussels concerts in March 1855.

scenes and the depictions of nature, whether calm or stormy, but there are scenes too of which you cannot possibly have any conception. Among these is the ensemble in which all the characters and the chorus express their horror and fear as they learn that Laocoön has met his death devoured by snakes,[1] also the finale of the third act and Aeneas' last scene in the fifth. I've decided to make a piano arrangement of the whole work. I think it will be a useful exercise as a critical study of the full score, forcing me to look closely at its most secret places.

It doesn't matter what happens to the work after that, whether it's staged or not. My passion for Virgil and for music will have been satisfied and I shall at least have shown what I think can be done in the way of treating an antique subject on a large scale.

Adieu, my dear Samuel, patience and perseverance, and I will even go so far as to add indifference. What does it all matter?

Yours sincerely, if sadly,

Hector Berlioz

357 *To his sister Adèle Suat*   Paris, 11 March 1858

Dear sister,

Don't be cross with me for this late reply. I'm finishing my score and haven't been able to leave it for some days now. I'm glueing myself to it all the more furiously because I had to lose seventeen whole days at the end of last month. A friend of mine from Germany (Litolff) descended on me, coming to get a hearing for his compositions in Paris.[2] He was counting on me for *everything*, and as he is a man of very considerable musical gifts I gave him all the help I possibly could. I introduced him to all my friends, I wrote to those of my fellow-members of the press whom we didn't manage to meet, in short I piloted him round Paris. He had an immediate, brilliant success and is in the seventh heaven. Have you read my article on him? I have a little more free time now. [. . .]

I can assure you, dear little sister, that the music of *Les Troyens* is something noble and grand. What is more, there's a poignant truthfulness about it and it contains some new ideas which will make composers the length and breadth of Europe prick up their ears, and perhaps make their hair stand on end, unless I'm grossly mistaken. I think that if Gluck were to return to earth, he would say to me when he

1 *Ottetto et chœur* in Act I, no. 8.
2 Henry Litolff, born in London of French parents, pursued a career as pianist, composer and publisher, mostly in Germany. He gave a series of concerts at the Conservatoire, the first of which Berlioz reviewed on 5 March, the third of which, on 2 May, he took part in.

heard it: 'Without question, that is my son.' Not exactly a modest remark, I know. But at least I have the modesty to admit that I have the failing of lacking modesty. [. . .]

We shall soon be running out of wine. If your husband could send me soon the two casks he has ready for me, I should receive them with an open cellar, indeed a practically empty one.

I'm absolutely exhausted this morning. We got back at one o'clock in the morning in the midst of appalling snow and mud after visiting the Théâtre-Lyrique and undergoing the revival of poor Félicien David's opera *La perle du Brésil*, in which he has produced a curious specimen of stupidity in music, believing it to be simplicity. All the ex-Saint-Simonians were there, they assured him of a grotesque success.[1] The libretto is as dull as the score.

Not long ago, on the other hand, Gounod gave us his *Médecin malgré lui*, a real little masterpiece of taste, wit, verve and classicism.[2] A work in this style puts to shame those bunglers, large and small, of the Parisian school! I had a large grey parrot ten years ago who, with a slight lisp, used to pronounce very distinctly the word 'Cochon!' The gentlemen of the Parisian school always make me think of that poor bird.

Adieu, dear sister, embrace your daughters on my behalf, and my nieces on your own; I shake your husband by the hand. My wife is a little better, she's been in great pain with her neuralgia.

H. Berlioz

358 *To Princess Carolyne Sayn-Wittgenstein*   Paris, 6 May 1858

It is always with excuses, dear Princess, that I have to begin my letters. This time I appear more inexcusable than ever not to have replied sooner to all the charming things you wrote to me in your last one. When I am ill in spirit, in body, in heart, in head, as I have just been for nearly a month, I'm careful not to write to people in whose eyes I am afraid of appearing in an unfavourable light. Then I'm like a wounded wolf, and there's nothing for me to do but huddle in a corner and let my wounds bleed. I didn't send you the manuscript of *Les Troyens* because I knew you intended to come to Paris with Liszt next July.[3] I

1 David began his career as a leading musician of the Saint-Simonian movement in the years 1831–3.
2 First performed at the Théâtre-Lyrique on 15 January 1858. Berlioz's review appeared on 22 January.
3 The last page of *Les Troyens* was finished and dated on 12 April.

shall ask your permission then to read you my five acts and give you some indications as to what I've been aiming at in the music of certain scenes. *I shall present you with my report*, because it was a mission you entrusted me with and I'm anxious to prove to you that I've done everything in my power to fulfil it worthily.

With regard to this work, I'm on the brink of an important step. Last Monday I was at the Tuileries. On seeing me, the Emperor came up and asked what I was working on. The answer was simple: 'I have just finished, etc, etc, and I should be very happy to be able to submit at least the libretto to Your Majesty.'

'But I should be extremely interested.'

'How should I proceed, Sire?'

'How? You must tell the Duc de Bassano that I am granting you an audience for next week. He will send you a letter of appointment. You will bring me your work and we will talk about it.' I did just that.

So in a week's time I will go and take *Les Troyens* to the Emperor. But will he really read it? I find it hard to believe. And will he then, if he likes the work, take definite sides and give actual *orders*, to spare me the Lilliputians at the Opéra? I find that even harder. There are absolutely serious plans for next year to put on a grand opera in five acts by Prince Poniatowski!![1] If that project comes to fruition, you can see what follows... [...]

Yours most sincerely,

Hector Berlioz

359 *To his sister Adèle Suat*   Paris, 10 May 1858

Dear little sister,

It's almost culpable of me to give in to my desire to write to you this evening; I have an article to write.[2] For three days now I've been keeping the pen of vitriol at a distance. I ought finally to take hold of it, but I'll work later on into the night. I was so happy to have your letter this morning! When I converse with you, I seem to breathe fresh air that restores me. I'm fearfully sad ... I should like to be near you, to speak to you. Now that your spirit and your heart seem intuitively to understand the world of art, my affection for you grows. If you only knew how lonely I am. Let me kiss your hand, *la tua man pietosa*,

1 A politician and part-time composer, nephew of one of Napoleon's marshals. His *Pierre de Médicis* was staged at the Opéra in 1860.

2 He had a notice to write on operas by Massé and Hérold.

which wrote such a sweet letter. If you didn't live in the provinces, how quickly your charming instincts would reveal to you a thousand divine things which now you catch only a glimpse of. [...]

You mention the book on Mozart; I know it.[1] Parts of it are very moving, but in others I get impatient with father Leopold. He did his son a great disservice in keeping a whole host of compositions by the infant prodigy which are nothing more than ridiculous and which he ought to have burnt. You'll never guess what, among other things, is making me so gloomy today: the newspapers, which are violently enthusiastic about last Sunday's concert.[2] There they are writing about *Roméo et Juliette* as a colossal work which has been revealed to them during these last few days. It's been in existence for twenty years and they're responding to the impression produced by a *single* movement when the score contains fourteen!!...[3] A composer in France has to live a couple of hundred years to get himself known! [...]

I spoke to your husband two years ago about a rather important work (my *Mémoires*) which I should like to entrust to him. I'll send it to him shortly. I've been correcting and recorrecting the style for six years now without managing to make it anything like satisfactory. I'm going to polish it again for the twentieth time. Nothing is as difficult as writing good prose.

Never mention this in your letters. I'll tell your husband what needs to be done with it when I send him the manuscript. I'm leaving these three volumes to Louis, with a plea to publish them as they are, without the slightest alteration. But I'll talk to you about them again. Don't read them, it would be too heart-rending for you and would revive too many painful memories. I can't re-read them myself without shedding floods of bitter tears. [...]

My best wishes to your husband. I wish I could be with the four of you for at least an hour, my hands in yours, without saying a word, letting my wounds bleed silently and loving you face to face.

H. Berlioz

---

1 *Mozart: la vie d'un artiste chrétien au XVIIIe siècle* by the Abbé Isidore Goschler.
2 Sharing a concert with Litolff on 2 May, Berlioz conducted *La captive* and the *Fête* from *Roméo et Juliette*.
3 Berlioz usually divided *Roméo et Juliette* into seven movements, not fourteen.

Dear little sister,

[...] As for me, I'm living in hell; my neuralgia doesn't leave me a moment's respite. Every day at nine in the morning I have violent colics which last until two or three in the afternoon; spasms in the chest; in the evening pains in the neck of the bladder and redoubled spasms. And depression to darken the rising sun, disgust with everything! . . . Oh please write to me, your letters do me good.

I saw the Emperor, but it was a meaningless audience; there were forty-two of us. [...]

H. Berlioz

361 *To his uncle Félix Marmion*   Paris, 5 September 1858

Dear uncle,

I arrived at one o'clock this morning, very tired and exhausted, but also very happy with my journey.[1] It was very kind of you to ask me to tell you about this excursion; it would have been even better to come to the concert. It was splendid, everything, chorus and orchestra, went like a first-class quartet; it was marvellous. I'd had *eleven* rehearsals for the first four movements of *Roméo et Juliette*, and there was no doing with less to get this work into the minds and fingers of the performers. The impact was enormous; I was recalled I don't know how many times, then the orchestra gave me an ovation, with fanfares on the brass, the violins tapping their bows, etc.

There were tears (in the Adagio, the love scene) and next day the Countess Kalergis (a well-known amateur virtuoso) said to my wife, 'I was so overwhelmed, I'm still crying today.'[2]

Bénazet gave a large dinner, in the middle of which Méry offered me a singularly witty and moving toast. A few days later, the poet did better still. They were putting on a comedy of his, before which he had added a prologue. In this prologue, in verse, after describing the charms of life in Baden-Baden and the mountains and woods of that delightful town, he went on to draw attention to the importance of music in the season's festivities, and in the course of so doing aimed a dozen lines in my direction which the audience received with extended

1 In August Berlioz went again to Baden-Baden where he gave a concert on the 27th.
2 The Countess Kalergis, niece of the Russian Chancellor Count Nesselrode and a pupil of Chopin, was also one of Wagner's patrons.

applause. Mme Bénazet made Marie a gift of a beautiful diamond brooch.

Amateurs and professionals came to the concert from all parts of Germany, not to mention those from Paris, London, St Petersburg (the Russians outnumbered everybody) and Switzerland.

Finally we had to leave, but we stayed for two days in Strasbourg at the house of M. Kastner, who had invited us to visit his large, beautiful estate. M. Kastner is a knowledgeable musician and theorist; he's married to M. Boursault's daughter and as a result has an immense fortune. His wife is one of the most distinguished people in France, for her wit, her unusual depth of learning and above all for the modest reserve with which she hides so many fine qualities. She's a considerable musician, what's more, and knows almost all my works by heart. They had both attended the concert in Baden and two of the rehearsals. In Strasbourg, another large dinner, more presents; we were overwhelmed with attention. Now I'm back again and I find your letter together with two from Louis. He's still in Bombay and will be there for another three or four months. He's enjoying himself there, working hard and he's popular; he's often asked to do the honours on board when the Captain gives a party. He's keeping well. He won't be back home until 1860.

I wrote to my sister before leaving Baden-Baden; I don't know why she hasn't replied; Joséphine, after all, has been out of danger for some time.[1] So there, dear uncle, you have a description (in auctioneer's style) of my musical travels. Forgive me, exhaustion has had a serious dulling effect on my brain, I'm afraid.

Remember me to my aunt,
Yours affectionately,
H. Berlioz

362 *To his sister Adèle Suat*   [Paris,] 20 September [1858]

Dear sister,

[...] Last evening I went to the Théâtre-Français to see the first performance of a translation of Sophocles' *Oedipus Rex*. It's very fine, but very exhausting; and for me, Shakespeare is still more astonishing than that, if not greater. When the wretched King, having torn out his eyes and before leaving Thebes for ever, asks his two daughters aged twelve and fourteen to be brought to him, it provoked floods of tears.

---

1 Joséphine Suat was struck down with an unnamed illness in July and August.

It is a work of sublime art. Shakespeare is a God, Sophocles is a great man.

H. Berlioz

363 *To Baron Wilhelm von Donop*   Paris, 2 October 1856

Monsieur,

[...] You ask me for details of my new opera (not *Didon* but *Les Troyens*). I will answer you in all naivety: it seems to me to be very grand and to contain a great variety of colours. The principal merit of the work, in my opinion, is its *truthfulness of expression*. There are, especially in the fifth act, phrases which should rend the heart ... of those who have one ...

But will it ever be performed? And how? Where shall I find a Cassandra? Or a Dido? Or an Aeneas? And where shall I find a theatre director intelligent enough to hand over to me his entire authority and leave me free to stage my opera as I think it ought to be staged? These are wild dreams. Female singers are blockheads, tenors are churls and directors are vain fools, pretty well everywhere.

About the timpani passage in the overture *Le roi Lear*

here's my answer:

It was the custom at the French court, as recently as 1830 under Charles X, to announce the King's entrance into his apartments (after Sunday Mass) with the sound of an enormous drum which beat out a bizarre rhythm in quintuple metre that had been handed down as a tradition from the most distant times. That gave me the idea of using a timpani effect of the same kind to accompany Lear's entrance into his council for the scene of the division of his kingdom. I did not intend to suggest his madness until the middle of the Allegro, when the basses repeat the theme of the introduction in the middle of the storm. It needs a first-class orchestra to perform this overture. I haven't heard it since my last journey to Hanover; it's the King's favourite piece.

I'm delighted to learn that you like *Les nuits d'été*, especially if you mean the full score and not the edition with piano. The only pieces I've ever heard from this collection are *Le spectre de la rose* and *Absence*, and those rarely played well. I've also written another collection

entitled *Tristia*, containing a *Hymne* for six voices on a text by
Moore,[1] a *Ballade* for women's chorus on the death of Ophelia, and
the *Marche funèbre* with invisible chorus and large orchestra for the
final scene of *Hamlet*; I've never heard a bar of it. It's published in full
score, but who's interested in that?

May I thank you again, dear Monsieur, for your sympathy; it is a
source of much pride and happiness for me. [. . .]

Yours most sincerely,

Hector Berlioz

364 *To Humbert Ferrand*   Paris, 26 November 1858

Dear Humbert,

All I have to say to you is this: I feel the need to write to you, so why
shouldn't I yield to it? You'll forgive me, won't you? I am ill, gloomy
(observe how many 'I's there are in such a few lines!), how sad it is!
Always *I*! Always *me*! One has friends only for *oneself*! And one
should exist only for one's friends.

That's how it is. *I* am a beast, a leopard, a cat, if you prefer; there are
cats who really love their friends, I won't say their masters, cats don't
recognize any masters . . .

Writing to you helps lift my depression; please don't let us go for
years, as we have, without writing to one another.

Just think how we're moving towards death at a terrifying speed . . .
Your letters do me so much good! You've received the score of *L'enfance du Christ*, haven't you? There's no way to make music here,
unless one is rich like your *friend* Mirès.[2] This was the subject of my
dreams last night (music, that is, not Mirès). This morning my dream
came back to me; in my mind I was performing, as we did three years
ago in Baden-Baden, the Adagio from Beethoven's Fourth Symphony:[3]

1 Its title is *Méditation religieuse*.
2 A millionaire with interests in railways and newspapers.
3 Berlioz, writing from memory, slightly misquotes Beethoven's melody.

and gradually, still awake, I fell into one of those unearthly ecstasies
... I wept all the tears of my soul, listening to those smiles in sound
such as the angels alone can give forth. Believe me, dear Humbert, the
being who wrote such a marvel of heavenly inspiration was not a man.
That is the kind of song the archangel Michael sings when, lost in
thought, he gazes down at the world, standing upon the threshold of
the empyrean ... Oh, not to be able to have an orchestra there under
my hand and sing to myself that archangelic poem!

Back to earth ... Ah! someone's come to disturb me. Banality,
vulgarisms, the tedious business of living! No more inspired orchestra!
I should like to have a hundred cannons and let them all off at once.

Adieu; I feel a little calmer now. Pardon me, pardon me!

H. Berlioz

365 *To his brother-in-law Camille Pal*   Paris, 7 January 1859

My dear Camille,

[...] I'm still ill, and from time to time in utter despair. I've tried
another doctor who's the talk of Paris at the moment with his marvellous cures.[1] If we'd got to know of him earlier, our poor Nanci would
still be alive. Among other medicaments he uses, and which he alone
knows about, is a specific against cancer. Our friend Sax had had a
terrible pain in his upper lip for four years, and gradually a horrible
tumour formed there, a cancerous growth, malignant and purulent.
Velpeau, Ricord and all the princes of science declared that he was lost,
that the only way might be to cut off his left cheek, but without any
certainty at all that the disease might not reappear elsewhere. Sax
refused to have this horrible operation; he was introduced to Dr Vries,
who inspected the tumour and said: 'There's still time, I can save him.'

And indeed, after three months' treatment, his specific against cancer
worked, the tumour fell off bit by bit, all the symptoms of gangrene
disappeared, and his lip today is as healthy and natural-looking as it
ever was.

I know of two other similar cases which have had the same outcome.
He was born in Java, I think, and these medicines which are known to
the Malays were passed on to him by his mother. The whole medical
fraternity is astonished.

1 Jan Hendrick Vries, known as 'Dr Noir', achieved some remission of Berlioz's illness, in
return for which the composer wrote a *Hymne pour la consécration du nouveau tabernacle*
for the temple which the self-styled doctor proposed to erect in the Champs-Elysées.

Poor Nanci, she might still be alive!

Adieu, my dear Camille, we have to take the rough with the smooth in this world, unlike in the other one where there is nothing at all.

H. Berlioz

366 *To Princess Carolyne Sayn-Wittgenstein*   Paris, 7 January 1859

On my knees I thank you, Princess, a thousand times for your compassionate letter. Allow me to kiss the hand (*la man pietosa* – the adjective doesn't exist in French) that wrote it. I'm suffering to such a degree that I value expressions of sympathy, yours especially! You give me leave to write nonsense to you; alas, I must not avail myself of this permission. The doctors say that I have a general inflammation of the nervous system, of the nervous *stem* ... that I must live like an oyster, not thinking, not feeling (that's to say, dead, to be strictly accurate). The nervous stem, since stem there is, produces bitter fruit ... Imagine, I have days when I'm hysterical like a young girl. Then the slightest thing can lead to strange occurrences. The day before yesterday I was having a quiet conversation with some friends by the fire when someone brought me a newspaper in which I saw announced a new biography of Christopher Columbus. Instantly, the entire life of that great man rose up before my mind. I saw it as one sees at a single glance the whole of a picture. My heart contracted at the memory of that famous, epic story, and I fell into a fit of indescribable despair, to the amazement of those present. They blamed it all on my illness. I wasn't going to court ridicule by owning up to my feeling for Columbus, whose name alone was responsible for my fit. It's a network of effects and causes, in which the most knowledgeable physiologists, aided by the most distinguished psychologists, would lose their way and their command of Latin. [. . .]

Yours most sincerely,

H. Berlioz

367 *To his sister Adèle Suat*   Paris, 10 January 1859

Dear little sister,

[. . .] I've just finished a book commissioned from me by the director of the Nouvelle Librairie; it's called *Les grotesques de la musique*. It's about to be sent to press. It's a series of comic stories and jokes of an acid gaiety . . .¹

The success of my *Mémoires* (or at least the extracts from them published in *Le monde illustré*)² is growing all the time; everyone's talking about them. Distractions seem to be presenting themselves uninvited, to bring me relief. This evening I'm having dinner with my neighbours M. and Mme Viardot, a charming family with whom I can breathe freely. Both of them are so intelligent and so good, and their children are so graceful and well brought up! Added to which the flower of art fills the house with its scent. There they love what I love, they admire what I admire in music, in literature and in all matters of the spirit.

The day after tomorrow I'm having dinner with Meyerbeer, again with friends or people with whom I feel at ease. [. . .]

Hector Berlioz

368 *To Princess Carolyne Sayn-Wittgenstein*   Paris, 22 January 1859

Dear Princess,

[. . .] You are perhaps entertaining a reservation about *Les Troyens*, thinking that you are the cause of my innermost troubles because you urged me to write this work. Please believe that this is not true in any way. On the contrary, I am deeply indebted to you for the passionate life I have led these last two years while composing it.

When I think about it, I can hardly manage to summon up a fit of volcanic anger. I've only to go to the Opéra to listen to a performance of anything whatever and I congratulate myself on not being dragged through the mud like that. In fact I only rarely think about it. Prince Napoleon is in Sardinia and his receptions have ceased. He's going to get married and is not taking any interest in literature or music. The Emperor has invited me to spend the evening at the Tuileries next Tuesday. I don't know whether I'll be able to speak to him.

Paris for me is a cemetery and its paving slabs tombstones. I live entirely in the past. On every hand I find mementos of friends or enemies who are no longer with us. There I met Balzac for the last time; here I went for a walk with Paganini; there I escorted the Duchesse d'Abrantès, a good woman, even if absurd; there's the house where

1 Berlioz's latest collection of writings *Les grotesques de la musique* was published in March by Bourdilliat. Its tone is mordant and humorous, with accounts of his travels to Marseille, Lyon, Lille and Baden-Baden.
2 Between September 1858 and September 1859 *Le monde illustré* published thirty-three extracts from the *Mémoires*.

Mme de Girardin used to live, a witty woman who thought I was an imbecile; there's the pavement on which I talked with Adolphe Nourrit the day before he left for Naples; that dilapidated house belonged to poor Rachel, etc, etc. They're all dead! All of them dead! Why are we not yet dead [. . .]

Your most devoted and grateful invalid,
H. Berlioz

369 *To Princess Carolyne Sayn-Wittgenstein*   Paris, 8 February 1859

Dear Princess,

[. . .] Last Sunday the Conservatoire put on Haydn's *The Creation* in its entirety. I abstained; I've always been profoundly antipathetic to this work. I make you this confession . . . too bad. His lowing cattle, his buzzing gnats, his light *in C major* shining like an oil lamp, and then his Adam, his Uriel, his Gabriel, and the flute solos and all his effects of *bonhomie* get on my nerves and make me want to hit someone. The English like their pudding well surrounded by a lake of fat, I hate it. It's precisely this fat which surrounds the musical pudding of Papa Haydn. One needs naivety, but not too much! I wouldn't give a fig to meet Eve in the woods; I'm sure she was stupid enough to make God ashamed of himself and entirely worthy to be the wife of her husband . . . [. . .]

Yours most sincerely,
H. Berlioz

370 *To George Alexander Osborne*[1]   Paris, 23 February 1859

My dear Osborne,

I see your name on the list of committee members of the Musical Society of London and I'm writing to ask an important favour. A German musician has written to me during the last few days to say that there was vague talk of performing my *Symphonie fantastique* at one of this new Society's concerts. Certainly it's one of the works of mine that I should most dearly like to introduce to the English public, but it's also one of the most difficult and one of the most impossible to perform well without a certain number of rehearsals. To play it after a single rehearsal, as is the custom in London, would be to commit downright

1 An Irish pianist who spent many years in Paris and had known Berlioz since his student days.

murder. I beg you, therefore, to dissuade the committee from this idea, if it exists. Benedict, Davison, Beale, Molique and Henry Smart will second you, I hope. Ask them to do so for me. The orchestration of this symphony is very complicated and demands a wide variety of instrumental groupings. It even requires the presence of certain instruments which are not to be found in ordinary orchestras: an E flat clarinet, four harps, a piano (which is easier), and four timpanists playing a pair of timpani each.[1]

I'm told that London does not possess four good timpanists capable of doing the delicate roll without which the Adagio (*Scène aux champs*) and the *Marche* don't come off. I'm sure the Society has a good orchestra and that M. Mellon[2] is an excellent conductor. But time and practice are necessary for a work of this kind if it is to be well performed. If I had to conduct it myself, I should not be confident of a good performance with only two rehearsals. Imagine for a moment what sort of performance might ensue with one rehearsal and with a conductor who did not know the score by heart! Do everything you can to prevent my symphony being put into the programme. I repeat, it would be murder. I am convinced of the kind intentions of your Society towards me.[3]

Adieu. Send me a brief word.

Yours sincerely,

H. Berlioz

371 *To Princess Carolyne Sayn-Wittgenstein*   Paris, 10 March 1859

Dear Princess,

[...] You ask me what the subject is of the opera I'm going to write for the new theatre in Baden-Baden. Unfortunately it's neither *Columbus* nor *Roméo*. It's a slightly fantastic drama, taken from German history; I've seen no more than a rough sketch. The author, M. Plouvier, was supposed to have brought me the libretto during the last few days and has not kept his word.[4] He's in ecstasies about his success at the Porte St-Martin. The drama he's just produced at that theatre (*L'outrage*) is a great sensation. I cannot tell you the vexation I feel at

---

1 Actually four timpanists on two pairs of timpani.
2 Alfred Mellon, conductor of the New Philharmonic Society.
3 The Society did not perform the *Symphonie fantastique* but chose the *Roi Lear* overture instead.
4 At Baden-Baden in August Berlioz agreed to compose an opera for the new theatre being built there. The librettist was to be Edouard Plouvier and the setting the Thirty Years War.

having been forced to sign this engagement with M. Bénazet. Perhaps I'm mistaken! Perhaps the fire will light itself as I compose. But there would be no perhaps if it was a question of dealing with the subjects you mentioned. The fire has long been lit; it burns, it smoulders, like those mines of underground coal which one knows to be on fire only by the burning waters they bring forth. Oh yes! One could make a marvellous opera out of *Roméo*, beside the symphony. But for whom? Who would sing it? Who would put it on? Who would appreciate it? Let's not talk of that. [. . .]

H. Berlioz

372 *To Enrico Tamberlick*[1]   Paris, 2 April 1859

My dear Tamberlick,

I've been so ill these last few days that I haven't been able to shake you by the hand and give you some idea of the emotions I felt, as did the whole audience, hearing you in *Il trovatore*. Never have you seemed to me to be so vehement in your passion, so irresistible in your tenderness, so powerful, in a word so great.

Certainly if you ever came to feel, rightly or wrongly, that you were approaching your final hour, you would have the right (forgive the comparison, *caro imperatore del canto*) to say like Nero: QUALIS ARTIFEX PEREO!!!

Adieu, adieu, I embrace you with all my heart.

Yours most sincerely,

Hector Berlioz

373 *To Humbert Ferrand*   Paris, 28 April 1859

My dearest Humbert,

Ill as I am, I still have the strength to feel great happiness when I receive your news. Your letter has revived me. It caught me even so in the middle of the uproar of preparing a sacred concert which I gave last Saturday (23rd) at the Opéra-Comique. *L'enfance du Christ* was better performed there than it had ever been before. The choice of singers and players was excellent. I was sorry you were not in the audience. The third part in particular (*L'arrivée à Saïs*) produced a highly emotional

---

1 Tenor who sang the role of Cellini in London in 1853. He appeared in *Il trovatore* at the Théâtre-Italien on 26 March and was so pleased with Berlioz's letter that he published it in *La France musicale* on 17 April.

effect. The solo by the father of the family 'Entrez, pauvres Hébreux', the trio of young Ishmaelites, the dialogue 'Comment vous nomme-t-on?' – 'Elle a pour nom Marie', etc, all that seemed to touch the audience greatly. They wouldn't stop applauding. But, between ourselves, what touched me far more and what, I hope, would have touched your heart, is the mystic chorus at the end, 'O mon âme', which for the first time was performed with the nuances and accents I asked for. This vocal peroration sums up the whole work. I think it carries a feeling of the infinite, of divine love ... I thought of you as I listened to it. [...]

In answer to your questions about the three new operatic productions of the moment, I will say that Gounod's *Faust*[1] contains extremely beautiful passages and extremely mediocre ones, and that the libretto has removed some admirably musical situations which would have had to be invented, if Goethe himself hadn't already done so.

The music of *Herculanum*[2] is feeble and depressingly *uncoloured* (pardon the neologism). That of *Le pardon de Ploërmel*[3] is, on the contrary, written magisterially, ingeniously, delicately, piquantly and often poetically!

There is a great gulf between Meyerbeer and these young people. One can see he is not a PARISIAN. With David and Gounod one sees the opposite.

Adieu, *most noble brother,*
  Let us be patient
  Your for ever[4]
H. Berlioz

---

374 *To Princess Carolyne Sayn-Wittgenstein*   Paris, 20 June 1859

[...] I should like you to be in no doubt of my gratitude, Princess, for the insistence you have shown that I should undertake this work and finish it. Whatever fate has in store for it, I now feel entirely happy at having brought it to a conclusion. I can now judge it with a cool head, and I think I can say that the score contains things worthy of being offered to you. There are even things that are new, such as the chorus of Trojan women in the second act, built on this strange scale:

1 Premiered at the Théâtre-Lyrique on 19 March.
2 By David, premiered at the Opéra on 4 March.
3 By Meyerbeer, premiered at the Opéra-Comique on 4 April.
4 The salutation is in English.

and the tone of desolation which results from the continual pre-
dominance of the G in relation to the D flat is something curious. It
reminds me of the despairing cries of Virgil's *feminae ululantes*, and
it's no more uncouth than Niobe dishevelled. The description of
Laocoon's death and especially the ensemble that follows it are, I
think, two terrifying set pieces which would make your heart beat
faster. As for the work's main objective, the expression of passion and
feelings and the musical reproduction of character, this was from the
beginning the easiest part of my task. I have spent my life with this
race of demigods. I imagine they knew me, I know them so well. And
that reminds me of a childhood impression which proves how deeply
these ancient figures exerted an instant fascination on me. In the days
when, in the course of my classical studies, I was construing the
twelfth book of the *Aeneid* under my father's guidance, my brain was
in turmoil over the characters of that masterpiece: Lavinia, Turnus,
Aeneas, Mezentius, Lausus, Pallas, Evander, Amata, Latinus, Camilla,
etc, etc. I began to sleepwalk and, to adapt a line by Victor Hugo:

> I walked wide awake in my dream beneath the stars.[1]

One Sunday I was taken to Vespers; the sad, monotonous chant of
the Psalm 'In exitu Israel' produced on me the magnetic effect it still
produces today and plunged me into the most palpable retrospective
reveries. I rejoined my Virgilian heroes, I heard the sound of their
weapons, I saw the beautiful Amazon Camilla running, I admired the
restrained blush on the cheeks of the weeping Lavinia, and poor
Turnus and his father Aunus, and his sister Juturna, I heard the bustle
in the great palace of Laurentum ... An immeasurable sadness took
hold of me, I left the church in floods of tears and remained weeping
for the rest of the day, unable to contain my epic sorrow, and no one
was ever able to get me to admit the reason for it. My parents never
knew nor even guessed the miseries that overwhelmed my childish
heart that day.

Is that not one of the strangest and most glorious manifestations of
the power of genius? A poet, dead for thousands of years, throwing
the soul of a young, ignorant, naive boy into disarray by a story
transmitted across the centuries and by pictures whose colouring
remains untouched by the beating wings of time ...

1 From *Ruy Blas.*

I have often asked myself what could be the point of this mystification we call life. It is to recognize what is beautiful, it is to love. Those who do not love and do not recognize beauty are really and truly the mystified ones. As for us, we have the right to whistle at the great mystificator. [...]

I remain always, and increasingly

your devoted Iopas,

H. Berlioz

375 *To Princess Carolyne Sayn-Wittgenstein*   Paris, 10 August 1859

[...] Last week two scenes from *Les Troyens* were sung (with piano) in the Salle Beethoven before an audience of around twenty; I may say that the effect was much greater that I had ever dared hope. Cassandra's aria and her great scene with Chorebus, which follows it, stirred the emotions of our small audience quite violently.

I must admit, from now on the thought of the quarantine into which this work is being put (if, indeed, it ever comes out of it) tortures me day and night. I had never heard any of it before, and those long phrases, brought to life by Mme Charton-Demeur's splendid voice, made me feel drunk.[1] I can already see the effect it would make in the theatre, and, try as I may to remain calm, this inert resistance on the part of the imbeciles who direct the Opéra breaks my heart. I know I promised to cultivate a resignation that was proof against anything, and here I am going back on my word completely. I'm in the grip of the bitterest disenchantment ... I shan't for long be able to support the physical ills brought on by such a combination of mental pressures. [...]

H. Berlioz

376 *To Auguste Morel*   Paris, 9 September 1859

My dear Morel,

[...] I'm back from Baden-Baden, ill and exhausted, but very happy with the enormous success of my scenes from *Les Troyens* and the four movements of *Roméo et Juliette*. Mme Viardot was a magnificent and moving Cassandra, and the love duet between Dido and Aeneas had to be repeated. I've already had an offer from Leipzig to buy the piano

---

1 Mme Charton-Demeur's performance convinced Berlioz that she was the only singer capable of singing the role of Dido when *Les Troyens à Carthage* was finally staged in 1863.

score of *Les Troyens*, a proposition which I don't think I should accept.

All sorts of things happened to me over this in Baden-Baden ... Read my article next Tuesday on Bellini's *Roméo* and Mme Vestvali's debut at the Opéra.[1]

Adieu, I've got more than fifteen letters to answer. I must leave you; all best wishes to Lecourt and my respects to Mme Morel. Louis is at Dieppe where he's on a course for his forthcoming examination.

Yours ever,
H. Berlioz

377 *To his son Louis Berlioz*   Paris, 23 September 1859

It's a quarter past eleven in the evening, I've just received your letter and I'm answering it at once. Yes, dear Louis, I ought to have written to you recently, but forgive me, I've been in such pain ... I went to spend two days at Courtavenel with Mme Viardot, where I was taken terribly ill; they tried to prevent me leaving. But the strain of seeing the whole of that charming family giving me their attention, and of upsetting such good friends, was too much. When I got back to Paris, I did no more than call in at the house; then I left again at once for St-Germain, where Marie was waiting for me at the house of M. Delaroche.

Next day I came back on my own, still in agony and preoccupied with four or five corrections I wanted to make in the second act of my score of *Les Troyens*. I worked on that for the rest of the day until eleven o'clock. Next day Rocquemont came bringing me the work I'd given him to do for the score of *Orphée*.[2] As they're waiting for the first act of this piece at the Théâtre-Lyrique, I had to get down to it at once and correct copying mistakes. Then I was struck down again with fits of crying and cardiac convulsions, so I could only have written you nonsense or things that would have depressed you horribly. This evening I feel a little better. I've finished putting in order the first act of *Orphée*; Carvalho will come and collect it tomorrow morning. He (Carvalho) is enthusiastic about my libretto for *Les Troyens*, which I lent him. He'd like to put it on at his theatre. But how? There's no tenor for Aeneas ... Mme Viardot is suggesting to

1 Berlioz bitterly criticized the Opéra's decision to mount Bellini's *I Capuleti e i Montecchi* with an act of Vaccai's *Giulietta e Romeo* interpolated, all sung in French.
2 Carvalho, director of the Théâtre-Lyrique, invited Berlioz to arrange Gluck's *Orphée* for Mme Viardot's mezzo voice, restoring elements of the Vienna version of the opera.

me that she should herself play the two roles in succession; the Cassandra of the first two acts would thus become the Dido of the last three. I think the public would accept this eccentricity, which is not without precedent, after all, and the two roles would be played in a heroic manner by that great artist.

This would take place next year in a new theatre which is to be built on the Place du Châtelet, by the Seine. Let's wait and see. On the other hand, there are numerous representations being made from all sides to the directors of the Opéra. My article put an end to their *Roméo et Juliette*; it's not making any money and the run has already been interrupted.

We must be patient and see what transpires. Mme Viardot, who is also a fine pianist, looked through my first two acts while I was with her. 'How wonderful', she said, 'that it's so good! If only I could now play Cassandra instead of Orpheus!' You must be patient on your own behalf, my dearest Louis; be patient on mine too. I have friends and devoted spirits ... But I see you in a mood of excitement and anger, whereas you need calm and tranquillity of mind in order to work fruitfully. Please think of your career above everything else and don't worry about me. We talked a lot about you the other day at Courtavenel, where they know how much we love one another. ...

Adieu, dear Louis, I embrace you with all my heart. I love you as you love me; what more could you want?

378 *To Pauline Viardot*   Paris, 7 October 1859

In obedience to the adorable despotism of your kindness I send you this bulletin on my wretched health. It is your wish. Very well. I can tell you that this morning I was electrocuted; an English doctor placed me between the pads of his machine. The negative and the positive pole launched into a furious battle along my sympathetic nervous system. There has been no noticeable result as yet.[1] Only I warn you all that, when we next meet, if you hold out a friendly hand to me as usual, you'll get a shock and see sparks flying from mine. It'll be the discharge of electric fluid, a positive fluid, naturally, since nothing on earth is more positive than my affection for you.

---

1 Berlioz continued electrotherapy at least until December.

The plays on words are coming back, could that be a good sign? We must hope so.

Yours most sincerely,

H. Berlioz

379 *To Princess Carolyne Sayn-Wittgenstein*   Paris, 28 October 1859

Dear Princess,

I didn't think of your departure as being so definitely fixed as to preclude the hope of seeing you today.[1] As a result, I have just been to the Hôtel du Rhin, only to find that you'd left this morning. I wanted to thank you again for all your kind words, all your encouragement, so many kind thoughts and so many charming illusions that you have been willing to share with me . . . How admirably good you are, you know how to talk to the ill and the dying and how to heal the wounded; perhaps you might even know how to bury the dead, given your ways with devoted care . . . I wish I could put your knowledge to the test. Vain knowledge, useless care! It's better to save the life of a single dolt than to bury twenty Emperors.

You want to tempt me with Cleopatra! Indeed, I think one could do something great with that subject, but also rather bitter. There's no example I know of a love more poisoned than Antony's for the Queen of Egypt. I feel that no man has ever been as wretched as that wretch after losing the battle of Actium, running away and then being callously abandoned by his infernal mistress, his Serpent of the Nile. I cannot envisage the scene of this ocean of miseries without dread. But never mind, if I regain some strength, I'll try.[2] First, though, I must work on Plouvier's opera. Do tell me what you think of that. [. . .]

H. Berlioz

380 *To his brother-in-law Marc Suat*   Paris, 25 November 1859

My dear Suat,

[. . .] You will have seen from the newspapers that I've been very busy recently with the production of Gluck's *Orphée* at the Théâtre-

---

1 The Princess spent a week in Paris at this time. Berlioz arranged a soirée at which Mme Viardot and the tenor Lefort sang several scenes from *Les Troyens*.
2 Berlioz never embarked on a Cleopatra opera.

Lyrique.[1] This masterpiece has had a triumphant success. Every evening there's a crush at the theatre door, then storms of emotion, tears, curtain calls for Mme Viardot ... The theatre is booked for six performances in advance. The entire press is wild with enthusiasm. You can imagine the good this revolution (for that's what it is) is doing me, as well as this return to ancient subjects. Did you read *Le constitutionnel*[2] last Monday and my article on Tuesday?

Carvalho (the director of the Théâtre-Lyrique) is more determined than ever to put on *Les Troyens* for the opening of his new theatre. But the cast is still lacking. Where are we to find an Aeneas or a Cassandra, if Mme Viardot plays Dido? [. . .]

Adieu, my dear Suat. I shake you by the hand and tenderly embrace all your dear people, my sister and my nieces.

H. Berlioz

381 *To Franz Liszt*   Paris, *c.*20 December 1859

Dear Liszt,

You have been struck a cruel blow;[3] you must know how much I feel for you in your sorrow. You had, I think, for some time been expecting the loss of this poor child and I know that he died without pain. But Fate, until now, had spared you; you had never experienced heartache of this kind. You were very young when you lost your father, and since then you have not endured the death of a brother, sister, child or any other loved one, and it is this inexperience of sorrow that makes me apprehensive on your behalf.

I should be glad to know that your daughters are with you in Weimar. Both of them are highly gifted in every respect. I have known them only since a year ago. A few weeks ago I spent the evening with the elder one and her husband at Wagner's house.[4]

Mme Ollivier always speaks of her father with a tender admiration which charms those who hear her. I have not seen her sister[5] so often, nonetheless I believe her to be a person of rare distinction and her devotion to you is evident in her every word.

---

1 *Orphée* opened on 18 November. Berlioz wrote about Mme Viardot's interpretation of the role in the *Débats* on 22 November.
2 An article by Fiorentino.
3 Liszt's son Daniel died on 13 December aged twenty.
4 Blandine and her husband Emile Ollivier. Wagner had recently arrived in Paris for a stay of eighteen months.
5 Cosima, Mme von Bülow.

Adieu, dear Liszt, you are surrounded by affection, let me embrace you and assure you once again of mine.

H. Berlioz

382 *To Adolphe Samuel*   Paris, 29 January 1860

My dear Samuel,

[...] I write to you rarely and laconically because I'm continually ill; my neuralgia is getting worse and allows me no respite. What's more, I'm anxious and unsettled in spirit ... My life is all on the surface, my home surroundings are exhausting, irritating, almost impossible, quite the opposite of yours. There's not a day, not an hour, when I'm not ready to risk my life and take the most desperate decisions. I say again, I am living in my thoughts and in my overwhelming affections, far from home ... I can't tell you any more.

I've signed a contract with Carvalho, by which he promises to put on *Les Troyens* in his new opera house as soon as it's built. That means another two years' delay. Meanwhile I'm constantly revising details of my score, simplifying the style and clarifying it, and I keep up the refrain 'Superanda omnis fortuna ferendo est'.[1]

Orphée continues to be a success. It's sublimely beautiful, and it's already moved me to tears on more than a score of occasions. Mme Viardot's beautiful performance is ideal for this role. Wagner has just given a concert which exasperated three quarters of the audience and enthused the rest.[2] Personally, I found a lot of it painful, even though I admired the vehemence of his musical feelings in certain instances. But the diminished sevenths, the discords and the crude modulations made me feverish, and I have to say that I find this sort of music loathsome and revolting.

Adieu, my dear Samuel, let me know your news every now and then, and never doubt my unchanging affection.

Yours sincerely,

H. Berlioz

---

1 'Destiny is to be overcome by enduring it' (*Aeneid*), the line which Berlioz inscribed on the last page of *Les Troyens*.
2 Wagner gave the first of three Paris concerts on 25 January, including the Prelude to *Tristan und Isolde*. Berlioz's article on it appeared on 9 February, after the last concert, and was reprinted in *A travers chants* in 1862.

My dear Wagner,

Although I'm still unwell, that is not what prevented me from coming to your second concert, and I can assure you it was still less a lack of interest in your compositions.[1] But I had an unbreakable appointment that evening and had to give the tickets you sent me to two ladies, both excellent musicians, who were very keen to hear you. I have not yet been able to write my article, but I'll get down to it shortly and tell you sincerely all my thoughts and impressions.

Yours ever,
H. Berlioz

384 *To Eduard Silas*[2]   Paris, 3 March 1860

My dear Silas,

I am very flattered by your wish to dedicate your oratorio to me and I gratefully accept the honour you do me.[3] But your son shouldn't have a godfather who's a long way away, that would be unrealistic. And then I neither believe in nor profess the Catholic religion, I even *protest* that I don't believe in it, so in that sense I'm a Protestant. The truth is, I'm a Nothingist, like so many excellent Americans. Only my Nothingism isn't a religion.

I can't abide any of that nonsense – philosophies, theories, beliefs, extravagances, stupidities, idiocies, japes, old wives' tales, twaddle and balderdash. I believe in nothing, I'm a sick man, I vomit them all up. Bring your son up to be truly Gallic, and let him be afraid of nothing except the sky falling on his head. In particular, let him not be afraid of God. And if, when he grows up, he falls in love with a Jewish Negress, the bastard daughter of a hangman, and wants to marry her, let him do so.

You see what a fine godfather you wanted to give him!

Adieu. Yours ever,
H. Berlioz

---

1 Wagner's second concert, on 1 February, coincided with a performance of *Orphée*.
2 A Dutch pianist and composer living in London.
3 Silas dedicated his oratorio *Joash* to Berlioz, and invited him also to be godfather to his son.

My dear Morel,

I've had good news today, but some terrible news three days ago. Your piece has had a brilliant success[1] and . . . my sister is dead.[2]

We loved each other like twins. She was a really close friend. I travelled to Vienne last week to see her again and I left with the assurance of a well-known doctor from Lyon that her convalescence would now begin. I cannot describe to you how painful this loss is to me. [. . .]

Adieu, dear Morel, I'm broken-hearted and cannot write any more.

Louis is in Vienne with his cousins and his uncle. He has borne the weight of all this fearful sorrow on his own shoulders. I'm so grateful to the poor boy for hurrying from Dieppe to support the grieving family.

Adieu, adieu, with my strong, sincere and unchanging affection,

H. Berlioz

386 *To Richard Wagner*   Paris, 23 May 1860

My dear Wagner,

I'm delighted you liked my articles on *Fidelio*.[3] I took care over writing them, but without expecting them to be the least bit helpful. I no longer believe in the idea of the public being educated by means of critical writings, or at least I think it needs a very long time for such writings to bear fruit. I don't know whether you still harbour illusions; as for me, for years now I've seen things as they are . . . You at least are full of enthusiasm, ready for the fight, whereas I am ready only to sleep and die. Even so, I still feel a twinge of feverish joy if, when I cry out in my love for what is beautiful, a voice answers me from afar and sends me, over the muttering of the mob, its supportive, friendly greeting. Thankyou then for your letter; I felt better for it. I thought you were still in Belgium.[4] Since we saw each other, I've been very ill, very miserable, and very much tormented in thousands of ways. Why, when you write, do you address me so formally as

---

1 Morel's opera *Jugement de Dieu* was played in Marseille that same day, 9 March.
2 Adèle Suat died on 2 March, aged forty-five.
3 Following the success of *Orphée*, Carvalho put on *Fidelio* at the Théâtre-Lyrique, again with Mme Viardot. It opened on 5 May. Berlioz devoted two articles to it in the *Débats*, on 19 and 22 May.
4 Wagner had just given two concerts there.

'cher maître'? There's no call for that, between us.

So yesterday was your birthday? You Germans, you pay a lot of attention to birthdays. It's true, it's an opportunity for showing family feelings, when you have a family, and friendly feelings, when you have friends. Well, you can see what sort of person I am: I have a family and I have excellent friends, but even if I had thirty birthdays a year, no one would dream of celebrating a single one of them, because they know I can't stand the idea . . . Don't laugh, I'm so unwell.

Adieu, goodbye, take heart; and no more 'cher maître'! I find it irritating. With all best wishes,

Yours sincerely,
Hector Berlioz

387 *To François-Joseph Fétis*   Paris, 22 July 1860

My dear Monsieur Fétis,

I have just read the article about me in your *Biographie des musiciens*.[1] May I thank you for the obvious goodwill with which you wrote it? I very much appreciate it and am sorry not to be able to come to Brussels to shake you by the hand.

What's more, it's so well written, and I'm such a lover of stylish prose, that I read your six columns with a pleasure in which the satisfaction of my *amour-propre* played no part whatever. You have committed only one insignificant error of fact, and another of opinion, when you claim that I have less regard for *La damnation de Faust* than for my other works. This score is, on the contrary, one of the ones I like best, and if I have performed it in Paris less often than the others, it's not for any artistic reason but for an economic one. Rehearsing the choruses for this work is too long a job and *costs too much*. Furthermore I couldn't find in Paris the tenor who is vital for the role of Faust. The performances of *La damnation de Faust* in Dresden, Weimar, Berlin, St Petersburg, Moscow and London have all been extremely happy occasions for me, even though I've never been able to find *the tenor* in those cities either.

There's just one further observation I have to make: the piece you mention under the title *Concert de sylphes* was not based on any programme; it was part of various scenes from Goethe's *Faust* which I

---

1 Fétis's article on Berlioz in the first edition of his dictionary (1837) was ample but reserved and inaccurate. For the second edition, in 1860, Fétis provided a much fuller and more sympathetic entry.

composed (*very badly*) some thirty-five years ago.[1] As the public in those days was not very familiar with the German poem, it's possible (I can't remember) that I may have issued some explanations about the subject of this piece, as is often done for extracts from certain operas which are unknown to the public. In that case I would not have written my music to a programme, but a programme to my music.

I should be happy to have an opportunity of talking to you about the art which we both love and respect so much. The only people I see love or hate depending on whether the wind of their passions, their prejudices or their interests is blowing in one direction or another. I am ill and very gloomy, and the bright gleams of your intelligence would no doubt dissipate the clouds which loom over mine. But then ... we do very little of what we should like to, and most of the time for reasons different from those the world imagines.

In any case, allow me to ask for a small measure of your friendship. As for your esteem, I have always had it, I think; you know that *I love music with a love that is noble.*

Yours most sincerely,
Hector Berlioz

388 *To his son Louis Berlioz*   Paris, 23 October 1860

I've received your two letters with details in the first one about your next position. It's better than I'd expected. With 200 francs a month, plus board and lodging (because your ship is your house when you're at sea), you'll be quite comfortably off. But you don't say what guarantee you have of being a second lieutenant. 'When I've set sail', you say, 'I shall have everything.' Who has been able to tell you anything positive about this? You've left me completely in the dark about it. Try and follow the diet when your stomach pains strike; it seems to be the best way of dealing with them.

Yesterday I worked for seven hours on a little one-act piece I've begun; I don't know if I mentioned it to you.[2] It's very attractive, but very difficult to set properly. There's a lot of work still to be done on the libretto; it so rarely happens that I can think about it at any length.

---

1 The *Huit scènes de Faust* of 1829.
2 Berlioz lost interest in Plouvier's libretto the previous winter (it was set by Litolff instead). During his summer visit to Baden-Baden in August 1860 Bénazet reiterated his commission since Berlioz offered to write a one-act *opéra comique* on *Much Ado About Nothing*, eventually entitled *Béatrice et Bénédict* and eventually in two acts. He began it in October 1860.

Then it'll be the music's turn. No news about *Les Troyens*, except that the Théâtre-Lyrique is getting nearer and nearer bankruptcy, while its new auditorium is being built. I wish the catastrophe was already over; then we should have a new administration that was less unlucky and less tactless than the present one. So you heard the finale of *La vestale*? You say the 'duet', but you're wrong. The phrase you quote in your letter comes from the finale, unless the people in Marseille made a potpourri of the two. [. . .]

389 *To his niece Nanci Suat*[1]   Paris, 28 November 1860

My dear Nanci,

[. . .] I've just sent Louis the news that he has a place in the Messageries Impériales; he'll get his nomination next Saturday, the Director General has just informed me. So poor Louis is finally settled in a firm career (even though the sea is its field of action).

Nothing new here, my dear Nanci, we're still just about as disagreeably unwell as ever. I'm working hard and go out as little as possible. I'm writing a one-act opera[2] (I don't know if I told you), a charming piece of frivolity . . .

I'm correcting piles of proofs of *Les Troyens*.[3] I write an article every now and then. I shall have one to write towards the end of this week on a poor work by a *poor*, very ambitious composer, who also has the misfortune to be a 'jettatore', that's to say to have the evil eye, to bring bad luck.[4] Everyone avoids him like the plague. This wretched fellow has also written a ballet which was put on the day before yesterday at the Opéra,[5] and the members of the audience were wearing *horns made of coral* to ward off the *jettatura*. It was known that at his rehearsal at the Opéra-Comique the other day, at the moment he entered the theatre a stage-hand fell and broke his thigh. Three days later, at his rehearsal of the ballet at the Opéra, a dancer was almost burnt alive when the gauze of her dress caught fire, and the librettist, M. de St-Georges, was also badly burnt coming to her aid. Finally, on the evening of the first performance, Mlle Livry, who was dancing the principal role, hurt her foot. I've never seen anything so funny as all

1 The younger daughter of Berlioz's sister Adèle, born in 1842.
2 *Béatrice et Bénédict*.
3 Berlioz had begun in September to have the vocal score engraved at his own expense.
4 The poor composer was Offenbach, whose *Barkouf* was played at the Opéra-Comique on 24 December.
5 The ballet was *Le papillon*.

these people who believe in the *jettatura*. The poor devil whom they're all avoiding in terror is even funnier.

How is Joséphine, and how is she behaving? You travelled to Tournon together, didn't you? Did you discover a new island on the journey? A savage, unknown tribe? A mine of gold, or silver, or merely copper? A diamond the size of an egg? Or some curious trifle? You'll let me know.

Adieu, my dear little niece.

I embrace your sister so that she can embrace you on my behalf.

All best wishes to your father.

H. Berlioz

390 *To his son Louis Berlioz*   Paris, 14 February 1861

Dear Louis,

Thank you for your letter which I had been looking forward to every day. But I'm upset by the state of mind I see you in; I don't know what dreams you've been cherishing to make you unhappy with your present position. All I can tell you is that at your age I was far from being as well treated by fate as you are.

More than that; I didn't expect that when you were appointed captain you would have even a modest post so soon. Your impatience to get on is perfectly natural, but it's exaggerated. You need to have this said to you again and again. A year sometimes leads to more unexpected changes in a man's life than ten years of feverish efforts.

What can I say to persuade you to be patient? You're bothering your head over fancies, and your matrimoniomania would make me laugh if it weren't so sad to see you hankering so passionately after the heaviest chain a man can bear and the burdens and tribulations of a ménage which are the most depressing and also the most exasperating things I know. At twenty-six you have a salary of 1800 francs and the possibility of rapid advancement. I, when I married your mother, was thirty. I had nothing but 300 francs lent me by my friend Gounet and the remainder of my Prix de Rome scholarship which had only eighteen months still to run. Apart from that nothing except a debt incurred by your mother of around 14,000 francs (which I paid off gradually). From time to time I had to send money to her mother, who was living in England, and I'd quarrelled with my family, who didn't want to hear my name mentioned. And in the middle of all these trials I had to make the first opening for myself in the world of music. Compare, just for a moment, what I had to suffer then with the situation you find so unsatisfactory today.

As for the present, do you think it is amusing to be forcibly tied to this infernal chain of writing articles which colours the whole of my existence? I'm so ill that the pen constantly falls out of my hand, but even so I have to steel myself to write in order to earn my miserable hundred francs and keep my position defended against an army of blackguards who would destroy me if they weren't so frightened. And my head is full of projects and ideas which I can't realize because of this bondage! Your health is good, while I am racked from morning till night with endless pain for which there is no cure.

For the last month I've been unable to find a single day to work on my score of *Béatrice*. Luckily I have plenty of time in which to finish it. I went and read the libretto to M. Bénazet, who appeared delighted. This opera is to be put on at Baden-Baden, then, in the new theatre. The fate of *Les Troyens* remains uncertain. I had a long talk a week ago with the Minister of State on this subject. I told him all the plotting I'd been the victim of. He asked to be shown my libretto. I took it along next day and since then I've had no news. Public opinion is becoming more and more indignant at seeing me left out at the Opéra when the protection of the Austrian ambassador's wife has allowed Wagner to be let in so easily.[1]

Meanwhile the engraving of my score goes slowly on: it probably won't be finished inside the next three months. I don't know whether I told you that I'd just written a double chorus for two nations each singing in its own language.[2] It's for the French choral singers who are going over in June to make a second visit to the singers in London; the English will sing in English and the French in French. They're already rehearsing the French chorus here and all these young people are in a state of wild enthusiasm which I should be only too happy to see continue until the performance. It'll be a curiosity, a duet sung in the Crystal Palace by eight or ten thousand men, but I shan't be going to hear it. I haven't the money to spare on pleasure jaunts.[3]

The Société des Concerts du Conservatoire, so I've been told, is going to ask my permission to play a fragment of *La damnation de Faust* at one of its forthcoming sessions. As it won't cost them anything, it'll come off.[4]

---

1 At the urging of Princess Metternich, wife of the Austrian ambassador, Napoleon III gave orders for *Tannhäuser* to be staged at the Opéra. It opened, after many postponements, on 13 March.
2 *Le temple universel* on a text (in French) by J.-F. Vaudin.
3 The mass visit to London did not take place and the work was not performed.
4 Four excerpts were played on 7 April.

That's how things stand at the moment. Marie thanks you for your kind wishes; she too is constantly ill.

I've had no more news from over there than you have. Every man for himself and God for no one, as the proverb so truly says. But you at least have a father, a friend, a comrade and a devoted brother who loves you more than you seem to realize, but who would be happy to see your character growing more solid and becoming more clear-sighted.

391 *To his son Louis Berlioz*   Paris, 21 February 1861

Dear Louis,

[...] The duet for the two national choruses is finished; it's being rehearsed in Paris and London. At the Opéra Wagner is turning the singers, chorus and orchestra upside down. They can't get round this *Tannhäuser* music. The last dress rehearsal was apparently atrocious and didn't finish until one o'clock in the morning. They'll have to get through it, though. Liszt is due to arrive to support the partisans of this circus.[1] I shan't write the article on *Tannhäuser*, I've asked d'Ortigue to do it. It's a better idea in every respect and will be more of a disappointment to them. Never have I had so many windmills to battle against as I have this year. I'm surrounded by fools of every complexion. There are times when my anger suffocates me.

Adieu, I must try and get on my feet and go out. If I can't, I'll come back and go to bed.

392 *To his son Louis Berlioz*   Paris, 21 March 1861

Dear Louis,

I don't know whether this note will reach you. I'm writing to you even so to wish you a safe journey and to embrace you before you leave. I'm taking advantage of a moment's solitude in the jury room.[2] This jury session is an abominable burden for me. This morning I had such an effort getting out of bed that I was overcome by vomiting. At the moment I'm feeling better. The second performance of *Tannhäuser* was worse than the first. There wasn't so much laughter; the audience was furious, and the whistling was enough to bring the house down, despite the presence of the Emperor and Empress in their box. The

1 Liszt did not in the end arrive in time for the performances.
2 Berlioz was serving on a jury set up to examine military bandmasters.

Emperor finds it entertaining. On the stairs, after the performance, poor Wagner was being treated as a scoundrel, an upstart and an idiot. If they go on like this, one of these days the performance will come to a halt and that will be the end of it all.[1] The press are unanimous in wanting to exterminate it. For my part, I am cruelly avenged.

393 *To his son Louis Berlioz*   Paris, 2 June 1861

[. . .] The rehearsals of *Der Freischütz* have been abandoned.[2] I've had a month wasted. As compensation I've been asked to put on *Alceste*, as I did *Orphée* at the Théâtre-Lyrique, retaining full author's rights; for musical reasons it would take too long to explain, I've refused. Those people think that by means of money they can persuade artists to do things in direct opposition to their conscience; I've just proved to them that this idea is false.[3]

Les Troyens has definitely been accepted by the Opéra. But Gounod and Gevaert have to have their turn before me; that'll take two years.[4] Gounod has walked over the body of Gevaert, who was due to be performed first. And neither of them is ready, whereas I could go into rehearsal tomorrow. Gounod can't be performed until March 1862 at the earliest.

My determined refusal to put on *Alceste* is causing a stir and upsetting a lot of people. They'd do better not to enjoy themselves wasting time and money insulting a masterpiece by Gluck but to put on *Les Troyens* right away. But as that is what's indicated by common sense, that's what will not happen. Liszt has just made a conquest of the Emperor: he played at court last week, and yesterday he was made a Commandeur de la Légion d'Honneur. Ah, when one plays the piano! . . .

I haven't yet finished my score of *Béatrice*; I can so rarely get down to work on it. Even so, it's progressing gradually.

1 There were only three performances, and in May Wagner left Paris for the last time.
2 In April, after the *Tannhäuser* débâcle, the Opéra proposed a revival of *Der Freischütz* with Berlioz's recitatives, originally mounted in 1841, but the plan was soon dropped.
3 Berlioz's role in the revival of Gluck's *Alceste* at the Opéra is not entirely clear. Despite his public refusal to be the 'arranger' of the opera for Mme Viardot's voice, he in fact edited the score and supervised the performances.
4 The operas which had precedence over Berlioz's were Gounod's *La reine de Saba*, which was still unfinished, and an opera by Gevaert that was never composed at all.

So you're back, you vagabonds! You think of nothing but running, jumping, flying, leaping, roaming, wandering and climbing! Heavens above, what wild legs and indefatigable brains!

To make you sensible, serious, solid and immobile it is imperative that your father brings you to Baden-Baden in August, because once there you'll never want to leave. It's a garden, an oasis, a paradise, and just for you we shall be performing some great music *on 26 August*. It's only a short journey from Plombières, and staying there is no more expensive than elsewhere.

If you're fond of flowers, that's the country, they're everywhere. And what mountains and ruins! What donkey rides! What lunches at the goat farm (where there are seventy white goats) and in addition a whole society of Parisians, Russians, Italians and Germans who will be asking me to introduce them to you.

And sulphur baths which restore one's health in five minutes!

It's agreed, you're coming! You must let me know when you're arriving and we'll meet you off the train. There'll be balls to make you gasp in wonder; when M. Bénazet finds out that my nieces and my brother-in-law are in Baden-Baden, he'll be sure to invite them. Likewise to the dramatic offerings in the Salle Louis XV, where the temperature is 48 degrees. But you will brave the heat. If you don't come, I shan't write to you again for another sixty years.[1]

Adieu, and I look forward to seeing all three of you soon. I embrace you with all my heart.

H. Berlioz

395 *To Humbert Ferrand*   Paris, 6 July 1861

You're right, my dear Humbert, I ought to have written to you despite your long silence, as I knew from Penet[2] the effort it costs you to pen the briefest letter. But I have to tell you that I too am racked by a persistent intestinal neuralgia. Some days I can't manage to write ten consecutive lines. Now it sometimes takes me four days to finish an article. I'm in less pain today and will take advantage of the fact to answer your questions.

---

1 To Berlioz's disappointment the Suats did not go to Baden-Baden.
2 A childhood friend of Berlioz's, now a lawyer.

Yes, *Les Troyens* has been accepted at the Opéra *by the director*; but the production depends now on the Minister of State. As it happens, although Count Walewski has been very gracious and well-disposed towards me, he is at the moment very displeased because I've refused to direct the rehearsals of *Alceste* at the Opéra. I've declined this honour because of the transpositions and alterations that have had to be made so that Mme Viardot can sing the role. Such practices are irreconcilable with the views I have held all my life. But ministers, and especially today's ministers, don't really understand such artistic scruples and won't accept for an instant that one of their wishes should be thwarted. So for the moment I'm unpopular at court. Not that that prevents the whole musical world in Paris and Germany from agreeing with me. I'll do no more than go to a few rehearsals and give instructions to the producer, to show the minister I'm not putting up any opposition. The director thinks this show of compliance will be enough to assuage Count Walewski's ill-humour.

The first production is to be a five-act opera by Gounod (which is not finished), then another by Gevaert (a little-known Belgian composer), after which work will probably begin on *Les Troyens*. Public opinion and the press are so firmly on my side that there are no real grounds for resistance. In any case, I've made an important change to the first act to fit in with the wishes of Royer (the director). The work is now down to the dimensions he wanted to reduce it to; I was not the least inflexible in the situation arising from this incident.[1] All I can do now is fold my arms and wait until my two rivals have had their turn.

I've made up my mind not to torture myself any longer. I no longer run after fortune, I wait for it in bed.

Even so I couldn't help making a somewhat over-frank reply to the Empress when she asked me, a few weeks ago at the Tuileries, when she would be able to hear *Les Troyens*: 'I couldn't say, Madame, but I'm beginning to think one has to live to be a hundred to be performed at the Opéra.'

One tiresome and unhelpful thing about these delays is that the work acquires an advance reputation which may detract from its success. I've given a few readings of the libretto here and there; two months ago fragments of the score were given at the house of M. Edouard Bertin;[2] there's been a good deal of talk about it. That worries me.

In the meantime I'm having the vocal score engraved, not to publish

---

1 Berlioz removed a complete scene, involving the Greek spy Sinon, from Act I.
2 Son of Armand Bertin and proprietor of the *Journal des débats*.

it, but so that it'll be ready when the work is staged. Do you know who I've dedicated it to? I was sent the title-page yesterday. At the head of it stand the two words: *Divo Virgilio.*

I assure you, dear Humbert, it's written stylishly, on a large scale but simply. I mean the style of the *music*. It would be the greatest pleasure for me to be able to let you hear at least a few scenes. But how?

For the moment the question is which of the ladies from the Olympus of song will be given the role of Cassandra or that of Dido; the roles of Aeneas and Chorebus mean that I'm surrounded by tenors and baritones.

I'm gradually finishing a one-act *opéra comique* for the new theatre in Baden-Baden, which they're putting the finishing touches to at the moment. I've carved this act for myself out of Shakespeare's tragicomedy called *Much Ado About Nothing.*

It's sensibly entitled *Béatrice et Bénédict.* In any case, I maintain there isn't much *ado*. Bénazet (the king of Baden-Baden) is having it produced next year (if I think that's the right moment, which isn't certain). We shall have singers from Paris and Strasbourg. It needs a woman with so much spirit about her to play Beatrice! Will we find her in Paris? . . .

I leave for Baden-Baden a month from now to organize and conduct the annual festival there. This time I'm unleashing two movements from the *Requiem* on them, the *Tuba mirum* and the *Offertoire*. I'd like to allow myself this pleasure; and then there's no harm in getting all those rich idlers to give an occasional thought to death . . .

396 To Humbert Ferrand   Paris, 14 July 1861

Dear Humbert,

[. . .] An American entrepreneur has suggested engaging me for the Disunited States this year.[1] But his offers have come to nothing in the face of antipathies I'm unable to overcome and a lack of keenness in my appreciation of money. I don't know whether your love for this great people and its *utilitarian* attitudes is a good deal stronger than mine . . . I doubt it.

In any case, it would be the height of folly for me to leave Paris for a year. I might be asked for *Les Troyens* at any moment. If some serious

---

1 News of the opening engagements of the Civil War had been reaching Europe since April. The impresario was probably Max Maretzek, manager of the Italian Opera Company in New York.

upset occurred at the Opéra, they'd have to turn to me. It would be wrong of me to be elsewhere.

Adieu, dear Humbert; I shake you by the hand.

Your devoted,

H. Berlioz

397 *To Richard Pohl*[1]   Baden-Baden, 28 August 1861

My dear Pohl,

Liszt told me you were wanting a triangle;[2] here's one made by Sax which has just been used for the first time here in the introduction to *Harold*. It's made in the image of God, like all triangles, but better than any other triangles, better than God, come to that, it plays true.

Yours ever,

Hector Berlioz

398 *To his niece Nanci Suat*   Paris, 1 October 1861

Dear Nanci,

You don't know why I haven't replied to you? It's because I was told by Mme Delaroche that you had said to her: 'My uncle won't reply to me!' So I couldn't prove you wrong by replying immediately and turn you into a slanderess, a niece without reverence.

And then also I've had much work and much pain. Now you're back under the paternal roof, with the prospect of a winter in Vienne!! You must realize, not everyone can live in Tahiti or Japan; paradises on earth are not made for us Europeans.

And you, Joséphine, as a philosopher, what do you think?

Even so, there are still fine places and fine days to be found near Paris, on M. Delaroche's country estate, for example, where we often go.[3] Marie's there at the moment, busy gathering grapes. I came back the day before yesterday. I should have come back the day before by the nine o'clock train, but I was overcome by laziness and preferred to spend the night in the country.

How lucky I did! M. and Mme Arban[4] and their pretty little daughter Valentine were with us at St-Germain and decided to leave.

1 German art critic and disciple of Liszt and Berlioz.
2 The, triangle was needed by von Bülow, who was planning performances of *Harold en Italie* in Leipzig and Berlin.
3 In St-Germain-en-Laye, west of Paris.
4 Arban was the leading cornettist of his day, see p. 351.

But on the way down from Le Vésinet the train was derailed and everybody was killed except two dogs! Well, I exaggerate slightly, no one was killed, but the Arban family and many others had to remain on the track until two o'clock in the morning. [. . .]

Adieu, dear niece. Embrace your father and embrace each other for me.
H. Berlioz

399 *To his son Louis Berlioz*   Paris, 28 October 1861

Dear Louis,

If I didn't know what a dreadful influence unhappiness can have on the finest characters, I should be able to answer you with some melancholy truths; you have wounded me to the heart, painfully and with a cool deliberation that is evident from your choice of words. But I forgive and embrace you; you are not a bad son, despite everything. Anyone who read your letter without knowing anything of our two positions in the world would think that I was without *real affection* for you, that people say *you aren't my son*; that I could have found, and still *could* find you a *better position, if I wanted to*, that I am wrong not to encourage you to *come to Paris* and look for A JOB, and leave the one you have; and that I have *humiliated* you by comparing you with some hero out of Béranger that you refer to. Come now, frankly and without wanting to resort to recrimination, you've gone too far, and I feel sad in a way I never have before. Honestly, is it my fault if I'm not rich, if I don't have the wherewithal to allow you to live a life of peace and leisure in Paris with your wife and child, or children, if you have others?[1] . . . Is there a shred of justice in such a reproach? You sent a letter to me in Baden-Baden in the middle of August; since then, not a word. You've let me go for two and a half months without knowing what was happening to you; Alexis[2] didn't know either. And now you write sarcastic remarks. Ah! poor dear Louis, it's not good.

Don't worry about what you owe your tailor; the bill will be paid when I receive it. If you want me to pay off this debt before then, send me the tailor's address and I will go and deal with it. It's true I thought you were younger; are you going to put it down as a crime that I haven't got a memory for dates? Do I know how old my father, my mother, my sisters and my brother were when they died? Are we to

1 The inference of this remark is very unclear; a woman in Le Havre later claimed to have had a child by Louis, with the fascinating possibility of a direct line of descent from the composer. It is not clear what the cause of Louis's recriminations against his father was.
2 Alexis Berchtschold, Louis's friend in Paris.

conclude from that that I didn't love them? Really . . . But I sound as though I'm justifying myself. Yes, I repeat, unhappiness is making you delirious, and that is why I can only love you and pity you more. You talk of my putting in a word for you, but with whom? And to obtain what? You know perfectly well there's nobody clumsier than I am at putting in words for people. Tell me precisely what I can do and I'll do it. [. . .]

I embrace you with all my heart and await your news by the next post.

H. Berlioz

400 *To Auguste de Gasperini*[1]   Paris, 10 November 1861

My dear Gasperini,

I have just read your article in *Le ménestrel* on the concerts given last week and was surprised to find this sentence:[2] 'I shall always be sorry that the *Invitation à la valse*, as orchestrated by Berlioz, stops before the Andante which concludes this beautiful piece by Weber. I do not know whether Berlioz omitted this final section of the waltz deliberately with a view to making an effect in the concert hall, but I very much doubt it,' etc.

Well, there should have been no question of doubt. You're not one of those who could possibly believe me capable of a lack of respect for a beautiful work and a great master in the puerile interests of what, in France and Italy, is called *effect*. I orchestrated Weber's piece as it stands, without omitting a single bar. This is clear from the engraved orchestral parts, as used everywhere, and when I have had the opportunity to conduct this delightful and characterful fantasy in France, England and Germany, the final Andante has never been omitted.

Yours ever,

Hector Berlioz

401 *To his niece Joséphine Suat*   Paris, 27 November 1861

Dear Joséphine,

[. . .] There was a large festival at the Opéra the other day, for which I was asked to provide a piece (the *Fête* from *Roméo et Juliette*).[3] I was

1 Music critic of *La France musicale*, *Le ménestrel* and *Le Figaro*, Gasperini was an ardent champion of both Berlioz and Wagner.
2 The concert was given by Pasdeloup in his Concerts Populaires.
3 A concert for the benefit of retired Opéra employees on 23 November.

given an ovation at the dress rehearsal. Next day at the concert, four blackguards came and *hissed* the piece, which provoked the whole audience and the 400 performers who filled the stage to protest in my favour. Everyone's talking about it, and it shows the furious hatreds to which I am now prey. Deliberately to choose a stirring piece like that, which is nearly always encored everywhere it's performed, in Germany, in England, and even at the Paris Conservatoire! So much for the fruits of criticism.[1] They're capable of sending emissaries to Baden-Baden next year to whistle at the first performance of my *Béatrice*. [. . .]

I embrace you all,

H. Berlioz

402 *To his brother-in-law Camille Pal*   Paris, 4 February 1862

My dear Camille,

[. . .] I should be very happy to be able to come and shake you by the hand and spend some days in your company; we would gossip like one-eyed magpies. But to find a way of leaving Paris! I'm busy at the moment with preliminary rehearsals of my two-act opera for the inauguration of the theatre in Baden-Baden.[2] It'll be performed on either the 5th or the 8th of this coming August. Bénazet, as always, has been the perfect gentleman; he asked me which actors I wanted, I gave him the list and he has engaged them all. The chorus will come from Strasbourg. God knows the money that involves, and for two performances! The Strasbourg theatre wants to put this little work on after Baden-Baden, but I doubt whether it'll be able to.

As for Paris, that's not in my thoughts, I can't take the smallest risk in the theatre until my great ship is launched, which is due to happen, so they say at the Opéra, in thirteen months' time (in March 1863). The minister is still as supportive as can be. I think I told you that he wrote a very gracious letter thanking me for producing *Alceste* and conducting the rehearsals of this wonderful masterpiece. [. . .]

Your sincerely,

H. Berlioz

1 Berlioz refers to his own work as a critic and the many enemies it made.
2 *Béatrice et Bénédict* was complete, except for the overture then in progress.

My dear Morel,

Be good enough to give me news of Louis. Has he sailed for the Indies? What I expected has come about: he hasn't written me a line. I can't say anything on this subject that you haven't guessed a long time ago, but I admit the unhappiness is one of the bitterest I've ever felt. I write in the middle of one of those abominable articles which defy all one's efforts. I'm trying to give a little support to this wretched Gounod who has just had the worst fiasco ever seen.[1] There's nothing in his score, absolutely nothing. How does one support something which has no bones or muscles? All the same, I have to find something to praise. The libretto is beneath everything. It hasn't a glimmer of interest or common sense. And it's his third fiasco at the Opéra.[2] No doubt he'll go on to a fourth! Nobody any more writes dozens of operas ... that are *good*. Paisiello wrote a hundred and seventy of them; but what operas! And what's left of them now?[3]

In the field of the symphony Mozart wrote seventeen, of which three are good, and how! Only good old Haydn wrote a large quantity of *attractive* things in this medium. Beethoven wrote seven masterpieces. But Beethoven isn't a man. And when one is only a man, one mustn't set oneself up as a god. [...]

Adieu.

Your devoted

H. Berlioz

Dear Louis,

You will have received a telegram and, this morning, a letter from me.[4] I'm writing to you again this morning to tell you that I'm managing fairly well some of the time and that there's no necessity for you to come. My nieces have also offered to come. But I feel it's better for the moment if I remain on my own. What I should like would be for you to come and see me in Baden-Baden on 6 or 7 August; I know you

1 *La reine de Saba* opened at the Opéra on 28 February.
2 *Sapho* (1851) and *La nonne sanglante* (1854) – in a version of the Scribe libretto Berlioz had abandoned – had both failed there.
3 Berlioz's estimate of Paisiello's operas is about twice too high.
4 Berlioz's wife Marie died on 13 June 1862 in St-Germain while visiting the Delaroches. Henceforth Berlioz was cared for, for the rest of his life, by his mother-in-law.

would also enjoy being present at the final rehearsals and the first performance of my opera. At least, you could keep me company in between my periods of forced activity; I could introduce you to my friends, in short we should be together. The question is whether you'll be able safely to leave your ship when it's just about to sail. You could be on your way back to Marseille on 11 August, as the first performance takes place on the 9th.

I don't know, either, what money I shall have available to send you; the expenses of the melancholy ceremony bringing her body from St-Germain are considerable and I don't yet know what they will be. And then I'm nervous of getting you to come to that city of gambling and gamblers.[1] But provided you give me your word of honour not to risk so much as a florin, I'll trust you and resign myself to the pain of our separation when you leave for your ship: a pain which will be all the sharper under these new circumstances. Tell me what you think on the subject.

Adieu, dear Louis. Yesterday my mother-in-law came back from a visit to St-Germain. Seeing that I didn't arrive for dinner on Tuesday, she suspected something was wrong. She arrived there when M. and Mme Delaroche and I had just left, only to find her daughter a corpse ... Since then she's remained there half out of her mind and has been looked after by one of her friends who came to comfort her, and I hadn't seen her again. You can imagine the distressing scene there was when we did.

Write to me, dearest Louis.
H. Berlioz

405 *To Emile Deschamps*   Paris, 19 June 1862

Thank you, my dear Deschamps, for your kind letter. Yes, it has been a terrible blow. She was prepared for this death, but I was very far from being so. I'm not sure how I shall manage life now on my own. My friends are my only hope. You have just proved to me that I am not mistaken in counting on them. As soon as I can, I shall come and see you, because I know that you too are on your own and, what's more, ill and in pain.

Yours in friendship and gratitude,
H. Berlioz

1 Baden-Baden.

Dear Princess,

Your kind and friendly letter made me almost happy for a few hours. The trouble is, these clear intervals don't last. I am nonetheless profoundly grateful for all your comforting words. Like you, I possess one of the theological virtues, Charity, but I do not, as you do, possess the other two.

The insoluble enigma of the world, the existence of evil and pain, the furious madness of the human race, and its stupid ferocity which it slakes by turning it at all times and places upon the most inoffensive of mortals and upon itself, these have reduced me to the glum, despairing resignation of the scorpion surrounded by burning coals. All I can do is refrain from wounding myself with my own sting.

And then I suffer physically, every day, from seven in the morning to four in the afternoon, so terribly that during these crises my thoughts are in complete confusion.

That is what prevented me from writing to you yesterday; I was quite incapable of doing so. You can imagine whether or not I can think of composing in any continuous fashion . . .

You ask how it is that you know nothing of the existence of this two-act opera we are putting on in Baden-Baden. The reason is that it's a long time since I wrote to you.

I couldn't bring myself to set to music the full-scale melodrama that you read,[1] so, as I wanted to give Bénazet proof of my goodwill, I took as my text a part of Shakespeare's tragi-comedy *Much Ado About Nothing* and musical ideas came in due order, but at long intervals, again because of my infernal neuralgia. These intervals of forced inactivity were so long and so frequent that when it came to the first rehearsals I made, as it were, the acquaintance of music of which I no longer had the smallest recollection. It's going well, and Beatrice and Benedict jeer and nibble at each other gracefully. There's also the sentimental couple, Hero and Claudio, who make an excellent contrast with the other two. In addition to the roles provided by Shakespeare, I've invented a musical caricature, a grotesque choirmaster called Somarone ('fat ass') whose asininities are ridiculous. I'd give a lot to be able to let you hear them. Best of all is the final scherzo, in which the characters of the two principals are summed up and which makes a curious effect. [. . .]

1 Plouvier's libretto on the Thirty Years War.

It's taken time to train the singers, now I shall have a hard time training the orchestra, because it's a caprice written with the point of a needle and has to be played with extreme delicacy.

Adieu, dear Princess, I'll keep you informed as to how it's received in performance.

The score of *Les Troyens*[1] was sent to Liszt yesterday.

Yours sincerely,

H. Berlioz

---

407 *To his son Louis Berlioz*   Baden-Baden, 10 August 1862

Dear Louis,

A great success! *Béatrice* was applauded from beginning to end, and I was recalled I don't know how many times.[2] All my friends are delighted. Personally, I remained impervious to the whole business; it was one of my painful days, and I couldn't bring myself to care about anything.

Today I'm feeling better and I'm very pleased to see the friends who are coming to congratulate me. Mme Charton-Demeur was the epitome of charm, and Montaubry gave us an elegant and refined Benedict. The duet, which you know, was sung by Mlle Montrose and Mme Geoffroy with pretty scenery and moonlight very successfully evoked by the lighting technician, and it made an astonishing impact; they wouldn't stop clapping. So I embrace you, I'm sure you're pleased. But it's been a long time since you wrote. Why are they moving you from ship to ship like this? I'll try and get back to Paris within the next few days, so don't write to me any more at Baden-Baden.

I've no time to do more than embrace you: I'm besieged from all quarters. I must go and thank my actors, who are also in a state of exhilaration.

---

408 *To Humbert Ferrand*   Paris, 21 August 1862

My dear Humbert,

I'm back from Baden-Baden where my opera *Béatrice et Bénédict* has just had a huge success. The French, Belgian and German press are unanimous in its praise. For better or worse, I still can't wait to tell you

---

1 The vocal score, of which fifteen copies were printed.
2 The first performance of *Béatrice et Bénédict* took place on 9 August, with a second on 11 August. Mme Charton-Demeur sang the role of Beatrice.

about it, certain as I am of the affectionate interest with which you will receive the news. Unfortunately you weren't there; the performance would have reminded you of *L'enfance du Christ*. The cliques and detractors stayed in Paris. Instead, a large number of writers and musicians had made the journey. The performance, with myself conducting, was excellent and Mme Charton-Demeur especially (as Beatrice) had some splendid moments as a singer and as an actress. But, believe it or not, my neuralgia was so bad that day that I couldn't take any interest in anything, and I mounted the rostrum, before an audience of Russians, Germans and Frenchmen, to conduct the first performance of an opera for which I had written both the words and the music, without feeling the slightest emotion. This bizarre sang-froid meant that I conducted better than usual. I was much more nervous at the second performance.

Bénazet always does things on a grand scale, and he spent enormous sums on costumes, scenery, actors and chorus for this opera. He was determined to make the inauguration of the new theatre a splendid occasion. It's made a huge splash here. They'd like to put *Béatrice* on at the Opéra-Comique, but there's no Beatrice. The Paris theatres don't have a woman capable of singing and acting the part, and Mme Charton is leaving for America.

You'd laugh if you could read the idiotically favourable notices given me by the critics. They've discovered that I can write melodies, that I can write happy music, even comic music. It's the story of the surprises caused by *L'enfance du Christ* all over again. They realized I wasn't a *noise*-maker when they saw that the more brutal instruments had been omitted from the orchestra. How patient I should need to be, if I weren't so apathetic!

Dear Humbert, I'm a martyr to pain *every* day now, from four in the morning until four in the afternoon. How will it end? I say this not to lend you patience for your own sufferings; I'm well aware that mine won't be any compensation for you. I cry out to you as one is always tempted to cry out to those one loves and by whom one is loved in return.

Adieu, adieu.

Hector Berlioz

409 To Vladimir Vasilyevich Stasov[1]   Paris, 10 September 1862

Monsieur,

I have, fortunately, found one of my manuscripts in reasonably good condition, and I am happy to be able to offer it to the Public Library of St Petersburg; it is, indeed, that of the *Te Deum* which you mentioned to me. If you would be good enough to do me the honour of a second visit tomorrow, Thursday, at midday, I will let you have it.[2]

At the time I wrote it, I had faith and hope; today no other virtue is left to me except resignation. I am nonetheless deeply grateful for the sympathy shown me by true friends of art, such as yourself.

Yours most sincerely,
Hector Berlioz

410 To Princess Carolyne Sayn-Wittgenstein   Paris,
21 September 1862
Still 4, Rue de Calais

Dear Princess,

Yes, I must seem to you decidedly neglectful and ungrateful; but then, a change of address, a house that threatens to fall down,[3] a great lad of twenty-eight who has left the navy and has moved in with me until he finds what he calls a 'position', a whole host of unbearable and expensive *business* matters and periodic recurrences of my neuralgia, together with the composition of two scenes I've added to the second act of *Béatrice*,[4] and finally the fear of boring you . . .

First of all, I must ask you for news of Liszt. How is he, how has he weathered the blow he has just received?[5] It's heart-rending! Now it's his turn; death is striking everywhere. The poor young woman used to idolize her father! Is it true that he's taken up religious ideas again? If so, so much the better, he'll be stronger in the face of the torments and tempests of this world. As for me, I'm simply not in a state to be able to respond to the kindly, comforting arguments which your good nature

---

1 Russian critic and principal polemicist for the 'Five'. He was librarian of the St Petersburg Imperial Library.
2 The autograph of the *Te Deum* is still today is St Petersburg, the only substantial Berlioz manuscript (apart from those of the *Messe solennelle* and *Le roi Lear*) outside Paris.
3 Berlioz had to move temporarily while his apartment was being repaired.
4 On his return from Baden-Baden Berlioz composed two extra numbers for Act II of *Béatrice et Bénédict*, the *Trio* and the *Chœur lointain*. Printing of the vocal score was held up while he completed them.
5 Liszt's daughter Blandine Ollivier died at St-Tropez on 11 September aged twenty-six.

and your lofty spirit have persuaded you to put to me. As you know, I
have for a long time nursed a hatred of philosophy and everything that
resembles it, whether it's religious philosophy or not; and if such
thoughts could make me weep, my eyes (as Shakespeare said) would
bring forth nothing but millstones.[1] [. . .]

Now, I have finished. Yesterday I wrote the last note of an orchestral
score to sully a piece of paper in my lifetime. 'No more of that.
Othello's occupation's gone.'[2] I wanted to have nothing more to do,
nothing, absolutely nothing. I've succeeded; and at any time I can say
to death, the grim reaper: 'When you like!' I've only one further
ambition: to be rich enough to be able to resign from writing articles
for the *Journal des débats*, which bring me in twelve hundred francs a
year. I have the ambition to stop being a servant, to stop being a
coachman to fools and idiots, and to be able instead to throw stones at
them, if I want to. But the witches in *Macbeth* have made no predic-
tions for me. I shall never be Thane of Cawdor or Thane of Glamis or
King hereafter; and for a long time yet I shall be praising the men and
the works I most despise. It is God's will! [. . .]

Yours,
H. Berlioz

411 *To Gustave Flaubert*   Paris, 4 December 1862

My dear Monsieur Flaubert,

I wanted to rush and see you today but, as I was not able to, I cannot
wait any longer to tell you that your book[3] has filled me with admiration, astonishment, even with terror . . . It has frightened me and I have
been dreaming of it these last few nights. What style! What arch-
aeological knowledge! What imagination! Your mysterious Salammbô,
with her secret love, unbidden and full of terror, for the enemy who has
raped her, is an invention of the highest poetry, while remaining
completely on the level of reality.

Allow me to shake your mighty hand and to call myself your devoted
admirer,

Hector Berlioz

1 'Your eyes drop millstones when fools' eyes drop tears' (*Richard III*, Act I, sc. 3); or
perhaps Pandarus: 'Queen Hecuba laughed that her eyes ran o'er.' Cressida: 'With millstones.' (*Troilus and Cressida*, Act I, sc. 2).
2 Berlioz combines two lines from *Othello*: 'I have done the state some service and they
know't; No more of that.' (Act V, sc. 2), and 'Farewell! Othello's occupation's gone!' (Act III,
sc. 3).
3 *Salammbô*, just published.

412 *To his uncle Félix Marmion*   [Paris,] 9 December 1862

Dear uncle,

[. . .] The Opéra is continuing in its refusal to put on any new work
of importance, partly for economic reasons, and the standards of
performance are becoming ever more deplorable. The Théâtre-Lyrique,
which had pretensions of putting on *Les Troyens* and which then fell
back on *Béatrice*, is unable to do anything and is as incapable of
performing my large opera as it is my small one. There's no point
thinking about it; music in Paris is in a dreadful state.

I'm sending you my book *A travers champs* in the next post.[1] It's
having a great success; it's being translated into German, and the
English and American papers are full of extracts from its serious
sections, while the French papers on the other hand only quote the
jokes and funny stories.

Adieu, dear uncle, write to me from Hyères, and while you're
enjoying your warm sunshine spare a thought for the poor people
drowning in the Paris fog. Remember me to my aunt.

H. Berlioz

413 *To Emile Perrin*[2]   Paris, 10 January 1863

My dear Monsieur Perrin,

Would you kindly allow me to draw your attention to a work about
which you may have formed a vague idea and in which you appeared
to take some interest at a time when you were free of all the cares that
beset a theatre director. I shall not swell the ranks of petitioners who
must, especially at the moment, be harassing you. Allow me merely to
beg you not to ignore a work which, by its very nature, is clearly suited
to the Opéra, which would lend an unrivalled brilliance to its repertoire and which would stun the audience, if only by the splendid variety
of its staging, in which your particular talents could be given free rein.

Would you care to re-read the libretto of *Les Troyens*? Unfortunately I have no way of letting you hear the music, but I truly believe
that this score contains a fair number of items likely to become popular, in the best sense of the word, in the week after the first performance.

1 Its real title is *A travers chants*, the third compilation of feuilletons, published in September
1862.
2 Painter and theatre director, Perrin managed the Opéra-Comique from 1848 to 1857 and
in December 1862 took over the Opéra from Royer.

It's totally free of musical hair-splitting; it's a bold work, that's true, but also grand and simple and its clarity is incontestable.

Why be for ever doubting? Why for ever distrustful? Why have confidence only in idols of clay or wood and pray only to deaf gods, gods that are old and unyielding?

Put yourself in a position to be able to refute the calumnies that have already spread about the forces required for this work. It's been said there are twenty-two roles; there are nine. It's been said the work lasts eight hours (which no one can possibly know, since it's the music and not the text that determines the length of an opera, and no one knows either of them). In fact, according to a meticulous timing, and including sixty-six minutes for intervals, the score is no longer than that of *Les Huguenots*.

It would be possible at the moment to cast it reasonably well, although one couldn't expect to do so superbly. Besides, the Opéra has to stay alive, and at the moment it hasn't anything to chew on. Not that I'm suggesting *Les Troyens* as bread rations to assuage its hunger; certainly not, on the contrary, I'm proud enough to believe that I'm offering it a splendid feast. This will become clear sooner or later. So I say to you, in the words of my hero:

Arma citi properate viro[1]

and we shall capture Latium.

Yours very sincerely,
Hector Berlioz

414 *To his brother-in-law Camille Pal*   Paris, 3 February 1863

My dear Camille,

[...] Tired as I am of awaiting the pleasure of the Minister who won't make a decision, I'm on the point of leaving the Opéra to its haughty inertia and signing a contract for *Les Troyens* with the director of the new Théâtre-Lyrique.[2] He's urging me very keenly. I've given the Opéra administration until the 15th of this month to decide.

At the Théâtre-Lyrique I'm being promised everything I could wish for; they'd engage Mme Charton (who's coming back from America) for the role of Dido; I'd have a large orchestra, a colossal chorus and the goodwill of all and sundry. I think, and my friends do too, that I ought to accept.

1 'Quickly bring the man arms!' (*Aeneid*, II. 425).
2 Carvalho resumed the direction of the Théâtre-Lyrique in October 1862 in its new building in the Place du Châtelet.

Béatrice et Bénédict is being put on at Weimar; the Grand Duchess has asked for this opera for the gala performance to mark her birthday on 8 April. I've been invited to go and conduct it. In June I'm also going to conduct the Lower Rhine Festival at Strasbourg, where they're giving *L'enfance du Christ*. Finally, in August I'll be returning to Baden-Baden to revive *Béatrice* with Mme Charton-Demeur.

That's all my musical news; though not quite, because I'm giving half a programme next Sunday at the concert of the Société Nationale des Beaux-Arts, and the Conservatoire are asking me for a fragment of *Béatrice* for March.

Adieu, yours ever,

H. Berlioz

415 *To James William Davison*   5 February 1863

Dear Davison,

[...] As to the events which preoccupy me the most, I shall say nothing, it would take too long. I live like a man who may die at any moment, who no longer believes in anything and who behaves as though he believes in everything.

I'm like a warship on fire, with flames leaping through the rigging, calmly waiting for the powder kegs to explode ... I wish I could see you and talk with you openly; it took me a long time to get to know you and now I understand you. I appreciate your excellent character, as man and artist! I've so often been accused of being intolerant and vehement that I'm all sympathy for intolerance and vehemence. The people for whom I feel an insurmountable antipathy are the cold reasoners without heart or guts and the idiots who, as well as lacking those items, haven't got any brains either.

I've just received a letter from New York which has affected me deeply; it's from a young American musician[1] who asks me to write to him because he's finding it hard to carve out a career for himself and disappointment is killing him. He's made a poor choice of comforter; even so, I'll answer him as best I can.

This letter may perhaps find you in some difficulty, or some sadness, because we all have a large share of such things in this cruel world. If ill-fortune dictates that it be so, wait for a lifting of the clouds before replying; the weather is not always stormy.

1 Hopkins (see the next letter).

Adieu, dear Davison, forgive these ramblings, and believe in the sincere and lively affection of your devoted

H. Berlioz

416 *To Edward Jerome Hopkins*[1]   Paris, 6 February 1863

Dear colleague,

I read with deep emotion the letter which you did me the honour of sending me. You are suffering for art, you say. Unfortunately, I am not the right person to offer you consolation. You probably harbour a very false idea of how artists (worthy of the name) live in Paris. If for you New York is the musicians' purgatory, for me who knows it, Paris is their hell. So do not be too discouraged. To begin with, you are young; this is a great joy, a great advantage, a great power, a supreme attribute. I should be delighted to see you and to make your acquaintance. But, if you were to come to Paris (to this hell) perhaps, despite my desire to be nice to you, you might regard my welcome as inadequate, cold and not cordial. Perhaps you might find me distracted, preoccupied and buffeted by some storm or other, or by some feeling of bitterness, such as often comes over me. At such moments my behaviour, the look of me even, gives a false picture of inner feelings and anyone would be bound to form an unfavourable impression of me. I should certainly be sorry if such a thing occurred. Let us hope it will not. I'm only afraid you may arrive too late, because every day I get up in the hope that that day will be my last. My physical and psychological torments allow me practically no respite; I have said farewell to my musical illusions and I am no longer composing. I have arranged my life so that I can at any moment say to death: 'When you like!'

If I write at such length about myself, my dear Monsieur, it is to establish a contrast between our two destinies, which may make yours more bearable.

Music is the greatest of the arts; it is also the one which, in the present state of civilization, brings the greatest misery to those who understand it in all its facets and who respect and honour it. One must, nonetheless, continue to honour it, respect it and love it. Yes, love it, with that mighty *love* which contains the essence of the most noble passions of the human heart. One must in consequence despise the mob and its prejudices, attach no value to successes won at the cost of base

1 A prolific young American composer active in New York in many spheres.

concessions, and protect oneself from the advances of fools, idiots and sophists who know how to make folly look like reason.

But I beg your pardon, Sir, if I give you this counsels,[1] which you haven't asked me for. I conclude by thanking you for the sympathy you have been kind enough to show me, and assure you of mine in return.

Allow me to shake you by the hand and to leave you with the final words of the Ghost in *Hamlet*:

'Farewell , farewell, remember me.'

Hector Berlioz

417 *To Humbert Ferrand*   Paris, 3 March 1863

Dear Humbert,

[. . .] Your suppositions as to the cause of my misery are happily unfounded. Alas! Yes, my poor Louis has been a cruel torment to me, but I've completely forgiven him! We both of us followed your programme. Those torments came to an end three months ago. Louis is back on board ship and hopes to be a captain soon. He's now in Mexico, ready to return to France which he'll reach in a month's time.

The matter in question is one of love, a love which came to me wreathed in smiles, which I didn't seek out and which for some time I even tried to resist.[2] But the isolation I live in and the inexorable need for affection which is killing me were too strong. I allowed myself to fall in love, then I fell in love more deeply and a voluntary separation of the two parties became necessary and essential, a separation complete and without compensation, as final as death . . . That's all there is to it. And I'm recovering bit by bit; but good health is a sad state.

Let's say no more about it. [. . .]

Yours,

H. Berlioz

---

1 Berlioz attempts English here.
2 Since the previous summer Berlioz had established a liaison with a woman of twenty-six called Amélie, although very little is known about her.

419 *To Louis-Albert Bourgault-Ducoudray*[1]   Paris,
late April 1863

My dear Bourgault,

[. . .] I am of course delighted that you liked my score of *Béatrice*, but there was no need to go to the trouble of writing at such length on the subject. It's practically an article! And without being driven to it! Ah, unhappy man, beware the article! If ever I blow my brains out, it'll certainly be the article that provokes me to such extreme measures.

It wasn't the final *Duo-scherzo* which they played at the Conservatoire, but the *Duo-nocturne*, the one you prefer.[2] Personally, the two items I prefer are that duet and Beatrice's aria, 'Dieu! que viens-je d'entendre!' That's also the piece the public likes best, which almost makes me think I'm wrong. A Greek orator used to say, 'The mob are applauding. Could I have said something stupid?' [. . .]

When I receive letters like yours, it upsets me considerably; they awaken the enthusiasm which I'm trying hard to extinguish. I must become cold and indifferent, otherwise I shan't be able to survive. A young American recently wrote to me from New York and among his other confidences admitted that it was one of his dreams to see me *reorchestrate* Beethoven's 'Pastoral' Symphony, especially the Storm. 'With your specialized knowledge of brass instruments,' he wrote, 'you would turn this piece into an everlasting monument.' One has to have been born on the shores of Lake Ontario to have such monstrous ideas! I was furious. I waited a week before replying, to give myself time to calm down. At first I thought I'd made a mistake and that my understanding of English was at fault, but when I re-read his *proposal* slowly, I realized that that was indeed what he meant and I wrote back in such a way as to bring a blush to his cheeks and (I now fear) perhaps to cause him considerable distress.

So then, when you write, don't let me have any more letters about music. I shall have to become a philistine and a philosopher of optimism. Adieu.

H. Berlioz

1 A young composer who had just won the Prix de Rome and was living at the Villa Medici. He was later a distinguished historian of music.
2 At a concert of the Société des Concerts on 22 March with Mmes Viardot and Vandenheuvel.

Dear uncle,

I'm now back from Germany[1] and I find on my table your letter
dated the 10th. I left on the first. I've just spent a month of veritable
musical ecstasy. I conducted the first two performances of *Béatrice* at
the theatre in Weimar (in German) with astonishing success and the
compliments of the Grand Duke and of the Grand Duchess who had
chosen my opera for her birthday, with even warmer congratulations
from the Queen of Prussia, curtain calls for the composer after both
acts, and a supper organized by the musicians of Weimar and by those
who had travelled from Leipzig, Dresden, Jena, etc. Charming flattery
from the Duke who drank my health from the other end of the room at
a grand dinner on the day of the Gala (with 300 guests) at the same
time as a military band in the gallery was playing my *Marche hon-
groise*. A few days later came an invitation from the Prince of Hohenzollern to go to Löwenberg, where he lives, to conduct a concert. He
was responsible for the programme and it consisted entirely of works
by myself. The prince has an excellent orchestra *of his own*, which has
known nearly all my works for some time. There's a charming concert
hall in his castle; there he *gives* concerts of good music to which he
invites the German aristocracy from fifty miles around and all those
whom he knows to be lovers of music or musicians of intelligence. He
had given me a fine apartment next to the hall. Every day when it was
time for rehearsal someone came and said to me: 'Monsieur, the
orchestra is ready.' I would open a couple of doors and find my fifty
players with their instruments in their hands, *already tuned up*, and in
silence; I would step up on to the podium, give the first downbeat and
everyone would begin absolutely together. For someone coming from
Paris it seemed like a dream. The instrumental concert included the
overture *Le roi Lear*, two extracts from *Roméo et Juliette*, *Le carnaval
romain* and *Harold en Italie* (complete). There was wild enthusiasm,
tears, etc. After the first part on the day of the concert, the Prince's
aide-de-camp made an appearance in the middle of the orchestra and,
in the name of His Highness, presented me with the Cross of the Order
of Hohenzollern. After the second part, it was the resident conductor
who offered me a wreath on behalf of the orchestra. More applause
from the audience and a trumpet fanfare. Another supper followed

1 Berlioz conducted two performances of *Béatrice et Bénédict* in Weimar and a concert in
Löwenberg, in Silesia.

next day, at which I had to reply to German toasts in French. The Prince overwhelmed me with friendly gestures of every kind, accompanied by *serious* financial rewards. But this journey has left me very tired. Conducting *Béatrice* was no more than an entertainment, but conducting the Löwenberg concert brought me to a state of delirious over-excitement that I'm quite unable to describe.

So there, dear uncle, is an outline of my activities this month. I find a pile of letters on my table which need answering. Louis had left again by the time I returned. He's at St-Nazaire waiting for his ship to leave again for Mexico. I'm very pleased with him. All best wishes to my aunt. As for you, I hope you are in the very best of health. Adieu, dear uncle.

H. Berlioz

420 *To Humbert Ferrand*   Paris, 27 June 1863

Dear Humbert,

I'm just back from Strasbourg,[1] aching and overwhelmed with emotion ... *L'enfance du Christ*, performed in front of a truly *popular* audience, made an enormous impact. The concert hall, put up for the occasion on the Place Kléber, held eight and a half thousand people, but even so you could hear from every part of it. They wept, shouted and interrupted several of the movements without meaning to. You can't imagine the impression made by the final mystic chorus: 'O mon âme'! It really was that religious ecstasy I'd dreamed of and felt when I wrote it. An unaccompanied choir of two hundred men and two hundred and fifty young women who had been rehearsing for three months! The pitch didn't drop by so much as a quarter of a semitone. Such things are unknown in Paris. In the final 'amen', at the *pianissimo* which seems to dissolve mysteriously into the distance, cheering broke out the like of which I've never heard; sixteen thousand hands were clapping. Then a torrent of flowers and all kinds of expressions of enthusiasm. I looked to see whether you were in the crowd.

I was extremely ill and exhausted by the pain of my neuralgia ... everything has to be paid for. How are your own pains? From your last letter you seem to be in poor health. Let me have your news in three lines.

---

1 Berlioz spent from 16 to 23 June in Strasbourg, where he presided over an enormous choral festival and made a speech about Franco–German harmony. He conducted *L'enfance du Christ* in the specially constructed hall on the 22nd.

I'm now immersed again in two sets of rehearsals, for *Béatrice* and for *Les Troyens*.[1] Mme Charton-Demeur is so excited by the role of Dido, she can't sleep. May the gods support and inspire her! [...]

H. Berlioz

421 *To Gustave Flaubert*   Paris, 6 July 1863

Learned poet,

I came to call on you today to ask you a favour. We are busy at the moment staging my opera *Les Troyens à Carthage*.[2] The director of the Théâtre-Lyrique and I would be very grateful if you could give us some advice about the Phoenician and Carthaginian costumes. Certainly there is no one who knows as much about the subject as you do.[3] Please, when you get back, would you let me know a time when we could meet. Carvalho will come with me and we shall listen to you as to the oracle at Delphi.

With deep admiration,

Yours most sincerely,

Hector Berlioz

422 *To Humbert Ferrand*   Paris, 8 July 1863

Dear Humbert,

[...] I leave you to go and rehearse my *Anna soror*, who is making me anxious.[4] This young woman is beautiful and she has a magnificent contralto voice, but she is antimusicality incarnate. I didn't know such a singular breed of monster existed. She has to be taught everything, note by note, a hundred times over. And I have to get her in some kind of shape for a rehearsal in my house in a few days' time with Mme Charton-Demeur. Dido would be annoyed if the *soror* didn't know her duet 'Reine d'un jeune empire', which she herself sings so superbly. After which, Carvalho and I are going to see Flaubert, the author of *Salammbô*, to consult him about the Carthaginian costumes.

Don't give me more cause for regret . . . I've had to resign myself to it

---

1 *Béatrice and Bénédict* was to be revived at Baden-Baden in August, and *Les Troyens* had gone into rehearsal at the Théâtre-Lyrique.

2 Under pressure from Carvalho, Berlioz divided *Les Troyens* into two operas. Only the second, *Les Troyens à Carthage*, was to be staged. The first two acts were entitled *La prise de Troie*.

3 *Salammbô* is set in Carthage.

4 The role of Anna was sung by Marie Dubois.

– there's no more Cassandra. We shan't be putting on *La prise de Troie*; the first two acts are in abeyance for the moment. I've had to replace them by a prologue, and we begin only at Carthage. The Théâtre-Lyrique isn't large or rich enough, and it was too long. Added to which I couldn't find a Cassandra.

In its present mutilated state the work with its prologue, and still divided into five acts, will last from eight o'clock until midnight because of the complicated scenery for the virgin forest[1] and for the final tableau, the pyre and the apotheosis of the Roman Capitol. [. . .]

Yours,

H. Berlioz

423 To Humbert Ferrand   Paris, 28 July 1863

What a splendid thing the post is! For four sous we can talk to one another at a distance. What could be nicer? [. . .]

My son arrived yesterday from Mexico and, as he's got three weeks' holiday, I'm taking him with me to Baden-Baden. The poor boy is never in Paris when any of my works is performed. All he's ever heard was one performance of the *Requiem* when he was twelve. You can imagine how thrilled he is to be coming to the two performances of *Béatrice*. He's sailing to Vera Cruz when he leaves Baden-Baden, but he'll be back in France in November for the première of *Les Troyens*. [. . .]

Adieu, dear Humbert, I'm leaving on Sunday.

H. Berlioz

424 To his uncle Félix Marmion   Paris, 23 August 1863

Dear uncle,

I've only been back for a couple of days.[2] I was taken ill in Baden-Baden with a quinsy which nearly turned into angina and which kept me in bed for several days. As a result I was unable to conduct the first dress rehearsal of *Béatrice* and I had to ask the conductor of the theatre[3] to replace me. But the singers were in consternation after this experience and gave me to understand that it was better not to perform

1 The *Chasse royale et orage*, no. 29.
2 Berlioz and Louis were in Baden-Baden for the two performances of *Béatrice et Bénédict* on the 14th and 18th.
3 Koenneman.

the work rather than do so under such a conductor; he turned everything upside down. I made an effort to get up, and conducted both
the second rehearsal and the performance, despite finding it hard to
talk, and everything came back into place. Mme Charton was even
more admirable than last year, her voice is more beautiful than anyone has ever heard it. But the two other female singers nearly wrecked
the well-known duet, thanks to their ugly voices and ugly style. Even
so I was cheered and applauded by the whole audience and by the
orchestra. Beatrice's aria made an enormous impact. Jourdan (Bénédict) (who's a good musician, in fact) had his mind elsewhere for
almost the whole of the first act. [. . .]

Adieu, dear uncle, best wishes to my aunt.

Yours sincerely,

H. Berlioz

425 *To Aglaé Massart*[1]   Paris, 23 September 1863
                                           in the evening, by my fireside

Dear Madame Massart,

You're imagining perhaps, because I'm no longer enjoying cups of
chocolate at your house, or Beethoven sonatas or quartets, that I'm
no longer thinking of you? ... You're quite capable of it; you've
imbibed the poison of Rochefoucauld's *Maximes*; you think all our
actions have an ulterior motive! Alas! You could be right.

Even so, what makes me write to you this evening? What forces me
to send your husband a friendly greeting? What leads me to feel sorry
for your plight? Because I'm sure you're having a miserable time in
your little pinewood box, so grandly entitled a 'country house', where
there's just room for a piano (an upright), where the smell of the sea
is always with you, where the wind is blowing hard enough to strip
the horns off an ox, where, when you play the F minor sonata,[2] you
bore yourself, 'possessing naught but crabs for audience'.

One has to say: Mme Massart is in the country, at her villa; she's
bathing in the sea, dancing about on the beach, breathing the sea air
and the 'emanations of the infinite'. What colossal, puerile rubbish! I
sympathize with you, but charlatans have to keep their hand in ...

Still, I sympathize with you again.

1 Aglaé Massart and her husband Lambert were close friends and neighbours of Berlioz in
his last years. She was a distinguished pianist and he a violinist.
2 Beethoven's 'Appassionata'.

When are you coming back? So, it looks as though I'm expecting news of you, and I'm sure neither Massart nor yourself will venture to write me three lines. I know how modest you are, you won't permit yourselves that honour. [. . .]

I'm totally preoccupied with our rehearsals at the Théâtre-Lyrique. They're going well. Luckily you won't yet be back from your estate in November and won't be irritating me by wanting to come to the first performance; I shan't have any tickets to give you. Massart, that well-known whipper-up of audiences, will no doubt blame me. That'll severely reduce my chances of success and could cost me four or five hundred performances; I'm resigned to it.

You imagine perhaps that I'm going to say to you: 'Ah, the fifth act! Ah, Dido's farewell! Ah, the chorus of Pluto's priests! Ah, this! Ah, that! . . .' Well, yes, you're right. I'm not so vain as to think myself modest; far from it, I'm modest enough to think myself puffed up with vanity. Yes, I'm bursting with 'Ah!'s. If your crab could hear them, they'd make him tremble inside his shell.

A very good day to you! I'm told Massart is enjoying some splendid hunting; rumour has it that he's killed *a goldfinch*.[1] For all that you pride yourself on your English, I'm sure you didn't know the name the British give to that charming bird.

Adieu, adieu! The only reason for this letter is to let you know that I'm in very poor health; I hope it finds you in the same state. That will be some consolation for me.

426 *To Humbert Ferrand*   Paris, 25 October 1863

I have your letter and there's time to tell you that the rehearsals of *Les Troyens* are a wild success. Yesterday I came out of the theatre so overwhelmed I could hardly speak or walk.

I'm quite likely not to write to you on the evening of the first performance; I shan't be in my right mind.

Adieu.

H. Berlioz

1 Which Berlioz writes in English.

427 *To James William Davison*   Paris, 29 October 1863

Come, it's on Wednesday, 4 November. I had a terrific success at this morning's rehearsal. It's all going well.[1]
  Yours,
  H. Berlioz

428 *To Humbert Ferrand*   Paris, 5 November 1863

My dear Humbert,
  Magnificent success! The audience were deeply affected, with tears and interminable applause. Just *one* person whistled when my name was called at the end. The septet and the love duet knocked them sideways; the septet had to be repeated. Mme Charton was superb, she's a true queen. She was transformed; no one knew she had such dramatic talent. I'm quite giddy from so many embraces. I missed having your hand to shake.
  Adieu.
  All best wishes.
  H. Berlioz

429 *To his niece Joséphine Suat*   Paris, 15 November 1863

Dear Joséphine,
  I'm ill in bed with bronchitis I caught at rehearsals, which is why I didn't reply earlier to your charming letter. And then all the other letters, visits and congratulations have rather made my head spin. Everything's going better and better. Louis and some friends came at midnight to tell me about the fifth performance, which was superb. Large takings, a full house, immense enthusiasm, tears, applause, nothing was missing.
  More than thirty newspapers have covered it, and all of them (apart from three barking dogs heaping insults on my head) praise the work and its composer to the skies. Some of them contain two articles, one for and one against (see *Le monde illustré*).
  It's hard, you must admit, not being able to get out and attend these wonderful performances. But I must get better. [. . .]
  All best wishes,
  H. Berlioz

1 *Les Troyens à Carthage* received its first performance at the Théâtre-Lyrique on 4 November. There were twenty-one performances, concluding on 20 December.

No indeed, dear Princess, I had not forgotten you in the midst of all this agitation! But I'm becoming excessively reticent. I'm always nervous these days about throwing myself at my friends' heads (not to mention that, in certain cases, one doesn't throw oneself at the head but at the heart of true friends). So many thanks, dear Princess, for your reassurance. Robinson Crusoe's great canoe has been launched! And you were the one who, five years ago, made me choose the tree and inspired me with the courage to hollow it out. But I'm ill and have been in bed for ten days; the anxiety of the rehearsals gave me a violent attack of bronchitis which can only be soothed and cured by rest. As a result I've been unable to see the last four performances. I've just been told that yesterday's was splendid and that the whole of the third act had an extraordinary effect. My enemies couldn't be angrier. Yesterday two young men were shouting furiously in the theatre corridors: 'We cannot, we must not *permit* music like this!' Don't you think the word 'permit' is charming? On the other hand, two women were leaving the theatre after the fifth act and one was saying to the other: 'Yes, I'm sure, it's fine, it's very fine, I'm not denying it, but that's no reason to get in such a state. You must learn to *control* yourself. Crying like this, you're making us the centre of attention, it's not *proper*.'

More than thirty newspapers have published superb articles, full of fire and enthusiasm; four or five others have heaped the most tedious invective and the most ridiculous criticism on my head. I've had to wipe away this downpour of muck. Even so, it hurts me, a secret hurt that I'm ashamed of. I will admit to you that things I should expect in my position, but which do violence to the *artist* in me, give me pain. So I suffer martyrdom at seeing myself dismembered by my publisher and at learning that my score is available on his stall in slabs, like meat on a butcher's stall, aimed at large-scale and small-scale consumers, and that for a couple of sous one can even buy lights to feed the concierge's cat . . . Ah! Commerce and art are locked in appalling mutual hatred.[1]

As you know, I have had to split the work into two parts, the first of which, *La prise de Troie*, makes a three-act opera, while the second, *Les Troyens à Carthage*, is the one that has just been staged. I had to replace the first three acts with an explicatory prologue, mixing music and recited verse. This makes a grandiose and novel impression. The

1 Choudens issued vocal scores of both *La prise de Troie* and *Les Troyens à Carthage*, but the latter was quickly reissued with cuts to correspond with cuts in the performance.

instrumental *Lamento*, the invisible choir and the summoning up of memories of the disaster of Troy, all make a forcible effect. The staging in general is excellent, but the theatre isn't large enough, although at certain moments we got nearly a hundred and fifty people on stage. Monjauze (Aeneas) is generally good and attractive, one day out of two. Mme Charton is always superb; irreproachable as a singer, she has become a real tragic actress, thanks to her willingness and her desire to scale the heights of the subject; she has some sublime moments. I've never heard anything as beautiful as her way of singing the final grand monologue: 'Je vais mourir, dans ma douleur immense submergée!' And her exit at the end of the aria on the words: 'Je ne vous verrai plus, ma carrière est finie!', holding her last note without looking at the audience, is absolutely antique, Aeschylean. I have the most charming *puer Ascanius* you can imagine,[1] and when his father embraces him and covers him with his shield the illusion is complete. I've had to cut out several passages for various reasons. But would you believe that in an opera of this length I have not been asked to change a *note*? The orchestra is managing capably, but I needed the Opéra orchestra; the wind instruments are not brilliant enough. As for putting on *La prise de Troie* now (a three-act opera, as I said), despite Carvalho's wish to do so, I shan't agree to it. Parisians are not of a sufficiently epic nature, they'd say: 'Enough Trojans!' In any case, the libretto of this part is more severe in style than that of the other; Cassandra, too, is a longer role than Dido and I shouldn't have Mme Charton, who won't be staying in Paris next year.

The misery of the human heart! Mme Viardot, who is doing nothing in Baden-Baden, didn't come; Mme Stoltz, who was in Paris, didn't come; neither of them have written to me. *Both* of them wanted to play Dido! They won't forgive me. Roger[2] was furious not to be given the role of Aeneas, but he has only one arm and no voice! At least, after the first performance, Roger wrote me a charming letter (with his left hand, poor boy).

And you weren't there, and Liszt wasn't there . . .

Among the numerous letters I received, one begins with a quotation from Shakespeare: 'Well roared, Lion!' Isn't that nice?[3]

But now let me place myself at your feet, grasp both your hands and thank you with all my heart (which is a good deal, I may say) for your

1 Mlle Estagel.
2 Roger, formerly the leading tenor at the Opéra, sang *Faust* in the first performance of *La damnation de Faust* in 1846.
3 The letter was from Auguste Barbier.

sympathetic words, your kind wishes, your greatness of soul and for your vibrations in tune with the distant echo of *our* work. Thankyou, thank you, dear intellect, with the profound gratitude of your devoted
H. Berlioz

431 *To Alexey Fyodorovich Lvov*   Paris, 13 December 1863

I was delighted to read your letter. Thank you for all the kind thoughts it contains. It was charming and thoughtful of you to send me your congratulations on *Les Troyens*. I have in fact been forced to stay in bed for the last three weeks, following the torments I endured during rehearsals.

What are they, compared with the misfortune you have suffered?[1] It is strange that so many great musicians have been struck by a similar calamity: Beethoven, Onslow, Lvov and Paganini, who in his case couldn't make himself *heard*.

Thank you for your kind offer of an opera subject, but I can't accept it as I've made a firm decision not to do any more composing. I still have *three* opera scores which the Parisians don't know,[2] and I shall never find a favourable opportunity to familiarize audiences with them. *Les Troyens* was completed four years ago and only the second part, *Les Troyens à Carthage*, has just been performed. *La prise de Troie* remains to be done. I shall only ever write for a theatre where I'm obeyed blindly, without comment, where I am the *absolute master*. And that will probably never happen.[3]

Theatres are (as I wrote somewhere) the places of ill repute of the musical world, and the chaste muse who finds herself dragged along there cannot enter without a shudder. Or if you like: opera houses are to music *sicut amori lupanar*.[4]

And the imbeciles and idiots who swarm there, the firemen, the lamplighters, the sub-candlesnuffers, and the dressers who give *advice* to composers and influence the director! . . .

Adieu, dear maître; God preserve you from contact with that race! What I write to you about theatres in general is in complete confidence,

1 Lvov was suffering from deafness.
2 Berlioz presumably means *La prise de Troie*, *Béatrice et Bénédict* and the Weimar version of *Benvenuto Cellini*.
3 Having missed eleven performances through illness, Berlioz returned to the theatre on 7 December and was appalled by what he saw. The *Mémoires* record his disgust at the production about which he had at first been so enthusiastic.
4 'As the brothel is to love'.

especially as everyone at the Théâtre-Lyrique, from the director down to the lowliest member of the orchestra, has shown me nothing but devotion and goodwill.

And yet . . .

And nonetheless . . .

I'm still ill with it all.

432 *To Princess Carolyne Sayn-Wittgenstein* Paris,
23 December 1863

Dear Princess,

[. . .] So now our performances are at an end and Mme Charton is leaving us; she had already made quite a large financial sacrifice in agreeing to be paid no more than 6000 francs a month. She's going back to her Verdi roles at the Théâtre-Italien. She (like all the other singers, indeed) was obedience itself during rehearsals and neither she nor any of the others made me change a note. But the director, while protesting that his only wish was to realize my intentions, inflicted on me a martyrdom to which I shall never submit again, by asking for passages to be cut and for frightful alterations in the staging. In the final analysis, nine passages were cut. When he didn't dare ask me for a mutilation himself, he got my friends to do it, one face to face, another by letter. He was *afraid* of his own shadow. Afraid! As if anyone could do anything on a large scale without boldness and a cool head! But he was risking his *money*, so I gave in. No, I shall never do anything worthwhile in any theatre unless I'm the absolute master. I must be obeyed without comment, and conflict with another person's will makes me suffer the torments of death, paralyses me and makes me stupid.

Never mind, these twenty-two performances[1] have sown an enthusiasm in the musical world which I should like you to have witnessed. I had never before seen such demonstrations of emotion. The only comparison can be with my enemies' explosions of anger.

What marvellous letters I've received, and how many people I saw in floods of tears! Last Friday (a splendid evening in every respect) I confess that I myself was overwhelmed by certain passages in Dido's last aria, 'Adieu, fière cité', and especially by the end 'Je ne vous verrai plus, ma carrière est finie!', which the soprano sang admirably.

1 Actually twenty-one.

I tell you this, Princess, to give you confidence and make you think the work worthy of being offered to you.[1]

By way of answering the kind questions in your letter, I tell you as follows: I am living in absolute emotional isolation, I do nothing but suffer for eight or nine hours a day, without hope of any sort, with no ambitions beyond sleep, and appreciating the truth of the Chinese proverb: 'Better sitting than standing, better lying than sitting, better asleep than awake, and better dead than asleep.' [. . .]

H. Berlioz

433 *To his nieces Joséphine and Nanci Suat*   12 February 1864

Dear nieces,

[. . .] As for concerts and theatre performances, everything here is so wretched and so bad that for three months I've kept away from them completely. I've resigned from the *Journal des débats*[2] and I'm taking advantage of the fact to stay by my fireside or in bed. In the evening I sometimes go and visit friends in the neighbourhood, M. Damcke, M. Kreutzer or M. Massart. There I'm left completely free to do as I like. I stretch out on a sofa, I talk if I want to, I keep quiet if I want to, and I laugh if I want to at the silly jokes people round me are telling. Sometimes Mme Massart plays us a Beethoven sonata, then I shed every tear in my body. If anyone mentions cards or charades or any other stupid thing, I take my hat and disappear. When I get home, I go to bed, read a Shakespeare play and spend part of the night ruminating on the sublime. Yesterday I went to M. Edouard Bertin's house and had a long talk with Mme Janin, who is charming. Her husband said to me after this long conversation, 'My wife is monopolizing you. Never mind, she's an excellent woman, a veritable angel. Imagine, my dear fellow, she spent three hours today writing at my dictation. I've taught her to correct my proofs. Ah, the poor girl, marrying me was a damned awful thing for her to have done!'

On the way home I looked in at the Massarts'. The drawing-room was full of people doing embroidery and playing whist and dominoes. I went out again as fast as I could. This morning it's snowing in great

1 In addition to the dedication 'Divo Virgilio', *Les Troyens* was also dedicated to the Princess.
2 The sale of the scores of *Les Troyens* and *Benvenuto Cellini* to Choudens allowed Berlioz to give up writing feuilletons. His last article was devoted to Bizet's *Les pêcheurs de perles* in October 1863.

flakes ('drops of ass's milk', as my mother-in-law says). Paris is a sewer and, as I sit happily in front of my fire, I think of those wretched Austro-Prussian, Danish and American soldiers spread over both hemispheres, lying in the mud, wracked by hunger and wounds, camped in icy woods, rocked by sharp winds, and trying to get some sleep before being woken by cannonfire.[1] What a miserable race of idiots and wild animals!

I also think I won't go to the ball at the Hôtel de Ville this evening. I was to have had Dido and her husband to supper, but in the event the Queen of Carthage has a cold and doesn't dare go out. The day before yesterday she accepted a three-year contract with the director of the Théâtre-Italien, so that's *Les Troyens* gone to the devil. It doesn't bother me, nothing bothers me. Adieu, my dear nieces, that's my news; I'm still sick. To the devil with life and death!

H. Berlioz

434 To his brother-in-law Camille Pal   Paris, 1 March 1864

My dear Camille,

I am writing no more feuilletons. I've had enough of dramatic criticism, though I am reserving the possibility of writing on general topics now and again if I feel like it. I've been doing that detestable job for long enough. My music gets played *with* all over the place these days. Yesterday the love duet from *Les Troyens* was sung in the salon of the Princess Mathilde, who loves music like I love being whipped. The septet is to be done one day soon in a concert at the Hôtel de Ville. I've been asked for some scenes from *Roméo et Juliette* for the final concert at the Conservatoire. The same work has just been performed in Basle in Switzerland, *Harold en Italie* in Weimar, *Le carnaval romain* in Vienna and *Harold* again in New York. Those are all the ones I know of; happily, I shan't hear any of them because, with very few exceptions, the performances won't be marvellous.

Adieu, with all best wishes,

Yours very sincerely,

H. Berlioz

---

1 Austria and Prussia, under Bismarck's leadership, had invaded Schleswig-Holstein on 1 February, while in America Union forces were moving in on the South after victories at Gettysburg and Vicksburg.

435 *To his son Louis Berlioz*   Paris, 20 March 1864

Dear Louis,

I'm sending this to St-Nazaire on the off-chance. The box has just arrived. You must explain to us what all these fruits are which it contains. You shouldn't have spent your money on them all, although I see they're exotica that you wanted us to know about.

I went to bed this morning at half-past one. I'd come back from listening to Gounod's *Mireille* at the Théâtre-Lyrique. At half-past twelve, as the fifth act hadn't yet begun, I left. I couldn't take any more. It's a mixture of beautiful things and cheap, vulgar clichés. Everything in the latter category was applauded wildly. But the overall effect was debilitating and monotonous. I've no idea whether it'll be a success. Mme Carvalho sings sharp, Ismael sings sharp, Morini sings sharp.[1] But the audience approves of this delightful shortcoming.

Don't hold it against me that I've given up my post as a critic; I shouldn't be able to write a review of this opera. Carvalho and all his crowd are furious that I shan't be showering them with praises as usual.

Adieu, I embrace you with all my heart,

H. Berlioz

436 *To James William Davison*   Paris, 22 April 1864

Dear Davison,

[. . .] How are you, you poor slave, how are you managing with your chain-and-ball, you poor convict?[2] Myself, I can hardly believe in my deliverance, and the first performances of operas in Paris still fill me with terror . . . out of habit. And how happily and tenaciously I refrain from going to them!

Won't you come and spend a few days in Paris this summer? We could go for walks in the country with the least annoying of our friends or even without friends at all. But you won't have the time, poor fellow! Because it's true of you more than anyone that *The Times* is money. But help me earn a million, and if I don't immediately give you seven eighths of it, call me a scoundrel.

Good day, I shake your hand.

H. Berlioz

1 Carvalho's wife sang many principal roles at the Théâtre Lyrique. Ismael and Morini sang the roles of Vincent and Ourrias. There were only ten performances.
2 For Davison, unlike Berlioz, criticism was a vocation.

How are you, my dear Humbert? In the night? In the daytime? I'm taking advantage of a few hours' respite from my afflictions to ask after yours.

It's cold, it's raining; there's something indefinably sad and prosaic floating in the air. [...] Half of our little musical world (including myself) is sad; the other half is cheerful, because Meyerbeer has just died. We were to have dined together last week; he didn't keep the appointment.[1]

Tell me if I've sent you a score called *Tristia*, with this epigraph from Ovid:

Qui viderit illas
De lacrymis factas sentiet esse meis.[2]

If you haven't got it, I'll send it to you, as you like reading jolly things. I've never heard the work. I think the opening chorus in prose, 'Ce monde entier n'est qu'une ombre fugitive', is worth something. I wrote it in Rome in 1831.

If we could talk to each other, I feel that by being close to your armchair I'd be able to make you forget your sufferings. Voices and looks have a certain power which paper doesn't have. Have you at least got flowers and new foliage in front of your windows? I've got nothing but walls in front of mine. On the side facing the street, a mongrel has been barking for a good hour, a parrot is screeching and a parakeet is imitating the tweeting of the sparrows; on the side facing the courtyard, washerwomen are singing and another parrot is producing continual cries of: 'Portez ... arrrm!' What can one do? The days are very long. [...]

Adieu, write me just six lines so as not to tire yourself.
    H. Berlioz

438 *To his son Louis Berlioz* Paris, 22 July 1864

Dear Louis,

[...] There are still some honest people around. At the same time as I received your letter this morning one came from my Leipzig publisher

---

1 Meyerbeer died on 2 May.
2 'Whoever sees any [blemishes] will know they were made with my tears', Ovid, *Tristia*, 1.1.14.

telling me that all my volumes translated into German have appeared and that my *Traité d'instrumentation* is coming to the end of its first edition.[1] On the publication of the second one, and of all subsequent ones, he says, he'll send me a hundred thalers, which I wasn't expecting. So now this work is published in French, English, Italian, Spanish and German in several editions, and is flooding music shops all over the world. When I'd just written it I travelled ineffectually all over Germany, offering it everywhere, and I couldn't find a publisher who'd take it even for nothing.[2] My Paris publisher[3] breaks his promises to me all the time, he's incurable and I've stopped worrying about him.

We gave the Prix de Rome the other day to a young man who wasn't expecting to win it and who went almost mad with joy.[4] We were all expecting the prize to go to Camille Saint-Saëns, who had the strange notion of competing. I confess I was sorry to vote against a man who is truly a great artist and one who is already well known, practically a celebrity. But the other man, who is still a student, has that inner fire, inspiration, he feels, he can do things that can't be learnt and the rest he'll learn more or less. So I voted for him, sighing at the thought of the unhappiness this failure must cause Saint-Saëns. But, whatever else, one must be honest. A week ago I finished a postscript to my *Mémoires*. It's a very brief recital of some of the things that have happened to me in the course of the last ten years, and it brings the work to a definite conclusion.[5] I never thought I'd get to the end of it, it's all been so exhausting.

Adieu, dear Louis, I must go back to bed. I'll try and read, that'll help me a little to forget the pain.

Adieu, adieu, I'll see you soon,

I embrace you.

439 *To Princess Carolyne Sayn-Wittgenstein* Paris, mid-August 1864

Dear Princess,

Thank you for your kindly sermon. Unfortunately I am as incapable of making a medicine out of faith as I am of having faith in medicine,

---

1 The Leipzig publisher was Gustav Heinze.
2 In fact the *Grand traité d'instrumentation* was published in Germany and Italy as well as in France in 1844; it was English and Russian editions he was unable to arrange.
3 Choudens.
4 The winner was Victor Sieg, whose career was surpassingly obscure.
5 He had still one more chapter to add.

and I must put up with my troubles with or without patience as best I can. But it's very good of you even so to send me so many words which give off the hollow harmony of consolation! We look up at the sky when we hear the sound of bells! We sigh, and for a moment we feel calmer.

I'm more or less on my own; my son goes back the day after tomorrow. I have nothing to do, not even proofs to correct. My publisher, who was to have brought out the full score of *Les Troyens* this summer, has gone back on his word, as everyone always does. Should I dedicate it to the Emperor, who didn't even deign to come to a single performance? No, no, why should I? It would be meaningless. *Divo Virgilio solo*. Even so, the Emperor has appointed me Officier de la Légion d'Honneur, and Marshal Vaillant informed me of the fact in a very gracious letter which has enraged a large number of people.

I have to tell you, and you will not be surprised, that the people of Paris have gone totally insane. All of them, men, women and children, have been gripped by an inexplicable mania which leads them to shout at the tops of their voices in the streets, in the public gardens, on foot, in carriages, on horseback: 'Eh! Lambert! Ohé! Lambert! Have you seen Lambert?' No one knows what it means and everyone is shouting it. Yesterday evening, right up to midnight, the whole of Paris was ringing with the words 'Ohé! Lambert!' Madness has many forms! How stupid people can be! And these manias have a way of spreading. I too now feel the urge to shout 'Ohé! Lambert!' It's fun, it's charming. You try shouting 'Ohé! Lambert!' as well. You'll see how enjoyable it is. I gather the cry of Lambert is already to be heard in Le Havre, in Rouen and at Versailles. The whole of France is going to be saying it. Heavens above! The human brain is turning to liquid.

Adieu, dear Princess, I prostrate myself at your feet and kiss your hands.

H. Berlioz

440 *To Auguste Morel*   Paris, 21 August 1864

My dear Morel,

[...] I'm almost alone here. Louis left the day before yesterday for St-Nazaire and all my friends and neighbours are in Switzerland, Italy, England or Baden-Baden. The only person I see from time to time is Heller; we're going to have dinner at Asnières, we're as happy as larks. I read and re-read. In the evening I walk past opera houses to give myself the pleasure of not going in. The day before yesterday I spent two hours in the Montmartre cemetery. I found a very comfortable seat there on a sumptuous tomb and went to sleep.

From time to time I go to Mme Erard's at Passy where there's a colony of good-hearted people who make me very welcome. I'm savouring the pleasure of not writing articles and of not doing anything at all. If I weren't attached to Paris by various minor interests, I'd travel despite my physical problems, but I have to stay here. In any case, Paris is becoming more beautiful every day; it's a pleasure to see it flourishing so rapidly.[1] The day after tomorrow there's a big festival in Karlsruhe; Liszt has arrived there from Rome. They're going to perform music of a kind to make your ears fall off. It's the young German council presided over by Hans von Bülow.

You know Scudo[2] has been declared mad and locked away. His madness was obvious a long time ago, like Wagner's is, like Schumann's was and Jullien's and so many others. What a dreadful thing!

Adieu, my best wishes to you and to Lecourt.

H. Berlioz

441 *To Princess Carolyne Sayn-Wittgenstein*   Paris, 30 August 1864

Dear Princess,

You made use of some most eloquent lines in your last letter to preach to the converted. I am and have always been one of the Emperor's admirers, I don't see why you appear to doubt the fact. He himself is well aware of it. But that does not prevent me from recognizing his contempt for great art or from being sensitive to it. His uncle was the same, he found the most sublime passages of Homer vulgar and barbarous. Your letter also contains parables and allusions which I don't understand. Who is this 'musician of our acquaintance who thinks he's also a composer'? I can't guess.

I must say I'm sorry to see how ready you are in artistic matters to support the claims of 'personal interest'. You find it quite straightforward that we shouldn't admire someone who doesn't admire us and vice versa. That's terrible and represents the complete negation of art. I can no more not admire a sublime work by my greatest enemy than not detest a frightful nonsense by my dearest friend. I swear that in my case this is true, because I am an artist, and whoever doubts the fact insults me. [...]

1 Haussmann's grand rebuilding of Paris's boulevards was at its height.
2 A critic who most bitterly attacked Berlioz in his early years.

May I take you into my confidence once more? No, it would be too childish and would take too long. I'll merely tell you that my favourite walk, especially when it's raining, when the heavens open, is in the Montmartre cemetery, near where I live. I go there often, I have many connections there. Recently I even discovered there a grave of whose opening and closing I had been unaware. She had been dead for six months and no one had thought or been able to tell me that she was dying; she was twenty-six years old, she was beautiful and she wrote like an angel. I had, *we* had agreed it was wiser not to see each other, not to write to each other any more and to live totally separate lives. It was not easy. We caught sight of each other in the distance at the theatre one evening, a motion of the head . . . that was all . . . She was already dying and I didn't know it. Six weeks later she was dead. I didn't know that either. Only six months later . . . Enough, enough.[1]

I read a lot of travel books, I keep up (why?) with all the activities of the pernicious insects with which the earth, this great, fat lump, is populated. If my health weren't so bad, and if seasickness weren't so unpleasant, I'd travel, I'd go to Tahiti; there's a small tribe of charming children there, heavenly scenery, a refreshing climate, they speak French (and Kanak, the most gentle of languages), and there's no second-rate music. [. . .]

There are some odd fragments in my scores where I think I have succeeded in expressing certain feelings in a quite exceptional manner, but those are precisely the passages you know either imperfectly or not at all. As for my literary style, if I have one indeed, it's that of a writer who searches for the word capable of describing what he feels without ever finding it. There's too much violence in me, I've tried to keep calm and I haven't succeeded; that gives something unsteady and lurching to the motion of my prose, like the walk of a drunkard. [. . .]

H. Berlioz

In September 1864 Berlioz visited his nieces and brother-in-law Suat in Vienne and was seized, as he had been in 1848, by an intense desire to revisit his childhood love Estelle, who was then living in Lyon. He went to Meylan first and immersed himself in childhood memories of her, and then went on to Lyon and called on her, sending ahead the first of a long series of letters, some of which were reprinted in the Mémoires.

1 This is evidently the Amélie to whom Berlioz became attached in the summer of 1862.

Madame,

I have come back once more from Meylan. This second pilgrimage to the places inhabited by my childhood dreams was more painful than the first, which I made sixteen years ago and after which I took the liberty of writing to you at Vif, where you were then living. Today I take a still greater liberty and ask you to let me come and see you.

I shall manage to control myself; you need not be afraid of any outbursts from a heart in revolt against the constraints of pitiless reality.

Grant me a few moments, let me see you again, I beg you.[1]

Hector Berlioz

443 *To Princess Carolyne Sayn-Wittgenstein* Paris, 24 September 1864

Dear Princess,

I spent last night in a train. I come back from a visit to the Dauphiné, I find a pile of letters, I read yours and I find that the heart, the soul and the spirit I knew are even greater than before. I don't think I shall ever do anything to merit the loss of your affection, but in any case, as one can never swear to anything with wretches like me, I beg and plead with you to let me retain it come what may. My heart is, if not broken, at least wounded and crushed by the blows dealt by memory in the course of this journey. I'll relate the sad details of this pilgrimage another time and at length. For the moment, speaking of it is unbelievably painful. Forgive me, allow me to count on you. The effect of the sublime scenery of the Alps and the mountains that lead up to them, the silence of that immense orchard through which the Isère makes its tortuous way, the solitude of those rocky paths, all of these made me drink deep draughts of a sorrow which no one can understand without knowing the whole story of my life. There was the sad, solemn episode of my visit to Lyon ... Forgive me, dear Princess, I'm stupid, but please continue to be your indulgent, kind and intuitive self.

I have no faith in the future, but the past tortures me. I suffer, I suffer, I see clearly that I'm absurd, but my lucidity of mind does not relieve my suffering in the slightest.

1 Estelle received him graciously and assented to his wish to write to her and visit her occasionally. She was to be at the centre of his emotional life for the next four years.

Even you and your gentle words are powerless. Adieu, eloquent Princess, conserve your strength.

Ah, how I should like to die!

Yours,

H. Berlioz

I go from one misery to another. Blessings to you for your prayers on behalf of the dead girl; her name was Amélie.

444 *To Princess Carolyne Sayn-Wittgenstein*   Paris, 19 October 1864

[...] I write to you today, dear Princess, in a sort of tranquil despondency. I recently received a letter from *her* that I wasn't expecting; it gave the promise of others to follow, and I feel calmer. Even so, I shan't go to Lyon this month; I'm sure I should worry and upset her. She's marrying off her son this very day, then she'll begin her preparations to go and live with the newly married couple in Geneva. No doubt she's disconcerted by the strange depth of my feelings, but she understands them up to a point and she hasn't decided I'm mad. But of course the twelve-year-old boy who fell so heavily in love with her did not and could not inspire any feelings in the sublime girl of eighteen, who barely guessed at the anguish he was going through. She has no vivid memories and she thinks as you do that my imagination is largely responsible, and no doubt she knows as well as you do that the imagination *tells lies*. But I think, perhaps unwittingly, she's beginning to believe it is the *other* which is the dominant strain, and that the *other* will keep the upper hand to the end; because it's the *truth*. Be that as it may, I'll do everything I can not to be intrusive or tactless or alarming; I shall be as cautious as possible and perhaps one day she will find herself saying, in the recesses of her heart, 'It would be a pity not to be loved like this.'

The years have destroyed practically everything about her; one has to reconstruct her splendid beauty almost entirely from memories. Only her goddess-like carriage remains. But when I see her, I feel such extraordinary rapture that I lose hold on reality almost completely ... Ah! dear sister, pardon; my calmness is deserting me. Speaking to you about her like this ... What torment not to be master of oneself any longer!

Impossible! Adieu. I had so much to tell you.

H. Berlioz

My dear Humbert,

[...] My monotonous existence was somewhat lightened three days ago. Mme Erard, Mme Spontini and their niece[1] asked me if, one morning when I was free, I would read Shakespeare's *Othello* to them. We arranged a time. The gate of the Château de la Muette, where these ladies live, was firmly closed. All the bourgeois and cretins who might have disturbed us were sent on their way, and I read the masterpiece from one end to the other, letting myself go as though I were alone. There were no more than six people in the audience and all of them wept splendidly.

My God, what a terrifying revelation of the abysses of the human heart! Desdemona, what a sublime angel! Othello, how noble and tragic! And Iago, what a loathsome devil! And to think a creature of our own species wrote that! [...]

Liszt came to spend a week in Paris.[2] We dined together twice and, as we sensibly avoided all talk of music, it was an enjoyable occasion. He's gone back to Rome, where he's playing some 'music of the future' for the Pope, who would like to know what that phrase means. [...]

Yours ever,

H. Berlioz

Berlioz included the first exchange of letters between himself and Estelle in the final chapter of the Mémoires, *which he concluded on 1 January 1865. The correspondence was to continue about once a month for another three years.*

446 *To Estelle Fornier*   Paris, 16 February 1865

[...] I've spent the last week in bed. The homoeopathy you recommended has had no more effect than its elder sister. I no longer have any faith in medicines or doctors, especially not doctors. I concentrate a little each day on correcting the proofs of my *Mémoires*, of which I should like to bring you a copy. It's a finicky job, and I should find it totally overwhelming if your name did not figure so often in the course of it.

1 Mmes Erard and Spontini were sisters-in-law living in the Château de la Muette in Passy.
2 Liszt was now living in Rome.

Fate has kept me at a distance from you all my life! I could have died twenty times over *without seeing you again*, without opening my heart to you ... And you allow me to write to you, and sometimes you write to me, and you forgive me for taking up your time! Oh, it's a source of happiness which I never expected, an inexpressible, barely believable happiness. It is as if Virgil, Shakespeare, Gluck and Beethoven returned to earth and all four of them said in chorus, 'You have understood and loved us; come and let us bless you!' Oh, Madame!!!!

I told you in my last letter that my overture *Les francs-juges* was to be performed at a concert in the Cirque, and that M. Gasperini was going to give a lecture on my score for *Les Troyens*.[1] In addition, M. Deschanel also gave a lecture in another room on Shakespeare's *Romeo and Juliet*, in which he mentioned my name because of my grand choral symphony on this story. Both speakers were loudly applauded. As for the overture, it produced a sort of riot. After the last bar a huge acclamation broke out, and after the third salvo my three faithful whistlers, true to their habit over the last two years, did not pass up the opportunity of giving two powerful shrieks. At that the applause redoubled, four thousand pairs of hands beating with fury. There was waving of handkerchiefs and hats. The Cirque presented a curious sight. On the way out I was stopped in the street: people I didn't know came and shook me by the hand. Women introduced themselves to me and offered their compliments. One of them said, 'What energy! What knowledge of the orchestra it shows! It must be one of your recent works!'

'Alas! Madame,' I replied, 'that work was written *thirty-seven* years ago. It was my first orchestral piece!' [...]

Adieu, Madame. May all the angels in heaven bless you for your kind heart, your gracious and stately simplicity, your indulgent spirit, your divine modesty and for everything that makes me admire you and makes me remain yours devotedly unto death.

Hector Berlioz

---

1 These were two separate but simultaneous events on 22 January; the concert was one of Pasdeloup's Concerts Populaires.

Dear Princess, most admirable of women! Thank you for the interest you take in my personal feelings, which may well seem ridiculous to you but which you examine nonetheless with an indulgent eye. Believe me, dear Princess, this indulgence on your part redoubles the affection I had for you. But why do you say in your letter, 'Is it *still* continuing?' Did you really think we were talking about one of those will-o'-the-wisps which flit over the marshes at night? No, it is my childhood that is being relived, my youth, my earliest impressions, my feeling for the infinite ... I love her as though she were still young and beautiful. Sometimes I don't dare to write to her for fear of tiring her by provoking a reply; I know only too well the embarrassment these replies must cause her. She does not feel what I feel; and what's more, as she admits, she's afraid to write to me. So a month has passed without my sending her so much as a couple of lines. But last week I could hold out no longer. I bought a lovely bouquet of violets, had it put in a box and sent it to her – *without any message*. That made me feel very much better and I'm sure my flowers were welcome. She is the reason why I'm having my *Mémoires* printed. She was reproaching me one day for my decision not to produce anything else and she ended up by saying, 'I hope you'll make an exception for your *Mémoires* and have them published soon; I have something of the daughter of Eve in me and I confess that before I die I should like to read your life story.' I delivered the manuscript to the printer immediately. [. . .]

Adieu, dear Princess, don't be angry with me. You know I'm right.

Yours truly,

H. Berlioz

448 *To Humbert Ferrand*   Paris, 26 April 1865

My dear Ferrand,

[. . .] What can I tell you about what's cooking in the musical tavern of Paris? I've left it and I practically never go back. I heard a dress rehearsal of Meyerbeer's *L'africaine*, from half-past seven to half-past one in the morning.[1] I don't think I shall ever return.

The famous German violinist Joachim came to spend ten days here; he was asked to play almost every evening in various salons. I thus heard him and some other fine artists playing the B flat Piano Trio, the

1 *L'africaine* opened at the Opéra on 28 April, put together posthumously after many years' gestation on Meyerbeer's desk. It was very successful.

A major Sonata and the E minor Quartet by Beethoven.[1] It's the music of the starry spheres ... As you can well understand, it's impossible, after hearing such inspired miracles, to put up with everyday music, patented products or works recommended by the mayor or the Minister of Education. [. . .]

Adieu, I embrace you with all my heart.

H. Berlioz

449 *To Estelle Fornier*   Paris, 27 April 1865

Dear, a thousand times dear Madame,

[. . .] There are moments when I'm filled with the desire to write a vast symphonic poem for you. The orchestra is the only means by which I could express what I feel. But it would not be worthy of the subject; my physical sufferings would paralyse me and I don't wish to run the risk of producing a mediocre work in such a situation. And then you would never hear it, so it would remain a dead letter for you. It's madness, it's too late. In any case many passages in my earlier works, in *Harold en Italie* and in the *Symphonie fantastique*, were in fact inspired by my memories of the star, the pale blue star that lit up the morning of my life.[2] I should repeat myself, and God preserve me from warming up old musical ideas. In singing to *you*, inspiration is an absolute requirement. And then music lives only by means of contrasts, and I see no possibility of any in a musical epic inspired by such a muse. You have never done me any harm. Never has a bitter thought entered my heart on your account, and when I had sung of my admiration and infinite enthusiasm for la Stella in every key and with every inflexion imaginable, and painted with the brightest colours that part of the sky where she shone, and the delightful countryside 'honoured by your footsteps and illuminated by your eyes' (as La Fontaine might have said), I could only begin again, and again and again. [. . .]

Adieu.

H. Berlioz

1 The 'Archduke', the 'Kreutzer', and 'Rasumovsky' no. 2.
2 In childhood Berlioz thought of Estelle as his 'stella montis', his mountain star.

450 *To his son Louis Berlioz*   Paris, 11 July 1865

Yes, my dear Louis, let us correspond, when we can, as often as we can. Your letter this morning was very welcome. But I spent an abominable day yesterday. I went out and wandered for a couple of hours on the Boulevard des Capucines. At half-past eight I started to feel hungry. I went into the Café Cardinal to eat something and I immediately heard someone calling me and saw a cheerful face smiling at me; it was Balfe, the Irish composer, who had just arrived from London and who asked me to have dinner with him. Then we went to the Grand Hôtel where he's staying, to smoke a really excellent cigar, though it's made me feel ill this morning. We talked endlessly about Shakespeare whom, he says, he's only understood properly these last ten or twelve years. [. . .]

451 *To M. and Madame Damcke*[1]   Geneva, Hôtel de la Métropole,
                                                      22 August 1865

My dear friends,

Here are just three lines, so that you don't accuse me of forgetting you. As you know, I don't forget easily and, if I could, I should take great care not to forget friends like you.

I am here in a state of uneasiness that I shan't attempt to describe to you;[2] there are moments of sublime calm, but many others full of anxiety and sorrow. I've been welcomed with the utmost warmth and cordiality; I'm asked to treat the house as my own and there are grumbles when I don't appear. I pay calls lasting four hours and we go for long walks round the edge of the lake. Yesterday we drove to a village some way off called Yvonne with her daughter-in-law and her youngest son, who has just arrived. But I haven't been able to get a single moment alone with her. I've been able to speak only of *other things* and that has made my heart feel as though it's going to burst.

What am I to do? I haven't a breath of reason on my side, I'm being unfair and stupid. Everyone in the family has read and re-read the *Mémoires*. *She* has gently upbraided me for having printed three of her letters, but her daughter-in-law has said I was right to do so and I don't think *she* is angry any more. Her second son, whom I have met in Paris, is a fine young man, and the baptism of the child his young wife has

1 Berthold Damcke and his wife were neighbours and very close friends of Berlioz in his last years. He was a German composer, violinist, pianist and critic who settled in Paris in 1859.
2 Berlioz was in Geneva to visit Estelle, who now lived with her son and daughter-in-law. He took with him a printed copy of the *Mémoires*.

just given him will take place the day after tomorrow. Mme Fornier is to be the godmother. It will be a family day.

Thinking of the time when I shall have to leave already makes me tremble. The scenery is charming, the lake is utterly pure, beautiful and deep. But I know something still deeper, purer and more beautiful.

Adieu, dear friends.

H. Berlioz

452 *To Estelle Fornier*   Vienne, Place de la Halle
                                                 30 August 1865

My dear doctor,

This time you have made an excursion into the field of surgery, and the operation you've conducted has, unfortunately, been successful.

You have rooted out for ever an idea which I had never expressed and which you must have guessed at. But during the operation you looked severe and disapproving. And yet it was not my fault if the chaste ambition of spending the rest of my life with you inserted itself into my heart. It grew from the intoxication caused by your presence. I'm not yet accustomed to seeing you and the anticipated misery of saying goodbye made me delirious. But it's over.

Read the last pages of my *Mémoires* and you will see that my dearest hopes have been for many a year enclosed within the limits which you yourself assigned to them the other day: to see you sometimes, to exchange letters, to retain your interest, your goodwill, and that is all (those are your own words).

I shall therefore remain inside this circle. I shall come two or three times a year to adore you at close quarters, for twenty-four hours, to see you, to hear you and to breathe the air you breathe. Then I shall return at once to Paris, as proud and happy as a bee carrying off his honey and, more than the bee, full of tender gratitude.

I wait for your reply and beg you to try not to make it disapproving or severe, so as to heal the wound which is bleeding still.

I arrived here yesterday, after various excursions to the environs of Grenoble during which I gave myself up to all the distractions that were offered me. I was careful not to go back to Meylan, and I think it better that I never do go back. Adieu, dear Madame, dear friend, forgive me for loving you to this extent.

All my best wishes to the young couple who were so kind to me.

Yours sincerely,

H. B.

Dear Madame, adorable friend,

[...] Now the director of the Théâtre-Lyrique[1] is making proposals to Mme Charton for a revival of *Les Troyens*. I have just pleaded with her not to accept. I shall use all the power at my command to oppose this renewed slaughter. The work's too large and the theatre's too small, it doesn't have the necessary equipment. I prefer to have no performance than one like that. Oh God! If only I could be left in peace! I have nothing in common, nor do I wish to have, with the world of entrepreneurs, directors, merchants, tradesmen, shopkeepers and philistines of every description, disguised under a variety of titles.

Adieu Madame, dear Madame. I ask you to give me your hand; I press it to my forehead, where there are no ideas, and to my heart, where there are too many, and you will forgive me.

Yours truly,

H. Berlioz

454 *To Estelle Fornier*   Paris, 4 November 1865

Dear Madame,

[...] I have a study next to my bedroom, with a table on which is placed the morning's post. For the last few weeks I've been getting up every day to glance at it, hoping to catch sight of your handwriting. But nothing ... Then last Monday I recognized the Geneva stamp ... Perhaps you think I rushed forward to seize the letter; on the contrary, I went back into my bedroom and paced round it any number of times saying to myself: 'There's a letter! There's a letter!' Then finally I went back, read it, devoured it, and uttered infinite thanks to you ...

I can see you laughing at what you term my childish behaviour. Well, laugh away, that doesn't hurt me, I know how very kind you are. Perhaps you think I'm unlucky enough to be what's called a *susceptible* person? A stupid remark I made to you one day in Geneva, when you seemed to avoid giving me your hand as you got down from your carriage, must have given you that impression. But you're wrong, I'm not, or rather I am only in your case. I'd do better, I know, not to reserve the bad sides of my character for you: that's what you were going to say. But the truth is, if I speak to you or write to you, I'm like a

1 Carvalho.

man who has recently discovered a hidden treasure – he counts it again and again, and every time it comes to the same amount he's amazed it hasn't grown. You are my million! And I'm such a miser!!! [. . .]

Yours truly,

Hector Berlioz

455 *To his son Louis Berlioz*   Paris, 13 November 1865

Dear Louis,

It's one o'clock. I've just received your letter and I'm replying to it before I go back to bed. I know you'll be very busy on the 15th and today's the 13th. I hope you'll find your way through the mass of soldiers and passengers. I very much approve of your idea of having a home, a place of your own, and of buying some furniture; but aren't you worried that your ship may be stationed somewhere other than St-Nazaire? In any case, it's something to bear in mind. I don't know what you could have written to Mme X,[1] but I have a good idea of what she might have replied. One would need money even if there were none left in the world! You need to stay on land, in Grenoble, in Claix, be a magistrate and a worthy citizen, sell your corn, your sheep, your wine, etc. Then you have everything going your way, you play *boules* on Sundays, you have a mob of dirty children that the grandparents think are very badly brought up, you get bored enough to turn into a vegetable, you have a wife who gets fat, then obese, until finally you can't stand her, and you say to yourself, 'Ah, if only I could start all over again!'

And then you feel a fury penetrating to your very marrow because you're getting older and you see your life draining uselessly away. You have plenty of money which has come too late and which you don't know what to do with, and then you die the same as everybody else.

Mine is a wretched life. If I could, I'd run away to Palermo, or at least to Nice! But the goat must be tethered where it can graze. The weather's appalling. The lamps have to be lit at half past three! It's our Monday dinner this evening,[2] so I'll get up to go to it. I'm going to try and sleep for two or three hours. I haven't had any letters from Geneva recently, though it's true I wasn't expecting any. When a letter does arrive, it gives my heart and spirit a lift.

Ah, my poor Louis, if I hadn't had you! . . . Believe it or not, I loved

1 The name is not given in the only available text. Was Louis asking for a loan, or contemplating marriage?
2 At the Tuileries.

you even when you were very small and it's so difficult for me to love little children! There was something about you I found attractive. Later it diminished when you reached the awkward age and were lacking in common sense, and since then it's returned and it's grown. You know how I love you and it can only become greater.

456 *To Humbert Ferrand*   Paris, 17 January 1866

My dear Humbert,

I'm writing to you this evening, alone by my fireside. Louis let me know this morning that he had arrived in France and mentioned you. He has read some of your letters and he appreciates your great friendship for his father. But on top of that, this morning I suffered a violent disturbance. They're reviving *Armide* at the Théâtre-Lyrique and the director has asked me to supervise the preliminary rehearsals, which are rather beyond the powers of his gang of philistines.

Mme Charton-Demeur, who is playing the exhausting role of Armide, is now coming every day to rehearse with M. Saint-Saëns, a fine pianist and a fine musician who knows his Gluck almost as well as I do. It's a curious experience to see this poor woman floundering about in the sublime, and her understanding growing little by little. This morning, in the Hatred scene, Saint-Saëns and I shook each other by the hand ... We were suffocating. Never has a man discovered such expression. And to think that people everywhere are blaspheming against this work, as much by their admiration as by the attacks they make on it. They disembowel it, cover it with mud, vilify it and insult it in every quarter, – important people, unimportant people, singers, directors, *conductors*, publishers ... everyone![1] [...]

That's another world. How I should like to have had you there! You won't believe it, but since I've been immersed again in the world of music my pains have gradually vanished. I get up every day now, like the rest of the world. But I'm going to have some fierce pains to endure in dealing with the other singers, and especially with the conductor. That'll be in April. [...]

Adieu.

H. Berlioz

---

1 Berlioz here quoted five lines from *Armide*. The project was abandoned in March 1866.

Dear Madame,

I see you are serious in wanting me to destroy your letters in the fear that prying eyes might read them after me. I shall obey you. The sorrow I feel at the thought of this sacrifice is immense, I won't hide the fact from you. But your wishes and your peace of mind come before everything.

I am sorry you should have taken the trouble to write four pages to me, as that is tiring for you.

Please don't forget to let me have the address of the house in the country that you're going to live in when you leave the Quai des Eaux-Vives.

Adieu, my heart is heavy. I am not well. It seems that total deprivation and abandonment are my lot.

H. Berlioz

P.S. – It's done! Everything has been burnt. *I have nothing now* except the envelopes.

My dear Humbert,

[...] I've waited till this morning before replying to you because I wanted to tell you what happened yesterday at an extraordinary grand concert at triple prices in the Cirque Napoléon for the benefit of a charitable society, with Pasdeloup conducting.

It included the first performance there of the septet from *Les Troyens*. Mme Charton was singing; there was a chorus of a hundred and fifty and a fine, large orchestra. Apart from the march from Wagner's *Lohengrin*, everything in the programme was terribly badly received by the audience. The overture to Meyerbeer's *Le prophète* was hissed outrageously; the police intervened to remove the whistlers ...

Finally came the septet. Huge applause; cries of 'encore'. Better performance the second time. I was spotted up in my three-franc seat (no one had sent me a single ticket), then there were renewed shouts and calls of 'encore' and much waving of hats and handkerchiefs. 'Long live Berlioz! Stand up, we want to get a look at you!' while I did my best to hide! Out on the street, after the concert, I was surrounded. This morning I've had visitors and a charming letter from Legouvé's daughter.

Liszt was there. I saw him from my perch. He's just back from Rome and didn't know a note of *Les Troyens*. Why weren't you there? There were at least three thousand people in the audience. Years ago I'd have been delighted by it . . .

It made a grand effect, especially the passage with the sea noises, which you can't get on the piano:

Et la mer endormie
Murmure en sommeillant les accords les plus doux.

I was profoundly moved by it. The people next to me in the amphitheatre didn't know me, but when they found out I was the composer, they shook my hand and thanked me in all kinds of ways . . . curious. Why weren't you there? It's sad, but beautiful! [. . .]

Adieu, dear Humbert.

Yours,

H. Berlioz

459 *To Estelle Fornier*   Paris, 29 May 1866

How kind you are! I've just received your letter and I wasn't expecting it for another eight or ten days. I write merely to thank you. Your advice, in a slightly complaining tone, always does me some good. I shall re-read your letter for a little before burning it, as we agreed.

I thank you, then, for bringing comfort to a heart in trouble. I've been seriously disturbed these last few days; a troupe of Italian actors has arrived to give performances of Shakespeare translated (unworthily) into Italian. I saw *Amleto* (*Hamlet*) which affected me dreadfully, despite everything. This evening the great actor Rossi is going to play Othello, not the squalid opera Rossini set to squalid music, but the prodigious masterpiece of the greatest of poets, and I can't resist the painful pleasure of going to have my heart torn apart. I shall be ill tomorrow, no doubt. But so what! Can we not go and greet the sun, even when it burns us? [. . .]

Your inexhaustible goodness redoubles my gratitude.

Hector Berlioz

Dear Princess,

[...] You were kind enough to ask what I am doing, thinking and reading. [...] I'm reading some old volumes from the library. On Saturdays I go early to the Institut and there, before the meeting, I spend a longish time in the library reading the entries in the *Biographie universelle*. I'm beginning to get tired of the non-artistic celebrities. Those poor little wretches called great men fill me with an irresistible horror. Caesar, Augustus, Antony, Alexander, Philip, Peter and all the others are no more than bandits. And then the biographers contradict each other; you can see they aren't sure about anything and that they don't really know anything.

When I think that I myself have forgotten certain events and crucial details of my life, I wonder how an alien pen, at a distance of two thousand years, could retrace the details of the lives of men the writer has never seen or known. History is a fraud, like so much received wisdom.

As for the war, yes, it's the right moment to discuss it.[1] Let's discuss those hundreds of thousands of idiots who are tearing out each other's throats and stomachs, firing point blank at each other and dying furiously in the mud and blood out of obedience to three or four good-for-nothings who are very careful not to get involved personally in the fighting, but without really understanding the reasons they're given for being led to the slaughter!!! ...

As Horace said a long time ago, 'Quidquid delirant reges, plectuntur Achivi.'[2]

How I'd like to see a small planet, only five hundred miles in circumference, bumping into ours during some great battle and bringing those petty monsters who were killing each other to see reason by crushing them all! What a pulp! And well deserved! It'd be a sublime display of Nature's indifference! It happened with other animals, in prehistoric times. They discovered proof of it on the banks of the Mississippi not long ago, in a strange area called the 'bad lands'. But those enormous numbers of animals were only drowned in water and mud.[3] And it's the crushing I'd like, so that all that was left would be a red stain once the planet had passed on, like when you really crush an ant-hill.

1 The Austro-Prussian War, then at its height.
2 'The Greek people suffer for the follies of kings', *Epistles*, 1.2.14.
3 The discovery of dinosaurs was one of the sensations of the 1850s.

Adieu, dear Princess, I'm writing to you from bed. I'm tired, I'm going to go back to sleep, if I can.

Yours truly,

H. Berlioz

461 *To Estelle Fornier*   Paris, 25 July 1866

Dear Madame Fornier,

[. . .] I've just come back from Louvain where, as a result of some little pressure, I went to sit on a musical jury. We were awarding a prize for a religious composition. So I had to read through seventy-three masses in full score and choose, not the best, but the least bad. There were fourteen of us on the jury, Belgians, Flemings, Germans, Englishmen and Frenchmen. I can assure you we all found our job a tough one. But it was fulfilled conscientiously and, unlike what happens in most competitions, there was no skulduggery or unfair bestowing of favours. When we opened the envelope with the number of the winner on, I was delighted to find that he was a young Dutch friend of mine who lives in London, and who's extremely poor.[1] So he'll be thrilled with the one thousand francs prize money. In Paris, nothing new. Only that next Saturday we're going to appoint a new member at the Institut (a sculptor), and there have been the usual intrigues to gain votes. You will ask how it comes about that I'm voting on such an occasion and what I know about sculpture. Nothing, alas! But those are the rules. In the Beaux-Arts section we all vote, so sculptors judge composers, painters judge architects, etc, etc. I think it's crazy, but that's how it is. [. . .]

Your ever devoted

Hector Berlioz

426 *To his uncle Félix Marmion*   Paris, 31 July 1866

Dear uncle,

I'm writing to you at Tournon on the off-chance, not knowing whether you're still there. You haven't come to Paris this summer and I haven't heard your news for a very long time. I'm very sorry about that, because I'm very fond of you, dear uncle, and we're almost the only two survivors of two generations of our family. It's upsetting, isn't it, to be living isolated like this, as though you were on the island of

---

1 Eduard Silas.

Tahiti and I was in Tobolsk? My activities in Paris can be summed up in two words: I'm bored and I'm unwell. I don't know how I survive this miserable existence. Even so there are happy moments now and again when, exceptionally, great art manifests itself in a particular quarter. I've seen Mozart's *Don Giovanni* eight times in succession at the Théâtre-Lyrique, while it was being murdered at the Théâtre-Italien and the Opéra. Mozart could never have foreseen in his lifetime that his masterpiece would be so popular in Paris where he was so totally despised.

I've also seen five or six performances of Shakespeare's *Hamlet* and *Othello*, mutilated in an Italian translation, but played by a tragic actor of genius called Rossi. I suffered all sorts of convulsions of admiration and tears, because the more I go the more violent my admiration becomes, not that I have any illusions any more. I see more and more clearly that Shakespeare was right when he said,

> Glory is like a circle in the water
> Which never ceaseth to enlarge itself
> Till by broad spreading it disperse to nought.[1]

[. . .] Louis was here last week; he's coming back tomorrow. He has just been given the command of a vessel of the Compagnie Transatlantique. He now earns about 12,000 francs and is therefore much richer than I am. He is leaving soon for the Antilles where I fear he will have to stay for nearly a year.[2] [. . .]

Yours very truly,
H. Berlioz

463 *To François-Joseph Fétis*   Paris, 14 October 1866

My dear Monsieur Fétis,

Thank you for the letter you were good enough to send me about the revival of *Alceste*;[3] I was delighted by it, as you may imagine. The performance of this masterpiece struck you as a good one because I found a director and singers who were as intelligent as they were dedicated. I played a very small part in their success. The monumental heights of Gluck's inspiration bowled them over to begin with, but then it brought them to their feet and made them acquire stature.

1 *Henry VI Part I*, Act I sc. 2.
2 Louis left soon afterwards, the last time he and his father were together.
3 *Alceste*, which Berlioz had supervised at the Opéra in 1861, was revived there on 12 October 1866. The title role was sung by Marie Battu.

Nonetheless, if there were anything that could give me a courage I no longer have use for, it would be support such as yours.

I defend our gods.

But in the small army (*nullam sperante salutem*)[1] which is fighting against the Myrmidons, you are still a lance while I am no more than a shield.

With all respects,
Yours sincerely,
Hector Berlioz

464 *To Humbert Ferrand* Paris, 10 November 1866

My dear Humbert,

[...] The rehearsals of *Alceste* brought some improvement in my health. Never had this masterpiece seemed to me so grandly beautiful, and never, I'm sure, did Gluck hear such a worthy performance of any of his works. A whole generation is hearing this marvel for the first time and prostrating itself with love before the master's inspiration. The other day I had near me in the auditorium a woman who was weeping explosively, so that people in the audience were gazing at her. I've had a heap of letters of thanks for the trouble I've taken with Gluck's score. Perrin[2] now wants to revive *Armide*. Ingres isn't the only member of the Institut who makes a habit of coming to the performances of *Alceste*; most of the painters and sculptors have a feeling for antiquity, a feeling for beauty undeformed by sorrow.

The Queen of Thessaly is another Niobe. And yet, in her final aria in the second act 'Ah! malgré moi mon faible cœur partage', the expression rises to such a height as to make one giddy.

I'll send you the new vocal score. You'll read it easily and it'll give you a few good moments.

Adieu, I've no more strength.

H. Berlioz

465 *To Marie d'Agoult* Paris, 20 November 1866

Thank you, Madame, for bringing a thing of beauty to my attention. I have read your book[3] with an avidity that would surprise you if you

---

1 'Without hope of salvation', the phrase from Virgil adopted in Act II of *Les Troyens*.
2 Director of the Opéra.
3 Under the name 'Daniel Stern' Marie d'Agoult published a volume of *Esquisses morales* in 1849, with a second edition in 1856.

knew that I have never been able to tolerate the works of La Rochefoucault nor those of La Bruyère, Vauvenargues, Epictetus[1] or any other compiler of sentences.

How did you bring this miracle about? I don't know, but once I'd read the opening chapter I stopped only in order to go back and appreciate certain pages more fully. My thirst grew. But you haven't dared to say everything; you haven't even begun to tackle certain questions round which all the others crucially revolve. You do not, I believe, have any religious viewpoint, and yet in certain places you write as though you had. If any criticism could be made of your book, your book itself would provide the material for it. You say on page 149: 'There is nothing more dangerous or more hateful in politics' (and so in philosophy as well?) 'than vague words'. Is there anything vaguer than words such as 'perfection', 'God', 'liberty', and any number of others which you use? But everything you say about art and about the various kinds of love is admirable! Time after time one comes across those luminous truths one feels one had been in possession of all one's life, but which nevertheless strike home like a sudden flash of lightning.

I won't presume to praise the purity and naturalness of your style, so free of all affectation and so elegantly correct. This will strike you as a merit of secondary importance; even so it's very rare and particularly indispensable in books about philosophy. But to return to the fearful question you haven't even touched on, have you read the story of the settling of the Pitcairn Islands by the mutinous crew of an English ship[2] and some Tahitians whom they had kidnapped? The earth is a large island in the midst of space, from which the human mob covering it cannot escape.

I thank you, Madame, once again and remain your sincere admirer and servant

Hector Berlioz

Prompted by a singer Berlioz had known in Weimar, Mlle Falconi, and the conductor Herbeck, the Gesellschaft der Musikfreunde in Vienna invited Berlioz to conduct a performance of La damnation de Faust. *Despite the season and his chronic ill-health, Berlioz accepted, saying 'I am in need of music'. He left Paris on 5 December.*

1 La Rochefoucault and La Bruyère were French philosophers of the seventeenth century, Vauvenargues of the eighteenth century. Epictetus was a Greek philosopher born AD 60.
2 The mutiny of the *Bounty*, which happened in 1789.

My dear Gasperini,

Yesterday *La damnation de Faust* was given in the Redoutensaal before an enormous audience and in the midst of an excitement such as I have never witnessed in my life. I was recalled more than ten times, and there were interminable encores which would have been more numerous still if the work hadn't been so long.

I had 400 performers and the best singers the Opéra could provide; among others the charming Mlle Bettelheim (Marguerite) and Walter (Faust), a delightful tenor. Their love duet was interrupted three times by applause, and Walter sang particularly well in his aria in Marguerite's bedroom. And Marguerite after she'd been abandoned!! Ah! The chorus had been well trained by Herbeck, a well-known conductor, and they sang with incomparable ensemble and nuances.

Already this morning there's a very nice article in the *Wanderer*; I'm told I can expect a slating from M. Hanslick,[1] but on the other hand a highly laudatory article from M. Schelle in the *Presse ancienne* the day after tomorrow.

I may tell you, it's the greatest success of my life. I know that you'll be delighted. Some of the audience came from as far as Munich and Leipzig. They're putting on a large party for me this evening; I must go and get dressed for it. My room is continually full of people complimenting and embracing me. The concert finished at three o'clock, and the audience stayed till the last bar: normally, when it gets to two o'clock, they leave. This was much commented upon.

Adieu, adieu. I'm very happy to have been adopted by the Viennese like this.

H. Berlioz

467 To *Estelle Fornier*   Paris, 4 March 1867

I must profoundly beg your pardon for the last letter I was unwise enough to send you. I was so ill that I no longer knew what I was saying. But your indulgence and kindness will have led you to forgive me.

Now, even though I'm still in considerable pain, I feel my spirit is a

1 Hanslick, an ardent champion of Berlioz's music in Prague in 1846, had become the leader of resistance to all manifestations of the new music, which included Berlioz, Liszt and Wagner. His notice of *La damnation de Faust* was very lukewarm.

little freer. I've just come back from Cologne, where I'd been invited to go and conduct two of my works in the concert on 26 February. I refused twice; they insisted a third time and finally, even though I wasn't sure what the journey might lead to, I made the decision to undertake it. I had some violent crises, it's true, but in the end I managed nonetheless to conduct three rehearsals and the evening concert. The Kapellmeister, M. Hiller, once a friend of mine but whose inner sentiments I inveighed against, proved on the contrary to be frank and cordial.[1] We came together again. His orchestra was marvellous and the audience enthusiastic. My scene from *Béatrice et Bénédict* and my grand symphony *Harold en Italie* were performed splendidly. As in Vienna, I was given a brilliant supper, with fanfares, speeches, etc.

Now, here, absolute rest, distaste for music, horror of hearing it, sadness at not seeing you, fear of troubling you, revival of physical pains and problems of all kinds, life weighing me down. However philosophical your outlook, I'm very afraid you may be feeling much the same. It cannot be that you are spared anxieties in your solitude, in winter, beneath the tall, bare trees, in that isolated park, with that monotonous existence to which you are no more than resigned; and boredom . . . I hope I may be wrong! [. . .]

Forgive me, I'm weeping again. I'd better stop and beg your forgiveness for my digressions, respectfully kissing your hand.

Hector Berlioz

468 *To Auguste Morel*   Paris, 12 May 1867

My dear Morel,

Thank you for your cordial letter; but your enthusiasm on the subject of music rather amazed me, such is my indifference these days for all that kind of thing. Even so, when I see enthusiastic souls busying themselves passionately with it, I do feel some revival of the spirit, but it doesn't last long. Everything now seems to me so puerile and dull. I'm suffering increasingly from my neuralgia and nothing else has any interest for me. Carvalho and Gounod didn't send me a ticket to go and see their production, so I haven't seen it.[2] Despite that, Gounod embraced me the other day at the Institut, I don't know why.

1 Hiller, Berlioz's friend from 1829, had been Kapellmeister in Cologne since 1850. He was now associated with the school of Schumann and Brahms in opposition to Liszt and Wagner, although he remained loyal to Berlioz.
2 Gounod's *Roméo et Juliette* opened at the Théâtre-Lyrique on 27 April.

I haven't any scores to send you, but there is something else: tell me whether you possess the full score of the *Requiem*. A thoroughly corrected edition has just been made in Milan and I've asked Ricordi to send me some copies. So if you'd like, I'll send you the new edition free of engraving mistakes and some mistakes of Latin prosody which had escaped me, all of which I've corrected with the utmost care. It puts Schlesinger's French edition in the shade.[1]

Roméo et Juliette was put on some time ago in Basle in Switzerland:[2] von Bülow directed the director. Mme von Bülow wrote to tell me that. Yesterday they performed *L'enfance du Christ* in Copenhagen and it had been given a month earlier in Lausanne in Switzerland. My music's being played here and there these days, even in America, but not in Paris, though Pasdeloup tears some of my works to shreds from time to time.

Louis is still in Mexico. I shall be writing to him soon and I know he will be very touched by Mme Morel's kind thoughts. Like you, he's passionately interested in my little musical activities. [. . .]

Yours very truly,

H. Berlioz

469 *To Humbert Ferrand*   Paris, 11 June 1867

Dear Humbert,

Thank you for your letter; it made me feel much better. Yes, I'm in Paris, but still so unwell, I hardly have the strength to write to you. I'm ill on every front; I'm tormented by anxiety. Louis is still in the region of Mexico, and I haven't had any news from him for a long time. I'm afraid those Mexican brigands are capable of anything.[3]

The Exhibition has turned Paris into a hell.[4] I haven't been to it yet. I can hardly walk, and now it's very difficult to find carriages. Yesterday there was a large celebration at court. I was invited, but at the crucial moment I didn't feel strong enough to get dressed.

I quite realize that you are in no better health than I am, and I thank you most earnestly for being kind enough to let me have your news from time to time.

1 Schlesinger's edition appeared in 1838. Ricordi published a revised edition in 1853 and a corrected second edition in 1867.
2 The Basle performance was on 14 December 1866.
3 Napoleon III's dismal meddling in Mexican affairs had been going on since 1861, but in 1867 he abandoned the puppet king Maximilian to his fate. Maximilian was captured on 15 May 1867 and executed on 19 June.
4 The 1867 Exposition Universelle.

I wrote you these lines at the Conservatoire, where the jury I'm on has been sitting to decide the Exhibition's composition prize. I had to stop for the meeting and the presentation. Over the last few days we've heard a hundred and four cantatas, and I've had the pleasure of seeing the prize awarded (unanimously) to my young friend Camille Saint-Saëns, one of the greatest composers of our time.[1]

You haven't read the large number of newspapers that mentioned my *Roméo et Juliette* in discussing Gounod's opera and in a way that he can't have enjoyed reading. I haven't taken any part in this success, which has surprised me considerably. [. . .]

Adieu, dear Humbert. I shake you by the hand.

H. Berlioz

470 To Estelle Fornier   Paris, 29 June 1867

Dear Madame,

Forgive me for turning to you at the moment when I have suffered the cruellest blow of my life. My poor son has died in Havana, at the age of thirty-three.[2]

Yours sincerely,

H. Berlioz

471 To Louise Damcke   Paris, 24 September 1867

Dear Madame Damcke,

I would certainly have written to you since my return,[3] but I didn't know where to send my letter. A double thankyou therefore for yours.

My laconic reply is: I'm still unwell.

When I got to Néris, I took five baths. While I was taking the fifth the doctor, hearing me talk, took my pulse and said, 'Come out at once, the waters don't agree with you. You're going to contract laryngitis. You must go somewhere you can look after your throat. It's not something to take lightly!'

I left the same evening. I almost suffocated on the railway journey from a coughing fit. Then I reached Vienne where my nieces overwhelmed me with solicitude. I spent almost all the time in bed.

---

1 The cantata was entitled *Les noces de Prométhée*.
2 Louis died in Havana on 5 June of yellow fever.
3 He had returned from two weeks at Néris, a spa near Vichy, followed by a stay with the Suats in Vienne. Estelle Fornier was living again near Lyon, so he called on her three times, their last meetings. She too had recently lost a son.

Finally my voice returned more or less to normal and the pain in my throat subsided, but my neuralgia returned too, fiercer than ever.

I had to stay in Vienne for a month because the elder of my nieces was getting married and she wanted me to be a witness.[1] She knows what a good witness I am ... She was marrying a major in the army, a charming fellow in every respect, otherwise I wouldn't have been a witness. After the wedding dinner, they left for a long tour of the south of France, otherwise, again, I wouldn't have been a witness.

There were thirty-two of us at the wedding from every side of the family, from Grenoble, from Tournon, from St-Geoire, etc, etc. We all met there, except *one*, alas ...

The one I was most pleased to see again was the oldest, my uncle the colonel, aged eighty-four.[2] We wept copiously when we saw each other again. He seemed ashamed to be alive ... I am far more so.

During my stay in Vienne I went to St-Symphorien three times to see Mme Fornier. These visits did me so much good. But she's very unhappy and bored and longs, as she says, to *rest*. She received me most graciously and her son and daughter-in-law were thoughtful enough to leave us alone several times ...

I'm back in Paris now, most of the time in bed, as in Vienne. And just recently the Grand Duchess Yelena of Russia has got round me to go to St Petersburg.[3] She wanted to see me, and finally I agreed. I shall leave on 15 November to go and conduct six concerts at the Conservatoire, including one of my own music.

The Princess is paying for my return journey, putting one of her carriages at my disposal, having me to stay at the Mikhailovsky Palace and giving me 15,000 francs. At least if I die of it all I'll know it was worth the trouble.

I wrote to your husband the other day, but didn't post the letter because I had no address. It was to ask whether I had lent him my Leipzig score of *Orphée*. I can't find it. I called on Heller and left him my card; I have no news of him.

Adieu, Madame; I shake you by the hand and send you both all my best wishes.

H. Berlioz

1 Joséphine Suat married Marc-Antoine-Auguste Chapot on 9 September.
2 Félix Marmion.
3 The Grand Duchess Yelena Pavlovna, the Tsar's German-born aunt, was the patroness of the Russian Musical Society.

[. . .] I must tell you too that an American,[1] whose offers I had refused six weeks ago, when he found out that I was accepting the one from Russia, came back three days ago and offered me a hundred thousand francs if I would go to New York next year. What do you say to that? Meanwhile he's having a bronze bust of me made here for a superb concert hall he's having built over there;[2] and I'm going to pose every day. If I weren't so old, I should enjoy all that. [. . .]

Berlioz left Paris on 12 November and devoted five days to the journey to St Petersburg. Few of his Russian acquaintances from 1847 were still there: only General Lvov, now deaf. But the new generation of Russian musicians – Cui, Stasov, Balakirev and Rimsky-Korsakov – were enthusiastically devoted to his music. He gave six concerts in St Petersburg and two concerts in Moscow and arrived back in Paris on 19 February after an absence of over three months.

473 *To Estelle Fornier*   St Petersburg, 13 December 1867
                                             Mikhailovsky Palace

Dear, beloved Madame,

Don't be annoyed at my writing to you. I don't ask for an answer, but I think I should give you at least a little idea of my life in this great capital of snow and frost. I'm conducting my third concert tomorrow. The audience and the musicians are overwhelming me with demonstrations of affection and enthusiasm. Each time I appear, there's applause that makes you wonder how it will all end. I have a superb orchestra to conduct which is completely devoted to me and with which I can do as I like. For my second concert, the music-lovers of Petersburg asked me for my *Symphonie fantastique*, which was not on the programme, and I gave it after a large number of rehearsals. It was an enormous success; there was applause after every movement and the fourth one had to be repeated. At the end I was overwhelmed with embraces, handshakes, vivats, etc, etc. What harm, after all, is there in my telling you this? I don't know, but I tell you without compunction.

Tomorrow I only have two works in the programme, my overture *Le*

1 Theodore Steinway.
2 The sculptor was Perraud.

carnaval romain and my romance *Rêverie et caprice* for violin.[1] The main part of the programme is taken up by the second act of Gluck's *Orphée* which, at this morning's rehearsal, moved me to the very bone. The Grand Duchess wanted me to have a very large chorus for this masterpiece and I have a body of 130 voices. Her Imperial Highness has overwhelmed me with kindnesses. The day before yesterday she sent me an album bound in malachite; I didn't realize why. It was my birthday, I don't know how she knew. That evening the musicians gave a dinner for me with 150 guests. I leave you to imagine all the toasts. There were a lot of men of letters there, all of them able to speak French. The Grand Duchess Yelena asked me recently to come one evening and read *Hamlet* to her. Her knowledge of Shakespeare is such as to inspire the reader with confidence. The poor woman has an income of eight million roubles (32 million francs); she is immensely generous to the poor and to artists. Even so I often feel bored in the fine apartment she's given me and I can't always accept the invitations she offers me. I spend much of my time in bed, especially after the rehearsals and concerts, which exhaust me. She has *your* regal carriage and way of walking, but then she's born to it.

When shall I be able to see you? There are days, mornings especially, when the pain is worst, when I feel it will never be possible . . . Then music revives me, and conducting masterpieces restores my strength. Beethoven's 'Pastoral' Symphony the other day put me absolutely back on my feet. A great man! A great poet! . . . They want me to go on to Moscow. I shan't accept.[2] In any case I have three more concerts to conduct here, after the one tomorrow, and by the third one I shall probably be at the end of my strength. The cold and snow are appalling and I've no desire to make another train journey just for a few hundred roubles. Goodbye, Madame, goodbye dear, beloved Madame. May I kneel at your feet and kiss your hand and tell you that I am your devoted slave unto death.

Hector Berlioz

474 *To Aglaé Massart*   St Petersburg, 22 December 1867

Dear Madame Massart,

I'm as ill as eighteen horses; I'm coughing like six donkeys with glanders, but even so I want to write to you before I go back to bed.

1 The soloist was the Polish virtuoso Wieniawski.
2 He changed his mind and went to Moscow.

Our concerts are going marvellously. Next Saturday we're performing the 'Eroica' and the second act of *Alceste*, with the *Offertoire* from
my *Requiem* (the chorus on two notes). At the one after that (the fifth
concert) I'm giving the first three (instrumental) movements of Beethoven's 'Choral' Symphony. I don't dare risk the vocal part since the
singers I have at my disposal don't inspire me with sufficient confidence. People from Moscow have come to fetch me; the Grand
Duchess has given her permission and I'll be going there after the fifth
concert. The arguments of these gentlemen of the mid-Asiatic capital
are irresistible, whatever Wieniawski may say; he thinks I shouldn't
simply have accepted their first offer. But I don't know how to haggle
and I'd be ashamed to do so. Someone has just come into my salon,
where I'm alone writing to you, because the Grand Duchess is giving a
musical soirée this evening at which she wants to hear the duet from
my *Béatrice et Bénédict*. The accompanist and the two singers know it
perfectly (in French), so I've just sent the score to Her Highness's
apartment asking the three virtuosi not to be nervous, because they
know perfectly well what they're about. As for me, I'm going back to
bed; it's nine o'clock and I'm not used to being out of bed at such
unseemly hours. [. . .]

475 *To Berthold Damcke*   Moscow, 10 January 1868

My dear Damcke,
    I've been so exhausted these last few days I haven't had the strength
to write to you, but I've had a great musical experience. The directors
of the Moscow Conservatoire came to see me in St Petersburg and
obtained from the Grand Duchess a twelve-day leave of absence for
me. I've agreed to conduct two concerts. As they couldn't find a hall
large enough for the first one, they had the idea of giving it in the
Riding School, a place as big as the hall in the middle of our Palais de
l'Industrie in the Champs-Elysées. I thought it was a crazy idea, but it
had the most incredible success. There were five hundred performers
and, according to the calculations of the police, an audience of twelve
and a half thousand. I won't try to describe the applause for the *Fête* in
Roméo et Juliette and the *Offertoire* from the *Requiem*. But I had an
attack of mortal anguish when this last movement began (they insisted
on having it because of the effect it had produced in St Petersburg).
When I heard this choir of three hundred voices incessantly repeating
those two notes, I suddenly imagined the audience getting more and
more bored and I was afraid I wouldn't be allowed to finish the piece.

But they understood what I was aiming at. They redoubled their concentration and were struck by the expression of resigned humility. After the final bar huge applause broke out from every quarter. I was recalled four times and the orchestra and chorus then joined in. I didn't know where to put myself. It was the biggest impact I've ever produced in my life. A telegram was immediately sent to the Grand Duchess to inform her of the feeling of the people. [. . .]

Adieu, my dear friend.

H. Berlioz

476 *To Alfred Holmes*[1]   St Petersburg, 1 February 1868

My dear Holmes,

[. . .] Despite all the offers being made to keep me here, I intend to leave; the cold and the snow are driving me out; with my health, I can't stand this kind of temperature. I have a rehearsal this evening and it makes me shiver just to think about it. [. . .]

Forgive me for such a disorganized letter. I haven't the strength to collect my thoughts. The journey to Moscow finished me off. [. . .] The plan at the moment is to put on a fearful programme approved by the Grand Duchess for my leavetaking. The concert they were to have given *for me* in March would have kept me here for more than another month but I prefer to sacrifice eight thousand francs and return home immediately. The kindnesses of everybody, musicians and audiences the dinners and presents, none of that makes any difference. I want the sun; I want to go to Nice or Monaco.

Adieu, my dear Holmes, give my regards to your wife who will need plenty of courage to support yours.

Six days ago there were 32 degrees of frost. The birds were falling out of the air and the coachmen off their seats. What a country! And in my symphonies I sing of Italy and sylphs and rosebeds on the banks of the Elbe!!!

477 *To Vladimir Vasilyevich Stasov*   Paris, 1 March 1868

Dear Stasov,

I haven't written to you since my return. I've been in terrible pain. Today I feel a little better and I greet you with the news that I'm leaving

1 English violinist and composer who settled in Paris in 1864. His symphony *Joan of Arc* was played in St Petersburg in 1867.

for Monaco. I go this evening at seven o'clock. I don't know why I don't die. But since I don't, I'm going to see my favourite coast round Nice once again and the rocks at Villefranche and the sun in Monaco. Yesterday I dragged myself off to the Académie, where I saw my sculptor colleague Perraud. He told me that the American, Steinway, had finally paid him for my bust and that they are at this moment busy casting three copies, larger than life-size, for New York and Paris. I think it was you who said you'd like to have one in bronze for the St Petersburg Conservatoire. If it wasn't you it was Kologrivov or Cui or Balakirev. In any case, now you know, so tell them M. Perraud has informed me that further copies of the bust could still be cast and that they will cost 280 francs. Write to me at 4, Rue de Calais, Paris. Your letter will be forwarded to me in Nice or Monaco. But it would be better still to write to M. Perraud, sculptor, member of the Académie des Beaux-Arts, at the Institut, Paris. You can tell him what you want and when you want it. And it'll be quicker. Oh, when I think that I'm going to stretch out on the marble steps of Monaco, in the sun, by the sea!!! ...

Don't be too niggardly, write to me despite my laconic efforts. Remember that I'm ill and that your letter will do me good, and don't talk to me about composing or say anything stupid ...

Reassure me that you've given my regards to your charming sister-in-law, to your delightful daughter and to your brother. I can see all three of them as though they were here in front of me.

Music ... Ah! I was going to tell you something about music, but I'll refrain.

Adieu, write to me soon. Your letter will bring me to life again as well as the SUN ... You poor wretch! You dwell amid the snows! ... Adieu again.

Yours truly,
Hector Berlioz

478 *To Estelle Fornier*   Paris, 25 March 1868

Dear, beloved Madame,

I am writing to you instead of coming to see you.[1] I am in my bed in Paris. I spent a week in bed in Nice. It's quite bizarre, I made an absurd journey. My niece knows nothing, my brother-in-law knows nothing,

1 Berlioz had planned to visit Estelle on his way home from Nice.

no one at Grenoble knows anything either, but I can't leave you in ignorance of my accident any longer.

I'd been in Monaco two days and was getting bored when, one morning, I decided to go down to the sea over some difficult rocks. After three steps my lack of common sense became all too clear. I couldn't stop moving forwards and I fell head first on my face. I stayed there a long time on the ground, alone, unable to get up and pouring with blood. Finally, after a quarter of an hour, I was able to drag myself to the villa where they wiped me and bandaged me as best they could.

I'd reserved my seat in the bus to return to Nice next day. I did return, but now listen to this: when I got to Nice I decided, disfigured though I was, to go and see the terrace overlooking the sea which I used to be so fond of years ago, and I climbed up there. I went to sit on a seat, but as I couldn't see the sea very well from there, I got up to change seats and hardly had I gone three steps than I fell headlong, on my face again, and began to pour blood worse than the day before. Two young people who were walking on the terrace came in panic to pick me up and led me by the arm to the Hôtel des Etrangers, near to where I'd fallen over. I stayed there in bed immobile for a week and, when I was strong enough, I came back to Paris without worrying what a sight I made on the train. My mother-in-law and my maid both screamed when they saw me come in. Since then I haven't left my bed and for a fortnight I've been in constant pain. My nose and eyes are in a dreadful state; the doctor has tried to console me by saying that it was lucky I shed all that blood, otherwise I'd have stayed where I fell, the second time especially.

Adieu, dear Madame, I needed to tell you why I didn't come and see you. My niece knows nothing of this, but I'll write to her later. You at least are well, I hope. Adieu once again.

Yours sincerely,
Hector Berlioz

479 *To Estelle Fornier*   Paris, 19 July 1868

Dear Madame,

[...] My life is uniform; my mother-in-law accompanies me almost everywhere. When I leave the house, it's in a carriage and she takes my arm. I go to the Institut every Saturday to sign the attendance book, after which I come away. I'm not able to stay for the meeting. I go to bed at nine o'clock. Impossible to read. I should really like to get some of my strength back. I feel I could make good use of it. Perhaps it will return. Meanwhile I thank you for making me feel better this morning.

Adieu, Madame, adieu. Write to me again, take care of me. I bless you with all my strength. Perhaps my courage will come back.

Yours sincerely,

Hector Berlioz

480 *To Vladimir Vasilyevich Stasov*   Paris, 21 August 1868

My dear Stasov,

As you see, I leave out the 'Monsieur'. I've just come back from Grenoble where I was more or less forced to go to preside over some sort of choral festival and to attend the inauguration of a statue of the Emperor Napoleon I.

We ate, we drank, we painted the town red and I still felt ill. I was collected in a carriage and was the subject of toasts to which I didn't know what to reply. The mayor of Grenoble overwhelmed me with compliments and gave me a gilded wreath, but I had to stay for a whole hour at the start of the banquet. I left the next day; I arrived home exhausted at eleven o'clock in the evening . . .

I can't do any more, and people write to me from Russia and Löwenberg with impossible requests. They want me to say kind things about a German musician, kind things which I do in fact believe, but on condition that I say unkind things about a Russian musician whom they want to replace by the German but who, on the contrary, deserves the highest praise; that I won't do. What sort of infernal world is that?[1]

I feel I'm going to die. I no longer believe in anything. I should like to see you; perhaps you'd raise my spirits; Cui and you would perhaps make my blood flow again. What can one do? I'm exorbitantly bored. There's no one in Paris; all my friends are away, in the country, on their bits of country, hunting; some of them have invited me to stay. I haven't the strength.

How are you? And your brother? And the charming ladies? Oh, please write to me as briefly as you wish. I'm still suffering repercussions from my fall on the rocks in Monaco; Nice has left a legacy too.

Perhaps you'll be away when this letter arrives; I'm prepared for

1 This refers to intrigues in St Petersburg, where the Grand Duchess and others wanted to oust Balakirev from the conductorship of the Russian Musical Society and replace him with Seifriz. Balakirev was forced to resign early in 1869 and was replaced by Naprávnik.

anything. If you're in St Petersburg, write me six lines; I'd be infinitely grateful.

All the best to Balakirev.

Adieu, I find it very difficult to write. You're a good friend, prove it to me once again.

I shake you by the hand.

Yours sincerely,

Hector Berlioz

481 *To his brother-in-law Camille Pal*   Paris, 28 December 1868

My dear Camille,

I haven't had any news from you, please give me your news. I'm still unwell, my nights are terrible, please give me some news as I haven't had any. I'm anxious to find a way out of my problems over money, you are a support for me, help me to find a way out. Help me. A letter doesn't take very long.

Adieu.

H. Berlioz

Berlioz lived on for little more than two months after writing this. He died at his home, 4, Rue de Calais, on 8 March 1869 and was buried in the Cimetière Montmartre.

Index

[475]